Family Maps
of
Washington County, Missouri
Deluxe Edition

With Homesteads, Roads, Waterways, Towns, Cemeteries, Railroads, and More

Family Maps of Washington County, Missouri

Deluxe Edition

With Homesteads, Roads, Waterways, Towns, Cemeteries, Railroads, and More

by Gregory A. Boyd, J.D.

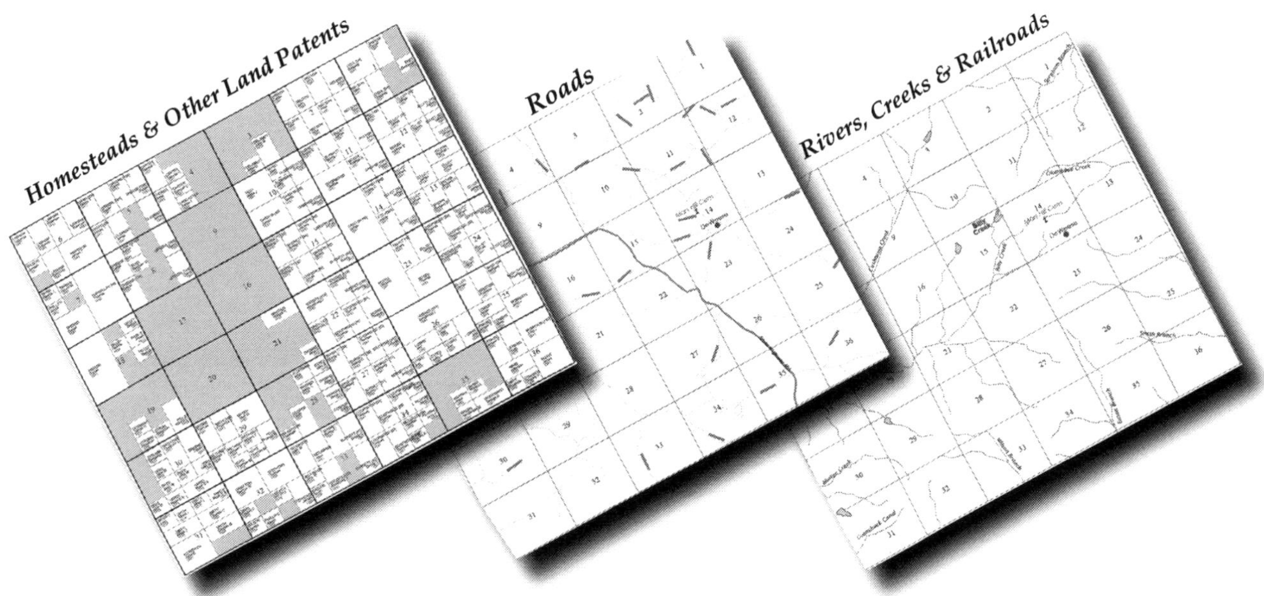

Featuring 3 Maps Per Township...

Arphax Publishing Co.
www.arphax.com

Family Maps of Washington County, Missouri, Deluxe Edition: With Homesteads, Roads, Waterways, Towns, Cemeteries, Railroads, and More.
by Gregory A. Boyd, J.D.

ISBN 1-4203-1210-3

Printed in the United States of America

Published by Arphax Publishing Co., 2210 Research Park Blvd., Norman, Oklahoma, USA 73069
www.arphax.com

First Edition

ATTENTION HISTORICAL & GENEALOGICAL SOCIETIES, UNIVERSITIES, COLLEGES, CORPORATIONS, FAMILY REUNION COORDINATORS, AND PROFESSIONAL ORGANIZATIONS: Quantity discounts are available on bulk purchases of this book. For information, please contact Arphax Publishing Co., at the address listed above, or at (405) 366-6181, or visit our web-site at www.arphax.com and contact us through the "Bulk Sales" link.

This book is dedicated to my wonderful family:

Vicki, Jordan, & Amy Boyd

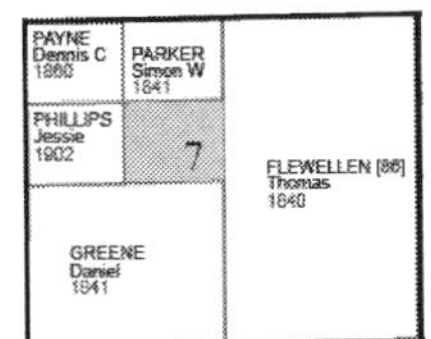

Contents

- Part I -

The Big Picture

- Part II -

Township Map Groups

(each Map Group contains a Patent Index, Patent Map, Road Map, & Historical Map)

Appendices

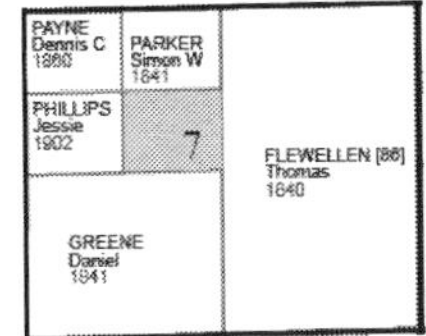

Preface

The quest for the discovery of my ancestors' origins, migrations, beliefs, and life-ways has brought me rewards that I could never have imagined. The *Family Maps* series of books is my first effort to share with historical and genealogical researchers, some of the tools that I have developed to achieve my research goals. I firmly believe that this effort will allow many people to reap the same sorts of treasures that I have.

Our Federal government's General Land Office of the Bureau of Land Management (the "GLO") has given genealogists and historians an incredible gift by virtue of its enormous database housed on its web-site at glorecords.blm.gov. Here, you can search for and find millions of parcels of land purchased by our ancestors in about thirty states.

This GLO web-site is one of the best FREE on-line tools available to family researchers. But, it is not for the faint of heart, nor is it for those unwilling or unable to to sift through and analyze the thousands of records that exist for most counties.

My immediate goal with this series is to spare you the hundreds of hours of work that it would take you to map the Land Patents for this county. Every Washington County homestead or land patent that I have gleaned from public GLO databases is mapped here. Consequently, I can usually show you in an instant, where your ancestor's land is located, as well as the names of nearby land-owners.

Originally, that was my primary goal. But after speaking to other genealogists, it became clear that there was much more that they wanted. Taking their advice set me back almost a full year, but I think you will agree it was worth the wait. Because now, you can learn so much more.

Now, this book answers these sorts of questions:

- Are there any variant spellings for surnames that I have missed in searching GLO records?
- Where is my family's traditional home-place?
- What cemeteries are near Grandma's house?
- My Granddad used to swim in such-and-such-Creek—where is that?
- How close is this little community to that one?
- Are there any other people with the same surname who bought land in the county?
- How about cousins and in-laws—did they buy land in the area?

And these are just for starters!

The rules for using the *Family Maps* books are simple, but the strategies for success are many. Some techniques are apparent on first use, but many are gained with time and experience. Please take the time to notice the roads, cemeteries, creek-names, family names, and unique first-names throughout the whole county. You cannot imagine what YOU might be the first to discover.

I hope to learn that many of you have answered age-old research questions within these pages or that you have discovered relationships previously not even considered. When these sorts of things happen to you, will you please let me hear about it? I would like nothing better. My contact information can always be found at www.arphax.com.

One more thing: please read the "How To Use This Book" chapter; it starts on the next page. This will give you the very best chance to find the treasures that lie within these pages.

My family and I wish you the very best of luck, both in life, and in your research. Greg Boyd

How to Use This Book - A Graphical Summary

Part I

"The Big Picture"

Map A ▸ *Counties in the State*
Map B ▸ *Surrounding Counties*
Map C ▸ *Congressional Townships (Map Groups) in the County*
Map D ▸ *Cities & Towns in the County*
Map E ▸ *Cemeteries in the County*
Surnames in the County ▸ *Number of Land-Parcels for Each Surname*
Surname/Township Index ▸ Directs you to Township Map Groups in Part II

The Surname/Township Index can direct you to any number of **Township Map Groups**

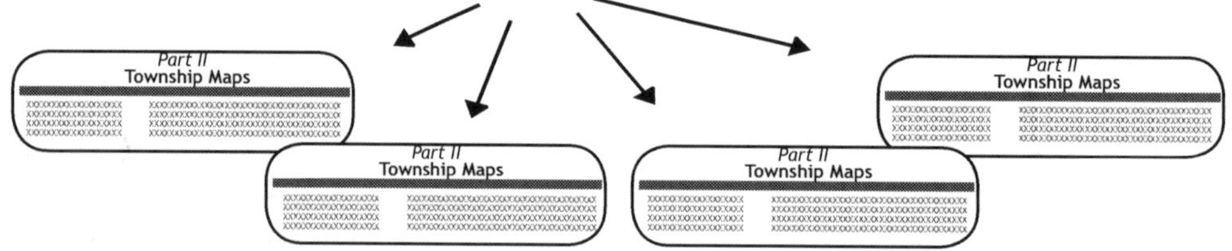

Part II

Township Map Groups

(1 for each Township in the County)

Each Township Map Group contains all four of of the following tools . . .

Land Patent Index ▸ *Every-name Index of Patents Mapped in this Township*
Land Patent Map ▸ *Map of Patents as listed in above Index*
Road Map ▸ *Map of Roads, City-centers, and Cemeteries in the Township*
Historical Map ▸ *Map of Railroads, Lakes, Rivers, Creeks, City-Centers, and Cemeteries*

Appendices

Appendix A ▸ *Congressional Authority enabling Patents within our Maps*
Appendix B ▸ *Section-Parts / Aliquot Parts (a comprehensive list)*
Appendix C ▸ *Multi-patentee Groups (Individuals within Buying Groups)*

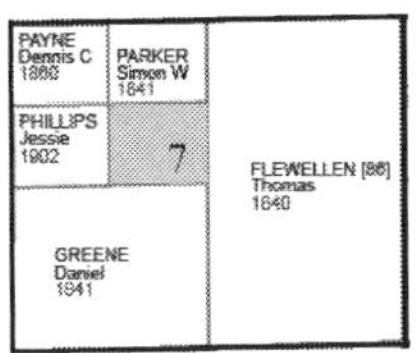

How to Use This Book

The two "Parts" of this *Family Maps* volume seek to answer two different types of questions. Part I deals with broad questions like: what counties surround Washington County, are there any ASHCRAFTs in Washington County, and if so, in which Townships or Maps can I find them? Ultimately, though, Part I should point you to a particular Township Map Group in Part II.

Part II concerns itself with details like: where exactly is this family's land, who else bought land in the area, and what roads and streams run through the land, or are located nearby. The Chart on the opposite page, and the remainder of this chapter attempt to convey to you the particulars of these two "parts", as well as how best to use them to achieve your research goals.

Part I
"The Big Picture"

Within Part I, you will find five "Big Picture" maps and two county-wide surname tools.

These include:

- Map A - Where Washington County lies within the state
- Map B - Counties that surround Washington County
- Map C - Congressional Townships of Washington County (+ Map Group Numbers)
- Map D - Cities & Towns of Washington County (with Index)
- Map E - Cemeteries of Washington County (with Index)
- Surnames in Washington County Patents (with Parcel-counts for each surname)
- Surname/Township Index (with Parcel-counts for each surname by Township)

The five "Big-Picture" Maps are fairly self-explanatory, yet should not be overlooked. This is particularly true of Maps "C", "D", and "E", all of which show Washington County and its Congressional Townships (and their assigned Map Group Numbers).

Let me briefly explain this concept of Map Group Numbers. These are a device completely of our own invention. They were created to help you quickly locate maps without having to remember the full legal name of the various Congressional Townships. It is simply easier to remember "Map Group 1" than a legal name like: "Township 9-North Range 6-West, 5th Principal Meridian." But the fact is that the TRUE legal name for these Townships IS terribly important. These are the designations that others will be familiar with and you will need to accurately record them in your notes. This is why both Map Group numbers AND legal descriptions of Townships are almost always displayed together.

Map "C" will be your first intoduction to "Map Group Numbers", and that is all it contains: legal Township descriptions and their assigned Map Group Numbers. Once you get further into your research, and more immersed in the details, you will likely want to refer back to Map "C" from time to time, in order to regain your bearings on just where in the county you are researching.

Remember, township boundaries are a completely artificial device, created to standardize land descriptions. But do not let them become a boundary in your mind when choosing which townships to research. Your relative's in-laws, children, cousins, siblings, and mamas and papas, might just as easily have lived in the township next to the one your grandfather lived in—rather than in the one where he actually lived. So Map "C" can be your guide to which other Townships/ Map Groups you likewise ought to analyze.

Of course, the same holds true for County lines; this is the purpose behind Map "B". It shows you surrounding counties that you may want to consider for further reserarch.

Map "D", the Cities and Towns map, is the first map with an index. Map "E" is the second (Cemeteries). Both, Maps "D" and "E" give you broad views of City (or Cemetery) locations in the County. But they go much further by pointing you toward pertinent Township Map Groups so you can locate the patents, roads, and waterways located near a particular city or cemetery.

Once you are familiar with these *Family Maps* volumes and the county you are researching, the "Surnames In Washington County" chapter (or its sister chapter in other volumes) is where you'll likely start your future research sessions. Here, you can quickly scan its few pages and see if anyone in the county possesses the surnames you are researching. The "Surnames in Washington County" list shows only two things: surnames and the number of parcels of land we have located for that surname in Washington County. But whether or not you immediately locate the surnames you are researching, please do not go any further without taking a few moments to scan ALL the surnames in these very few pages.

You cannot imagine how many lost ancestors are waiting to be found by someone willing to take just a little longer to scan the "Surnames In Washington County" list. Misspellings and typographical errors abound in most any index of this sort. Don't miss out on finding your Kinard that was written Rynard or Cox that was written Lox. If it looks funny or wrong, it very often is. And one of those little errors may well be your relative.

Now, armed with a surname and the knowledge that it has one or more entries in this book, you are ready for the "Surname/Township Index." Unlike the "Surnames In Washington County", which has only one line per Surname, the "Surname/Township Index" contains one line-item for each Township Map Group in which each surname is found. In other words, each line represents a different Township Map Group that you will need to review.

Specifically, each line of the Surname/Township Index contains the following four columns of information:

1. Surname
2. Township Map Group Number (these Map Groups are found in Part II)
3. Parcels of Land (number of them with the given Surname within the Township)
4. Meridian/Township/Range (the legal description for this Township Map Group)

The key column here is that of the Township Map Group Number. While you should definitely record the Meridian, Township, and Range, you can do that later. Right now, you need to dig a little deeper. That Map Group Number tells you where in Part II that you need to start digging.

But before you leave the "Surname/Township Index", do the same thing that you did with the "Surnames in Washington County" list: take a moment to scan the pages of the Index and see if there are similarly spelled or misspelled surnames that deserve your attention. Here again, is an easy opportunity to discover grossly misspelled family names with very little effort. Now you are ready to turn to . . .

Part II
"Township Map Groups"

You will normally arrive here in Part II after being directed to do so by one or more "Map Group Numbers" in the Surname/Township Index of Part I.

Each Map Group represents a set of four tools dedicated to a single Congressional Township that is either wholly or partially within the county. If you are trying to learn all that you can about a particular family or their land, then these tools should usually be viewed in the order they are presented.

These four tools include:

1. a Land Patent Index
2. a Land Patent Map
3. a Road Map, and
4. an Historical Map

As I mentioned earlier, each grouping of this sort is assigned a Map Group Number. So, let's now move on to a discussion of the four tools that make up one of these Township Map Groups.

Land Patent Index

Each Township Map Group's Index begins with a title, something along these lines:

MAP GROUP 1: Index to Land Patents
Township 16-North Range 5-West (2nd PM)

The Index contains seven (7) columns. They are:

1. ID (a unique ID number for this Individual and a corresponding Parcel of land in this Township)
2. Individual in Patent (name)
3. Sec. (Section), and
4. Sec. Part (Section Part, or Aliquot Part)
5. Date Issued (Patent)
6. Other Counties (often means multiple counties were mentioned in GLO records, or the section lies within multiple counties).
7. For More Info . . . (points to other places within this index or elsewhere in the book where you can find more information)

While most of the seven columns are self-explanatory, I will take a few moments to explain the "Sec. Part." and "For More Info" columns.

The "Sec. Part" column refers to what surveryors and other land professionals refer to as an Aliquot Part. The origins and use of such a term mean little to a non-surveyor, and I have chosen to simply call these sub-sections of land what they are: a "Section Part". No matter what we call them, what we are referring to are things like a quarter-section or half-section or quarter-quarter-section. See Appendix "B" for most of the "Section Parts" you will come across (and many you will not) and what size land-parcel they represent.

The "For More Info" column of the Index may seem like a small appendage to each line, but please recognize quickly that this is not so. And to understand the various items you might find here, you need to become familiar with the Legend that appears at the top of each Land Patent Index.

Here is a sample of the Legend . . .

LEGEND

"For More Info . . . " column

A = Authority (Legislative Act, See Appendix "A")
B = Block or Lot (location in Section unknown)
C = Cancelled Patent
F = Fractional Section
G = Group (Multi-Patentee Patent, see Appendix "C")
V = Overlaps another Parcel
R = Re-Issued (Parcel patented more than once)

Most parcels of land will have only one or two of these items in their "For More Info" columns, but when that is not the case, there is often some valuable information to be gained from further investigation. Below, I will explain what each of these items means to you you as a researcher.

A = Authority
(Legislative Act, See Appendix "A")

All Federal Land Patents were issued because some branch of our government (usually the U.S. Congress) passed a law making such a transfer of title possible. And therefore every patent within these pages will have an "A" item next to it in the index. The number after the "A" indicates which item in Appendix "A" holds the citation to the particular law which authorized the transfer of land to the public. As it stands, most of the Public Land data compiled and released by our government, and which serves as the basis for the patents mapped here, concerns itself with "Cash Sale" homesteads. So in some Counties, the law which authorized cash sales will be the primary, if not the only, entry in the Appendix.

B = Block or Lot (location in Section unknown)

A "B" designation in the Index is a tip-off that the EXACT location of the patent within the map is not apparent from the legal description. This Patent will nonetheless be noted within the proper

Section along with any other Lots purchased in the Section. Given the scope of this project (many states and many Counties are being mapped), trying to locate all relevant plats for Lots (if they even exist) and accurately mapping them would have taken one person several lifetimes. But since our primary goal from the onset has been to establish relationships between neighbors and families, very little is lost to this goal since we can still observe who all lived in which Section.

C = Cancelled Patent

A Cancelled Patent is just that: cancelled. Whether the original Patentee forfeited his or her patent due to fraud, a technicality, non-payment, or whatever, the fact remains that it is significant to know who received patents for what parcels and when. A cancellation may be evidence that the Patentee never physically re-located to the land, but does not in itself prove that point. Further evidence would be required to prove that. *See also*, Re-issued Patents, *below*.

F = Fractional Section

A Fractional Section is one that contains less than 640 acres, almost always because of a body of water. The exact size and shape of land-parcels contained in such sections may not be ascertainable, but we map them nonetheless. Just keep in mind that we are not mapping an actual parcel to scale in such instances. Another point to consider is that we have located some fractional sections that are not so designated by the Bureau of Land Management in their data. This means that not all fractional sections have been so identified in our indexes.

G = Group
(Multi-Patentee Patent, see Appendix "C")

A "G" designation means that the Patent was issued to a GROUP of people (Multi-patentees). The "G" will always be followed by a number. Some such groups were quite large and it was impractical if not impossible to display each individual in our maps without unduly affecting readability. EACH person in the group is named in the Index, but they won't all be found on the Map. You will find the name of the first person in such a Group on the map with the Group number next to it, enclosed in [square brackets].

To find all the members of the Group you can either scan the Index for all people with the same Group Number or you can simply refer to Appendix "C" where all members of the Group are listed next to their number.

O = Overlaps another Parcel

An Overlap is one where PART of a parcel of land gets issued on more than one patent. For genealogical purposes, both transfers of title are important and both Patentees are mapped. If the ENTIRE parcel of land is re-issued, that is what we call it, a Re-Issued Patent (*see below*). The number after the "O" indicates the ID for the overlapping Patent(s) contained within the same Index. Like Re-Issued and Cancelled Patents, Overlaps may cause a map-reader to be confused at first, but for genealogical purposes, all of these parties' relationships to the underlying land is important, and therefore, we map them.

R = Re-Issued (Parcel patented more than once)

The label, "Re-issued Patent" describes Patents which were issued more than once for land with the EXACT SAME LEGAL DESCRIPTION. Whether the original patent was cancelled or not, there were a good many parcels which were patented more than once. The number after the "R" indicates the ID for the other Patent contained within the same Index that was for the same land. A quick glance at the map itself within the relevant Section will be the quickest way to find the other Patentee to whom the Parcel was transferred. They should both be mapped in the same general area.

I have gone to some length describing all sorts of anomalies either in the underlying data or in their representation on the maps and indexes in this book. Most of this will bore the most ardent reseracher, but I do this with all due respect to those researchers who will inevitably (and rightfully) ask: *"Why isn't so-and-so's name on the exact spot that the index says it should be?"*

In most cases it will be due to the existence of a Multi-Patentee Patent, a Re-issued Patent, a Cancelled Patent, or Overlapping Parcels named in separate Patents. I don't pretend that this discussion will answer every question along these lines, but I hope it will at least convince you of the complexity of the subject.

Not to despair, this book's companion web-site will offer a way to further explain "odd-ball" or errant data. Each book (County) will have its own web-page or pages to discuss such situations. You can go to www.arphax.com to find the relevant web-page for Washington County.

Land Patent Map

On the first two-page spread following each Township's Index to Land Patents, you'll find the corresponding Land Patent Map. And here lies the real heart of our work. For the first time anywhere, researchers will be able to observe and analyze, on a grand scale, most of the original land-owners for an area AND see them mapped in proximity to each one another.

We encourage you to make vigorous use of the accompanying Index described above, but then later, to abandon it, and just stare at these maps for a while. This is a great way to catch misspellings or to find collateral kin you'd not known were in the area.

Each Land Patent Map represents one Congressional Township containing approximately 36-square miles. Each of these square miles is labeled by an accompanying Section Number (1 through 36, in most cases). Keep in mind, that this book concerns itself solely with Washington County's patents. Townships which creep into one or more other counties will not be shown in their entirety in any one book. You will need to consult other books, as they become available, in order to view other countys' patents, cities, cemeteries, etc.

But getting back to Washington County: each Land Patent Map contains a Statistical Chart that looks like the following:

Township Statistics

Parcels Mapped	:	173
Number of Patents	:	163
Number of Individuals	:	152
Patentees Identified	:	151
Number of Surnames	:	137
Multi-Patentee Parcels	:	4
Oldest Patent Date	:	11/27/1820
Most Recent Patent	:	9/28/1917
Block/Lot Parcels	:	0
Parcels Re-Issued	:	3
Parcels that Overlap	:	8
Cities and Towns	:	6
Cemeteries	:	6

This information may be of more use to a social statistician or historian than a genealogist, but I think all three will find it interesting.

Most of the statistics are self-explanatory, and what is not, was described in the above discussion of the Index's Legend, but I do want to mention a few of them that may affect your understanding of the Land Patent Maps.

First of all, Patents often contain more than one Parcel of land, so it is common for there to be more Parcels than Patents. Also, the Number of Individuals will more often than not, not match the number of Patentees. A Patentee is literally the person or PERSONS named in a patent. So, a Patent may have a multi-person Patentee or a single-person patentee. Nonetheless, we account for all these individuals in our indexes.

On the lower-righthand side of the Patent Map is a Legend which describes various features in the map, including Section Boundaries, Patent (land) Boundaries, Lots (numbered), and Multi-Patentee Group Numbers. You'll also find a "Helpful Hints" Box that will assist you.

One important note: though the vast majority of Patents mapped in this series will prove to be reasonably accurate representations of their actual locations, we cannot claim this for patents lying along state and county lines, or waterways, or that have been platted (lots).

Shifting boundaries and sparse legal descriptions in the GLO data make this a reality that we have nonetheless tried to overcome by estimating these patents' locations the best that we can.

Road Map

On the two-page spread following each Patent Map you will find a Road Map covering the exact same area (the same Congressional Township).

For me, fully exploring the past means that every once in a while I must leave the library and travel to the actual locations where my ancestors once walked and worked the land. Our Township Road Maps are a great place to begin such a quest.

Keep in mind that the scaling and proportion of these maps was chosen in order to squeeze hundreds of people-names, road-names, and place-names into tinier spaces than you would traditionally see. These are not professional road-maps, and like any secondary genealogical source, should be looked upon as an entry-way to original sources—in this case, original patents and applications, professionally produced maps and surveys, etc.

Both our Road Maps and Historical Maps contain cemeteries and city-centers, along with a listing of these on the left-hand side of the map. I should note that I am showing you city center-points, rather than city-limit boundaries, because in many instances, this will represent a place where settlement began. This may be a good time to mention that many cemeteries are located on private property, Always check with a local historical or genealogical society to see if a particular cemetery is publicly accessible (if it is not obviously so). As a final point, look for your surnames among the road-names. You will often be surprised by what you find.

Historical Map

The third and final map in each Map Group is our attempt to display what each Township might have looked like before the advent of modern roads. In frontier times, people were usually more determined to settle near rivers and creeks than they were near roads, which were often few and far between. As was the case with the Road Map, we've included the same cemeteries and city-centers. We've also included railroads, many of which came along before most roads.

While some may claim "Historical Map" to be a bit of a misnomer for this tool, we settled for this label simply because it was almost as accurate as saying "Railroads, Lakes, Rivers, Cities, and Cemeteries," and it is much easier to remember.

In Closing . . .

By way of example, here is *A Really Good Way to Use a Township Map Group*. First, find the person you are researching in the Township's Index to Land Patents, which will direct you to the proper Section and parcel on the Patent Map. But before leaving the Index, scan all the patents within it, looking for other names of interest. Now, turn to the Patent Map and locate your parcels of land. Pay special attention to the names of patent-holders who own land surrounding your person of interest. Next, turn the page and look at the same Section(s) on the Road Map. Note which roads are closest to your parcels and also the names of nearby towns and cemeteries. Using other resources, you may be able to learn of kin who have been buried here, plus, you may choose to visit these cemeteries the next time you are in the area.

Finally, turn to the Historical Map. Look once more at the same Sections where you found your research subject's land. Note the nearby streams, creeks, and other geographical features. You may be surprised to find family names were used to name them, or you may see a name you haven't heard mentioned in years and years—and a new research possibility is born.

Many more techniques for using these *Family Maps* volumes will no doubt be discovered. If from time to time, you will navigate to Washington County's web-page at www.arphax.com (use the "Research" link), you can learn new tricks as they become known (or you can share ones you have employed). But for now, you are ready to get started. So, go, and good luck.

– Part I –

The Big Picture

Map A - Where Washington County, Missouri Lies Within the State

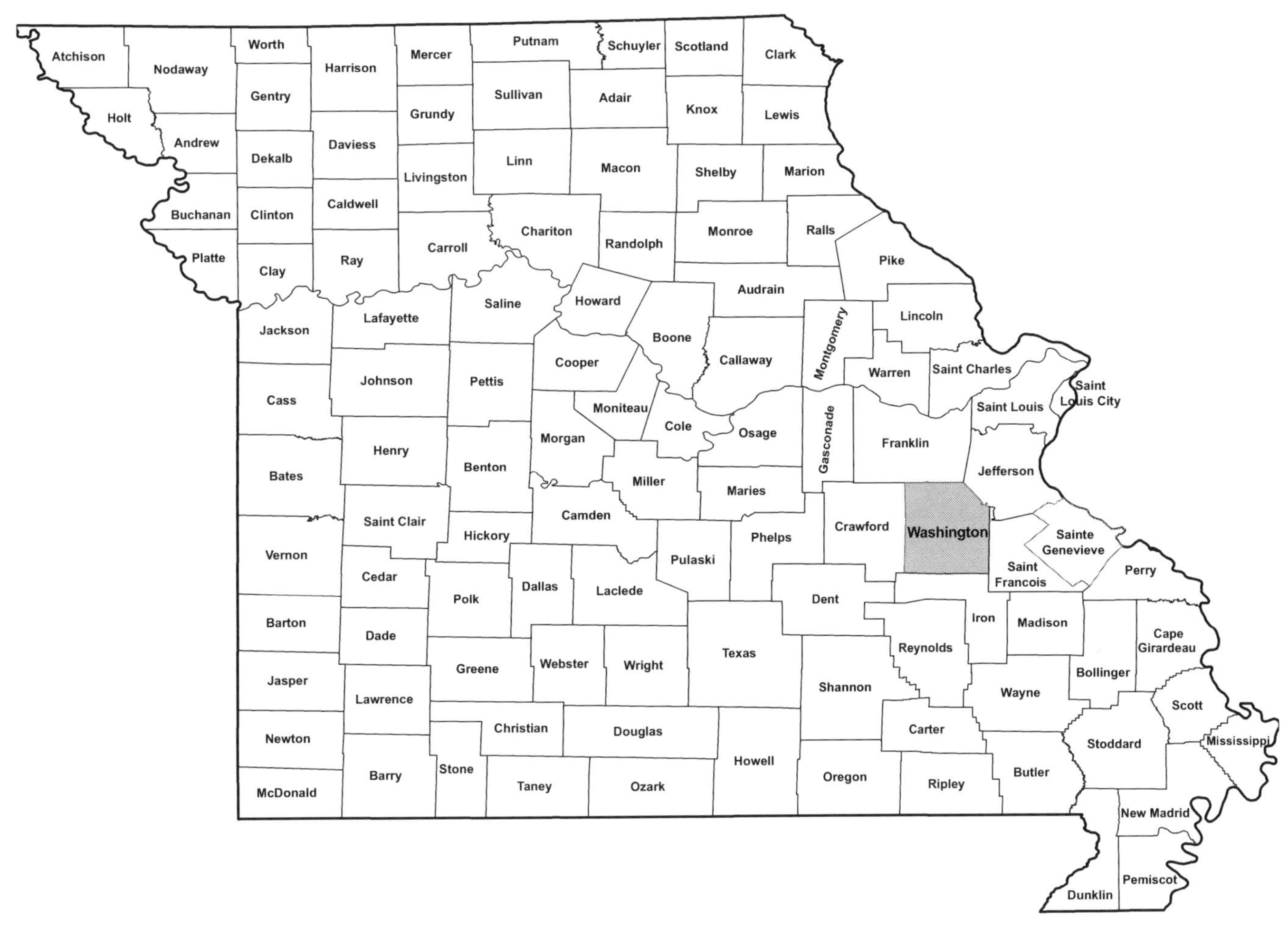

Legend

State Boundary

County Boundaries

Washington County, Missouri

Helpful Hints

1 We start with Map "A" which simply shows us where within the State this county lies.

2 Map "B" zooms in further to help us more easily identify surrounding Counties.

3 Map "C" zooms in even further to reveal the Congressional Townships that either lie within or intersect Washington County.

Map B - Washington County, Missouri and Surrounding Counties

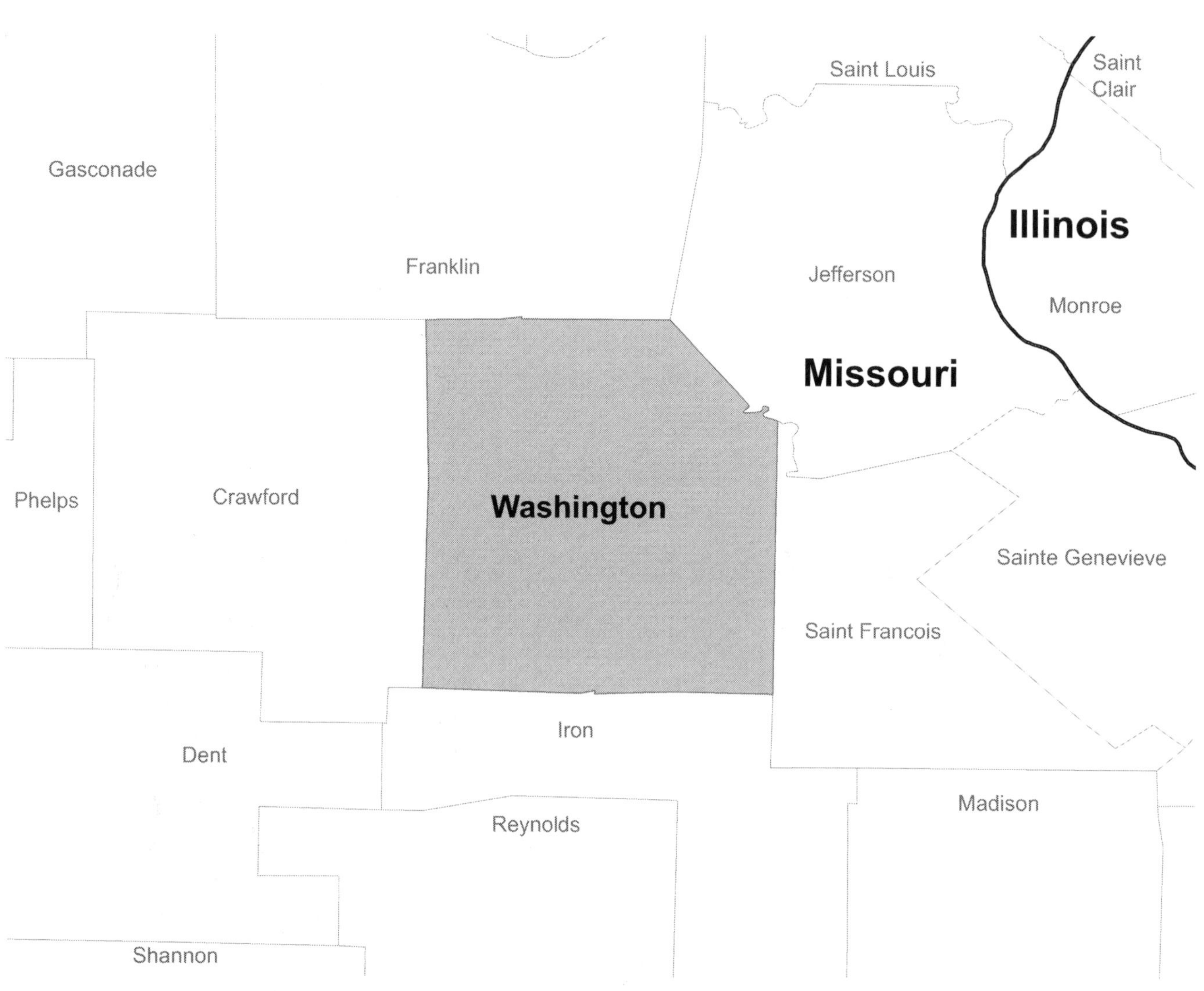

Legend

State Boundaries (when applicable)

County Boundary

Helpful Hints

1 Many Patent-holders and their families settled across county lines. It is always a good idea to check nearby counties for your families.

2 Refer to Map "A" to see a broader view of where this County lies within the State, and Map "C" to see which Congressional Townships lie within Washington County.

Map C - Congressional Townships of Washington County, Missouri

Legend

Washington County, Missouri

Congressional Townships

Helpful Hints

1 Many Patent-holders and their families settled across county lines. It is always a good idea to check nearby counties for your families (See Map "B").

2 Refer to Map "A" to see a broader view of where this county lies within the State, and Map "B" for a view of the counties surrounding Washington County.

Map D Index: Cities & Towns of Washington County, Missouri

The following represents the Cities and Towns of Washington County, along with the corresponding Map Group in which each is found. Cities and Towns are displayed in both the Road and Historical maps in the Group.

City/Town	Map Group No.
Adelbert (historical)	15
Anthonies Mill	7
Aptus	14
Baryties	10
Bates Creek Camp	19
Belgrade	24
Bellefontaine	15
Berryman	16
Bliss	10
Brazil	22
Cadet	15
Caledonia	29
Camp Lakewood	18
Cannon Mines	15
Courtois	27
Cruise Mill	10
Delbridge	22
Ebo	13
Fertile	10
Floyd	18
Fountain Farm	15
Fourche a Renault (historical)	13
French Town	20
Frogtown	14
Happy Hollow	15
Holiday Shores	30
Hopewell	20
Horton Town	28
Hulsey	2
Hurricane	4
Irondale	25
Ishmael	22
Latty	14
Levy	18
Maddens Richwoods	10
Mineral Point	20
Mud Town	15
Northcut	8
Old Mines	14
Palmer	22
Pea Ridge	7
Peoria	28
Potosi	19
Quaker	27
Rabbitville	10
Racola	14
Richwoods	4
Robidoux	14
Shibboleth	15
Shirley	18
Springtown	19
Summit	20
Sunlight	28
Theabeau Town	15
Tiff	15
White (historical)	15

Map D - Cities & Towns of Washington County, Missouri

Legend

Washington County, Missouri

Congressional Townships

Helpful Hints

1 Cities and towns are marked only at their center-points as published by the USGS and/or NationalAtlas.gov. This often enables us to more closely approximate where these might have existed when first settled.

2 To see more specifically where these Cities & Towns are located within the county, refer to both the Road and Historical maps in the Map-Group referred to above. See also, the Map "D" Index on the opposite page.

Map E Index: Cemeteries of Washington County, Missouri

The following represents many of the Cemeteries of Washington County, along with the corresponding Township Map Group in which each is found. Cemeteries are displayed in both the Road and Historical maps in the Map Groups referred to below.

Cemetery	Map Group No.
Anthonie's Mill Cem.	7
Antioch Cem.	27
Aquilla Cole Cem.	15
Arnold Cem.	3
Asplin Cem.	3
Barlow Cem.	15
Bates Creek Cem.	19
Belgrade Methodist Cem.	24
Bellvue Cem.	29
Bennett Bryan Cem.	24
Big River Cem.	25
Blount Cem.	18
Boas Cem.	20
Brick Cem.	15
Caledonia Cem.	29
Calvary Cem.	19
Carson Cem.	29
Chadbourne Cem.	19
City Cem.	19
Cresswell Cem.	17
Davis Cem.	24
Davis Cem.	30
Dry Branch Cem.	8
Emily Cem.	4
Fourche a Renault Cem.	13
Furnace Creek Cem.	24
Goff Cem.	15
Grassy Hollow Baptist Church Cem.	18
Griggs Cem.	8
Hazel Creek Cem.	23
Hickory Grove Cem.	25
Higginbotham Cem.	14
High Point-Missionary Ridge Cem.	18
Horine Cem.	4
Horton Cem.	28
Hughes Cem.	25
Jane Bryan Cem.	24
Jarvis Farm Cem.	20
Jenkins Family Cem.	23
Jinkerson Cem.	27
Jones Cem.	4
Joseph Chapel Cem.	27
Liberty Cem.	13
Lost Creek Cem.	17
Martin Cem.	13
Masonic Cem.	10
McClain Cem.	27
McGready Family Cem.	20
Metcalf Cem.	12
New Hope Cem.	2
Nicholson Cem.	19
Old Baptist Church Cem.	14
Palmer Cem.	22
Pea Ridge Cem.	2
Perry-McGready Cem.	19
Pleasant Hill Cem.	14
Potosi Colored Cem.	19
Potosi New Masonic Cem.	19
Potosi Old Masonic Cem.	19
Potosi Presbyterian Cem.	19
Redbud Memorial Gardens	19
Saint James Catholic Cem.	19
Saint Joachim Cem. Number 1	14
Saint Joachim Cem. Number 2	14
Saint Joachim Cem. Number 3	14
Saint Joseph Cem.	15
Saint Stephens Cem.	4
Scott Cem.	23
Scott-Reynolds Cem.	7
Shirley Union Church Cem.	18
Silvey Cem.	18
Sitton Cem.	23
Smith Cem.	8
Souls Chapel Cem.	13
Stephens Cem.	13
Sunlight Cem.	28
Sunset Hill Cem.	19
Swan Cem.	7
Thomas Chapel Cem.	29
Trinity Cem.	19
Tullock Cem.	29
Wallen Cem.	30
Whitby-Ellis Cem.	17
White Oak Grove Cem.	18
Wilson Family Cem.	18
Wright Cem.	23
Yarbrough Cem.	8

Map E - Cemeteries of Washington County, Missouri

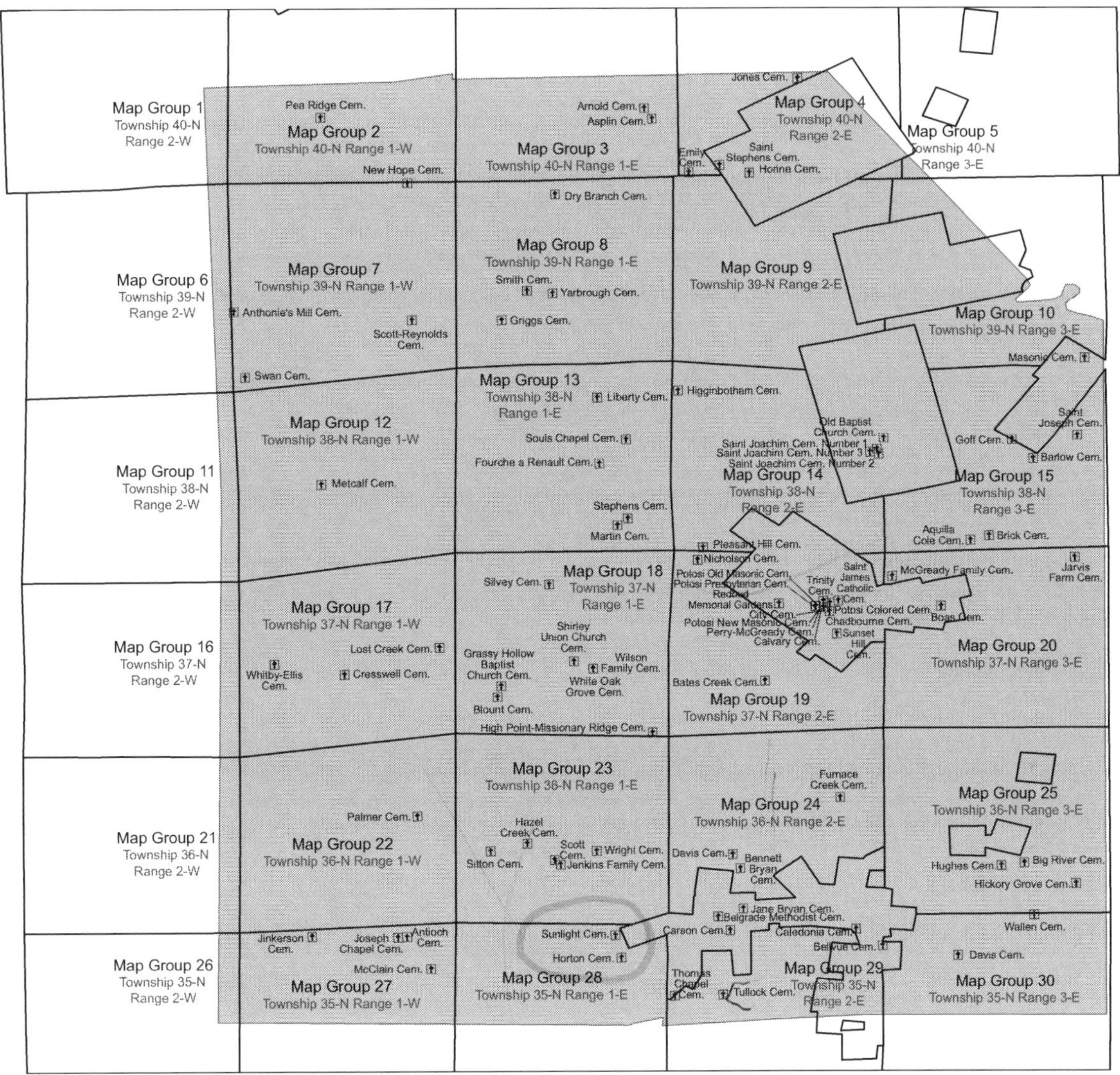

Legend

Washington County, Missouri

Congressional Townships

Helpful Hints

1 Cemeteries are marked at locations as published by the USGS and/or NationalAtlas.gov.

2 To see more specifically where these Cemeteries are located, refer to the Road & Historical maps in the Map-Group referred to above. See also, the Map "E" Index on the opposite page to make sure you don't miss any of the Cemeteries located within this Congressional township.

Surnames in Washington County, Missouri Patents

The following list represents the surnames that we have located in Washington County, Missouri Patents and the number of parcels that we have mapped for each one. Here is a quick way to determine the existence (or not) of Patents to be found in the subsequent indexes and maps of this volume.

Surname	# of Land Parcels
ADAMS	2
AGGUS	1
AKINSON	1
ALDERSON	1
ALDRIDGE	15
ALEXANDER	12
ALLADICE	3
ALLEN	8
ALLISON	3
ALMOND	2
AMELIN	1
AMELY	5
AMES	1
AMONETT	1
ANDERSON	7
ANDRES	1
ANTHONY	3
ANTON	1
ARCHAMBO	3
ARNDT	3
ARNOLD	4
ASHLEY	1
ATKINSON	4
ATTWOOD	1
AUBUCHON	1
AUGHEY	2
AUSTIN	5
BACON	5
BAILEY	1
BAIRD	2
BAIZE	2
BAKER	9
BALEW	1
BARBOUR	3
BARGER	2
BARKER	2
BARNES	1
BARRETT	2
BARRON	1
BARROW	2
BASS	8
BASSETT	1
BASSNETT	2
BATCHELDER	4
BATEMAN	6
BATTERSON	3
BATTREAL	1
BAUGHER	1
BAYS	1
BEACH	3
BEAN	2
BEAR	2
BELEW	4
BELFIELD	1
BELL	58
BELLFIELD	1
BENNETT	6
BENNING	3
BENOIST	1
BENOIT	2
BENSON	2
BENTON	1
BEQUETTE	13
BERGESCH	3
BERRY	5
BERRYMAN	6
BIBO	1
BIRCHFIELD	1
BLACK	4
BLACKFORD	2
BLACKWELL	5
BLAIN	1
BLAIR	3
BLANTON	11
BLEDSOE	1
BLICKBORN	1
BLOUNT	3
BLOW	5
BLUNT	8
BOAS	20
BOCKENKAMP	5
BOGGS	3
BOGY	2
BOHANNAN	2
BOHANNON	2
BOISAUBIN	4
BOLDUC	1
BOLLINGER	2
BOLTON	1
BOND	1
BONE	4
BOOTHE	4
BORGE	1
BORING	1
BORMAN	1
BOSWELL	1
BOTTO	1
BOUCHARD	1
BOULLIER	2
BOURBON	2
BOUSIN	1
BOWMAN	1
BOYD	2
BOYER	21
BOYLE	1
BOYNTON	4
BOZARTH	1
BRADLEY	1
BRADSHAW	1
BRAGG	2
BRAKEFIELD	1
BREDELL	7
BREDOLL	5
BREMAN	1
BREWINGTON	4
BRICKEY	6
BRIGGS	1
BRINCKWIRTH	4
BRINKER	2
BROCK	4
BROLASKI	16
BRONDAMOUR	4
BRONSON	2
BROOKS	3
BROWN	20
BROWNE	1
BRUCE	3
BRUEL	3
BRYAN	10
BRYNE	1
BUCHARD	2
BUCKLAND	2
BUCKLIN	1
BUFORD	1
BUGG	2
BUNYARD	3
BURDION	3
BUREN	3
BURGESS	3
BURK	5
BURNET	2
BURNETT	5
BURNS	2
BURROSSA	1
BURROWES	6
BURTON	3
BUSCH	1
BUSH	4
BUXTON	4
BYRD	2
BYRNE	1
CAIN	5
CAINE	1
CALLAWAY	3
CALVERD	2
CALVIRD	3
CAMERON	2
CAMMIER	1
CAMP	1
CAMPBELL	22
CANTRELL	1
CARPENTER	3
CARR	1
CARROLL	4
CARSON	12
CARTER	7
CARVER	1
CASEBOLT	1
CASEY	17
CASH	1
CASTLEMAN	4
CASWELL	1
CATEN	2
CATLETT	2
CATLIFF	1
CAVANAH	1
CAYCE	1
CAYLE	1
CHADBOURN	1
CHALFANT	6
CHAMBERS	1
CHANCE	2
CHANDLER	1
CHAPMAN	1
CHAPPEL	4
CHARBANO	1
CHARBONEAU	3
CHARBONO	1
CHARLEVILLE	1
CHEATHAM	3
CHICKEN	3
CHOUTEAU	1
CHRISTY	2
CLARK	17
CLARKSON	30
CLAUSEY	1
CLEMENT	1
CLEUFF	1
CLOUDY	1
CLUFF	1
COALMAN	2
COATWAY	1
COBURN	10
COCK	1
COE	2
COFFMAN	2
COLE	49
COLEMAN	12
COLEMANT	1
COLLIER	1
COLMAN	3
COMFORT	4
COMPTON	28
COMSTOCK	1
CONAWAY	1
CONNER	2
COOK	3
CORDIER	1
CORDIES	1
CORNELL	3
COTTARD	2
COUNTS	1
COURTIOL	1
COVER	5
COWAN	3
COXE	2
CRABTREE	1
CRAHAN	3
CRAIG	4
CRESSWELL	24
CRESWELL	16
CRISWELL	3
CROSSWELL	1
CROW	4
CROZIER	3
CRUMP	1
CULL	1
CULTON	2
CUMMINGS	1
CUMMINS	2
CUMPTON	2
CUNDIFF	2
CUNIFF	1
CUNNINGHAM	1
CURD	1
CURRY	4
CURTIN	1
DACE	2

Surname	# of Land Parcels
DANIEL	1
DANKLIN	1
DARBY	1
DARRAH	5
DAVIDSON	5
DAVIS	11
DAVISON	1
DAY	7
DAYTON	1
DE BOW	3
DE CLOUS	2
DEAN	2
DEANE	1
DECLOIS	5
DECLOS	1
DEEGAN	1
DEGURRIA	1
DELAFIELD	6
DELAURIERE	20
DELCOR	1
DELCOUR	2
DELY	1
DEMOSS	4
DENNING	4
DENNY	2
DENT	2
DENTON	1
DESLOGE	7
DETCHMENDY	1
DEVALIN	7
DIAMOND	3
DICKEY	12
DIKEMAN	1
DINGUID	2
DINNIDDIE	1
DINNISTON	1
DINWIDDIE	2
DOBKINS	1
DOLAN	3
DOLL	1
DONNA	3
DOTSON	6
DOTY	1
DOUGHERTY	9
DOUGLASS	3
DOWNARD	2
DOWNER	1
DOWNEY	1
DOYEN	2
DOYLE	2
DUCKWORTH	7
DUCLOS	3
DUCLOUS	1
DUDLEY	3
DUFF	3
DUNCAN	3
DUNKIN	2
DUNKLIN	5
DUPAVILLON	1
DURHAM	1
DUTY	3
DWANE	2
DYKE	1
EARS	1
EASOM	1
EASTIN	1
EATON	9
EDGAR	3
EDMANDS	1
EDMONDS	1

Surname	# of Land Parcels
EDMUNDS	1
EDWARDS	2
EFFINGER	3
EIDSON	1
ELLEDGE	1
ELLIOTT	2
ELLISON	2
ELMER	1
ENDLY	1
ENGLEDOW	2
ENLOE	3
ENOCH	4
ESTABROOK	3
ESTES	3
EUSTIS	5
EVANS	29
EVENS	34
EVERSOLE	1
EYE	2
FARISH	1
FARMER	1
FARQUHAR	2
FARRELL	15
FARRINGTON	2
FARRIS	7
FARRISS	3
FARROW	3
FASSETT	4
FEA	3
FELL	3
FENISON	2
FENNISON	2
FERGUSON	4
FERIE	1
FEROLL	1
FICKES	8
FIEDELDEY	5
FIELD	3
FIFER	2
FINISON	2
FINK	4
FINLEY	4
FISHER	9
FITCH	2
FITZWATER	5
FLANAGAN	1
FLEMING	2
FLEMMING	2
FLINN	1
FLOTTEMSCH	6
FLOWERS	6
FLYNN	8
FOGARTY	2
FORD	4
FORESTER	3
FORREST	3
FORRESTER	4
FORTNER	2
FORTUNE	1
FOSTER	9
FRAME	2
FRAYSER	1
FRAZER	2
FRENCH	5
FRISSEL	1
FRISSELL	11
FRITTS	1
FRITZ	1
FRIZZLE	1
GALE	6

Surname	# of Land Parcels
GALLAGHER	4
GALLAHER	1
GALLAUGHER	2
GALLEY	1
GALLOWAY	1
GAMACHE	1
GAMBLE	5
GAN	2
GARRETT	4
GARRISON	1
GARRISSON	1
GARRITY	1
GARTSIDE	9
GARVIN	1
GATES	1
GATY	2
GAUGH	3
GAY	5
GELLENBECK	1
GENERELLY	3
GENSIL	2
GEORGE	1
GEZZI	3
GHOLSON	3
GIBSON	17
GILCHRIST	9
GILLAM	5
GILLIAM	10
GILMORE	2
GIPSON	1
GIRARDIER	5
GLENN	6
GLORE	6
GOADE	5
GOBBETT	1
GODARD	1
GODAT	1
GOFF	4
GOFORTH	6
GOGAY	1
GOLDEN	3
GOLDING	5
GOLDSBERG	1
GOODRICH	1
GOULD	1
GOVRO	1
GRADE	1
GRADON	1
GRAGG	3
GRANT	2
GRAVES	4
GREEN	2
GREENE	1
GREENLEE	1
GREGG	3
GREGORY	8
GRIDER	2
GRIFFIN	3
GRIFFITH	2
GRIMES	3
GRINEA	2
GRISHAM	1
GROGG	1
GROOM	2
GROOMS	3
GROSS	2
GUINN	5
GUSHEE	4
GUT	1
GUY	1

Surname	# of Land Parcels
HAAS	3
HAEFNER	8
HAENSSLER	1
HAGGARD	2
HAIGH	1
HALL	7
HALLIDAY	2
HAMBLETON	1
HAMILTON	1
HANCOCK	4
HANGER	2
HANS	1
HANSON	5
HARGES	1
HARGIS	1
HARGRAVE	2
HARLOW	1
HARMAN	8
HARMON	1
HARPER	14
HARRINGTON	1
HARRIS	15
HARRISON	20
HARRTY	1
HARVER	2
HARVEY	1
HATHORN	1
HAUS	1
HAVEN	1
HAWKINS	19
HAY	1
HAYNES	1
HAYS	14
HEARST	4
HEARTY	1
HEINE	2
HEITZ	1
HELLIARD	2
HELMICK	1
HENDERSON	9
HENRY	3
HENSLEE	1
HENSLEY	5
HENSON	3
HENWOOD	4
HERELSON	1
HERSHEY	1
HESSE	4
HEWIT	6
HIBBARD	2
HIBLER	9
HICKERSON	1
HICKLEY	1
HICKS	6
HIGGENBOTHAM	4
HIGGINBOTHAM	14
HIGGINBOTHOM	2
HIGGINS	2
HIGHLEY	2
HIGHLY	2
HIGHT	6
HILL	19
HILLEN	8
HIMMLEY	4
HINCH	7
HINDRICKER	1
HINDS	2
HINKSON	3
HINSON	1
HIRSH	1

Surname	# of Land Parcels
HOBAN	1
HOFF	5
HOGAN	4
HOLDEN	2
HOLLINGSWORTH	2
HOLLINSWORTH	3
HOLMES	4
HOLT	10
HOOTER	1
HOPKINS	2
HORBISON	1
HORINE	3
HORNEY	3
HORNSEY	2
HORROCKS	2
HORTON	10
HOUK	1
HOUSE	4
HOUSEMAN	6
HOWARD	11
HOWE	8
HOWELL	1
HUDLESTON	1
HUDSON	6
HUDSPETH	22
HUFF	6
HUFSTETTER	1
HUGHES	33
HUITT	7
HULL	2
HULSEY	6
HUNT	19
HUNTER	9
HURD	1
HUTCHINGS	13
HUTCHISON	1
HYNSON	2
HYPOLITE	2
HYPOTITE	1
IMBODEN	7
INGE	4
IRVIN	1
IRVINE	4
ISGRIG	6
ISRAEL	1
JACKSON	14
JACO	1
JACOBS	2
JACOMELLA	2
JAMISON	19
JANIS	2
JANNEY	2
JARDIN	4
JARRELL	1
JARVIS	22
JENKINS	3
JENNINGS	2
JETT	2
JIMMERSON	1
JINKERSON	2
JINKINS	3
JOHNSON	74
JOHNSTON	15
JOLLIN	1
JONES	17
JORDAN	2
JUDD	4
KANE	2
KAVANAUGH	1
KEAN	1

Surname	# of Land Parcels
KEARNS	1
KEAUGH	1
KEENE	2
KEISEN	2
KELLEHER	3
KELLER	2
KELLY	3
KENDALL	1
KENNER	2
KENNETT	2
KEOUGH	1
KERDER	1
KERSEY	1
KERSHAW	5
KESSLER	1
KIESEN	3
KILLPACK	1
KIMBERLIN	5
KIMBERLING	1
KING	16
KINKAID	1
KINKEAD	2
KINSEY	1
KIRBY	4
KIRKPATRICK	11
KIRKWOOD	5
KIRTLAND	1
KLEIN	7
KNIGHT	3
KRAFT	1
KULKE	1
KUMER	3
LA BARGE	2
LABAUME	2
LABRAUME	2
LACY	2
LAMARAQUE	1
LAMARQUE	12
LANCASTER	8
LAND	2
LANGE	1
LANINS	2
LANIUS	1
LARAMORE	11
LARGENT	1
LARUE	1
LASWELL	1
LATIMER	1
LATTIMER	1
LATUNIO	1
LE BOURGEOIS	4
LEA	4
LEAGUE	3
LEAKY	1
LECLARE	2
LECLERE	3
LEFFINGWELL	1
LEFFLER	2
LEGERET	2
LEONARD	2
LERSHALL	1
LEVENS	1
LEVY	4
LEWIS	8
LIBBY	3
LIBHART	1
LIGHTFOOT	1
LINK	1
LINN	3
LITTEN	4

Surname	# of Land Parcels
LITTLE	1
LIVERMORE	2
LIVINGSTON	5
LOCKE	1
LOGAN	4
LONDON	5
LONG	45
LOOMIS	1
LORE	3
LOWERY	1
LUCAS	14
LUMPKINS	1
LUPTON	6
LUTS	2
LYNCH	5
LYON	1
MACK	3
MACKAY	3
MACKENZIE	1
MACKY	1
MADDEN	4
MADDIN	1
MADDY	1
MAHENY	2
MAIDES	5
MAIRAT	1
MAJOR	6
MALLE	1
MALLOW	2
MANES	6
MANESS	7
MANEY	4
MANION	7
MANN	2
MANNING	42
MANSFIELD	1
MANWARING	1
MARA	1
MARAS	1
MARCILLE	1
MARGETTS	1
MARLE	1
MARLEE	1
MARLER	8
MARQUESS	1
MARSH	1
MARSHALL	10
MARTIN	17
MARTINDALE	1
MASHMEYER	2
MASON	16
MASSIE	1
MATCHELL	1
MATHEWS	4
MATHIS	2
MATLOCK	8
MATTHEWS	42
MAUL	1
MAUNDER	1
MAURICE	3
MAXWELL	7
MAYGER	3
MAYHEW	1
MCANULTY	8
MCBRIDE	5
MCCABE	4
MCCANTEY	1
MCCAUSLAND	4
MCCHESNEY	5
MCCLAIN	1

Surname	# of Land Parcels
MCCLOWNY	1
MCCORMICK	4
MCCRACKEN	4
MCCREARY	4
MCCREERY	1
MCCUNE	3
MCCURDY	1
MCCURRY	1
MCDONALD	3
MCDONOUGH	2
MCDOWELL	2
MCEWIN	1
MCGAHAN	4
MCGINN	1
MCGRADY	4
MCGREADY	14
MCGREW	1
MCGUIRE	1
MCILVAIN	5
MCILVAINE	8
MCINTIRE	1
MCKEAN	1
MCKEE	2
MCKENZIE	1
MCKEON	6
MCLANE	1
MCMANUS	1
MCMILLEN	1
MCMURTREY	3
MCNABB	1
MCNALLY	1
MCNEAL	2
MCPEAKE	1
MCPHAILL	1
MCSPADEN	1
MELVIN	1
MERCEILLE	7
MERCER	2
MERCILE	2
MERRY	8
MERRYMAN	1
MESEY	1
MESPLAY	7
METCALF	5
MEYER	1
MEYERS	3
MIDGETT	1
MIDYETT	5
MILLER	6
MILLIGAN	4
MINCK	2
MISEY	1
MISPLAY	1
MITCHELL	7
MOLLY	1
MONDAY	1
MONTGOMERY	12
MOODY	4
MOORE	11
MOREL	1
MORELAND	3
MORGAN	4
MORRIS	2
MORRISON	8
MORRISSON	1
MORROW	3
MOSES	2
MOSHER	1
MOSLANDER	3
MOTHERSHEAD	6

Surname	# of Land Parcels	Surname	# of Land Parcels	Surname	# of Land Parcels	Surname	# of Land Parcels
MOULTRAY	1	PEASE	6	RELFE	22	SHOTWELL	1
MOUNT	1	PECK	2	REMY	1	SHOULTS	1
MOUTRAY	3	PEEBLES	4	RENFRO	3	SHUMATE	5
MUDD	1	PEERY	2	RENN	1	SHURTLEFF	1
MUNDAY	2	PEIRCE	1	REVES	2	SHUTTE	1
MUNDY	2	PELICAN	1	REYBURN	1	SIGNAIGO	5
MURPHEY	6	PENROSE	1	REYNOLDS	4	SILENCE	3
MURPHY	19	PENYMAN	2	RICE	8	SILVER	1
MURRILL	2	PERKINS	1	RICHARDSON	2	SILVERS	11
MYERS	10	PERKS	2	RIDGWAY	2	SILVEY	9
NAUMAN	1	PERRY	28	RIENDO	1	SILVY	2
NAVE	1	PERRYMAN	3	RILEY	1	SIMMONS	2
NEALY	1	PERSHALL	7	RISSER	1	SIMONS	1
NEFF	3	PETER	2	ROBERSON	2	SIMPSON	6
NETTLETON	2	PETERS	1	ROBERT	1	SIMS	1
NEUSE	2	PETERSON	2	ROBERTS	2	SINEX	1
NEVES	1	PETTIGREW	4	ROBINSON	34	SITTON	5
NEVISON	2	PHILLIPS	1	RODDA	1	SKEWES	5
NICHOLAS	2	PHILPOT	1	RODERICK	2	SLOAN	12
NICHOLS	2	PICKERING	1	ROGERS	4	SLOANE	1
NICHOLSON	10	PICKLES	4	ROLFE	1	SLOSS	3
NIEHANS	5	PIERCE	5	ROLL	3	SMITH	166
NIEHAUS	3	PINSON	9	ROMAINE	1	SMITHER	1
NILEND	2	POINDEXTER	1	RONGEY	2	SONSUCIE	2
NOEL	1	POLITTE	1	RONGY	1	SOUCI	1
NORP	3	POLLARD	1	ROONEY	7	SOULARD	4
NORRIS	3	POPE	1	ROOT	2	SPEAR	2
NORTHCUT	2	PORTAIS	1	ROSE	2	SPEERS	1
NORTRUP	1	PORTEL	2	ROSS	1	SPENCER	1
NORVELL	2	PORTELL	2	ROUSAN	1	SPRINGER	18
NUESE	5	PORTER	3	ROUSIN	6	STACEY	1
OBRIEN	2	POUND	1	ROUSSIN	12	STAFFORD	4
OBUCHAN	1	POWELL	8	ROZIER	4	STAMM	1
OBUCHON	6	POWER	1	RUGGLES	2	STANDEFER	2
OCHELTREE	1	POWERS	4	RULO	3	STAPLES	5
OFARRELL	1	PRADER	5	RUMELL	1	STAPPLES	1
OFARROLL	3	PRATHER	3	RUSS	1	STATLER	3
OGDEN	1	PRATT	2	RUSSELL	3	STEAD	1
OHANLIN	2	PRATTE	1	RUTLEDGE	1	STEERMAN	4
OHANLON	3	PREWETT	2	SANDERS	4	STEMBER	1
OHARVER	1	PREWITT	1	SANSOCIE	2	STEPHENS	4
OLIVER	2	PRICE	1	SAPPINGTON	2	STEPHENSON	3
OMARA	1	PROFFETT	1	SAUNDERS	6	STEVENS	2
ONEIL	2	PROFIT	1	SAWYER	1	STEVENSON	7
ORCHARD	2	PROFITT	2	SCHANE	1	STEWART	13
ORCHARDS	1	PROSS	3	SCHARIT	2	STOFER	1
ORME	3	PROVENCE	1	SCHENCK	1	STOLLE	1
OTTMAN	1	PRUDEN	1	SCHIEBEL	1	STONE	19
OUTLAY	1	PRUETT	1	SCHNEIDER	1	STONER	4
OWENS	11	PRYOR	1	SCHOOL	1	STONG	1
PAGE	8	PUCKETT	7	SCHUTTE	1	STOVALL	2
PAINE	2	PULLAM	1	SCHWICE	2	STOW	2
PALMATORY	3	PULLIAM	1	SCOTT	39	STRAUSER	2
PALMER	1	PURSLEY	7	SELF	6	STROHBECK	3
PARK	3	PYATT	5	SENSENDERFER	2	STRONG	2
PARKER	7	QUEEN	1	SERVICE	1	STROTHER	1
PARKIN	6	RACINE	1	SEYMOUR	8	STUART	2
PARKINSON	8	RAMBO	1	SHAW	1	STUDLEY	4
PARKS	2	RAMSEY	14	SHEPHERD	7	SUHR	1
PARMER	2	RANDALL	1	SHERLOCK	4	SUICOCK	2
PARTENAY	2	RANEY	3	SHIELDS	2	SULLIVAN	2
PATCH	2	RANNEY	2	SHIMIN	1	SULLIVANTE	2
PATTEN	1	RATLEY	2	SHIRLEY	4	SUMMERS	9
PATTERSON	2	RAY	3	SHIRLOCK	1	SUMPTER	1
PATTON	6	READING	1	SHMELL	1	SUTTON	11
PAUL	2	REANDEAU	1	SHOLAR	1	SWAIN	1
PAWLING	1	REANDO	3	SHONBACKER	3	SWAN	5
PEAK	2	RECTOR	1	SHOOK	3	SWENDT	1
PEARSHALL	2	REED	14	SHOOKS	1	SWIER	1
PEARSON	3	REID	3	SHORE	13	SWOFFORD	2

Surname	# of Land Parcels
TALBOT	2
TANEY	2
TASCHETTA	2
TAUSSIG	2
TAYLOR	17
TEAS	2
TEDDER	6
TEMBY	2
TENISON	1
TENNESON	2
TENNISON	6
THAYER	3
THEBEAU	4
THIBEAU	2
THODD	1
THOMAS	16
THOMPSON	18
THORP	5
THURMOND	2
THWING	1
TIBEAN	2
TIBEAU	1
TIFFT	2
TILLSON	7
TINISON	7
TINKERSON	2
TODD	14
TORINI	1
TOWNSEND	1
TRAMMELL	1
TREMLETT	1
TRIMBLE	2
TRIPP	1
TRIPPE	1
TROKY	1
TROUTT	1
TROXELL	2
TRUDAU	1
TUCKER	6
TUFLY	1
TULLOCK	3
TURNBAUGH	1
TURNBOUGH	3
TURNER	8
TURPIN	1
TWITTY	2
TYREY	1
TYZACK	1
ULLMAN	4
VALENTIN	1
VALLE	3
VALLEY	3
VAN FRANK	1
VAN HOUTEN	2
VAN REED	11
VANDIVER	1
VARNER	1
VERNER	2
VICTOR	1
VIENNA	3
VILLEMAR	1
VILLMARE	2
VILMAIN	1
VILMAR	3
VINEYARD	1
VINYARD	2
VIVRETT	1
VORNBERG	5
WADE	1
WALKER	4
WALLEN	27
WALSER	2
WALTHALL	1
WALTON	70
WARD	11
WARDEN	1
WARE	5
WARNER	3
WARSON	1
WATERS	3
WATKINS	1
WATSON	1
WAUGH	1
WEIDLE	1
WEIGER	1
WEIGHER	1
WELKER	6
WELLS	1
WELSH	1
WESTENFELT	3
WESTHOVER	1
WESTOVER	9
WETER	1
WHALEY	1
WHAYLEY	1
WHEALAN	2
WHEALEY	4
WHITBY	1
WHITE	38
WHITEHEAD	1
WHITENER	11
WHITLEY	2
WHITMIRE	1
WHYERS	3
WIATT	4
WICKERS	4
WICKS	3
WIGGER	9
WILCOX	2
WILDER	3
WILDMAN	3
WILKERSON	3
WILKINSON	8
WILKSON	3
WILLARD	10
WILLIAMS	19
WILLOUGHBY	1
WILMESHERR	1
WILSON	9
WIMER	1
WINDER	1
WINEOUR	3
WISDOM	2
WOLLIN	1
WOOD	13
WOODARD	4
WOODRUFF	2
WOODS	9
WOOLFORD	2
WOOLSAY	1
WORTHAM	2
WORTHINGTON	3
WRIGHT	25
WYATT	1
XENO	1
YATES	5
YEATES	1
YEAUGHBERRY	1
YELLER	2
YODER	3
YOUGHBERRY	1
YOUNG	1
YOUNT	10
ZENT	1
ZOLMAN	2

Surname/Township Index

This Index allows you to determine which *Township Map Group(s)* contain individuals with the following surnames. Each *Map Group* has a corresponding full-name index of all individuals who obtained patents for land within its Congressional township's borders. After each index you will find the Patent Map to which it refers, and just thereafter, you can view the township's Road Map and Historical Map, with the latter map displaying streams, railroads, and more.

So, once you find your Surname here, proceed to the Index at the beginning of the **Map Group** indicated below.

Surname	Map Group	Parcels of Land	Meridian/Township/Range
ADAMS	**23**	2	5th PM 36-N 1-E
AGGUS	**25**	1	5th PM 36-N 3-E
AKINSON	**14**	1	5th PM 38-N 2-E
ALDERSON	**10**	1	5th PM 39-N 3-E
ALDRIDGE	**28**	11	5th PM 35-N 1-E
" "	**23**	3	5th PM 36-N 1-E
" "	**24**	1	5th PM 36-N 2-E
ALEXANDER	**30**	8	5th PM 35-N 3-E
" "	**9**	3	5th PM 39-N 2-E
" "	**14**	1	5th PM 38-N 2-E
ALLADICE	**3**	3	5th PM 40-N 1-E
ALLEN	**12**	5	5th PM 38-N 1-W
" "	**18**	2	5th PM 37-N 1-E
" "	**19**	1	5th PM 37-N 2-E
ALLISON	**9**	3	5th PM 39-N 2-E
ALMOND	**27**	2	5th PM 35-N 1-W
AMELIN	**4**	1	5th PM 40-N 2-E
AMELY	**9**	4	5th PM 39-N 2-E
" "	**8**	1	5th PM 39-N 1-E
AMES	**2**	1	5th PM 40-N 1-W
AMONETT	**24**	1	5th PM 36-N 2-E
ANDERSON	**13**	3	5th PM 38-N 1-E
" "	**16**	2	5th PM 37-N 2-W
" "	**3**	1	5th PM 40-N 1-E
" "	**2**	1	5th PM 40-N 1-W
ANDRES	**8**	1	5th PM 39-N 1-E
ANTHONY	**6**	3	5th PM 39-N 2-W
ANTON	**10**	1	5th PM 39-N 3-E
ARCHAMBO	**10**	3	5th PM 39-N 3-E
ARNDT	**10**	3	5th PM 39-N 3-E
ARNOLD	**20**	3	5th PM 37-N 3-E
" "	**28**	1	5th PM 35-N 1-E
ASHLEY	**7**	1	5th PM 39-N 1-W
ATKINSON	**18**	4	5th PM 37-N 1-E
ATTWOOD	**14**	1	5th PM 38-N 2-E
AUBUCHON	**15**	1	5th PM 38-N 3-E
AUGHEY	**23**	2	5th PM 36-N 1-E
AUSTIN	**28**	5	5th PM 35-N 1-E
BACON	**30**	4	5th PM 35-N 3-E
" "	**22**	1	5th PM 36-N 1-W
BAILEY	**1**	1	5th PM 40-N 2-W
BAIRD	**23**	1	5th PM 36-N 1-E
" "	**22**	1	5th PM 36-N 1-W
BAIZE	**18**	2	5th PM 37-N 1-E

Surname	Map Group	Parcels of Land	Meridian/Township/Range
BAKER	**10**	4	5th PM 39-N 3-E
" "	**7**	2	5th PM 39-N 1-W
" "	**26**	1	5th PM 35-N 2-W
" "	**20**	1	5th PM 37-N 3-E
" "	**9**	1	5th PM 39-N 2-E
BALEW	**17**	1	5th PM 37-N 1-W
BARBOUR	**3**	3	5th PM 40-N 1-E
BARGER	**28**	2	5th PM 35-N 1-E
BARKER	**28**	1	5th PM 35-N 1-E
" "	**3**	1	5th PM 40-N 1-E
BARNES	**7**	1	5th PM 39-N 1-W
BARRETT	**13**	2	5th PM 38-N 1-E
BARRON	**18**	1	5th PM 37-N 1-E
BARROW	**20**	2	5th PM 37-N 3-E
BASS	**13**	5	5th PM 38-N 1-E
" "	**3**	2	5th PM 40-N 1-E
" "	**14**	1	5th PM 38-N 2-E
BASSETT	**2**	1	5th PM 40-N 1-W
BASSNETT	**28**	2	5th PM 35-N 1-E
BATCHELDER	**23**	4	5th PM 36-N 1-E
BATEMAN	**27**	3	5th PM 35-N 1-W
" "	**21**	3	5th PM 36-N 2-W
BATTERSON	**28**	3	5th PM 35-N 1-E
BATTREAL	**10**	1	5th PM 39-N 3-E
BAUGHER	**3**	1	5th PM 40-N 1-E
BAYS	**14**	1	5th PM 38-N 2-E
BEACH	**16**	3	5th PM 37-N 2-W
BEAN	**22**	2	5th PM 36-N 1-W
BEAR	**23**	1	5th PM 36-N 1-E
" "	**22**	1	5th PM 36-N 1-W
BELEW	**12**	3	5th PM 38-N 1-W
" "	**16**	1	5th PM 37-N 2-W
BELFIELD	**20**	1	5th PM 37-N 3-E
BELL	**22**	50	5th PM 36-N 1-W
" "	**24**	3	5th PM 36-N 2-E
" "	**13**	2	5th PM 38-N 1-E
" "	**16**	1	5th PM 37-N 2-W
" "	**14**	1	5th PM 38-N 2-E
" "	**10**	1	5th PM 39-N 3-E
BELLFIELD	**20**	1	5th PM 37-N 3-E
BENNETT	**9**	3	5th PM 39-N 2-E
" "	**18**	2	5th PM 37-N 1-E
" "	**14**	1	5th PM 38-N 2-E
BENNING	**24**	2	5th PM 36-N 2-E
" "	**23**	1	5th PM 36-N 1-E
BENOIST	**2**	1	5th PM 40-N 1-W
BENOIT	**4**	2	5th PM 40-N 2-E
BENSON	**7**	1	5th PM 39-N 1-W
" "	**6**	1	5th PM 39-N 2-W
BENTON	**4**	1	5th PM 40-N 2-E
BEQUETTE	**10**	9	5th PM 39-N 3-E
" "	**15**	2	5th PM 38-N 3-E
" "	**9**	2	5th PM 39-N 2-E
BERGESCH	**12**	3	5th PM 38-N 1-W
BERRY	**4**	3	5th PM 40-N 2-E
" "	**12**	1	5th PM 38-N 1-W
" "	**9**	1	5th PM 39-N 2-E
BERRYMAN	**17**	4	5th PM 37-N 1-W
" "	**22**	1	5th PM 36-N 1-W
" "	**16**	1	5th PM 37-N 2-W

Surname	Map Group	Parcels of Land	Meridian/Township/Range
BIBO	**8**	1	5th PM 39-N 1-E
BIRCHFIELD	**1**	1	5th PM 40-N 2-W
BLACK	**28**	3	5th PM 35-N 1-E
" "	**30**	1	5th PM 35-N 3-E
BLACKFORD	**29**	2	5th PM 35-N 2-E
BLACKWELL	**15**	3	5th PM 38-N 3-E
" "	**22**	2	5th PM 36-N 1-W
BLAIN	**20**	1	5th PM 37-N 3-E
BLAIR	**27**	1	5th PM 35-N 1-W
" "	**10**	1	5th PM 39-N 3-E
" "	**1**	1	5th PM 40-N 2-W
BLANTON	**12**	7	5th PM 38-N 1-W
" "	**2**	3	5th PM 40-N 1-W
" "	**29**	1	5th PM 35-N 2-E
BLEDSOE	**18**	1	5th PM 37-N 1-E
BLICKBORN	**14**	1	5th PM 38-N 2-E
BLOUNT	**18**	2	5th PM 37-N 1-E
" "	**17**	1	5th PM 37-N 1-W
BLOW	**9**	5	5th PM 39-N 2-E
BLUNT	**18**	4	5th PM 37-N 1-E
" "	**23**	2	5th PM 36-N 1-E
" "	**17**	2	5th PM 37-N 1-W
BOAS	**20**	9	5th PM 37-N 3-E
" "	**22**	4	5th PM 36-N 1-W
" "	**15**	3	5th PM 38-N 3-E
" "	**24**	2	5th PM 36-N 2-E
" "	**30**	1	5th PM 35-N 3-E
" "	**17**	1	5th PM 37-N 1-W
BOCKENKAMP	**8**	5	5th PM 39-N 1-E
BOGGS	**20**	2	5th PM 37-N 3-E
" "	**19**	1	5th PM 37-N 2-E
BOGY	**3**	2	5th PM 40-N 1-E
BOHANNAN	**18**	2	5th PM 37-N 1-E
BOHANNON	**18**	2	5th PM 37-N 1-E
BOISAUBIN	**23**	4	5th PM 36-N 1-E
BOLDUC	**10**	1	5th PM 39-N 3-E
BOLLINGER	**17**	1	5th PM 37-N 1-W
" "	**16**	1	5th PM 37-N 2-W
BOLTON	**2**	1	5th PM 40-N 1-W
BOND	**8**	1	5th PM 39-N 1-E
BONE	**20**	4	5th PM 37-N 3-E
BOOTHE	**17**	3	5th PM 37-N 1-W
" "	**18**	1	5th PM 37-N 1-E
BORGE	**10**	1	5th PM 39-N 3-E
BORING	**20**	1	5th PM 37-N 3-E
BORMAN	**27**	1	5th PM 35-N 1-W
BOSWELL	**23**	1	5th PM 36-N 1-E
BOTTO	**27**	1	5th PM 35-N 1-W
BOUCHARD	**8**	1	5th PM 39-N 1-E
BOULLIER	**14**	2	5th PM 38-N 2-E
BOURBON	**8**	1	5th PM 39-N 1-E
" "	**4**	1	5th PM 40-N 2-E
BOUSIN	**5**	1	5th PM 40-N 3-E
BOWMAN	**12**	1	5th PM 38-N 1-W
BOYD	**12**	1	5th PM 38-N 1-W
" "	**10**	1	5th PM 39-N 3-E
BOYER	**15**	12	5th PM 38-N 3-E
" "	**10**	4	5th PM 39-N 3-E
" "	**8**	2	5th PM 39-N 1-E
" "	**9**	2	5th PM 39-N 2-E

Surname	Map Group	Parcels of Land	Meridian/Township/Range
BOYER (Cont'd)	**14**	1	5th PM 38-N 2-E
BOYLE	**15**	1	5th PM 38-N 3-E
BOYNTON	**12**	4	5th PM 38-N 1-W
BOZARTH	**25**	1	5th PM 36-N 3-E
BRADLEY	**25**	1	5th PM 36-N 3-E
BRADSHAW	**22**	1	5th PM 36-N 1-W
BRAGG	**24**	1	5th PM 36-N 2-E
" "	**18**	1	5th PM 37-N 1-E
BRAKEFIELD	**22**	1	5th PM 36-N 1-W
BREDELL	**1**	4	5th PM 40-N 2-W
" "	**7**	2	5th PM 39-N 1-W
" "	**2**	1	5th PM 40-N 1-W
BREDOLL	**6**	5	5th PM 39-N 2-W
BREMAN	**28**	1	5th PM 35-N 1-E
BREWINGTON	**30**	4	5th PM 35-N 3-E
BRICKEY	**20**	2	5th PM 37-N 3-E
" "	**23**	1	5th PM 36-N 1-E
" "	**17**	1	5th PM 37-N 1-W
" "	**19**	1	5th PM 37-N 2-E
" "	**14**	1	5th PM 38-N 2-E
BRIGGS	**13**	1	5th PM 38-N 1-E
BRINCKWIRTH	**12**	4	5th PM 38-N 1-W
BRINKER	**29**	1	5th PM 35-N 2-E
" "	**25**	1	5th PM 36-N 3-E
BROCK	**18**	3	5th PM 37-N 1-E
" "	**17**	1	5th PM 37-N 1-W
BROLASKI	**24**	8	5th PM 36-N 2-E
" "	**19**	5	5th PM 37-N 2-E
" "	**20**	2	5th PM 37-N 3-E
" "	**25**	1	5th PM 36-N 3-E
BRONDAMOUR	**23**	4	5th PM 36-N 1-E
BRONSON	**20**	2	5th PM 37-N 3-E
BROOKS	**29**	3	5th PM 35-N 2-E
BROWN	**23**	5	5th PM 36-N 1-E
" "	**8**	5	5th PM 39-N 1-E
" "	**22**	4	5th PM 36-N 1-W
" "	**25**	2	5th PM 36-N 3-E
" "	**9**	2	5th PM 39-N 2-E
" "	**15**	1	5th PM 38-N 3-E
" "	**1**	1	5th PM 40-N 2-W
BROWNE	**3**	1	5th PM 40-N 1-E
BRUCE	**21**	3	5th PM 36-N 2-W
BRUEL	**17**	3	5th PM 37-N 1-W
BRYAN	**24**	6	5th PM 36-N 2-E
" "	**25**	3	5th PM 36-N 3-E
" "	**2**	1	5th PM 40-N 1-W
BRYNE	**3**	1	5th PM 40-N 1-E
BUCHARD	**9**	1	5th PM 39-N 2-E
" "	**10**	1	5th PM 39-N 3-E
BUCKLAND	**7**	2	5th PM 39-N 1-W
BUCKLIN	**3**	1	5th PM 40-N 1-E
BUFORD	**29**	1	5th PM 35-N 2-E
BUGG	**19**	2	5th PM 37-N 2-E
BUNYARD	**17**	3	5th PM 37-N 1-W
BURDION	**25**	2	5th PM 36-N 3-E
" "	**23**	1	5th PM 36-N 1-E
BUREN	**3**	2	5th PM 40-N 1-E
" "	**10**	1	5th PM 39-N 3-E
BURGESS	**18**	2	5th PM 37-N 1-E
" "	**5**	1	5th PM 40-N 3-E

Surname	Map Group	Parcels of Land	Meridian/Township/Range
BURK	**12**	5	5th PM 38-N 1-W
BURNET	**5**	2	5th PM 40-N 3-E
BURNETT	**8**	5	5th PM 39-N 1-E
BURNS	**7**	1	5th PM 39-N 1-W
" "	**1**	1	5th PM 40-N 2-W
BURROSSA	**9**	1	5th PM 39-N 2-E
BURROWES	**23**	4	5th PM 36-N 1-E
" "	**24**	1	5th PM 36-N 2-E
" "	**18**	1	5th PM 37-N 1-E
BURTON	**20**	3	5th PM 37-N 3-E
BUSCH	**16**	1	5th PM 37-N 2-W
BUSH	**25**	4	5th PM 36-N 3-E
BUXTON	**24**	3	5th PM 36-N 2-E
" "	**29**	1	5th PM 35-N 2-E
BYRD	**23**	1	5th PM 36-N 1-E
" "	**24**	1	5th PM 36-N 2-E
BYRNE	**7**	1	5th PM 39-N 1-W
CAIN	**20**	4	5th PM 37-N 3-E
" "	**19**	1	5th PM 37-N 2-E
CAINE	**4**	1	5th PM 40-N 2-E
CALLAWAY	**10**	3	5th PM 39-N 3-E
CALVERD	**2**	2	5th PM 40-N 1-W
CALVIRD	**1**	2	5th PM 40-N 2-W
" "	**2**	1	5th PM 40-N 1-W
CAMERON	**11**	2	5th PM 38-N 2-W
CAMMIER	**4**	1	5th PM 40-N 2-E
CAMP	**3**	1	5th PM 40-N 1-E
CAMPBELL	**24**	8	5th PM 36-N 2-E
" "	**23**	3	5th PM 36-N 1-E
" "	**22**	3	5th PM 36-N 1-W
" "	**15**	3	5th PM 38-N 3-E
" "	**19**	2	5th PM 37-N 2-E
" "	**25**	1	5th PM 36-N 3-E
" "	**16**	1	5th PM 37-N 2-W
" "	**13**	1	5th PM 38-N 1-E
CANTRELL	**2**	1	5th PM 40-N 1-W
CARPENTER	**15**	2	5th PM 38-N 3-E
" "	**22**	1	5th PM 36-N 1-W
CARR	**17**	1	5th PM 37-N 1-W
CARROLL	**18**	4	5th PM 37-N 1-E
CARSON	**23**	7	5th PM 36-N 1-E
" "	**24**	3	5th PM 36-N 2-E
" "	**29**	2	5th PM 35-N 2-E
CARTER	**7**	4	5th PM 39-N 1-W
" "	**12**	2	5th PM 38-N 1-W
" "	**10**	1	5th PM 39-N 3-E
CARVER	**24**	1	5th PM 36-N 2-E
CASEBOLT	**26**	1	5th PM 35-N 2-W
CASEY	**20**	8	5th PM 37-N 3-E
" "	**19**	2	5th PM 37-N 2-E
" "	**13**	2	5th PM 38-N 1-E
" "	**14**	2	5th PM 38-N 2-E
" "	**7**	1	5th PM 39-N 1-W
" "	**9**	1	5th PM 39-N 2-E
" "	**3**	1	5th PM 40-N 1-E
CASH	**23**	1	5th PM 36-N 1-E
CASTLEMAN	**24**	3	5th PM 36-N 2-E
" "	**30**	1	5th PM 35-N 3-E
CASWELL	**22**	1	5th PM 36-N 1-W
CATEN	**10**	2	5th PM 39-N 3-E

Surname	Map Group	Parcels of Land	Meridian/Township/Range		
CATLETT	**15**	2	5th PM	38-N	3-E
CATLIFF	**9**	1	5th PM	39-N	2-E
CAVANAH	**7**	1	5th PM	39-N	1-W
CAYCE	**20**	1	5th PM	37-N	3-E
CAYLE	**8**	1	5th PM	39-N	1-E
CHADBOURN	**14**	1	5th PM	38-N	2-E
CHALFANT	**17**	6	5th PM	37-N	1-W
CHAMBERS	**8**	1	5th PM	39-N	1-E
CHANCE	**7**	2	5th PM	39-N	1-W
CHANDLER	**24**	1	5th PM	36-N	2-E
CHAPMAN	**11**	1	5th PM	38-N	2-W
CHAPPEL	**24**	4	5th PM	36-N	2-E
CHARBANO	**4**	1	5th PM	40-N	2-E
CHARBONEAU	**3**	2	5th PM	40-N	1-E
" "	**12**	1	5th PM	38-N	1-W
CHARBONO	**3**	1	5th PM	40-N	1-E
CHARLEVILLE	**2**	1	5th PM	40-N	1-W
CHEATHAM	**10**	2	5th PM	39-N	3-E
" "	**15**	1	5th PM	38-N	3-E
CHICKEN	**3**	3	5th PM	40-N	1-E
CHOUTEAU	**10**	1	5th PM	39-N	3-E
CHRISTY	**3**	1	5th PM	40-N	1-E
" "	**2**	1	5th PM	40-N	1-W
CLARK	**2**	10	5th PM	40-N	1-W
" "	**22**	2	5th PM	36-N	1-W
" "	**1**	2	5th PM	40-N	2-W
" "	**12**	1	5th PM	38-N	1-W
" "	**7**	1	5th PM	39-N	1-W
" "	**3**	1	5th PM	40-N	1-E
CLARKSON	**24**	15	5th PM	36-N	2-E
" "	**19**	11	5th PM	37-N	2-E
" "	**18**	4	5th PM	37-N	1-E
CLAUSEY	**7**	1	5th PM	39-N	1-W
CLEMENT	**1**	1	5th PM	40-N	2-W
CLEUFF	**20**	1	5th PM	37-N	3-E
CLOUDY	**7**	1	5th PM	39-N	1-W
CLUFF	**20**	1	5th PM	37-N	3-E
COALMAN	**10**	2	5th PM	39-N	3-E
COATWAY	**9**	1	5th PM	39-N	2-E
COBURN	**15**	10	5th PM	38-N	3-E
COCK	**13**	1	5th PM	38-N	1-E
COE	**2**	2	5th PM	40-N	1-W
COFFMAN	**23**	2	5th PM	36-N	1-E
COLE	**20**	17	5th PM	37-N	3-E
" "	**14**	10	5th PM	38-N	2-E
" "	**15**	8	5th PM	38-N	3-E
" "	**24**	7	5th PM	36-N	2-E
" "	**27**	6	5th PM	35-N	1-W
" "	**22**	1	5th PM	36-N	1-W
COLEMAN	**15**	5	5th PM	38-N	3-E
" "	**24**	2	5th PM	36-N	2-E
" "	**3**	2	5th PM	40-N	1-E
" "	**20**	1	5th PM	37-N	3-E
" "	**9**	1	5th PM	39-N	2-E
" "	**10**	1	5th PM	39-N	3-E
COLEMANT	**4**	1	5th PM	40-N	2-E
COLLIER	**1**	1	5th PM	40-N	2-W
COLMAN	**10**	3	5th PM	39-N	3-E
COMFORT	**18**	2	5th PM	37-N	1-E
" "	**13**	2	5th PM	38-N	1-E

Surname	Map Group	Parcels of Land	Meridian/Township/Range
COMPTON	**13**	14	5th PM 38-N 1-E
" "	**18**	8	5th PM 37-N 1-E
" "	**23**	3	5th PM 36-N 1-E
" "	**17**	3	5th PM 37-N 1-W
COMSTOCK	**8**	1	5th PM 39-N 1-E
CONAWAY	**28**	1	5th PM 35-N 1-E
CONNER	**9**	2	5th PM 39-N 2-E
COOK	**14**	2	5th PM 38-N 2-E
" "	**19**	1	5th PM 37-N 2-E
CORDIER	**8**	1	5th PM 39-N 1-E
CORDIES	**9**	1	5th PM 39-N 2-E
CORNELL	**28**	3	5th PM 35-N 1-E
COTTARD	**3**	1	5th PM 40-N 1-E
" "	**4**	1	5th PM 40-N 2-E
COUNTS	**27**	1	5th PM 35-N 1-W
COURTIOL	**8**	1	5th PM 39-N 1-E
COVER	**22**	5	5th PM 36-N 1-W
COWAN	**24**	1	5th PM 36-N 2-E
" "	**25**	1	5th PM 36-N 3-E
" "	**13**	1	5th PM 38-N 1-E
COXE	**3**	2	5th PM 40-N 1-E
CRABTREE	**18**	1	5th PM 37-N 1-E
CRAHAN	**8**	3	5th PM 39-N 1-E
CRAIG	**10**	4	5th PM 39-N 3-E
CRESSWELL	**13**	7	5th PM 38-N 1-E
" "	**14**	7	5th PM 38-N 2-E
" "	**8**	6	5th PM 39-N 1-E
" "	**9**	4	5th PM 39-N 2-E
CRESWELL	**13**	6	5th PM 38-N 1-E
" "	**14**	5	5th PM 38-N 2-E
" "	**8**	5	5th PM 39-N 1-E
CRISWELL	**8**	2	5th PM 39-N 1-E
" "	**13**	1	5th PM 38-N 1-E
CROSSWELL	**14**	1	5th PM 38-N 2-E
CROW	**7**	3	5th PM 39-N 1-W
" "	**1**	1	5th PM 40-N 2-W
CROZIER	**23**	3	5th PM 36-N 1-E
CRUMP	**22**	1	5th PM 36-N 1-W
CULL	**7**	1	5th PM 39-N 1-W
CULTON	**15**	2	5th PM 38-N 3-E
CUMMINGS	**15**	1	5th PM 38-N 3-E
CUMMINS	**15**	2	5th PM 38-N 3-E
CUMPTON	**23**	2	5th PM 36-N 1-E
CUNDIFF	**10**	2	5th PM 39-N 3-E
CUNIFF	**10**	1	5th PM 39-N 3-E
CUNNINGHAM	**13**	1	5th PM 38-N 1-E
CURD	**12**	1	5th PM 38-N 1-W
CURRY	**27**	4	5th PM 35-N 1-W
CURTIN	**3**	1	5th PM 40-N 1-E
DACE	**3**	2	5th PM 40-N 1-E
DANIEL	**13**	1	5th PM 38-N 1-E
DANKLIN	**9**	1	5th PM 39-N 2-E
DARBY	**6**	1	5th PM 39-N 2-W
DARRAH	**13**	5	5th PM 38-N 1-E
DAVIDSON	**25**	4	5th PM 36-N 3-E
" "	**2**	1	5th PM 40-N 1-W
DAVIS	**24**	8	5th PM 36-N 2-E
" "	**19**	2	5th PM 37-N 2-E
" "	**27**	1	5th PM 35-N 1-W
DAVISON	**25**	1	5th PM 36-N 3-E

Surname	Map Group	Parcels of Land	Meridian/Township/Range
DAY	**13**	3	5th PM 38-N 1-E
" "	**30**	2	5th PM 35-N 3-E
" "	**20**	2	5th PM 37-N 3-E
DAYTON	**2**	1	5th PM 40-N 1-W
DE BOW	**25**	3	5th PM 36-N 3-E
DE CLOUS	**13**	2	5th PM 38-N 1-E
DEAN	**9**	2	5th PM 39-N 2-E
DEANE	**19**	1	5th PM 37-N 2-E
DECLOIS	**8**	3	5th PM 39-N 1-E
" "	**13**	2	5th PM 38-N 1-E
DECLOS	**8**	1	5th PM 39-N 1-E
DEEGAN	**8**	1	5th PM 39-N 1-E
DEGURRIA	**19**	1	5th PM 37-N 2-E
DELAFIELD	**23**	5	5th PM 36-N 1-E
" "	**24**	1	5th PM 36-N 2-E
DELAURIERE	**9**	11	5th PM 39-N 2-E
" "	**3**	6	5th PM 40-N 1-E
" "	**8**	2	5th PM 39-N 1-E
" "	**2**	1	5th PM 40-N 1-W
DELCOR	**4**	1	5th PM 40-N 2-E
DELCOUR	**8**	2	5th PM 39-N 1-E
DELY	**7**	1	5th PM 39-N 1-W
DEMOSS	**2**	4	5th PM 40-N 1-W
DENNING	**28**	4	5th PM 35-N 1-E
DENNY	**4**	2	5th PM 40-N 2-E
DENT	**30**	1	5th PM 35-N 3-E
" "	**4**	1	5th PM 40-N 2-E
DENTON	**25**	1	5th PM 36-N 3-E
DESLOGE	**23**	3	5th PM 36-N 1-E
" "	**24**	2	5th PM 36-N 2-E
" "	**19**	2	5th PM 37-N 2-E
DETCHMENDY	**10**	1	5th PM 39-N 3-E
DEVALIN	**16**	7	5th PM 37-N 2-W
DIAMOND	**3**	3	5th PM 40-N 1-E
DICKEY	**26**	6	5th PM 35-N 2-W
" "	**23**	5	5th PM 36-N 1-E
" "	**28**	1	5th PM 35-N 1-E
DIKEMAN	**27**	1	5th PM 35-N 1-W
DINGUID	**2**	2	5th PM 40-N 1-W
DINNIDDIE	**14**	1	5th PM 38-N 2-E
DINNISTON	**9**	1	5th PM 39-N 2-E
DINWIDDIE	**17**	2	5th PM 37-N 1-W
DOBKINS	**16**	1	5th PM 37-N 2-W
DOLAN	**4**	3	5th PM 40-N 2-E
DOLL	**19**	1	5th PM 37-N 2-E
DONNA	**25**	2	5th PM 36-N 3-E
" "	**22**	1	5th PM 36-N 1-W
DOTSON	**26**	4	5th PM 35-N 2-W
" "	**27**	2	5th PM 35-N 1-W
DOTY	**2**	1	5th PM 40-N 1-W
DOUGHERTY	**9**	8	5th PM 39-N 2-E
" "	**10**	1	5th PM 39-N 3-E
DOUGLASS	**23**	3	5th PM 36-N 1-E
DOWNARD	**19**	2	5th PM 37-N 2-E
DOWNER	**4**	1	5th PM 40-N 2-E
DOWNEY	**14**	1	5th PM 38-N 2-E
DOYEN	**4**	2	5th PM 40-N 2-E
DOYLE	**16**	2	5th PM 37-N 2-W
DUCKWORTH	**13**	6	5th PM 38-N 1-E
" "	**7**	1	5th PM 39-N 1-W

Surname	Map Group	Parcels of Land	Meridian/Township/Range
DUCLOS	**9**	2	5th PM 39-N 2-E
" "	**14**	1	5th PM 38-N 2-E
DUCLOUS	**9**	1	5th PM 39-N 2-E
DUDLEY	**30**	2	5th PM 35-N 3-E
" "	**29**	1	5th PM 35-N 2-E
DUFF	**20**	2	5th PM 37-N 3-E
" "	**14**	1	5th PM 38-N 2-E
DUNCAN	**22**	2	5th PM 36-N 1-W
" "	**30**	1	5th PM 35-N 3-E
DUNKIN	**23**	2	5th PM 36-N 1-E
DUNKLIN	**24**	1	5th PM 36-N 2-E
" "	**13**	1	5th PM 38-N 1-E
" "	**12**	1	5th PM 38-N 1-W
" "	**15**	1	5th PM 38-N 3-E
" "	**1**	1	5th PM 40-N 2-W
DUPAVILLON	**7**	1	5th PM 39-N 1-W
DURHAM	**20**	1	5th PM 37-N 3-E
DUTY	**28**	3	5th PM 35-N 1-E
DWANE	**12**	2	5th PM 38-N 1-W
DYKE	**7**	1	5th PM 39-N 1-W
EARS	**23**	1	5th PM 36-N 1-E
EASOM	**17**	1	5th PM 37-N 1-W
EASTIN	**2**	1	5th PM 40-N 1-W
EATON	**25**	7	5th PM 36-N 3-E
" "	**22**	1	5th PM 36-N 1-W
" "	**19**	1	5th PM 37-N 2-E
EDGAR	**25**	3	5th PM 36-N 3-E
EDMANDS	**4**	1	5th PM 40-N 2-E
EDMONDS	**24**	1	5th PM 36-N 2-E
EDMUNDS	**14**	1	5th PM 38-N 2-E
EDWARDS	**4**	2	5th PM 40-N 2-E
EFFINGER	**25**	3	5th PM 36-N 3-E
EIDSON	**23**	1	5th PM 36-N 1-E
ELLEDGE	**4**	1	5th PM 40-N 2-E
ELLIOTT	**18**	1	5th PM 37-N 1-E
" "	**9**	1	5th PM 39-N 2-E
ELLISON	**27**	2	5th PM 35-N 1-W
ELMER	**30**	1	5th PM 35-N 3-E
ENDLY	**20**	1	5th PM 37-N 3-E
ENGLEDOW	**15**	2	5th PM 38-N 3-E
ENLOE	**1**	3	5th PM 40-N 2-W
ENOCH	**13**	4	5th PM 38-N 1-E
ESTABROOK	**9**	3	5th PM 39-N 2-E
ESTES	**16**	3	5th PM 37-N 2-W
EUSTIS	**23**	5	5th PM 36-N 1-E
EVANS	**29**	10	5th PM 35-N 2-E
" "	**20**	6	5th PM 37-N 3-E
" "	**25**	4	5th PM 36-N 3-E
" "	**24**	3	5th PM 36-N 2-E
" "	**18**	3	5th PM 37-N 1-E
" "	**15**	2	5th PM 38-N 3-E
" "	**4**	1	5th PM 40-N 2-E
EVENS	**18**	15	5th PM 37-N 1-E
" "	**24**	9	5th PM 36-N 2-E
" "	**25**	4	5th PM 36-N 3-E
" "	**20**	4	5th PM 37-N 3-E
" "	**29**	1	5th PM 35-N 2-E
" "	**15**	1	5th PM 38-N 3-E
EVERSOLE	**29**	1	5th PM 35-N 2-E
EYE	**18**	2	5th PM 37-N 1-E

Surname	Map Group	Parcels of Land	Meridian/Township/Range
FARISH	**7**	1	5th PM 39-N 1-W
FARMER	**28**	1	5th PM 35-N 1-E
FARQUHAR	**24**	2	5th PM 36-N 2-E
FARRELL	**23**	7	5th PM 36-N 1-E
" "	**9**	5	5th PM 39-N 2-E
" "	**14**	3	5th PM 38-N 2-E
FARRINGTON	**8**	2	5th PM 39-N 1-E
FARRIS	**25**	4	5th PM 36-N 3-E
" "	**24**	3	5th PM 36-N 2-E
FARRISS	**24**	3	5th PM 36-N 2-E
FARROW	**3**	2	5th PM 40-N 1-E
" "	**9**	1	5th PM 39-N 2-E
FASSETT	**27**	4	5th PM 35-N 1-W
FEA	**7**	3	5th PM 39-N 1-W
FELL	**6**	3	5th PM 39-N 2-W
FENISON	**27**	2	5th PM 35-N 1-W
FENNISON	**27**	2	5th PM 35-N 1-W
FERGUSON	**9**	3	5th PM 39-N 2-E
" "	**20**	1	5th PM 37-N 3-E
FERIE	**12**	1	5th PM 38-N 1-W
FEROLL	**9**	1	5th PM 39-N 2-E
FICKES	**19**	7	5th PM 37-N 2-E
" "	**24**	1	5th PM 36-N 2-E
FIEDELDEY	**8**	5	5th PM 39-N 1-E
FIELD	**27**	3	5th PM 35-N 1-W
FIFER	**18**	2	5th PM 37-N 1-E
FINISON	**17**	2	5th PM 37-N 1-W
FINK	**23**	4	5th PM 36-N 1-E
FINLEY	**21**	4	5th PM 36-N 2-W
FISHER	**3**	5	5th PM 40-N 1-E
" "	**23**	3	5th PM 36-N 1-E
" "	**24**	1	5th PM 36-N 2-E
FITCH	**18**	1	5th PM 37-N 1-E
" "	**19**	1	5th PM 37-N 2-E
FITZWATER	**13**	2	5th PM 38-N 1-E
" "	**8**	2	5th PM 39-N 1-E
" "	**12**	1	5th PM 38-N 1-W
FLANAGAN	**3**	1	5th PM 40-N 1-E
FLEMING	**17**	1	5th PM 37-N 1-W
" "	**12**	1	5th PM 38-N 1-W
FLEMMING	**25**	2	5th PM 36-N 3-E
FLINN	**9**	1	5th PM 39-N 2-E
FLOTTEMSCH	**12**	6	5th PM 38-N 1-W
FLOWERS	**22**	6	5th PM 36-N 1-W
FLYNN	**9**	4	5th PM 39-N 2-E
" "	**18**	1	5th PM 37-N 1-E
" "	**16**	1	5th PM 37-N 2-W
" "	**14**	1	5th PM 38-N 2-E
" "	**15**	1	5th PM 38-N 3-E
FOGARTY	**16**	2	5th PM 37-N 2-W
FORD	**22**	2	5th PM 36-N 1-W
" "	**18**	1	5th PM 37-N 1-E
" "	**9**	1	5th PM 39-N 2-E
FORESTER	**5**	2	5th PM 40-N 3-E
" "	**17**	1	5th PM 37-N 1-W
FORREST	**8**	3	5th PM 39-N 1-E
FORRESTER	**29**	2	5th PM 35-N 2-E
" "	**5**	2	5th PM 40-N 3-E
FORTNER	**30**	2	5th PM 35-N 3-E
FORTUNE	**28**	1	5th PM 35-N 1-E

Surname	Map Group	Parcels of Land	Meridian/Township/Range
FOSTER	**27**	4	5th PM 35-N 1-W
" "	**7**	4	5th PM 39-N 1-W
" "	**8**	1	5th PM 39-N 1-E
FRAME	**7**	2	5th PM 39-N 1-W
FRAYSER	**4**	1	5th PM 40-N 2-E
FRAZER	**12**	2	5th PM 38-N 1-W
FRENCH	**18**	5	5th PM 37-N 1-E
FRISSEL	**5**	1	5th PM 40-N 3-E
FRISSELL	**19**	5	5th PM 37-N 2-E
" "	**15**	3	5th PM 38-N 3-E
" "	**24**	1	5th PM 36-N 2-E
" "	**20**	1	5th PM 37-N 3-E
" "	**10**	1	5th PM 39-N 3-E
FRITTS	**2**	1	5th PM 40-N 1-W
FRITZ	**2**	1	5th PM 40-N 1-W
FRIZZLE	**25**	1	5th PM 36-N 3-E
GALE	**18**	6	5th PM 37-N 1-E
GALLAGHER	**11**	2	5th PM 38-N 2-W
" "	**6**	2	5th PM 39-N 2-W
GALLAHER	**2**	1	5th PM 40-N 1-W
GALLAUGHER	**22**	2	5th PM 36-N 1-W
GALLEY	**8**	1	5th PM 39-N 1-E
GALLOWAY	**22**	1	5th PM 36-N 1-W
GAMACHE	**9**	1	5th PM 39-N 2-E
GAMBLE	**2**	4	5th PM 40-N 1-W
" "	**1**	1	5th PM 40-N 2-W
GAN	**30**	2	5th PM 35-N 3-E
GARRETT	**15**	3	5th PM 38-N 3-E
" "	**2**	1	5th PM 40-N 1-W
GARRISON	**16**	1	5th PM 37-N 2-W
GARRISSON	**16**	1	5th PM 37-N 2-W
GARRITY	**30**	1	5th PM 35-N 3-E
GARTSIDE	**7**	6	5th PM 39-N 1-W
" "	**3**	3	5th PM 40-N 1-E
GARVIN	**24**	1	5th PM 36-N 2-E
GATES	**30**	1	5th PM 35-N 3-E
GATY	**19**	2	5th PM 37-N 2-E
GAUGH	**7**	3	5th PM 39-N 1-W
GAY	**27**	5	5th PM 35-N 1-W
GELLENBECK	**25**	1	5th PM 36-N 3-E
GENERELLY	**12**	3	5th PM 38-N 1-W
GENSIL	**2**	2	5th PM 40-N 1-W
GEORGE	**25**	1	5th PM 36-N 3-E
GEZZI	**15**	3	5th PM 38-N 3-E
GHOLSON	**22**	2	5th PM 36-N 1-W
" "	**17**	1	5th PM 37-N 1-W
GIBSON	**18**	8	5th PM 37-N 1-E
" "	**21**	4	5th PM 36-N 2-W
" "	**10**	3	5th PM 39-N 3-E
" "	**29**	1	5th PM 35-N 2-E
" "	**25**	1	5th PM 36-N 3-E
GILCHRIST	**23**	4	5th PM 36-N 1-E
" "	**24**	3	5th PM 36-N 2-E
" "	**19**	2	5th PM 37-N 2-E
GILLAM	**22**	4	5th PM 36-N 1-W
" "	**27**	1	5th PM 35-N 1-W
GILLIAM	**27**	7	5th PM 35-N 1-W
" "	**22**	2	5th PM 36-N 1-W
" "	**26**	1	5th PM 35-N 2-W
GILMORE	**17**	2	5th PM 37-N 1-W

Surname	Map Group	Parcels of Land	Meridian/Township/Range
GIPSON	**28**	1	5th PM 35-N 1-E
GIRARDIER	**9**	3	5th PM 39-N 2-E
" "	**4**	2	5th PM 40-N 2-E
GLENN	**22**	3	5th PM 36-N 1-W
" "	**7**	2	5th PM 39-N 1-W
" "	**14**	1	5th PM 38-N 2-E
GLORE	**20**	2	5th PM 37-N 3-E
" "	**18**	1	5th PM 37-N 1-E
" "	**14**	1	5th PM 38-N 2-E
" "	**15**	1	5th PM 38-N 3-E
" "	**8**	1	5th PM 39-N 1-E
GOADE	**22**	5	5th PM 36-N 1-W
GOBBETT	**14**	1	5th PM 38-N 2-E
GODARD	**8**	1	5th PM 39-N 1-E
GODAT	**8**	1	5th PM 39-N 1-E
GOFF	**15**	4	5th PM 38-N 3-E
GOFORTH	**28**	6	5th PM 35-N 1-E
GOGAY	**8**	1	5th PM 39-N 1-E
GOLDEN	**8**	2	5th PM 39-N 1-E
" "	**9**	1	5th PM 39-N 2-E
GOLDING	**8**	5	5th PM 39-N 1-E
GOLDSBERG	**8**	1	5th PM 39-N 1-E
GOODRICH	**11**	1	5th PM 38-N 2-W
GOULD	**7**	1	5th PM 39-N 1-W
GOVRO	**25**	1	5th PM 36-N 3-E
GRADE	**22**	1	5th PM 36-N 1-W
GRADON	**4**	1	5th PM 40-N 2-E
GRAGG	**29**	2	5th PM 35-N 2-E
" "	**28**	1	5th PM 35-N 1-E
GRANT	**13**	2	5th PM 38-N 1-E
GRAVES	**24**	2	5th PM 36-N 2-E
" "	**12**	2	5th PM 38-N 1-W
GREEN	**29**	1	5th PM 35-N 2-E
" "	**1**	1	5th PM 40-N 2-W
GREENE	**6**	1	5th PM 39-N 2-W
GREENLEE	**13**	1	5th PM 38-N 1-E
GREGG	**29**	3	5th PM 35-N 2-E
GREGORY	**25**	5	5th PM 36-N 3-E
" "	**17**	3	5th PM 37-N 1-W
GRIDER	**24**	2	5th PM 36-N 2-E
GRIFFIN	**6**	2	5th PM 39-N 2-W
" "	**9**	1	5th PM 39-N 2-E
GRIFFITH	**22**	2	5th PM 36-N 1-W
GRIMES	**21**	2	5th PM 36-N 2-W
" "	**26**	1	5th PM 35-N 2-W
GRINEA	**25**	2	5th PM 36-N 3-E
GRISHAM	**28**	1	5th PM 35-N 1-E
GROGG	**29**	1	5th PM 35-N 2-E
GROOM	**23**	2	5th PM 36-N 1-E
GROOMS	**10**	3	5th PM 39-N 3-E
GROSS	**29**	2	5th PM 35-N 2-E
GUINN	**28**	5	5th PM 35-N 1-E
GUSHEE	**20**	4	5th PM 37-N 3-E
GUT	**2**	1	5th PM 40-N 1-W
GUY	**14**	1	5th PM 38-N 2-E
HAAS	**3**	3	5th PM 40-N 1-E
HAEFNER	**13**	3	5th PM 38-N 1-E
" "	**18**	2	5th PM 37-N 1-E
" "	**24**	1	5th PM 36-N 2-E
" "	**25**	1	5th PM 36-N 3-E

Surname	Map Group	Parcels of Land	Meridian/Township/Range		
HAEFNER (Cont'd)	**20**	1	5th PM	37-N	3-E
HAENSSLER	**24**	1	5th PM	36-N	2-E
HAGGARD	**17**	2	5th PM	37-N	1-W
HAIGH	**18**	1	5th PM	37-N	1-E
HALL	**18**	3	5th PM	37-N	1-E
" "	**19**	3	5th PM	37-N	2-E
" "	**17**	1	5th PM	37-N	1-W
HALLIDAY	**8**	2	5th PM	39-N	1-E
HAMBLETON	**1**	1	5th PM	40-N	2-W
HAMILTON	**8**	1	5th PM	39-N	1-E
HANCOCK	**18**	4	5th PM	37-N	1-E
HANGER	**29**	2	5th PM	35-N	2-E
HANS	**2**	1	5th PM	40-N	1-W
HANSON	**14**	3	5th PM	38-N	2-E
" "	**12**	2	5th PM	38-N	1-W
HARGES	**13**	1	5th PM	38-N	1-E
HARGIS	**13**	1	5th PM	38-N	1-E
HARGRAVE	**28**	2	5th PM	35-N	1-E
HARLOW	**13**	1	5th PM	38-N	1-E
HARMAN	**7**	5	5th PM	39-N	1-W
" "	**12**	2	5th PM	38-N	1-W
" "	**6**	1	5th PM	39-N	2-W
HARMON	**12**	1	5th PM	38-N	1-W
HARPER	**12**	9	5th PM	38-N	1-W
" "	**24**	3	5th PM	36-N	2-E
" "	**21**	1	5th PM	36-N	2-W
" "	**7**	1	5th PM	39-N	1-W
HARRINGTON	**25**	1	5th PM	36-N	3-E
HARRIS	**24**	3	5th PM	36-N	2-E
" "	**30**	2	5th PM	35-N	3-E
" "	**18**	2	5th PM	37-N	1-E
" "	**17**	2	5th PM	37-N	1-W
" "	**19**	2	5th PM	37-N	2-E
" "	**29**	1	5th PM	35-N	2-E
" "	**14**	1	5th PM	38-N	2-E
" "	**15**	1	5th PM	38-N	3-E
" "	**3**	1	5th PM	40-N	1-E
HARRISON	**20**	12	5th PM	37-N	3-E
" "	**25**	3	5th PM	36-N	3-E
" "	**14**	2	5th PM	38-N	2-E
" "	**16**	1	5th PM	37-N	2-W
" "	**7**	1	5th PM	39-N	1-W
" "	**6**	1	5th PM	39-N	2-W
HARRTY	**9**	1	5th PM	39-N	2-E
HARVER	**10**	2	5th PM	39-N	3-E
HARVEY	**17**	1	5th PM	37-N	1-W
HATHORN	**19**	1	5th PM	37-N	2-E
HAUS	**2**	1	5th PM	40-N	1-W
HAVEN	**10**	1	5th PM	39-N	3-E
HAWKINS	**20**	13	5th PM	37-N	3-E
" "	**25**	3	5th PM	36-N	3-E
" "	**15**	2	5th PM	38-N	3-E
" "	**10**	1	5th PM	39-N	3-E
HAY	**20**	1	5th PM	37-N	3-E
HAYNES	**4**	1	5th PM	40-N	2-E
HAYS	**25**	9	5th PM	36-N	3-E
" "	**29**	4	5th PM	35-N	2-E
" "	**14**	1	5th PM	38-N	2-E
HEARST	**10**	4	5th PM	39-N	3-E
HEARTY	**9**	1	5th PM	39-N	2-E

Surname	Map Group	Parcels of Land	Meridian/Township/Range
HEINE	**3**	2	5th PM 40-N 1-E
HEITZ	**27**	1	5th PM 35-N 1-W
HELLIARD	**23**	2	5th PM 36-N 1-E
HELMICK	**28**	1	5th PM 35-N 1-E
HENDERSON	**23**	6	5th PM 36-N 1-E
" "	**28**	1	5th PM 35-N 1-E
" "	**30**	1	5th PM 35-N 3-E
" "	**25**	1	5th PM 36-N 3-E
HENRY	**27**	1	5th PM 35-N 1-W
" "	**25**	1	5th PM 36-N 3-E
" "	**12**	1	5th PM 38-N 1-W
HENSLEE	**26**	1	5th PM 35-N 2-W
HENSLEY	**26**	3	5th PM 35-N 2-W
" "	**16**	2	5th PM 37-N 2-W
HENSON	**24**	3	5th PM 36-N 2-E
HENWOOD	**13**	4	5th PM 38-N 1-E
HERELSON	**10**	1	5th PM 39-N 3-E
HERSHEY	**29**	1	5th PM 35-N 2-E
HESSE	**9**	4	5th PM 39-N 2-E
HEWIT	**27**	4	5th PM 35-N 1-W
" "	**22**	2	5th PM 36-N 1-W
HIBBARD	**15**	2	5th PM 38-N 3-E
HIBLER	**2**	4	5th PM 40-N 1-W
" "	**7**	2	5th PM 39-N 1-W
" "	**1**	2	5th PM 40-N 2-W
" "	**3**	1	5th PM 40-N 1-E
HICKERSON	**24**	1	5th PM 36-N 2-E
HICKLEY	**7**	1	5th PM 39-N 1-W
HICKS	**14**	3	5th PM 38-N 2-E
" "	**25**	2	5th PM 36-N 3-E
" "	**24**	1	5th PM 36-N 2-E
HIGGENBOTHAM	**10**	3	5th PM 39-N 3-E
" "	**15**	1	5th PM 38-N 3-E
HIGGINBOTHAM	**10**	12	5th PM 39-N 3-E
" "	**15**	2	5th PM 38-N 3-E
HIGGINBOTHOM	**10**	2	5th PM 39-N 3-E
HIGGINS	**10**	2	5th PM 39-N 3-E
HIGHLEY	**25**	2	5th PM 36-N 3-E
HIGHLY	**30**	2	5th PM 35-N 3-E
HIGHT	**18**	2	5th PM 37-N 1-E
" "	**14**	2	5th PM 38-N 2-E
" "	**13**	1	5th PM 38-N 1-E
" "	**9**	1	5th PM 39-N 2-E
HILL	**13**	7	5th PM 38-N 1-E
" "	**18**	3	5th PM 37-N 1-E
" "	**12**	3	5th PM 38-N 1-W
" "	**28**	1	5th PM 35-N 1-E
" "	**23**	1	5th PM 36-N 1-E
" "	**19**	1	5th PM 37-N 2-E
" "	**14**	1	5th PM 38-N 2-E
" "	**7**	1	5th PM 39-N 1-W
" "	**9**	1	5th PM 39-N 2-E
HILLEN	**23**	8	5th PM 36-N 1-E
HIMMLEY	**9**	4	5th PM 39-N 2-E
HINCH	**9**	7	5th PM 39-N 2-E
HINDRICKER	**8**	1	5th PM 39-N 1-E
HINDS	**26**	2	5th PM 35-N 2-W
HINKSON	**13**	2	5th PM 38-N 1-E
" "	**14**	1	5th PM 38-N 2-E
HINSON	**3**	1	5th PM 40-N 1-E

Surname	Map Group	Parcels of Land	Meridian/Township/Range
HIRSH	**23**	1	5th PM 36-N 1-E
HOBAN	**9**	1	5th PM 39-N 2-E
HOFF	**9**	3	5th PM 39-N 2-E
" "	**17**	1	5th PM 37-N 1-W
" "	**3**	1	5th PM 40-N 1-E
HOGAN	**27**	3	5th PM 35-N 1-W
" "	**7**	1	5th PM 39-N 1-W
HOLDEN	**28**	2	5th PM 35-N 1-E
HOLLINGSWORTH	**18**	2	5th PM 37-N 1-E
HOLLINSWORTH	**18**	3	5th PM 37-N 1-E
HOLMES	**7**	3	5th PM 39-N 1-W
" "	**17**	1	5th PM 37-N 1-W
HOLT	**19**	6	5th PM 37-N 2-E
" "	**18**	1	5th PM 37-N 1-E
" "	**20**	1	5th PM 37-N 3-E
" "	**13**	1	5th PM 38-N 1-E
" "	**14**	1	5th PM 38-N 2-E
HOOTER	**5**	1	5th PM 40-N 3-E
HOPKINS	**22**	1	5th PM 36-N 1-W
" "	**15**	1	5th PM 38-N 3-E
HORBISON	**7**	1	5th PM 39-N 1-W
HORINE	**12**	3	5th PM 38-N 1-W
HORNEY	**8**	3	5th PM 39-N 1-E
HORNSEY	**19**	2	5th PM 37-N 2-E
HORROCKS	**9**	2	5th PM 39-N 2-E
HORTON	**3**	5	5th PM 40-N 1-E
" "	**28**	3	5th PM 35-N 1-E
" "	**30**	1	5th PM 35-N 3-E
" "	**25**	1	5th PM 36-N 3-E
HOUK	**15**	1	5th PM 38-N 3-E
HOUSE	**19**	2	5th PM 37-N 2-E
" "	**20**	2	5th PM 37-N 3-E
HOUSEMAN	**9**	4	5th PM 39-N 2-E
" "	**12**	2	5th PM 38-N 1-W
HOWARD	**30**	11	5th PM 35-N 3-E
HOWE	**25**	7	5th PM 36-N 3-E
" "	**24**	1	5th PM 36-N 2-E
HOWELL	**19**	1	5th PM 37-N 2-E
HUDLESTON	**20**	1	5th PM 37-N 3-E
HUDSON	**18**	2	5th PM 37-N 1-E
" "	**17**	1	5th PM 37-N 1-W
" "	**13**	1	5th PM 38-N 1-E
" "	**14**	1	5th PM 38-N 2-E
" "	**6**	1	5th PM 39-N 2-W
HUDSPETH	**22**	14	5th PM 36-N 1-W
" "	**16**	5	5th PM 37-N 2-W
" "	**24**	2	5th PM 36-N 2-E
" "	**17**	1	5th PM 37-N 1-W
HUFF	**20**	5	5th PM 37-N 3-E
" "	**3**	1	5th PM 40-N 1-E
HUFSTETTER	**19**	1	5th PM 37-N 2-E
HUGHES	**25**	27	5th PM 36-N 3-E
" "	**7**	3	5th PM 39-N 1-W
" "	**30**	2	5th PM 35-N 3-E
" "	**24**	1	5th PM 36-N 2-E
HUITT	**27**	6	5th PM 35-N 1-W
" "	**22**	1	5th PM 36-N 1-W
HULL	**25**	1	5th PM 36-N 3-E
" "	**19**	1	5th PM 37-N 2-E
HULSEY	**8**	2	5th PM 39-N 1-E

Surname	Map Group	Parcels of Land	Meridian/Township/Range		
HULSEY (Cont'd)	**2**	2	5th PM	40-N	1-W
" "	**7**	1	5th PM	39-N	1-W
" "	**3**	1	5th PM	40-N	1-E
HUNT	**14**	10	5th PM	38-N	2-E
" "	**9**	4	5th PM	39-N	2-E
" "	**10**	2	5th PM	39-N	3-E
" "	**24**	1	5th PM	36-N	2-E
" "	**13**	1	5th PM	38-N	1-E
" "	**15**	1	5th PM	38-N	3-E
HUNTER	**24**	6	5th PM	36-N	2-E
" "	**25**	3	5th PM	36-N	3-E
HURD	**6**	1	5th PM	39-N	2-W
HUTCHINGS	**24**	8	5th PM	36-N	2-E
" "	**25**	3	5th PM	36-N	3-E
" "	**23**	2	5th PM	36-N	1-E
HUTCHISON	**22**	1	5th PM	36-N	1-W
HYNSON	**5**	2	5th PM	40-N	3-E
HYPOLITE	**15**	2	5th PM	38-N	3-E
HYPOTITE	**15**	1	5th PM	38-N	3-E
IMBODEN	**30**	6	5th PM	35-N	3-E
" "	**24**	1	5th PM	36-N	2-E
INGE	**20**	2	5th PM	37-N	3-E
" "	**1**	2	5th PM	40-N	2-W
IRVIN	**6**	1	5th PM	39-N	2-W
IRVINE	**12**	2	5th PM	38-N	1-W
" "	**8**	1	5th PM	39-N	1-E
" "	**6**	1	5th PM	39-N	2-W
ISGRIG	**12**	6	5th PM	38-N	1-W
ISRAEL	**13**	1	5th PM	38-N	1-E
JACKSON	**9**	5	5th PM	39-N	2-E
" "	**14**	3	5th PM	38-N	2-E
" "	**8**	3	5th PM	39-N	1-E
" "	**2**	3	5th PM	40-N	1-W
JACO	**21**	1	5th PM	36-N	2-W
JACOBS	**9**	2	5th PM	39-N	2-E
JACOMELLA	**9**	2	5th PM	39-N	2-E
JAMISON	**25**	14	5th PM	36-N	3-E
" "	**20**	3	5th PM	37-N	3-E
" "	**15**	2	5th PM	38-N	3-E
JANIS	**24**	2	5th PM	36-N	2-E
JANNEY	**22**	2	5th PM	36-N	1-W
JARDIN	**9**	4	5th PM	39-N	2-E
JARRELL	**28**	1	5th PM	35-N	1-E
JARVIS	**23**	17	5th PM	36-N	1-E
" "	**22**	4	5th PM	36-N	1-W
" "	**27**	1	5th PM	35-N	1-W
JENKINS	**18**	2	5th PM	37-N	1-E
" "	**20**	1	5th PM	37-N	3-E
JENNINGS	**10**	2	5th PM	39-N	3-E
JETT	**22**	2	5th PM	36-N	1-W
JIMMERSON	**25**	1	5th PM	36-N	3-E
JINKERSON	**17**	2	5th PM	37-N	1-W
JINKINS	**22**	3	5th PM	36-N	1-W
JOHNSON	**24**	14	5th PM	36-N	2-E
" "	**13**	13	5th PM	38-N	1-E
" "	**10**	7	5th PM	39-N	3-E
" "	**30**	6	5th PM	35-N	3-E
" "	**19**	6	5th PM	37-N	2-E
" "	**7**	6	5th PM	39-N	1-W
" "	**12**	4	5th PM	38-N	1-W

Surname	Map Group	Parcels of Land	Meridian/Township/Range
JOHNSON (Cont'd)	**17**	3	5th PM 37-N 1-W
" "	**20**	3	5th PM 37-N 3-E
" "	**23**	2	5th PM 36-N 1-E
" "	**18**	2	5th PM 37-N 1-E
" "	**14**	2	5th PM 38-N 2-E
" "	**8**	2	5th PM 39-N 1-E
" "	**6**	2	5th PM 39-N 2-W
" "	**9**	1	5th PM 39-N 2-E
" "	**3**	1	5th PM 40-N 1-E
JOHNSTON	**14**	9	5th PM 38-N 2-E
" "	**13**	4	5th PM 38-N 1-E
" "	**27**	1	5th PM 35-N 1-W
" "	**4**	1	5th PM 40-N 2-E
JOLLIN	**20**	1	5th PM 37-N 3-E
JONES	**25**	5	5th PM 36-N 3-E
" "	**28**	3	5th PM 35-N 1-E
" "	**7**	3	5th PM 39-N 1-W
" "	**9**	2	5th PM 39-N 2-E
" "	**29**	1	5th PM 35-N 2-E
" "	**19**	1	5th PM 37-N 2-E
" "	**12**	1	5th PM 38-N 1-W
" "	**10**	1	5th PM 39-N 3-E
JORDAN	**25**	2	5th PM 36-N 3-E
JUDD	**27**	4	5th PM 35-N 1-W
KANE	**20**	1	5th PM 37-N 3-E
" "	**9**	1	5th PM 39-N 2-E
KAVANAUGH	**2**	1	5th PM 40-N 1-W
KEAN	**9**	1	5th PM 39-N 2-E
KEARNS	**19**	1	5th PM 37-N 2-E
KEAUGH	**22**	1	5th PM 36-N 1-W
KEENE	**8**	2	5th PM 39-N 1-E
KEISEN	**13**	2	5th PM 38-N 1-E
KELLEHER	**7**	3	5th PM 39-N 1-W
KELLER	**12**	2	5th PM 38-N 1-W
KELLY	**15**	2	5th PM 38-N 3-E
" "	**17**	1	5th PM 37-N 1-W
KENDALL	**19**	1	5th PM 37-N 2-E
KENNER	**14**	1	5th PM 38-N 2-E
" "	**9**	1	5th PM 39-N 2-E
KENNETT	**14**	2	5th PM 38-N 2-E
KEOUGH	**22**	1	5th PM 36-N 1-W
KERDER	**8**	1	5th PM 39-N 1-E
KERSEY	**8**	1	5th PM 39-N 1-E
KERSHAW	**3**	5	5th PM 40-N 1-E
KESSLER	**8**	1	5th PM 39-N 1-E
KIESEN	**13**	3	5th PM 38-N 1-E
KILLPACK	**9**	1	5th PM 39-N 2-E
KIMBERLIN	**3**	3	5th PM 40-N 1-E
" "	**2**	2	5th PM 40-N 1-W
KIMBERLING	**2**	1	5th PM 40-N 1-W
KING	**27**	6	5th PM 35-N 1-W
" "	**26**	5	5th PM 35-N 2-W
" "	**8**	5	5th PM 39-N 1-E
KINKAID	**25**	1	5th PM 36-N 3-E
KINKEAD	**30**	2	5th PM 35-N 3-E
KINSEY	**30**	1	5th PM 35-N 3-E
KIRBY	**18**	3	5th PM 37-N 1-E
" "	**3**	1	5th PM 40-N 1-E
KIRKPATRICK	**25**	5	5th PM 36-N 3-E
" "	**3**	3	5th PM 40-N 1-E

Surname	Map Group	Parcels of Land	Meridian/Township/Range
KIRKPATRICK (Cont'd)	**2**	2	5th PM 40-N 1-W
" "	**8**	1	5th PM 39-N 1-E
KIRKWOOD	**7**	5	5th PM 39-N 1-W
KIRTLAND	**12**	1	5th PM 38-N 1-W
KLEIN	**7**	7	5th PM 39-N 1-W
KNIGHT	**21**	3	5th PM 36-N 2-W
KRAFT	**8**	1	5th PM 39-N 1-E
KULKE	**8**	1	5th PM 39-N 1-E
KUMER	**9**	3	5th PM 39-N 2-E
LA BARGE	**13**	2	5th PM 38-N 1-E
LABAUME	**4**	2	5th PM 40-N 2-E
LABRAUME	**3**	1	5th PM 40-N 1-E
" "	**4**	1	5th PM 40-N 2-E
LACY	**19**	2	5th PM 37-N 2-E
LAMARAQUE	**14**	1	5th PM 38-N 2-E
LAMARQUE	**14**	7	5th PM 38-N 2-E
" "	**9**	3	5th PM 39-N 2-E
" "	**15**	2	5th PM 38-N 3-E
LANCASTER	**15**	7	5th PM 38-N 3-E
" "	**22**	1	5th PM 36-N 1-W
LAND	**8**	2	5th PM 39-N 1-E
LANGE	**8**	1	5th PM 39-N 1-E
LANINS	**29**	2	5th PM 35-N 2-E
LANIUS	**29**	1	5th PM 35-N 2-E
LARAMORE	**27**	11	5th PM 35-N 1-W
LARGENT	**13**	1	5th PM 38-N 1-E
LARUE	**1**	1	5th PM 40-N 2-W
LASWELL	**23**	1	5th PM 36-N 1-E
LATIMER	**15**	1	5th PM 38-N 3-E
LATTIMER	**30**	1	5th PM 35-N 3-E
LATUNIO	**25**	1	5th PM 36-N 3-E
LE BOURGEOIS	**9**	2	5th PM 39-N 2-E
" "	**4**	2	5th PM 40-N 2-E
LEA	**7**	4	5th PM 39-N 1-W
LEAGUE	**17**	3	5th PM 37-N 1-W
LEAKY	**9**	1	5th PM 39-N 2-E
LECLARE	**20**	2	5th PM 37-N 3-E
LECLERE	**20**	3	5th PM 37-N 3-E
LEFFINGWELL	**9**	1	5th PM 39-N 2-E
LEFFLER	**18**	2	5th PM 37-N 1-E
LEGERET	**3**	2	5th PM 40-N 1-E
LEONARD	**28**	2	5th PM 35-N 1-E
LERSHALL	**12**	1	5th PM 38-N 1-W
LEVENS	**13**	1	5th PM 38-N 1-E
LEVY	**4**	4	5th PM 40-N 2-E
LEWIS	**19**	3	5th PM 37-N 2-E
" "	**13**	3	5th PM 38-N 1-E
" "	**9**	1	5th PM 39-N 2-E
" "	**4**	1	5th PM 40-N 2-E
LIBBY	**23**	3	5th PM 36-N 1-E
LIBHART	**2**	1	5th PM 40-N 1-W
LIGHTFOOT	**25**	1	5th PM 36-N 3-E
LINK	**24**	1	5th PM 36-N 2-E
LINN	**25**	3	5th PM 36-N 3-E
LITTEN	**13**	4	5th PM 38-N 1-E
LITTLE	**20**	1	5th PM 37-N 3-E
LIVERMORE	**12**	2	5th PM 38-N 1-W
LIVINGSTON	**8**	4	5th PM 39-N 1-E
" "	**9**	1	5th PM 39-N 2-E
LOCKE	**10**	1	5th PM 39-N 3-E

Surname	Map Group	Parcels of Land	Meridian/Township/Range
LOGAN	**7**	4	5th PM 39-N 1-W
LONDON	**17**	3	5th PM 37-N 1-W
" "	**24**	2	5th PM 36-N 2-E
LONG	**15**	22	5th PM 38-N 3-E
" "	**20**	7	5th PM 37-N 3-E
" "	**13**	4	5th PM 38-N 1-E
" "	**23**	3	5th PM 36-N 1-E
" "	**14**	3	5th PM 38-N 2-E
" "	**2**	2	5th PM 40-N 1-W
" "	**22**	1	5th PM 36-N 1-W
" "	**18**	1	5th PM 37-N 1-E
" "	**12**	1	5th PM 38-N 1-W
" "	**10**	1	5th PM 39-N 3-E
LOOMIS	**17**	1	5th PM 37-N 1-W
LORE	**20**	2	5th PM 37-N 3-E
" "	**18**	1	5th PM 37-N 1-E
LOWERY	**8**	1	5th PM 39-N 1-E
LUCAS	**24**	10	5th PM 36-N 2-E
" "	**28**	3	5th PM 35-N 1-E
" "	**2**	1	5th PM 40-N 1-W
LUMPKINS	**14**	1	5th PM 38-N 2-E
LUPTON	**14**	3	5th PM 38-N 2-E
" "	**7**	2	5th PM 39-N 1-W
" "	**8**	1	5th PM 39-N 1-E
LUTS	**29**	2	5th PM 35-N 2-E
LYNCH	**13**	4	5th PM 38-N 1-E
" "	**8**	1	5th PM 39-N 1-E
LYON	**13**	1	5th PM 38-N 1-E
MACK	**27**	3	5th PM 35-N 1-W
MACKAY	**25**	2	5th PM 36-N 3-E
" "	**30**	1	5th PM 35-N 3-E
MACKENZIE	**24**	1	5th PM 36-N 2-E
MACKY	**8**	1	5th PM 39-N 1-E
MADDEN	**15**	3	5th PM 38-N 3-E
" "	**10**	1	5th PM 39-N 3-E
MADDIN	**10**	1	5th PM 39-N 3-E
MADDY	**18**	1	5th PM 37-N 1-E
MAHENY	**12**	2	5th PM 38-N 1-W
MAIDES	**12**	5	5th PM 38-N 1-W
MAIRAT	**8**	1	5th PM 39-N 1-E
MAJOR	**13**	5	5th PM 38-N 1-E
" "	**6**	1	5th PM 39-N 2-W
MALLE	**10**	1	5th PM 39-N 3-E
MALLOW	**22**	2	5th PM 36-N 1-W
MANES	**10**	4	5th PM 39-N 3-E
" "	**9**	1	5th PM 39-N 2-E
" "	**5**	1	5th PM 40-N 3-E
MANESS	**5**	5	5th PM 40-N 3-E
" "	**10**	2	5th PM 39-N 3-E
MANEY	**28**	4	5th PM 35-N 1-E
MANION	**8**	7	5th PM 39-N 1-E
MANN	**13**	2	5th PM 38-N 1-E
MANNING	**22**	24	5th PM 36-N 1-W
" "	**17**	8	5th PM 37-N 1-W
" "	**13**	6	5th PM 38-N 1-E
" "	**23**	4	5th PM 36-N 1-E
MANSFIELD	**11**	1	5th PM 38-N 2-W
MANWARING	**15**	1	5th PM 38-N 3-E
MARA	**9**	1	5th PM 39-N 2-E
MARAS	**10**	1	5th PM 39-N 3-E

Surname	Map Group	Parcels of Land	Meridian/Township/Range		
MARCILLE	**9**	1	5th PM	39-N	2-E
MARGETTS	**8**	1	5th PM	39-N	1-E
MARLE	**20**	1	5th PM	37-N	3-E
MARLEE	**20**	1	5th PM	37-N	3-E
MARLER	**20**	6	5th PM	37-N	3-E
" "	**22**	2	5th PM	36-N	1-W
MARQUESS	**1**	1	5th PM	40-N	2-W
MARSH	**7**	1	5th PM	39-N	1-W
MARSHALL	**23**	5	5th PM	36-N	1-E
" "	**17**	3	5th PM	37-N	1-W
" "	**22**	1	5th PM	36-N	1-W
" "	**3**	1	5th PM	40-N	1-E
MARTIN	**22**	4	5th PM	36-N	1-W
" "	**24**	3	5th PM	36-N	2-E
" "	**13**	2	5th PM	38-N	1-E
" "	**2**	2	5th PM	40-N	1-W
" "	**1**	2	5th PM	40-N	2-W
" "	**21**	1	5th PM	36-N	2-W
" "	**19**	1	5th PM	37-N	2-E
" "	**14**	1	5th PM	38-N	2-E
" "	**9**	1	5th PM	39-N	2-E
MARTINDALE	**30**	1	5th PM	35-N	3-E
MASHMEYER	**8**	2	5th PM	39-N	1-E
MASON	**23**	6	5th PM	36-N	1-E
" "	**26**	4	5th PM	35-N	2-W
" "	**22**	3	5th PM	36-N	1-W
" "	**18**	2	5th PM	37-N	1-E
" "	**8**	1	5th PM	39-N	1-E
MASSIE	**10**	1	5th PM	39-N	3-E
MATCHELL	**22**	1	5th PM	36-N	1-W
MATHEWS	**24**	2	5th PM	36-N	2-E
" "	**17**	1	5th PM	37-N	1-W
" "	**20**	1	5th PM	37-N	3-E
MATHIS	**30**	2	5th PM	35-N	3-E
MATLOCK	**13**	8	5th PM	38-N	1-E
MATTHEWS	**17**	28	5th PM	37-N	1-W
" "	**13**	6	5th PM	38-N	1-E
" "	**23**	4	5th PM	36-N	1-E
" "	**18**	2	5th PM	37-N	1-E
" "	**22**	1	5th PM	36-N	1-W
" "	**20**	1	5th PM	37-N	3-E
MAUL	**19**	1	5th PM	37-N	2-E
MAUNDER	**11**	1	5th PM	38-N	2-W
MAURICE	**25**	3	5th PM	36-N	3-E
MAXWELL	**17**	3	5th PM	37-N	1-W
" "	**23**	2	5th PM	36-N	1-E
" "	**29**	1	5th PM	35-N	2-E
" "	**24**	1	5th PM	36-N	2-E
MAYGER	**10**	3	5th PM	39-N	3-E
MAYHEW	**8**	1	5th PM	39-N	1-E
MCANULTY	**15**	8	5th PM	38-N	3-E
MCBRIDE	**27**	5	5th PM	35-N	1-W
MCCABE	**20**	3	5th PM	37-N	3-E
" "	**18**	1	5th PM	37-N	1-E
MCCANTEY	**8**	1	5th PM	39-N	1-E
MCCAUSLAND	**24**	4	5th PM	36-N	2-E
MCCHESNEY	**12**	5	5th PM	38-N	1-W
MCCLAIN	**27**	1	5th PM	35-N	1-W
MCCLOWNY	**19**	1	5th PM	37-N	2-E
MCCORMICK	**25**	4	5th PM	36-N	3-E

Surname	Map Group	Parcels of Land	Meridian/Township/Range
MCCRACKEN	**13**	3	5th PM 38-N 1-E
" "	**7**	1	5th PM 39-N 1-W
MCCREARY	**25**	3	5th PM 36-N 3-E
" "	**19**	1	5th PM 37-N 2-E
MCCREERY	**3**	1	5th PM 40-N 1-E
MCCUNE	**7**	3	5th PM 39-N 1-W
MCCURDY	**8**	1	5th PM 39-N 1-E
MCCURRY	**14**	1	5th PM 38-N 2-E
MCDONALD	**3**	3	5th PM 40-N 1-E
MCDONOUGH	**13**	1	5th PM 38-N 1-E
" "	**7**	1	5th PM 39-N 1-W
MCDOWELL	**6**	1	5th PM 39-N 2-W
" "	**2**	1	5th PM 40-N 1-W
MCEWIN	**2**	1	5th PM 40-N 1-W
MCGAHAN	**9**	4	5th PM 39-N 2-E
MCGINN	**27**	1	5th PM 35-N 1-W
MCGRADY	**18**	4	5th PM 37-N 1-E
MCGREADY	**18**	11	5th PM 37-N 1-E
" "	**20**	2	5th PM 37-N 3-E
" "	**19**	1	5th PM 37-N 2-E
MCGREW	**24**	1	5th PM 36-N 2-E
MCGUIRE	**13**	1	5th PM 38-N 1-E
MCILVAIN	**14**	3	5th PM 38-N 2-E
" "	**15**	2	5th PM 38-N 3-E
MCILVAINE	**15**	4	5th PM 38-N 3-E
" "	**19**	2	5th PM 37-N 2-E
" "	**25**	1	5th PM 36-N 3-E
" "	**20**	1	5th PM 37-N 3-E
MCINTIRE	**7**	1	5th PM 39-N 1-W
MCKEAN	**5**	1	5th PM 40-N 3-E
MCKEE	**22**	1	5th PM 36-N 1-W
" "	**17**	1	5th PM 37-N 1-W
MCKENZIE	**13**	1	5th PM 38-N 1-E
MCKEON	**13**	3	5th PM 38-N 1-E
" "	**8**	3	5th PM 39-N 1-E
MCLANE	**19**	1	5th PM 37-N 2-E
MCMANUS	**19**	1	5th PM 37-N 2-E
MCMILLEN	**17**	1	5th PM 37-N 1-W
MCMURTREY	**28**	2	5th PM 35-N 1-E
" "	**17**	1	5th PM 37-N 1-W
MCNABB	**29**	1	5th PM 35-N 2-E
MCNALLY	**14**	1	5th PM 38-N 2-E
MCNEAL	**20**	2	5th PM 37-N 3-E
MCPEAKE	**10**	1	5th PM 39-N 3-E
MCPHAILL	**23**	1	5th PM 36-N 1-E
MCSPADEN	**12**	1	5th PM 38-N 1-W
MELVIN	**2**	1	5th PM 40-N 1-W
MERCEILLE	**9**	7	5th PM 39-N 2-E
MERCER	**12**	2	5th PM 38-N 1-W
MERCILE	**9**	2	5th PM 39-N 2-E
MERRY	**23**	4	5th PM 36-N 1-E
" "	**14**	2	5th PM 38-N 2-E
" "	**17**	1	5th PM 37-N 1-W
" "	**19**	1	5th PM 37-N 2-E
MERRYMAN	**8**	1	5th PM 39-N 1-E
MESEY	**10**	1	5th PM 39-N 3-E
MESPLAY	**28**	4	5th PM 35-N 1-E
" "	**20**	3	5th PM 37-N 3-E
METCALF	**12**	5	5th PM 38-N 1-W
MEYER	**8**	1	5th PM 39-N 1-E

Surname	Map Group	Parcels of Land	Meridian/Township/Range
MEYERS	**30**	3	5th PM 35-N 3-E
MIDGETT	**22**	1	5th PM 36-N 1-W
MIDYETT	**22**	5	5th PM 36-N 1-W
MILLER	**19**	3	5th PM 37-N 2-E
" "	**6**	2	5th PM 39-N 2-W
" "	**14**	1	5th PM 38-N 2-E
MILLIGAN	**7**	4	5th PM 39-N 1-W
MINCK	**15**	2	5th PM 38-N 3-E
MISEY	**10**	1	5th PM 39-N 3-E
MISPLAY	**20**	1	5th PM 37-N 3-E
MITCHELL	**10**	5	5th PM 39-N 3-E
" "	**13**	1	5th PM 38-N 1-E
" "	**15**	1	5th PM 38-N 3-E
MOLLY	**19**	1	5th PM 37-N 2-E
MONDAY	**19**	1	5th PM 37-N 2-E
MONTGOMERY	**18**	8	5th PM 37-N 1-E
" "	**23**	2	5th PM 36-N 1-E
" "	**25**	1	5th PM 36-N 3-E
" "	**19**	1	5th PM 37-N 2-E
MOODY	**30**	4	5th PM 35-N 3-E
MOORE	**20**	7	5th PM 37-N 3-E
" "	**30**	3	5th PM 35-N 3-E
" "	**7**	1	5th PM 39-N 1-W
MOREL	**24**	1	5th PM 36-N 2-E
MORELAND	**20**	2	5th PM 37-N 3-E
" "	**19**	1	5th PM 37-N 2-E
MORGAN	**29**	2	5th PM 35-N 2-E
" "	**28**	1	5th PM 35-N 1-E
" "	**27**	1	5th PM 35-N 1-W
MORRIS	**29**	1	5th PM 35-N 2-E
" "	**30**	1	5th PM 35-N 3-E
MORRISON	**7**	3	5th PM 39-N 1-W
" "	**13**	2	5th PM 38-N 1-E
" "	**12**	1	5th PM 38-N 1-W
" "	**6**	1	5th PM 39-N 2-W
" "	**10**	1	5th PM 39-N 3-E
MORRISSON	**10**	1	5th PM 39-N 3-E
MORROW	**2**	3	5th PM 40-N 1-W
MOSES	**22**	2	5th PM 36-N 1-W
MOSHER	**13**	1	5th PM 38-N 1-E
MOSLANDER	**3**	3	5th PM 40-N 1-E
MOTHERSHEAD	**10**	6	5th PM 39-N 3-E
MOULTRAY	**15**	1	5th PM 38-N 3-E
MOUNT	**12**	1	5th PM 38-N 1-W
MOUTRAY	**17**	2	5th PM 37-N 1-W
" "	**6**	1	5th PM 39-N 2-W
MUDD	**20**	1	5th PM 37-N 3-E
MUNDAY	**19**	1	5th PM 37-N 2-E
" "	**4**	1	5th PM 40-N 2-E
MUNDY	**19**	2	5th PM 37-N 2-E
MURPHEY	**15**	4	5th PM 38-N 3-E
" "	**20**	1	5th PM 37-N 3-E
" "	**10**	1	5th PM 39-N 3-E
MURPHY	**22**	4	5th PM 36-N 1-W
" "	**20**	4	5th PM 37-N 3-E
" "	**14**	4	5th PM 38-N 2-E
" "	**17**	2	5th PM 37-N 1-W
" "	**9**	2	5th PM 39-N 2-E
" "	**12**	1	5th PM 38-N 1-W
" "	**7**	1	5th PM 39-N 1-W

Surname	Map Group	Parcels of Land	Meridian/Township/Range
MURPHY (Cont'd)	**1**	1	5th PM 40-N 2-W
MURRILL	**10**	2	5th PM 39-N 3-E
MYERS	**19**	9	5th PM 37-N 2-E
" "	**13**	1	5th PM 38-N 1-E
NAUMAN	**8**	1	5th PM 39-N 1-E
NAVE	**30**	1	5th PM 35-N 3-E
NEALY	**13**	1	5th PM 38-N 1-E
NEFF	**2**	3	5th PM 40-N 1-W
NETTLETON	**11**	1	5th PM 38-N 2-W
" "	**8**	1	5th PM 39-N 1-E
NEUSE	**22**	2	5th PM 36-N 1-W
NEVES	**20**	1	5th PM 37-N 3-E
NEVISON	**12**	2	5th PM 38-N 1-W
NICHOLAS	**30**	2	5th PM 35-N 3-E
NICHOLS	**21**	1	5th PM 36-N 2-W
" "	**13**	1	5th PM 38-N 1-E
NICHOLSON	**19**	7	5th PM 37-N 2-E
" "	**18**	2	5th PM 37-N 1-E
" "	**14**	1	5th PM 38-N 2-E
NIEHANS	**12**	4	5th PM 38-N 1-W
" "	**8**	1	5th PM 39-N 1-E
NIEHAUS	**12**	3	5th PM 38-N 1-W
NILEND	**27**	2	5th PM 35-N 1-W
NOEL	**3**	1	5th PM 40-N 1-E
NORP	**8**	3	5th PM 39-N 1-E
NORRIS	**7**	3	5th PM 39-N 1-W
NORTHCUT	**14**	1	5th PM 38-N 2-E
" "	**7**	1	5th PM 39-N 1-W
NORTRUP	**16**	1	5th PM 37-N 2-W
NORVELL	**22**	2	5th PM 36-N 1-W
NUESE	**19**	5	5th PM 37-N 2-E
OBRIEN	**19**	2	5th PM 37-N 2-E
OBUCHAN	**9**	1	5th PM 39-N 2-E
OBUCHON	**19**	3	5th PM 37-N 2-E
" "	**24**	1	5th PM 36-N 2-E
" "	**20**	1	5th PM 37-N 3-E
" "	**15**	1	5th PM 38-N 3-E
OCHELTREE	**13**	1	5th PM 38-N 1-E
OFARRELL	**9**	1	5th PM 39-N 2-E
OFARROLL	**9**	3	5th PM 39-N 2-E
OGDEN	**7**	1	5th PM 39-N 1-W
OHANLIN	**19**	2	5th PM 37-N 2-E
OHANLON	**19**	3	5th PM 37-N 2-E
OHARVER	**10**	1	5th PM 39-N 3-E
OLIVER	**17**	1	5th PM 37-N 1-W
" "	**14**	1	5th PM 38-N 2-E
OMARA	**19**	1	5th PM 37-N 2-E
ONEIL	**8**	2	5th PM 39-N 1-E
ORCHARD	**22**	2	5th PM 36-N 1-W
ORCHARDS	**22**	1	5th PM 36-N 1-W
ORME	**13**	2	5th PM 38-N 1-E
" "	**18**	1	5th PM 37-N 1-E
OTTMAN	**12**	1	5th PM 38-N 1-W
OUTLAY	**7**	1	5th PM 39-N 1-W
OWENS	**15**	6	5th PM 38-N 3-E
" "	**9**	4	5th PM 39-N 2-E
" "	**18**	1	5th PM 37-N 1-E
PAGE	**29**	2	5th PM 35-N 2-E
" "	**15**	2	5th PM 38-N 3-E
" "	**8**	2	5th PM 39-N 1-E

Surname	Map Group	Parcels of Land	Meridian/Township/Range
PAGE (Cont'd)	**9**	2	5th PM 39-N 2-E
PAINE	**28**	2	5th PM 35-N 1-E
PALMATORY	**21**	3	5th PM 36-N 2-W
PALMER	**9**	1	5th PM 39-N 2-E
PARK	**3**	3	5th PM 40-N 1-E
PARKER	**13**	4	5th PM 38-N 1-E
" "	**10**	2	5th PM 39-N 3-E
" "	**30**	1	5th PM 35-N 3-E
PARKIN	**18**	4	5th PM 37-N 1-E
" "	**23**	2	5th PM 36-N 1-E
PARKINSON	**14**	5	5th PM 38-N 2-E
" "	**13**	1	5th PM 38-N 1-E
" "	**6**	1	5th PM 39-N 2-W
" "	**1**	1	5th PM 40-N 2-W
PARKS	**30**	2	5th PM 35-N 3-E
PARMER	**10**	2	5th PM 39-N 3-E
PARTENAY	**9**	2	5th PM 39-N 2-E
PATCH	**27**	2	5th PM 35-N 1-W
PATTEN	**4**	1	5th PM 40-N 2-E
PATTERSON	**19**	2	5th PM 37-N 2-E
PATTON	**3**	2	5th PM 40-N 1-E
" "	**4**	2	5th PM 40-N 2-E
" "	**8**	1	5th PM 39-N 1-E
" "	**7**	1	5th PM 39-N 1-W
PAUL	**18**	1	5th PM 37-N 1-E
" "	**17**	1	5th PM 37-N 1-W
PAWLING	**2**	1	5th PM 40-N 1-W
PEAK	**28**	2	5th PM 35-N 1-E
PEARSHALL	**18**	2	5th PM 37-N 1-E
PEARSON	**17**	2	5th PM 37-N 1-W
" "	**24**	1	5th PM 36-N 2-E
PEASE	**19**	6	5th PM 37-N 2-E
PECK	**28**	2	5th PM 35-N 1-E
PEEBLES	**19**	3	5th PM 37-N 2-E
" "	**30**	1	5th PM 35-N 3-E
PEERY	**29**	1	5th PM 35-N 2-E
" "	**24**	1	5th PM 36-N 2-E
PEIRCE	**9**	1	5th PM 39-N 2-E
PELICAN	**9**	1	5th PM 39-N 2-E
PENROSE	**13**	1	5th PM 38-N 1-E
PENYMAN	**15**	2	5th PM 38-N 3-E
PERKINS	**9**	1	5th PM 39-N 2-E
PERKS	**8**	2	5th PM 39-N 1-E
PERRY	**14**	15	5th PM 38-N 2-E
" "	**19**	7	5th PM 37-N 2-E
" "	**25**	2	5th PM 36-N 3-E
" "	**23**	1	5th PM 36-N 1-E
" "	**20**	1	5th PM 37-N 3-E
" "	**13**	1	5th PM 38-N 1-E
" "	**15**	1	5th PM 38-N 3-E
PERRYMAN	**15**	2	5th PM 38-N 3-E
" "	**20**	1	5th PM 37-N 3-E
PERSHALL	**18**	7	5th PM 37-N 1-E
PETER	**3**	2	5th PM 40-N 1-E
PETERS	**3**	1	5th PM 40-N 1-E
PETERSON	**30**	2	5th PM 35-N 3-E
PETTIGREW	**18**	2	5th PM 37-N 1-E
" "	**17**	2	5th PM 37-N 1-W
PHILLIPS	**2**	1	5th PM 40-N 1-W
PHILPOT	**28**	1	5th PM 35-N 1-E

Surname	Map Group	Parcels of Land	Meridian/Township/Range
PICKERING	**22**	1	5th PM 36-N 1-W
PICKLES	**12**	4	5th PM 38-N 1-W
PIERCE	**9**	4	5th PM 39-N 2-E
" "	**14**	1	5th PM 38-N 2-E
PINSON	**10**	5	5th PM 39-N 3-E
" "	**12**	4	5th PM 38-N 1-W
POINDEXTER	**7**	1	5th PM 39-N 1-W
POLITTE	**9**	1	5th PM 39-N 2-E
POLLARD	**13**	1	5th PM 38-N 1-E
POPE	**2**	1	5th PM 40-N 1-W
PORTAIS	**5**	1	5th PM 40-N 3-E
PORTEL	**15**	2	5th PM 38-N 3-E
PORTELL	**15**	2	5th PM 38-N 3-E
PORTER	**23**	3	5th PM 36-N 1-E
POUND	**3**	1	5th PM 40-N 1-E
POWELL	**13**	5	5th PM 38-N 1-E
" "	**17**	2	5th PM 37-N 1-W
" "	**22**	1	5th PM 36-N 1-W
POWER	**16**	1	5th PM 37-N 2-W
POWERS	**27**	4	5th PM 35-N 1-W
PRADER	**13**	5	5th PM 38-N 1-E
PRATHER	**2**	3	5th PM 40-N 1-W
PRATT	**27**	1	5th PM 35-N 1-W
" "	**7**	1	5th PM 39-N 1-W
PRATTE	**14**	1	5th PM 38-N 2-E
PREWETT	**29**	2	5th PM 35-N 2-E
PREWITT	**29**	1	5th PM 35-N 2-E
PRICE	**27**	1	5th PM 35-N 1-W
PROFFETT	**25**	1	5th PM 36-N 3-E
PROFIT	**25**	1	5th PM 36-N 3-E
PROFITT	**25**	2	5th PM 36-N 3-E
PROSS	**3**	3	5th PM 40-N 1-E
PROVENCE	**25**	1	5th PM 36-N 3-E
PRUDEN	**23**	1	5th PM 36-N 1-E
PRUETT	**29**	1	5th PM 35-N 2-E
PRYOR	**28**	1	5th PM 35-N 1-E
PUCKETT	**13**	7	5th PM 38-N 1-E
PULLAM	**22**	1	5th PM 36-N 1-W
PULLIAM	**22**	1	5th PM 36-N 1-W
PURSLEY	**30**	7	5th PM 35-N 3-E
PYATT	**22**	5	5th PM 36-N 1-W
QUEEN	**29**	1	5th PM 35-N 2-E
RACINE	**15**	1	5th PM 38-N 3-E
RAMBO	**15**	1	5th PM 38-N 3-E
RAMSEY	**28**	12	5th PM 35-N 1-E
" "	**23**	2	5th PM 36-N 1-E
RANDALL	**30**	1	5th PM 35-N 3-E
RANEY	**13**	3	5th PM 38-N 1-E
RANNEY	**7**	2	5th PM 39-N 1-W
RATLEY	**30**	1	5th PM 35-N 3-E
" "	**25**	1	5th PM 36-N 3-E
RAY	**15**	3	5th PM 38-N 3-E
READING	**9**	1	5th PM 39-N 2-E
REANDEAU	**15**	1	5th PM 38-N 3-E
REANDO	**15**	3	5th PM 38-N 3-E
RECTOR	**13**	1	5th PM 38-N 1-E
REED	**19**	5	5th PM 37-N 2-E
" "	**10**	4	5th PM 39-N 3-E
" "	**15**	3	5th PM 38-N 3-E
" "	**8**	1	5th PM 39-N 1-E

Surname	Map Group	Parcels of Land	Meridian/Township/Range
REED (Cont'd)	**7**	1	5th PM 39-N 1-W
REID	**25**	3	5th PM 36-N 3-E
RELFE	**30**	7	5th PM 35-N 3-E
" "	**24**	6	5th PM 36-N 2-E
" "	**25**	6	5th PM 36-N 3-E
" "	**29**	3	5th PM 35-N 2-E
REMY	**7**	1	5th PM 39-N 1-W
RENFRO	**23**	1	5th PM 36-N 1-E
" "	**13**	1	5th PM 38-N 1-E
" "	**7**	1	5th PM 39-N 1-W
RENN	**30**	1	5th PM 35-N 3-E
REVES	**18**	2	5th PM 37-N 1-E
REYBURN	**24**	1	5th PM 36-N 2-E
REYNOLDS	**13**	3	5th PM 38-N 1-E
" "	**30**	1	5th PM 35-N 3-E
RICE	**28**	6	5th PM 35-N 1-E
" "	**23**	1	5th PM 36-N 1-E
" "	**2**	1	5th PM 40-N 1-W
RICHARDSON	**18**	1	5th PM 37-N 1-E
" "	**15**	1	5th PM 38-N 3-E
RIDGWAY	**7**	2	5th PM 39-N 1-W
RIENDO	**15**	1	5th PM 38-N 3-E
RILEY	**2**	1	5th PM 40-N 1-W
RISSER	**7**	1	5th PM 39-N 1-W
ROBERSON	**23**	2	5th PM 36-N 1-E
ROBERT	**15**	1	5th PM 38-N 3-E
ROBERTS	**15**	2	5th PM 38-N 3-E
ROBINSON	**23**	15	5th PM 36-N 1-E
" "	**24**	5	5th PM 36-N 2-E
" "	**19**	5	5th PM 37-N 2-E
" "	**18**	4	5th PM 37-N 1-E
" "	**30**	3	5th PM 35-N 3-E
" "	**22**	1	5th PM 36-N 1-W
" "	**25**	1	5th PM 36-N 3-E
RODDA	**8**	1	5th PM 39-N 1-E
RODERICK	**7**	2	5th PM 39-N 1-W
ROGERS	**4**	4	5th PM 40-N 2-E
ROLFE	**24**	1	5th PM 36-N 2-E
ROLL	**13**	3	5th PM 38-N 1-E
ROMAINE	**10**	1	5th PM 39-N 3-E
RONGEY	**20**	2	5th PM 37-N 3-E
RONGY	**20**	1	5th PM 37-N 3-E
ROONEY	**9**	7	5th PM 39-N 2-E
ROOT	**18**	2	5th PM 37-N 1-E
ROSE	**8**	2	5th PM 39-N 1-E
ROSS	**8**	1	5th PM 39-N 1-E
ROUSAN	**5**	1	5th PM 40-N 3-E
ROUSIN	**9**	4	5th PM 39-N 2-E
" "	**10**	2	5th PM 39-N 3-E
ROUSSIN	**9**	3	5th PM 39-N 2-E
" "	**10**	3	5th PM 39-N 3-E
" "	**3**	3	5th PM 40-N 1-E
" "	**4**	3	5th PM 40-N 2-E
ROZIER	**19**	2	5th PM 37-N 2-E
" "	**20**	2	5th PM 37-N 3-E
RUGGLES	**24**	2	5th PM 36-N 2-E
RULO	**9**	3	5th PM 39-N 2-E
RUMELL	**8**	1	5th PM 39-N 1-E
RUSS	**19**	1	5th PM 37-N 2-E
RUSSELL	**30**	2	5th PM 35-N 3-E

Surname	Map Group	Parcels of Land	Meridian/Township/Range
RUSSELL (Cont'd)	**19**	1	5th PM 37-N 2-E
RUTLEDGE	**13**	1	5th PM 38-N 1-E
SANDERS	**22**	4	5th PM 36-N 1-W
SANSOCIE	**9**	2	5th PM 39-N 2-E
SAPPINGTON	**6**	2	5th PM 39-N 2-W
SAUNDERS	**15**	6	5th PM 38-N 3-E
SAWYER	**17**	1	5th PM 37-N 1-W
SCHANE	**13**	1	5th PM 38-N 1-E
SCHARIT	**12**	2	5th PM 38-N 1-W
SCHENCK	**7**	1	5th PM 39-N 1-W
SCHIEBEL	**3**	1	5th PM 40-N 1-E
SCHNEIDER	**6**	1	5th PM 39-N 2-W
SCHOOL	**13**	1	5th PM 38-N 1-E
SCHUTTE	**14**	1	5th PM 38-N 2-E
SCHWICE	**13**	2	5th PM 38-N 1-E
SCOTT	**25**	11	5th PM 36-N 3-E
" "	**22**	6	5th PM 36-N 1-W
" "	**30**	5	5th PM 35-N 3-E
" "	**20**	5	5th PM 37-N 3-E
" "	**15**	4	5th PM 38-N 3-E
" "	**18**	3	5th PM 37-N 1-E
" "	**27**	1	5th PM 35-N 1-W
" "	**17**	1	5th PM 37-N 1-W
" "	**16**	1	5th PM 37-N 2-W
" "	**13**	1	5th PM 38-N 1-E
" "	**9**	1	5th PM 39-N 2-E
SELF	**25**	6	5th PM 36-N 3-E
SENSENDERFER	**9**	2	5th PM 39-N 2-E
SERVICE	**16**	1	5th PM 37-N 2-W
SEYMOUR	**23**	3	5th PM 36-N 1-E
" "	**22**	2	5th PM 36-N 1-W
" "	**18**	2	5th PM 37-N 1-E
" "	**19**	1	5th PM 37-N 2-E
SHAW	**11**	1	5th PM 38-N 2-W
SHEPHERD	**18**	6	5th PM 37-N 1-E
" "	**8**	1	5th PM 39-N 1-E
SHERLOCK	**30**	4	5th PM 35-N 3-E
SHIELDS	**12**	1	5th PM 38-N 1-W
" "	**9**	1	5th PM 39-N 2-E
SHIMIN	**19**	1	5th PM 37-N 2-E
SHIRLEY	**22**	2	5th PM 36-N 1-W
" "	**13**	2	5th PM 38-N 1-E
SHIRLOCK	**30**	1	5th PM 35-N 3-E
SHMELL	**3**	1	5th PM 40-N 1-E
SHOLAR	**20**	1	5th PM 37-N 3-E
SHONBACKER	**28**	3	5th PM 35-N 1-E
SHOOK	**8**	2	5th PM 39-N 1-E
" "	**4**	1	5th PM 40-N 2-E
SHOOKS	**3**	1	5th PM 40-N 1-E
SHORE	**13**	10	5th PM 38-N 1-E
" "	**17**	3	5th PM 37-N 1-W
SHOTWELL	**22**	1	5th PM 36-N 1-W
SHOULTS	**22**	1	5th PM 36-N 1-W
SHUMATE	**13**	5	5th PM 38-N 1-E
SHURTLEFF	**15**	1	5th PM 38-N 3-E
SHUTTE	**14**	1	5th PM 38-N 2-E
SIGNAIGO	**9**	5	5th PM 39-N 2-E
SILENCE	**12**	3	5th PM 38-N 1-W
SILVER	**14**	1	5th PM 38-N 2-E
SILVERS	**13**	9	5th PM 38-N 1-E

Surname	Map Group	Parcels of Land	Meridian/Township/Range
SILVERS (Cont'd)	**14**	2	5th PM 38-N 2-E
SILVEY	**18**	8	5th PM 37-N 1-E
" "	**17**	1	5th PM 37-N 1-W
SILVY	**18**	2	5th PM 37-N 1-E
SIMMONS	**17**	1	5th PM 37-N 1-W
" "	**2**	1	5th PM 40-N 1-W
SIMONS	**24**	1	5th PM 36-N 2-E
SIMPSON	**24**	3	5th PM 36-N 2-E
" "	**14**	2	5th PM 38-N 2-E
" "	**8**	1	5th PM 39-N 1-E
SIMS	**15**	1	5th PM 38-N 3-E
SINEX	**19**	1	5th PM 37-N 2-E
SITTON	**23**	5	5th PM 36-N 1-E
SKEWES	**3**	5	5th PM 40-N 1-E
SLOAN	**25**	8	5th PM 36-N 3-E
" "	**29**	3	5th PM 35-N 2-E
" "	**24**	1	5th PM 36-N 2-E
SLOANE	**25**	1	5th PM 36-N 3-E
SLOSS	**12**	3	5th PM 38-N 1-W
SMITH	**23**	27	5th PM 36-N 1-E
" "	**14**	20	5th PM 38-N 2-E
" "	**15**	19	5th PM 38-N 3-E
" "	**10**	14	5th PM 39-N 3-E
" "	**19**	12	5th PM 37-N 2-E
" "	**18**	11	5th PM 37-N 1-E
" "	**22**	10	5th PM 36-N 1-W
" "	**17**	10	5th PM 37-N 1-W
" "	**20**	10	5th PM 37-N 3-E
" "	**8**	9	5th PM 39-N 1-E
" "	**12**	7	5th PM 38-N 1-W
" "	**26**	6	5th PM 35-N 2-W
" "	**28**	3	5th PM 35-N 1-E
" "	**24**	2	5th PM 36-N 2-E
" "	**2**	2	5th PM 40-N 1-W
" "	**1**	2	5th PM 40-N 2-W
" "	**25**	1	5th PM 36-N 3-E
" "	**13**	1	5th PM 38-N 1-E
SMITHER	**13**	1	5th PM 38-N 1-E
SONSUCIE	**8**	2	5th PM 39-N 1-E
SOUCI	**9**	1	5th PM 39-N 2-E
SOULARD	**3**	2	5th PM 40-N 1-E
" "	**2**	2	5th PM 40-N 1-W
SPEAR	**22**	2	5th PM 36-N 1-W
SPEERS	**22**	1	5th PM 36-N 1-W
SPENCER	**24**	1	5th PM 36-N 2-E
SPRINGER	**13**	17	5th PM 38-N 1-E
" "	**12**	1	5th PM 38-N 1-W
STACEY	**12**	1	5th PM 38-N 1-W
STAFFORD	**10**	4	5th PM 39-N 3-E
STAMM	**22**	1	5th PM 36-N 1-W
STANDEFER	**8**	2	5th PM 39-N 1-E
STAPLES	**17**	2	5th PM 37-N 1-W
" "	**16**	2	5th PM 37-N 2-W
" "	**18**	1	5th PM 37-N 1-E
STAPPLES	**17**	1	5th PM 37-N 1-W
STATLER	**21**	3	5th PM 36-N 2-W
STEAD	**8**	1	5th PM 39-N 1-E
STEERMAN	**22**	3	5th PM 36-N 1-W
" "	**23**	1	5th PM 36-N 1-E
STEMBER	**14**	1	5th PM 38-N 2-E

Surname	Map Group	Parcels of Land	Meridian/Township/Range
STEPHENS	**28**	3	5th PM 35-N 1-E
" "	**17**	1	5th PM 37-N 1-W
STEPHENSON	**23**	2	5th PM 36-N 1-E
" "	**29**	1	5th PM 35-N 2-E
STEVENS	**28**	1	5th PM 35-N 1-E
" "	**2**	1	5th PM 40-N 1-W
STEVENSON	**25**	3	5th PM 36-N 3-E
" "	**23**	2	5th PM 36-N 1-E
" "	**30**	1	5th PM 35-N 3-E
" "	**22**	1	5th PM 36-N 1-W
STEWART	**30**	5	5th PM 35-N 3-E
" "	**18**	4	5th PM 37-N 1-E
" "	**28**	2	5th PM 35-N 1-E
" "	**27**	2	5th PM 35-N 1-W
STOFER	**30**	1	5th PM 35-N 3-E
STOLLE	**25**	1	5th PM 36-N 3-E
STONE	**22**	10	5th PM 36-N 1-W
" "	**17**	5	5th PM 37-N 1-W
" "	**23**	3	5th PM 36-N 1-E
" "	**25**	1	5th PM 36-N 3-E
STONER	**23**	4	5th PM 36-N 1-E
STONG	**10**	1	5th PM 39-N 3-E
STOVALL	**13**	1	5th PM 38-N 1-E
" "	**14**	1	5th PM 38-N 2-E
STOW	**20**	2	5th PM 37-N 3-E
STRAUSER	**2**	2	5th PM 40-N 1-W
STROHBECK	**12**	3	5th PM 38-N 1-W
STRONG	**10**	2	5th PM 39-N 3-E
STROTHER	**18**	1	5th PM 37-N 1-E
STUART	**10**	2	5th PM 39-N 3-E
STUDLEY	**28**	4	5th PM 35-N 1-E
SUHR	**8**	1	5th PM 39-N 1-E
SUICOCK	**13**	2	5th PM 38-N 1-E
SULLIVAN	**2**	2	5th PM 40-N 1-W
SULLIVANTE	**1**	2	5th PM 40-N 2-W
SUMMERS	**13**	5	5th PM 38-N 1-E
" "	**12**	3	5th PM 38-N 1-W
" "	**14**	1	5th PM 38-N 2-E
SUMPTER	**23**	1	5th PM 36-N 1-E
SUTTON	**30**	11	5th PM 35-N 3-E
SWAIN	**23**	1	5th PM 36-N 1-E
SWAN	**14**	4	5th PM 38-N 2-E
" "	**7**	1	5th PM 39-N 1-W
SWENDT	**20**	1	5th PM 37-N 3-E
SWIER	**16**	1	5th PM 37-N 2-W
SWOFFORD	**22**	2	5th PM 36-N 1-W
TALBOT	**14**	2	5th PM 38-N 2-E
TANEY	**14**	2	5th PM 38-N 2-E
TASCHETTA	**2**	2	5th PM 40-N 1-W
TAUSSIG	**15**	2	5th PM 38-N 3-E
TAYLOR	**30**	6	5th PM 35-N 3-E
" "	**25**	3	5th PM 36-N 3-E
" "	**28**	2	5th PM 35-N 1-E
" "	**9**	2	5th PM 39-N 2-E
" "	**3**	2	5th PM 40-N 1-E
" "	**27**	1	5th PM 35-N 1-W
" "	**14**	1	5th PM 38-N 2-E
TEAS	**23**	1	5th PM 36-N 1-E
" "	**22**	1	5th PM 36-N 1-W
TEDDER	**28**	5	5th PM 35-N 1-E

Surname	Map Group	Parcels of Land	Meridian/Township/Range
TEDDER (Cont'd)	**30**	1	5th PM 35-N 3-E
TEMBY	**9**	2	5th PM 39-N 2-E
TENISON	**23**	1	5th PM 36-N 1-E
TENNESON	**23**	2	5th PM 36-N 1-E
TENNISON	**23**	6	5th PM 36-N 1-E
THAYER	**7**	3	5th PM 39-N 1-W
THEBEAU	**8**	4	5th PM 39-N 1-E
THIBEAU	**9**	2	5th PM 39-N 2-E
THODD	**7**	1	5th PM 39-N 1-W
THOMAS	**29**	8	5th PM 35-N 2-E
" "	**9**	5	5th PM 39-N 2-E
" "	**12**	2	5th PM 38-N 1-W
" "	**25**	1	5th PM 36-N 3-E
THOMPSON	**20**	6	5th PM 37-N 3-E
" "	**25**	4	5th PM 36-N 3-E
" "	**29**	2	5th PM 35-N 2-E
" "	**23**	2	5th PM 36-N 1-E
" "	**24**	1	5th PM 36-N 2-E
" "	**16**	1	5th PM 37-N 2-W
" "	**8**	1	5th PM 39-N 1-E
" "	**2**	1	5th PM 40-N 1-W
THORP	**7**	4	5th PM 39-N 1-W
" "	**23**	1	5th PM 36-N 1-E
THURMOND	**10**	1	5th PM 39-N 3-E
" "	**2**	1	5th PM 40-N 1-W
THWING	**4**	1	5th PM 40-N 2-E
TIBEAN	**9**	2	5th PM 39-N 2-E
TIBEAU	**9**	1	5th PM 39-N 2-E
TIFFT	**20**	2	5th PM 37-N 3-E
TILLSON	**13**	7	5th PM 38-N 1-E
TINISON	**23**	7	5th PM 36-N 1-E
TINKERSON	**22**	2	5th PM 36-N 1-W
TODD	**19**	6	5th PM 37-N 2-E
" "	**7**	5	5th PM 39-N 1-W
" "	**13**	1	5th PM 38-N 1-E
" "	**12**	1	5th PM 38-N 1-W
" "	**3**	1	5th PM 40-N 1-E
TORINI	**9**	1	5th PM 39-N 2-E
TOWNSEND	**27**	1	5th PM 35-N 1-W
TRAMMELL	**30**	1	5th PM 35-N 3-E
TREMLETT	**8**	1	5th PM 39-N 1-E
TRIMBLE	**15**	2	5th PM 38-N 3-E
TRIPP	**25**	1	5th PM 36-N 3-E
TRIPPE	**14**	1	5th PM 38-N 2-E
TROKY	**10**	1	5th PM 39-N 3-E
TROUTT	**13**	1	5th PM 38-N 1-E
TROXELL	**24**	2	5th PM 36-N 2-E
TRUDAU	**15**	1	5th PM 38-N 3-E
TUCKER	**16**	3	5th PM 37-N 2-W
" "	**24**	1	5th PM 36-N 2-E
" "	**12**	1	5th PM 38-N 1-W
" "	**7**	1	5th PM 39-N 1-W
TUFLY	**13**	1	5th PM 38-N 1-E
TULLOCK	**25**	2	5th PM 36-N 3-E
" "	**18**	1	5th PM 37-N 1-E
TURNBAUGH	**21**	1	5th PM 36-N 2-W
TURNBOUGH	**21**	3	5th PM 36-N 2-W
TURNER	**27**	4	5th PM 35-N 1-W
" "	**8**	2	5th PM 39-N 1-E
" "	**7**	2	5th PM 39-N 1-W

Surname	Map Group	Parcels of Land	Meridian/Township/Range
TURPIN	**20**	1	5th PM 37-N 3-E
TWITTY	**9**	2	5th PM 39-N 2-E
TYREY	**4**	1	5th PM 40-N 2-E
TYZACK	**8**	1	5th PM 39-N 1-E
ULLMAN	**23**	2	5th PM 36-N 1-E
" "	**19**	2	5th PM 37-N 2-E
VALENTIN	**18**	1	5th PM 37-N 1-E
VALLE	**20**	2	5th PM 37-N 3-E
" "	**25**	1	5th PM 36-N 3-E
VALLEY	**4**	2	5th PM 40-N 2-E
" "	**9**	1	5th PM 39-N 2-E
VAN FRANK	**20**	1	5th PM 37-N 3-E
VAN HOUTEN	**7**	2	5th PM 39-N 1-W
VAN REED	**10**	10	5th PM 39-N 3-E
" "	**15**	1	5th PM 38-N 3-E
VANDIVER	**20**	1	5th PM 37-N 3-E
VARNER	**18**	1	5th PM 37-N 1-E
VERNER	**18**	1	5th PM 37-N 1-E
" "	**19**	1	5th PM 37-N 2-E
VICTOR	**12**	1	5th PM 38-N 1-W
VIENNA	**2**	3	5th PM 40-N 1-W
VILLEMAR	**20**	1	5th PM 37-N 3-E
VILLMARE	**15**	2	5th PM 38-N 3-E
VILMAIN	**15**	1	5th PM 38-N 3-E
VILMAR	**15**	2	5th PM 38-N 3-E
" "	**9**	1	5th PM 39-N 2-E
VINEYARD	**28**	1	5th PM 35-N 1-E
VINYARD	**29**	2	5th PM 35-N 2-E
VIVRETT	**10**	1	5th PM 39-N 3-E
VORNBERG	**12**	5	5th PM 38-N 1-W
WADE	**15**	1	5th PM 38-N 3-E
WALKER	**27**	1	5th PM 35-N 1-W
" "	**30**	1	5th PM 35-N 3-E
" "	**16**	1	5th PM 37-N 2-W
" "	**13**	1	5th PM 38-N 1-E
WALLEN	**25**	13	5th PM 36-N 3-E
" "	**30**	12	5th PM 35-N 3-E
" "	**24**	2	5th PM 36-N 2-E
WALSER	**13**	2	5th PM 38-N 1-E
WALTHALL	**20**	1	5th PM 37-N 3-E
WALTON	**18**	44	5th PM 37-N 1-E
" "	**23**	12	5th PM 36-N 1-E
" "	**24**	6	5th PM 36-N 2-E
" "	**17**	3	5th PM 37-N 1-W
" "	**25**	2	5th PM 36-N 3-E
" "	**20**	2	5th PM 37-N 3-E
" "	**4**	1	5th PM 40-N 2-E
WARD	**13**	4	5th PM 38-N 1-E
" "	**9**	4	5th PM 39-N 2-E
" "	**21**	3	5th PM 36-N 2-W
WARDEN	**15**	1	5th PM 38-N 3-E
WARE	**25**	3	5th PM 36-N 3-E
" "	**19**	2	5th PM 37-N 2-E
WARNER	**23**	1	5th PM 36-N 1-E
" "	**18**	1	5th PM 37-N 1-E
" "	**8**	1	5th PM 39-N 1-E
WARSON	**13**	1	5th PM 38-N 1-E
WATERS	**21**	3	5th PM 36-N 2-W
WATKINS	**20**	1	5th PM 37-N 3-E
WATSON	**13**	1	5th PM 38-N 1-E

Surname	Map Group	Parcels of Land	Meridian/Township/Range		
WAUGH	**20**	1	5th PM	37-N	3-E
WEIDLE	**15**	1	5th PM	38-N	3-E
WEIGER	**25**	1	5th PM	36-N	3-E
WEIGHER	**20**	1	5th PM	37-N	3-E
WELKER	**23**	6	5th PM	36-N	1-E
WELLS	**3**	1	5th PM	40-N	1-E
WELSH	**3**	1	5th PM	40-N	1-E
WESTENFELT	**3**	3	5th PM	40-N	1-E
WESTHOVER	**2**	1	5th PM	40-N	1-W
WESTOVER	**20**	2	5th PM	37-N	3-E
" "	**9**	2	5th PM	39-N	2-E
" "	**1**	2	5th PM	40-N	2-W
" "	**25**	1	5th PM	36-N	3-E
" "	**7**	1	5th PM	39-N	1-W
" "	**2**	1	5th PM	40-N	1-W
WETER	**11**	1	5th PM	38-N	2-W
WHALEY	**23**	1	5th PM	36-N	1-E
WHAYLEY	**25**	1	5th PM	36-N	3-E
WHEALAN	**22**	2	5th PM	36-N	1-W
WHEALEY	**25**	2	5th PM	36-N	3-E
" "	**20**	2	5th PM	37-N	3-E
WHITBY	**11**	1	5th PM	38-N	2-W
WHITE	**14**	9	5th PM	38-N	2-E
" "	**22**	6	5th PM	36-N	1-W
" "	**13**	4	5th PM	38-N	1-E
" "	**12**	4	5th PM	38-N	1-W
" "	**15**	4	5th PM	38-N	3-E
" "	**23**	3	5th PM	36-N	1-E
" "	**20**	3	5th PM	37-N	3-E
" "	**7**	3	5th PM	39-N	1-W
" "	**17**	2	5th PM	37-N	1-W
WHITEHEAD	**24**	1	5th PM	36-N	2-E
WHITENER	**18**	6	5th PM	37-N	1-E
" "	**17**	5	5th PM	37-N	1-W
WHITLEY	**2**	2	5th PM	40-N	1-W
WHITMIRE	**2**	1	5th PM	40-N	1-W
WHYERS	**8**	3	5th PM	39-N	1-E
WIATT	**20**	2	5th PM	37-N	3-E
" "	**24**	1	5th PM	36-N	2-E
" "	**25**	1	5th PM	36-N	3-E
WICKERS	**22**	3	5th PM	36-N	1-W
" "	**17**	1	5th PM	37-N	1-W
WICKS	**10**	3	5th PM	39-N	3-E
WIGGER	**23**	4	5th PM	36-N	1-E
" "	**19**	3	5th PM	37-N	2-E
" "	**24**	2	5th PM	36-N	2-E
WILCOX	**4**	2	5th PM	40-N	2-E
WILDER	**2**	3	5th PM	40-N	1-W
WILDMAN	**20**	2	5th PM	37-N	3-E
" "	**25**	1	5th PM	36-N	3-E
WILKERSON	**22**	3	5th PM	36-N	1-W
WILKINSON	**15**	4	5th PM	38-N	3-E
" "	**22**	2	5th PM	36-N	1-W
" "	**17**	1	5th PM	37-N	1-W
" "	**1**	1	5th PM	40-N	2-W
WILKSON	**13**	2	5th PM	38-N	1-E
" "	**7**	1	5th PM	39-N	1-W
WILLARD	**23**	6	5th PM	36-N	1-E
" "	**27**	4	5th PM	35-N	1-W
WILLIAMS	**25**	8	5th PM	36-N	3-E

Surname	Map Group	Parcels of Land	Meridian/Township/Range
WILLIAMS (Cont'd)	**28**	4	5th PM 35-N 1-E
" "	**13**	3	5th PM 38-N 1-E
" "	**24**	2	5th PM 36-N 2-E
" "	**8**	1	5th PM 39-N 1-E
" "	**7**	1	5th PM 39-N 1-W
WILLOUGHBY	**19**	1	5th PM 37-N 2-E
WILMESHERR	**12**	1	5th PM 38-N 1-W
WILSON	**18**	5	5th PM 37-N 1-E
" "	**17**	2	5th PM 37-N 1-W
" "	**23**	1	5th PM 36-N 1-E
" "	**13**	1	5th PM 38-N 1-E
WIMER	**2**	1	5th PM 40-N 1-W
WINDER	**8**	1	5th PM 39-N 1-E
WINEOUR	**15**	3	5th PM 38-N 3-E
WISDOM	**18**	2	5th PM 37-N 1-E
WOLLIN	**25**	1	5th PM 36-N 3-E
WOOD	**25**	6	5th PM 36-N 3-E
" "	**12**	4	5th PM 38-N 1-W
" "	**16**	3	5th PM 37-N 2-W
WOODARD	**23**	4	5th PM 36-N 1-E
WOODRUFF	**27**	2	5th PM 35-N 1-W
WOODS	**29**	4	5th PM 35-N 2-E
" "	**19**	2	5th PM 37-N 2-E
" "	**14**	2	5th PM 38-N 2-E
" "	**28**	1	5th PM 35-N 1-E
WOOLFORD	**29**	2	5th PM 35-N 2-E
WOOLSAY	**18**	1	5th PM 37-N 1-E
WORTHAM	**28**	1	5th PM 35-N 1-E
" "	**25**	1	5th PM 36-N 3-E
WORTHINGTON	**8**	3	5th PM 39-N 1-E
WRIGHT	**23**	19	5th PM 36-N 1-E
" "	**29**	2	5th PM 35-N 2-E
" "	**13**	2	5th PM 38-N 1-E
" "	**14**	1	5th PM 38-N 2-E
" "	**10**	1	5th PM 39-N 3-E
WYATT	**14**	1	5th PM 38-N 2-E
XENO	**4**	1	5th PM 40-N 2-E
YATES	**10**	5	5th PM 39-N 3-E
YEATES	**29**	1	5th PM 35-N 2-E
YEAUGHBERRY	**9**	1	5th PM 39-N 2-E
YELLER	**13**	2	5th PM 38-N 1-E
YODER	**27**	3	5th PM 35-N 1-W
YOUGHBERRY	**8**	1	5th PM 39-N 1-E
YOUNG	**14**	1	5th PM 38-N 2-E
YOUNT	**27**	9	5th PM 35-N 1-W
" "	**23**	1	5th PM 36-N 1-E
ZENT	**23**	1	5th PM 36-N 1-E
ZOLMAN	**25**	2	5th PM 36-N 3-E

– Part II –

Township Map Groups

Map Group 1: Index to Land Patents

Township 40-North Range 2-West (5th PM)

After you locate an individual in this Index, take note of the Section and Section Part then proceed to the Land Patent map on the pages immediately following. You should have no difficulty locating the corresponding parcel of land.

The "For More Info" Column will lead you to more information about the underlying Patents. See the *Legend* at right, and the "How to Use this Book" chapter, for more information.

LEGEND

"For More Info . . . " column

- **A** = Authority (Legislative Act, See Appendix "A")
- **B** = Block or Lot (location in Section unknown)
- **C** = Cancelled Patent
- **F** = Fractional Section
- **G** = Group (Multi-Patentee Patent, see Appendix "C")
- **V** = Overlaps another Parcel
- **R** = Re-Issued (Parcel patented more than once)

(A & G items require you to look in the Appendixes referred to above. All other Letter-designations followed by a number require you to locate line-items in this index that possess the ID number found after the letter).

ID	Individual in Patent	Sec.	Sec. Part	Date Issued	Other Counties	For More Info . . .
17	BAILEY, James H	36	NWNE	1870-09-09	Crawford	A1
21	BIRCHFIELD, John	24	NENW	1835-09-09	Crawford	A1
28	BLAIR, Stephen W	25	SWSE	1874-03-20	Crawford	A3
10	BREDELL, Edward	13	SW	1848-07-01	Crawford;Franklin	A1 G29 F R34
11	" "	24	S½NW	1848-07-01	Crawford	A1 G30 F
9	" "	24	SESE	1849-06-01	Crawford	A1 G31
8	" "	25	NESE	1856-09-01	Crawford	A1
22	BROWN, Joseph H	25	NENE	1875-03-01	Crawford	A3 V27
34	BURNS, Uriah	13	SW	1825-07-15	Crawford;Franklin	A1 F R10
31	CALVIRD, Thomas	13	SWNE	1838-09-07	Crawford;Franklin	A1
30	" "	13	N½NE	1844-08-01	Crawford;Franklin	A1 F
15	CLARK, Jacob	25	NWSE	1849-06-01	Crawford	A1 G62
16	" "	25	SESE	1851-11-01	Crawford	A1 G63
1	CLEMENT, Barclay	24	SENW	1848-07-01	Crawford	A1 F
10	COLLIER, George	13	SW	1848-07-01	Crawford;Franklin	A1 G29 F R34
24	CROW, Ross M	25	NWNE	1867-05-01	Crawford	A1 V27
11	DUNKLIN, Stephen T	24	S½NW	1848-07-01	Crawford	A1 G30 F
4	ENLOE, Benjamin	24	W½NW	1838-09-07	Crawford	A1 F
3	" "	13	SENE	1850-06-01	Crawford;Franklin	A1
20	ENLOE, Jesse	24	SE	1825-07-15	Crawford	A1 F
9	GAMBLE, Archibald	24	SESE	1849-06-01	Crawford	A1 G31
23	GREEN, Obediah	24	W½SE	1840-10-01	Crawford	A1 G119 F
18	HAMBLETON, James	24	NW	1840-10-01	Crawford	A1 F
5	HIBLER, Daniel	13	S½NW	1859-05-02	Crawford;Franklin	A1
6	" "	25	SENE	1859-05-02	Crawford	A1 V27
15	INGE, Chesley B	25	NWSE	1849-06-01	Crawford	A1 G62
12	INGE, George R	13	W½SE	1837-11-07	Crawford;Franklin	A1
25	LARUE, Samuel	13	NE	1840-10-01	Crawford;Franklin	A1 F
19	MARQUESS, James	25	SWNE	1835-09-09	Crawford	A1 V27
2	MARTIN, Bartlett	25	SW	1825-07-15	Crawford	A1
16	MARTIN, Thomas J	25	SESE	1851-11-01	Crawford	A1 G63
29	MURPHY, Thomas C	13	SESE	1860-10-01	Crawford;Franklin	A1 G188
29	MURPHY, William S	13	SESE	1860-10-01	Crawford;Franklin	A1 G188
23	PARKINSON, John	24	W½SE	1840-10-01	Crawford	A1 G119 F
32	SMITH, Turner	24	NESE	1848-07-01	Crawford	A1 F
33	" "	24	SENE	1848-07-01	Crawford	A1
26	SULLIVANTE, Stephen	24	SW	1825-07-15	Crawford	A1 F
27	" "	25	NE	1840-10-01	Crawford	A1 V19, 6, 24, 22
13	WESTOVER, George T	25	NW	1848-07-01	Crawford	A1 F
14	" "	36	SWSW	1851-11-01	Crawford	A1
7	WILKINSON, Daniel	25	N½NW	1866-06-01	Crawford	A1 F

HIBLER
Daniel
1859

CALVIRD
Thomas
1838

LARUE
Samuel
1840

ENLOE
Benjamin
1850

13

BREDELL [29]
Edward
1848

INGE
George R
1837

BURNS
Uriah
1825

MURPHY [188]
Thomas C
1860

BIRCHFIELD
John
1835

Washington County

ENLOE
Benjamin
1838

HAMBLETON
James
1840

BREDELL [30]
Edward
1848

CLEMENT
Barclay
1848

SMITH
Turner
1848

24

GREEN [119]
Obediah
1840

SMITH
Turner
1848

SULLIVANTE
Stephen
1825

ENLOE
Jesse
1825

BREDELL [31]
Edward
1849

WILKINSON
Daniel
1866

CROW
Ross M
1867

BROWN
Joseph H
1875

WESTOVER
George T
1848

SULLIVANTE
Stephen
1840

Crawford County

MARQUESS
James
1835

HIBLER
Daniel
1859

25

CLARK [62]
Jacob
1849

BREDELL
Edward
1856

MARTIN
Bartlett
1825

BLAIR
Stephen W
1874

CLARK [63]
Jacob
1851

BAILEY
James H
1870

36

WESTOVER
George T
1851

Patent Map

T40-N R2-W
5th PM Meridian

Map Group 1

Township Statistics

Parcels Mapped	:	34
Number of Patents	:	33
Number of Individuals	:	31
Patentees Identified	:	28
Number of Surnames	:	27
Multi-Patentee Parcels	:	7
Oldest Patent Date	:	7/15/1825
Most Recent Patent	:	3/1/1875
Block/Lot Parcels	:	0
Parcels Re - Issued	:	1
Parcels that Overlap	:	5
Cities and Towns	:	0
Cemeteries	:	0

Note: the area contained in this map amounts to far less than a full Township. Therefore, its contents are completely on this single page (instead of a "normal" 2-page spread).

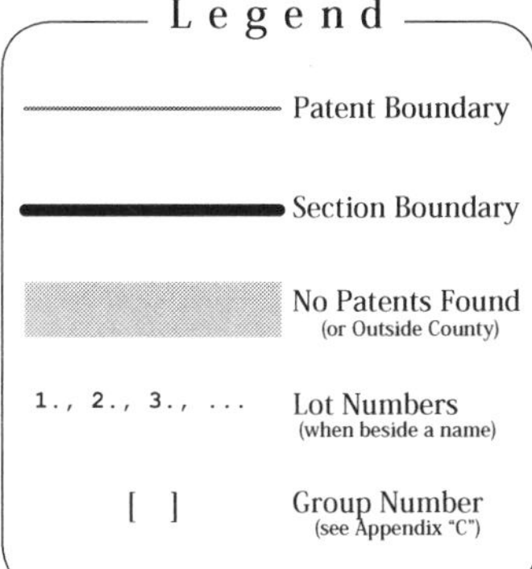

Scale: Section = 1 mile X 1 mile
(generally, with some exceptions)

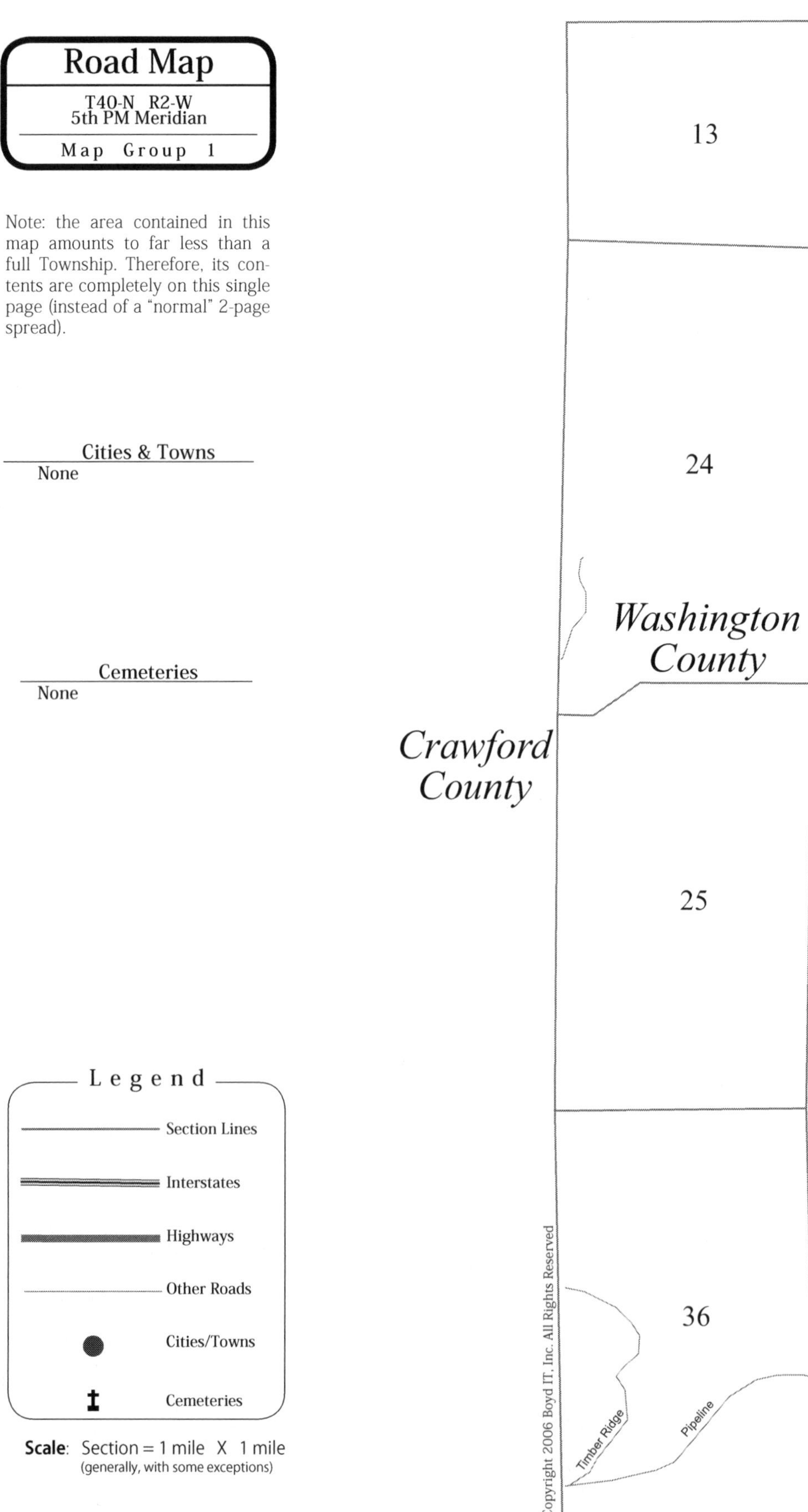
Road Map
T40-N R2-W
5th PM Meridian
Map Group 1
Note: the area contained in this map amounts to far less than a full Township. Therefore, its contents are completely on this single page (instead of a "normal" 2-page spread).
Cities & Towns
None
Cemeteries
None
Legend
Section Lines
Interstates
Highways
Other Roads
Cities/Towns
Cemeteries
Scale: Section = 1 mile X 1 mile
(generally, with some exceptions)
13
24
Washington County
Crawford County
25
36
Timber Ridge
Pipeline
Copyright 2006 Boyd IT, Inc. All Rights Reserved

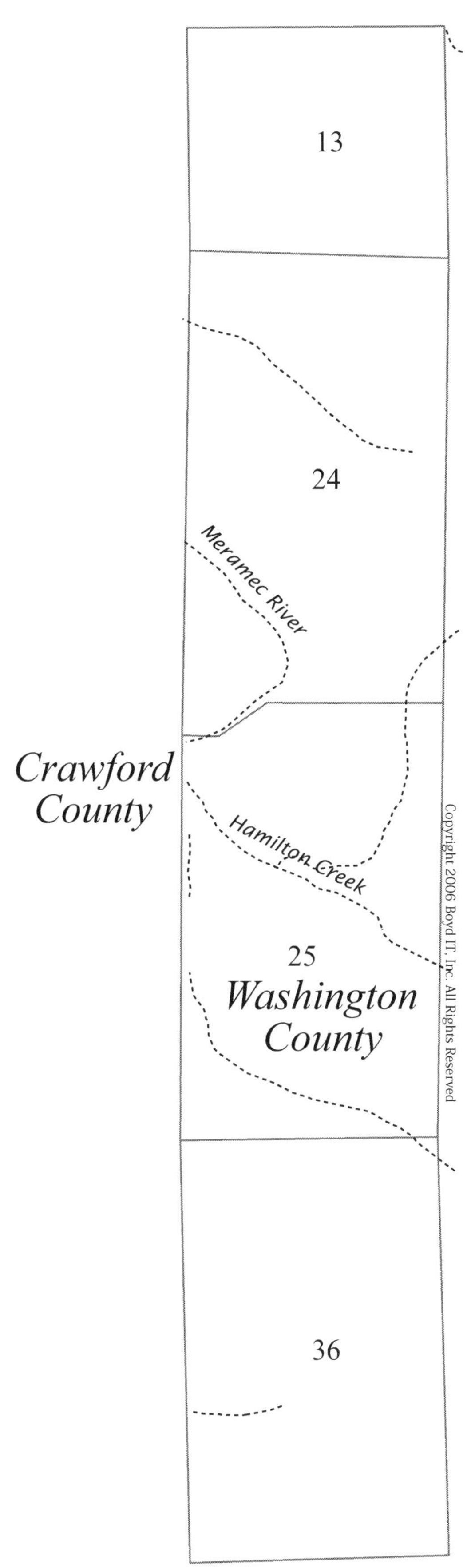

Historical Map

T40-N R2-W
5th PM Meridian

Map Group 1

Note: the area contained in this map amounts to far less than a full Township. Therefore, its contents are completely on this single page (instead of a "normal" 2-page spread).

Cities & Towns

None

Cemeteries

None

Legend

- Section Lines
- Railroads
- Large Rivers & Bodies of Water
- Streams/Creeks & Small Rivers
- Cities/Towns
- Cemeteries

Scale: Section = 1 mile X 1 mile
(there are some exceptions)

Map Group 2: Index to Land Patents

Township 40-North Range 1-West (5th PM)

After you locate an individual in this Index, take note of the Section and Section Part then proceed to the Land Patent map on the pages immediately following. You should have no difficulty locating the corresponding parcel of land.

The "For More Info" Column will lead you to more information about the underlying Patents. See the *Legend* at right, and the "How to Use this Book" chapter, for more information.

LEGEND

"For More Info . . . " column

A = Authority (Legislative Act, See Appendix "A")
B = Block or Lot (location in Section unknown)
C = Cancelled Patent
F = Fractional Section
G = Group (Multi-Patentee Patent, see Appendix "C")
V = Overlaps another Parcel
R = Re-Issued (Parcel patented more than once)

(A & G items require you to look in the Appendixes referred to above. All other Letter-designations followed by a number require you to locate line-items in this index that possess the ID number found after the letter).

ID	Individual in Patent	Sec.	Sec. Part	Date Issued	Other Counties	For More Info . . .
61	AMES, Edgar	31	N½NE	1859-05-02		A1 G3
61	AMES, Henry	31	N½NE	1859-05-02		A1 G3
38	ANDERSON, Alexander C	33	E½	1857-06-10		A1
135	BASSETT, William W	31	SESE	1849-06-01		A1
66	BENOIST, Eugene H	21	SWSW	1905-06-26		A1
35	BLANTON, Absalom	29	SWNW	1856-11-01		A1 G20
37	BLANTON, Absolom	32	SWNW	1849-06-01		A1 G21
65	BLANTON, Elbert S	29	N½SE	1871-11-25		A1
51	BOLTON, Charles	15	SWNW	1868-06-01	Franklin	A1
35	BREDELL, Edward	29	SWNW	1856-11-01		A1 G20
36	BRYAN, Absalom	35	SESE	1838-09-07		A1
110	CALVERD, Peter	18	N½2NW	1849-06-01	Franklin	A1 G41
108	CALVERD, Peter C	19	NENE	1850-01-01		A1 G40
109	CALVIRD, Peter C	30	N½1SW	1849-06-01		A1
77	CANTRELL, Henry J	35	NENE	1856-09-01		A1
127	CHARLEVILLE, Victor	17	N½SE	1874-09-10	Franklin	A3
134	CHRISTY, William T	19	SWSW	1849-06-20		A1 F
44	CLARK, Austin	18	S½1NW	1851-11-01	Franklin	A1 G58
45	CLARK, Austin W	29	SESE	1871-11-25		A1
85	CLARK, Jacob	33	W½NW	1845-10-01		A1 G60
88	" "	22	SENE	1849-06-01		A1 G64
83	" "	23	SWNW	1849-06-01		A1 G60
84	" "	30	S½2NW	1849-06-01		A1 G60
86	" "	30	SWSE	1849-06-01		A1 G61
87	" "	18	N½1SW	1851-11-01	Franklin	A1 G65
44	" "	18	S½1NW	1851-11-01	Franklin	A1 G58
82	" "	30	N½1NW	1851-11-01		A1
35	" "	29	SWNW	1856-11-01		A1 G20
78	COE, Henry J	29	E½NW	1869-07-01		A1
79	" "	29	NWNW	1869-07-01		A1
76	DAVIDSON, Henry	21	W½SE	1875-05-20		A3
90	DAYTON, John	17	NW	1859-05-02	Franklin	A1
52	DELAURIERE, Charles F	23	SENW	1856-06-03		A2
91	DEMOSS, John	25	E½SW	1857-06-10		A1
92	" "	25	N½NW	1857-06-10		A1
93	" "	25	SENW	1857-06-10		A1
94	" "	25	W½SE	1857-06-10		A1
67	DINGUID, Fannie B	21	NWSW	1900-07-21		A3
68	" "	21	SWNW	1900-07-21		A3
104	DOTY, Lot	29	NE	1897-08-24		A3
116	EASTIN, Robert	25	SWNW	1840-10-01		A1
132	FRITTS, William M	17	W½SW	1896-03-25	Franklin	A3
80	FRITZ, Henry J	21	N½NE	1892-04-09		A3
107	GALLAHER, Patrick	17	S½SE	1873-10-15	Franklin	A3
40	GAMBLE, Archibald	31	N½1NW	1856-09-01		A1
41	" "	31	N½2NW	1856-09-01		A1

ID	Individual in Patent	Sec.	Sec. Part	Date Issued	Other Counties	For More Info . . .
42	GAMBLE, Archibald (Cont'd)	31	S½1NW	1857-07-28		A1
43	" "	31	S½4NW	1857-07-28		A1
103	GARRETT, Levi	29	N½SW	1873-05-22		A3
72	GENSIL, George R	21	N½NW	1866-11-01		A1
73	" "	21	SENW	1866-11-01		A1
62	GUT, Edward F	35	W½	1857-06-10		A1
99	HANS, Jordan C	17	NESW	1875-07-30	Franklin	A3
100	HAUS, Jordan C	15	N½SW	1875-02-01	Franklin	A3
85	HIBLER, Daniel	33	W½NW	1845-10-01		A1 G60
83	" "	23	SWNW	1849-06-01		A1 G60
84	" "	30	S½2NW	1849-06-01		A1 G60
86	" "	30	SWSE	1849-06-01		A1 G61
86	HIBLER, Isaac	30	SWSE	1849-06-01		A1 G61
130	HULSEY, William	24	E½NW	1835-09-02		A1
131	" "	25	NWSW	1840-10-01		A1
55	JACKSON, Clark	21	E½SW	1899-04-17		A3
120	JACKSON, Smith	27	S½SE	1857-06-10		A1
121	" "	27	SESW	1857-06-10		A1
125	KAVANAUGH, Thomas	15	NWNW	1868-06-01	Franklin	A1
114	KIMBERLIN, Renard	17	SESW	1848-02-01	Franklin	A1
37	" "	32	SWNW	1849-06-01		A1 G21
49	KIMBERLING, Benjamin	24	W½NE	1826-05-01		A1
70	KIRKPATRICK, Francis W	29	SESW	1849-06-01		A1 G159
69	" "	29	SWSW	1849-06-01		A1 G158
128	LIBHART, William H	15	S½SW	1875-02-01	Franklin	A3
63	LONG, Edwin A	32	NESE	1845-10-01		A1
64	" "	33	SWSW	1845-10-01		A1
117	LUCAS, Samuel W	33	NWSW	1845-10-01		A1
105	MARTIN, Mulford	27	NW	1860-03-01		A1
106	" "	27	W½SW	1860-03-01		A1
88	MCDOWELL, William	22	SENE	1849-06-01		A1 G64
97	MCEWIN, John	13	E½SW	1826-05-01	Franklin	A1
39	MELVIN, Alfred	30	S½2SW	1851-11-01		A1 G180
59	MORROW, David	31	NWSE	1856-10-01		A1
60	" "	31	SWNE	1856-10-01		A1
58	" "	31	N½1SW	1857-07-28		A1
53	NEFF, Charles	31	NESE	1904-09-28		A3
54	" "	31	SENE	1904-09-28		A3
81	NEFF, Isaiah	19	S½NE	1903-10-01		A3
50	PAWLING, Benjamin M	24	E½SE	1838-09-07		A1
111	PHILLIPS, Peter	18	S½2NW	1854-10-02	Franklin	A1
115	POPE, Richard	15	E½NW	1875-09-20	Franklin	A3
57	PRATHER, Daniel	13	W½NE	1843-04-10	Franklin	A1
56	" "	13	SWSW	1856-01-15	Franklin	A1
133	PRATHER, William	13	SENW	1840-10-01	Franklin	A1
89	RICE, Joel T	15	E½	1858-05-03	Franklin	A1
126	RILEY, Thomas	35	W½SE	1860-03-01		A1
98	SIMMONS, John	35	W½NE	1857-06-10		A1
95	SMITH, John E	13	NENW	1849-06-01	Franklin	A1
129	SMITH, William H	18	N½2SW	1851-11-01	Franklin	A1
69	SOULARD, Benjamin A	29	SWSW	1849-06-01		A1 G158
70	SOULARD, Benjamin S	29	SESW	1849-06-01		A1 G159
70	SOULARD, James G	29	SESW	1849-06-01		A1 G159
69	" "	29	SWSW	1849-06-01		A1 G158
88	STEVENS, Richard H	22	SENE	1849-06-01		A1 G64
101	STRAUSER, Josiah	21	E½SE	1890-02-18		A3
102	" "	21	S½NE	1890-02-18		A3
110	SULLIVAN, Stephen	18	N½2NW	1849-06-01	Franklin	A1 G41
39	" "	30	S½2SW	1851-11-01		A1 G180
112	TASCHETTA, Peter	13	E½NE	1859-11-01	Franklin	A1
113	" "	13	SE	1859-11-01	Franklin	A1
71	THOMPSON, Francis W	23	E½	1857-06-10		A1
108	THURMOND, Bennett	19	NENE	1850-01-01		A1 G40
122	VIENNA, Stephen	27	N½SE	1860-03-01		A1
123	" "	27	NE	1860-03-01		A1
124	" "	27	NESW	1860-03-01		A1
74	WESTHOVER, George T	18	NWSE	1851-11-01	Franklin	A1
75	WESTOVER, George T	30	N½2SW	1849-06-20		A1
118	WHITLEY, Samuel	35	SENE	1837-11-07		A1
119	" "	36	SWNW	1837-11-07		A1
87	WHITMIRE, John	18	N½1SW	1851-11-01	Franklin	A1 G65
46	WILDER, Benjamin F	25	E½NE	1860-03-01		A1
47	" "	25	E½SE	1860-03-01		A1

ID	Individual in Patent	Sec.	Sec. Part	Date Issued	Other Counties	For More Info . . .
48	WILDER, Benjamin F (Cont'd)	25	SWNE	1860-03-01		A1
96	WIMER, John M	32	W½SW	1849-06-01		A1

Patent Map

T40-N R1-W
5th PM Meridian

Map Group 2

Township Statistics

Parcels Mapped	:	101
Number of Patents	:	85
Number of Individuals	:	82
Patentees Identified	:	75
Number of Surnames	:	69
Multi-Patentee Parcels	:	15
Oldest Patent Date	:	5/1/1826
Most Recent Patent	:	6/26/1905
Block/Lot Parcels	:	15
Parcels Re - Issued	:	0
Parcels that Overlap	:	0
Cities and Towns	:	1
Cemeteries	:	2

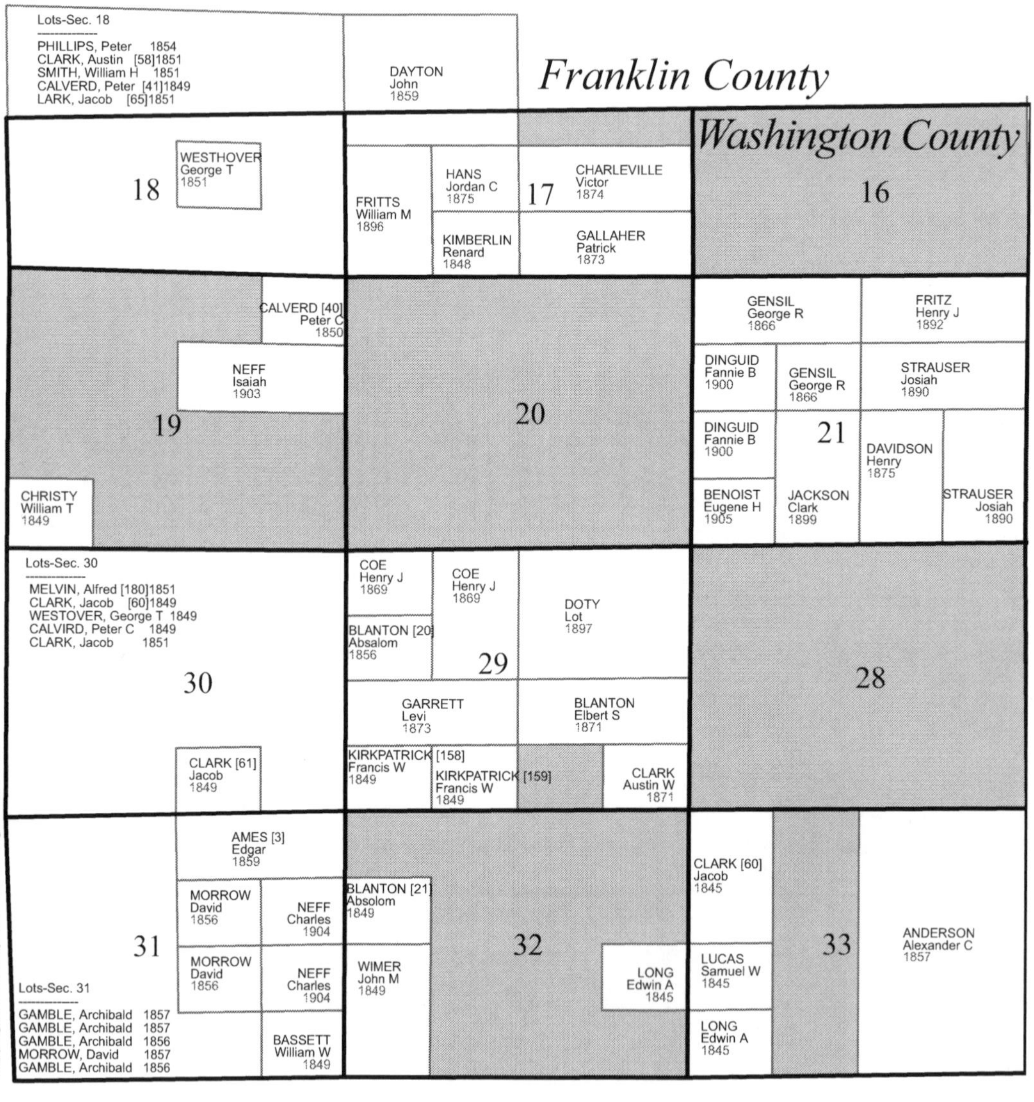

Franklin County

Washington County

Lots-Sec. 18
PHILLIPS, Peter 1854
CLARK, Austin [58]1851
SMITH, William H 1851
CALVERD, Peter [41]1849
LARK, Jacob [65]1851

DAYTON John 1859

18
WESTHOVER George T 1851

17
FRITTS William M 1896
HANS Jordan C 1875
KIMBERLIN Renard 1848
CHARLEVILLE Victor 1874
GALLAHER Patrick 1873

16

19
CALVERD [40] Peter C 1850
NEFF Isaiah 1903
CHRISTY William T 1849

20

21
GENSIL George R 1866
FRITZ Henry J 1892
DINGUID Fannie B 1900
GENSIL George R 1866
STRAUSER Josiah 1890
DINGUID Fannie B 1900
DAVIDSON Henry 1875
BENOIST Eugene H 1905
JACKSON Clark 1899
STRAUSER Josiah 1890

30
Lots-Sec. 30
MELVIN, Alfred [180]1851
CLARK, Jacob [60]1849
WESTOVER, George T 1849
CALVIRD, Peter C 1849
CLARK, Jacob 1851
CLARK [61] Jacob 1849

29
COE Henry J 1869
COE Henry J 1869
DOTY Lot 1897
BLANTON [20] Absalom 1856
GARRETT Levi 1873
BLANTON Elbert S 1871
KIRKPATRICK [158] Francis W 1849
KIRKPATRICK [159] Francis W 1849
CLARK Austin W 1871

28

31
AMES [3] Edgar 1859
MORROW David 1856
NEFF Charles 1904
MORROW David 1856
NEFF Charles 1904
BASSETT William W 1849
Lots-Sec. 31
GAMBLE, Archibald 1857
GAMBLE, Archibald 1857
GAMBLE, Archibald 1856
MORROW, David 1857
GAMBLE, Archibald 1856

32
BLANTON [21] Absolom 1849
WIMER John M 1849
LONG Edwin A 1845

33
CLARK [60] Jacob 1845
LUCAS Samuel W 1845
LONG Edwin A 1845
ANDERSON Alexander C 1857

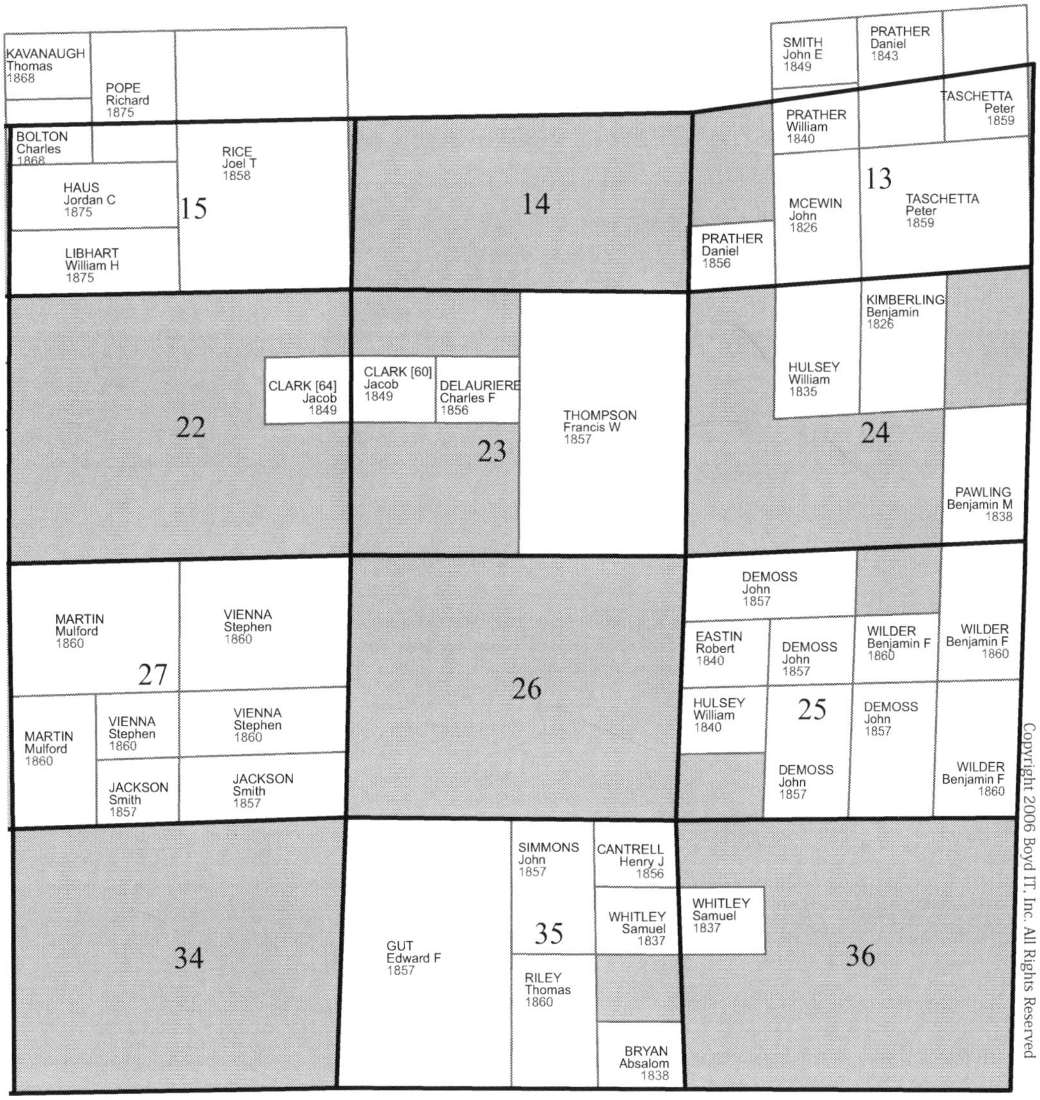

KAVANAUGH Thomas 1868
POPE Richard 1875
BOLTON Charles 1868
HAUS Jordan C 1875
LIBHART William H 1875
RICE Joel T 1858
15
14
SMITH John E 1849
PRATHER Daniel 1843
PRATHER William 1840
TASCHETTA Peter 1859
MCEWIN John 1826
13
TASCHETTA Peter 1859
PRATHER Daniel 1856
KIMBERLING Benjamin 1826
HULSEY William 1835
24
PAWLING Benjamin M 1838
CLARK [64] Jacob 1849
22
CLARK [60] Jacob 1849
DELAURIERE Charles F 1856
23
THOMPSON Francis W 1857
MARTIN Mulford 1860
VIENNA Stephen 1860
27
MARTIN Mulford 1860
VIENNA Stephen 1860
VIENNA Stephen 1860
JACKSON Smith 1857
JACKSON Smith 1857
26
DEMOSS John 1857
EASTIN Robert 1840
DEMOSS John 1857
WILDER Benjamin F 1860
WILDER Benjamin F 1860
HULSEY William 1840
25
DEMOSS John 1857
DEMOSS John 1857
WILDER Benjamin F 1860
34
GUT Edward F 1857
SIMMONS John 1857
CANTRELL Henry J 1856
WHITLEY Samuel 1837
35
WHITLEY Samuel 1837
RILEY Thomas 1860
BRYAN Absalom 1838
36

Helpful Hints

1. This Map's INDEX can be found on the preceding pages.
2. Refer to Map "C" to see where this Township lies within Washington County, Missouri.
3. Numbers within square brackets [ ] denote a multi-patentee land parcel (multi-owner). Refer to Appendix "C" for a full list of members in this group.
4. Areas that look to be crowded with Patentees usually indicate multiple sales of the same parcel (Re-issues) or Overlapping parcels. See this Township's Index for an explanation of these and other circumstances that might explain "odd" groupings of Patentees on this map.

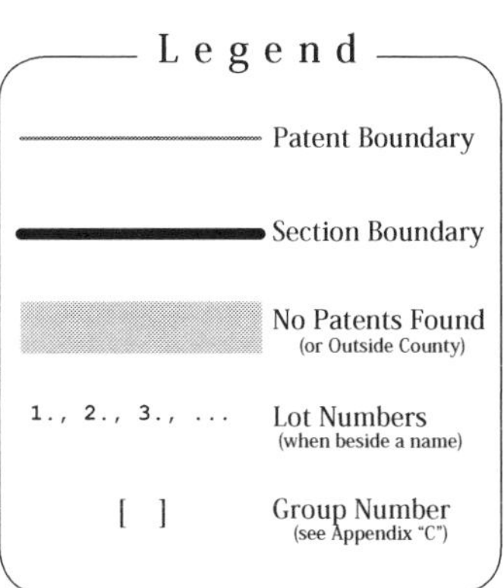

Scale: Section = 1 mile X 1 mile
(generally, with some exceptions)

Road Map

T40-N R1-W
5th PM Meridian

Map Group 2

Cities & Towns
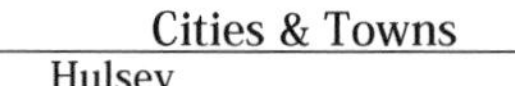
Hulsey

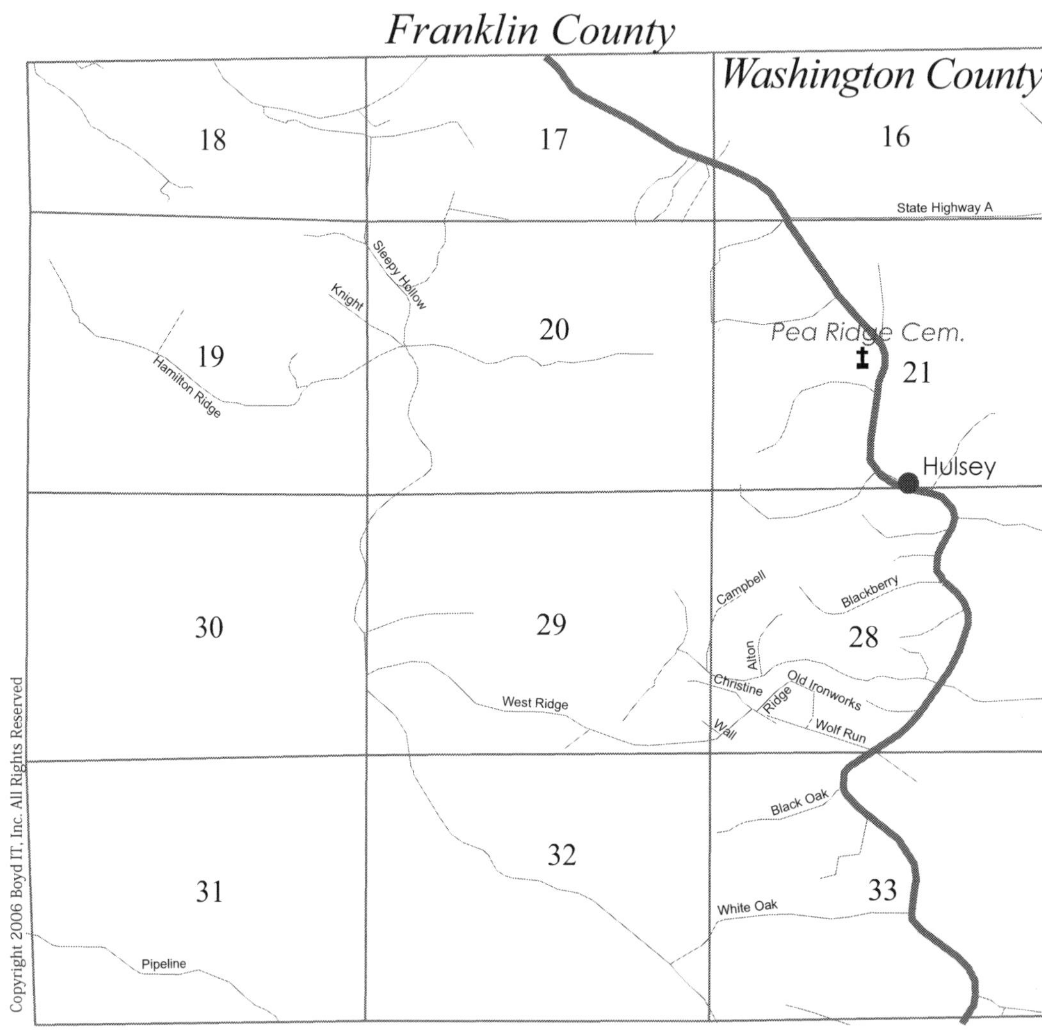

Cemeteries
New Hope Cemetery
Pea Ridge Cemetery

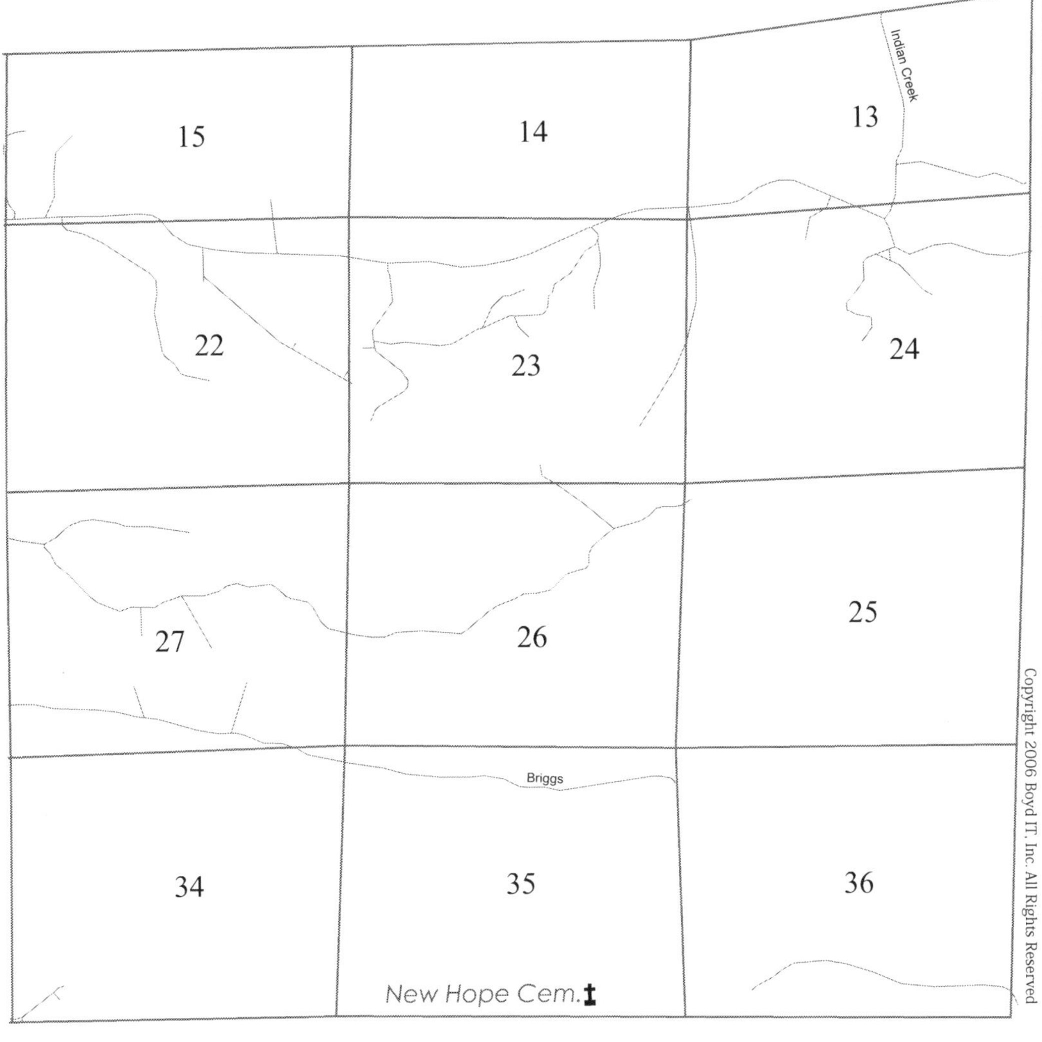

Helpful Hints

1. This road map has a number of uses, but primarily it is to help you: a) find the present location of land owned by your ancestors (at least the general area), b) find cemeteries and city-centers, and c) estimate the route/roads used by Census-takers & tax-assessors.

2. If you plan to travel to Washington County to locate cemeteries or land parcels, please pick up a modern travel map for the area before you do. Mapping old land parcels on modern maps is not as exact a science as you might think. Just the slightest variations in public land survey coordinates, estimates of parcel boundaries, or road-map deviations can greatly alter a map's representation of how a road either does or doesn't cross a particular parcel of land.

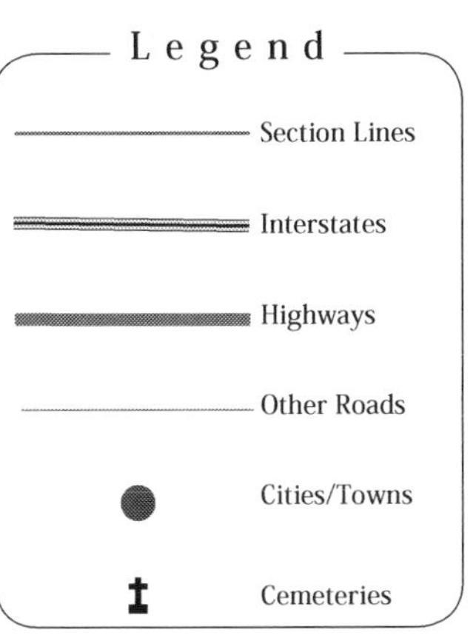

Scale: Section = 1 mile X 1 mile
(generally, with some exceptions)

Historical Map

T40-N R1-W
5th PM Meridian

Map Group 2

Cities & Towns
Hulsey

Cemeteries
New Hope Cemetery
Pea Ridge Cemetery

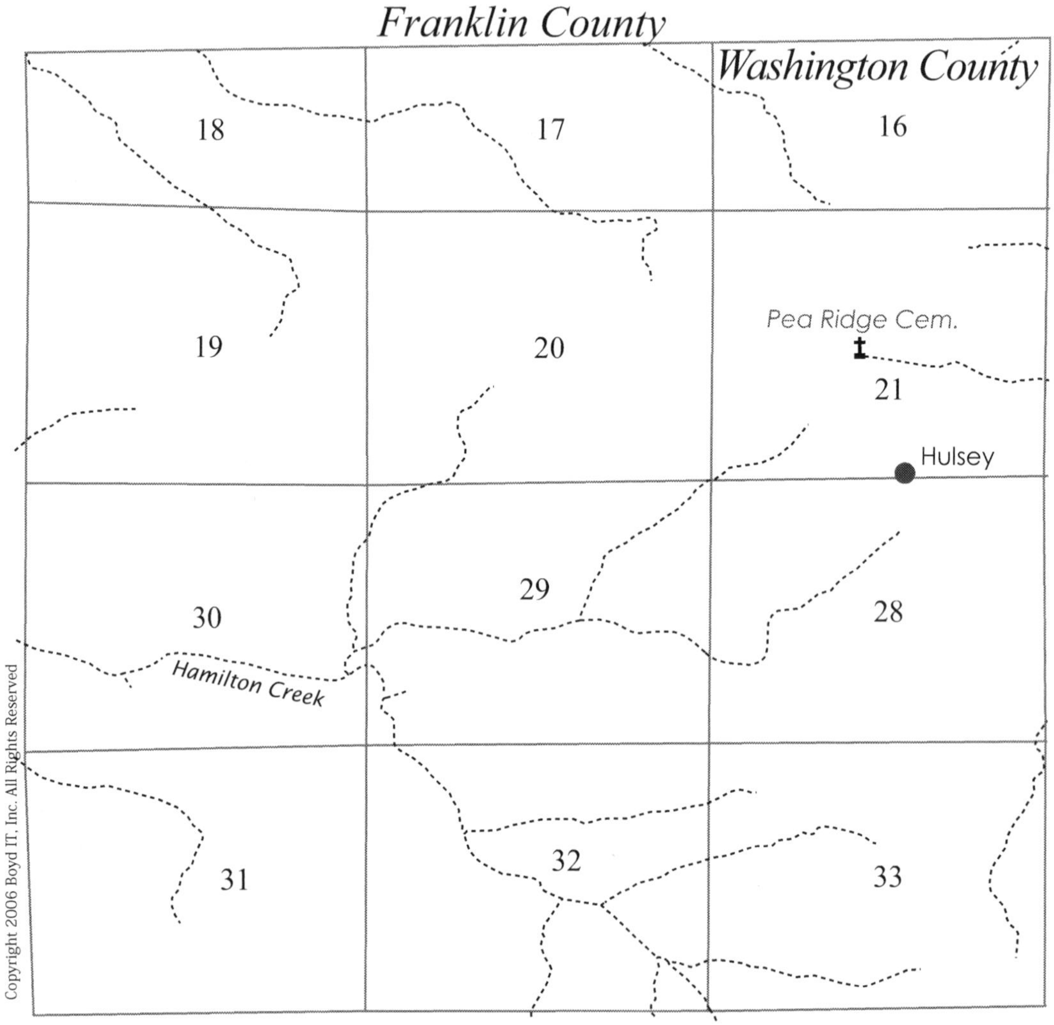

Franklin County
Washington County
18
17
16
19
20
Pea Ridge Cem.
21
Hulsey
30
29
28
Hamilton Creek
31
32
33

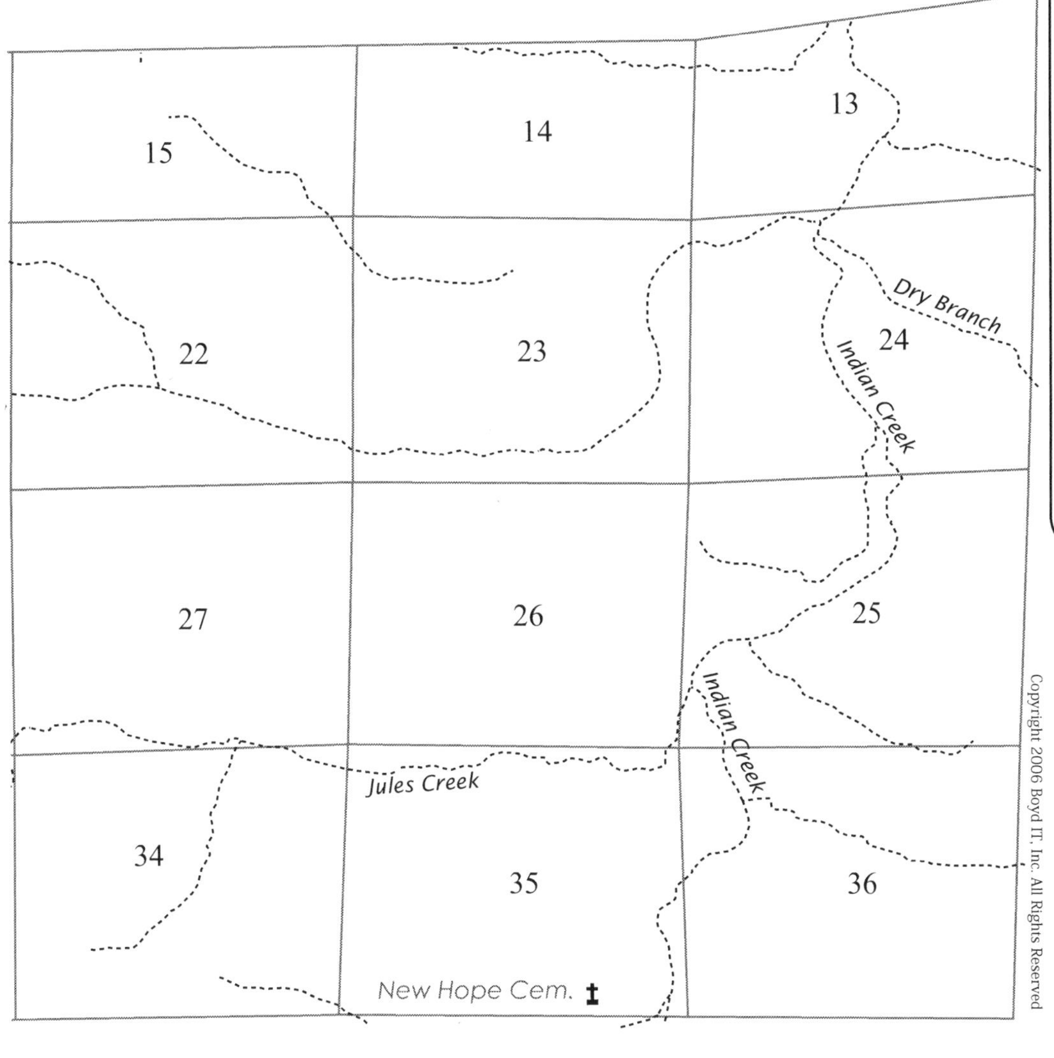

Helpful Hints

1. This Map takes a different look at the same Congressional Township displayed in the preceding two maps. It presents features that can help you better envision the historical development of the area: a) Water-bodies (lakes & ponds), b) Water-courses (rivers, streams, etc.), c) Railroads, d) City/town center-points (where they were oftentimes located when first settled), and e) Cemeteries.
2. Using this "Historical" map in tandem with this Township's Patent Map and Road Map, may lead you to some interesting discoveries. You will often find roads, towns, cemeteries, and waterways are named after nearby landowners: sometimes those names will be the ones you are researching. See how many of these research gems you can find here in Washington County.

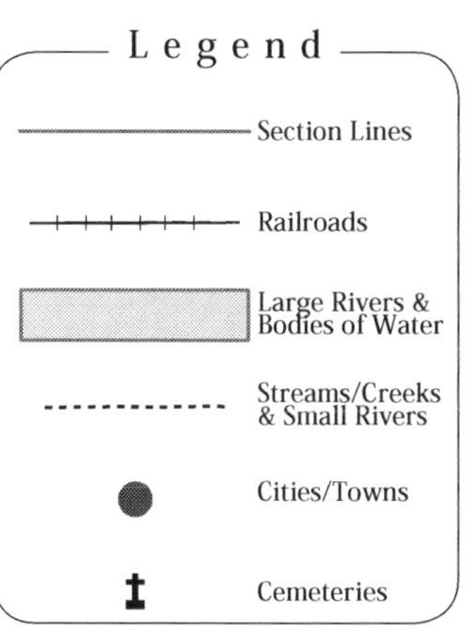

Scale: Section = 1 mile X 1 mile
(there are some exceptions)

Map Group 3: Index to Land Patents

Township 40-North Range 1-East (5th PM)

After you locate an individual in this Index, take note of the Section and Section Part then proceed to the Land Patent map on the pages immediately following. You should have no difficulty locating the corresponding parcel of land.

The "For More Info" Column will lead you to more information about the underlying Patents. See the *Legend* at right, and the "How to Use this Book" chapter, for more information.

LEGEND

"For More Info . . . " column

A = Authority (Legislative Act, See Appendix "A")
B = Block or Lot (location in Section unknown)
C = Cancelled Patent
F = Fractional Section
G = Group (Multi-Patentee Patent, see Appendix "C")
V = Overlaps another Parcel
R = Re-Issued (Parcel patented more than once)

(A & G items require you to look in the Appendixes referred to above. All other Letter-designations followed by a number require you to locate line-items in this index that possess the ID number found after the letter).

ID	Individual in Patent	Sec.	Sec. Part	Date Issued	Other Counties	For More Info . . .
236	ALLADICE, William	35	SESW	1858-01-13		A1
237	" "	35	W½NW	1858-01-13		A1
238	" "	35	W½SW	1858-01-13		A1
211	ANDERSON, Kirk	13	S½	1858-01-13	Franklin	A1
168	BARBOUR, Gabriel H	28	NWSE	1838-09-07		A1 G7
169	" "	33	SENE	1838-09-07		A1 G7
193	BARBOUR, James T	23	E½NE	1840-10-01		A1 G8
193	BARBOUR, William T	23	E½NE	1840-10-01		A1 G8
217	BARKER, Miles	19	E½	1857-06-10		A1
229	BASS, Stephen	32	SWNW	1853-05-10		A1
231	BASS, Thomas	31	NENE	1857-06-10		A1
158	BAUGHER, Edmund H	29	NE	1856-09-01		A1
213	BOGY, Louis V	25	SWSE	1848-07-01		A1
214	" "	36	NWNE	1848-07-01		A1
156	BROWNE, Davit	35	SWSE	1860-03-01		A1
171	BRYNE, George O	13	SWNW	1860-03-01	Franklin	A1
187	BUCKLIN, James M	20	NW	1849-06-01		A1
220	BUREN, Pascal H	28	SESE	1838-09-07		A1
221	" "	33	NENE	1838-09-07		A1
247	CAMP, William K	22	SESW	1849-06-01		A1 G42
155	CASEY, Daniel	14	SWNW	1843-04-10	Franklin	A1
239	CHARBONEAU, William	27	N½NW	1911-01-30		A3
240	" "	27	SWNW	1911-01-30		A3
235	CHARBONO, Tousin	25	E½SE	1827-05-01		A1
241	CHICKEN, William	35	E½SE	1857-06-10		A1
242	" "	35	NE	1857-06-10		A1
243	" "	35	NWSE	1857-06-10		A1
193	CHRISTY, Andrew	23	E½NE	1840-10-01		A1 G8
177	CLARK, Jacob	18	NENW	1849-06-01	Franklin	A1 G60
215	COLEMAN, Michael	19	NESW	1860-03-01		A1
216	" "	19	S½NW	1860-03-01		A1
164	COTTARD, Francis	36	E½SE	1821-09-24		A1 V160
168	COXE, Henry S	28	NWSE	1838-09-07		A1 G7
169	" "	33	SENE	1838-09-07		A1 G7
234	CURTIN, Timothy	15	NESE	1846-01-01	Franklin	A1
157	DACE, Dennis	15	NENE	1840-10-01	Franklin	A1
196	DACE, John	23	NESE	1840-10-01		A1
149	DELAURIERE, Charles F	14	NESE	1856-06-03	Franklin	A2
150	" "	14	SENE	1856-06-03		A2
151	" "	21	SENW	1856-06-03		A2
152	" "	21	SWNE	1856-06-03		A2
153	" "	24	SWNW	1856-06-03		A2
154	" "	36	SWNE	1856-06-03		A2
197	DIAMOND, John	31	SE	1861-04-04		A1
198	" "	31	SENE	1861-04-04		A1
199	" "	31	W½NE	1861-04-04		A1

ID	Individual in Patent	Sec.	Sec. Part	Date Issued	Other Counties	For More Info . . .
146	FARROW, Augustus	19	2SW	1857-06-10		A1
147	" "	19	S½1SW	1857-06-10		A1
141	FISHER, Anthony	23	SESW	1851-11-01		A1
142	" "	23	SWSE	1856-11-01		A1
170	FISHER, George	14	SESE	1848-07-01	Franklin	A1
173	FISHER, George W	23	NENW	1840-10-01		A1
208	FISHER, Joseph	23	W½NE	1824-05-10		A1
232	FLANAGAN, Thomas	23	NWSE	1856-09-01		A1
244	GARTSIDE, William	31	1SW	1857-06-10		A1
245	" "	31	N½2SW	1857-06-10		A1
246	" "	31	NW	1857-06-10		A1
226	HAAS, Sebastian	35	NENW	1859-05-02		A1
227	" "	35	NESW	1859-11-01		A1
228	" "	35	SENW	1859-11-01		A1
180	HARRIS, James	29	W½	1860-03-01		A1
209	HEINE, Joseph	13	NE	1859-11-01	Franklin	A1
210	" "	13	NENW	1859-11-01	Franklin	A1
177	HIBLER, Daniel	18	NENW	1849-06-01	Franklin	A1 G60
148	HINSON, Benoni	24	NWNW	1848-02-01		A1
179	HOFF, James G	17	SW	1848-05-04	Franklin	A1
181	HORTON, James	15	SENE	1857-06-10	Franklin	A1
182	" "	15	SENW	1857-06-10	Franklin	A1
183	" "	15	SESE	1857-06-10	Franklin	A1
184	" "	15	W½NE	1857-06-10	Franklin	A1
185	" "	15	W½SE	1857-06-10	Franklin	A1
247	HUFF, Powell	22	SESW	1849-06-01		A1 G42
186	HULSEY, James	14	E½SW	1840-10-01	Franklin	A1
222	JOHNSON, Pleasant S	33	SWSW	1856-09-01		A1
188	KERSHAW, James M	21	E½NE	1859-11-01		A1
189	" "	21	NENW	1859-11-01		A1
190	" "	21	NESE	1859-11-01		A1
191	" "	21	NWNE	1859-11-01		A1
192	" "	21	W½NW	1859-11-01		A1
178	KIMBERLIN, Jacob	30	SWSE	1840-10-01		A1
223	KIMBERLIN, Rinard	30	NENW	1840-10-01		A1
224	" "	30	SWNE	1840-10-01		A1
195	KIRBY, John C	29	SE	1859-11-01		A1
165	KIRKPATRICK, Francis W	23	SWSW	1849-06-01		A1
166	" "	28	SWNW	1849-06-01		A1 G159
167	" "	33	NESW	1849-06-01		A1 G159
230	LABRAUME, Theodore	36	NENE	1848-07-01		A1
136	LEGERET, Alphonse	25	SESW	1848-02-01		A1
137	LEGERET, Alphornse	25	NWSE	1848-07-01		A1
225	MARSHALL, Samuel	33	SE	1860-03-01		A1
160	MCCREERY, Elijah	36	SESE	1840-10-01		A1 V164
248	MCDONALD, William	15	NENW	1857-06-10	Franklin	A1
249	" "	15	SW	1857-06-10	Franklin	A1
250	" "	15	W½NW	1857-06-10	Franklin	A1
200	MOSLANDER, John	33	NW	1857-06-10		A1
201	" "	33	NWSW	1857-06-10		A1
202	" "	33	W½NE	1857-06-10		A1
219	NOEL, Noah	23	SESE	1856-11-01		A1
139	PARK, Andrew	18	S½SW	1849-06-01	Franklin	A1
140	" "	18	W½NE	1849-06-01	Franklin	A1
138	" "	17	SE	1859-05-02	Franklin	A1
203	PATTON, John	14	NENW	1835-10-08	Franklin	A1
233	PATTON, Thomas	14	SENW	1837-04-01	Franklin	A1
204	PETER, John	32	W½SE	1840-10-01		A1
205	" "	33	SESW	1840-10-01		A1
212	PETERS, Lewis	27	W½SW	1860-03-01		A1
218	POUND, Newman	25	NWNW	1840-10-01		A1
143	PROSS, August H	21	SESE	1857-06-10		A1
144	" "	21	SW	1857-06-10		A1
145	" "	21	W½SE	1857-06-10		A1
162	ROUSSIN, Etienne	25	E½NW	1831-10-01		A1
161	" "	24	W½SW	1835-09-09		A1
163	" "	25	SWNE	1835-09-09		A1
172	SCHIEBEL, George	13	NWNW	1857-06-10	Franklin	A1
206	SHMELL, John	31	S½2SW	1860-03-01		A1
207	SHOOKS, John	23	NWNW	1860-03-01		A1
251	SKEWES, William	25	E½NE	1858-10-30		A1
252	" "	25	NESW	1858-10-30		A1
253	" "	25	NWNE	1858-10-30		A1

ID	Individual in Patent	Sec.	Sec. Part	Date Issued	Other Counties	For More Info . . .
254	SKEWES, William (Cont'd)	25	SWNW	1858-10-30		A1
255	" "	25	W½SW	1858-10-30		A1
166	SOULARD, Benjamin S	28	SWNW	1849-06-01		A1 G159
167	" "	33	NESW	1849-06-01		A1 G159
166	SOULARD, James G	28	SWNW	1849-06-01		A1 G159
167	" "	33	NESW	1849-06-01		A1 G159
168	TAYLOR, Nathaniel P	28	NWSE	1838-09-07		A1 G7
169	" "	33	SENE	1838-09-07		A1 G7
256	TODD, William	14	NWSW	1840-10-01	Franklin	A1
159	WELLS, Edmund P	35	SESE	1840-10-01		A1 F
194	WELSH, James	17	N½NE	1860-03-01	Franklin	A1
174	WESTENFELT, Henry	27	NE	1857-06-10		A1
175	" "	27	SESW	1857-06-10		A1
176	" "	27	W½SE	1857-06-10		A1

Patent Map

T40-N R1-E
5th PM Meridian

Map Group 3

Township Statistics

Parcels Mapped	:	121
Number of Patents	:	80
Number of Individuals	:	78
Patentees Identified	:	71
Number of Surnames	:	67
Multi-Patentee Parcels	:	7
Oldest Patent Date	:	9/24/1821
Most Recent Patent	:	1/30/1911
Block/Lot Parcels	:	5
Parcels Re - Issued	:	0
Parcels that Overlap	:	2
Cities and Towns	:	0
Cemeteries	:	2

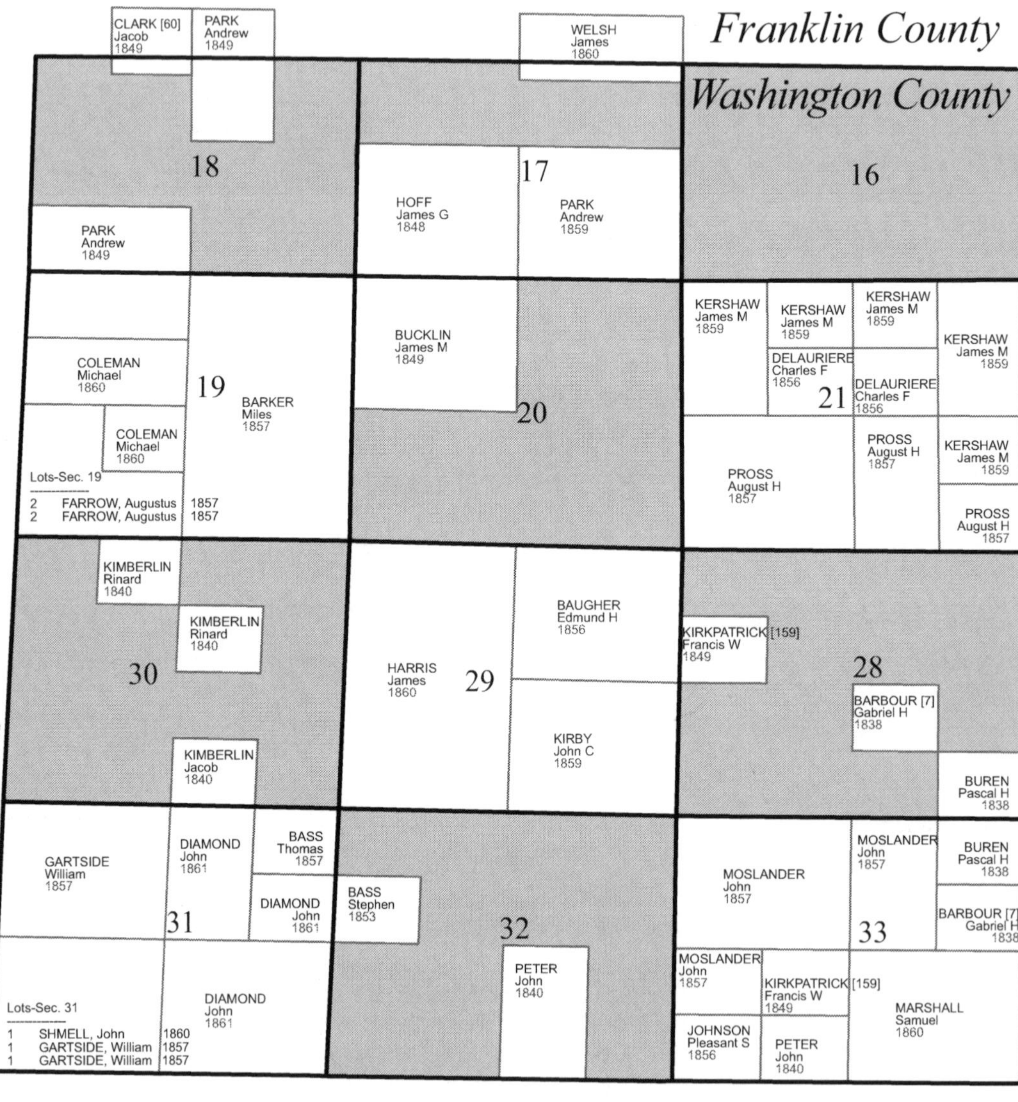

MCDONALD William 1857
HORTON James 1857
DACE Dennis 1840
PATTON John 1835
SCHIEBEL George 1857
HEINE Joseph 1859

MCDONALD William 1857
HORTON James 1857
HORTON James 1857
CASEY Daniel 1843
PATTON Thomas 1837
DELAURIERE Charles F 1856
BRYNE George O 1860
13
HEINE Joseph 1859

15
MCDONALD William 1857
HORTON James 1857
CURTIN Timothy 1846
HORTON James 1857
TODD William 1840
14
HULSEY James 1840
DELAURIERE Charles F 1856
FISHER George 1848
ANDERSON Kirk 1858

SHOOKS John 1860
FISHER George W 1840
FISHER Joseph 1824
BARBOUR [8] James T 1840
HINSON Benoni 1848
DELAURIERE Charles F 1856
22
23
24
FLANAGAN Thomas 1856
DACE John 1840
ROUSSIN Etienne 1835
CAMP [42] William K 1849
KIRKPATRICK Francis W 1849
FISHER Anthony 1851
FISHER Anthony 1856
NOEL Noah 1856

CHARBONEAU William 1911
WESTENFELT Henry 1857
POUND Newman 1840
ROUSSIN Etienne 1831
SKEWES William 1858
CHARBONEAU William 1911
27
26
SKEWES William 1858
25
ROUSSIN Etienne 1835
SKEWES William 1858
WESTENFELT Henry 1857
PETERS Lewis 1860
SKEWES William 1858
SKEWES William 1858
LEGERET Alphornse 1848
CHARBONO Tousin 1827
WESTENFELT Henry 1857
LEGERET Alphonse 1848
BOGY Louis V 1848

ALLADICE William 1858
HAAS Sebastian 1859
CHICKEN William 1857
BOGY Louis V 1848
LABRAUME Theodore 1848
HAAS Sebastian 1859
35
DELAURIERE Charles F 1856
34
36
ALLADICE William 1858
HAAS Sebastian 1859
CHICKEN William 1857
ALLADICE William 1858
BROWNE Davit 1860
CHICKEN William 1857
WELLS Edmund P 1840
MCCREERY Elijah 1840
COTTARD Francis 1821

Helpful Hints

1. This Map's INDEX can be found on the preceding pages.
2. Refer to Map "C" to see where this Township lies within Washington County, Missouri.
3. Numbers within square brackets [ ] denote a multi-patentee land parcel (multi-owner). Refer to Appendix "C" for a full list of members in this group.
4. Areas that look to be crowded with Patentees usually indicate multiple sales of the same parcel (Re-issues) or Overlapping parcels. See this Township's Index for an explanation of these and other circumstances that might explain "odd" groupings of Patentees on this map.

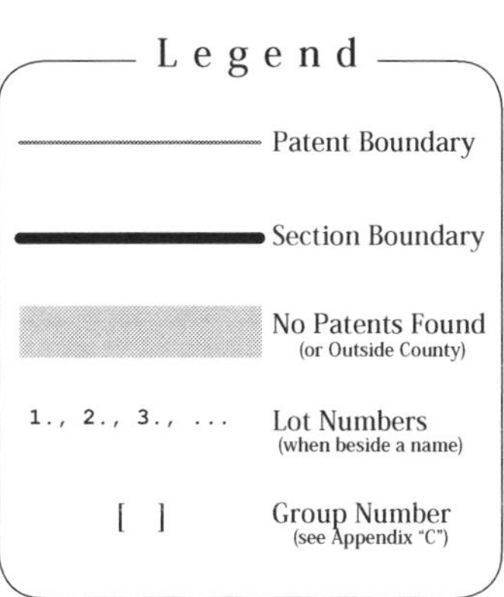

Scale: Section = 1 mile X 1 mile
(generally, with some exceptions)

Road Map

T40-N R1-E
5th PM Meridian

Map Group 3

Cities & Towns
None

Cemeteries
Arnold Cemetery
Asplin Cemetery

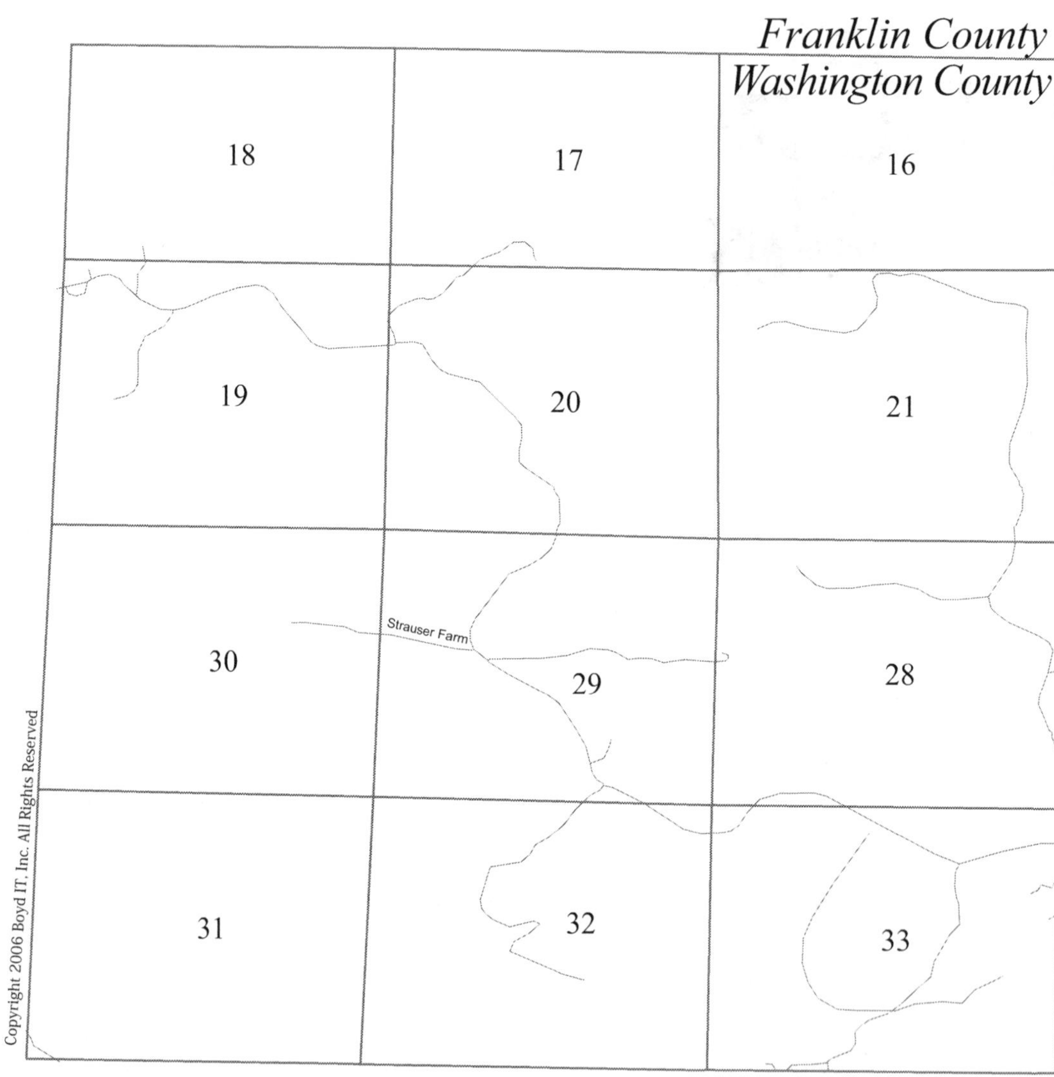

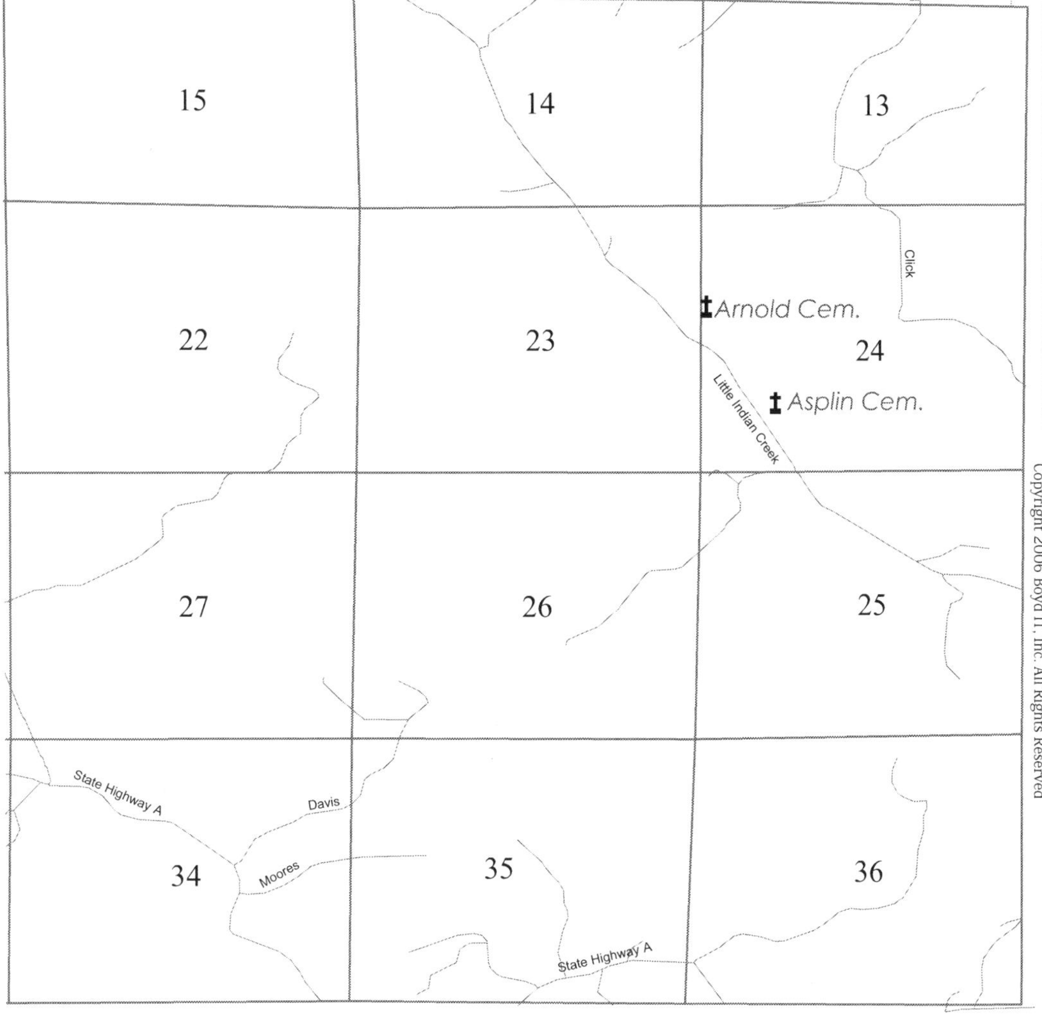

Helpful Hints

1. This road map has a number of uses, but primarily it is to help you: a) find the present location of land owned by your ancestors (at least the general area), b) find cemeteries and city-centers, and c) estimate the route/roads used by Census-takers & tax-assessors.
2. If you plan to travel to Washington County to locate cemeteries or land parcels, please pick up a modern travel map for the area before you do. Mapping old land parcels on modern maps is not as exact a science as you might think. Just the slightest variations in public land survey coordinates, estimates of parcel boundaries, or road-map deviations can greatly alter a map's representation of how a road either does or doesn't cross a particular parcel of land.

Legend

- Section Lines
- Interstates
- Highways
- Other Roads
- Cities/Towns
- Cemeteries

Scale: Section = 1 mile X 1 mile
(generally, with some exceptions)

Historical Map

T40-N R1-E
5th PM Meridian

Map Group 3

Cities & Towns
None

Cemeteries
Arnold Cemetery
Asplin Cemetery

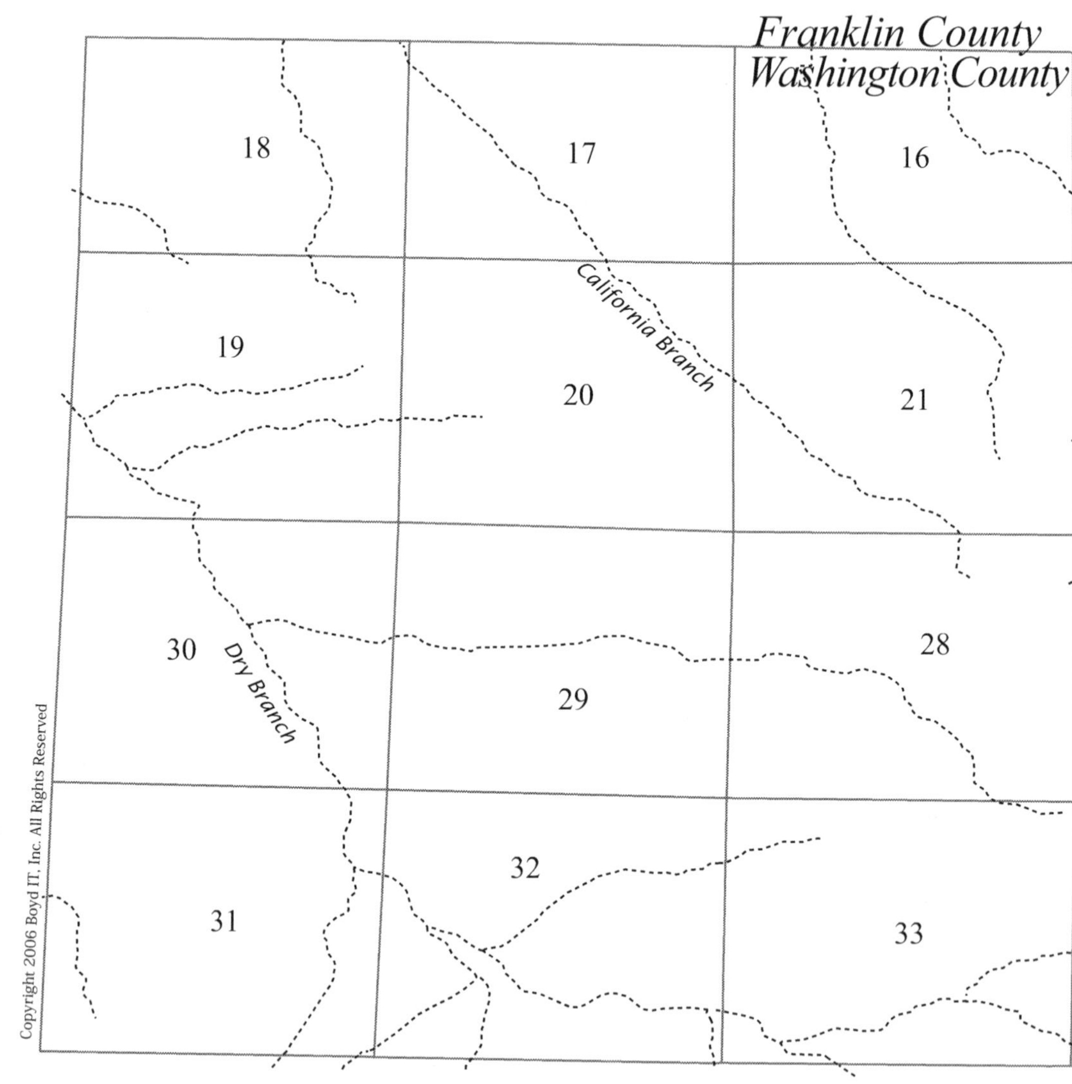

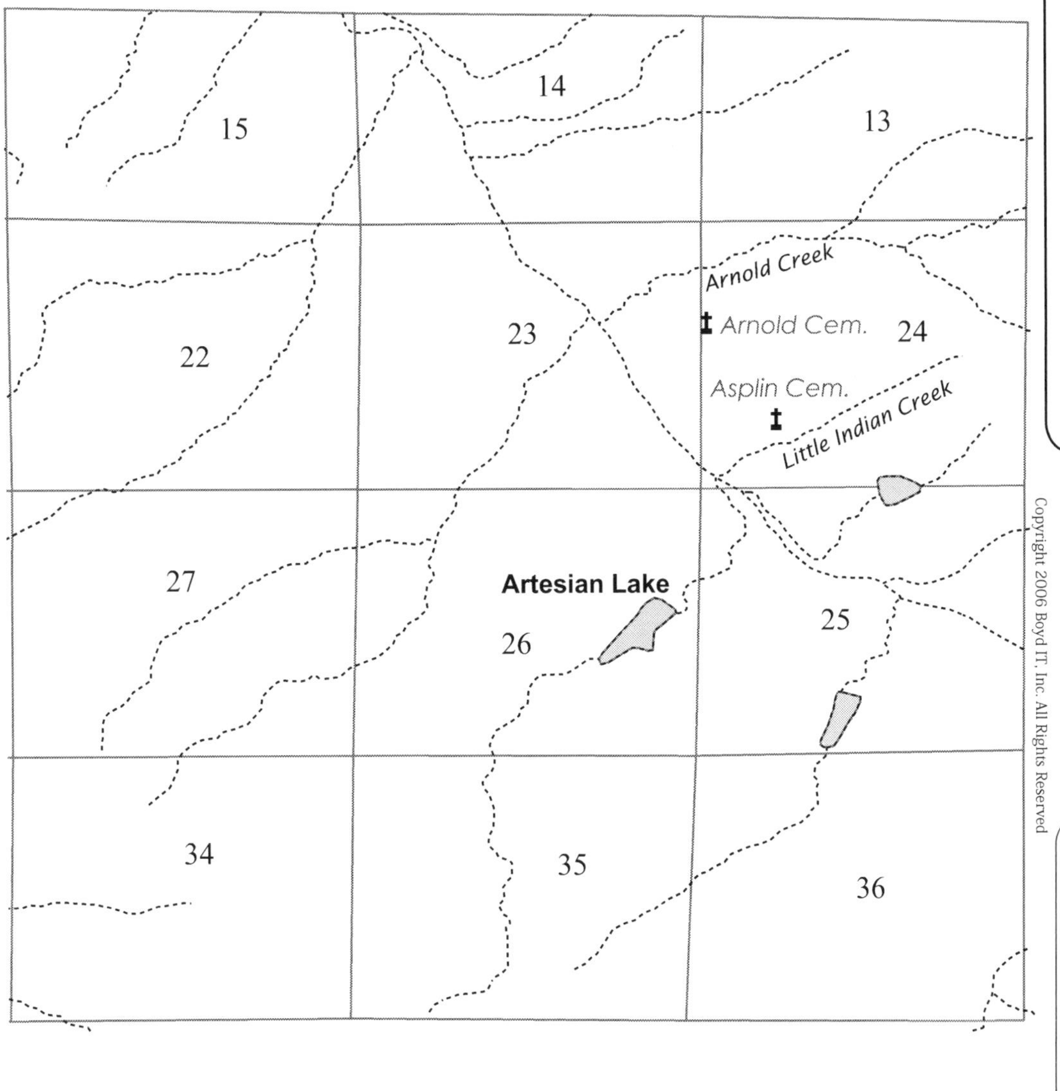

Helpful Hints

1. This Map takes a different look at the same Congressional Township displayed in the preceding two maps. It presents features that can help you better envision the historical development of the area: a) Water-bodies (lakes & ponds), b) Water-courses (rivers, streams, etc.), c) Railroads, d) City/town center-points (where they were oftentimes located when first settled), and e) Cemeteries.
2. Using this "Historical" map in tandem with this Township's Patent Map and Road Map, may lead you to some interesting discoveries. You will often find roads, towns, cemeteries, and waterways are named after nearby landowners: sometimes those names will be the ones you are researching. See how many of these research gems you can find here in Washington County.

Legend

- Section Lines
- Railroads
- Large Rivers & Bodies of Water
- Streams/Creeks & Small Rivers
- Cities/Towns
- Cemeteries

Scale: Section = 1 mile X 1 mile
(there are some exceptions)

Map Group 4: Index to Land Patents

Township 40-North Range 2-East (5th PM)

After you locate an individual in this Index, take note of the Section and Section Part then proceed to the Land Patent map on the pages immediately following. You should have no difficulty locating the corresponding parcel of land.

The "For More Info" Column will lead you to more information about the underlying Patents. See the *Legend* at right, and the "How to Use this Book" chapter, for more information.

LEGEND

"For More Info . . . " column

A = Authority (Legislative Act, See Appendix "A")
B = Block or Lot (location in Section unknown)
C = Cancelled Patent
F = Fractional Section
G = Group (Multi-Patentee Patent, see Appendix "C")
V = Overlaps another Parcel
R = Re-Issued (Parcel patented more than once)

(A & G items require you to look in the Appendixes referred to above. All other Letter-designations followed by a number require you to locate line-items in this index that possess the ID number found after the letter).

ID	Individual in Patent	Sec.	Sec. Part	Date Issued	Other Counties	For More Info . . .
301	AMELIN, Manuel	30	W½NE	1824-05-10		A1
277	BENOIT, F M	30	W½SE	1856-06-03		A2 F
278	" "	36	NE	1856-06-03		A2 F
257	BENTON, Abraham	30	S½2SW	1843-04-10		A1
302	BERRY, Richard	17	NESW	1896-07-27	Franklin	A1
303	" "	17	SENE	1896-07-27	Franklin	A1
304	" "	17	SENW	1896-07-27	Franklin	A1
281	BOURBON, Francis M	17	NWNW	1902-02-07	Franklin	A1
279	CAINE, Farrel	17	SWSE	1860-03-01	Franklin	A1
284	CAMMIER, Henry	30	E½SW	1845-10-01		A1 C F
312	CHARBANO, Touissaint	30	E½SE	1824-05-10		A1
282	COLEMANT, Francois B	36	E½SE	1826-05-01		A1
280	COTTARD, Francis	31	SW	1821-09-24		A1
298	DELCOR, Louis	31	S½2NW	1845-08-04		A1
307	DENNY, Samuel	24	SE	1860-03-01	Jefferson	A1 F
308	" "	24	SWNE	1860-03-01	Jefferson	A1 F
283	DENT, George W	24	NENE	1848-07-01	Jefferson	A1
313	DOLAN, William	19	S½1SW	1857-07-01		A1
314	" "	19	S½2SW	1857-07-01		A1
315	" "	19	S½SE	1857-07-01		A1
297	DOWNER, Joseph W	17	NWSE	1848-07-01	Franklin	A1
276	DOYEN, Eugene	31	N½NE	1855-06-15		A1 F
290	DOYEN, John B	31	S½NE	1848-12-01		A1 F
266	EDMANDS, Charles A	21	W½NW	1856-11-01		A1 F
267	EDWARDS, Charles A	17	N½NE	1861-01-21	Franklin	A1 G87
268	" "	17	NENW	1861-01-21	Franklin	A1 G87
316	ELLEDGE, William J	19	N½2SW	1906-06-30		A1
269	EVANS, Charles L	31	SWSE	1904-05-13		A1
305	FRAYSER, Robert B	21	SW	1848-07-01		A1 F
287	GIRARDIER, James L	29	E½NW	1848-05-04		A1 F
288	" "	29	SW	1848-05-04		A1 F
258	GRADON, Alexander	19	2NW	1860-03-01		A1
311	HAYNES, Thomas	17	NWSW	1856-09-01	Franklin	A1
306	JOHNSTON, Robert R	25	NE	1861-01-21	Jefferson	A1 F
260	LABAUME, Augustus	32	SE	1824-05-10		A1 F
261	" "	32	SW	1824-05-10		A1
310	LABRAUME, Theodore	31	N½2NW	1848-07-01		A1
299	LE BOURGEOIS, LOUIS S	35		1856-01-15		A1 F
300	" "	36	SW	1856-01-15		A1 F
270	LEVY, Charles	19	1NW	1859-11-01		A1
271	" "	19	N½1SW	1859-11-01		A1
272	" "	19	NE	1859-11-01		A1
273	" "	19	NWSE	1859-11-01		A1
293	LEWIS, John	24	SENE	1848-07-01	Jefferson	A1
289	MUNDAY, James	29	NE	1849-08-28		A1 F
317	PATTEN, William	17	SWNW	1848-02-01	Franklin	A1

ID	Individual in Patent	Sec.	Sec. Part	Date Issued	Other Counties	For More Info . . .
295	PATTON, Joseph	21	E½NW	1848-12-01		A1 F
296	" "	21	NE	1848-12-01		A1 F
263	ROGERS, Benjamin	15	SW	1847-07-22	Franklin	A1 F
264	" "	20	W½NE	1848-05-04		A1
275	ROGERS, Elijah S	15	NE	1857-06-10	Franklin	A1 F
294	ROGERS, John	17	E½SE	1856-10-01	Franklin	A1
262	ROUSSIN, Baptist	36	W½SE	1848-12-01		A1 F
265	ROUSSIN, Carpentier	31	E½SE	1848-12-01		A1 F
309	ROUSSIN, Siffroid E	31	NWSE	1848-07-01		A1
259	SHOOK, Amos C	32	E½NW	1824-05-10		A1
285	THWING, Henry G	24	NWNE	1849-06-01	Jefferson	A1
286	TYREY, Jacob F	17	S½SW	1857-06-10	Franklin	A1
291	VALLEY, John B	30	N½2SW	1835-10-01		A1
292	" "	30	S½1SW	1835-10-01		A1
318	WALTON, William	19	NESE	1848-02-01		A1
267	WILCOX, William L	17	N½NE	1861-01-21	Franklin	A1 G87
268	" "	17	NENW	1861-01-21	Franklin	A1 G87
274	XENO, Charles	31	1NW	1835-09-02		A1

Patent Map

T40-N R2-E
5th PM Meridian

Map Group 4

Township Statistics

Parcels Mapped	:	62
Number of Patents	:	48
Number of Individuals	:	47
Patentees Identified	:	46
Number of Surnames	:	42
Multi-Patentee Parcels	:	2
Oldest Patent Date	:	9/24/1821
Most Recent Patent	:	6/30/1906
Block/Lot Parcels	:	12
Parcels Re - Issued	:	0
Parcels that Overlap	:	0
Cities and Towns	:	2
Cemeteries	:	4

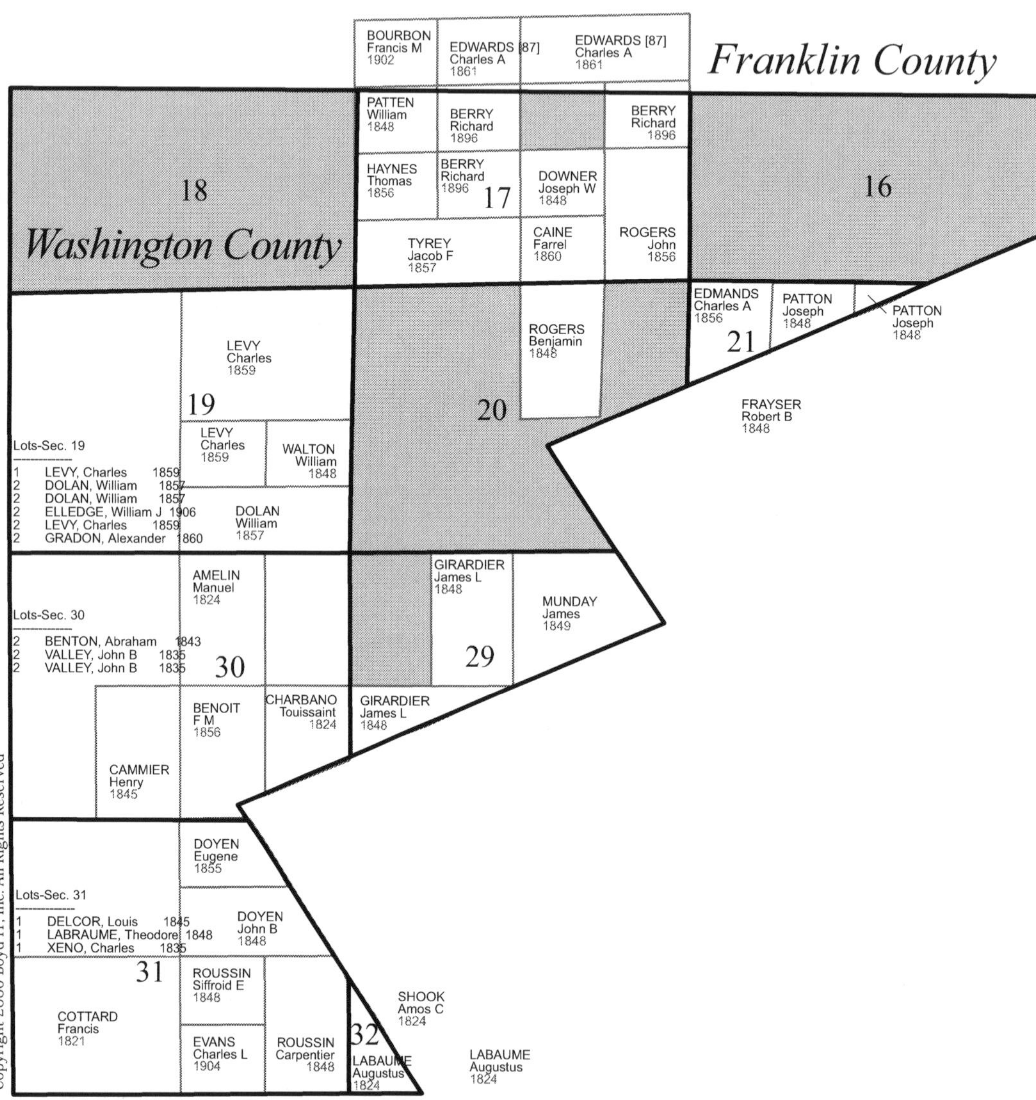

Helpful Hints

1. This Map's INDEX can be found on the preceding pages.
2. Refer to Map "C" to see where this Township lies within Washington County, Missouri.
3. Numbers within square brackets [ ] denote a multi-patentee land parcel (multi-owner). Refer to Appendix "C" for a full list of members in this group.
4. Areas that look to be crowded with Patentees usually indicate multiple sales of the same parcel (Re-issues) or Overlapping parcels. See this Township's Index for an explanation of these and other circumstances that might explain "odd" groupings of Patentees on this map.

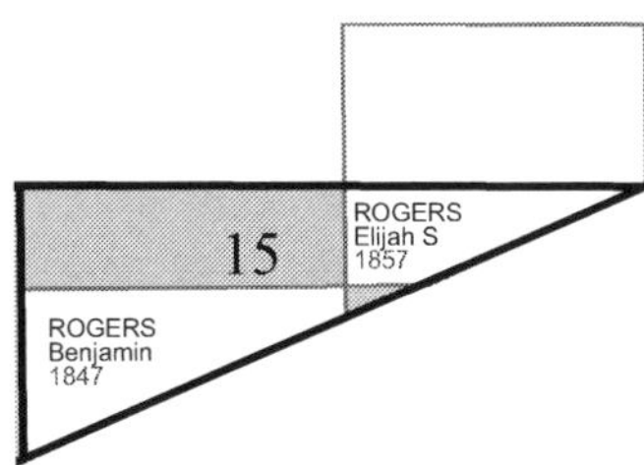

Jefferson County

THWING Henry G 1849

DENT George W 1848

DENNY Samuel 1860

LEWIS John 1848

DENNY Samuel 1860

JOHNSTON Robert R 1861

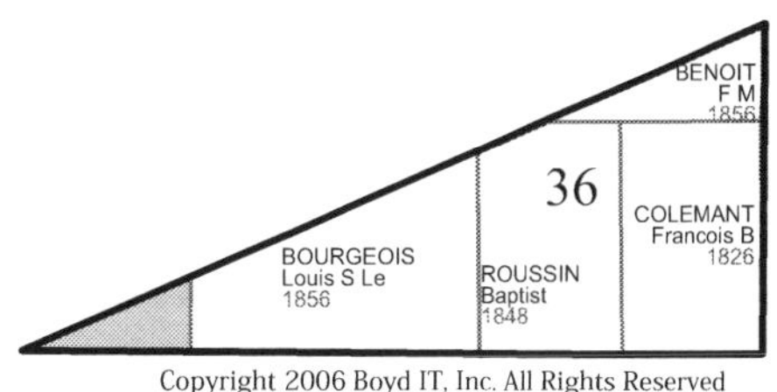

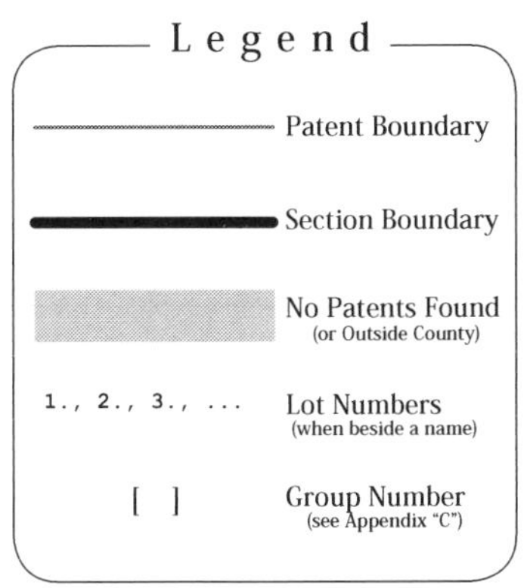

Scale: Section = 1 mile X 1 mile
(generally, with some exceptions)

Road Map

T40-N R2-E
5th PM Meridian

Map Group 4

Cities & Towns
- Hurricane
- Richwoods

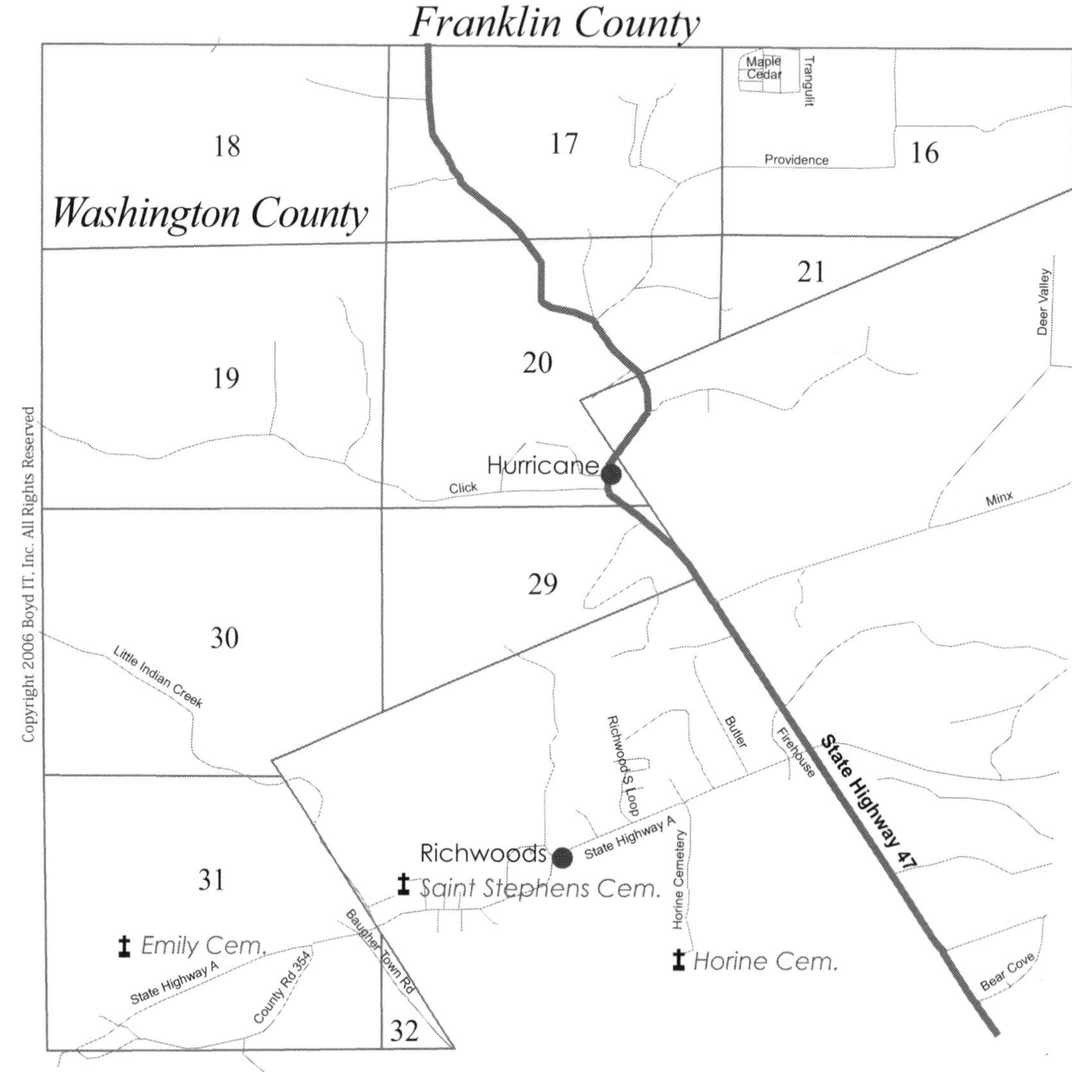

Cemeteries
- Emily Cemetery
- Jones Cemetery
- Horine Cemetery
- Saint Stephens Cemetery

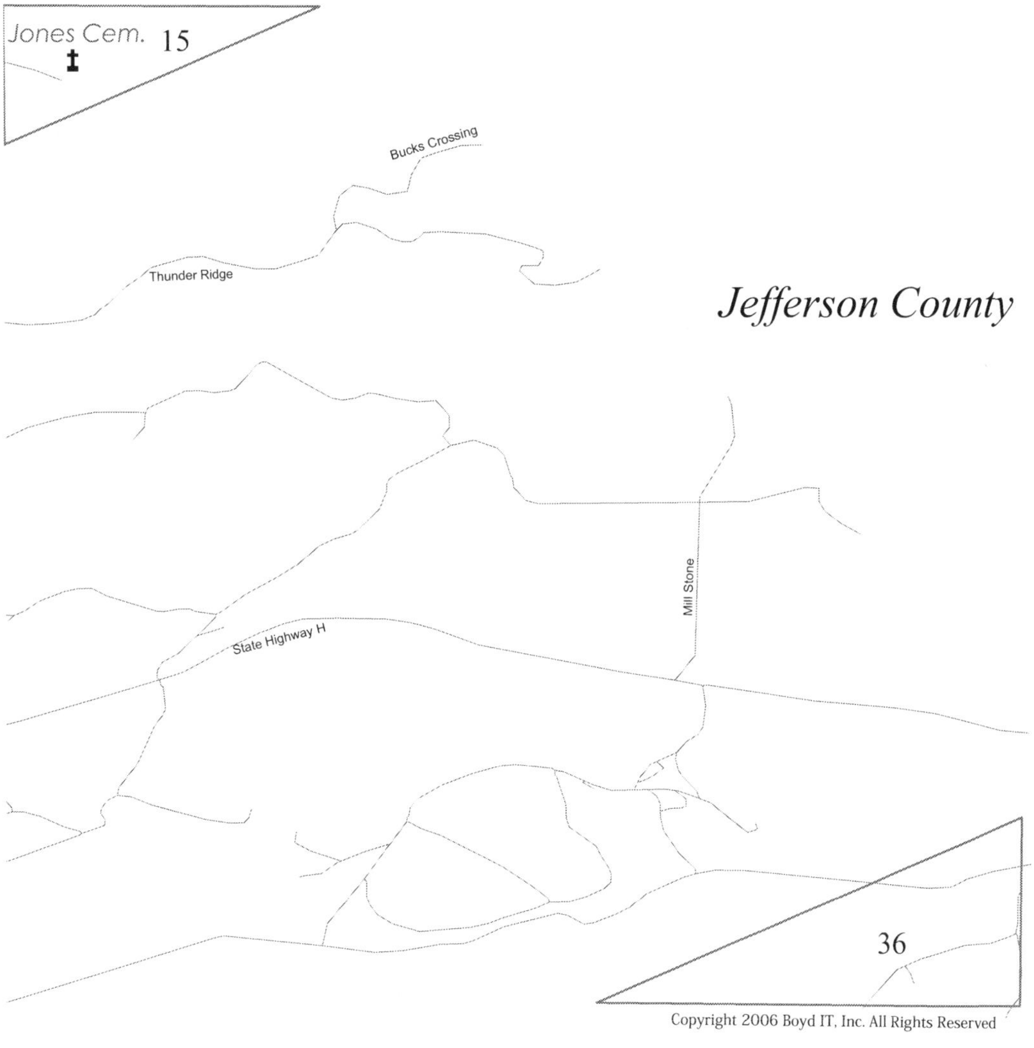

Jones Cem.
15
Bucks Crossing
Thunder Ridge
Jefferson County
Mill Stone
State Highway H
36

Helpful Hints

1. This road map has a number of uses, but primarily it is to help you: a) find the present location of land owned by your ancestors (at least the general area), b) find cemeteries and city-centers, and c) estimate the route/roads used by Census-takers & tax-assessors.
2. If you plan to travel to Washington County to locate cemeteries or land parcels, please pick up a modern travel map for the area before you do. Mapping old land parcels on modern maps is not as exact a science as you might think. Just the slightest variations in public land survey coordinates, estimates of parcel boundaries, or road-map deviations can greatly alter a map's representation of how a road either does or doesn't cross a particular parcel of land.

Legend

Section Lines
Interstates
Highways
Other Roads
Cities/Towns
Cemeteries

Scale: Section = 1 mile X 1 mile
(generally, with some exceptions)

Historical Map

T40-N R2-E
5th PM Meridian

Map Group 4

Cities & Towns
Hurricane
Richwoods

Cemeteries
Emily Cemetery
Jones Cemetery
Horine Cemetery
Saint Stephens Cemetery

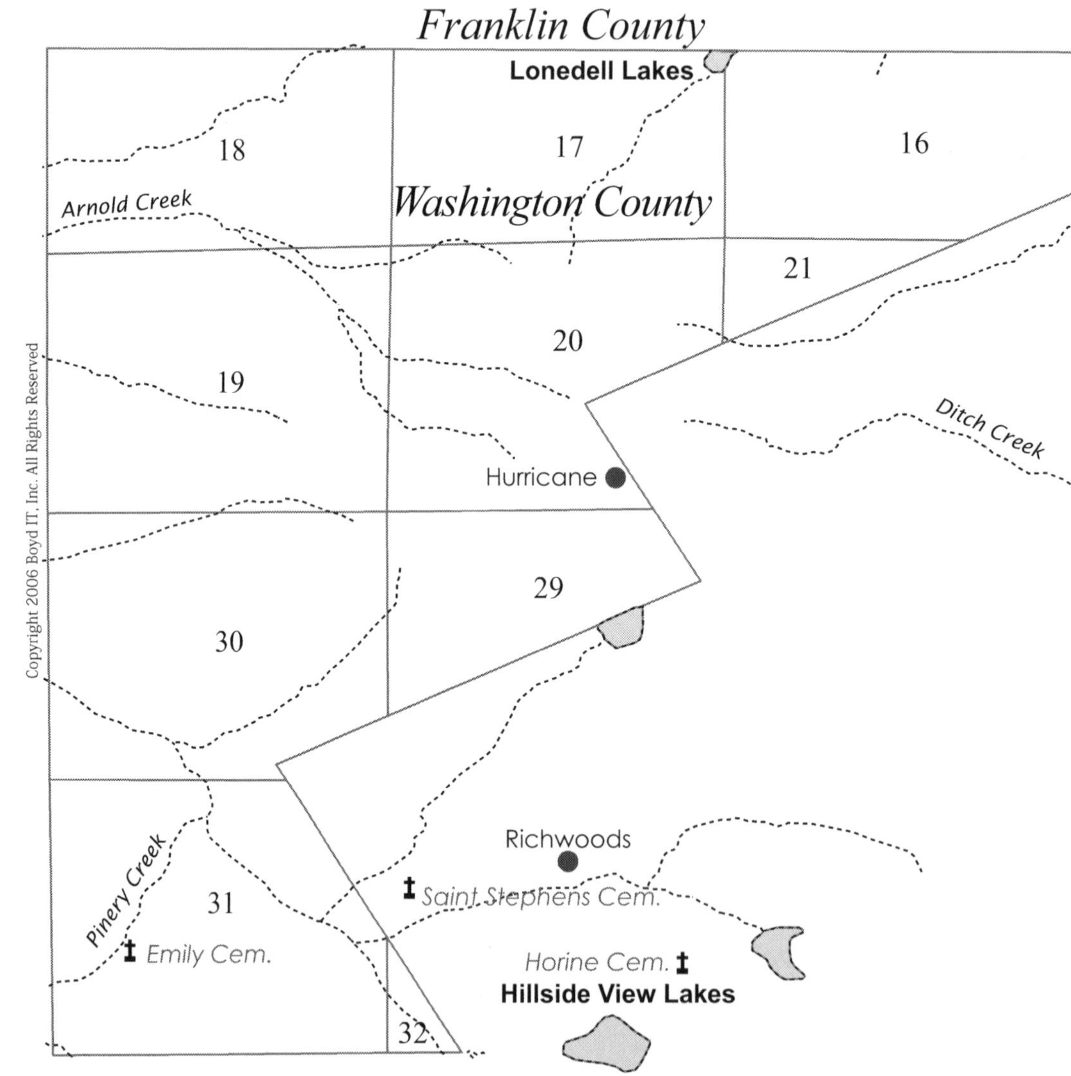

Helpful Hints

1. This Map takes a different look at the same Congressional Township displayed in the preceding two maps. It presents features that can help you better envision the historical development of the area: a) Water-bodies (lakes & ponds), b) Water-courses (rivers, streams, etc.), c) Railroads, d) City/town center-points (where they were oftentimes located when first settled), and e) Cemeteries.
2. Using this "Historical" map in tandem with this Township's Patent Map and Road Map, may lead you to some interesting discoveries. You will often find roads, towns, cemeteries, and waterways are named after nearby landowners: sometimes those names will be the ones you are researching. See how many of these research gems you can find here in Washington County.

Legend

- Section Lines
- Railroads
- Large Rivers & Bodies of Water
- Streams/Creeks & Small Rivers
- Cities/Towns
- Cemeteries

Scale: Section = 1 mile X 1 mile
(there are some exceptions)

Map Group 5: Index to Land Patents

Township 40-North Range 3-East (5th PM)

After you locate an individual in this Index, take note of the Section and Section Part then proceed to the Land Patent map on the pages immediately following. You should have no difficulty locating the corresponding parcel of land.

The "For More Info" Column will lead you to more information about the underlying Patents. See the *Legend* at right, and the "How to Use this Book" chapter, for more information.

LEGEND

"For More Info . . . " column

A = Authority (Legislative Act, See Appendix "A")
B = Block or Lot (location in Section unknown)
C = Cancelled Patent
F = Fractional Section
G = Group (Multi-Patentee Patent, see Appendix "C")
V = Overlaps another Parcel
R = Re-Issued (Parcel patented more than once)

(A & G items require you to look in the Appendixes referred to above. All other Letter-designations followed by a number require you to locate line-items in this index that possess the ID number found after the letter).

ID	Individual in Patent	Sec.	Sec. Part	Date Issued	Other Counties	For More Info . . .
319	BOUSIN, Belloni	31	N½1SW	1849-06-01	Jefferson	A1
336	BURGESS, Sanders	30	SENE	1848-07-01	Jefferson	A1 G39
326	BURNET, George	30	NWNW	1848-07-01	Jefferson	A1
338	BURNET, William K	30	NENE	1848-07-01	Jefferson	A1
329	FORESTER, Henry M	31	NENW	1857-06-10	Jefferson	A1 F
330	" "	31	W½NW	1857-06-10	Jefferson	A1
331	FORRESTER, Henry W	31	E½SE	1856-01-15	Jefferson	A1
332	" "	31	SWSE	1856-01-15	Jefferson	A1
337	FRISSEL, Willard	30	NENW	1848-07-01	Jefferson	A1
336	HOOTER, Louis C	30	SENE	1848-07-01	Jefferson	A1 G39
327	HYNSON, Harrison	30	SENW	1848-07-01	Jefferson	A1
328	" "	30	W½NW	1848-12-01	Jefferson	A1 F
325	MANES, Elisha	30	W½SE	1836-01-14	Jefferson	A1
321	MANESS, Elijah	30	SW	1848-05-04	Jefferson	A1 F
320	" "	30	SESE	1848-07-01	Jefferson	A1
322	" "	30	SWNE	1848-07-01	Jefferson	A1
324	" "	31	NWSE	1848-07-01	Jefferson	A1
323	" "	31	NE	1856-10-01	Jefferson	A1
333	MCKEAN, James	30	NESE	1837-11-07	Jefferson	A1
334	PORTAIS, John	31	2SW	1826-05-01	Jefferson	A1
335	ROUSAN, Mary L	31	SESW	1856-09-01	Jefferson	A1

Patent Map

T40-N R3-E
5th PM Meridian

Map Group 5

Township Statistics

Parcels Mapped	:	20
Number of Patents	:	18
Number of Individuals	:	14
Patentees Identified	:	13
Number of Surnames	:	13
Multi-Patentee Parcels	:	1
Oldest Patent Date	:	5/1/1826
Most Recent Patent	:	6/10/1857
Block/Lot Parcels	:	2
Parcels Re - Issued	:	0
Parcels that Overlap	:	0
Cities and Towns	:	0
Cemeteries	:	0

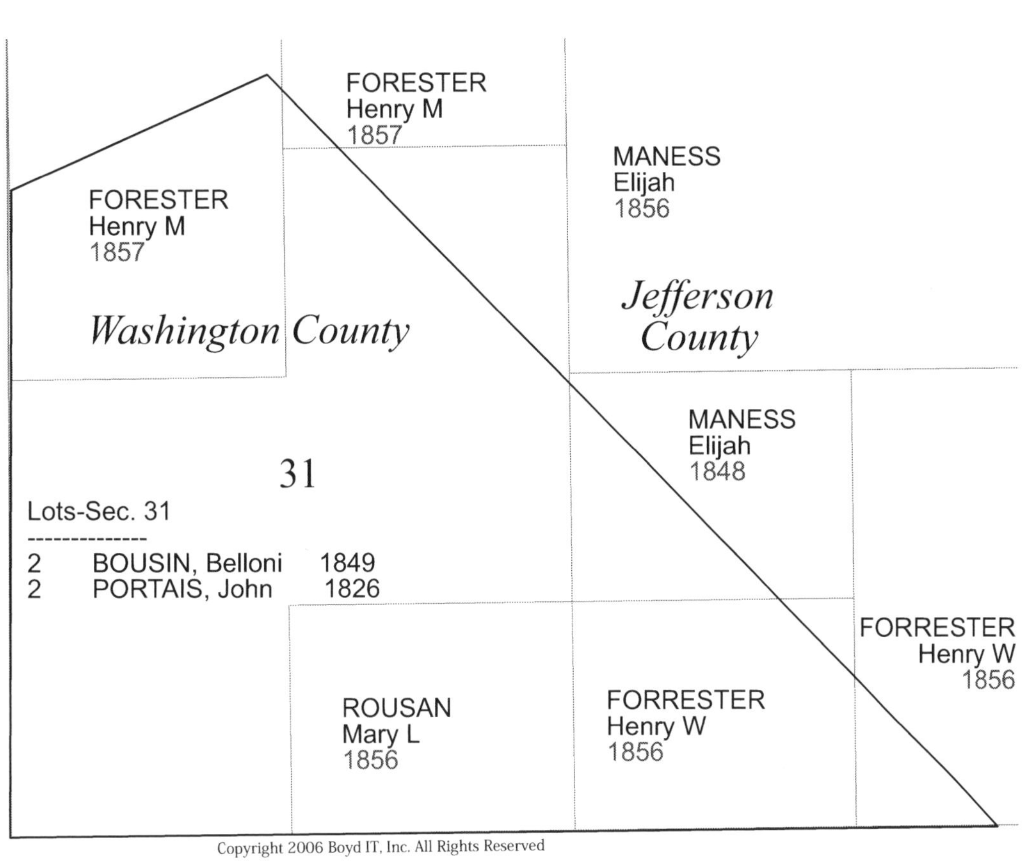

Note: the area contained in this map amounts to far less than a full Township. Therefore, its contents are completely on this single page (instead of a "normal" 2-page spread).

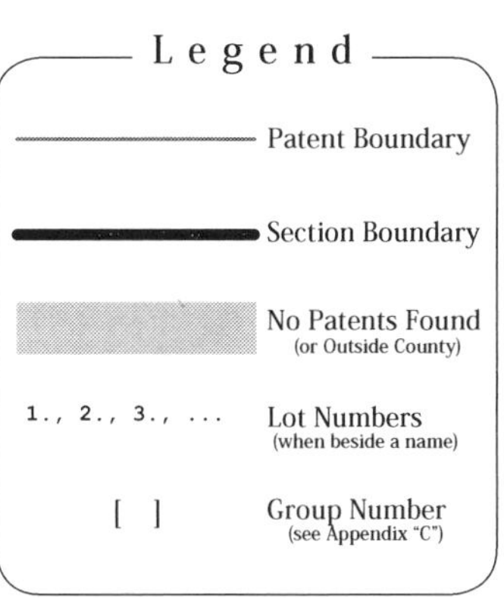

Scale: Section = 1 mile X 1 mile
(generally, with some exceptions)

Road Map

T40-N R3-E
5th PM Meridian

Map Group 5

Note: the area contained in this map amounts to far less than a full Township. Therefore, its contents are completely on this single page (instead of a "normal" 2-page spread).

Cities & Towns
None

Cemeteries
None

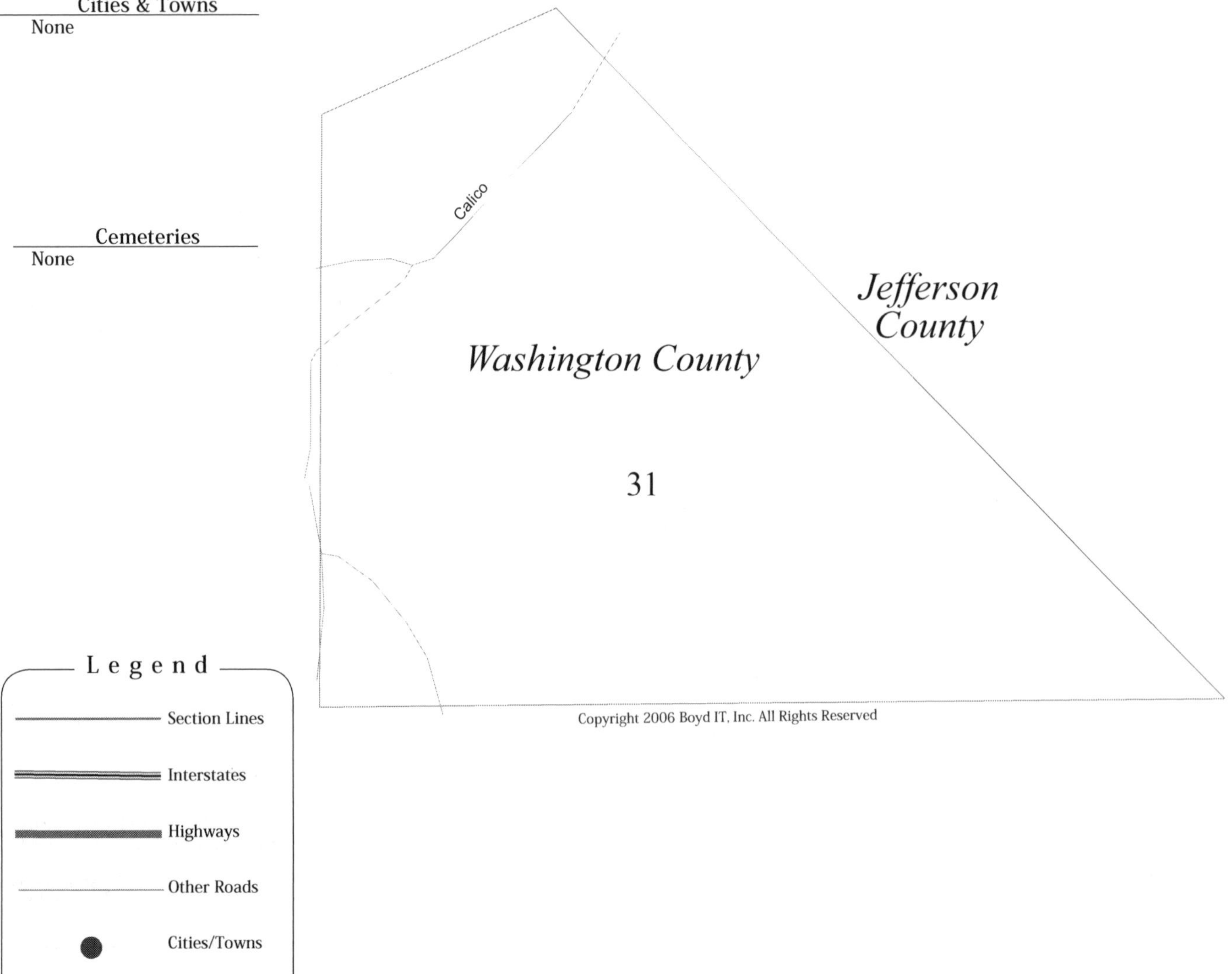

Legend

Section Lines
Interstates
Highways
Other Roads
Cities/Towns
Cemeteries

Scale: Section = 1 mile X 1 mile
(generally, with some exceptions)

Historical Map

T40-N R3-E
5th PM Meridian

Map Group 5

Note: the area contained in this map amounts to far less than a full Township. Therefore, its contents are completely on this single page (instead of a "normal" 2-page spread).

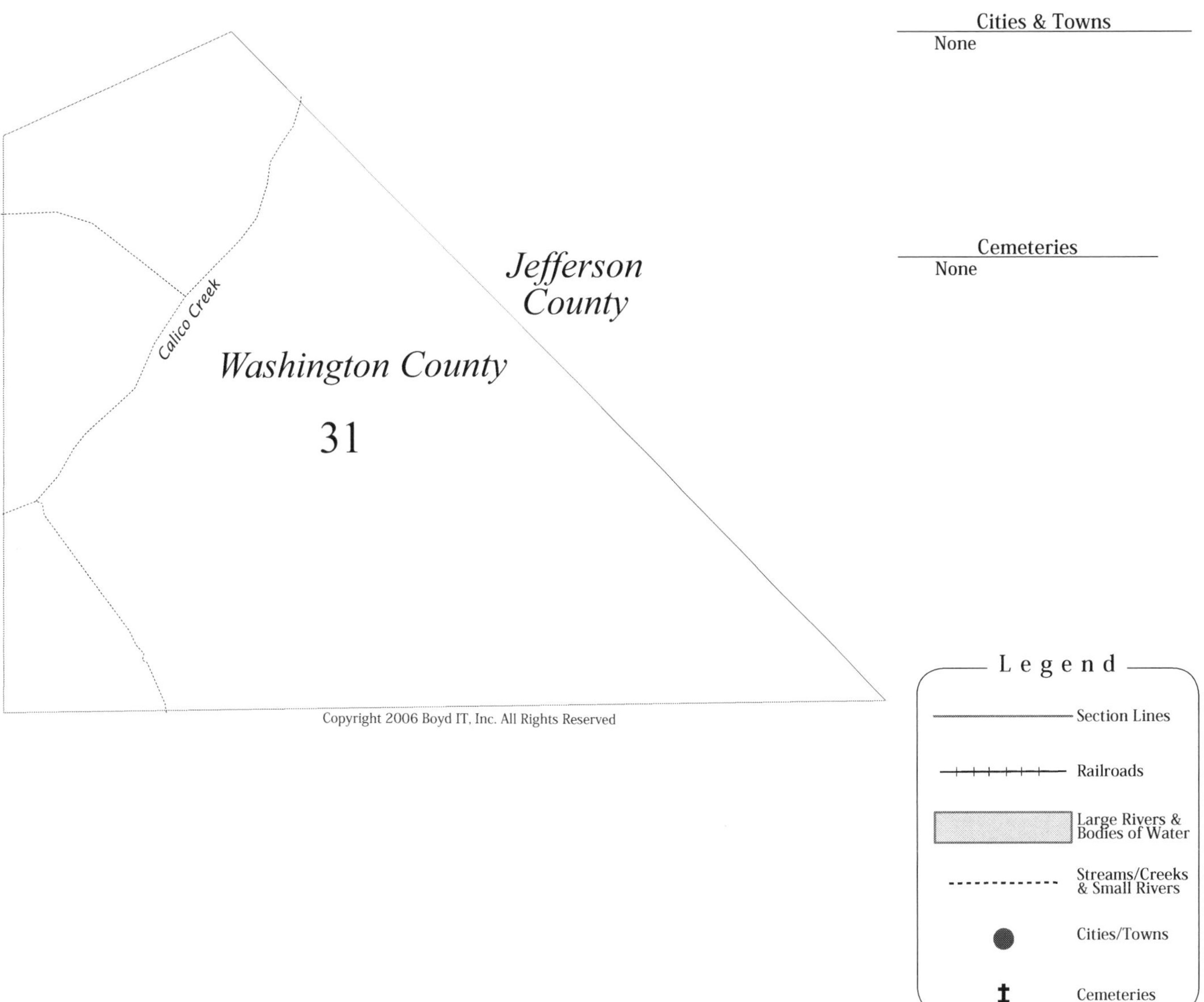

Cities & Towns

None

Cemeteries

None

Legend

- Section Lines
- Railroads
- Large Rivers & Bodies of Water
- Streams/Creeks & Small Rivers
- Cities/Towns
- Cemeteries

Scale: Section = 1 mile X 1 mile
(there are some exceptions)

Map Group 6: Index to Land Patents

Township 39-North Range 2-West (5th PM)

After you locate an individual in this Index, take note of the Section and Section Part then proceed to the Land Patent map on the pages immediately following. You should have no difficulty locating the corresponding parcel of land.

The "For More Info" Column will lead you to more information about the underlying Patents. See the *Legend* at right, and the "How to Use this Book" chapter, for more information.

LEGEND

"For More Info . . . " column

A = Authority (Legislative Act, See Appendix "A")
B = Block or Lot (location in Section unknown)
C = Cancelled Patent
F = Fractional Section
G = Group (Multi-Patentee Patent, see Appendix "C")
V = Overlaps another Parcel
R = Re-Issued (Parcel patented more than once)

(A & G items require you to look in the Appendixes referred to above. All other Letter-designations followed by a number require you to locate line-items in this index that possess the ID number found after the letter).

ID	Individual in Patent	Sec.	Sec. Part	Date Issued	Other Counties	For More Info . . .
361	ANTHONY, Jonas M	25	NESE	1835-10-01	Crawford	A1
362	" "	25	SESE	1836-01-14	Crawford	A1
363	" "	25	W½SE	1856-01-15	Crawford	A1
355	BENSON, Gilbert	13	E½SE	1857-06-10	Crawford	A1
347	BREDOLL, Edward	1	1NE	1856-01-15	Crawford	A1
348	" "	1	2NW	1856-01-15	Crawford	A1
349	" "	1	3NE	1856-01-15	Crawford	A1
350	" "	1	E½1NW	1856-01-15	Crawford	A1
351	" "	1	W½2NE	1856-01-15	Crawford	A1
359	DARBY, John F	1	6NW	1856-09-01	Crawford	A1 G78
343	FELL, Christian G	25	N½SW	1857-06-10	Crawford	A1
344	" "	25	NW	1857-06-10	Crawford	A1
345	" "	25	W½NE	1857-06-10	Crawford	A1
368	GALLAGHER, Thomas	1	E½SW	1859-11-01	Crawford	A1
369	" "	1	SE	1859-11-01	Crawford	A1
365	GREENE, Obadiah	1	W½SW	1840-10-01	Crawford	A1 G120
352	GRIFFIN, George M	13	SW	1859-11-01	Crawford	A1
353	" "	13	W½SE	1859-11-01	Crawford	A1
357	HARMAN, James L	1	E½2NE	1853-05-10	Crawford	A1 G126
360	HARRISON, John M	24	SWNE	1841-12-10	Crawford	A1
358	HUDSON, John B	36	SENW	1852-08-02	Crawford	A1
346	HURD, David	1	W½1NW	1860-07-20	Crawford	A1
339	IRVIN, Andrew	1	3NW	1848-07-01	Crawford	A1
340	IRVINE, Andrew	1	W½4NW	1850-06-01	Crawford	A1
359	JOHNSON, Isaac	1	6NW	1856-09-01	Crawford	A1 G78
356	" "	1	4NE	1857-06-10	Crawford	A1
371	MAJOR, William	25	S½SW	1859-11-01	Crawford	A1
357	MCDOWELL, John	1	E½2NE	1853-05-10	Crawford	A1 G126
341	MILLER, Andrew	24	E½SE	1835-10-08	Crawford	A1
342	" "	25	E½NE	1835-10-08	Crawford	A1
364	MORRISON, Lewis	36	W½NW	1843-04-10	Crawford	A1
354	MOUTRAY, George W	24	SENW	1841-12-10	Crawford	A1
365	PARKINSON, John	1	W½SW	1840-10-01	Crawford	A1 G120
366	SAPPINGTON, Philip	1	W½6NE	1882-04-29	Crawford	A3
370	SAPPINGTON, William I	1	5NE	1870-09-10	Crawford	A3
367	SCHNEIDER, Therese	13	N½	1857-06-10	Crawford	A1

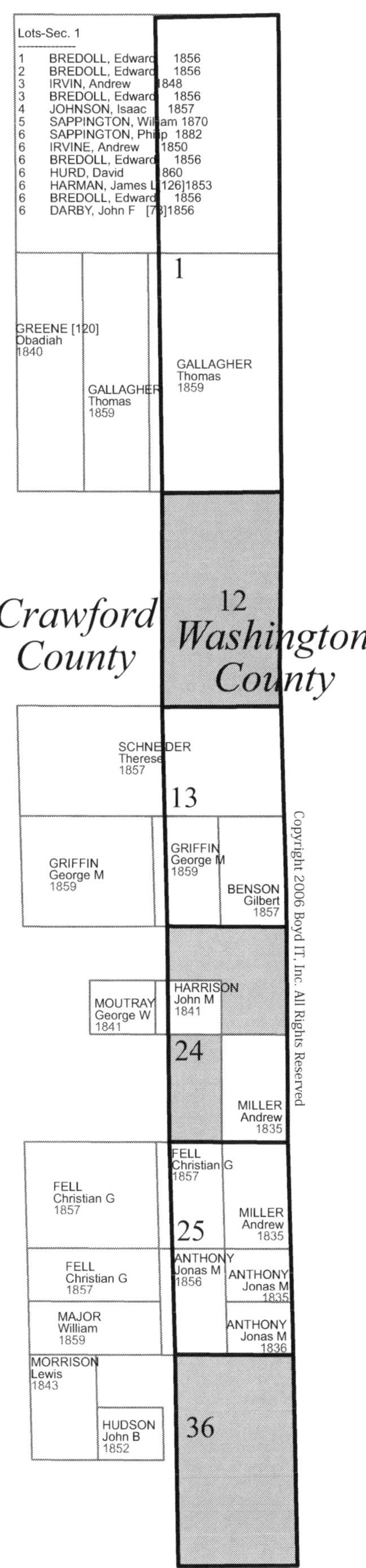

Patent Map

T39-N R2-W
5th PM Meridian

Map Group 6

Township Statistics

Parcels Mapped	:	33
Number of Patents	:	25
Number of Individuals	:	24
Patentees Identified	:	22
Number of Surnames	:	23
Multi-Patentee Parcels	:	3
Oldest Patent Date	:	10/1/1835
Most Recent Patent	:	4/29/1882
Block/Lot Parcels	:	13
Parcels Re - Issued	:	0
Parcels that Overlap	:	0
Cities and Towns	:	0
Cemeteries	:	0

Note: the area contained in this map amounts to far less than a full Township. Therefore, its contents are completely on this single page (instead of a "normal" 2-page spread).

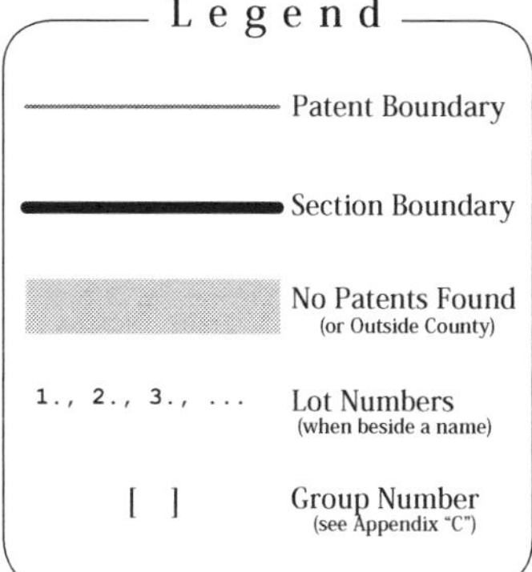

Scale: Section = 1 mile X 1 mile
(generally, with some exceptions)

Road Map

T39-N R2-W
5th PM Meridian

Map Group 6

Note: the area contained in this map amounts to far less than a full Township. Therefore, its contents are completely on this single page (instead of a "normal" 2-page spread).

Cities & Towns

None

Cemeteries

None

1

12

English Oak

Lost

Fair Acres

Indian Hill

Cimarron

Daybreak

Chiquita

Kickapoo

Chisholm

Chivvis

Crawford County

13

Washington County

24

25

36

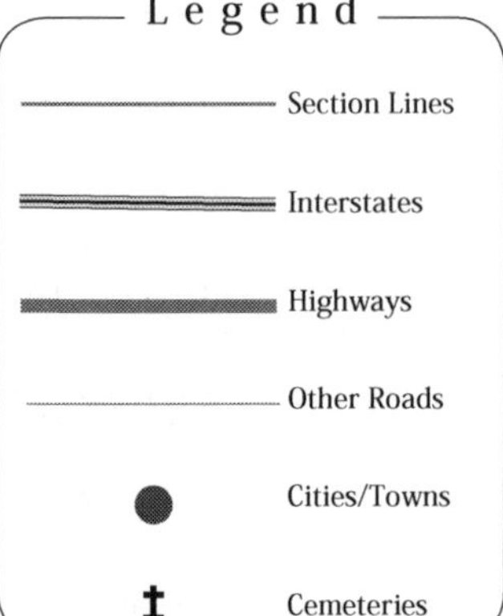

Scale: Section = 1 mile X 1 mile
(generally, with some exceptions)

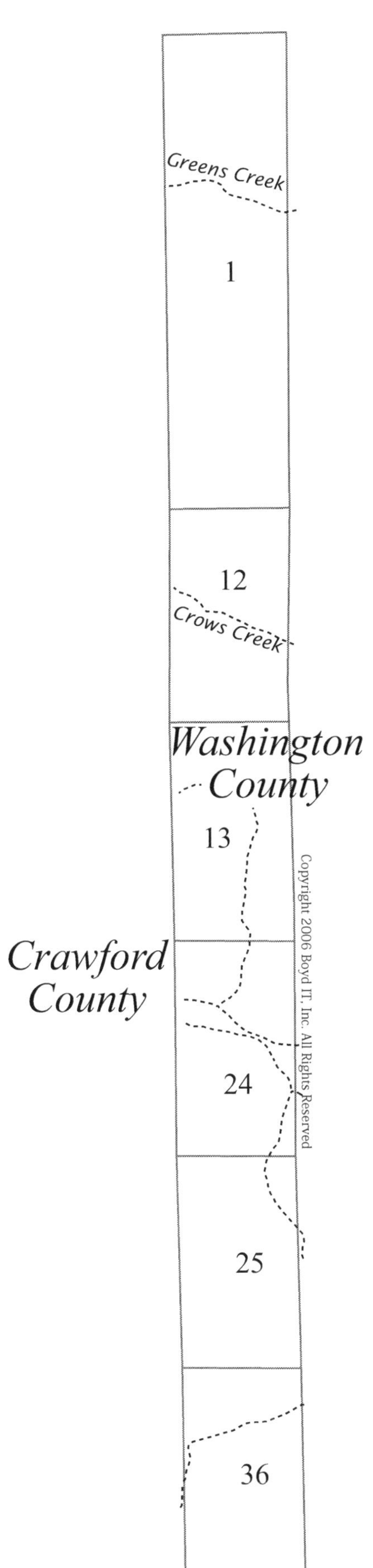

Historical Map

T39-N R2-W
5th PM Meridian

Map Group 6

Note: the area contained in this map amounts to far less than a full Township. Therefore, its contents are completely on this single page (instead of a "normal" 2-page spread).

Cities & Towns
None

Cemeteries
None

Legend

- Section Lines
- Railroads
- Large Rivers & Bodies of Water
- Streams/Creeks & Small Rivers
- Cities/Towns
- Cemeteries

Scale: Section = 1 mile X 1 mile
(there are some exceptions)

Map Group 7: Index to Land Patents

Township 39-North Range 1-West (5th PM)

After you locate an individual in this Index, take note of the Section and Section Part then proceed to the Land Patent map on the pages immediately following. You should have no difficulty locating the corresponding parcel of land.

The "For More Info" Column will lead you to more information about the underlying Patents. See the *Legend* at right, and the "How to Use this Book" chapter, for more information.

LEGEND

"For More Info . . . " column

- **A** = Authority (Legislative Act, See Appendix "A")
- **B** = Block or Lot (location in Section unknown)
- **C** = Cancelled Patent
- **F** = Fractional Section
- **G** = Group (Multi-Patentee Patent, see Appendix "C")
- **V** = Overlaps another Parcel
- **R** = Re-Issued (Parcel patented more than once)

(A & G items require you to look in the Appendixes referred to above. All other Letter-designations followed by a number require you to locate line-items in this index that possess the ID number found after the letter).

ID	Individual in Patent	Sec.	Sec. Part	Date Issued	Other Counties	For More Info . . .
439	ASHLEY, John	35	W½SW	1860-03-01		A1 R451
395	BAKER, Cyrus H	2	SWSW	1853-04-15		A1
397	BAKER, David N	11	W½NW	1856-06-10		A1
398	BARNES, David P	3	S½	1859-11-01		A1
518	BENSON, William	18	S½1SW	1844-08-01		A1
400	BREDELL, Edward	6	W½1NW	1849-06-01		A1
401	" "	6	W½3NW	1849-06-01		A1 F
501	BUCKLAND, Sarah	29	W½	1857-06-10		A1
504	BUCKLAND, Thomas A	31	E½	1857-06-10		A1
514	BURNS, Uriah	35	E½NE	1826-05-10		A1
515	BYRNE, Valentine	33	SW	1860-03-01		A1
409	CARTER, George	36	NWSW	1840-10-01		A1
412	CARTER, Harden T	6	E½3NW	1849-06-01		A1 G51
411	" "	6	W½3NE	1856-09-15		A1 G50
413	CARTER, Hardin T	6	W½4NW	1849-06-01		A1 G52
441	CASEY, John	7	NENE	1854-05-01		A1 G54
463	CAVANAH, Joseph	31	2NW	1836-01-14		A1
442	CHANCE, John	3	3NE	1859-11-01		A1
443	" "	3	3NW	1859-11-01		A1
411	CLARK, Jacob	6	W½3NE	1856-09-15		A1 G50
441	CLAUSEY, John	7	NENE	1854-05-01		A1 G54
488	CLOUDY, Norman S	35	NWNE	1858-01-13		A1 G68
412	CROW, Joseph	6	E½3NW	1849-06-01		A1 G51
464	" "	6	W½4NE	1849-06-01		A1 G76
412	CROW, William	6	E½3NW	1849-06-01		A1 G51
464	" "	6	W½4NE	1849-06-01		A1 G76
411	" "	6	W½3NE	1856-09-15		A1 G50
444	CULL, John	11	S½SW	1859-11-01		A1
445	DELY, John	31	S½1SW	1860-03-01		A1
517	DUCKWORTH, Wiley S	22	SESE	1843-04-10		A1
384	DUPAVILLON, Charles A	9	E½	1859-11-01		A1
408	DYKE, Frederick W	19	NENE	1860-03-01		A1
446	FARISH, John	25	E½	1859-11-01		A1 R447
447	" "	25	E½	1896-10-05		A1 R446
505	FEA, Thomas	21	NWNE	1860-03-01		A1 V402
506	" "	21	NWSE	1860-03-01		A1
507	" "	21	S½NE	1860-03-01		A1 V402
425	FOSTER, James H	15	NWSW	1859-11-01		A1
426	" "	15	S½SW	1859-11-01		A1
427	" "	15	SE	1859-11-01		A1
428	" "	15	SWNW	1859-11-01		A1
508	FRAME, Thomas	1	2NW	1859-11-01		A1
509	" "	1	E½3NW	1859-11-01		A1
422	GARTSIDE, James	13	NESE	1857-06-10		A1
423	" "	13	SW	1857-06-10		A1
424	" "	13	W½SE	1857-06-10		A1

ID	Individual in Patent	Sec.	Sec. Part	Date Issued	Other Counties	For More Info . . .
465	GARTSIDE, Joseph	13	NW	1857-06-10		A1
466	" "	13	SENE	1857-06-10		A1
467	" "	13	W½NE	1857-06-10		A1
386	GAUGH, Charles L	15	SENE	1856-06-10		A1
385	" "	15	NENE	1856-11-01		A1
387	" "	15	W½NE	1856-11-01		A1
502	GLENN, Smith And	19	2NW	1826-06-15		A1
503	" "	6	SW	1827-05-01		A1
402	GOULD, Edward J	21	NE	1860-03-01		A1 V505, 507
412	HARMAN, James	6	E½3NW	1849-06-01		A1 G51
464	" "	6	W½4NE	1849-06-01		A1 G76
495	HARMAN, Reuben	19	NESE	1857-06-10		A1
496	" "	19	SENE	1857-06-10		A1
497	" "	19	SESE	1883-07-10		A3
419	HARPER, Isaac	19	S½2SW	1858-01-13		A1
448	HARRISON, John	30	N½1NW	1840-10-01		A1
396	HIBLER, Daniel	7	SENE	1851-11-01		A1 G131
411	" "	6	W½3NE	1856-09-15		A1 G50
449	HICKLEY, John	11	SE	1859-11-01		A1
441	HILL, Jonas M	7	NENE	1854-05-01		A1 G54
441	HILL, Milton B	7	NENE	1854-05-01		A1 G54
480	HOGAN, Michael	21	NENW	1860-03-01		A1
519	HOLMES, William C	11	E½NW	1859-11-01		A1
520	" "	11	N½SW	1859-11-01		A1
521	" "	11	NE	1859-11-01		A1
413	HORBISON, Thomas	6	W½4NW	1849-06-01		A1 G52
522	HUGHES, William	18	N½1SW	1849-06-01		A1
524	" "	19	NWNE	1849-06-01		A1
523	" "	18	NESE	1853-04-15		A1
438	HULSEY, James W	1	W½SE	1840-10-01		A1
429	JOHNSON, James H	23	NWSW	1841-12-10		A1
430	JOHNSON, James J	13	SESE	1840-10-01		A1
431	JOHNSON, James M	1	NWSW	1859-11-01		A1
432	" "	1	S½SW	1859-11-01		A1
433	" "	1	W½1NW	1859-11-01		A1
488	JOHNSON, Uriah P	35	NWNE	1858-01-13		A1 G68
453	JONES, John	19	NWSE	1837-11-07		A1
454	" "	19	SWNE	1838-09-07		A1
452	" "	18	W½SE	1849-06-01		A1
392	KELLEHER, Cornelius	5	1NW	1862-05-24		A1
393	" "	5	2NW	1862-05-24		A1
394	" "	5	SW	1862-05-24		A1
375	KIRKWOOD, Allan	5	1NE	1862-01-28		A1
376	" "	5	2NE	1862-01-28		A1
377	" "	5	4NE	1862-01-28		A1
378	" "	5	E½3NE	1862-01-28		A1
379	" "	5	E½4NW	1862-01-28		A1
407	KLEIN, Felicite	17	N½	1857-06-10		A1
476	KLEIN, Mary A	7	NESE	1857-06-10		A1
477	" "	7	S½SE	1857-06-10		A1
478	" "	7	SW	1857-06-10		A1
489	KLEIN, Peter	7	NW	1857-06-10		A1
490	" "	7	NWSE	1857-06-10		A1
491	" "	7	W½NE	1857-06-10		A1
455	LEA, John	3	4NE	1859-11-01		A1
456	" "	3	4NW	1859-11-01		A1
457	" "	3	5NE	1859-11-01		A1
458	" "	3	5NW	1859-11-01		A1
510	LOGAN, Thomas	3	1NE	1859-11-01		A1
511	" "	3	1NW	1859-11-01		A1
512	" "	3	2NE	1859-11-01		A1
513	" "	3	2NW	1859-11-01		A1
461	LUPTON, Jonathan	23	NESE	1848-07-01		A1
462	" "	23	NESW	1848-07-01		A1
525	MARSH, William	31	N½1NW	1860-03-01		A1
526	MCCRACKEN, William	8	NESW	1843-04-10		A1
492	MCCUNE, Peter	5	W½4NW	1860-03-01		A1
493	" "	5	W½5NW	1860-03-01		A1
494	" "	5	W½6NW	1860-03-01		A1
516	MCDONOUGH, Walter	27	SESE	1860-03-01		A1
498	MCINTIRE, Robert N	15	NESW	1859-11-01		A1
403	MILLIGAN, Edward	27	E½NW	1859-11-01		A1
404	" "	27	N½NE	1859-11-01		A1

ID	Individual in Patent	Sec.	Sec. Part	Date Issued	Other Counties	For More Info . . .
405	MILLIGAN, Edward (Cont'd)	27	NESW	1859-11-01		A1
406	" "	27	SWNE	1859-11-01		A1
479	MOORE, Matthias	5	SE	1859-11-01		A1
471	MORRISON, Lewis	31	N½1SW	1857-06-10		A1
472	" "	31	N½2SW	1857-06-10		A1
473	" "	31	S½1NW	1857-06-10		A1
414	MURPHY, Henry	33	N½	1859-11-01		A1
380	NORRIS, Amos B	23	NE	1857-06-10		A1
381	" "	23	S½SW	1857-06-10		A1
382	" "	23	W½SE	1857-06-10		A1
410	NORTHCUT, George	1	W½3NW	1858-05-03		A1
418	OGDEN, Hiram	8	NENE	1860-03-01		A1
474	OUTLAY, Lorenzo	25	W½	1862-05-24		A1
468	PATTON, Joseph	1	NESW	1843-04-10		A1
413	POINDEXTER, Marcellus	6	W½4NW	1849-06-01		A1 G52
436	PRATT, James	19	N½2SW	1856-09-01		A1
499	RANNEY, Rowland R	27	NWSW	1859-11-01		A1
500	" "	27	W½NW	1859-11-01		A1
440	REED, John C	8	W½NW	1843-04-10		A1 G203
487	REMY, Nicholas	17	S½	1857-06-10		A1
399	RENFRO, David	19	1NW	1825-07-15		A1
469	RIDGWAY, Joseph	5	E½3NW	1849-06-01		A1
470	" "	5	W½3NE	1849-06-01		A1
475	RISSER, Ludwig	5	E½5NE	1860-03-01		A1
450	RODERICK, John J	35	W½NW	1858-05-03		A1
451	" "	35	W½SW	1858-05-03		A1 R439
372	SCHENCK, Addison V	13	NENE	1860-03-01		A1
460	SWAN, John	19	1SW	1826-06-15		A1
415	THAYER, Henry	35	E½NW	1858-01-13		A1
416	" "	35	SE	1858-01-13		A1
417	" "	35	SWNE	1858-01-13		A1
481	THODD, Moses	26	W½NW	1850-01-01		A1
388	THORP, Charles	1	1NE	1857-06-10		A1
389	" "	1	2NE	1857-06-10		A1
390	" "	1	3NE	1857-06-10		A1
391	" "	1	E½SE	1857-06-10		A1
482	TODD, Moses	26	NWSW	1850-06-01		A1
483	" "	27	NESE	1850-06-01		A1
484	" "	27	S½SW	1856-01-15		A1
485	" "	27	SENE	1856-01-15		A1
486	" "	27	W½SE	1856-01-15		A1
437	TUCKER, James	23	SESE	1840-10-01		A1
373	TURNER, Alfred	15	E½NW	1860-03-01		A1
374	" "	15	NWNW	1860-03-01		A1
420	VAN HOUTEN, JACOB	26	SWSE	1840-10-01		A1
421	" "	36	SESW	1840-10-01		A1
396	WESTOVER, George T	7	SENE	1851-11-01		A1 G131
434	WHITE, James M	6	E½SE	1843-04-10		A1
435	" "	8	E½NW	1843-04-10		A1
440	" "	8	W½NW	1843-04-10		A1 G203
383	WILKSON, Anthony	8	W½NE	1843-04-10		A1
459	WILLIAMS, John N	8	NWSW	1843-04-10		A1

Patent Map

T39-N R1-W
5th PM Meridian

Map Group 7

Township Statistics

Parcels Mapped	:	155
Number of Patents	:	100
Number of Individuals	:	97
Patentees Identified	:	88
Number of Surnames	:	84
Multi-Patentee Parcels	:	8
Oldest Patent Date	:	7/15/1825
Most Recent Patent	:	10/5/1896
Block/Lot Parcels	:	50
Parcels Re - Issued	:	2
Parcels that Overlap	:	3
Cities and Towns	:	2
Cemeteries	:	3

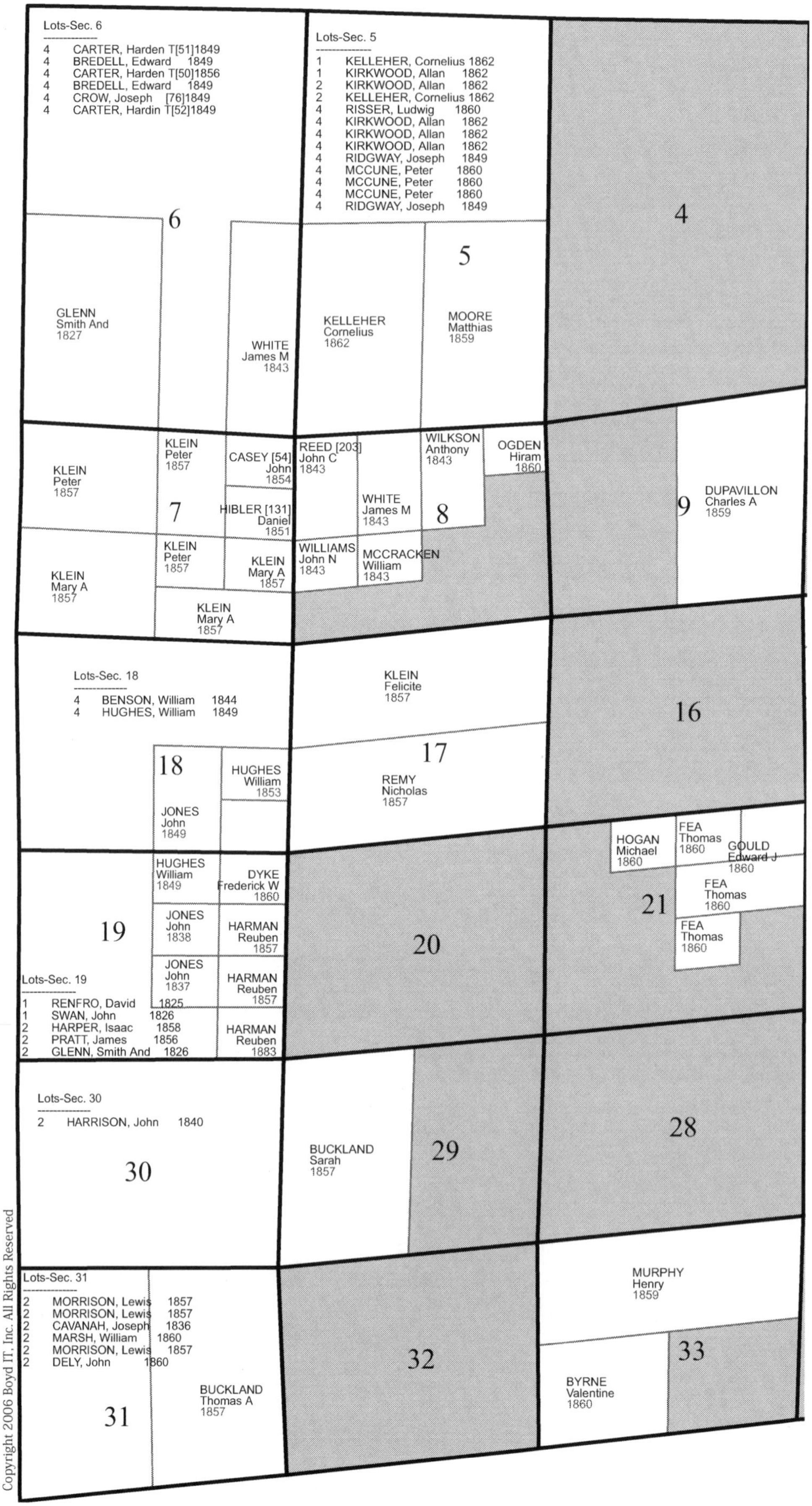

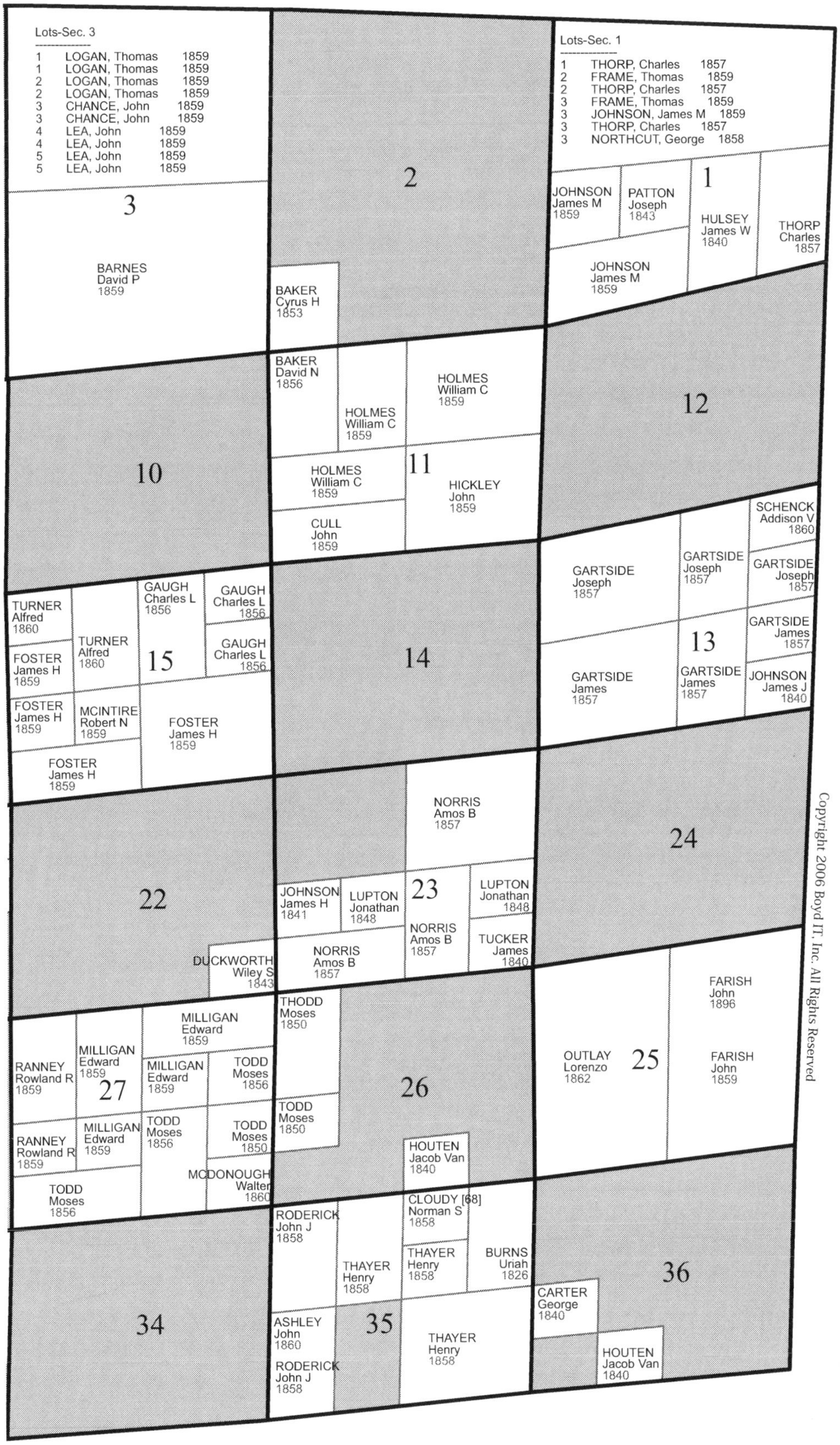

Lots-Sec. 3

1 LOGAN, Thomas 1859
1 LOGAN, Thomas 1859
2 LOGAN, Thomas 1859
2 LOGAN, Thomas 1859
3 CHANCE, John 1859
3 CHANCE, John 1859
4 LEA, John 1859
4 LEA, John 1859
5 LEA, John 1859
5 LEA, John 1859

3
BARNES David P 1859

2
BAKER Cyrus H 1853

Lots-Sec. 1

1 THORP, Charles 1857
2 FRAME, Thomas 1859
2 THORP, Charles 1857
3 FRAME, Thomas 1859
3 JOHNSON, James M 1859
3 THORP, Charles 1857
3 NORTHCUT, George 1858

1
JOHNSON James M 1859
PATTON Joseph 1843
HULSEY James W 1840
THORP Charles 1857
JOHNSON James M 1859

10

11
BAKER David N 1856
HOLMES William C 1859
HOLMES William C 1859
HOLMES William C 1859
HICKLEY John 1859
CULL John 1859

12

15
TURNER Alfred 1860
TURNER Alfred 1860
GAUGH Charles L 1856
GAUGH Charles L 1856
GAUGH Charles L 1856
FOSTER James H 1859
FOSTER James H 1859
MCINTIRE Robert N 1859
FOSTER James H 1859
FOSTER James H 1859

14

13
SCHENCK Addison V 1860
GARTSIDE Joseph 1857
GARTSIDE Joseph 1857
GARTSIDE Joseph 1857
GARTSIDE James 1857
GARTSIDE James 1857
GARTSIDE James 1857
JOHNSON James J 1840

22
DUCKWORTH Wiley S 1843

23
NORRIS Amos B 1857
JOHNSON James H 1841
LUPTON Jonathan 1848
LUPTON Jonathan 1848
NORRIS Amos B 1857
NORRIS Amos B 1857
TUCKER James 1840

24

27
MILLIGAN Edward 1859
RANNEY Rowland R 1859
MILLIGAN Edward 1859
MILLIGAN Edward 1859
TODD Moses 1856
RANNEY Rowland R 1859
MILLIGAN Edward 1859
TODD Moses 1856
TODD Moses 1850
MCDONOUGH Walter 1860
TODD Moses 1856

26
THODD Moses 1850
TODD Moses 1850
HOUTEN Jacob Van 1840

25
OUTLAY Lorenzo 1862
FARISH John 1896
FARISH John 1859

34

35
RODERICK John J 1858
CLOUDY [68] Norman S 1858
THAYER Henry 1858
THAYER Henry 1858
BURNS Uriah 1826
ASHLEY John 1860
RODERICK John J 1858
THAYER Henry 1858

36
CARTER George 1840
HOUTEN Jacob Van 1840

Helpful Hints

1. This Map's INDEX can be found on the preceding pages.
2. Refer to Map "C" to see where this Township lies within Washington County, Missouri.
3. Numbers within square brackets [ ] denote a multi-patentee land parcel (multi-owner). Refer to Appendix "C" for a full list of members in this group.
4. Areas that look to be crowded with Patentees usually indicate multiple sales of the same parcel (Re-issues) or Overlapping parcels. See this Township's Index for an explanation of these and other circumstances that might explain "odd" groupings of Patentees on this map.

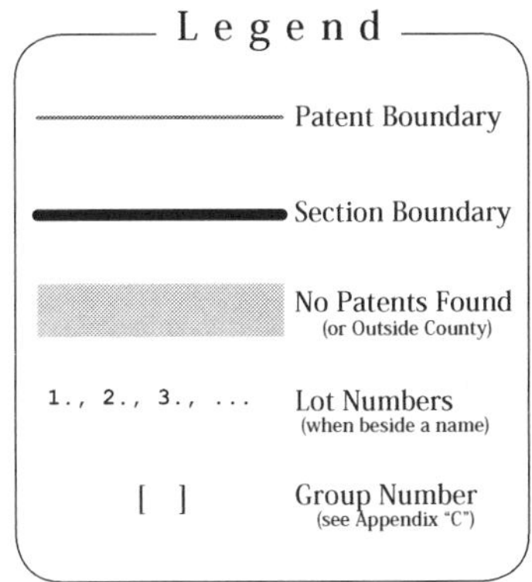

Scale: Section = 1 mile X 1 mile
(generally, with some exceptions)

Road Map

T39-N R1-W
5th PM Meridian

Map Group 7

Cities & Towns

Anthonies Mill
Pea Ridge

Cemeteries

Anthonie's Mill Cemetery
Scott-Reynolds Cemetery
Swan Cemetery

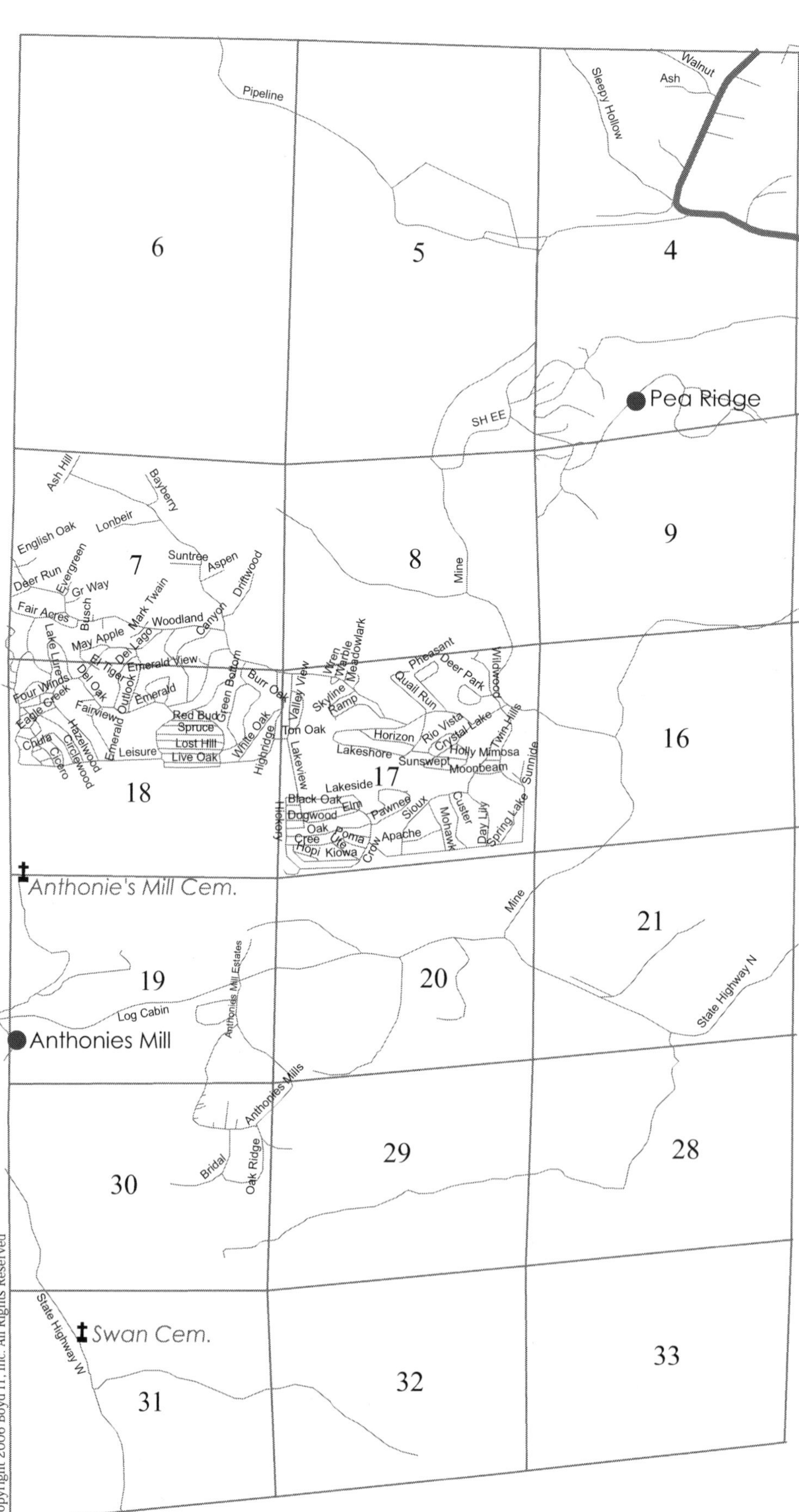

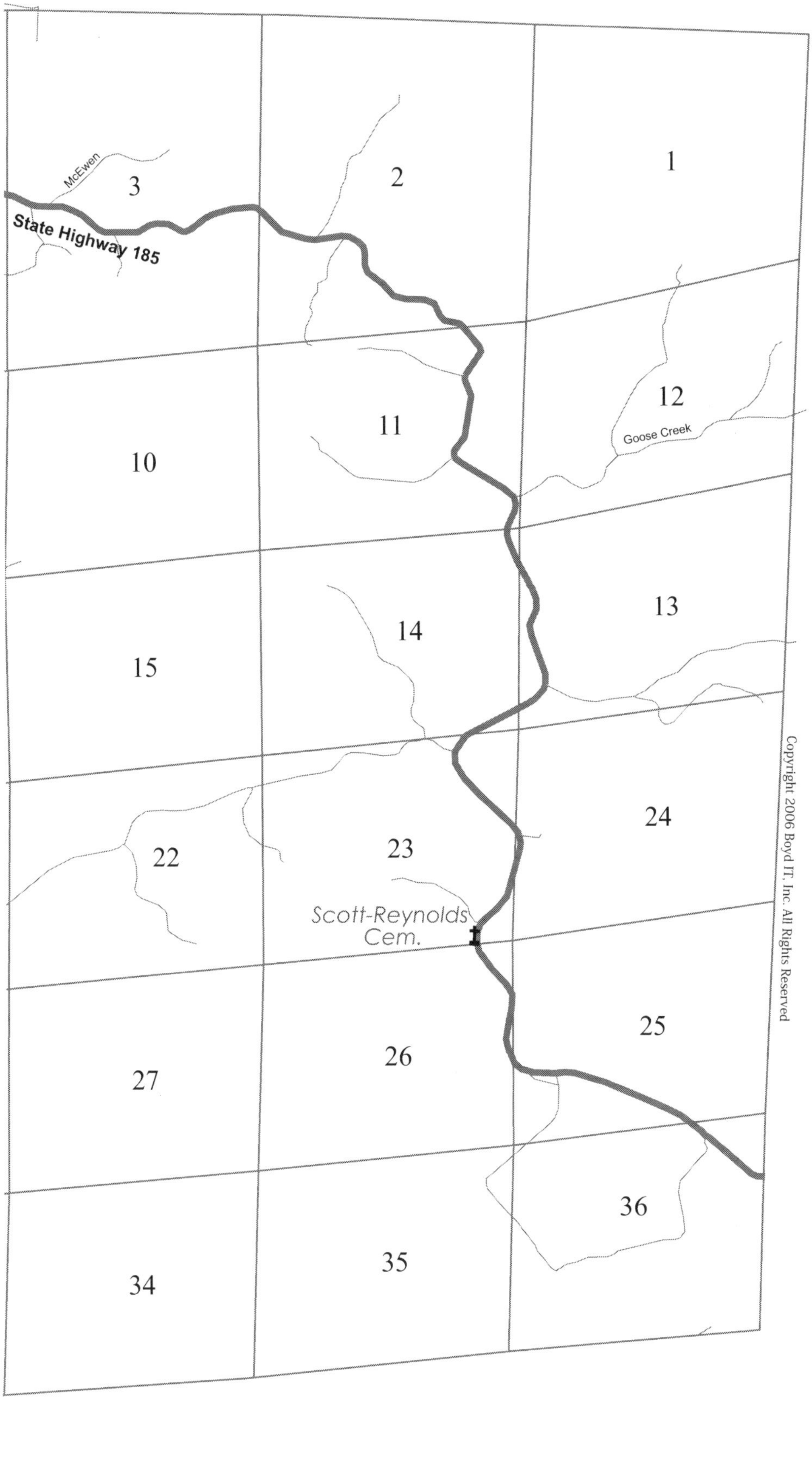

3
McEwen
State Highway 185
2
1
10
11
12
Goose Creek
15
14
13
22
23
24
Scott-Reynolds Cem.
27
26
25
34
35
36

Helpful Hints

1. This road map has a number of uses, but primarily it is to help you: a) find the present location of land owned by your ancestors (at least the general area), b) find cemeteries and city-centers, and c) estimate the route/roads used by Census-takers & tax-assessors.

2. If you plan to travel to Washington County to locate cemeteries or land parcels, please pick up a modern travel map for the area before you do. Mapping old land parcels on modern maps is not as exact a science as you might think. Just the slightest variations in public land survey coordinates, estimates of parcel boundaries, or road-map deviations can greatly alter a map's representation of how a road either does or doesn't cross a particular parcel of land.

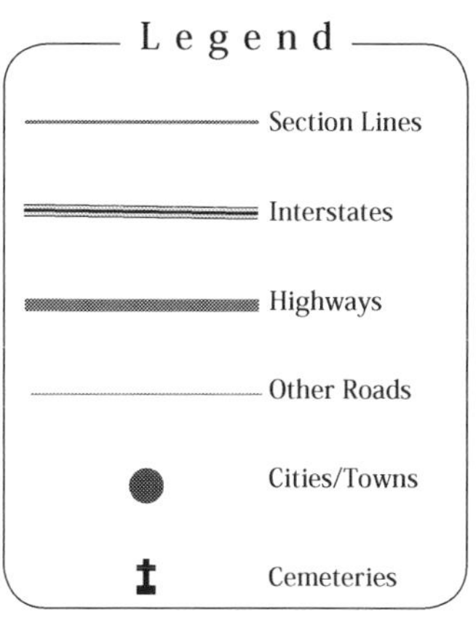

Scale: Section = 1 mile X 1 mile
(generally, with some exceptions)

Historical Map

T39-N R1-W
5th PM Meridian

Map Group 7

Cities & Towns

Anthonies Mill
Pea Ridge

Cemeteries

Anthonie's Mill Cemetery
Scott-Reynolds Cemetery
Swan Cemetery

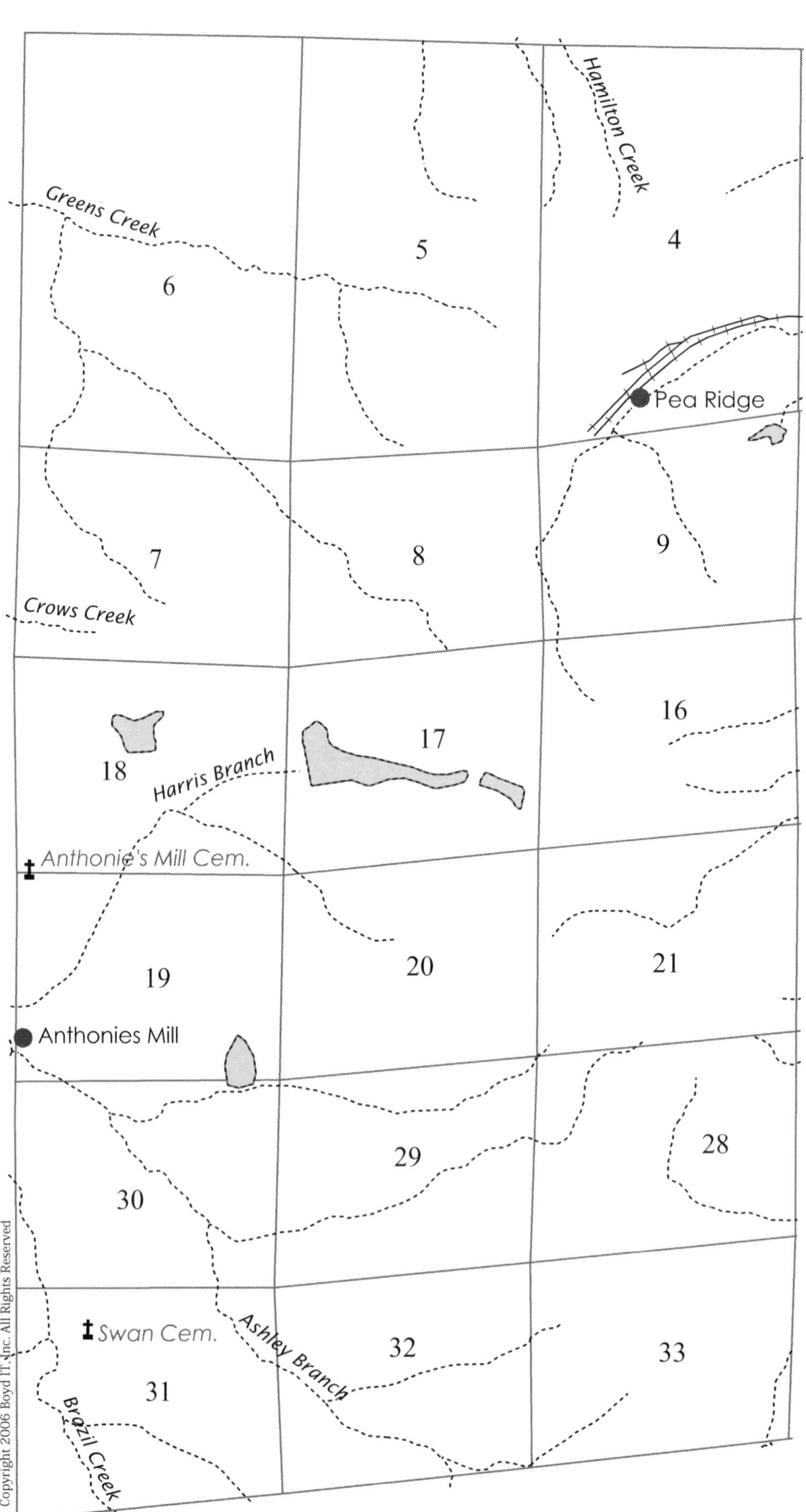

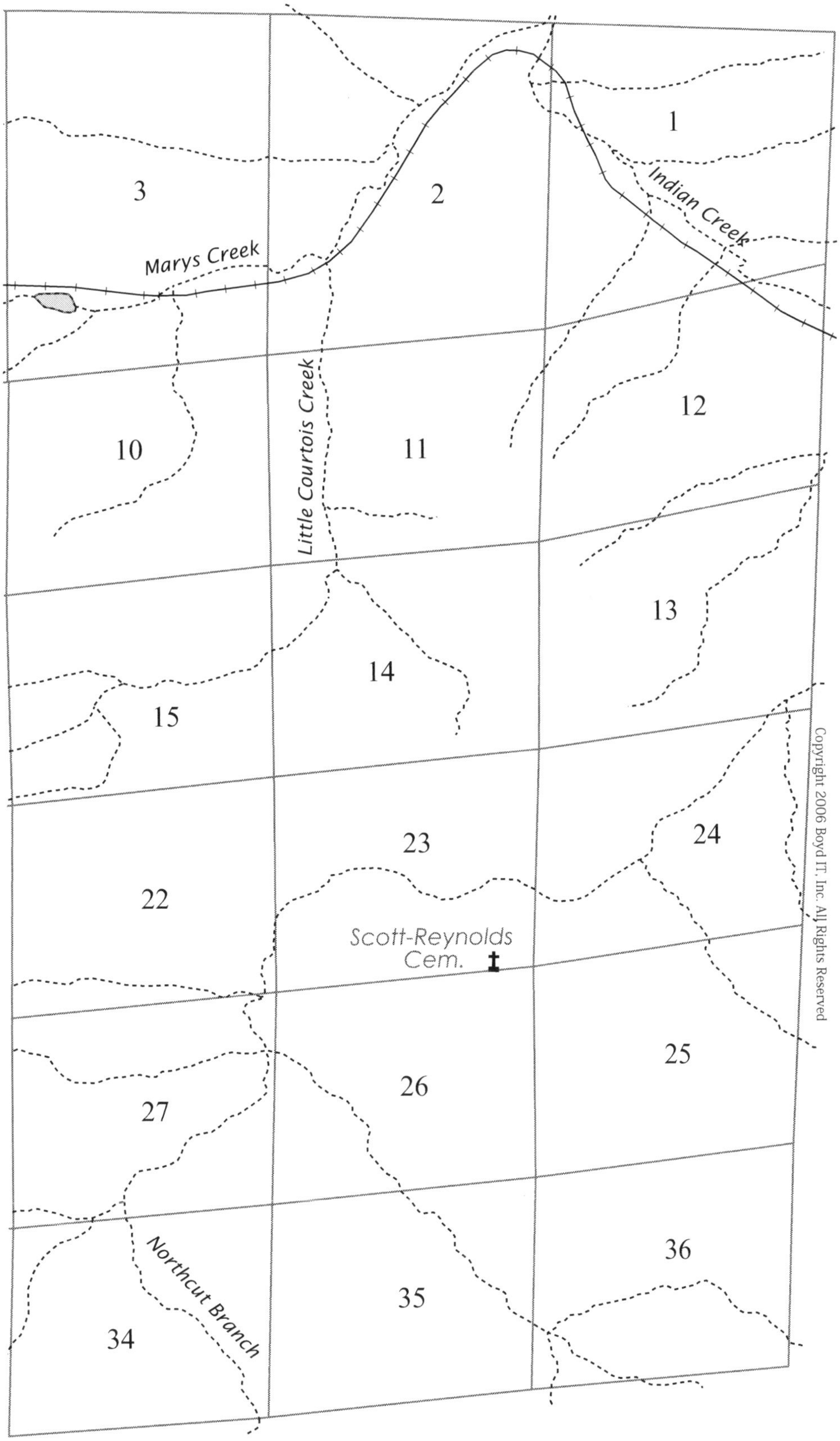

3
2
1
Marys Creek
Indian Creek
Little Courtois Creek
10
11
12
15
14
13
23
24
22
Scott-Reynolds Cem.
27
26
25
Northcut Branch
34
35
36

Helpful Hints

1. This Map takes a different look at the same Congressional Township displayed in the preceding two maps. It presents features that can help you better envision the historical development of the area: a) Water-bodies (lakes & ponds), b) Water-courses (rivers, streams, etc.), c) Railroads, d) City/town center-points (where they were oftentimes located when first settled), and e) Cemeteries.

2. Using this "Historical" map in tandem with this Township's Patent Map and Road Map, may lead you to some interesting discoveries. You will often find roads, towns, cemeteries, and waterways are named after nearby landowners: sometimes those names will be the ones you are researching. See how many of these research gems you can find here in Washington County.

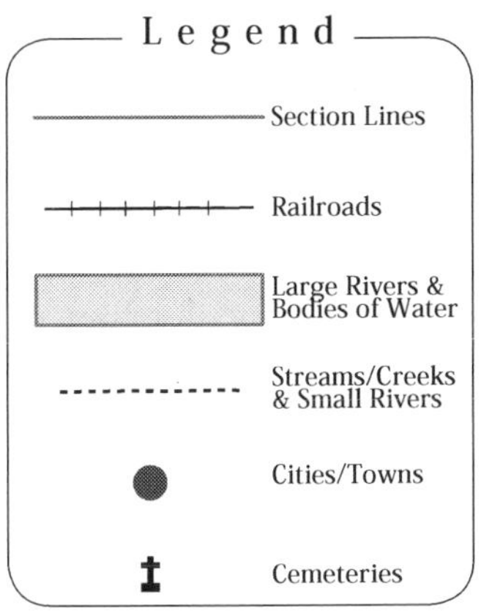

Scale: Section = 1 mile X 1 mile
(there are some exceptions)

Map Group 8: Index to Land Patents

Township 39-North Range 1-East (5th PM)

After you locate an individual in this Index, take note of the Section and Section Part then proceed to the Land Patent map on the pages immediately following. You should have no difficulty locating the corresponding parcel of land.

The "For More Info" Column will lead you to more information about the underlying Patents. See the *Legend* at right, and the "How to Use this Book" chapter, for more information.

LEGEND

"For More Info . . . " column

A = Authority (Legislative Act, See Appendix "A")
B = Block or Lot (location in Section unknown)
C = Cancelled Patent
F = Fractional Section
G = Group (Multi-Patentee Patent, see Appendix "C")
V = Overlaps another Parcel
R = Re-Issued (Parcel patented more than once)

(A & G items require you to look in the Appendixes referred to above. All other Letter-designations followed by a number require you to locate line-items in this index that possess the ID number found after the letter).

ID	Individual in Patent	Sec.	Sec. Part	Date Issued	Other Counties	For More Info . . .
531	AMELY, Antoine	1	SESW	1857-06-10		A1
695	ANDRES, Stephen	11	S½NE	1859-11-01		A1
540	BIBO, Bernhard	13	N½SW	1859-11-01		A1
608	BOCKENKAMP, Gerhard H	26	NWNW	1859-05-02		A1
609	" "	26	NWSW	1859-05-02		A1
610	" "	26	S½NW	1859-05-02		A1
611	" "	26	S½SW	1859-05-02		A1
612	" "	26	W½SE	1859-05-02		A1
565	BOND, Edward B	34	NE	1859-11-01		A1
706	BOUCHARD, Vetal	28	S½SW	1859-11-01		A1
649	BOURBON, John P	1	N½SW	1858-01-13		A1
562	BOYER, Derville	21	NENE	1859-11-01		A1
564	BOYER, Durville	21	NWNE	1859-05-02		A1
629	BROWN, John	29	NWNE	1860-03-01		A1
630	" "	29	S½NE	1860-03-01		A1
660	BROWN, Joseph A	12	NESE	1857-06-10		A1
661	" "	12	SESE	1858-05-03		A1
707	BROWN, William	29	NW	1859-11-01		A1
578	BURNETT, Francis	28	N½NE	1859-11-01		A1
579	" "	28	N½SE	1859-11-01		A1
580	" "	28	SWNE	1859-11-01		A1
581	" "	28	SWSE	1859-11-01		A1
582	" "	33	W½NE	1859-11-01		A1
538	CAYLE, Bernard	9	SE	1859-11-01		A1
594	CHAMBERS, George	7	2SW	1860-03-01		A1
614	COMSTOCK, Isaac	17	E½	1859-11-01		A1
694	CORDIER, Sophie	1	W½1NE	1853-04-15		A1
682	COURTIOL, Pierre	7	NWNE	1857-06-10		A1 V627
542	CRAHAN, Bryan	12	S½SW	1859-11-01		A1
543	" "	12	W½SE	1859-11-01		A1
675	CRAHAN, Patrick	14	S½NE	1859-11-01		A1
599	CRESSWELL, George	34	SWSE	1849-06-01		A1
600	" "	35	SESW	1849-06-01		A1
595	" "	23	S½SE	1856-06-10		A1
596	" "	24	SWSW	1856-06-10		A1
597	" "	25	E½NW	1856-06-10		A1
598	" "	26	NENW	1856-06-10		A1
601	CRESWELL, George	25	E½SW	1840-10-01		A1
602	" "	25	W½NW	1840-10-01		A1
603	" "	25	W½SW	1840-10-01		A1
604	" "	26	NE	1840-10-01		A1
605	" "	35	SWSE	1848-07-01		A1
696	CRISWELL, Stephen	34	SESE	1843-04-10		A1
697	" "	35	SWSW	1843-04-10		A1
583	DECLOIS, Francis	28	SESE	1857-06-10		A1
584	" "	33	E½NE	1857-06-10		A1

ID	Individual in Patent	Sec.	Sec. Part	Date Issued	Other Counties	For More Info . . .
585	DECLOIS, Francis (Cont'd)	33	E½SE	1857-06-10		A1
677	DECLOS, Paul	29	NENE	1857-06-10		A1
668	DEEGAN, Michael J	22	W½SW	1859-11-01		A1
546	DELAURIERE, Charles F	1	3NW	1856-06-03		A2
547	" "	3	S½SW	1856-06-03		A2
664	DELCOUR, Louis	1	2NE	1856-09-01		A1
665	" "	1	E½1NW	1856-09-01		A1
637	FARRINGTON, John	1	W½1NW	1860-03-01		A1
638	" "	1	W½2NW	1860-03-01		A1
639	FIEDELDEY, John G	27	SW	1859-05-02		A1
640	" "	34	NW	1859-05-02		A1
641	FIEDELDEY, John H	17	E½SW	1859-05-02		A1
642	" "	17	NW	1859-05-02		A1
643	" "	17	SWSW	1859-05-02		A1
689	FITZWATER, Robert H	25	NE	1859-11-01		A1
690	" "	30	N½NW	1859-11-01		A1
558	FORREST, David	5	1NW	1896-04-28		A1
559	" "	5	E½SW	1896-04-28		A1
560	" "	5	SE	1896-04-28		A1
678	FOSTER, Perry	15	W½	1859-11-01		A1
615	GALLEY, James	31	W½SE	1860-03-01		A1
669	GLORE, Morton J	25	SESE	1916-06-06		A1
573	GODARD, Eugene	20	NENW	1849-06-01		A1 G117
574	GODAT, Eugene	10	NWNW	1849-06-01		A1 G118
616	GOGAY, James	26	E½SE	1859-11-01		A1
553	GOLDEN, Daniel M	22	SESW	1859-05-02		A1
554	" "	22	W½SE	1859-05-02		A1
555	GOLDING, Daniel M	22	NESW	1857-06-10		A1
556	" "	22	SENW	1857-06-10		A1
708	GOLDING, William	27	NWNW	1857-06-10		A1
709	" "	27	SWNW	1857-06-10		A1
710	" "	28	SENE	1857-06-10		A1
670	GOLDSBERG, Moses	22	NE	1859-11-01		A1
644	HALLIDAY, John	7	NESE	1859-05-02		A1 G124
645	" "	7	SENE	1859-05-02		A1 G124
617	HAMILTON, James	7	SWNW	1840-10-01		A1
527	HINDRICKER, Adam	36	W½	1859-05-02		A1
685	HORNEY, Rees	34	N½SE	1859-11-01		A1
686	" "	34	SW	1859-11-01		A1
687	" "	35	N½SW	1859-11-01		A1
574	HULSEY, William	10	NWNW	1849-06-01		A1 G118
711	" "	7	N½1SW	1854-05-01		A1
530	IRVINE, Andrew	33	SENW	1849-06-01		A1 G148
680	JACKSON, Philip	18	NWNE	1848-07-01		A1
713	JACKSON, William P	7	S½1SW	1857-06-10		A1
714	" "	7	SWSE	1857-10-30		A1
683	JOHNSON, Pleasant S	5	E½3NW	1856-09-01		A1
684	" "	5	W½3NE	1856-09-01		A1
673	KEENE, Oliver	3	2NE	1860-03-01		A1
674	" "	3	3NE	1860-03-01		A1
646	KERDER, John N	11	NW	1859-11-01		A1
537	KERSEY, Benjamin	1	E½2NW	1852-08-02		A1
539	KESSLER, Bernard	33	SWSW	1860-03-01		A1
623	KING, James S	7	N½1NW	1896-08-26		A1
624	" "	7	N½2NW	1896-08-26		A1
625	" "	7	NENE	1896-08-26		A1
626	" "	7	NWSE	1896-08-26		A1
627	" "	7	W½NE	1896-08-26		A1 V682
548	KIRKPATRICK, Charles	9	N½	1859-11-01		A1
586	KRAFT, Francis	3	NW	1859-11-01		A1
606	KULKE, George	13	NW	1859-11-01		A1
667	LAND, Lucy	32	SENW	1857-06-10		A1
666	" "	32	N½SW	1859-05-02		A1
541	LANGE, Berthold	32	E½	1859-11-01		A1
699	LIVINGSTON, Thomas R	24	NESE	1859-05-02		A1
700	" "	24	S½SE	1859-05-02		A1
701	" "	24	SENE	1859-05-02		A1
702	" "	24	SESW	1859-05-02		A1
676	LOWERY, Patrick	13	NE	1859-11-01		A1
688	LUPTON, Richard C	17	NWSW	1840-10-01		A1
681	LYNCH, Philip	9	SW	1859-11-01		A1
618	MACKY, James	21	SWNW	1860-03-01		A1
563	MAIRAT, Donat	1	3NE	1857-06-10		A1

ID	Individual in Patent	Sec.	Sec. Part	Date Issued	Other Counties	For More Info . . .
653	MANION, John S	23	E½NW	1859-11-01		A1
654	" "	23	S½NE	1859-11-01		A1
655	" "	24	N½SW	1859-11-01		A1
656	" "	24	NWSE	1859-11-01		A1
657	" "	24	SWNW	1859-11-01		A1
691	MANION, Samuel S	21	SWNE	1840-10-01		A1
698	MANION, Sydney	20	NENE	1840-10-01		A1
607	MARGETTS, George	33	W½SE	1859-11-01		A1
544	MASHMEYER, Catrina	25	NESE	1859-11-01		A1
545	" "	25	W½SE	1859-11-01		A1
536	MASON, Bartholomew E	5	E½3NE	1860-03-01		A1
712	MAYHEW, William	22	SESE	1860-03-01		A1
679	MCCANTEY, Peter	23	W½NW	1860-03-01		A1
613	MCCURDY, Horace S	14	S½	1859-11-01		A1
551	MCKEON, Coleman	31	SESE	1859-05-02		A1
552	" "	32	S½SW	1859-05-02		A1
550	" "	31	NESE	1860-03-01		A1
589	MERRYMAN, Frank	27	SENE	1860-03-01		A1
628	MEYER, Johann H	31	W½	1859-11-01		A1
671	NAUMAN, Nathan	7	SESE	1860-03-01		A1
619	NETTLETON, James	5	W½SW	1860-03-01		A1
590	NIEHANS, Friedrich	36	E½	1859-05-02		A1
591	NORP, G H	13	S½SW	1859-11-01		A1
592	" "	13	SE	1859-11-01		A1
593	" "	24	N½NW	1859-11-01		A1
647	ONEIL, John	27	SE	1859-11-01		A1
648	" "	27	SWNE	1859-11-01		A1
574	PAGE, John B	10	NWNW	1849-06-01		A1 G118
573	" "	20	NENW	1849-06-01		A1 G117
572	PATTON, Eliza J	4	E½3NW	1845-08-04		A1
620	PERKS, James	28	N½SW	1860-03-01		A1
621	" "	28	SENW	1860-03-01		A1
622	REED, James	15	E½	1859-11-01		A1
703	RODDA, Thomas	19	W½	1859-11-01		A1
650	ROSE, John	5	2NW	1860-03-01		A1
651	" "	5	W½3NW	1860-03-01		A1
652	ROSS, John	11	SW	1859-11-01		A1
672	RUMELL, Nicholas	23	N½NE	1859-11-01		A1
561	SHEPHERD, David	1	W½SE	1857-06-10		A1
529	SHOOK, Amos C	18	NESW	1840-10-01		A1
530	" "	33	SENW	1849-06-01		A1 G148
704	SIMPSON, Thomas	35	N½SE	1859-11-01		A1
566	SMITH, Edward	21	SESW	1859-11-01		A1
567	" "	21	SWSE	1859-11-01		A1
568	" "	21	W½SW	1859-11-01		A1
631	SMITH, John E	21	E½NW	1856-06-10		A1
634	" "	21	NWNW	1856-06-10		A1
632	" "	21	NESE	1856-11-01		A1
633	" "	21	NESW	1856-11-01		A1
635	" "	21	NWSE	1856-11-01		A1
636	" "	21	SESE	1856-11-01		A1
588	SONSUCIE, Francis	1	NESE	1856-09-01		A1
587	" "	1	E½1NE	1857-06-10		A1
644	STANDEFER, David W	7	NESE	1859-05-02		A1 G124
645	" "	7	SENE	1859-05-02		A1 G124
549	STEAD, Charles	31	NE	1859-11-01		A1
658	SUHR, John	11	SE	1859-11-01		A1
532	THEBEAU, Antoine	33	E½SW	1859-11-01		A1
533	" "	33	N½NW	1859-11-01		A1
534	" "	33	NWSW	1859-11-01		A1
535	" "	33	SWNW	1859-11-01		A1
528	THOMPSON, Alexander	11	NENE	1860-03-01		A1
659	TREMLETT, John	29	S½	1859-11-01		A1
692	TURNER, Samuel	27	E½NW	1860-03-01		A1
693	" "	27	NWNE	1860-03-01		A1
662	TYZACK, Joseph W	19	E½	1859-11-01		A1
663	WARNER, Levi	35	N½	1859-11-01		A1
569	WHYERS, Elijah G	23	E½SW	1897-09-20		A1
570	" "	23	NESE	1897-09-20		A1
571	" "	23	SWSW	1897-09-20		A1
705	WILLIAMS, Thomas	35	SESE	1860-03-01		A1
715	WINDER, William	1	SWSW	1860-03-01		A1
575	WORTHINGTON, Fannie A	3	1NE	1859-11-01		A1

ID	Individual in Patent	Sec.	Sec. Part	Date Issued	Other Counties	For More Info . . .
576	WORTHINGTON, Fannie A (Cont'd)	3	N½SW	1859-11-01		A1
577	" "	3	SE	1859-11-01		A1
557	YOUGHBERRY, Daniel	21	SENE	1859-11-01		A1

Patent Map

T39-N R1-E
5th PM Meridian

Map Group 8

Township Statistics

Parcels Mapped	:	189
Number of Patents	:	123
Number of Individuals	:	113
Patentees Identified	:	111
Number of Surnames	:	103
Multi-Patentee Parcels	:	5
Oldest Patent Date	:	10/1/1840
Most Recent Patent	:	6/6/1916
Block/Lot Parcels	:	24
Parcels Re - Issued	:	0
Parcels that Overlap	:	2
Cities and Towns	:	1
Cemeteries	:	4

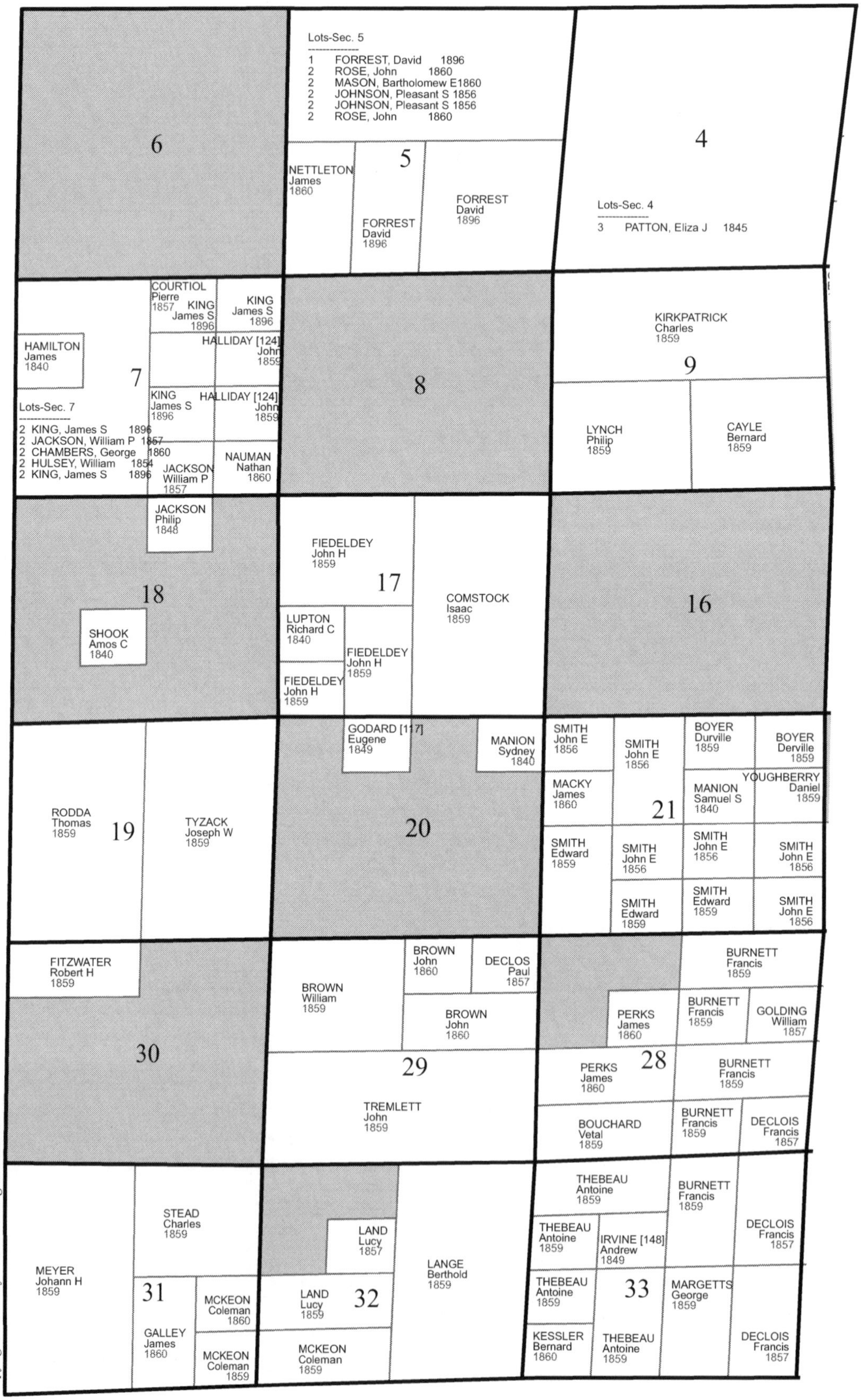

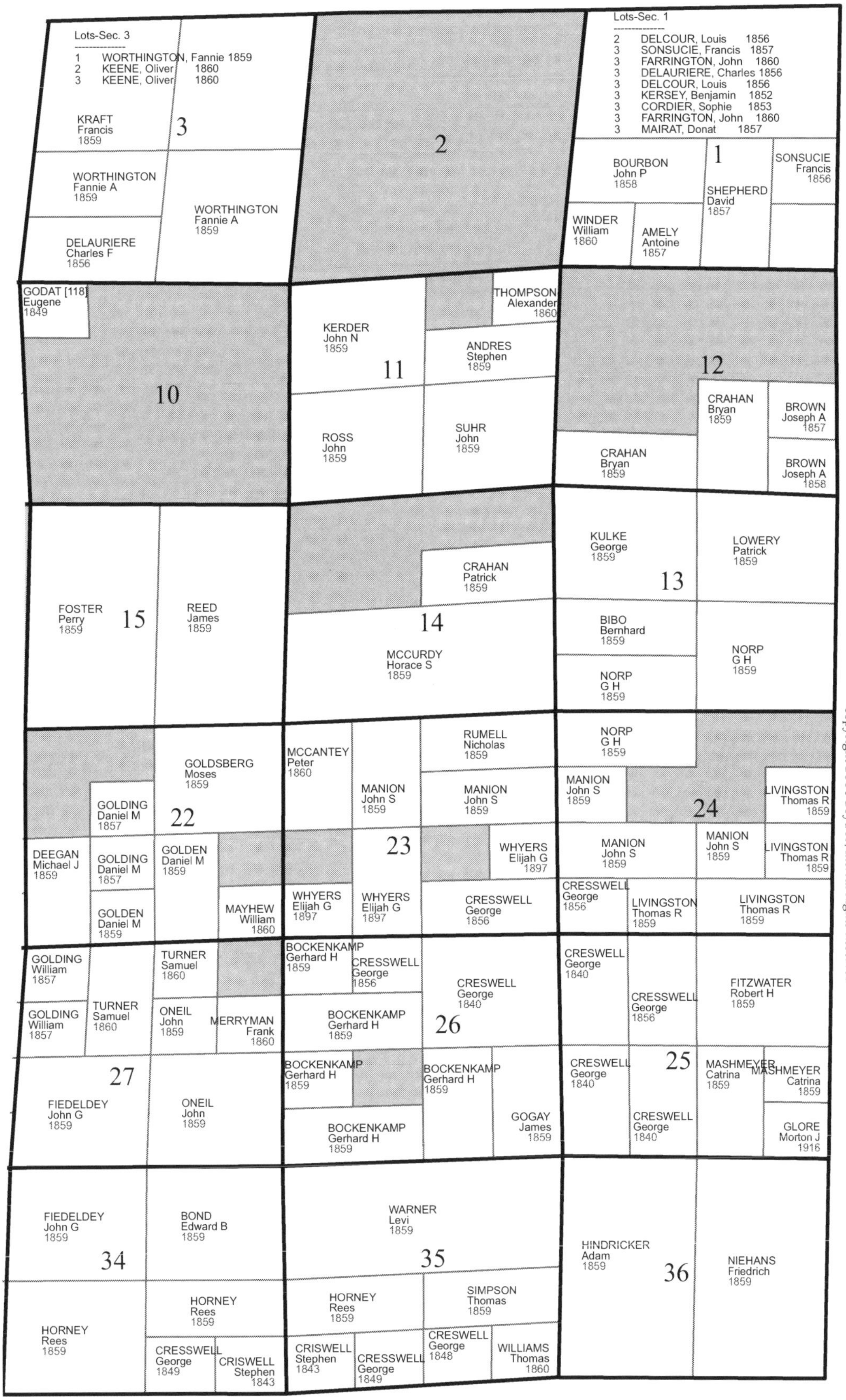

Helpful Hints

1. This Map's INDEX can be found on the preceding pages.
2. Refer to Map "C" to see where this Township lies within Washington County, Missouri.
3. Numbers within square brackets [ ] denote a multi-patentee land parcel (multi-owner). Refer to Appendix "C" for a full list of members in this group.
4. Areas that look to be crowded with Patentees usually indicate multiple sales of the same parcel (Re-issues) or Overlapping parcels. See this Township's Index for an explanation of these and other circumstances that might explain "odd" groupings of Patentees on this map.

Legend

Patent Boundary

Section Boundary

No Patents Found (or Outside County)

1., 2., 3., ... Lot Numbers (when beside a name)

[ ] Group Number (see Appendix "C")

Scale: Section = 1 mile X 1 mile (generally, with some exceptions)

Road Map

T39-N R1-E
5th PM Meridian

Map Group 8

Cities & Towns
Northcut

Cemeteries
Dry Branch Cemetery
Griggs Cemetery
Smith Cemetery
Yarbrough Cemetery

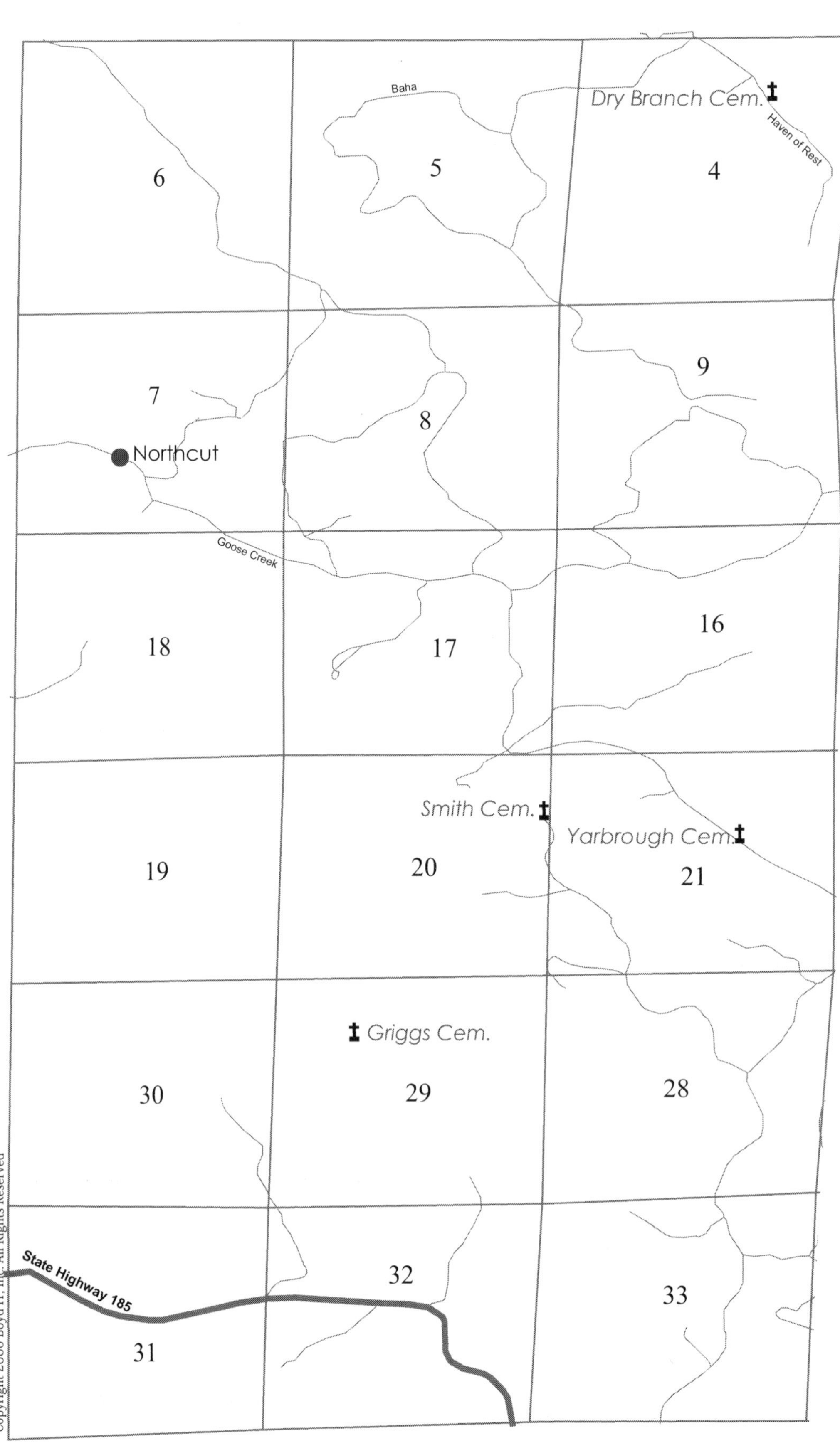

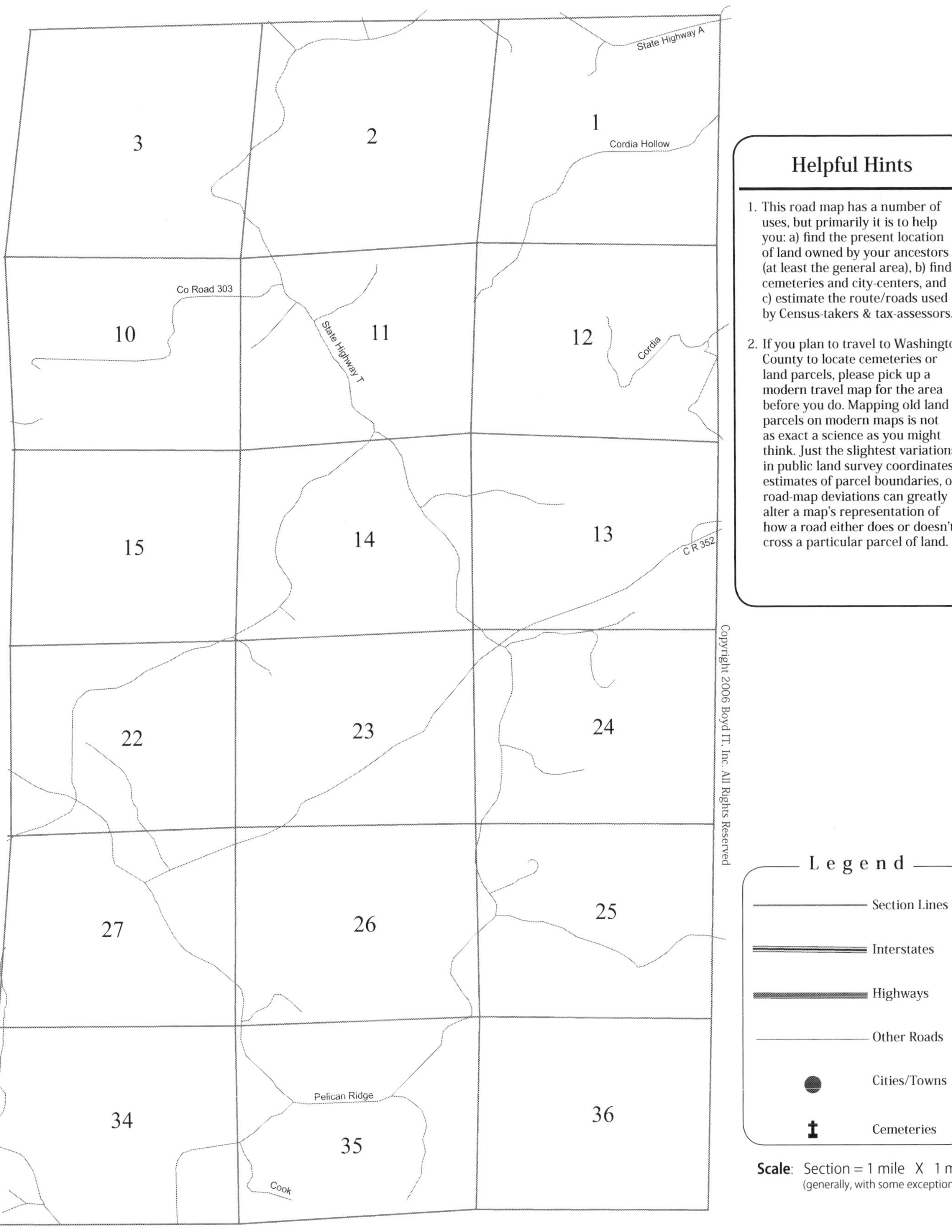

Helpful Hints

1. This road map has a number of uses, but primarily it is to help you: a) find the present location of land owned by your ancestors (at least the general area), b) find cemeteries and city-centers, and c) estimate the route/roads used by Census-takers & tax-assessors.
2. If you plan to travel to Washington County to locate cemeteries or land parcels, please pick up a modern travel map for the area before you do. Mapping old land parcels on modern maps is not as exact a science as you might think. Just the slightest variations in public land survey coordinates, estimates of parcel boundaries, or road-map deviations can greatly alter a map's representation of how a road either does or doesn't cross a particular parcel of land.

Legend

- Section Lines
- Interstates
- Highways
- Other Roads
- Cities/Towns
- Cemeteries

Scale: Section = 1 mile X 1 mile
(generally, with some exceptions)

Historical Map

T39-N R1-E
5th PM Meridian

Map Group 8

Cities & Towns

Northcut

Cemeteries

Dry Branch Cemetery
Griggs Cemetery
Smith Cemetery
Yarbrough Cemetery

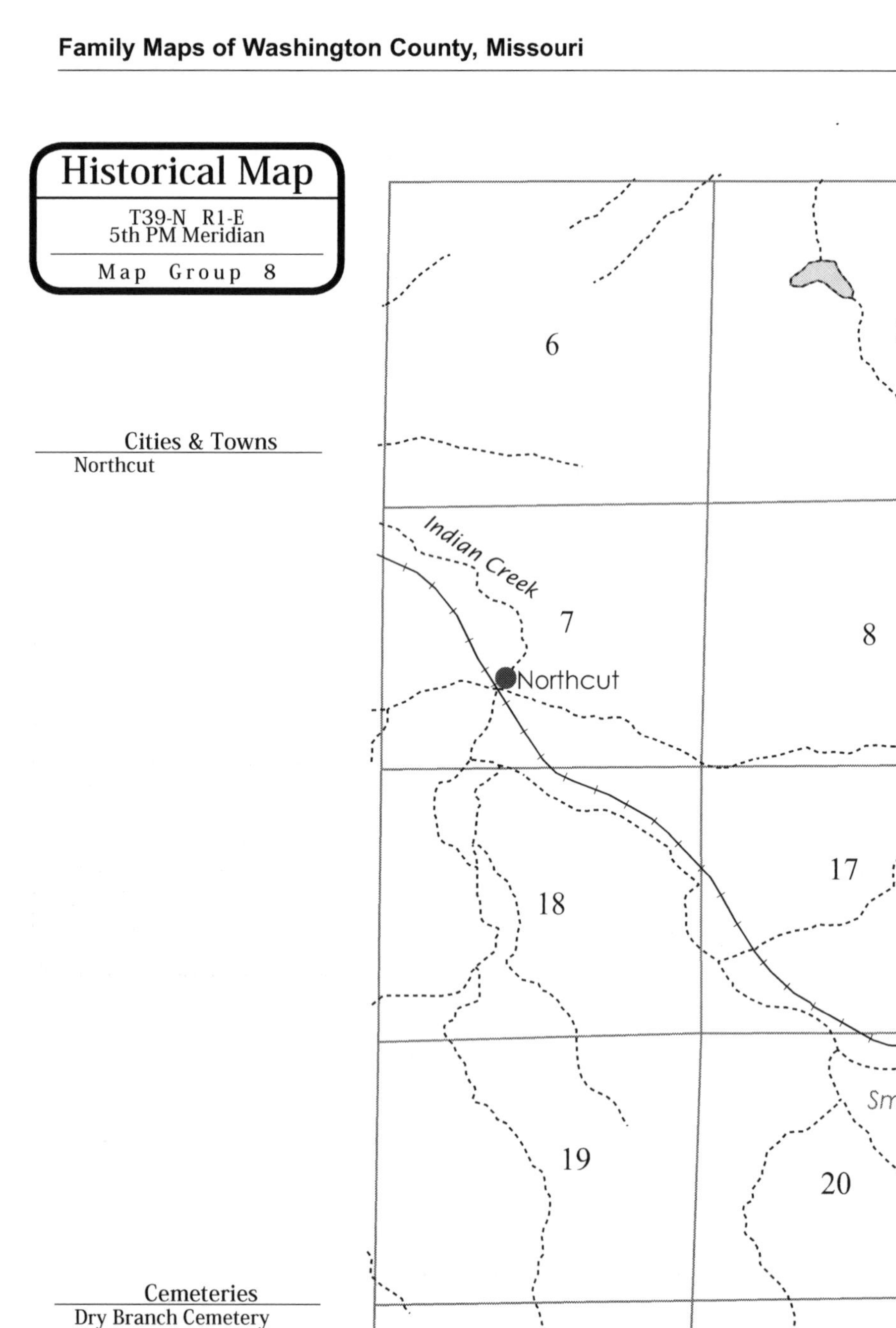

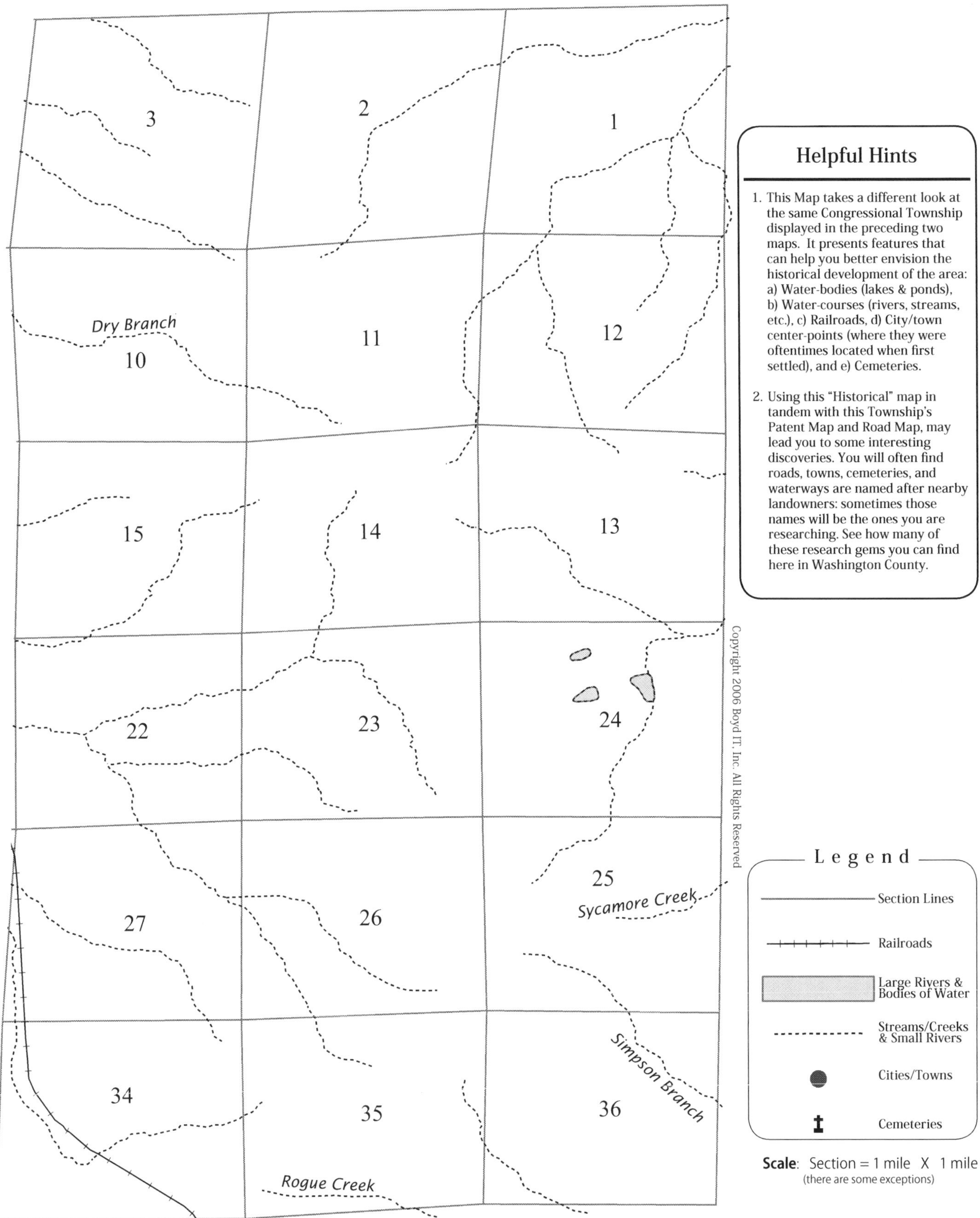

Helpful Hints

1. This Map takes a different look at the same Congressional Township displayed in the preceding two maps. It presents features that can help you better envision the historical development of the area: a) Water-bodies (lakes & ponds), b) Water-courses (rivers, streams, etc.), c) Railroads, d) City/town center-points (where they were oftentimes located when first settled), and e) Cemeteries.
2. Using this "Historical" map in tandem with this Township's Patent Map and Road Map, may lead you to some interesting discoveries. You will often find roads, towns, cemeteries, and waterways are named after nearby landowners: sometimes those names will be the ones you are researching. See how many of these research gems you can find here in Washington County.

Map Group 9: Index to Land Patents

Township 39-North Range 2-East (5th PM)

After you locate an individual in this Index, take note of the Section and Section Part then proceed to the Land Patent map on the pages immediately following. You should have no difficulty locating the corresponding parcel of land.

The "For More Info" Column will lead you to more information about the underlying Patents. See the *Legend* at right, and the "How to Use this Book" chapter, for more information.

LEGEND

"For More Info . . . " column

A = Authority (Legislative Act, See Appendix "A")
B = Block or Lot (location in Section unknown)
C = Cancelled Patent
F = Fractional Section
G = Group (Multi-Patentee Patent, see Appendix "C")
V = Overlaps another Parcel
R = Re-Issued (Parcel patented more than once)

(A & G items require you to look in the Appendixes referred to above. All other Letter-designations followed by a number require you to locate line-items in this index that possess the ID number found after the letter).

ID	Individual in Patent	Sec.	Sec. Part	Date Issued	Other Counties	For More Info . . .
716	ALEXANDER, Adolph	1	SWSE	1857-06-10		A1
913	ALEXANDER, Peter	10	SWSW	1848-07-01		A1
927	ALEXANDER, Siffroid	14	E½NW	1859-11-01		A1
932	ALLISON, Sylvanus	23	W½SE	1835-09-02		A1
934	ALLISON, Sylvanus M	27	NENE	1840-10-01		A1 C R935
933	" "	26	NWNW	1852-01-28		A1
935	" "	27	NENE	1852-01-28		A1 R934
881	AMELY, Manuel	18	NWNE	1856-11-01		A1
884	" "	7	SWSE	1856-11-01		A1
882	" "	7	NWSE	1857-06-10		A1
883	" "	7	SWNE	1857-06-10		A1
947	BAKER, William	22	SWNW	1860-03-01		A1
825	BENNETT, John	23	W½SW	1840-10-01		A1
824	" "	23	E½SW	1852-01-28		A1
826	" "	27	NWNE	1852-01-28		A1
745	BEQUETTE, Edward	29	SE	1848-07-01		A1 F
750	BEQUETTE, Eli	35	NE	1848-12-01		A1 F
922	BERRY, Richard	9	NWNW	1859-05-02		A1
914	BLOW, Peter E	1	3NW	1856-01-15		A1
915	" "	1	E½1NW	1856-01-15		A1
916	" "	1	E½2NW	1856-01-15		A1
917	" "	1	W½1NE	1856-01-15		A1
918	" "	2	4NE	1856-01-15		A1
718	BOYER, Antoine	21	SENW	1843-04-10		A1
780	BOYER, Godfrey	9	SESW	1859-11-01		A1
741	BROWN, Daniel E	4	SW	1859-11-01		A1 F
858	BROWN, Joseph A	7	N½SW	1857-06-10		A1 F
723	BUCHARD, Baptiste	12	NE	1857-06-10		A1 F
764	BURROSSA, Francis	3	SWSE	1851-11-01		A1 F
949	CASEY, William	17	SWSE	1860-03-01		A1
792	CATLIFF, James	17	SESW	1849-06-01		A1 G56
861	COATWAY, Joseph	5	SESE	1857-09-01		A1
912	COLEMAN, Paul	25	SW	1849-06-01		A1 F
746	CONNER, Edward R	34	NESW	1852-01-28		A1
831	CONNER, John H	34	SENW	1852-01-28		A1
789	CORDIES, Hypolite	6	NW	1854-11-15		A1
777	CRESSWELL, George	33	NENW	1849-06-01		A1
779	" "	34	SWSW	1853-05-10		A1
778	" "	33	SWSW	1857-10-30		A1
948	CRESSWELL, William C	19	SENE	1850-06-01		A1
740	DANKLIN, Daniel	26	W½NE	1848-07-01		A1
795	DEAN, James	9	NWSE	1859-11-01		A1
796	" "	9	S½SE	1859-11-01		A1
728	DELAURIERE, Charles F	1	SWSW	1856-06-03		A2
729	" "	11	NE	1856-06-03		A2 F
730	" "	20	SENW	1856-06-03		A2

ID	Individual in Patent	Sec.	Sec. Part	Date Issued	Other Counties	For More Info . . .
731	DELAURIERE, Charles F (Cont'd)	20	SWNE	1856-06-03		A2
732	" "	20	SWNW	1856-06-03		A2
733	" "	21	NENE	1856-06-03		A2
734	" "	22	NWNW	1856-06-03		A2
735	" "	8	E½NE	1856-06-03		A2
736	" "	9	NESW	1856-06-03		A2
737	" "	9	SWNW	1856-06-03		A2
738	" "	9	W½SW	1856-06-03		A2
950	DINNISTON, William	22	SE	1860-03-01		A1
782	DOUGHERTY, Henry	17	E½NE	1857-06-10		A1
783	" "	17	E½SE	1857-06-10		A1
902	DOUGHERTY, Owen	17	SENW	1840-10-01		A1
903	" "	17	SWNE	1840-10-01		A1
900	" "	17	NWSE	1848-02-01		A1
901	" "	17	NWSW	1849-06-01		A1
904	DOUGHERTY, Patrick	17	NESW	1840-10-01		A1
792	" "	17	SESW	1849-06-01		A1 G56
862	DUCLOS, Joseph	34	NWNW	1852-01-28		A1
887	DUCLOS, Michael	34	SWNE	1854-05-01		A1
781	DUCLOUS, Godfrey	34	SESW	1849-06-01		A1
923	ELLIOTT, Richard S	14	SWSE	1856-01-15		A1 G88
827	ESTABROOK, John D	33	NWSW	1860-03-01		A1
828	" "	33	SENW	1860-03-01		A1
829	" "	33	W½NW	1860-03-01		A1
724	FARRELL, Bernard O	29	E½SW	1857-09-01		A1
725	" "	29	W½SE	1857-09-01		A1
765	FARRELL, Francis O	21	NWSE	1856-11-01		A1
766	" "	32	NESW	1859-05-02		A1
767	" "	32	SENW	1859-05-02		A1
717	FARROW, Andrew D	36	SW	1849-06-01		A1
925	FERGUSON, Robert	26	E½NW	1835-09-02		A1 C R926
924	" "	23	SESE	1840-10-01		A1
926	" "	26	E½NW	1852-01-28		A1 R925
951	FERGUSON, William	14	NWSE	1840-10-01		A1
768	FEROLL, Francis O	32	SESW	1848-07-01		A1
888	FLINN, Michael	34	NWSW	1856-11-01		A1
889	FLYNN, Michael	33	E½SW	1856-01-15		A1
890	" "	33	N½SE	1856-01-15		A1
891	" "	33	NE	1856-01-15		A1
894	FLYNN, Michael M	4	4	1917-11-21		A1
942	FORD, Thomas	19	NENE	1860-03-01		A1
813	GAMACHE, Jean B	20	N½NE	1856-06-03		A2
802	GIRARDIER, James L	5	E½1NW	1860-03-01		A1
803	" "	5	W½1NE	1860-03-01		A1
804	" "	5	W½2NE	1860-03-01		A1
742	GOLDEN, Daniel M	32	SWSE	1848-07-01		A1
743	GRIFFIN, Dennis	20	SENE	1860-03-01		A1
744	HARRTY, Edmond	17	NWNE	1860-03-01		A1
832	HEARTY, John	22	E½SW	1825-07-15		A1
773	HESSE, Frederick	10	SENE	1857-06-10		A1
774	" "	11	SENW	1857-06-10		A1
775	" "	11	SW	1857-06-10		A1
776	" "	11	W½NW	1857-06-10		A1
833	HIGHT, John	22	SWSW	1843-04-10		A1
727	HILL, Britton	14	E½SE	1849-06-01		A1 G132 F
818	HIMMLEY, Johan C	31	SE	1859-11-01		A1
819	" "	31	SENE	1859-11-01		A1
820	" "	32	SWNW	1859-11-01		A1
821	" "	32	W½SW	1859-11-01		A1
835	HINCH, John	27	NENW	1849-06-01		A1
837	" "	27	SENW	1856-01-15		A1
838	" "	27	SWNE	1856-01-15		A1
839	" "	27	W½NW	1856-01-15		A1
834	" "	27	N½SW	1857-09-01		A1
836	" "	27	SENE	1859-05-02		A1
840	" "	28	SENE	1859-05-02		A1
841	HOBAN, John	1	NWSE	1860-03-01		A1
855	HOFF, Jonathan S	20	NENW	1849-06-01		A1
856	" "	8	NENW	1849-06-01		A1
857	" "	8	NWNE	1849-06-01		A1
859	HORROCKS, Joseph B	30	S½SW	1859-11-01		A1 F
860	" "	31	W½	1859-11-01		A1 F
727	HOUSEMAN, James	14	E½SE	1849-06-01		A1 G132 F

ID	Individual in Patent	Sec.	Sec. Part	Date Issued	Other Counties	For More Info . . .
797	HOUSEMAN, James (Cont'd)	26	SENE	1849-06-01		A1 G137 F
793	HOUSEMAN, James D	25	NWNW	1849-12-31		A1 G136 F
794	" "	26	NENE	1849-12-31		A1 G136
798	HUNT, James	25	S½NW	1849-06-01		A1 F
799	" "	26	SWNW	1850-06-01		A1
800	" "	25	NE	1854-05-01		A1 G147 F
923	" "	14	SWSE	1856-01-15		A1 G88
727	JACKSON, Smith	14	E½SE	1849-06-01		A1 G132 F
929	" "	34	NWNE	1850-01-01		A1 F
928	" "	33	SESE	1851-11-01		A1
930	JACKSON, Susan	27	SESW	1856-11-01		A1
931	" "	34	NENW	1856-11-01		A1
791	JACOBS, Jack B	8	SWNE	1848-02-01		A1
790	" "	8	SENW	1856-09-01		A1
885	JACOMELLA, Marco	7	E½NE	1857-06-10		A1
886	" "	8	W½NW	1857-06-10		A1
869	JARDIN, Junius	18	NW	1860-03-01		A1 F
870	" "	18	S½NE	1860-03-01		A1 F
871	" "	18	W½SE	1860-03-01		A1 F
872	" "	7	S½SW	1860-03-01		A1
921	JOHNSON, Pleasant S	14	N½NE	1869-09-01		A1 G156 V817
944	JONES, Thomas	10	SE	1857-06-10		A1
945	" "	15	NE	1857-06-10		A1
892	KANE, Michael	31	SWNE	1860-03-01		A1
784	KEAN, Henry	34	SWNW	1860-03-01		A1
830	KENNER, John G	33	SWSE	1841-12-10		A1
801	KILLPACK, James	5	3NW	1860-03-01		A1
785	KUMER, Henry	18	SW	1860-07-20		A1 F
786	" "	19	NW	1860-07-20		A1 F
787	" "	19	W½NE	1860-07-20		A1
753	LAMARQUE, Etiene	18	NESE	1850-06-01		A1
754	LAMARQUE, Etienne	23	NE	1831-10-01		A1 F
755	" "	24	SWNW	1835-10-01		A1 F
876	LE BOURGEOIS, LOUIS S	1	2NE	1856-01-15		A1
877	" "	1	3NE	1856-01-15		A1
893	LEAKY, Michael	32	NWNE	1860-03-01		A1
923	LEFFINGWELL, Hiram W	14	SWSE	1856-01-15		A1 G88
842	LEWIS, John	15	W½SE	1860-03-01		A1
946	LIVINGSTON, Thomas R	19	SW	1859-05-02		A1
751	MANES, Ephraim	2	W½NW	1848-05-04		A1 F
763	MARA, Eugene O	23	NESE	1835-10-08		A1
899	MARCILLE, Moyes	1	W½1NW	1857-06-10		A1
788	MARTIN, Henry S	11	NENW	1848-02-01		A1
843	MCGAHAN, John	28	W½NW	1857-06-10		A1
844	" "	28	W½SW	1857-06-10		A1
845	" "	29	E½NE	1857-06-10		A1
846	" "	29	E½SE	1857-06-10		A1
747	MERCEILLE, Edward V	10	N½NE	1857-06-10		A1
748	" "	10	SENW	1859-05-02		A1
749	" "	10	SWNE	1859-05-02		A1
752	MERCEILLE, Ertenne	9	E½NE	1857-06-10		A1 F
874	MERCEILLE, Louis	10	NWSW	1857-06-10		A1
875	" "	9	NESE	1857-06-10		A1
873	" "	10	NESW	1858-05-03		A1
863	MERCILE, Joseph	1	W½2NW	1850-06-01		A1
864	" "	2	3NE	1850-06-01		A1
940	MURPHY, Thomas C	34	NENE	1851-11-01		A1 F
941	" "	35	NW	1854-10-02		A1 G187 F
941	MURPHY, William	35	NW	1854-10-02		A1 G187 F
792	OBUCHAN, John M	17	SESW	1849-06-01		A1 G56
726	OFARRELL, Bernard	32	NENE	1859-11-01		A1
771	OFARROLL, Francis	32	SESE	1837-11-07		A1
769	" "	32	NESE	1856-01-15		A1
770	" "	32	S½NE	1856-01-15		A1
936	OWENS, Terence	10	NENW	1848-02-01		A1
937	" "	3	SW	1848-07-01		A1 F
938	" "	4	SE	1855-06-15		A1 F
939	OWENS, Terrence	10	NWNW	1843-04-10		A1
805	PAGE, James M	2	2NE	1850-06-01		A1
806	" "	2	E½NW	1850-06-01		A1
868	PALMER, Joseph W	1	NWSW	1882-11-20		A3
847	PARTENAY, John	5	NESE	1856-11-01		A1
848	" "	5	NWSE	1857-06-10		A1

ID	Individual in Patent	Sec.	Sec. Part	Date Issued	Other Counties	For More Info . . .
739	PEIRCE, Charles	14	S½NE	1849-06-01		A1 G194 F
849	PELICAN, John	32	NWSE	1859-05-02		A1
865	PERKINS, Joseph	27	SE	1849-06-01		A1
727	PIERCE, Charles	14	E½SE	1849-06-01		A1 G132 F
797	" "	26	SENE	1849-06-01		A1 G137 F
793	" "	25	NWNW	1849-12-31		A1 G136 F
794	" "	26	NENE	1849-12-31		A1 G136
772	POLITTE, Francis	3	NWSE	1851-11-01		A1 F
800	READING, James N	25	NE	1854-05-01		A1 G147 F
905	ROONEY, Patrick	21	SESE	1858-05-03		A1
906	" "	28	NENE	1858-05-03		A1
907	" "	28	NENW	1858-05-03		A1
908	" "	28	NESW	1858-05-03		A1
909	" "	28	SENW	1858-05-03		A1
910	" "	28	SESW	1858-05-03		A1
911	" "	28	W½NE	1858-05-03		A1
756	ROUSIN, Etienne	12	NW	1825-07-15		A1 F
757	" "	2	1NE	1825-07-15		A1
758	" "	2	E½SW	1825-07-15		A1
759	" "	2	W½SW	1831-03-01		A1
721	ROUSSIN, Augustus	1	E½1NE	1857-06-10		A1
722	" "	1	NESE	1858-01-13		A1
760	ROUSSIN, Etienne	2	SE	1825-07-15		A1
814	RULO, Jefferson	18	NENE	1857-06-10		A1
815	" "	7	SESE	1857-06-10		A1
919	RULO, Peter	8	SESE	1859-11-01		A1
822	SANSOCIE, John B	7	N½NW	1856-09-01		A1
823	" "	7	NWNE	1857-06-10		A1
812	SCOTT, Jane	5	SWSE	1860-03-01		A1
850	SENSENDERFER, John	22	NE	1857-06-10		A1
851	" "	23	NW	1857-06-10		A1
921	SHIELDS, James W	14	N½NE	1869-09-01		A1 G156 V817
807	SIGNAIGO, James	5	N½SW	1856-10-01		A1
808	" "	5	S½SW	1857-06-10		A1
809	" "	5	W½1NW	1857-06-10		A1
810	" "	6	E½1NE	1857-06-10		A1
811	" "	6	SE	1857-06-10		A1
866	SOUCI, Joseph San	5	E½1NE	1872-03-04		A1 F
719	TAYLOR, Archibald R	5	3NE	1848-12-01		A1 F
720	" "	5	E½2NE	1853-05-10		A1
953	TEMBY, William	8	NWSE	1856-11-01		A1
952	" "	8	NESE	1859-05-02		A1
878	THIBEAU, Louis	3	E½SE	1848-12-01		A1 F
879	" "	3	NE	1848-12-01		A1 F
727	THOMAS, Elihu	14	E½SE	1849-06-01		A1 G132 F
739	THOMAS, Elihu B	14	S½NE	1849-06-01		A1 G194 F
797	" "	26	SENE	1849-06-01		A1 G137 F
793	" "	25	NWNW	1849-12-31		A1 G136 F
794	" "	26	NENE	1849-12-31		A1 G136
761	TIBEAN, Ettienne	1	NESW	1856-09-01		A1
762	" "	1	SESW	1857-06-10		A1
852	TIBEAU, John	11	SE	1857-06-10		A1 F
867	TORINI, Joseph	5	2NW	1859-05-02		A1
853	TWITTY, John	9	E½NW	1848-12-01		A1 F
854	" "	9	W½NE	1848-12-01		A1 F
920	VALLEY, Peter	7	S½NW	1857-06-10		A1
880	VILMAR, Louis	34	W½SE	1860-03-01		A1 F
895	WARD, Michael	29	W½SW	1858-05-03		A1
896	" "	30	S½SE	1858-05-03		A1
897	" "	31	N½NE	1858-05-03		A1
898	" "	32	N½NW	1858-05-03		A1
816	WESTOVER, Job	14	E½SW	1824-05-20		A1
817	" "	14	W½NE	1824-05-20		A1 V921
943	YEAUGHBERRY, Thomas G	25	SE	1848-05-04		A1 F

Patent Map

T39-N R2-E
5th PM Meridian

Map Group 9

Township Statistics

Parcels Mapped	:	238
Number of Patents	:	168
Number of Individuals	:	136
Patentees Identified	:	130
Number of Surnames	:	112
Multi-Patentee Parcels	:	10
Oldest Patent Date	:	5/20/1824
Most Recent Patent	:	11/21/1917
Block/Lot Parcels	:	24
Parcels Re - Issued	:	2
Parcels that Overlap	:	2
Cities and Towns	:	0
Cemeteries	:	0

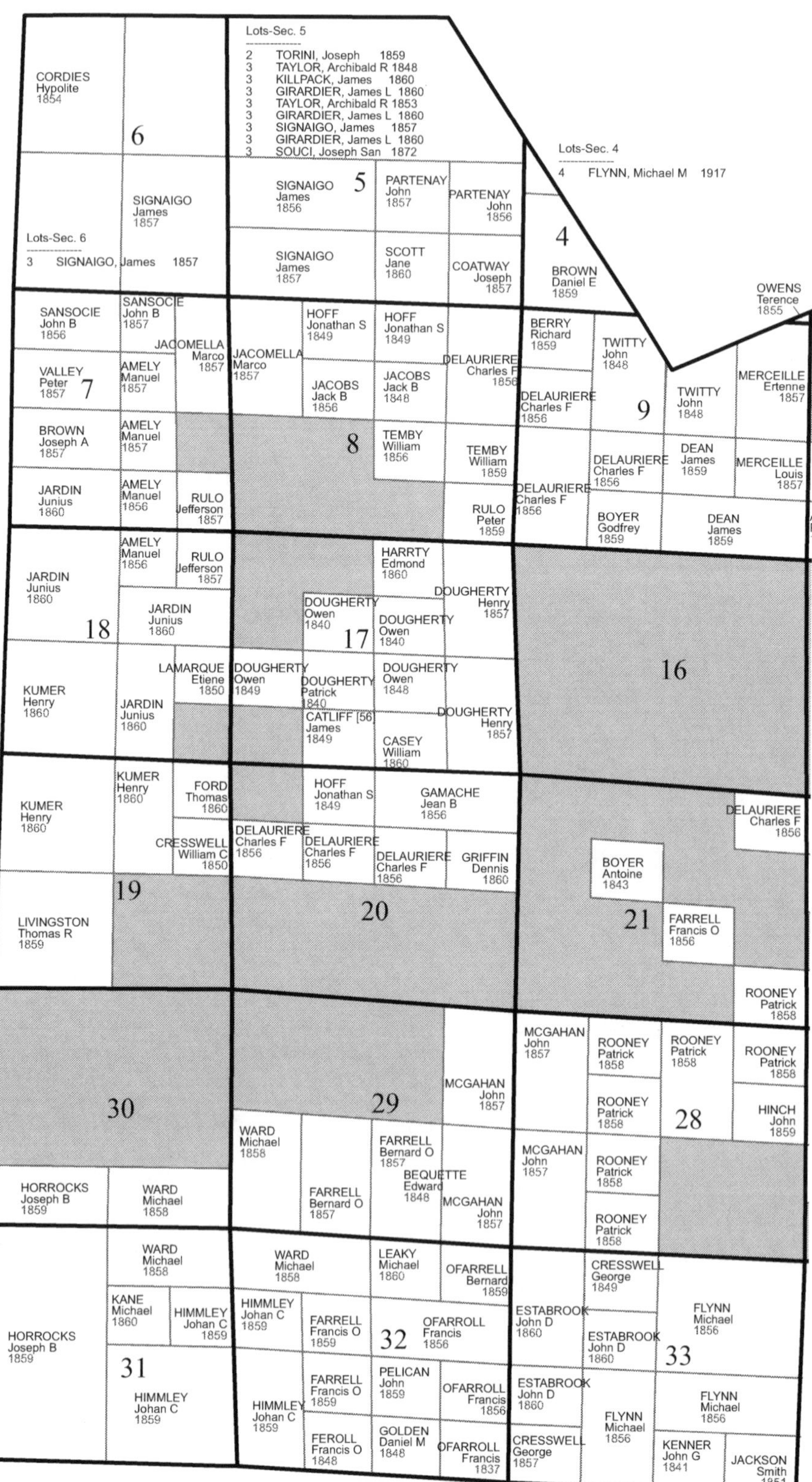

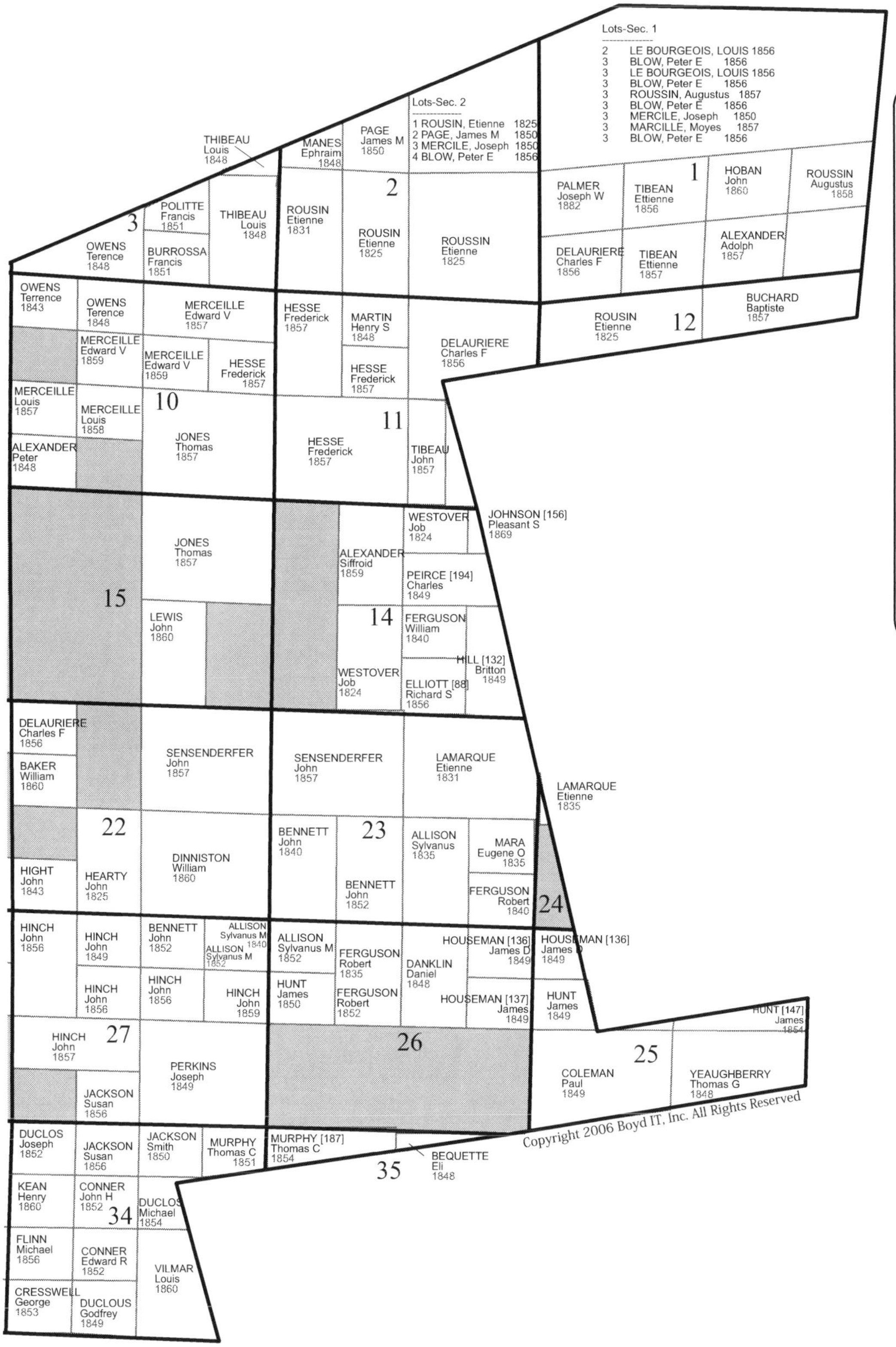

Lots-Sec. 1

2 LE BOURGEOIS, LOUIS 1856
3 BLOW, Peter E 1856
3 LE BOURGEOIS, LOUIS 1856
3 BLOW, Peter E 1856
3 ROUSSIN, Augustus 1857
3 BLOW, Peter E 1856
3 MERCILE, Joseph 1850
3 MARCILLE, Moyes 1857
3 BLOW, Peter E 1856

Lots-Sec. 2

1 ROUSIN, Etienne 1825
2 PAGE, James M 1850
3 MERCILE, Joseph 1850
4 BLOW, Peter E 1856

1
PALMER Joseph W 1882
TIBEAN Ettienne 1856
HOBAN John 1860
ROUSSIN Augustus 1858
DELAURIERE Charles F 1856
TIBEAN Ettienne 1857
ALEXANDER Adolph 1857

2
MANES Ephraim 1848
PAGE James M 1850
ROUSIN Etienne 1831
ROUSIN Etienne 1825
ROUSSIN Etienne 1825

3
THIBEAU Louis 1848
POLITTE Francis 1851
THIBEAU Louis 1848
OWENS Terence 1848
BURROSSA Francis 1851

10
OWENS Terrence 1843
OWENS Terence 1848
MERCEILLE Edward V 1857
MERCEILLE Edward V 1859
MERCEILLE Edward V 1859
HESSE Frederick 1857
MERCEILLE Louis 1857
MERCEILLE Louis 1858
ALEXANDER Peter 1848
JONES Thomas 1857

11
HESSE Frederick 1857
MARTIN Henry S 1848
DELAURIERE Charles F 1856
HESSE Frederick 1857
HESSE Frederick 1857
TIBEAU John 1857

12
ROUSIN Etienne 1825
BUCHARD Baptiste 1857

14
WESTOVER Job 1824
JOHNSON [156] Pleasant S 1869
ALEXANDER Siffroid 1859
PEIRCE [194] Charles 1849
FERGUSON William 1840
HILL [132] Britton 1849
WESTOVER Job 1824
ELLIOTT [88] Richard S 1856

15
JONES Thomas 1857
LEWIS John 1860

22
DELAURIERE Charles F 1856
BAKER William 1860
SENSENDERFER John 1857
HIGHT John 1843
HEARTY John 1825
DINNISTON William 1860

23
SENSENDERFER John 1857
LAMARQUE Etienne 1831
BENNETT John 1840
ALLISON Sylvanus 1835
MARA Eugene O 1835
BENNETT John 1852
FERGUSON Robert 1840

24
LAMARQUE Etienne 1835

25
HOUSEMAN [136] James D 1849
HUNT James 1849
HUNT [147] James 1854
COLEMAN Paul 1849
YEAUGHBERRY Thomas G 1848

26
ALLISON Sylvanus M 1852
FERGUSON Robert 1835
DANKLIN Daniel 1848
HOUSEMAN [136] James D 1849
HUNT James 1850
FERGUSON Robert 1852
HOUSEMAN [137] James 1849

27
HINCH John 1856
HINCH John 1849
BENNETT John 1852
ALLISON Sylvanus M 1840
ALLISON Sylvanus M 1852
HINCH John 1856
HINCH John 1856
HINCH John 1859
HINCH John 1857
PERKINS Joseph 1849
JACKSON Susan 1856

34
DUCLOS Joseph 1852
JACKSON Susan 1856
JACKSON Smith 1850
MURPHY Thomas C 1851
KEAN Henry 1860
CONNER John H 1852
DUCLOS Michael 1854
FLINN Michael 1856
CONNER Edward R 1852
VILMAR Louis 1860
CRESSWELL George 1853
DUCLOUS Godfrey 1849

35
MURPHY [187] Thomas C 1854
BEQUETTE Eli 1848

Helpful Hints

1. This Map's INDEX can be found on the preceding pages.
2. Refer to Map "C" to see where this Township lies within Washington County, Missouri.
3. Numbers within square brackets [ ] denote a multi-patentee land parcel (multi-owner). Refer to Appendix "C" for a full list of members in this group.
4. Areas that look to be crowded with Patentees usually indicate multiple sales of the same parcel (Re-issues) or Overlapping parcels. See this Township's Index for an explanation of these and other circumstances that might explain "odd" groupings of Patentees on this map.

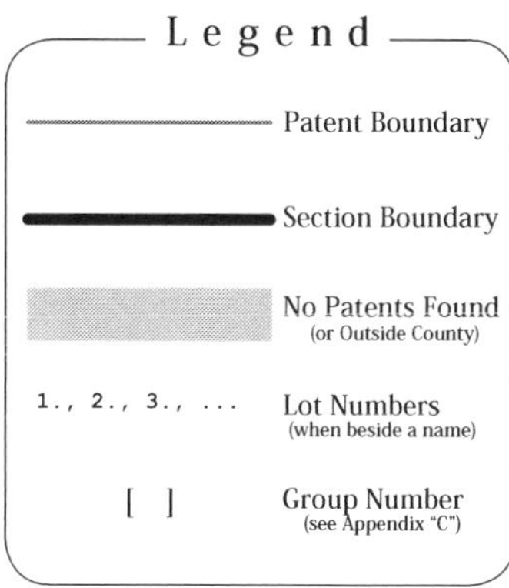

Scale: Section = 1 mile X 1 mile
(generally, with some exceptions)

Road Map

T39-N R2-E
5th PM Meridian

Map Group 9

Cities & Towns

None

Cemeteries

None

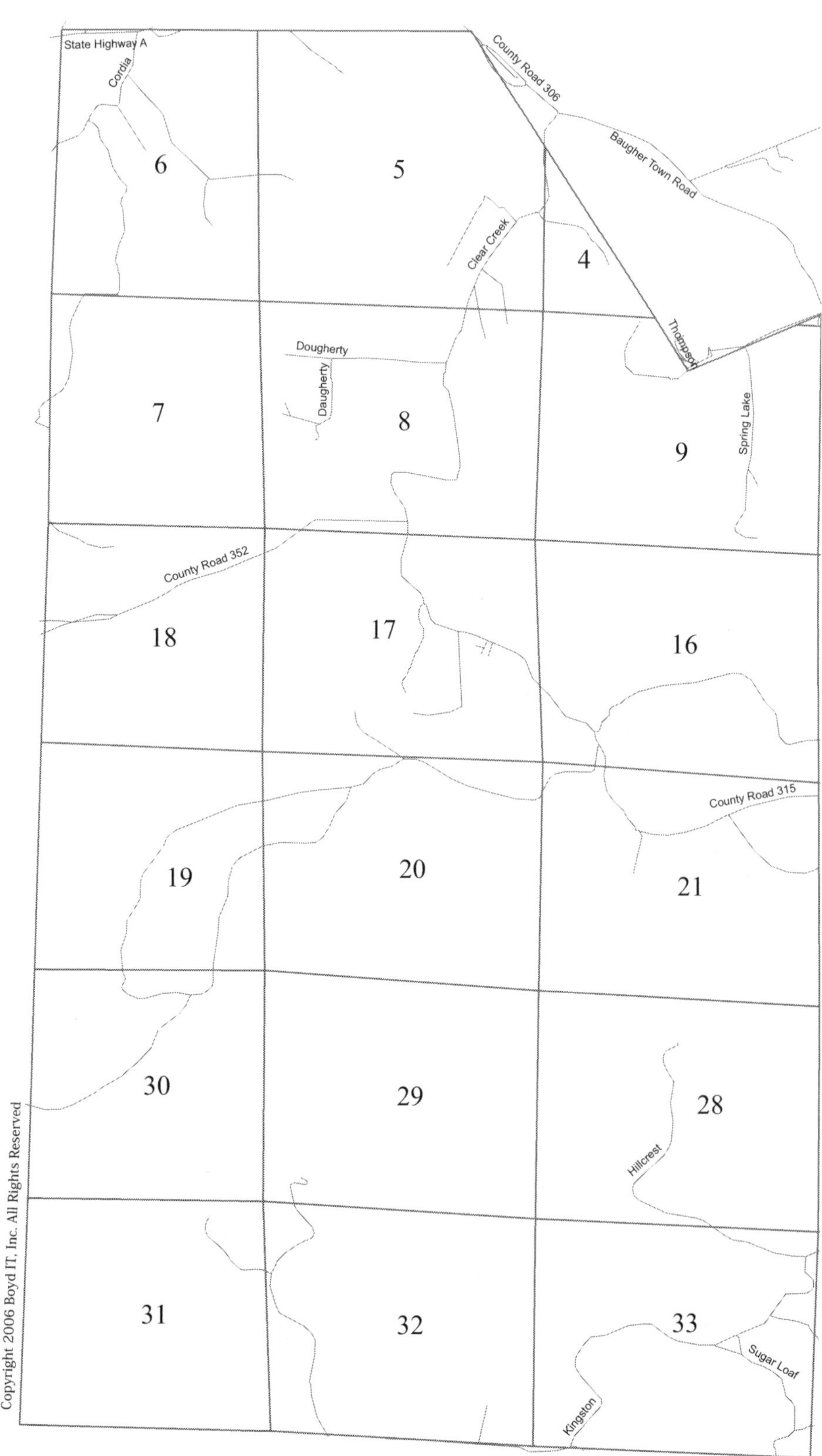

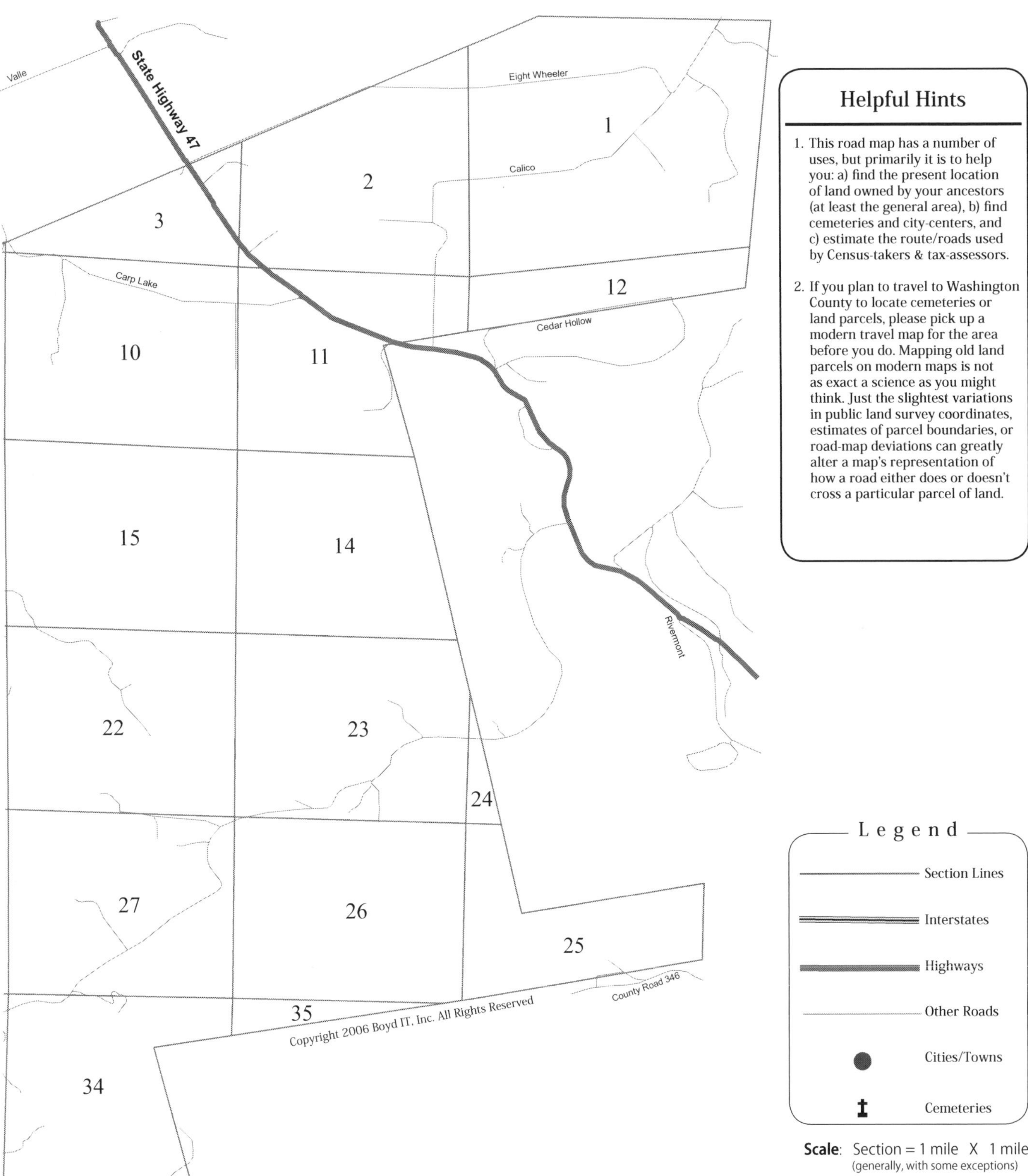

Helpful Hints

1. This road map has a number of uses, but primarily it is to help you: a) find the present location of land owned by your ancestors (at least the general area), b) find cemeteries and city-centers, and c) estimate the route/roads used by Census-takers & tax-assessors.

2. If you plan to travel to Washington County to locate cemeteries or land parcels, please pick up a modern travel map for the area before you do. Mapping old land parcels on modern maps is not as exact a science as you might think. Just the slightest variations in public land survey coordinates, estimates of parcel boundaries, or road-map deviations can greatly alter a map's representation of how a road either does or doesn't cross a particular parcel of land.

Historical Map

T39-N R2-E
5th PM Meridian

Map Group 9

Cities & Towns

None

Cemeteries

None

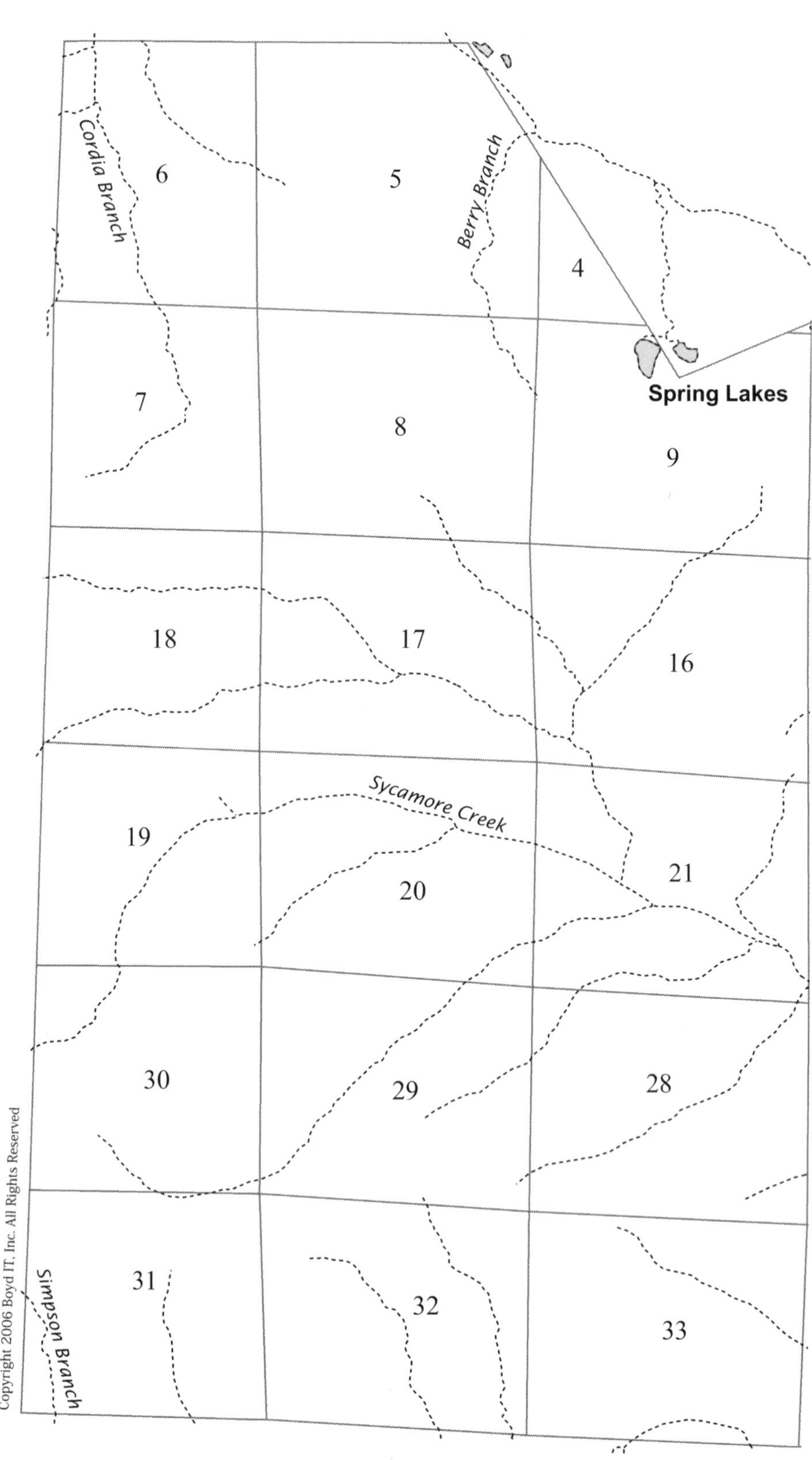

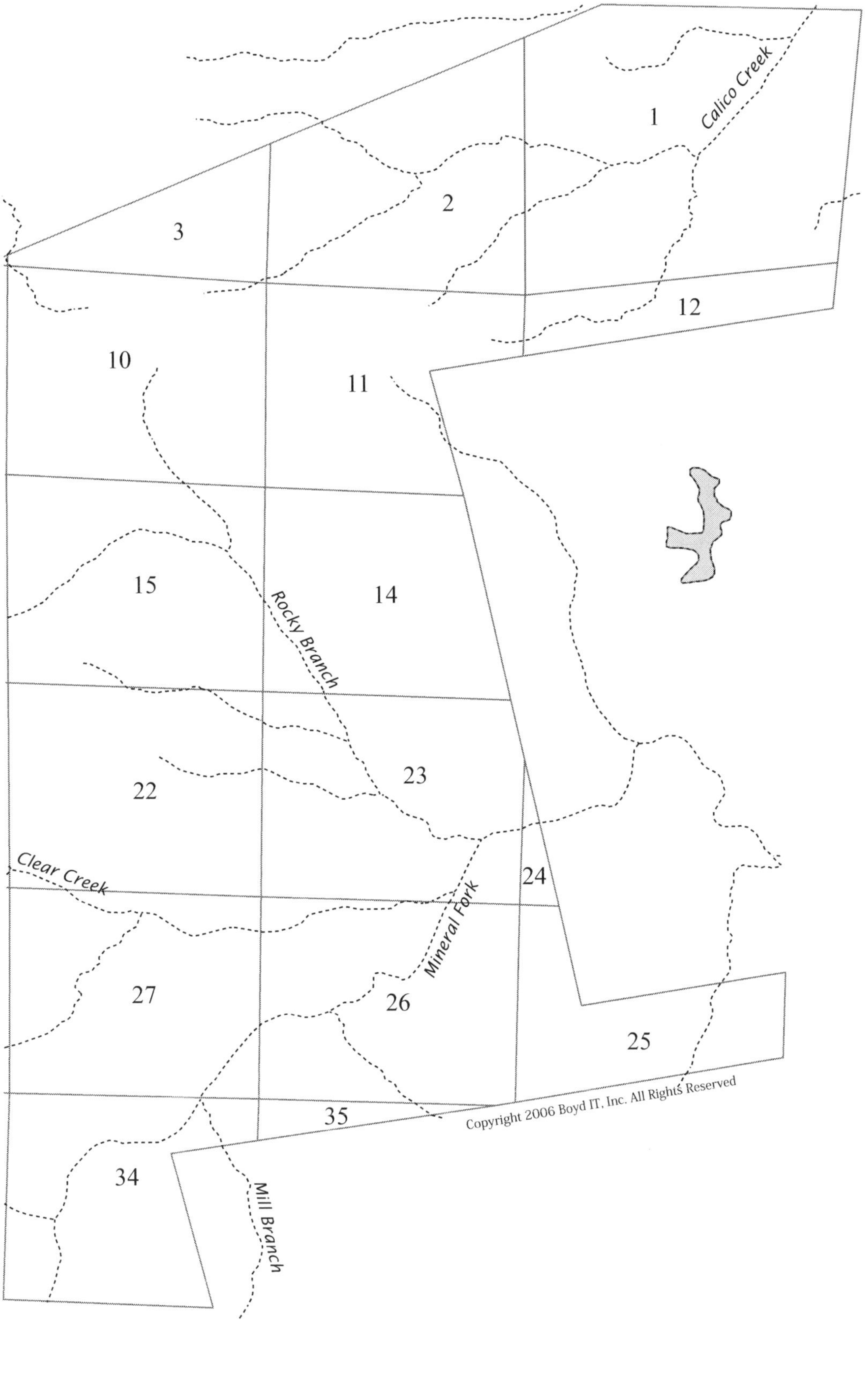

1
Calico Creek
2
3
12
10
11
15
14
Rocky Branch
22
23
Clear Creek
24
Mineral Fork
27
26
25
35
34
Mill Branch

Helpful Hints

1. This Map takes a different look at the same Congressional Township displayed in the preceding two maps. It presents features that can help you better envision the historical development of the area: a) Water-bodies (lakes & ponds), b) Water-courses (rivers, streams, etc.), c) Railroads, d) City/town center-points (where they were oftentimes located when first settled), and e) Cemeteries.
2. Using this "Historical" map in tandem with this Township's Patent Map and Road Map, may lead you to some interesting discoveries. You will often find roads, towns, cemeteries, and waterways are named after nearby landowners: sometimes those names will be the ones you are researching. See how many of these research gems you can find here in Washington County.

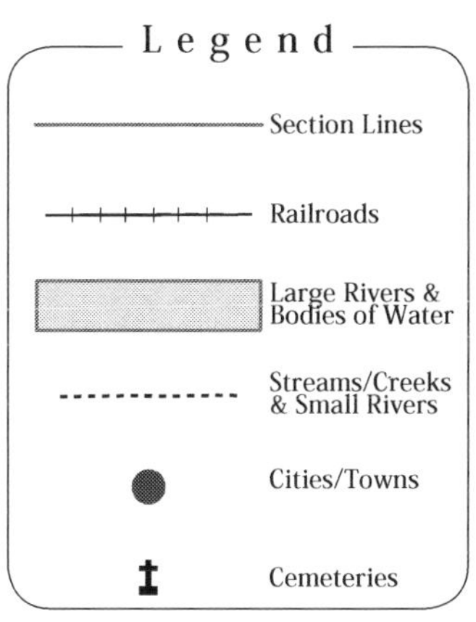

Scale: Section = 1 mile X 1 mile
(there are some exceptions)

Map Group 10: Index to Land Patents

Township 39-North Range 3-East (5th PM)

After you locate an individual in this Index, take note of the Section and Section Part then proceed to the Land Patent map on the pages immediately following. You should have no difficulty locating the corresponding parcel of land.

The "For More Info" Column will lead you to more information about the underlying Patents. See the *Legend* at right, and the "How to Use this Book" chapter, for more information.

LEGEND

"For More Info . . . " column

A = Authority (Legislative Act, See Appendix "A")
B = Block or Lot (location in Section unknown)
C = Cancelled Patent
F = Fractional Section
G = Group (Multi-Patentee Patent, see Appendix "C")
V = Overlaps another Parcel
R = Re-Issued (Parcel patented more than once)

(A & G items require you to look in the Appendixes referred to above. All other Letter-designations followed by a number require you to locate line-items in this index that possess the ID number found after the letter).

ID	Individual in Patent	Sec.	Sec. Part	Date Issued	Other Counties	For More Info . . .
1037	ALDERSON, John A	23	NESW	1853-10-10	Jefferson	A1
970	ANTON, Arnold C	4	4NE	1860-03-01	Jefferson	A1 F
1080	ARCHAMBO, Louis	6	W½1NE	1856-09-01		A1
1081	" "	6	W½2NE	1856-09-01		A1
1082	" "	6	W½3NE	1856-09-01		A1
983	ARNDT, Charles	14	E½NW	1857-06-10	Jefferson	A1
984	" "	14	NENE	1857-06-10	Jefferson	A1
985	" "	14	W½NE	1857-06-10	Jefferson	A1
976	BAKER, Austin	23	W½NW	1831-10-01	Jefferson	A1
975	" "	22	E½SE	1834-11-04	Jefferson	A1
974	BAKER, Austin A	22	W½SE	1840-10-01	Jefferson	A1
1003	BAKER, Elijah	10	NESE	1840-10-01	Jefferson	A1
1139	BATTREAL, William	6	3NW	1911-08-17		A1
1030	BELL, Henry	32	W½NE	1833-09-17		A1
999	BEQUETTE, Derville	32	NENW	1835-10-08		A1
1000	" "	32	NESE	1843-04-10		A1
997	" "	30	E½NE	1848-07-01		A1 F
998	" "	30	SE	1848-07-01		A1 F
1001	BEQUETTE, Edmund	29	SESW	1835-10-08		A1
1009	BEQUETTE, Felix	30	W½NE	1848-07-01		A1 F
1069	BEQUETTE, Joseph	29	NW	1824-05-01		A1
1070	" "	29	NWSW	1835-09-09		A1
1071	" "	29	SWSW	1836-01-14		A1
1140	BLAIR, William	22	NWNW	1840-10-01	Jefferson	A1
1083	BOLDUC, Louis	10	NWNE	1836-01-14	Jefferson	A1
1141	BORGE, William	4	E½1NE	1860-03-01	Jefferson	A1
1076	BOYD, Leard B	10	E½NE	1824-05-01	Jefferson	A1
1084	BOYER, Louis	29	NESW	1836-01-14		A1
1092	BOYER, Napolean	34	SWSW	1884-06-30		A3
1099	BOYER, Peter	4	SWSE	1856-01-15	Jefferson	A1
1100	" "	9	NWNE	1856-01-15	Jefferson	A1
977	BUCHARD, Baptiste	7	NW	1856-09-01		A1 F
1097	BUREN, Pascal H	25	NENE	1854-03-01	Jefferson	A1
1045	CALLAWAY, John	24	E½NE	1857-09-01	Jefferson	A1
1046	" "	24	E½SE	1857-09-01	Jefferson	A1
1047	" "	24	NWNE	1857-09-01	Jefferson	A1
1098	CARTER, Peggy	20	SE	1856-06-03		A2 G53 F
1107	CATEN, Samuel	26	NWNW	1862-06-18	Jefferson	A1
1108	" "	27	NE	1862-06-18		A1
968	CHEATHAM, Archer	34	NWNW	1897-08-16		A1
969	CHEATHAM, Archibald	14	W½NW	1833-05-01	Jefferson	A1 G57
971	CHOUTEAU, Auguste P	4	E½3NE	1856-06-03	Jefferson	A2
1013	COALMAN, Francois E	6	N½SW	1857-09-01		A1
1014	" "	6	NWSE	1857-09-01		A1
1038	COLEMAN, John B	6	E½SE	1856-09-01		A1
1039	COLMAN, John B	6	S½SW	1858-01-13		A1 F

ID	Individual in Patent	Sec.	Sec. Part	Date Issued	Other Counties	For More Info . . .
1040	COLMAN, John B (Cont'd)	6	SWSE	1858-01-13		A1 F
1041	" "	7	NE	1858-01-13		A1 F
956	CRAIG, Alexander	21	N½SW	1844-08-01		A1 F
957	" "	21	SWSE	1844-08-01		A1 F
1125	CRAIG, Samy B	21	SENE	1837-04-01		A1
1126	CRAIG, Sancy B	21	NENE	1840-10-01		A1
1033	CUNDIFF, James	36	SENE	1835-10-01		A1
1077	CUNDIFF, Lewis	34	SESE	1838-09-07		A1
1089	CUNIFF, Martin	21	S½SW	1861-02-01		A1 F
1127	DETCHMENDY, Sawveur	28	W½SW	1831-10-01		A1
1096	DOUGHERTY, Owen	32	W½SE	1835-09-02		A1
1090	FRISSELL, Mason	4	W½2NW	1846-01-01	Jefferson	A1
1036	GIBSON, James R	8	N½NE	1854-11-15		A1 G109 F
1036	GIBSON, Samuel D	8	N½NE	1854-11-15		A1 G109 F
1109	" "	8	S½NE	1896-07-27		A1 F
1110	" "	9	SWNW	1896-07-27	Jefferson	A1 F
1133	GROOMS, Timothy	5	E½1NW	1860-03-01	Jefferson	A1
1134	" "	5	N½SW	1860-03-01	Jefferson	A1
1135	" "	5	NWSE	1860-03-01	Jefferson	A1
1011	HARVER, Francis O	4	NWSW	1840-10-01	Jefferson	A1
1103	HARVER, Philip O	4	E½SW	1824-05-01	Jefferson	A1 V1105
1106	HAVEN, Rosanna O	4	NWSE	1854-11-15	Jefferson	A1
973	HAWKINS, Augustus	36	SWNE	1840-10-01		A1
1032	HEARST, Isabella	21	NW	1831-03-01		A1 F
1129	HEARST, Thomas	16	E½SE	1824-05-01		A1
1130	" "	21	W½NE	1824-05-01		A1
1142	HEARST, William	15	SWSW	1840-10-01	Jefferson	A1
1004	HERELSON, Elijah	36	S½NW	1844-08-01		A1 F
1019	HIGGENBOTHAM, George W	26	SWNW	1840-10-01	Jefferson	A1
1017	" "	26	NENW	1850-06-01	Jefferson	A1
1018	" "	26	NWNE	1850-06-01	Jefferson	A1
1024	HIGGINBOTHAM, George W	34	E½NW	1840-10-01		A1
1025	" "	34	NESE	1840-10-01		A1
1026	" "	34	W½SE	1840-10-01		A1
1020	" "	25	E½SW	1841-12-10	Jefferson	A1
1021	" "	25	W½SW	1849-06-01	Jefferson	A1
1023	" "	28	NESE	1849-06-01		A1
1027	" "	35	NESW	1849-06-01		A1
1028	" "	35	SESW	1849-06-01		A1 F
1029	" "	35	W½SW	1849-06-01		A1 F
1022	" "	26	SENW	1854-11-15	Jefferson	A1
1073	HIGGINBOTHAM, Joseph	9	SE	1912-02-05	Jefferson	A1 F
1104	HIGGINBOTHAM, Press G	28	SENW	1911-06-26		A1
1078	HIGGINBOTHOM, Lewis	9	SENW	1874-05-01	Jefferson	A3 F
1079	" "	9	SW	1874-05-01	Jefferson	A3 F
1075	HIGGINS, Julius	24	W½NW	1831-03-01	Jefferson	A1
1074	" "	23	SENE	1837-11-07	Jefferson	A1
1034	HUNT, James	30	W½NW	1849-06-01		A1 F
1035	" "	32	SW	1854-03-01		A1 F
1087	JENNINGS, Mark C	4	E½2NW	1856-06-10	Jefferson	A1
1088	" "	5	NESE	1856-06-10	Jefferson	A1
969	JOHNSON, Calvin	14	W½NW	1833-05-01	Jefferson	A1 G57
980	" "	4	NESE	1854-03-01	Jefferson	A1
981	" "	4	SESE	1859-05-02	Jefferson	A1
982	" "	9	NENE	1859-05-02	Jefferson	A1
979	" "	10	NENW	1860-03-01	Jefferson	A1
1085	JOHNSON, Luther	24	NENW	1840-10-01	Jefferson	A1
1086	" "	4	W½1NE	1840-10-01	Jefferson	A1
1098	JONES, Peggy	20	SE	1856-06-03		A2 G53 F
1072	LOCKE, Joseph H	14	SE	1857-06-10	Jefferson	A1
1143	LONG, William	31		1853-10-10		A1 F
1131	MADDEN, Thomas	23	NENE	1840-10-01	Jefferson	A1
1132	MADDIN, Thomas	23	E½SE	1831-10-01	Jefferson	A1
1010	MALLE, Francis	29	NWSE	1838-09-07		A1
963	MANES, Amos	4	W½3NW	1857-06-10	Jefferson	A1
964	" "	5	3NE	1857-06-10	Jefferson	A1
965	" "	5	4NE	1857-06-10	Jefferson	A1
1005	MANES, Elijah	5	E½3NW	1860-03-01	Jefferson	A1
1006	MANESS, Elijah	4	2NE	1848-07-01	Jefferson	A1
1007	" "	4	E½3NW	1860-03-01	Jefferson	A1
972	MARAS, Augustus A	30	SW	1848-12-01		A1 F
1138	MASSIE, Upshaw R	36	SE	1831-10-01		A1 F
1048	MAYGER, John	14	SW	1857-06-10	Jefferson	A1

ID	Individual in Patent	Sec.	Sec. Part	Date Issued	Other Counties	For More Info . . .
1049	MAYGER, John (Cont'd)	23	E½NW	1857-06-10	Jefferson	A1
1050	" "	23	W½NE	1857-06-10	Jefferson	A1
1091	MCPEAKE, Mathew	25	SENE	1840-10-01	Jefferson	A1
1101	MESEY, Peter	30	E½NW	1848-07-01		A1 F
967	MISEY, Aquilla	32	SENW	1854-03-01		A1
961	MITCHELL, Alfred	25	NENW	1854-03-01	Jefferson	A1
962	" "	25	NWNE	1854-03-01	Jefferson	A1
958	" "	24	SENW	1857-09-01	Jefferson	A1
959	" "	24	SWNE	1857-09-01	Jefferson	A1
960	" "	24	W½SE	1857-09-01	Jefferson	A1
991	MORRISON, Clarendon	24	NESW	1840-10-01	Jefferson	A1
992	MORRISSON, Clarendon	24	SESW	1843-04-10	Jefferson	A1
993	MOTHERSHEAD, Clifton	22	NWNE	1835-09-09	Jefferson	A1
1128	MOTHERSHEAD, Thomas E	14	SENE	1853-10-10	Jefferson	A1
1144	MOTHERSHEAD, William	15	E½NE	1824-05-01	Jefferson	A1
1146	" "	22	E½NE	1824-05-01	Jefferson	A1
1147	" "	22	E½NW	1824-05-01	Jefferson	A1
1145	" "	15	SE	1831-03-01	Jefferson	A1
1148	MURPHEY, William S	28	SWNW	1849-06-01		A1
978	MURRILL, Briggs	26	SWNE	1841-12-10	Jefferson	A1
1002	MURRILL, Elias	36	NWNW	1840-10-01		A1
1012	OHARVER, Francis	5	1NE	1840-10-01	Jefferson	A1
1095	PARKER, Nathaniel	23	W½SE	1824-05-01	Jefferson	A1
1105	PARKER, Robert	4	NESW	1860-03-01	Jefferson	A1 V1103
1136	PARMER, Upheme	6	1NW	1857-06-10		A1
1137	" "	6	2NW	1857-06-10		A1
954	PINSON, Aaron	25	E½SE	1856-01-15	Jefferson	A1
955	" "	36	NENE	1856-01-15		A1
1008	PINSON, Elizabeth J	25	NWSE	1841-12-10	Jefferson	A1
1093	PINSON, Nathan	25	SENW	1835-09-09	Jefferson	A1
1094	" "	25	SWNE	1840-10-01	Jefferson	A1
1112	REED, Samuel V	27	N½SW	1841-12-10		A1
1113	" "	28	E½NE	1851-11-01		A1
1114	" "	28	NWNE	1851-11-01		A1
1111	" "	22	NESW	1859-05-02	Jefferson	A1 F
1102	ROMAINE, Peter	23	W½SW	1835-09-02	Jefferson	A1
1051	ROUSIN, John R	6	E½2NE	1856-01-15		A1
1052	" "	6	W½1NW	1856-01-15		A1
1043	ROUSSIN, John B	5	W½2NW	1854-11-15	Jefferson	A1
1044	" "	6	E½1NE	1856-09-01		A1
1042	" "	5	E½2NW	1860-03-01	Jefferson	A1
1053	SMITH, John	26	SE	1856-11-01	Jefferson	A1 F
1054	" "	33	NESW	1856-11-01		A1
1057	" "	35	NE	1856-11-01		A1 F
1055	" "	34	NWSW	1858-03-02		A1
1056	" "	34	SWNW	1858-03-02		A1
1058	SMITH, John T	26	SW	1858-03-02	Jefferson	A1
1059	" "	27	SE	1858-03-02		A1
1060	" "	28	SWSE	1858-03-02		A1
1061	" "	33	E½	1858-03-02		A1
1062	" "	33	E½NW	1858-03-02		A1
1063	" "	34	NE	1858-03-02		A1
1064	" "	35	NW	1858-03-02		A1
1153	SMITH, William W	17		1835-09-02		A1 F
1154	" "	8	SE	1835-09-02		A1 F
1149	STAFFORD, William	4	SWSW	1857-06-10	Jefferson	A1
1151	" "	5	SESE	1857-06-10	Jefferson	A1
1152	" "	9	N½NW	1857-06-10	Jefferson	A1
1150	" "	5	2NE	1860-03-01	Jefferson	A1
994	STONG, David	26	E½NE	1833-05-01	Jefferson	A1
995	STRONG, David	24	W½SW	1824-05-01	Jefferson	A1
996	" "	25	W½NW	1824-05-20	Jefferson	A1
1015	STUART, George B	32	E½NE	1850-06-01		A1
1016	" "	33	W½NW	1850-06-01		A1
1065	THURMOND, John	4	1NW	1824-05-01	Jefferson	A1
966	TROKY, Anthony	32	W½NW	1848-12-01		A1 F
1119	VAN REED, SAMUEL	27	S½SW	1840-10-01		A1
1115	" "	21	E½SE	1849-06-01		A1 F
1116	" "	22	SESW	1849-06-01	Jefferson	A1
1117	" "	22	W½SW	1849-06-01	Jefferson	A1 F
1120	" "	27	SENW	1849-06-01		A1
1124	" "	29	SWSE	1849-06-01		A1
1118	" "	27	N½NW	1850-11-05		A1

ID	Individual in Patent	Sec.	Sec. Part	Date Issued	Other Counties	For More Info . . .
1121	VAN REED, SAMUEL (Cont'd)	27	SWNW	1850-11-05		A1
1122	" "	28	NWSE	1897-08-16		A1
1123	" "	28	SWNE	1897-08-16		A1
1031	VIVRETT, Henry	10	SWNE	1879-07-21	Jefferson	A1 F
1066	WICKS, Johnson H	25	SWSE	1857-09-01	Jefferson	A1
1067	" "	36	NENW	1857-09-01		A1
1068	" "	36	NWNE	1857-09-01		A1
1155	WRIGHT, William	23	SESW	1860-03-01	Jefferson	A1
988	YATES, Charles	29	E½NE	1825-07-15		A1
986	" "	28	E½SW	1835-09-02		A1
989	" "	29	E½SE	1843-04-10		A1
987	" "	28	N½NW	1856-09-01		A1
990	" "	29	W½NE	1856-09-01		A1

Patent Map

T39-N R3-E
5th PM Meridian

Map Group 10

Township Statistics

Parcels Mapped	:	202
Number of Patents	:	150
Number of Individuals	:	110
Patentees Identified	:	109
Number of Surnames	:	83
Multi-Patentee Parcels	:	3
Oldest Patent Date	:	5/1/1824
Most Recent Patent	:	2/5/1912
Block/Lot Parcels	:	27
Parcels Re - Issued	:	0
Parcels that Overlap	:	2
Cities and Towns	:	6
Cemeteries	:	1

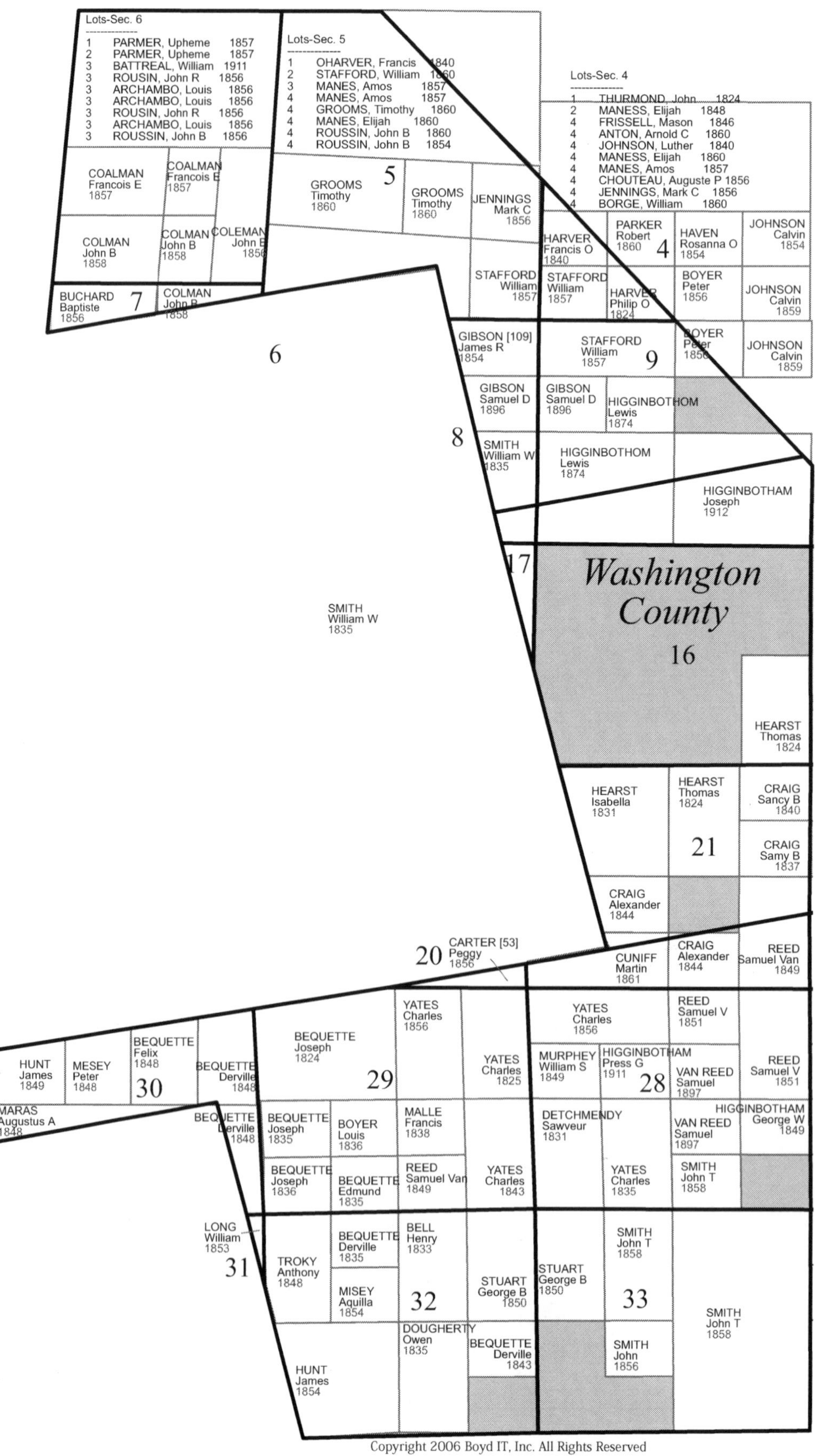

JOHNSON Calvin 1860
BOLDUC Louis 1836
VIVRETT Henry 1879
BOYD Leard B 1824
BAKER Elijah 1840

10

Jefferson County

CHEATHAM [57] Archibald 1833
ARNDT Charles 1857
ARNDT Charles 1857
ARNDT Charles 1857
MOTHERSHEAD William 1824
MOTHERSHEAD Thomas E 1853

15

HEARST William 1840
MOTHERSHEAD William 1831
MAYGER John 1857
LOCKE Joseph H 1857

BLAIR William 1840
MOTHERSHEAD Clifton 1835
MOTHERSHEAD William 1824
MOTHERSHEAD William 1824
22
REED Samuel V 1859
REED Samuel Van 1849
REED Samuel Van 1849
BAKER Austin A 1840
BAKER Austin 1834

BAKER Austin 1831
MAYGER John 1857
MAYGER John 1857
MADDEN Thomas 1840
HIGGINS Julius 1837
23
ROMAINE Peter 1835
ALDERSON John A 1853
PARKER Nathaniel 1824
MADDIN Thomas 1831
WRIGHT William 1860

JOHNSON Luther 1840
CALLAWAY John 1857
HIGGINS Julius 1831
MITCHELL Alfred 1857
MITCHELL Alfred 1857
CALLAWAY John 1857
STRONG David 1824
MORRISON Clarendon 1843
24
MITCHELL Alfred 1857
CALLAWAY John 1857
MORRISSON Clarendon 1843

REED Samuel Van 1850
CATEN Samuel 1862
REED Samuel Van 1850
REED Samuel Van 1849
27
REED Samuel V 1841
SMITH John T 1858
REED Samuel Van 1840

CATEN Samuel 1862
HIGGENBOTHAM George W 1850
HIGGENBOTHAM George W 1850
HIGGENBOTHAM George W 1840
HIGGINBOTHAM George W 1854
MURRILL Briggs 1841
STONG David 1833
26
SMITH John T 1858
SMITH John 1856

STRONG David 1824
MITCHELL Alfred 1854
MITCHELL Alfred 1854
BUREN Pascal H 1854
PINSON Nathan 1835
PINSON Nathan 1840
MCPEAKE Mathew 1840
25
HIGGINBOTHAM George W 1849
HIGGINBOTHAM George W 1841
PINSON Elizabeth J 1841
WICKS Johnson H 1857
PINSON Aaron 1856

CHEATHAM Archer 1897
HIGGINBOTHAM George W 1840
SMITH John T 1858
SMITH John 1858
34
SMITH John 1858
HIGGINBOTHAM George W 1840
HIGGINBOTHAM George W 1840
BOYER Napolean 1884
CUNDIFF Lewis 1838

SMITH John T 1858
SMITH John 1856
35
HIGGINBOTHAM George W 1849
HIGGINBOTHAM George W 1849
HIGGINBOTHAM George W 1849

MURRILL Elias 1840
WICKS Johnson H 1857
WICKS Johnson H 1857
PINSON Aaron 1856
HERELSON Elijah 1844
HAWKINS Augustus 1840
CUNDIFF James 1835
36
MASSIE Upshaw R 1831

Helpful Hints

1. This Map's INDEX can be found on the preceding pages.
2. Refer to Map "C" to see where this Township lies within Washington County, Missouri.
3. Numbers within square brackets [ ] denote a multi-patentee land parcel (multi-owner). Refer to Appendix "C" for a full list of members in this group.
4. Areas that look to be crowded with Patentees usually indicate multiple sales of the same parcel (Re-issues) or Overlapping parcels. See this Township's Index for an explanation of these and other circumstances that might explain "odd" groupings of Patentees on this map.

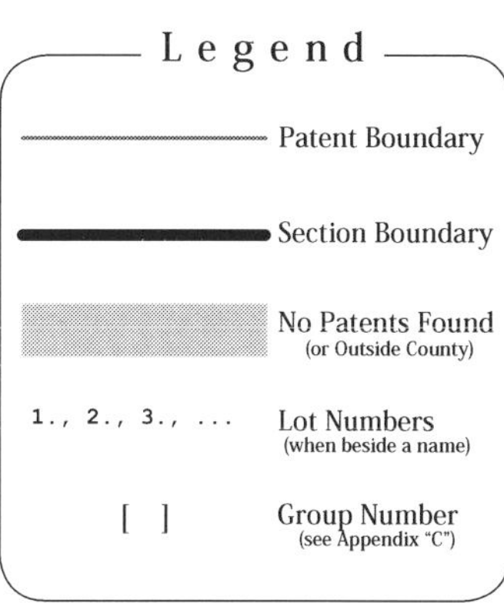

Scale: Section = 1 mile X 1 mile
(generally, with some exceptions)

Road Map

T39-N R3-E
5th PM Meridian

Map Group 10

Cities & Towns

Cruise Mill
Fertile
Baryties
Bliss
Maddens Richwoods
Rabbitville

Cemeteries

Masonic Cemetery

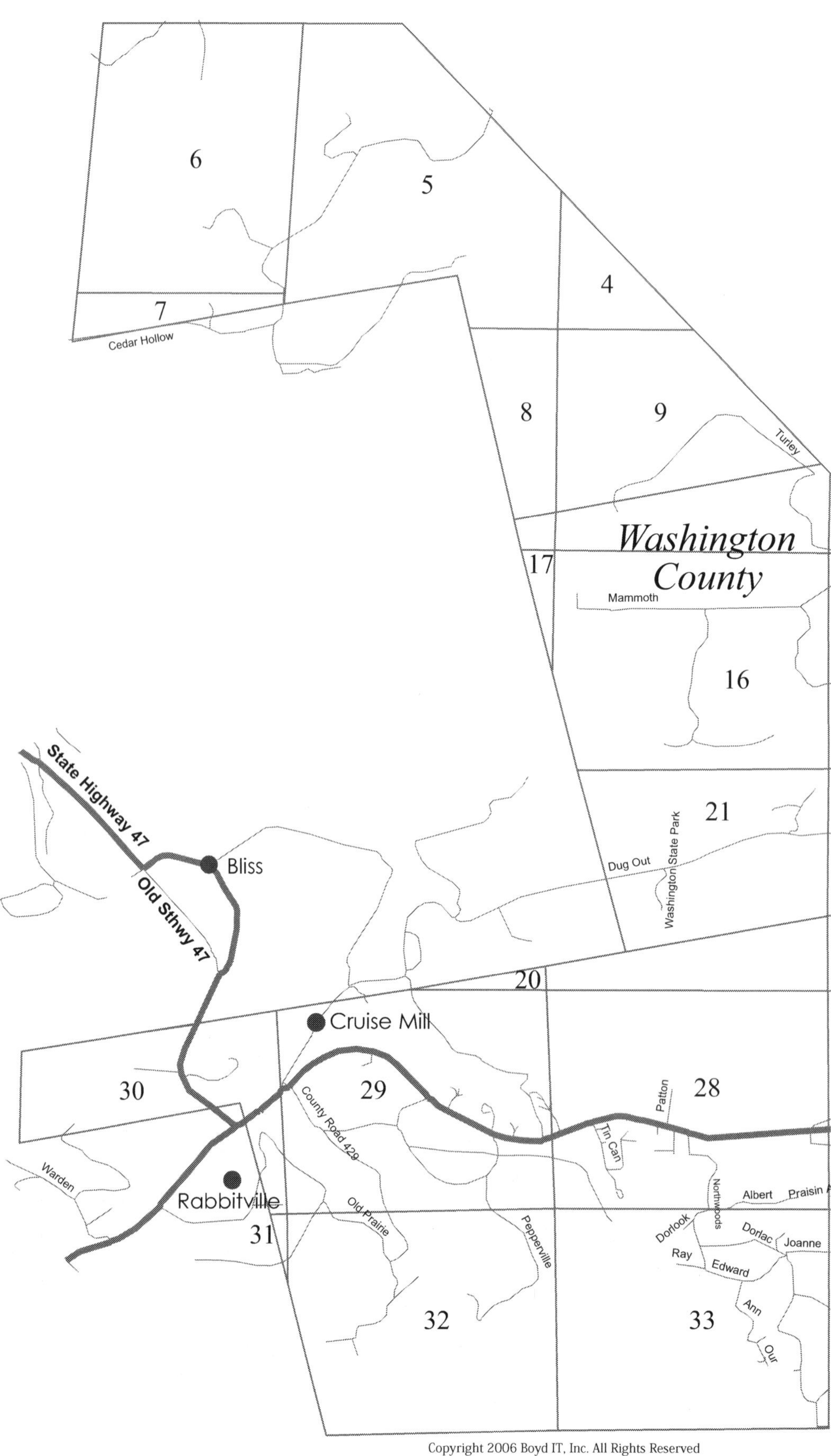

Helpful Hints

1. This road map has a number of uses, but primarily it is to help you: a) find the present location of land owned by your ancestors (at least the general area), b) find cemeteries and city-centers, and c) estimate the route/roads used by Census-takers & tax-assessors.

2. If you plan to travel to Washington County to locate cemeteries or land parcels, please pick up a modern travel map for the area before you do. Mapping old land parcels on modern maps is not as exact a science as you might think. Just the slightest variations in public land survey coordinates, estimates of parcel boundaries, or road-map deviations can greatly alter a map's representation of how a road either does or doesn't cross a particular parcel of land.

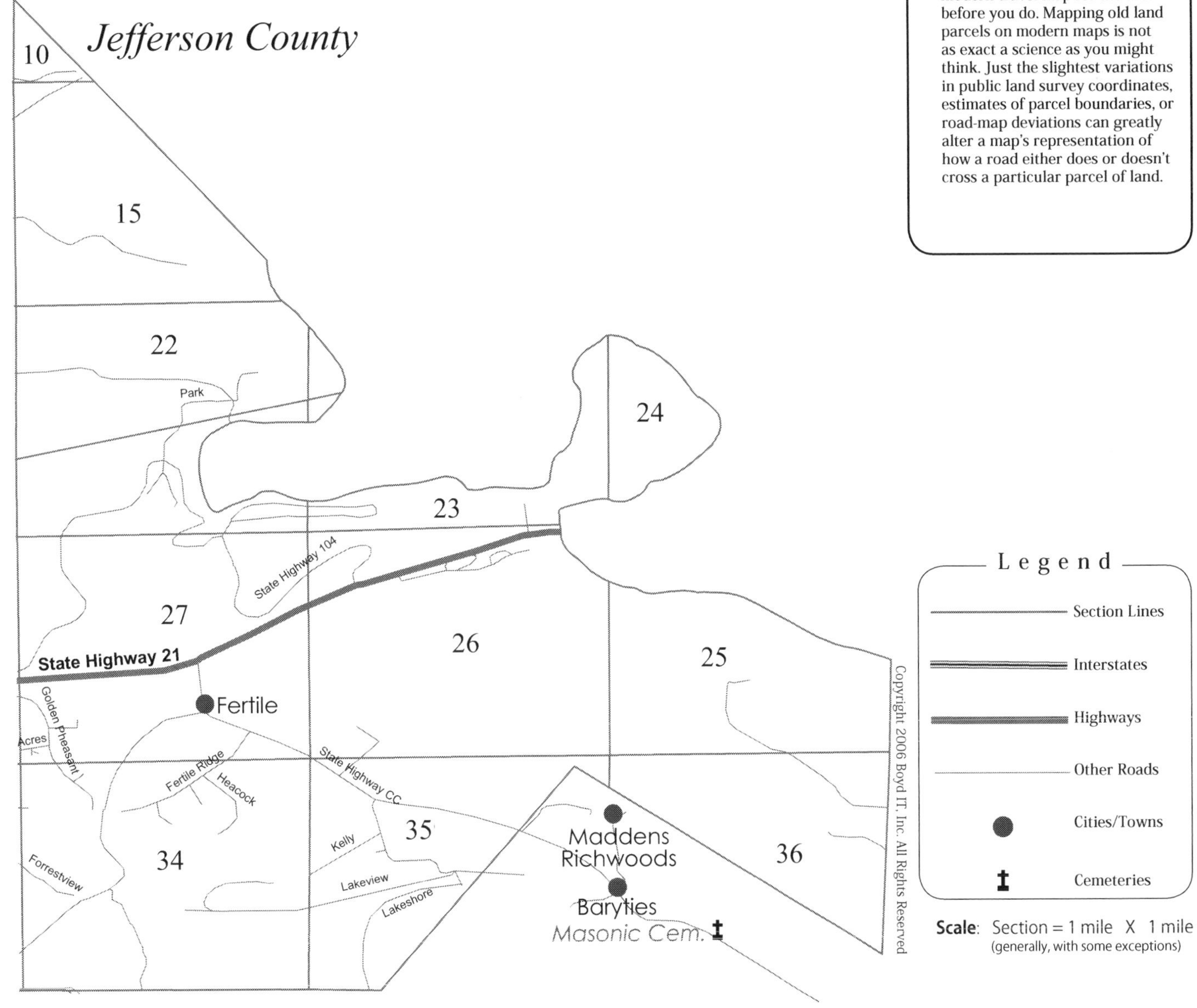

Historical Map

T39-N R3-E
5th PM Meridian

Map Group 10

Cities & Towns

- Cruise Mill
- Fertile
- Baryties
- Bliss
- Maddens Richwoods
- Rabbitville

Cemeteries

- Masonic Cemetery

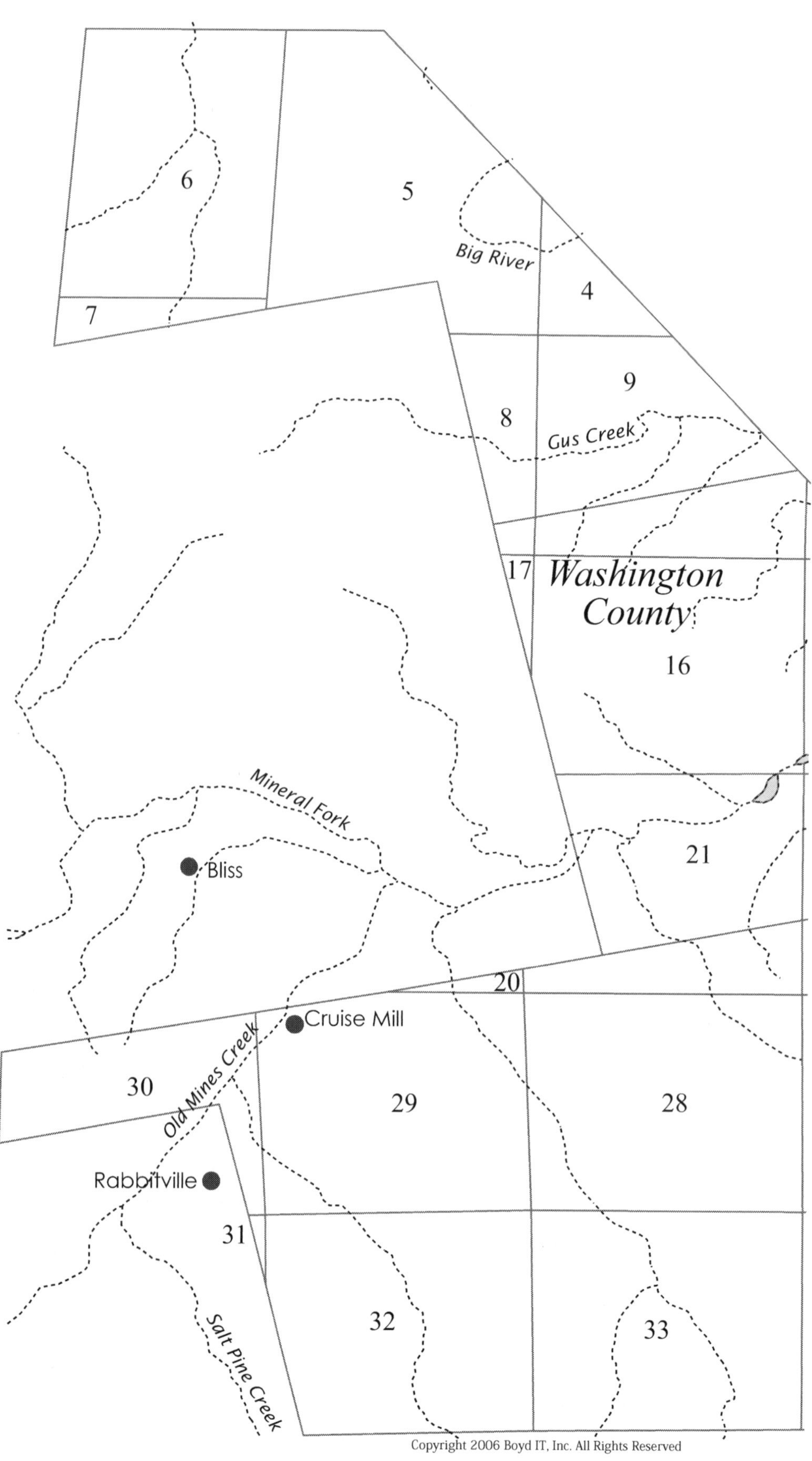

Helpful Hints

1. This Map takes a different look at the same Congressional Township displayed in the preceding two maps. It presents features that can help you better envision the historical development of the area: a) Water-bodies (lakes & ponds), b) Water-courses (rivers, streams, etc.), c) Railroads, d) City/town center-points (where they were oftentimes located when first settled), and e) Cemeteries.
2. Using this "Historical" map in tandem with this Township's Patent Map and Road Map, may lead you to some interesting discoveries. You will often find roads, towns, cemeteries, and waterways are named after nearby landowners: sometimes those names will be the ones you are researching. See how many of these research gems you can find here in Washington County.

Scale: Section = 1 mile X 1 mile
(there are some exceptions)

Map Group 11: Index to Land Patents

Township 38-North Range 2-West (5th PM)

After you locate an individual in this Index, take note of the Section and Section Part then proceed to the Land Patent map on the pages immediately following. You should have no difficulty locating the corresponding parcel of land.

The "For More Info" Column will lead you to more information about the underlying Patents. See the *Legend* at right, and the "How to Use this Book" chapter, for more information.

LEGEND

"For More Info . . . " column

A = Authority (Legislative Act, See Appendix "A")
B = Block or Lot (location in Section unknown)
C = Cancelled Patent
F = Fractional Section
G = Group (Multi-Patentee Patent, see Appendix "C")
V = Overlaps another Parcel
R = Re-Issued (Parcel patented more than once)

(A & G items require you to look in the Appendixes referred to above. All other Letter-designations followed by a number require you to locate line-items in this index that possess the ID number found after the letter).

ID	Individual in Patent	Sec.	Sec. Part	Date Issued	Other Counties	For More Info . . .
1159	CAMERON, John	25	E½NW	1859-11-01	Crawford	A1
1160	" "	25	W½NW	1859-11-01	Crawford	A1
1158	CHAPMAN, John A	12	SENW	1848-07-01	Crawford	A1
1161	GALLAGHER, John	1	NE	1859-11-01	Crawford	A1
1162	" "	1	NW	1859-11-01	Crawford	A1
1156	GOODRICH, Daniel W	13	S½	1859-11-01	Crawford	A1
1165	MANSFIELD, Solomon	36	E½NE	1860-03-01	Crawford	A1
1164	MAUNDER, Samuel	25	S½	1859-11-01	Crawford	A1
1166	NETTLETON, William H	1	S½	1859-11-01	Crawford	A1
1167	SHAW, William J	36	S½	1859-11-01	Crawford	A1
1157	WETER, James H	13	N½	1859-11-01	Crawford	A1
1163	WHITBY, Joseph	25	NE	1859-05-02	Crawford	A1

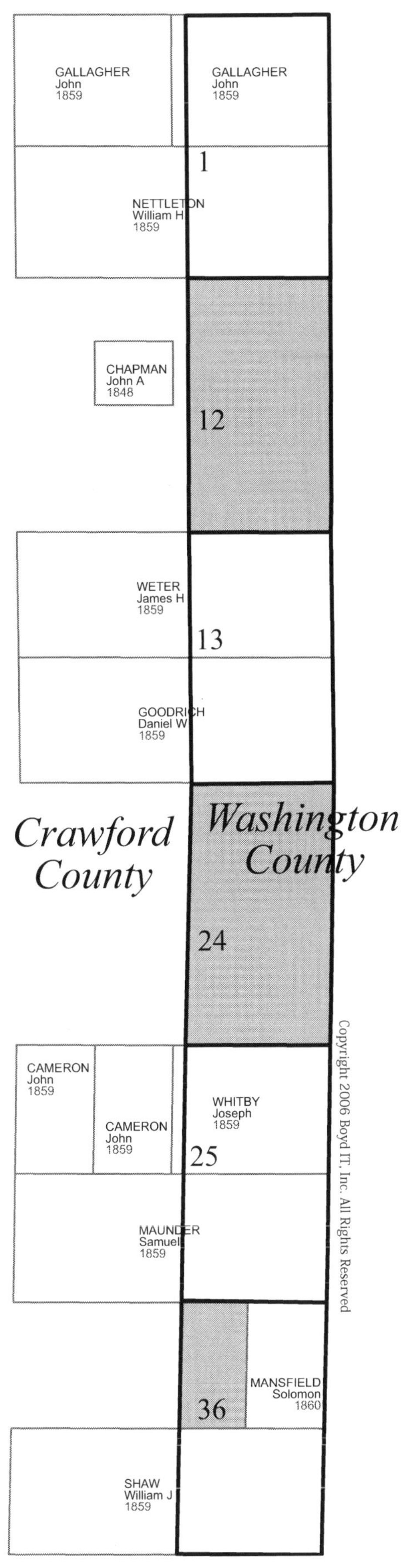

Patent Map

T38-N R2-W
5th PM Meridian

Map Group 11

Township Statistics

Parcels Mapped	:	12
Number of Patents	:	12
Number of Individuals	:	10
Patentees Identified	:	10
Number of Surnames	:	10
Multi-Patentee Parcels	:	0
Oldest Patent Date	:	7/1/1848
Most Recent Patent	:	3/1/1860
Block/Lot Parcels	:	0
Parcels Re - Issued	:	0
Parcels that Overlap	:	0
Cities and Towns	:	0
Cemeteries	:	0

Note: the area contained in this map amounts to far less than a full Township. Therefore, its contents are completely on this single page (instead of a "normal" 2-page spread).

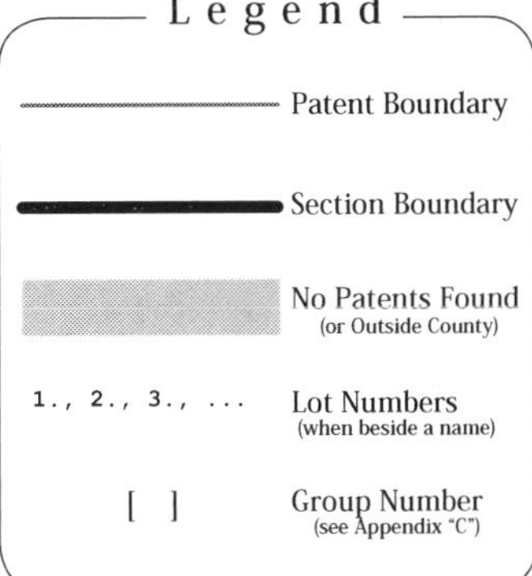

Scale: Section = 1 mile X 1 mile
(generally, with some exceptions)

Road Map

T38-N R2-W
5th PM Meridian

Map Group 11

Note: the area contained in this map amounts to far less than a full Township. Therefore, its contents are completely on this single page (instead of a "normal" 2-page spread).

Cities & Towns
None

Cemeteries
None

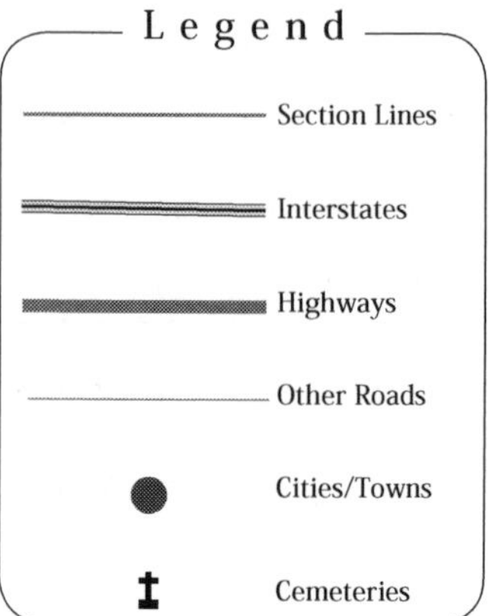

Scale: Section = 1 mile X 1 mile
(generally, with some exceptions)

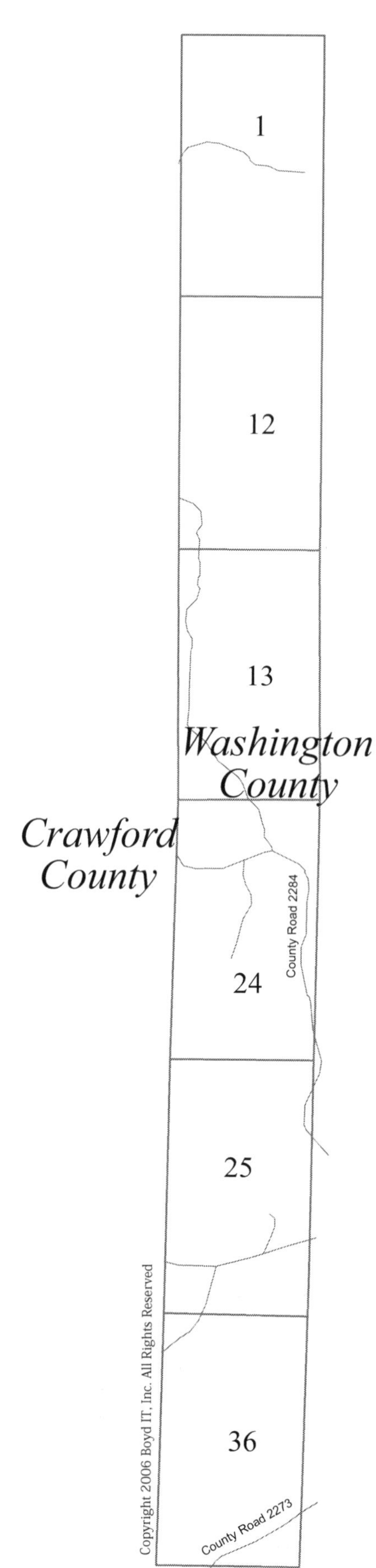

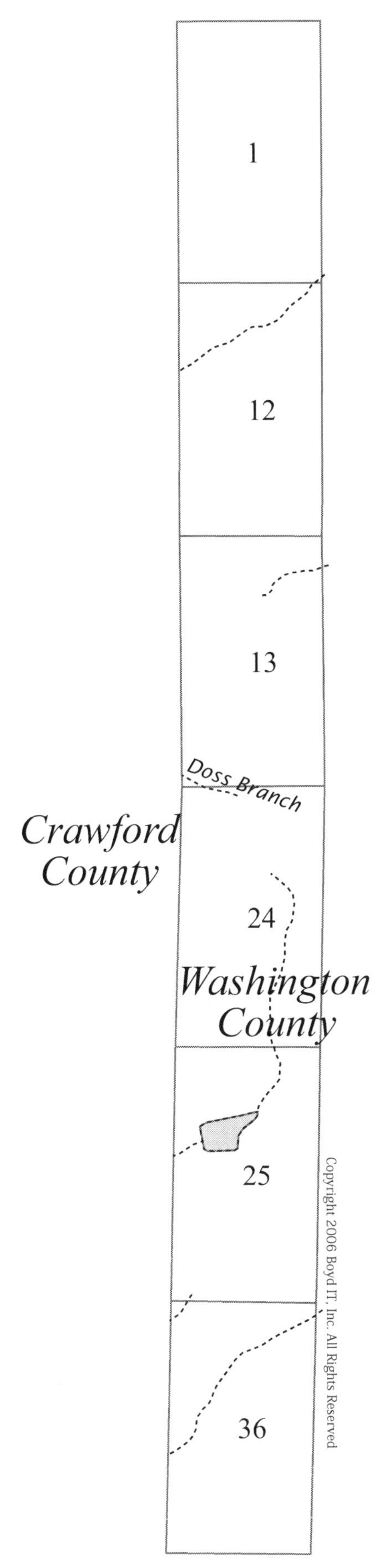

Historical Map

T38-N R2-W
5th PM Meridian

Map Group 11

Note: the area contained in this map amounts to far less than a full Township. Therefore, its contents are completely on this single page (instead of a "normal" 2-page spread).

Cities & Towns

None

Cemeteries

None

Legend

- Section Lines
- Railroads
- Large Rivers & Bodies of Water
- Streams/Creeks & Small Rivers
- Cities/Towns
- Cemeteries

Scale: Section = 1 mile X 1 mile
(there are some exceptions)

Map Group 12: Index to Land Patents

Township 38-North Range 1-West (5th PM)

After you locate an individual in this Index, take note of the Section and Section Part then proceed to the Land Patent map on the pages immediately following. You should have no difficulty locating the corresponding parcel of land.

The "For More Info" Column will lead you to more information about the underlying Patents. See the *Legend* at right, and the "How to Use this Book" chapter, for more information.

LEGEND

"For More Info . . . " column

A = Authority (Legislative Act, See Appendix "A")
B = Block or Lot (location in Section unknown)
C = Cancelled Patent
F = Fractional Section
G = Group (Multi-Patentee Patent, see Appendix "C")
V = Overlaps another Parcel
R = Re-Issued (Parcel patented more than once)

(A & G items require you to look in the Appendixes referred to above. All other Letter-designations followed by a number require you to locate line-items in this index that possess the ID number found after the letter).

ID	Individual in Patent	Sec.	Sec. Part	Date Issued	Other Counties	For More Info . . .
1319	ALLEN, Thomas	26	W½SW	1859-05-02		A1
1320	" "	27	N½SE	1859-05-02		A1
1321	" "	36	N½NW	1859-05-02		A1 R1190
1322	" "	36	NWNE	1859-05-02		A1 R1191
1323	" "	36	SWNW	1859-05-02		A1
1339	BELEW, William L	15	W½SW	1857-09-01		A1
1340	" "	21	NENE	1857-09-01		A1
1341	" "	22	NWNW	1857-09-01		A1
1216	BERGESCH, Herman H	19	1NW	1859-11-01		A1
1217	" "	19	E½SE	1859-11-01		A1
1218	" "	19	NE	1859-11-01		A1
1301	BERRY, Moses	3	W½2NE	1849-06-01		A1 G17
1244	BLANTON, John A	11	NENW	1858-05-03		A1
1245	" "	11	SESW	1858-05-03		A1
1246	" "	11	W½NW	1858-05-03		A1
1247	" "	11	W½SW	1858-05-03		A1
1311	BLANTON, Stephen H	11	E½NE	1858-05-03		A1
1312	" "	11	E½SE	1858-05-03		A1
1313	" "	11	SWSE	1858-05-03		A1
1172	BOWMAN, Albert F	31	NENE	1860-03-01		A1
1251	BOYD, John E	9	SESE	1860-07-20		A1
1252	BOYNTON, John F	33	E½NW	1859-11-01		A1
1253	" "	33	E½SW	1859-11-01		A1
1254	" "	33	W½NE	1859-11-01		A1
1255	" "	33	W½SE	1859-11-01		A1
1315	BRINCKWIRTH, Theodor	7	1SW	1859-11-01		A1
1316	" "	7	2NW	1859-11-01		A1
1317	" "	7	S½1NW	1859-11-01		A1
1318	" "	7	S½SE	1859-11-01		A1
1294	BURK, Michael	3	1NE	1858-05-03		A1
1295	" "	3	3NE	1858-05-03		A1
1296	" "	3	E½2NE	1858-05-03		A1
1297	" "	3	E½SE	1858-05-03		A1
1298	" "	3	SWSE	1858-05-03		A1
1206	CARTER, George	2	1NE	1840-10-01		A1
1207	" "	2	SE	1840-10-01		A1
1335	CHARBONEAU, William	34	E½NE	1910-07-21		A1
1178	CLARK, Austin	15	E½	1858-05-03		A1
1196	CURD, Edward	7	2SW	1860-03-01		A1
1314	DUNKLIN, Stephen T	36	S½NE	1848-02-01		A1 G83
1226	DWANE, James	21	NENW	1860-03-01		A1
1227	" "	21	NWNE	1860-03-01		A1
1276	FERIE, Joseph	17	W½	1859-05-02		A1
1219	FITZWATER, Humble	6	E½1NW	1850-06-01		A1
1256	FLEMING, John	17	SWSE	1860-03-01		A1
1186	FLOTTEMSCH, Bernard	26	SESE	1859-11-01		A1

ID	Individual in Patent	Sec.	Sec. Part	Date Issued	Other Counties	For More Info . . .
1187	FLOTTEMSCH, Bernard (Cont'd)	26	SWNE	1859-11-01		A1
1188	" "	26	W½SE	1859-11-01		A1
1189	" "	35	NENE	1859-11-01		A1
1190	" "	36	N½NW	1859-11-01		A1 R1321
1191	" "	36	NWNE	1859-11-01		A1 R1322
1277	FRAZER, Joseph	7	N½1NW	1860-03-01		A1
1278	" "	7	NWNE	1860-03-01		A1
1202	GENERELLY, Emile	3	1NW	1857-09-01		A1
1203	" "	3	2NW	1857-09-01		A1
1204	" "	3	SW	1857-09-01		A1
1288	GRAVES, Martin	5	2NE	1860-03-01		A1
1289	" "	5	2NW	1860-03-01		A1
1263	HANSON, John P	32	E½SE	1860-03-01		A1
1264	" "	33	W½SW	1860-03-01		A1
1270	HARMAN, Jonas	27	NWSW	1858-01-13		A1
1271	" "	27	SWNW	1858-01-13		A1
1234	HARMON, James L	21	NWNW	1848-07-01		A1
1248	HARPER, John A	21	NESW	1857-09-01		A1
1249	" "	21	NWSE	1857-09-01		A1
1250	" "	21	SWNE	1857-09-01		A1
1303	HARPER, Noah	27	S½SE	1857-06-10		A1
1304	" "	27	S½SW	1857-06-10		A1
1305	" "	28	SESE	1857-06-10		A1
1302	" "	27	NESW	1858-05-03		A1
1306	" "	34	NENW	1859-05-02		A1
1307	" "	34	NWNE	1859-05-02		A1
1310	HENRY, Sandford	1	SESE	1843-04-10		A1
1273	HILL, Jonas M	1	E½2NE	1860-03-01		A1
1272	" "	1	E½1NE	1874-05-06		A1
1300	HILL, Milton B	1	NESE	1849-06-01		A1
1197	HORINE, Elias	1	3NW	1857-06-10		A1
1198	" "	1	E½2NW	1857-06-10		A1
1199	" "	1	W½2NE	1857-06-10		A1
1224	HOUSEMAN, James D	25	SESE	1849-06-01		A1 G135
1225	" "	36	NENE	1849-06-01		A1 G135
1224	IRVINE, Andrew	25	SESE	1849-06-01		A1 G135
1225	" "	36	NENE	1849-06-01		A1 G135
1283	ISGRIG, Madison	21	SWSE	1843-04-10		A1
1282	" "	21	E½SE	1857-09-01		A1
1284	" "	22	E½NW	1859-05-02		A1 V1332
1285	" "	22	SWSW	1859-05-02		A1
1286	" "	27	NWNW	1859-05-02		A1
1287	" "	28	NWNE	1859-05-02		A1
1242	JOHNSON, Jeptha B	24	E½NE	1849-06-01		A1 G155
1243	" "	24	SWNE	1849-06-01		A1 G155
1241	" "	12	NWSE	1849-06-20		A1 G154
1241	JOHNSON, John H	12	NWSE	1849-06-20		A1 G154
1265	JOHNSON, John P	17	E½SE	1848-07-01		A1
1242	JOHNSON, Joseph	24	E½NE	1849-06-01		A1 G155
1243	" "	24	SWNE	1849-06-01		A1 G155
1241	JOHNSON, Joseph D	12	NWSE	1849-06-20		A1 G154
1220	JONES, Isaac H	19	SWSE	1848-07-01		A1
1221	KELLER, Jacob	31	2NW	1860-03-01		A1
1222	" "	31	2SW	1860-03-01		A1
1192	KIRTLAND, Charles B	36	SENW	1859-05-02		A1
1314	LERSHALL, Samuel	36	S½NE	1848-02-01		A1 G83
1174	LIVERMORE, Arthur	34	SE	1859-05-02		A1
1175	" "	35	SW	1859-05-02		A1
1342	LONG, William	1	NWNW	1860-03-01		A1
1308	MAHENY, Patrick	15	E½SW	1860-03-01		A1
1309	" "	15	SENW	1860-03-01		A1
1236	MAIDES, James	21	NWSW	1860-03-01		A1
1237	" "	21	S½SW	1860-03-01		A1
1238	" "	28	E½NW	1860-03-01		A1
1239	" "	28	NWNW	1860-03-01		A1
1240	" "	28	SWNE	1860-03-01		A1
1228	MCCHESNEY, James E	35	SENW	1896-10-05		A1
1229	" "	35	SESE	1896-10-05		A1
1230	" "	35	SWNE	1896-10-05		A1
1231	" "	35	W½SE	1896-10-05		A1
1232	" "	36	SWSW	1896-10-05		A1
1301	MCSPADEN, Moses M	3	W½2NE	1849-06-01		A1 G17
1274	MERCER, Joseph B	12	SESW	1850-06-01		A1

ID	Individual in Patent	Sec.	Sec. Part	Date Issued	Other Counties	For More Info . . .
1275	MERCER, Joseph B (Cont'd)	13	E½NW	1858-05-03		A1
1176	METCALF, Arthur	17	SENE	1856-01-15		A1
1177	" "	21	S½NW	1856-01-15		A1
1324	METCALF, Thomas	23	W½SW	1859-05-02		A1
1325	" "	26	W½NW	1859-05-02		A1
1326	" "	27	NE	1859-05-02		A1
1343	MORRISON, William	3	NWSE	1860-03-01		A1
1281	MOUNT, Lewis	25	SENW	1860-03-01		A1
1299	MURPHY, Michael	17	NENE	1860-03-01		A1
1261	NEVISON, John	36	E½SW	1859-11-01		A1
1262	" "	36	S½SE	1859-11-01		A1
1257	NIEHANS, John H	31	1NW	1859-05-02		A1
1258	" "	31	1SW	1859-05-02		A1
1259	" "	31	W½NE	1859-05-02		A1
1260	" "	31	W½SE	1859-05-02		A1
1193	NIEHAUS, Christopher	5	1NE	1859-11-01		A1
1194	" "	5	1NW	1859-11-01		A1
1195	" "	5	SW	1859-11-01		A1
1334	OTTMAN, Tobias	26	NESE	1861-08-30		A1
1290	PICKLES, Matthew F	19	1SW	1860-03-01		A1
1291	" "	19	2NW	1860-03-01		A1
1292	" "	19	2SW	1860-03-01		A1
1293	" "	19	NWSE	1860-03-01		A1
1201	PINSON, Elijah	17	W½NE	1857-06-10		A1
1200	" "	17	NWSE	1859-05-02		A1
1269	PINSON, John W	28	E½NE	1857-06-10		A1
1279	PINSON, Joseph	7	E½NE	1843-04-10		A1
1224	SCHARIT, Augustus W	25	SESE	1849-06-01		A1 G135
1225	" "	36	NENE	1849-06-01		A1 G135
1223	SHIELDS, James A	3	3NW	1911-02-01		A1
1327	SILENCE, Thomas	34	E½SW	1860-03-01		A1
1328	" "	34	SENW	1860-03-01		A1
1329	" "	34	SWNE	1860-03-01		A1
1266	SLOSS, John	1	W½1NE	1859-11-01		A1
1267	" "	1	W½SE	1859-11-01		A1
1268	" "	12	NWNE	1859-11-01		A1
1181	SMITH, Benjamin F	1	W½2NW	1857-09-01		A1
1179	" "	1	E½SW	1857-10-30		A1
1180	" "	1	SWSW	1857-10-30		A1
1182	" "	11	NESW	1857-10-30		A1
1183	" "	11	NWSE	1857-10-30		A1
1184	" "	11	SENW	1857-10-30		A1
1185	" "	11	W½NE	1857-10-30		A1
1235	SPRINGER, James M	12	NENE	1848-02-01		A1
1241	STACEY, Joseph	12	NWSE	1849-06-20		A1 G154
1208	STROHBECK, George H	12	S½SE	1859-11-01		A1
1209	" "	13	N½SE	1859-11-01		A1
1210	" "	13	NE	1859-11-01		A1
1338	SUMMERS, William H	8	NESW	1848-07-01		A1
1336	" "	7	N½SE	1857-09-01		A1
1337	" "	7	SWNE	1857-09-01		A1
1242	THOMAS, John	24	E½NE	1849-06-01		A1 G155
1243	" "	24	SWNE	1849-06-01		A1 G155
1280	TODD, Joseph	13	S½SE	1858-05-03		A1
1233	TUCKER, James G	32	W½SE	1840-10-01		A1
1173	VICTOR, Alexander	24	NWNE	1867-01-02		A1
1211	VORNBERG, Gerhard H	25	E½SW	1859-05-02		A1
1212	" "	25	N½SE	1859-05-02		A1
1213	" "	25	S½NE	1859-05-02		A1
1214	" "	25	SWSE	1859-05-02		A1
1215	" "	25	SWSW	1859-05-02		A1
1168	WHITE, Abraham C	33	E½NE	1859-11-01		A1
1169	" "	33	E½SE	1859-11-01		A1 R1205
1170	" "	34	NWSW	1859-11-01		A1
1171	" "	34	W½NW	1859-11-01		A1
1205	WILMESHERR, Frank A	33	E½SE	1904-01-28		A1 R1169
1330	WOOD, Thomas	21	SENE	1860-03-01		A1
1331	" "	22	N½SW	1860-03-01		A1
1332	" "	22	S½NW	1860-03-01		A1 V1284
1333	" "	22	SESW	1860-03-01		A1

Patent Map

T38-N R1-W
5th PM Meridian

Map Group 12

Township Statistics

Parcels Mapped	:	176
Number of Patents	:	85
Number of Individuals	:	82
Patentees Identified	:	74
Number of Surnames	:	72
Multi-Patentee Parcels	:	7
Oldest Patent Date	:	10/1/1840
Most Recent Patent	:	2/1/1911
Block/Lot Parcels	:	33
Parcels Re - Issued	:	3
Parcels that Overlap	:	2
Cities and Towns	:	0
Cemeteries	:	1

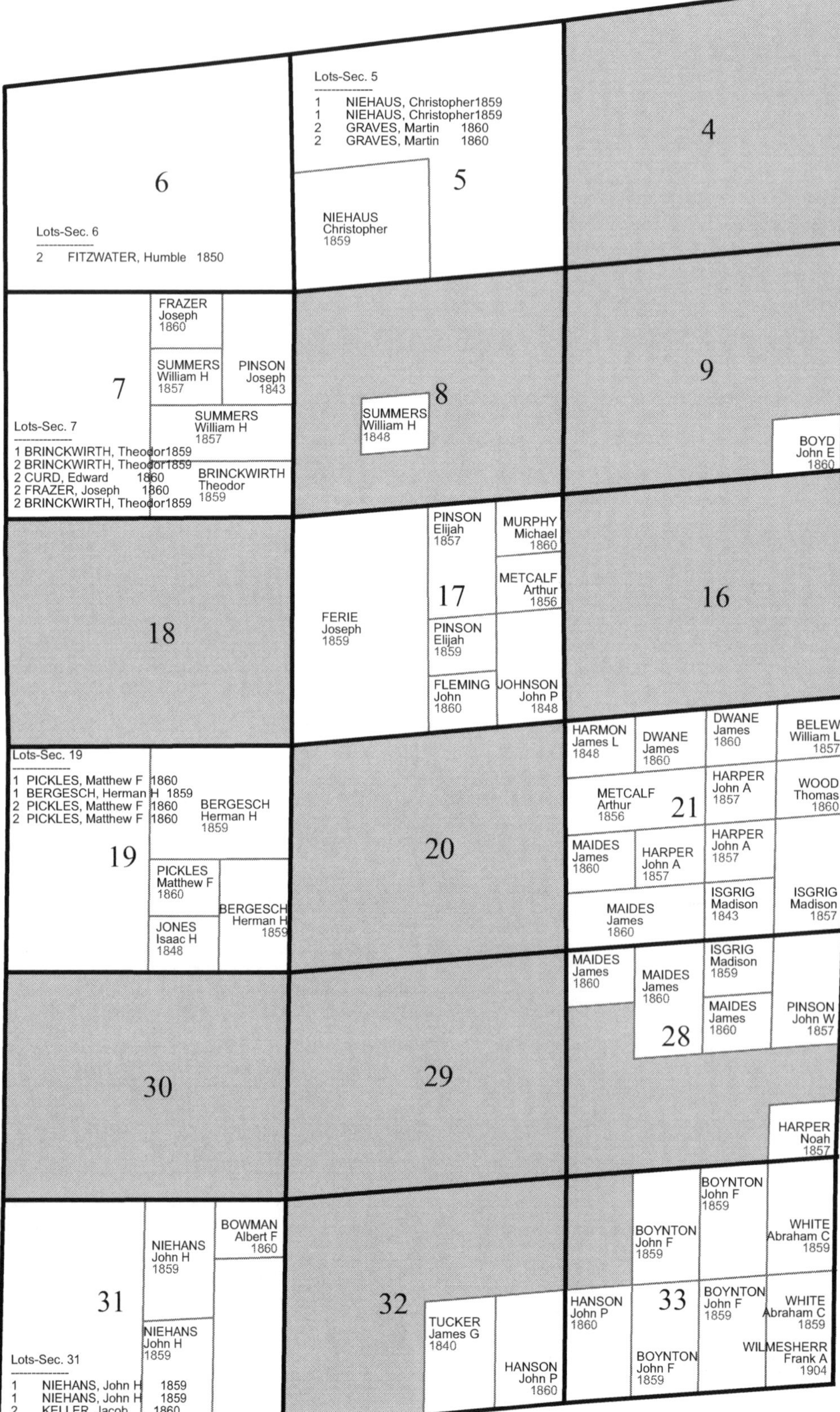

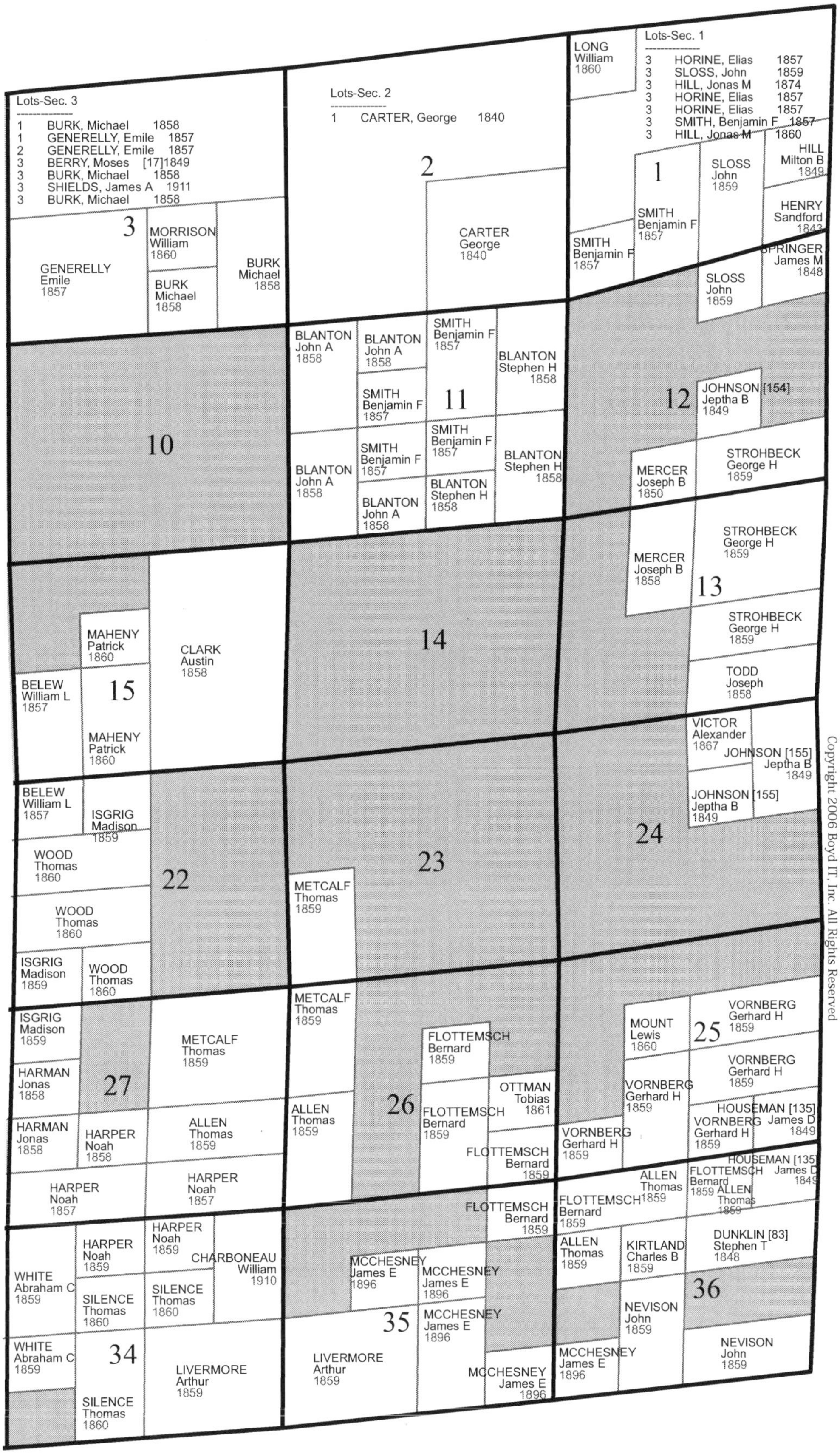

Lots-Sec. 3
1 BURK, Michael 1858
1 GENERELLY, Emile 1857
2 GENERELLY, Emile 1857
3 BERRY, Moses [17]1849
3 BURK, Michael 1858
3 SHIELDS, James A 1911
3 BURK, Michael 1858

3
GENERELLY Emile 1857
MORRISON William 1860
BURK Michael 1858
BURK Michael 1858

Lots-Sec. 2
1 CARTER, George 1840

2
CARTER George 1840

LONG William 1860

Lots-Sec. 1
3 HORINE, Elias 1857
3 SLOSS, John 1859
3 HILL, Jonas M 1874
3 HORINE, Elias 1857
3 HORINE, Elias 1857
3 SMITH, Benjamin F 1857
3 HILL, Jonas M 1860

1
HILL Milton B 1849
SLOSS John 1859
HENRY Sandford 1843
SMITH Benjamin F 1857
SMITH Benjamin F 1857
SPRINGER James M 1848
SLOSS John 1859

10

BLANTON John A 1858
BLANTON John A 1858
SMITH Benjamin F 1857
BLANTON Stephen H 1858
SMITH Benjamin F 1857
11
SMITH Benjamin F 1857
SMITH Benjamin F 1857
BLANTON Stephen H 1858
BLANTON John A 1858
BLANTON Stephen H 1858
BLANTON John A 1858

12
JOHNSON [154] Jeptha B 1849
MERCER Joseph B 1850
STROHBECK George H 1859

MAHENY Patrick 1860
CLARK Austin 1858
BELEW William L 1857
15
MAHENY Patrick 1860

14

MERCER Joseph B 1858
STROHBECK George H 1859
13
STROHBECK George H 1859
TODD Joseph 1858

BELEW William L 1857
ISGRIG Madison 1859
WOOD Thomas 1860
22
WOOD Thomas 1860
ISGRIG Madison 1859
WOOD Thomas 1860

23
METCALF Thomas 1859

VICTOR Alexander 1867
JOHNSON [155] Jeptha B 1849
JOHNSON [155] Jeptha B 1849
24

ISGRIG Madison 1859
METCALF Thomas 1859
HARMAN Jonas 1858
27
HARMAN Jonas 1858
HARPER Noah 1858
ALLEN Thomas 1859
HARPER Noah 1857
HARPER Noah 1857

METCALF Thomas 1859
FLOTTEMSCH Bernard 1859
ALLEN Thomas 1859
26
FLOTTEMSCH Bernard 1859
OTTMAN Tobias 1861
FLOTTEMSCH Bernard 1859
FLOTTEMSCH Bernard 1859

MOUNT Lewis 1860
25
VORNBERG Gerhard H 1859
VORNBERG Gerhard H 1859
VORNBERG Gerhard H 1859
HOUSEMAN [135] James D 1849
VORNBERG Gerhard H 1859
VORNBERG Gerhard H 1859
HOUSEMAN [135] James D 1849
ALLEN Thomas 1859
FLOTTEMSCH Bernard 1859
ALLEN Thomas 1859
FLOTTEMSCH Bernard 1859

HARPER Noah 1859
HARPER Noah 1859
CHARBONEAU William 1910
WHITE Abraham C 1859
SILENCE Thomas 1860
SILENCE Thomas 1860
WHITE Abraham C 1859
34
LIVERMORE Arthur 1859
SILENCE Thomas 1860

MCCHESNEY James E 1896
MCCHESNEY James E 1896
35
MCCHESNEY James E 1896
LIVERMORE Arthur 1859
MCCHESNEY James E 1896

ALLEN Thomas 1859
KIRTLAND Charles B 1859
DUNKLIN [83] Stephen T 1848
36
NEVISON John 1859
MCCHESNEY James E 1896
NEVISON John 1859

Helpful Hints

1. This Map's INDEX can be found on the preceding pages.
2. Refer to Map "C" to see where this Township lies within Washington County, Missouri.
3. Numbers within square brackets [ ] denote a multi-patentee land parcel (multi-owner). Refer to Appendix "C" for a full list of members in this group.
4. Areas that look to be crowded with Patentees usually indicate multiple sales of the same parcel (Re-issues) or Overlapping parcels. See this Township's Index for an explanation of these and other circumstances that might explain "odd" groupings of Patentees on this map.

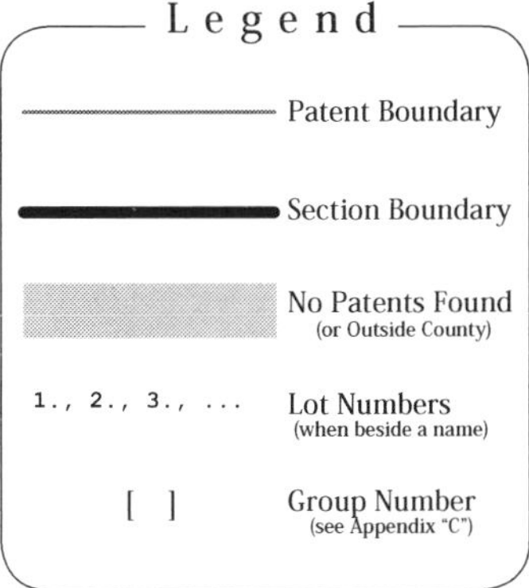

Scale: Section = 1 mile X 1 mile
(generally, with some exceptions)

Road Map

T38-N R1-W
5th PM Meridian

Map Group 12

Cities & Towns

None

Cemeteries

Metcalf Cemetery

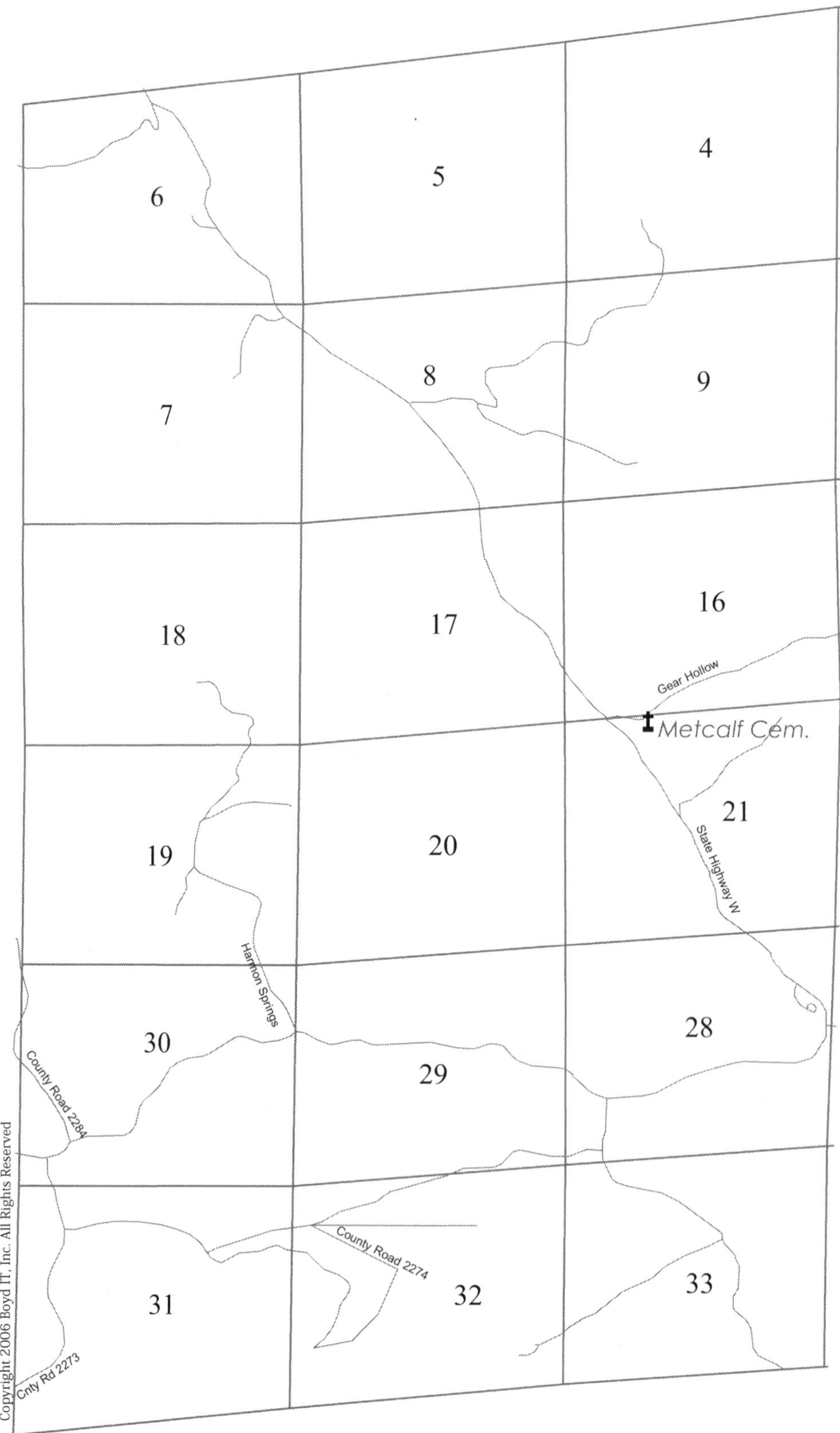

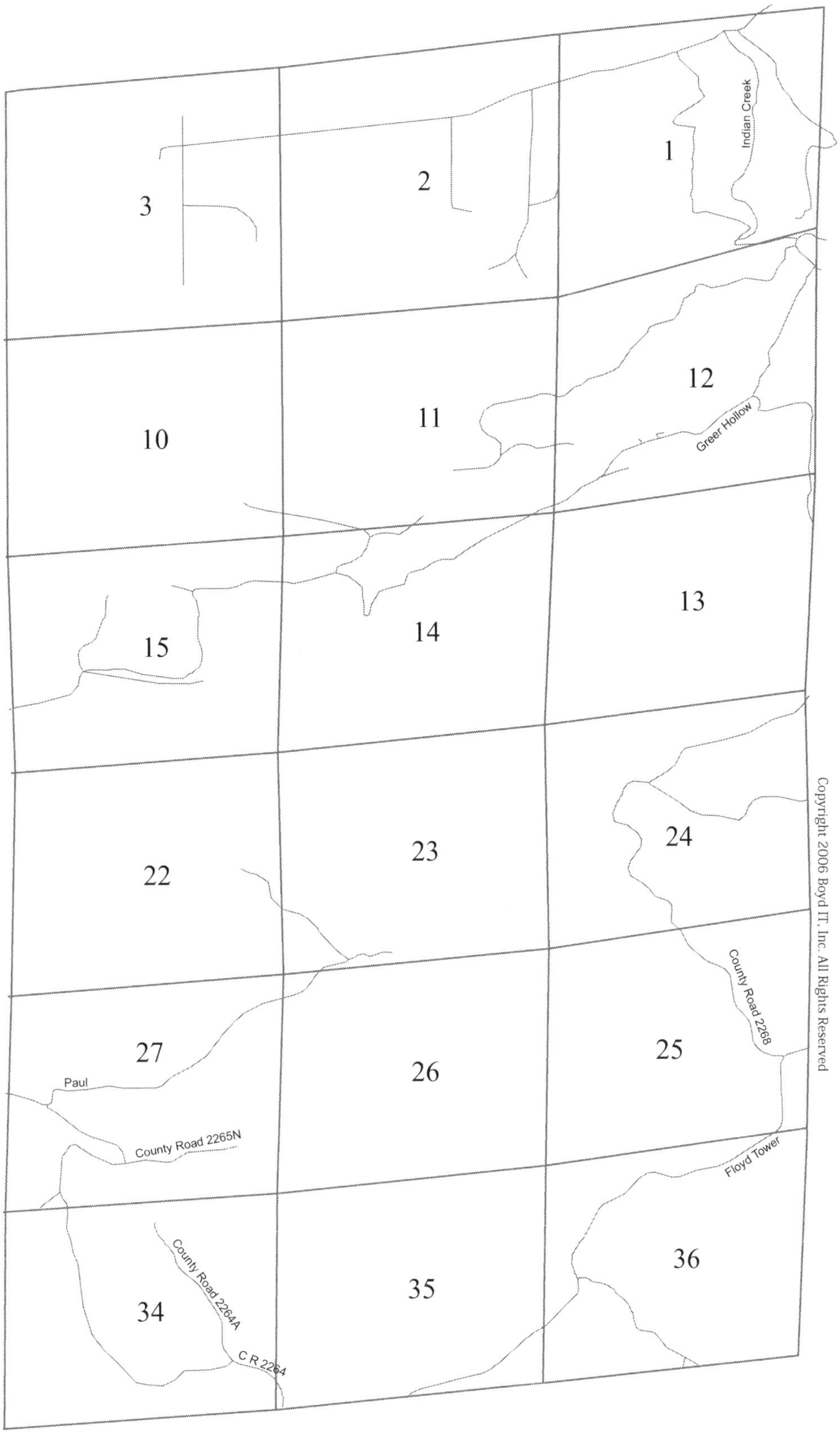

3
2
1
Indian Creek
12
11
10
Greer Hollow
15
14
13
24
23
22
County Road 2268
27
26
25
Paul
County Road 2265N
Floyd Tower
36
35
34
County Road 2264A
C R 2264

Helpful Hints

1. This road map has a number of uses, but primarily it is to help you: a) find the present location of land owned by your ancestors (at least the general area), b) find cemeteries and city-centers, and c) estimate the route/roads used by Census-takers & tax-assessors.

2. If you plan to travel to Washington County to locate cemeteries or land parcels, please pick up a modern travel map for the area before you do. Mapping old land parcels on modern maps is not as exact a science as you might think. Just the slightest variations in public land survey coordinates, estimates of parcel boundaries, or road-map deviations can greatly alter a map's representation of how a road either does or doesn't cross a particular parcel of land.

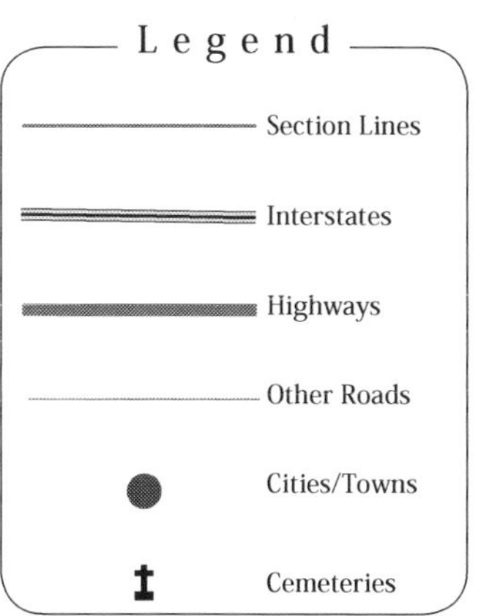

Scale: Section = 1 mile X 1 mile
(generally, with some exceptions)

Historical Map

T38-N R1-W
5th PM Meridian

Map Group 12

Cities & Towns
None

Cemeteries
Metcalf Cemetery

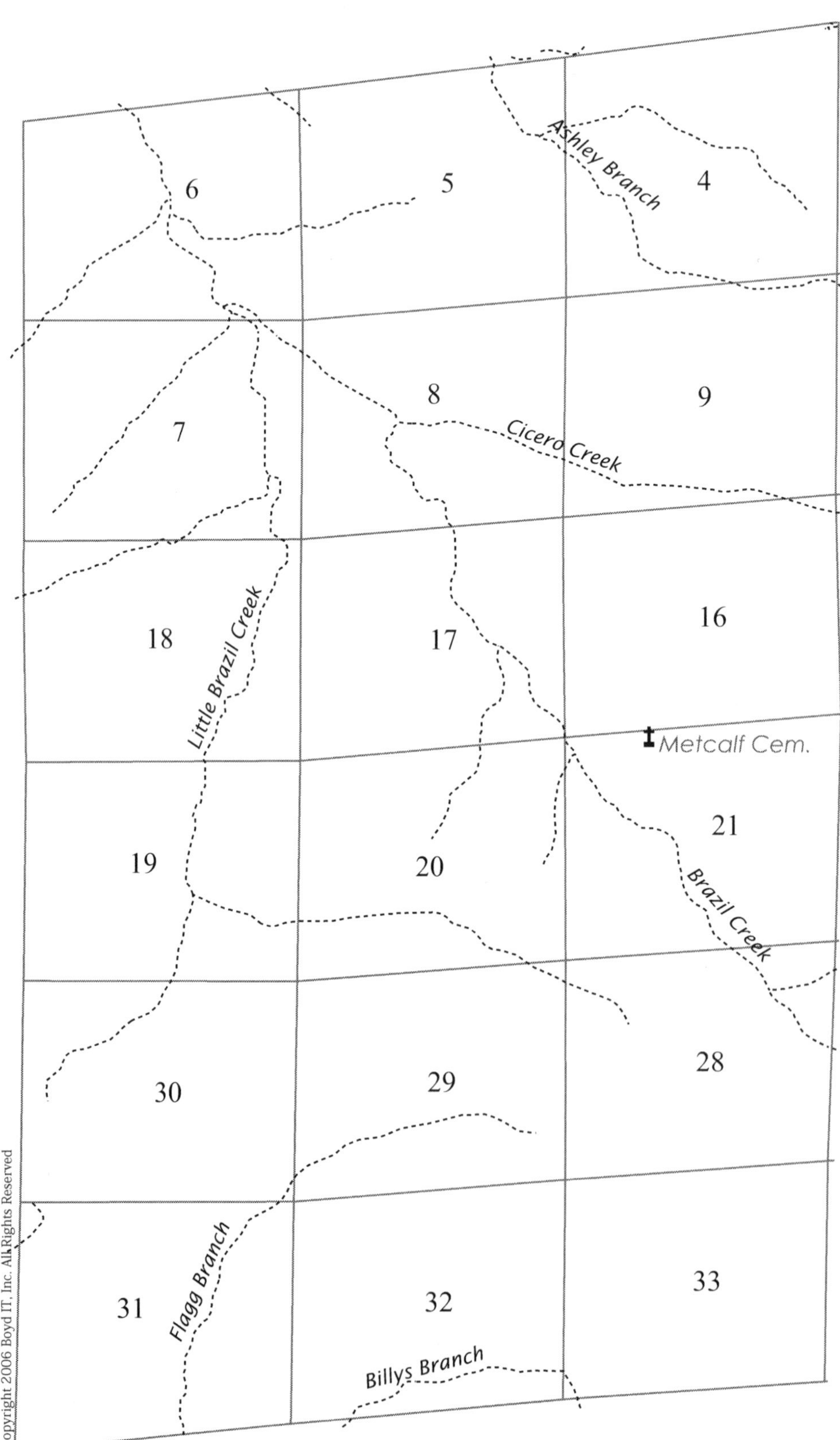

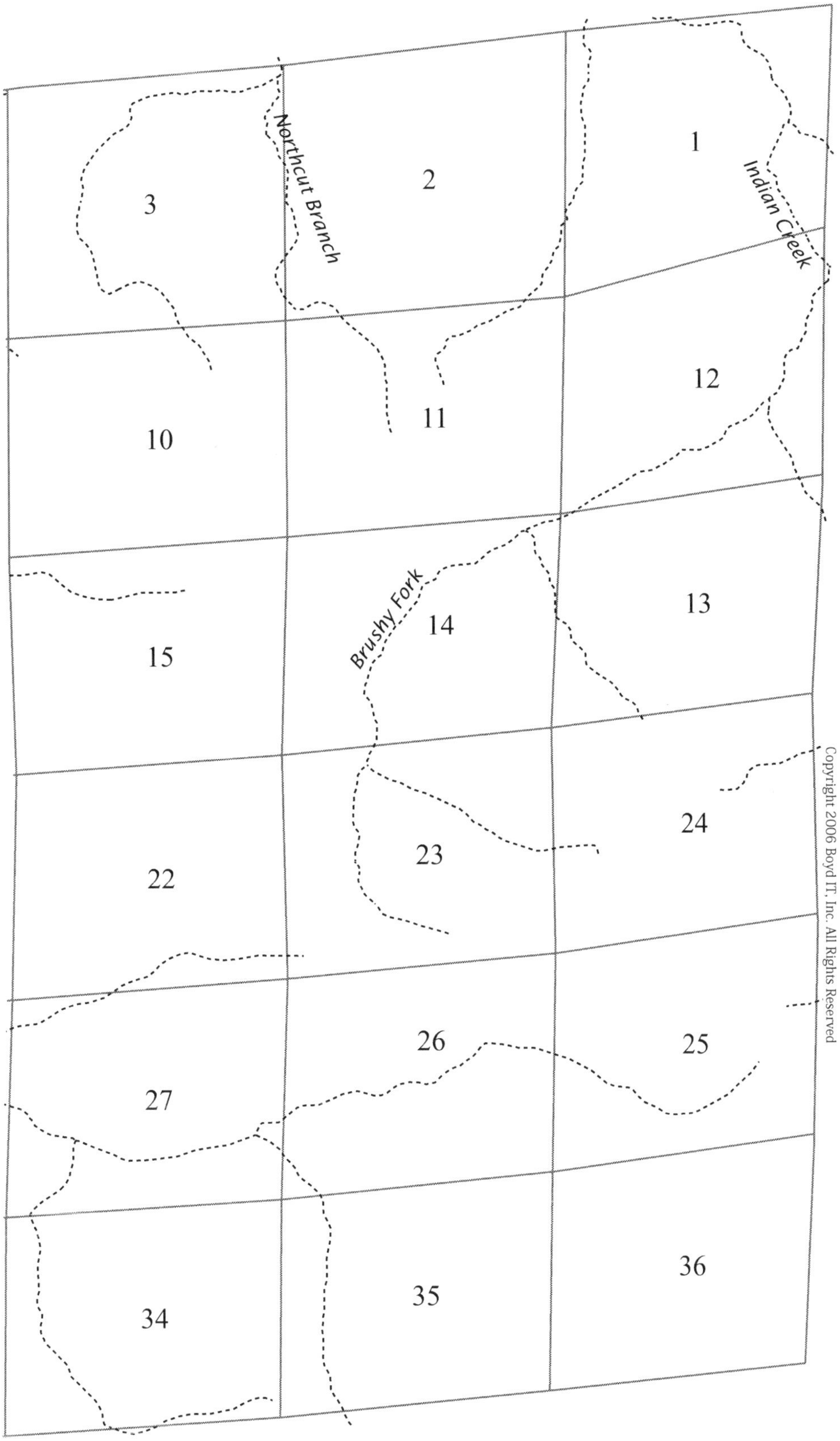

3
Northcut Branch
2
1
Indian Creek
10
11
12
15
Brushy Fork
14
13
22
23
24
27
26
25
34
35
36

Helpful Hints

1. This Map takes a different look at the same Congressional Township displayed in the preceding two maps. It presents features that can help you better envision the historical development of the area: a) Water-bodies (lakes & ponds), b) Water-courses (rivers, streams, etc.), c) Railroads, d) City/town center-points (where they were oftentimes located when first settled), and e) Cemeteries.

2. Using this "Historical" map in tandem with this Township's Patent Map and Road Map, may lead you to some interesting discoveries. You will often find roads, towns, cemeteries, and waterways are named after nearby landowners: sometimes those names will be the ones you are researching. See how many of these research gems you can find here in Washington County.

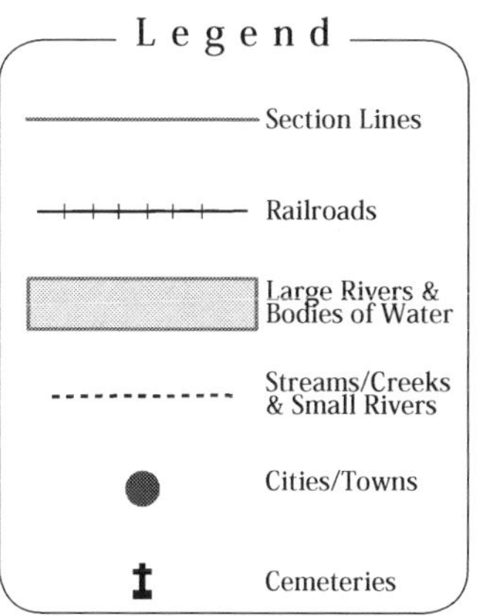

Scale: Section = 1 mile X 1 mile
(there are some exceptions)

Map Group 13: Index to Land Patents

Township 38-North Range 1-East (5th PM)

After you locate an individual in this Index, take note of the Section and Section Part then proceed to the Land Patent map on the pages immediately following. You should have no difficulty locating the corresponding parcel of land.

The "For More Info" Column will lead you to more information about the underlying Patents. See the *Legend* at right, and the "How to Use this Book" chapter, for more information.

LEGEND

"For More Info . . . " column

A = Authority (Legislative Act, See Appendix "A")
B = Block or Lot (location in Section unknown)
C = Cancelled Patent
F = Fractional Section
G = Group (Multi-Patentee Patent, see Appendix "C")
V = Overlaps another Parcel
R = Re-Issued (Parcel patented more than once)

(A & G items require you to look in the Appendixes referred to above. All other Letter-designations followed by a number require you to locate line-items in this index that possess the ID number found after the letter).

ID	Individual in Patent	Sec.	Sec. Part	Date Issued	Other Counties	For More Info . . .
1435	ANDERSON, James	18	E½SW	1860-03-01		A1
1436	" "	18	S½SE	1860-03-01		A1
1465	ANDERSON, John	2	E½SW	1834-11-04		A1
1460	BARRETT, Jesse W	8	NE	1859-11-01		A1
1461	" "	9	NW	1859-11-01		A1
1556	BASS, Nancy	13	E½NE	1848-06-01		A1
1555	" "	11	NWNE	1857-04-15		A1
1583	BASS, Richard	13	W½NE	1848-07-01		A1
1615	BASS, Thomas	2	W½3NE	1844-08-01		A1
1632	BASS, William	3	NWSE	1843-04-10		A1 G10
1422	BELL, Hugh	25	NESE	1840-10-01		A1
1423	" "	25	SENE	1840-10-01		A1
1632	BRIGGS, Oliver	3	NWSE	1843-04-10		A1 G10
1554	CAMPBELL, Moses	28	SENW	1860-03-01		A1
1472	CASEY, John	12	E½NE	1856-01-15		A1
1473	" "	12	NWNE	1856-01-15		A1
1517	COCK, Joseph	10	SESE	1860-03-01		A1
1438	COMFORT, James H	31	S½1SW	1859-05-02		A1
1439	" "	31	S½SE	1859-05-02		A1
1475	COMPTON, John	34	E½SW	1831-10-01		A1
1476	" "	34	SWSE	1840-10-01		A1
1477	" "	34	SWSW	1840-10-01		A1
1478	" "	31	2NW	1849-05-01		A1 G72
1474	" "	33	SESE	1849-06-01		A1
1516	COMPTON, Jonathan	34	NENW	1857-04-15		A1
1510	" "	28	SESE	1857-09-01		A1
1513	" "	33	NENE	1857-09-01		A1
1511	" "	28	SWSE	1859-05-02		A1
1512	" "	33	N½SE	1859-05-02		A1
1514	" "	33	NWNE	1859-05-02		A1
1515	" "	33	SENE	1859-05-02		A1
1518	COMPTON, Joseph	23	E½SE	1824-05-10		A1 G73
1584	COMPTON, Richard	24	E½NW	1824-05-10		A1
1434	COWAN, Jabez C	34	SWNW	1860-03-01		A1
1389	CRESSWELL, George	2	W½1NE	1849-06-01		A1
1390	" "	27	SESW	1856-09-01		A1
1391	" "	27	SWSW	1856-09-01		A1
1387	" "	17	SWNW	1858-05-03		A1
1386	" "	17	NWNW	1859-05-02		A1
1388	" "	2	2NE	1859-05-02		A1
1613	CRESSWELL, Stephen L	20	N½	1857-06-10		A1
1392	CRESWELL, George	2	NWNW	1835-10-08		A1
1394	" "	3	W½2NE	1848-02-01		A1
1393	" "	27	SWSE	1856-01-15		A1
1519	CRESWELL, Joseph	18	1NW	1861-01-30		A1
1520	" "	18	N½SE	1861-01-30		A1

ID	Individual in Patent	Sec.	Sec. Part	Date Issued	Other Counties	For More Info . . .
1521	CRESWELL, Joseph (Cont'd)	18	NE	1861-01-30		A1
1395	CRISWELL, George	12	E½SW	1848-07-01		A1
1633	CUNNINGHAM, William	35	E½NE	1824-05-10		A1
1494	DANIEL, John P	2	E½1NE	1860-03-01		A1
1417	DARRAH, Henry T	6	E½SW	1859-05-02		A1
1418	" "	6	SESE	1859-05-02		A1
1419	" "	6	W½SE	1859-05-02		A1
1420	" "	7	N½NE	1859-05-02		A1
1421	" "	7	NENW	1859-05-02		A1
1464	DAY, Job	29	NENE	1857-06-10		A1
1462	" "	20	E½SE	1858-05-03		A1
1463	" "	21	N½SW	1858-05-03		A1
1350	DE CLOUS, ANTHONY	23	E½SW	1856-09-01		A1
1351	" "	23	SWSW	1856-09-01		A1
1380	DECLOIS, Francis	4	E½1NE	1857-06-10		A1
1381	" "	4	E½2NE	1857-06-10		A1
1581	DUCKWORTH, Polaski	15	E½NW	1840-10-01		A1
1582	" "	15	E½SW	1840-10-01		A1
1577	DUCKWORTH, Polaski C	14	W½SW	1840-10-01		A1
1579	" "	15	SENE	1840-10-01		A1
1578	" "	15	N½SE	1857-06-10		A1
1580	" "	15	SWSW	1857-06-10		A1
1478	DUNKLIN, Stephen T	31	2NW	1849-05-01		A1 G72
1522	ENOCH, Joseph	8	NESE	1859-11-01		A1
1523	" "	9	SESE	1859-11-01		A1 F
1524	" "	9	SW	1859-11-01		A1 F
1525	" "	9	W½SE	1859-11-01		A1 F
1563	FITZWATER, Noah	36	E½NW	1838-09-07		A1
1619	FITZWATER, Uriah	36	NESW	1838-09-07		A1
1602	GRANT, Samuel B	7	S½1NW	1860-03-01		A1
1603	" "	7	SWNE	1860-03-01		A1
1374	GREENLEE, Elijah F	31	S½2SW	1911-02-03		A1
1527	HAEFNER, Joseph W	28	SWSW	1857-10-30		A1 G123
1528	" "	31	N½2SW	1857-10-30		A1 G123
1529	" "	33	NESW	1859-05-02		A1 G123
1616	HARGES, Thomas	35	E½SE	1824-05-20		A1
1637	HARGIS, William	11	SWSE	1843-04-10		A1
1344	HARLOW, Alden	34	NWSW	1844-01-19		A1 G125
1344	HARLOW, Josiah	34	NWSW	1844-01-19		A1 G125
1484	HENWOOD, John	7	SE	1859-05-02		A1
1485	" "	8	NESW	1859-05-02		A1
1486	" "	8	NWSE	1859-05-02		A1
1487	" "	8	W½SW	1859-05-02		A1
1346	HIGHT, Alfred D	1	E½SE	1836-01-14		A1
1347	HILL, Alfred	25	NENE	1856-01-15		A1
1348	" "	25	NWSE	1856-01-15		A1
1349	" "	25	SWNE	1856-01-15		A1
1345	HILL, Alfred A	25	NWNE	1859-05-02		A1
1459	HILL, Jesse	12	W½SW	1824-05-01		A1
1508	HILL, Jonas M	6	1NW	1874-05-06		A1
1509	" "	6	2SW	1874-05-06		A1
1488	HINKSON, John	35	W½SE	1824-05-10		A1
1638	HINKSON, William	35	W½NE	1821-09-24		A1
1489	HOLT, John	36	E½SE	1840-10-01		A1
1639	HUDSON, William	36	W½SE	1856-09-01		A1
1440	HUNT, James	25	SESE	1854-11-15		A1
1640	ISRAEL, William	24	NWSW	1835-10-01		A1
1457	JOHNSON, Jeptha B	34	NWSE	1840-10-01		A1
1458	" "	34	SENW	1840-10-01		A1
1454	" "	10	NWSE	1859-05-02		A1
1455	" "	10	W½NE	1859-05-02		A1
1456	" "	11	E½SW	1859-05-02		A1
1471	JOHNSON, John C	27	SESE	1840-10-01		A1
1482	JOHNSON, John H	24	NESW	1835-09-09		A1
1480	" "	10	NENW	1846-01-01		A1
1481	" "	10	NWNW	1856-03-10		A1
1483	" "	3	SWSE	1856-03-10		A1
1495	JOHNSON, John P	23	SWNE	1835-09-09		A1
1496	" "	23	SWSE	1835-10-01		A1
1620	JOHNSON, Uriah	3	E½SW	1845-10-01		A1
1531	JOHNSTON, Josiah	11	W½NW	1824-05-10		A1
1530	" "	10	E½NE	1825-07-15		A1
1621	JOHNSTON, Uriah	14	NE	1824-05-10		A1

ID	Individual in Patent	Sec.	Sec. Part	Date Issued	Other Counties	For More Info . . .
1622	JOHNSTON, Uriah (Cont'd)	14	W½NW	1824-05-10		A1
1414	KEISEN, Henry	28	SESW	1860-03-01		A1
1415	" "	28	SWNW	1860-03-01		A1
1411	KIESEN, Heinrich	28	N½SW	1858-05-03		A1
1412	" "	28	NWSE	1858-05-03		A1
1413	" "	28	W½NE	1858-05-03		A1 V1549
1466	LA BARGE, JOHN B	3	NW	1859-11-01		A1
1467	" "	3	W½SW	1859-11-01		A1
1562	LARGENT, Nisbet G	2	SWSE	1857-06-10		A1
1358	LEVENS, Bazil W	11	E½NW	1824-05-10		A1
1566	LEWIS, Oscar	4	E½1NW	1860-03-01		A1
1567	" "	4	W½1NE	1860-03-01		A1
1568	" "	4	W½2NE	1860-03-01		A1
1571	LITTEN, Patrick	7	2NW	1856-11-01		A1
1569	" "	18	2NW	1859-11-01		A1
1570	" "	7	1SW	1859-11-01		A1
1572	" "	7	2SW	1859-11-01		A1
1370	LONG, Edward	1	1NE	1859-11-01		A1
1371	" "	1	1NW	1859-11-01		A1
1372	" "	1	2NW	1859-11-01		A1
1373	" "	1	N½SW	1859-11-01		A1
1550	LYNCH, Michael M	25	S½NW	1857-06-10		A1
1551	" "	25	SW	1857-06-10		A1
1552	" "	25	SWSE	1857-06-10		A1
1553	" "	36	NWNW	1857-06-10		A1
1573	LYON, Peter	34	W½NE	1835-09-02		A1
1441	MAJOR, James M	15	S½SE	1857-04-15		A1
1442	" "	22	N½NE	1857-04-15		A1
1443	" "	22	S½NE	1859-05-02		A1
1444	" "	22	SENW	1859-05-02		A1
1445	" "	23	NWNW	1859-05-02		A1
1409	MANN, Harvey	14	SESW	1860-03-01		A1
1410	" "	23	NENW	1860-03-01		A1
1352	MANNING, Arthur	17	E½NW	1858-05-03		A1
1354	" "	17	W½NE	1858-05-03		A1
1357	" "	8	SWSE	1858-05-03		A1
1353	" "	17	NENE	1859-05-02		A1
1355	" "	8	SESE	1859-05-02		A1
1356	" "	8	SESW	1859-05-02		A1
1565	MARTIN, Noah	34	NENE	1835-09-09		A1
1564	" "	26	NWSW	1856-01-15		A1
1432	MATLOCK, Isom	27	SENE	1854-03-01		A1
1431	" "	27	NESE	1856-01-15		A1
1430	" "	26	SWNW	1856-09-01		A1
1433	" "	27	W½NE	1856-09-01		A1
1428	" "	22	NESW	1859-05-02		A1
1429	" "	22	NWSE	1859-05-02		A1
1490	MATLOCK, John	22	SESW	1859-05-02		A1
1491	" "	22	SWSE	1859-05-02		A1
1527	MATTHEWS, William A	28	SWSW	1857-10-30		A1 G123
1629	" "	30	E½SE	1857-10-30		A1
1528	" "	31	N½2SW	1857-10-30		A1 G123
1630	" "	31	N½SE	1857-10-30		A1
1631	" "	31	NE	1857-10-30		A1
1529	" "	33	NESW	1859-05-02		A1 G123
1641	MCCRACKEN, William	5	W½1NW	1859-11-01		A1
1642	" "	5	W½2NW	1859-11-01		A1
1643	" "	6	NE	1859-11-01		A1
1574	MCDONOUGH, Peter	36	SWNW	1860-03-01		A1
1575	MCGUIRE, Philip	1	2NE	1860-03-01		A1
1652	MCKENZIE, William W	34	NWNW	1840-10-01		A1
1367	MCKEON, Coleman	5	E½1NW	1859-05-02		A1
1368	" "	5	E½2NW	1859-05-02		A1
1369	" "	5	W½1NE	1859-05-02		A1
1644	MITCHELL, William	36	SENE	1852-08-02		A1
1492	MORRISON, John	14	E½NW	1824-06-01		A1
1545	MORRISON, Lewis	26	E½SW	1824-05-10		A1
1408	MOSHER, Guy	27	NWSW	1860-03-01		A1
1601	MYERS, Rufus P	33	SWNE	1860-03-01		A1
1645	NEALY, William	19	SWNE	1873-04-01		A1
1634	NICHOLS, William D	24	SWSW	1860-03-01		A1
1646	OCHELTREE, William	12	NW	1825-09-20		A1 G193
1493	ORME, John	36	SESW	1848-07-01		A1

ID	Individual in Patent	Sec.	Sec. Part	Date Issued	Other Counties	For More Info . . .
1576	ORME, Philip	36	W½SW	1848-07-01		A1
1500	PARKER, John T	4	2NW	1859-11-01		A1
1501	" "	4	W½1NW	1859-11-01		A1
1502	" "	5	2NE	1859-11-01		A1
1503	" "	5	E½1NE	1859-11-01		A1
1647	PARKINSON, William	35	E½SW	1840-10-01		A1
1384	PENROSE, Fred	27	SWNW	1904-12-29		A1
1437	PERRY, James F	13	NW	1824-05-10		A1 G195
1437	PERRY, Samuel	13	NW	1824-05-10		A1 G195
1468	POLLARD, John B	36	SWNE	1836-01-14		A1
1596	POWELL, Robert W	21	E½SE	1859-05-02		A1 V1548
1597	" "	22	W½SW	1859-05-02		A1
1598	" "	27	E½NW	1859-05-02		A1
1599	" "	27	NWNW	1859-05-02		A1
1600	" "	28	NENE	1859-05-02		A1 V1549
1385	PRADER, Georg	28	N½NW	1858-05-03		A1
1397	PRADER, George	21	S½SW	1857-06-10		A1
1399	" "	21	W½SE	1857-06-10		A1 V1548
1396	" "	21	NENW	1859-05-02		A1 R1383
1398	" "	21	SWNE	1859-05-02		A1
1375	PUCKETT, Elijah	2	NWSW	1856-01-15		A1
1376	" "	3	SESE	1856-01-15		A1
1497	PUCKETT, John	3	1NE	1857-09-01		A1
1498	" "	3	NESE	1857-09-01		A1
1595	PUCKETT, Robert	2	SWSW	1854-11-15		A1
1593	" "	11	NENE	1857-06-10		A1
1594	" "	2	SESE	1857-06-10		A1
1377	RANEY, Felix	10	SWSE	1835-09-09		A1
1379	" "	26	SWSW	1835-09-09		A1 G202
1378	" "	15	NENE	1840-10-01		A1
1379	RANEY, James	26	SWSW	1835-09-09		A1 G202
1379	RANEY, Valentine	26	SWSW	1835-09-09		A1 G202
1646	RECTOR, Elias	12	NW	1825-09-20		A1 G193
1479	RENFRO, John F	2	E½NW	1840-10-01		A1
1649	REYNOLDS, William	4	W½SW	1862-05-01		A1
1650	" "	5	E½SW	1862-05-01		A1
1651	" "	5	SE	1862-05-01		A1
1424	ROLL, Isaac	21	SENE	1857-09-01		A1
1425	" "	22	NWNW	1857-09-01		A1
1426	" "	22	SWNW	1857-09-01		A1
1400	RUTLEDGE, George	1	SWSW	1857-06-10		A1
1407	SCHANE, Gotleib	1	SESW	1860-03-01		A1
1416	SCHOOL, Henry	17	SENE	1860-03-01		A1
1548	SCHWICE, Marthis	21	SE	1857-06-10		A1 V1399, 1596
1549	" "	28	N½NE	1857-06-10		A1 V1413, 1600
1427	SCOTT, Isaac T	35	W½SW	1856-09-01		A1
1446	SHIRLEY, James M	33	W½NW	1857-06-10		A1
1447	" "	33	W½SW	1857-06-10		A1
1403	SHORE, Gilbert	24	SWNE	1835-09-09		A1
1404	" "	24	W½SE	1840-10-01		A1
1401	" "	24	E½SE	1857-04-15		A1
1402	" "	24	SESW	1857-04-15		A1
1405	" "	25	N½NW	1857-04-15		A1
1406	" "	26	NENE	1857-04-15		A1
1499	SHORE, John	2	N½SE	1859-05-02		A1
1610	SHORE, Stephen D	10	NESE	1849-06-01		A1
1611	" "	11	NWSW	1849-06-01		A1
1612	" "	11	SESE	1849-06-01		A1
1557	SHUMATE, Nathan	4	E½SW	1859-11-01		A1
1558	" "	4	NWSE	1859-11-01		A1
1559	" "	4	S½SE	1859-11-01		A1
1560	" "	9	NENE	1859-11-01		A1
1561	" "	9	W½NE	1859-11-01		A1
1534	SILVERS, Levi H	13	W½SE	1833-06-08		A1 G208
1535	" "	13	W½SW	1833-06-08		A1 G208
1533	" "	13	NESE	1835-09-09		A1 G208
1537	" "	24	NWNE	1835-09-09		A1 G208
1536	" "	24	E½NE	1840-10-01		A1 G208
1605	SILVERS, Samuel	13	E½SW	1821-09-24		A1
1534	SILVERS, Washington	13	W½SE	1833-06-08		A1 G208
1535	" "	13	W½SW	1833-06-08		A1 G208
1533	" "	13	NESE	1835-09-09		A1 G208
1537	" "	24	NWNE	1835-09-09		A1 G208

ID	Individual in Patent	Sec.	Sec. Part	Date Issued	Other Counties	For More Info . . .
1626	SILVERS, Washington (Cont'd)	13	SESE	1835-10-01		A1
1536	" "	24	E½NE	1840-10-01		A1 G208
1627	" "	14	E½SE	1857-04-15		A1
1628	" "	14	SWSE	1857-04-15		A1
1359	SMITH, Benjamin F	26	SENE	1856-01-15		A1
1518	SMITHER, Joel	23	E½SE	1824-05-10		A1 G73
1365	SPRINGER, Charles	24	W½NW	1821-09-24		A1
1364	" "	23	E½NE	1824-05-10		A1
1362	SPRINGER, Charles H	14	NESW	1857-09-01		A1
1363	" "	14	NWSE	1857-09-01		A1
1448	SPRINGER, James M	26	NWSE	1843-04-10		A1
1449	SPRINGER, James P	23	NWNE	1840-10-01		A1
1450	" "	23	NWSE	1840-10-01		A1
1451	" "	23	SENW	1840-10-01		A1
1546	SPRINGER, Margaret	33	SESW	1860-03-01		A1
1547	" "	33	SWSE	1860-03-01		A1
1589	SPRINGER, Robert F	26	SESE	1849-06-01		A1
1592	" "	35	S½NW	1856-01-15		A1
1588	" "	26	NWNE	1856-09-01		A1
1590	" "	34	E½SE	1856-09-01		A1
1591	" "	34	SENE	1856-09-01		A1
1587	" "	26	NESE	1859-05-02		A1
1636	SPRINGER, William H	26	SWNE	1856-06-10		A1
1614	STOVALL, Thomas B	2	SWNW	1843-04-10		A1
1617	SUICOCK, Thomas	1	3NW	1859-11-01		A1
1618	" "	2	E½3NE	1859-11-01		A1
1585	SUMMERS, Richard	26	E½NW	1824-05-10		A1
1586	" "	35	N½NW	1835-09-09		A1
1604	SUMMERS, Samuel R	27	NWSE	1835-09-09		A1
1623	SUMMERS, Valentine	26	NWNW	1835-09-09		A1 G218
1624	SUMMERS, Valentine T	26	SWSE	1835-09-09		A1 G217
1623	SUMMERS, William	26	NWNW	1835-09-09		A1 G218
1624	SUMMERS, William H	26	SWSE	1835-09-09		A1 G217
1538	TILLSON, Levi	10	E½SW	1856-01-15		A1
1540	" "	10	SENW	1856-01-15		A1
1542	" "	10	SWSW	1856-01-15		A1
1539	" "	10	NWSW	1859-05-02		A1
1541	" "	10	SWNW	1859-05-02		A1
1543	" "	9	NESE	1859-05-02		A1
1544	" "	9	SENE	1859-05-02		A1
1526	TODD, Joseph	18	2SW	1858-05-03		A1
1648	TROUTT, William R	4	NESE	1859-11-01		A1
1532	TUFLY, Josias	27	NESW	1857-06-10		A1
1635	WALKER, William G	33	E½NW	1840-10-01		A1
1469	WALSER, John B	11	N½SE	1856-11-01		A1
1470	" "	11	S½NE	1856-11-01		A1
1504	WARD, John	22	E½SE	1860-03-01		A1
1505	" "	23	NWSW	1860-03-01		A1
1506	" "	23	SWNW	1860-03-01		A1
1507	" "	27	NENE	1860-03-01		A1
1366	WARSON, Charles	19	2NW	1860-03-01		A1
1625	WATSON, Walter	15	W½NE	1824-05-10		A1
1607	WHITE, Samuel	17	NWSW	1857-06-10		A1
1606	" "	17	E½SW	1859-05-02		A1
1608	" "	17	SE	1859-05-02		A1
1609	" "	17	SWSW	1859-05-02		A1
1360	WILKSON, Bernard C	12	SWNE	1854-05-01		A1
1361	" "	12	W½SE	1854-05-01		A1
1653	WILLIAMS, William	15	NWNW	1838-09-07		A1
1655	" "	15	SWNW	1840-10-01		A1
1654	" "	15	NWSW	1856-09-01		A1
1656	WILSON, William	22	NENW	1840-10-01		A1
1452	WRIGHT, James	36	NENE	1848-07-01		A1
1453	" "	36	NWNE	1854-11-15		A1
1382	YELLER, Frantzes	21	N½NE	1860-03-01		A1
1383	" "	21	NENW	1860-03-01		A1 R1396

Patent Map

T38-N R1-E
5th PM Meridian

Map Group 13

Township Statistics

Parcels Mapped	:	313
Number of Patents	:	203
Number of Individuals	:	157
Patentees Identified	:	149
Number of Surnames	:	112
Multi-Patentee Parcels	:	17
Oldest Patent Date	:	9/24/1821
Most Recent Patent	:	2/3/1911
Block/Lot Parcels	:	40
Parcels Re - Issued	:	1
Parcels that Overlap	:	6
Cities and Towns	:	2
Cemeteries	:	5

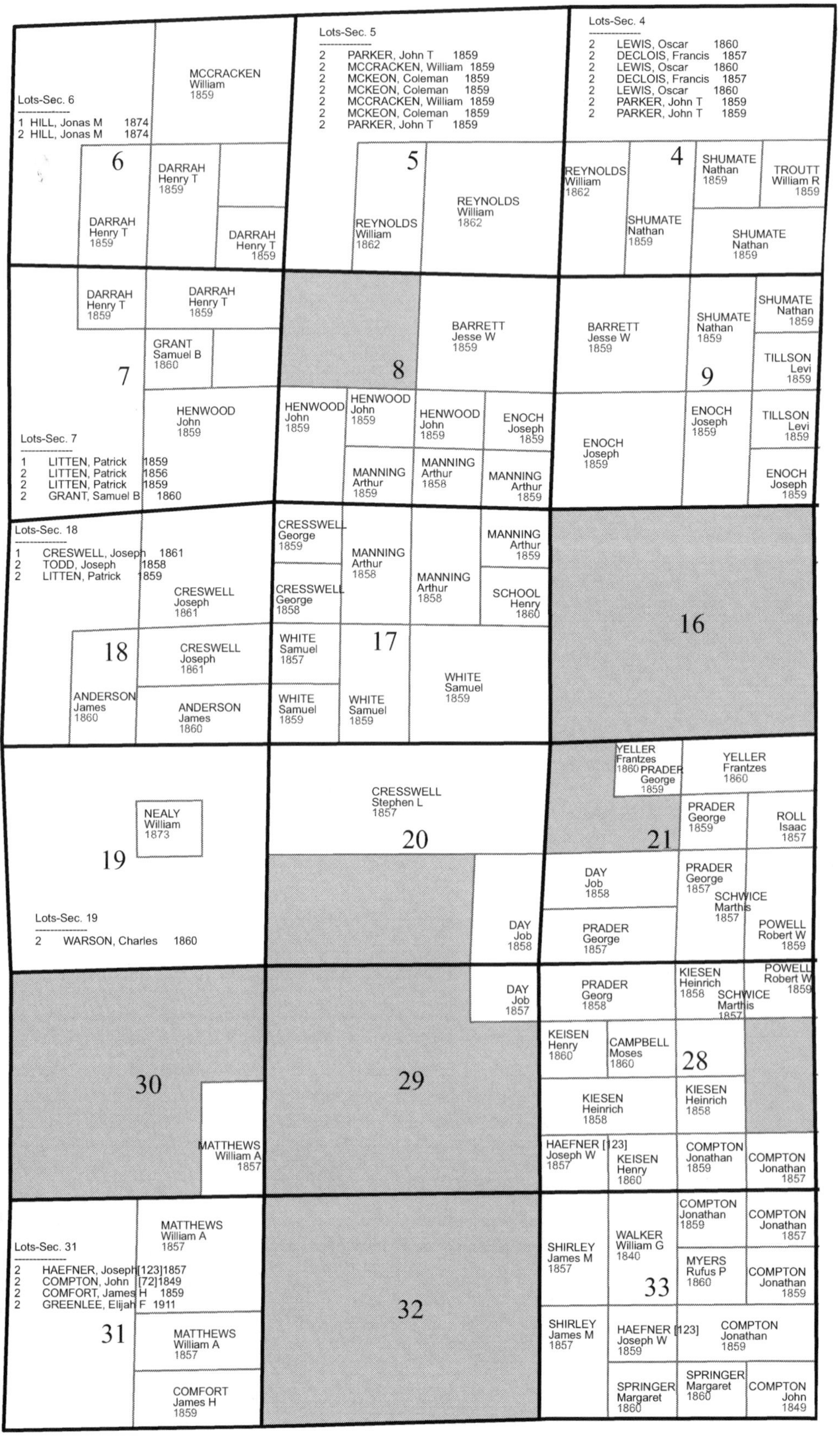

Lots-Sec. 6
1 HILL, Jonas M 1874
2 HILL, Jonas M 1874

MCCRACKEN William 1859

6
DARRAH Henry T 1859
DARRAH Henry T 1859
DARRAH Henry T 1859

Lots-Sec. 5
2 PARKER, John T 1859
2 MCCRACKEN, William 1859
2 MCKEON, Coleman 1859
2 MCKEON, Coleman 1859
2 MCCRACKEN, William 1859
2 MCKEON, Coleman 1859
2 PARKER, John T 1859

5
REYNOLDS William 1862
REYNOLDS William 1862

Lots-Sec. 4
2 LEWIS, Oscar 1860
2 DECLOIS, Francis 1857
2 LEWIS, Oscar 1860
2 DECLOIS, Francis 1857
2 LEWIS, Oscar 1860
2 PARKER, John T 1859
2 PARKER, John T 1859

4
REYNOLDS William 1862
SHUMATE Nathan 1859
TROUTT William R 1859
SHUMATE Nathan 1859
SHUMATE Nathan 1859

7
DARRAH Henry T 1859
DARRAH Henry T 1859
GRANT Samuel B 1860
HENWOOD John 1859

Lots-Sec. 7
1 LITTEN, Patrick 1859
2 LITTEN, Patrick 1856
2 LITTEN, Patrick 1859
2 GRANT, Samuel B 1860

8
BARRETT Jesse W 1859
HENWOOD John 1859
HENWOOD John 1859
HENWOOD John 1859
ENOCH Joseph 1859
MANNING Arthur 1859
MANNING Arthur 1858
MANNING Arthur 1859

9
BARRETT Jesse W 1859
SHUMATE Nathan 1859
SHUMATE Nathan 1859
TILLSON Levi 1859
ENOCH Joseph 1859
ENOCH Joseph 1859
TILLSON Levi 1859
ENOCH Joseph 1859

Lots-Sec. 18
1 CRESWELL, Joseph 1861
2 TODD, Joseph 1858
2 LITTEN, Patrick 1859

18
CRESWELL Joseph 1861
CRESWELL Joseph 1861
ANDERSON James 1860
ANDERSON James 1860

17
CRESSWELL George 1859
MANNING Arthur 1858
MANNING Arthur 1858
MANNING Arthur 1859
CRESSWELL George 1858
SCHOOL Henry 1860
WHITE Samuel 1857
WHITE Samuel 1859
WHITE Samuel 1859
WHITE Samuel 1859

16

19
NEALY William 1873

Lots-Sec. 19
2 WARSON, Charles 1860

20
CRESSWELL Stephen L 1857
DAY Job 1858

21
YELLER Frantzes 1860
PRADER George 1859
YELLER Frantzes 1860
PRADER George 1859
ROLL Isaac 1857
DAY Job 1858
PRADER George 1857
SCHWICE Marthis 1857
POWELL Robert W 1859
PRADER George 1857

30
MATTHEWS William A 1857

29
DAY Job 1857

28
PRADER Georg 1858
KIESEN Heinrich 1858
SCHWICE Marthis 1857
POWELL Robert W 1859
KEISEN Henry 1860
CAMPBELL Moses 1860
KIESEN Heinrich 1858
KIESEN Heinrich 1858
HAEFNER [123] Joseph W 1857
KEISEN Henry 1860
COMPTON Jonathan 1859
COMPTON Jonathan 1857

Lots-Sec. 31
2 HAEFNER, Joseph [123] 1857
2 COMPTON, John [72] 1849
2 COMFORT, James H 1859
2 GREENLEE, Elijah F 1911

31
MATTHEWS William A 1857
MATTHEWS William A 1857
COMFORT James H 1859

32

33
SHIRLEY James M 1857
WALKER William G 1840
COMPTON Jonathan 1859
COMPTON Jonathan 1857
MYERS Rufus P 1860
COMPTON Jonathan 1859
SHIRLEY James M 1857
HAEFNER [123] Joseph W 1859
COMPTON Jonathan 1859
SPRINGER Margaret 1860
SPRINGER Margaret 1860
COMPTON John 1849

Lots-Sec. 3
1 CRESWELL, George 1848
1 PUCKETT, John 1857

BARGE John B La 1859

3

BARGE John B La 1859
BASS [10] William 1843
PUCKETT John 1857
JOHNSON Uriah 1845
JOHNSON John H 1856
PUCKETT Elijah 1856

CRESWELL George 1835
STOVALL Thomas B 1843

Lots-Sec. 2
2 DANIEL, John P 1860
2 SUICOCK, Thomas 1859
2 CRESSWELL, George 1849
2 BASS, Thomas 1844
2 CRESSWELL, George 1859

RENFRO John F 1840

2

PUCKETT Elijah 1856
ANDERSON John 1834
SHORE John 1859
PUCKETT Robert 1854
LARGENT Nisbet G 1857
PUCKETT Robert 1857

Lots-Sec. 1
1 LONG, Edward 1859
1 LONG, Edward 1859
2 MCGUIRE, Philip 1860
2 LONG, Edward 1859
3 SUICOCK, Thomas 1859

1

LONG Edward 1859
HIGHT Alfred D 1836
RUTLEDGE George 1857
SCHANE Gotleib 1860

JOHNSON John H 1856
JOHNSON John H 1846
JOHNSON Jeptha B 1859
JOHNSTON Josiah 1825
TILLSON Levi 1859
TILLSON Levi 1856

10

TILLSON Levi 1859
JOHNSON Jeptha B 1859
SHORE Stephen D 1849
TILLSON Levi 1856
TILLSON Levi 1856
RANEY Felix 1835
COCK Joseph 1860

JOHNSTON Josiah 1824
BASS Nancy 1857
PUCKETT Robert 1857
LEVENS Bazil W 1824
WALSER John B 1856

11

SHORE Stephen D 1849
WALSER John B 1856
JOHNSON Jeptha B 1859
HARGIS William 1843
SHORE Stephen D 1849

CASEY John 1856
CASEY John 1856
OCHELTREE [193] William 1825
WILKSON Bernard C 1854

12

HILL Jesse 1824
WILKSON Bernard C 1854
CRISWELL George 1848

WILLIAMS William 1838
RANEY Felix 1840
DUCKWORTH Polaski 1840
WILLIAMS William 1840
WATSON Walter 1824
DUCKWORTH Polaski C 1840

15

WILLIAMS William 1856
DUCKWORTH Polaski 1840
DUCKWORTH Polaski C 1857
DUCKWORTH Polaski C 1857
MAJOR James M 1857

JOHNSTON Uriah 1824
MORRISON John 1824
JOHNSTON Uriah 1824

14

SPRINGER Charles H 1857
SPRINGER Charles H 1857
DUCKWORTH Polaski C 1840
SILVERS Washington 1857
MANN Harvey 1860
SILVERS Washington 1857

BASS Richard 1848
PERRY [195] James F 1824
BASS Nancy 1848

13

SILVERS [208] Levi H 1835
SILVERS [208] Levi H 1833
SILVERS [208] Levi H 1833
SILVERS Samuel 1821
SILVERS Washington 1835

ROLL Isaac 1857
WILSON William 1840
MAJOR James M 1857
ROLL Isaac 1857
MAJOR James M 1859

22

MAJOR James M 1859
POWELL Robert W 1859
MATLOCK Isom 1859
MATLOCK Isom 1859
MATLOCK John 1859
MATLOCK John 1859
WARD John 1860

MAJOR James M 1859
MANN Harvey 1860
SPRINGER James P 1840
WARD John 1860
SPRINGER James P 1840
JOHNSON John P 1835
SPRINGER Charles 1824
WARD John 1860

23

SPRINGER James P 1840
COMPTON [73] Joseph 1824
CLOUS Anthony De 1856
CLOUS Anthony De 1856
JOHNSON John P 1835

SILVERS [208] Levi H 1835
SPRINGER Charles 1821
SILVERS [208] Levi H 1840
COMPTON Richard 1824
SHORE Gilbert 1835

24

ISRAEL William 1835
JOHNSON John H 1835
SHORE Gilbert 1840
SHORE Gilbert 1857
NICHOLS William D 1860
SHORE Gilbert 1857

POWELL Robert W 1859
MATLOCK Isom 1856
WARD John 1860
PENROSE Fred 1904
POWELL Robert W 1859

27

MATLOCK Isom 1854
MOSHER Guy 1860
TUFLY Josias 1857
SUMMERS Samuel R 1835
MATLOCK Isom 1856
CRESSWELL George 1856
CRESSWELL George 1856
CRESWELL George 1856
JOHNSON John C 1840

SUMMERS [218] Valentine 1835
SPRINGER Robert F 1856
SHORE Gilbert 1857
MATLOCK Isom 1856
SUMMERS Richard 1824
SPRINGER William H 1856
SMITH Benjamin F 1856
MARTIN Noah 1856

26

SPRINGER James M 1843
SPRINGER Robert F 1859
MORRISON Lewis 1824
SUMMERS [217] Valentine T 1835
SPRINGER Robert F 1849
RANEY [202] Felix 1835

SHORE Gilbert 1857
HILL Alfred A 1859
HILL Alfred 1856
LYNCH Michael M 1857
HILL Alfred 1856
BELL Hugh 1840

25

HILL Alfred 1856
BELL Hugh 1840
LYNCH Michael M 1857
LYNCH Michael M 1857
HUNT James 1854

MCKENZIE William W 1840
COMPTON Jonathan 1857
LYON Peter 1835
MARTIN Noah 1835
COWAN Jabez C 1860
JOHNSON Jeptha B 1840

34

SPRINGER Robert F 1856
HARLOW [125] Alden 1844
JOHNSON Jeptha B 1840
COMPTON John 1831
SPRINGER Robert F 1856
COMPTON John 1840
COMPTON John 1840

SUMMERS Richard 1835
HINKSON William 1821
CUNNINGHAM William 1824
SPRINGER Robert F 1856
SCOTT Isaac T 1856

35

HINKSON John 1824
PARKINSON William 1840
HARGES Thomas 1824

LYNCH Michael M 1857
FITZWATER Noah 1838
WRIGHT James 1854
WRIGHT James 1848
MCDONOUGH Peter 1860

36

POLLARD John B 1836
MITCHELL William 1852
ORME Philip 1848
FITZWATER Uriah 1838
HUDSON William 1856
ORME John 1848
HOLT John 1840

Helpful Hints

1. This Map's INDEX can be found on the preceding pages.
2. Refer to Map "C" to see where this Township lies within Washington County, Missouri.
3. Numbers within square brackets [ ] denote a multi-patentee land parcel (multi-owner). Refer to Appendix "C" for a full list of members in this group.
4. Areas that look to be crowded with Patentees usually indicate multiple sales of the same parcel (Re-issues) or Overlapping parcels. See this Township's Index for an explanation of these and other circumstances that might explain "odd" groupings of Patentees on this map.

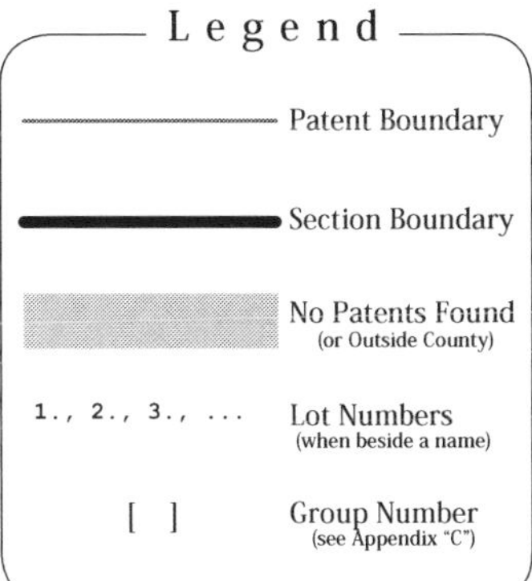

Scale: Section = 1 mile X 1 mile
(generally, with some exceptions)

Road Map

T38-N R1-E
5th PM Meridian

Map Group 13

Cities & Towns

Ebo
Fourche a Renault (historical)

Cemeteries

Fourche a Renault Cemetery
Liberty Cemetery
Martin Cemetery
Souls Chapel Cemetery
Stephens Cemetery

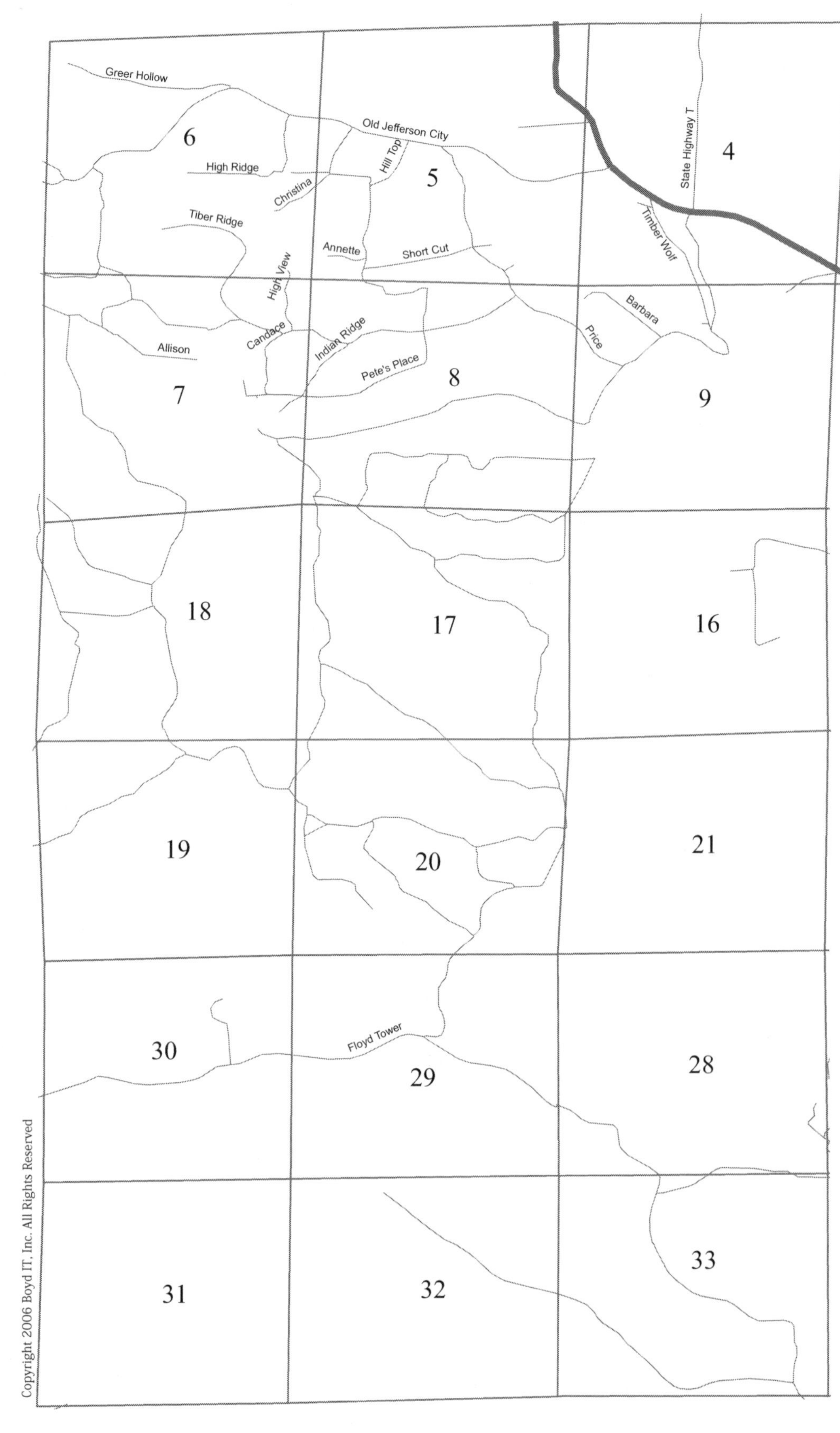

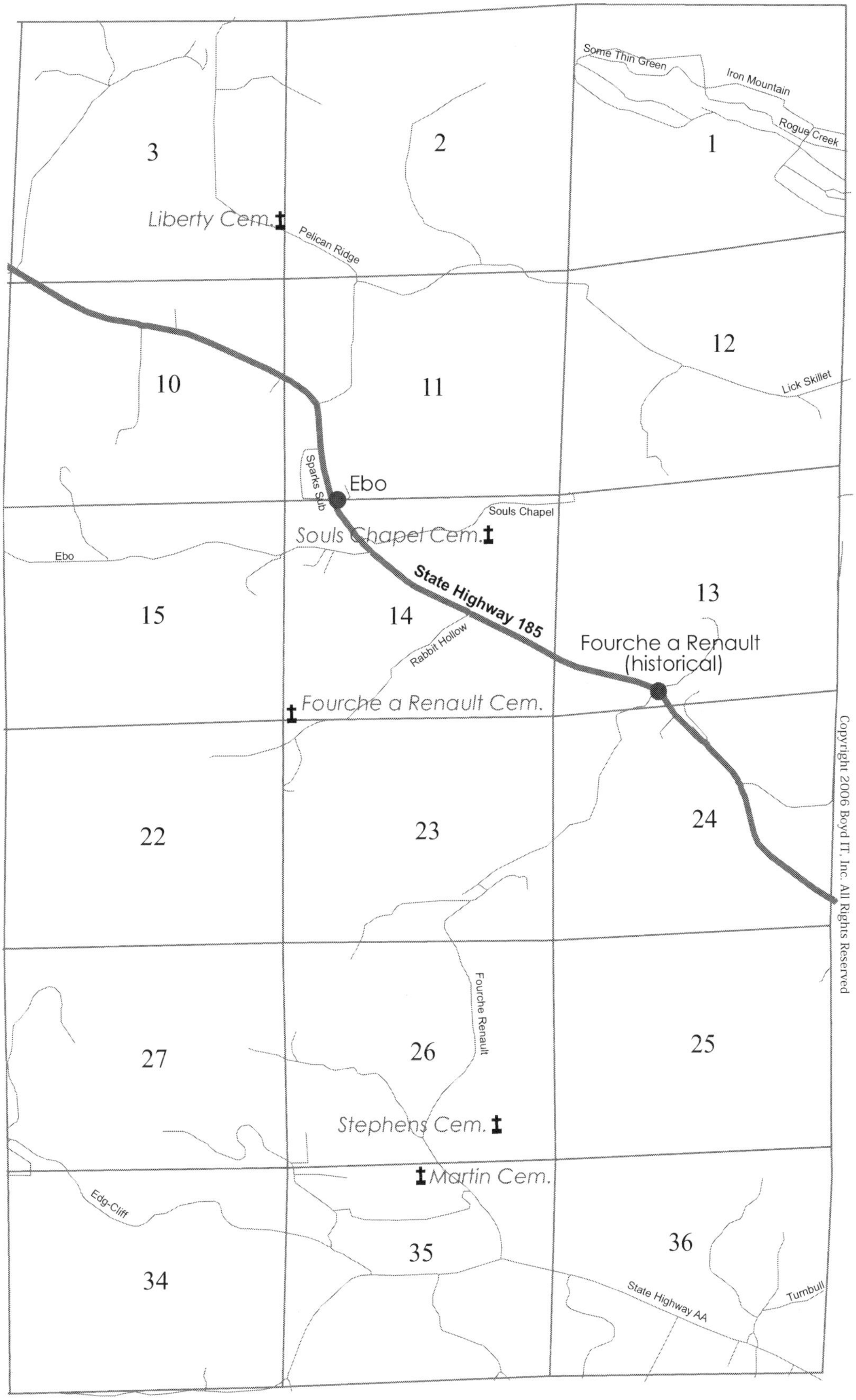

Some Thin Green
Iron Mountain
Rogue Creek
1
2
3
Liberty Cem.
Pelican Ridge
10
11
12
Lick Skillet
Sparks Sub
Ebo
Souls Chapel
Souls Chapel Cem.
Ebo
State Highway 185
15
14
13
Rabbit Hollow
Fourche a Renault
(historical)
Fourche a Renault Cem.
22
23
24
Fourche Renault
27
26
25
Stephens Cem.
Martin Cem.
Edg-Cliff
34
35
36
State Highway AA
Turnbull

Helpful Hints

1. This road map has a number of uses, but primarily it is to help you: a) find the present location of land owned by your ancestors (at least the general area), b) find cemeteries and city-centers, and c) estimate the route/roads used by Census-takers & tax-assessors.
2. If you plan to travel to Washington County to locate cemeteries or land parcels, please pick up a modern travel map for the area before you do. Mapping old land parcels on modern maps is not as exact a science as you might think. Just the slightest variations in public land survey coordinates, estimates of parcel boundaries, or road-map deviations can greatly alter a map's representation of how a road either does or doesn't cross a particular parcel of land.

Legend
Section Lines
Interstates
Highways
Other Roads
Cities/Towns
Cemeteries

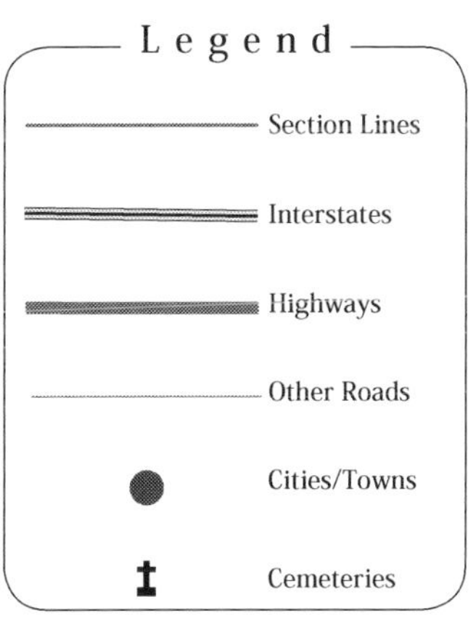

Scale: Section = 1 mile X 1 mile
(generally, with some exceptions)

Historical Map

T38-N R1-E
5th PM Meridian

Map Group 13

Cities & Towns
Ebo
Fourche a Renault (historical)

Cemeteries
Fourche a Renault Cemetery
Liberty Cemetery
Martin Cemetery
Souls Chapel Cemetery
Stephens Cemetery

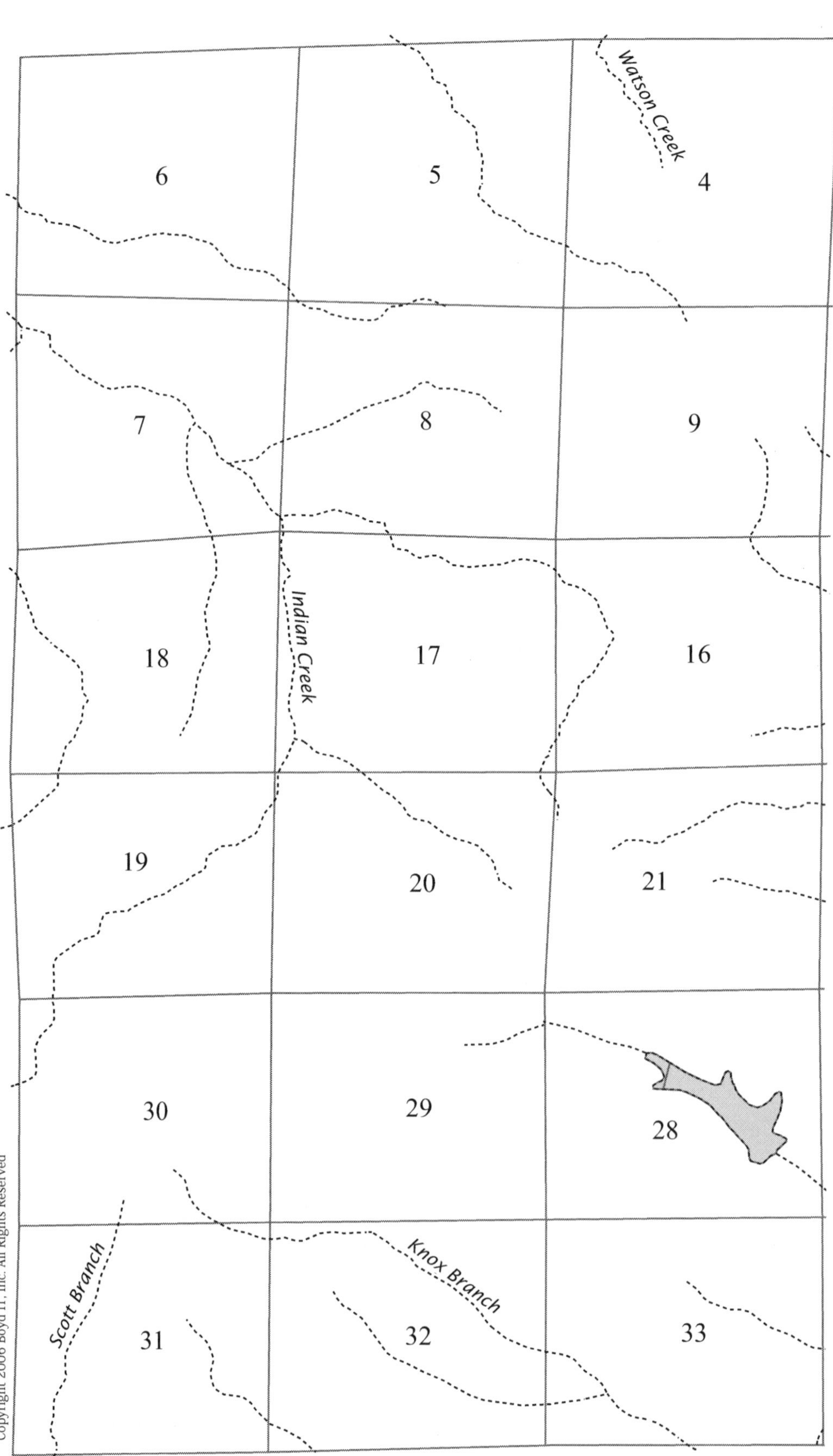

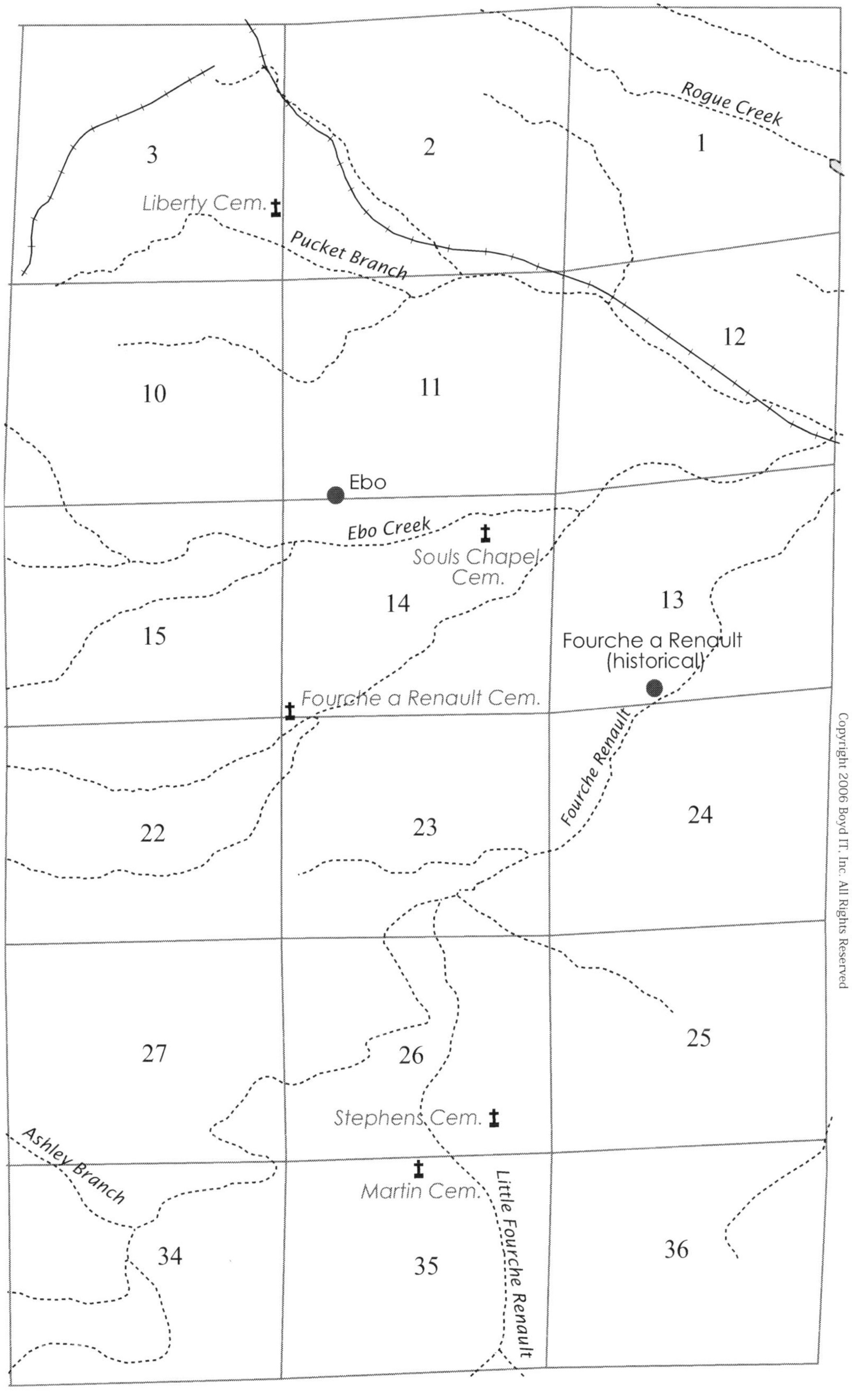

Rogue Creek

3 2 1

Liberty Cem.

Pucket Branch

12

10 11

Ebo

Ebo Creek

Souls Chapel Cem.

14 13

15

Fourche a Renault (historical)

Fourche a Renault Cem.

Fourche Renault

22 23 24

27 26 25

Stephens Cem.

Ashley Branch

Martin Cem.

Little Fourche Renault

34 35 36

Helpful Hints

1. This Map takes a different look at the same Congressional Township displayed in the preceding two maps. It presents features that can help you better envision the historical development of the area: a) Water-bodies (lakes & ponds), b) Water-courses (rivers, streams, etc.), c) Railroads, d) City/town center-points (where they were oftentimes located when first settled), and e) Cemeteries.

2. Using this "Historical" map in tandem with this Township's Patent Map and Road Map, may lead you to some interesting discoveries. You will often find roads, towns, cemeteries, and waterways are named after nearby landowners: sometimes those names will be the ones you are researching. See how many of these research gems you can find here in Washington County.

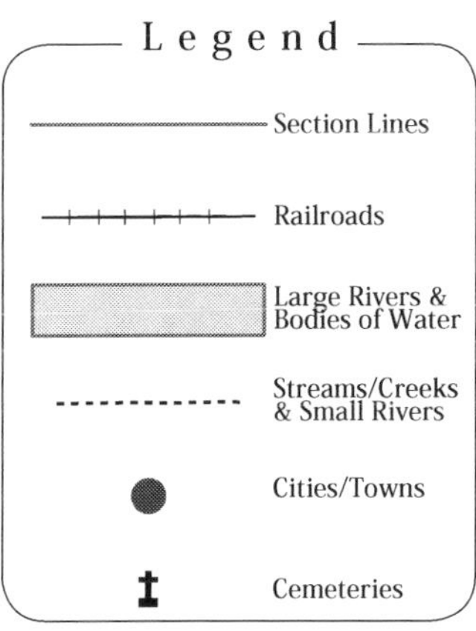

Scale: Section = 1 mile X 1 mile
(there are some exceptions)

Map Group 14: Index to Land Patents

Township 38-North Range 2-East (5th PM)

After you locate an individual in this Index, take note of the Section and Section Part then proceed to the Land Patent map on the pages immediately following. You should have no difficulty locating the corresponding parcel of land.

The "For More Info" Column will lead you to more information about the underlying Patents. See the *Legend* at right, and the "How to Use this Book" chapter, for more information.

LEGEND

"For More Info . . . " column

A = Authority (Legislative Act, See Appendix "A")
B = Block or Lot (location in Section unknown)
C = Cancelled Patent
F = Fractional Section
G = Group (Multi-Patentee Patent, see Appendix "C")
V = Overlaps another Parcel
R = Re-Issued (Parcel patented more than once)

(A & G items require you to look in the Appendixes referred to above. All other Letter-designations followed by a number require you to locate line-items in this index that possess the ID number found after the letter).

ID	Individual in Patent	Sec.	Sec. Part	Date Issued	Other Counties	For More Info . . .
1699	AKINSON, James	29	NE	1851-11-01		A1 F
1825	ALEXANDER, Walter B	36	NW	1824-05-10		A1
1783	ATTWOOD, Moses	4	SWSE	1849-06-01		A1 G4
1826	BASS, William	18	NW	1848-07-01		A1 F
1785	BAYS, Orval	18	W½NE	1848-07-01		A1
1698	BELL, Hugh	30	NW	1835-09-02		A1
1721	BENNETT, John	4	W½2NW	1840-10-01		A1
1700	BLICKBORN, James	6	3NE	1860-03-01		A1
1722	BOULLIER, John	14	SW	1840-10-01		A1
1723	" "	14	W½NW	1849-12-01		A1
1663	BOYER, Andrew	25	NE	1853-05-10		A1 F
1724	BRICKEY, John C	26	W½NW	1832-02-11		A1 G32
1664	CASEY, Andrew	28	E½NE	1840-10-01		A1
1725	CASEY, John	14	E½NW	1850-06-01		A1 F
1772	CHADBOURN, Joseph	28	SW	1907-02-12		A1 F
1683	COLE, George B	27	SE	1841-12-10		A1 F
1791	COLE, Philip	35	SE	1831-10-01		A1 F
1790	" "	35	NW	1832-02-11		A1 F
1789	" "	35	NENE	1835-09-09		A1
1787	" "	26	SE	1840-10-01		A1
1788	" "	26	W½SW	1840-10-01		A1 F
1792	" "	35	SENE	1840-10-01		A1
1793	" "	35	W½NE	1840-10-01		A1
1786	" "	26	E½SW	1849-06-01		A1 F
1794	COLE, Philip D	27	W½NE	1841-12-10		A1 G71
1672	COOK, David A	17	E½NW	1849-06-01		A1 F
1824	COOK, Valentine	17	W½NW	1824-05-01		A1
1684	CRESSWELL, George	4	NESE	1849-06-01		A1
1686	" "	8	E½NE	1849-07-23		A1
1685	" "	7	NW	1851-11-01		A1 F
1687	" "	8	W½SE	1853-10-10		A1
1688	" "	9	NENW	1853-10-10		A1
1815	CRESSWELL, Stephen G	7	NE	1849-06-01		A1
1827	CRESSWELL, William C	4	SESW	1849-06-20		A1
1691	CRESWELL, George	5	S½NE	1835-10-01		A1
1689	" "	4	W½SW	1840-10-01		A1
1692	" "	5	W½SE	1840-10-01		A1
1693	" "	8	SWSW	1848-02-01		A1
1690	" "	5	2NE	1848-07-01		A1
1694	CROSSWELL, George	3	E½1NW	1854-10-02		A1 G75
1728	DINNIDDIE, John	15	W½SE	1849-07-23		A1
1729	DOWNEY, John	11	NWNW	1850-06-01		A1 F
1657	DUCLOS, Alexander	3	NESE	1840-10-01		A1
1737	DUFF, John M	30	W½SE	1848-07-01		A1
1806	EDMUNDS, Samuel	9	NWNW	1849-06-01		A1
1669	FARRELL, Bernard O	5	3NE	1844-08-01		A1

ID	Individual in Patent	Sec.	Sec. Part	Date Issued	Other Counties	For More Info . . .
1668	FARRELL, Bernard O (Cont'd)	4	NWSE	1845-10-01		A1
1822	FARRELL, Thomas	28	NW	1857-06-10		A1 F
1778	FLYNN, Michael	28	W½NE	1840-10-01		A1
1701	GLENN, James	19	NW	1835-10-01		A1 G116 F
1782	GLORE, Morton C	36	W½SE	1840-10-01		A1
1702	GOBBETT, James	22	SENE	1840-10-01		A1
1730	GUY, John F	8	E½SW	1825-07-15		A1 G122
1734	HANSON, John	6	W½1NE	1856-09-01		A1
1732	" "	6	E½1NE	1856-11-01		A1
1733	" "	6	E½2NE	1860-03-01		A1
1777	HARRIS, Littleton W	6	N½SE	1840-10-01		A1
1828	HARRISON, William	19	W½SE	1821-09-24		A1
1829	" "	30	NE	1821-09-24		A1
1830	HAYS, William	19	NE	1824-05-10		A1 G130
1796	HICKS, Robert D	5	W½SW	1835-09-02		A1
1797	" "	6	SESE	1835-09-09		A1
1798	" "	6	SWSE	1837-11-07		A1
1658	HIGHT, Alfred D	6	N½SW	1836-01-14		A1 C R1659
1660	" "	6	S½SW	1836-01-14		A1 C R1661
1659	" "	6	N½SW	1852-01-28		A1 R1658
1661	" "	6	S½SW	1852-01-28		A1 R1660
1781	HILL, Milton B	9	SWSW	1850-06-01		A1
1671	HINKSON, Cicero N	29	SW	1848-05-04		A1 F
1735	HOLT, John	31	SW	1840-10-01		A1
1670	HUDSON, Calvin	31	E½NW	1835-10-08		A1
1703	HUNT, James	11	S½SW	1854-03-01		A1
1704	" "	14	SE	1854-11-15		A1 G146 F
1705	" "	15	NENE	1854-11-15		A1 G146
1706	" "	20	SENE	1854-11-15		A1 G146
1707	" "	20	SESW	1854-11-15		A1 G146
1708	" "	21	E½NW	1854-11-15		A1 G146
1709	" "	23	NE	1854-11-15		A1 G146 F
1710	" "	3	N½SW	1855-06-15		A1 G146
1711	" "	3	SWSE	1855-06-15		A1 G146
1712	" "	3	W½1NW	1855-06-15		A1 G146
1736	JACKSON, John	5	E½1NW	1848-02-01		A1
1814	JACKSON, Smith	4	SE2NW	1840-10-01		A1
1783	" "	4	SWSE	1849-06-01		A1 G4
1731	JOHNSON, John H	18	SW	1835-10-01		A1 F
1795	JOHNSON, Pleasant S	17	NESE	1855-06-15		A1 F
1704	JOHNSTON, Robert	14	SE	1854-11-15		A1 G146 F
1705	" "	15	NENE	1854-11-15		A1 G146
1706	" "	20	SENE	1854-11-15		A1 G146
1707	" "	20	SESW	1854-11-15		A1 G146
1708	" "	21	E½NW	1854-11-15		A1 G146
1709	" "	23	NE	1854-11-15		A1 G146 F
1710	" "	3	N½SW	1855-06-15		A1 G146
1711	" "	3	SWSE	1855-06-15		A1 G146
1712	" "	3	W½1NW	1855-06-15		A1 G146
1799	KENNER, Rosamunda	4	E½1NE	1841-12-10		A1
1681	KENNETT, Ferdinand	10	NENW	1854-05-01		A1
1682	" "	3	SESW	1854-05-01		A1
1673	LAMARAQUE, Etienne	25	NW	1850-06-01		A1 F
1678	LAMARQUE, Etienne	8	W½NE	1821-09-24		A1
1679	" "	22	E½SW	1825-07-15		A1 G160
1680	" "	22	W½SE	1825-07-15		A1 G160
1677	" "	5	SESW	1835-09-09		A1
1675	" "	22	E½SE	1840-10-01		A1
1674	" "	15	E½SE	1843-04-10		A1
1676	" "	26	NENE	1850-06-01		A1 F
1834	LONG, William	15	SENE	1849-06-20		A1 G166
1833	" "	25	N½SE	1854-03-01		A1
1832	" "	23	W½NW	1854-11-15		A1
1694	LUMPKINS, Charles B	3	E½1NW	1854-10-02		A1 G75
1697	LUPTON, Henry	5	E½SE	1835-10-01		A1 G169
1697	LUPTON, Jonathan	5	E½SE	1835-10-01		A1 G169
1770	" "	21	NWNW	1840-10-01		A1
1771	" "	20	W½NE	1844-08-01		A1 G170 R1836
1697	LUPTON, Joseph	5	E½SE	1835-10-01		A1 G169
1784	MARTIN, Noah	30	SW	1831-10-01		A1 F
1662	MCCURRY, Amos E	21	W½NE	1848-07-01		A1
1724	MCILVAIN, John	26	W½NW	1832-02-11		A1 G32
1738	" "	27	E½NE	1840-10-01		A1

ID	Individual in Patent	Sec.	Sec. Part	Date Issued	Other Counties	For More Info . . .
1739	MCILVAIN, John (Cont'd)	36	E½SE	1840-10-01		A1
1740	MCNALLY, John	21	W½SW	1850-06-01		A1
1808	MERRY, Samuel	21	SE	1840-10-01		A1 G181
1807	" "	26	E½NW	1840-10-01		A1
1665	MILLER, Andrew	31	SE	1821-09-24		A1
1817	MURPHY, Thomas C	3	NWSE	1854-10-02		A1 G187
1818	" "	3	2NE	1855-06-15		A1 G188
1819	" "	3	E½NW	1855-06-15		A1 G188
1820	" "	3	W½1NE	1855-06-15		A1 G188
1817	MURPHY, William	3	NWSE	1854-10-02		A1 G187
1818	MURPHY, William S	3	2NE	1855-06-15		A1 G188
1819	" "	3	E½NW	1855-06-15		A1 G188
1820	" "	3	W½1NE	1855-06-15		A1 G188
1823	NICHOLSON, Thomas	32	SW	1855-06-15		A1 G191 F
1823	NICHOLSON, William	32	SW	1855-06-15		A1 G191 F
1695	NORTHCUT, George	17	E½NE	1849-06-01		A1
1719	OLIVER, Jeremiah	20	NENE	1853-10-10		A1
1741	PARKINSON, John	19	SW	1840-10-01		A1 V1751
1811	PARKINSON, Sarah	20	NESW	1849-06-01		A1
1837	PARKINSON, William	4	2NE	1832-02-11		A1
1836	" "	20	W½NE	1836-01-14		A1 C R1771
1771	" "	20	W½NE	1844-08-01		A1 G170 R1836
1835	" "	17	W½NE	1854-11-15		A1 F
1713	PERRY, James	17	W½SW	1821-09-24		A1 G196
1714	" "	18	E½NE	1821-09-24		A1 G196
1715	" "	18	E½SE	1821-09-24		A1 G196
1716	" "	20	NW	1821-09-24		A1 G196
1717	" "	8	NW	1821-09-24		A1 G197
1713	PERRY, John	17	W½SW	1821-09-24		A1 G196
1714	" "	18	E½NE	1821-09-24		A1 G196
1715	" "	18	E½SE	1821-09-24		A1 G196
1716	" "	20	NW	1821-09-24		A1 G196
1742	" "	18	W½SE	1824-05-10		A1
1830	" "	19	NE	1824-05-10		A1 G130
1749	" "	20	W½SW	1824-05-10		A1 G199
1748	" "	21	E½SW	1824-05-20		A1 G200
1746	" "	36	NESW	1835-10-01		A1
1747	" "	36	NWSW	1835-10-01		A1
1808	" "	21	SE	1840-10-01		A1 G181
1744	" "	27	SW	1840-10-01		A1 F
1745	" "	28	SE	1840-10-01		A1 F
1743	" "	25	W½SW	1843-04-10		A1
1713	PERRY, Samuel	17	W½SW	1821-09-24		A1 G196
1714	" "	18	E½NE	1821-09-24		A1 G196
1715	" "	18	E½SE	1821-09-24		A1 G196
1716	" "	20	NW	1821-09-24		A1 G196
1717	" "	8	NW	1821-09-24		A1 G197
1713	PERRY, William	17	W½SW	1821-09-24		A1 G196
1714	" "	18	E½NE	1821-09-24		A1 G196
1715	" "	18	E½SE	1821-09-24		A1 G196
1716	" "	20	NW	1821-09-24		A1 G196
1749	" "	20	W½SW	1824-05-10		A1 G199
1748	PERRY, William M	21	E½SW	1824-05-20		A1 G200
1783	PIERCE, Charles	4	SWSE	1849-06-01		A1 G4
1750	PRATTE, John	3	SENE	1849-07-23		A1 F
1726	SCHUTTE, John D	4	NESW	1848-07-01		A1
1727	SHUTTE, John D	4	W½1NE	1846-07-03		A1
1831	SILVER, William J	29	NW	1849-06-01		A1 F
1809	SILVERS, Samuel	8	E½SE	1850-06-01		A1
1810	" "	9	NWSW	1850-06-01		A1
1774	SIMPSON, Joseph	6	W½2NE	1856-11-01		A1
1773	" "	6	NW	1857-06-10		A1
1701	SMITH, Jesse B	19	NW	1835-10-01		A1 G116 F
1755	SMITH, John T	10	W½NW	1858-03-02		A1
1756	" "	10	W½SW	1858-03-02		A1
1757	" "	15	SW	1858-03-02		A1
1758	" "	15	W½NW	1858-03-02		A1
1759	" "	21	E½NE	1858-03-02		A1
1760	" "	22	NW	1858-03-02		A1
1761	" "	22	W½NE	1858-03-02		A1
1762	" "	25	S½SE	1858-03-02		A1
1763	" "	3	SWSW	1858-03-02		A1
1764	" "	36	N½NE	1858-03-02		A1

ID	Individual in Patent	Sec.	Sec. Part	Date Issued	Other Counties	For More Info . . .
1765	SMITH, John T (Cont'd)	36	SESW	1858-03-02		A1
1766	" "	36	SWSW	1858-03-02		A1 F
1767	" "	4	SESE	1858-03-02		A1
1768	" "	9	E½NE	1858-03-02		A1
1769	" "	9	E½SE	1858-03-02		A1
1679	SMITH, Reuben	22	E½SW	1825-07-15		A1 G160
1680	" "	22	W½SE	1825-07-15		A1 G160
1838	SMITH, William W	3	W½2NW	1835-10-08		A1
1794	" "	27	W½NE	1841-12-10		A1 G71
1730	STEMBER, John	8	E½SW	1825-07-15		A1 G122
1816	STOVALL, Thomas B	8	NWSW	1848-02-01		A1
1839	SUMMERS, William W	10	SENE	1850-06-01		A1 G219
1751	SWAN, John	19	E½SW	1824-05-10		A1 V1741
1752	" "	30	E½SE	1831-10-01		A1
1753	" "	31	E½NE	1831-10-01		A1
1754	" "	31	W½NE	1835-10-01		A1
1666	TALBOT, Benjamin	10	NENE	1850-06-01		A1
1667	" "	2	SW	1850-06-01		A1 F
1779	TANEY, Michael	17	E½SW	1848-07-01		A1 F
1780	" "	17	S½SE	1848-07-01		A1 F
1720	TAYLOR, John B	26	W½NE	1854-11-15		A1
1696	TRIPPE, Henry D	25	E½SW	1843-04-10		A1
1834	WHITE, Samuel	15	SENE	1849-06-20		A1 G166
1804	WHITE, Samuel C	27	N½NW	1848-02-01		A1
1805	" "	27	S½NW	1848-07-01		A1
1803	" "	22	W½SW	1849-06-01		A1
1800	" "	11	N½SW	1851-11-01		A1 F
1801	" "	11	S½NW	1851-11-01		A1 F
1802	" "	21	SWNW	1854-05-01		A1
1821	WHITE, Thomas C	10	NESE	1851-11-01		A1
1839	WHITE, Thomas S	10	SENE	1850-06-01		A1 G219
1812	WOODS, Simeon	4	1NW	1835-09-02		A1
1813	" "	4	NE2NW	1835-10-01		A1
1718	WRIGHT, James	31	W½NW	1856-11-01		A1
1776	WYATT, Landing D	22	NENE	1850-06-01		A1
1775	YOUNG, Joseph	5	NESW	1836-01-14		A1

Patent Map

T38-N R2-E
5th PM Meridian

Map Group 14

Township Statistics

Parcels Mapped	:	183
Number of Patents	:	154
Number of Individuals	:	109
Patentees Identified	:	103
Number of Surnames	:	83
Multi-Patentee Parcels	:	35
Oldest Patent Date	:	9/24/1821
Most Recent Patent	:	2/12/1907
Block/Lot Parcels	:	20
Parcels Re - Issued	:	3
Parcels that Overlap	:	2
Cities and Towns	:	6
Cemeteries	:	6

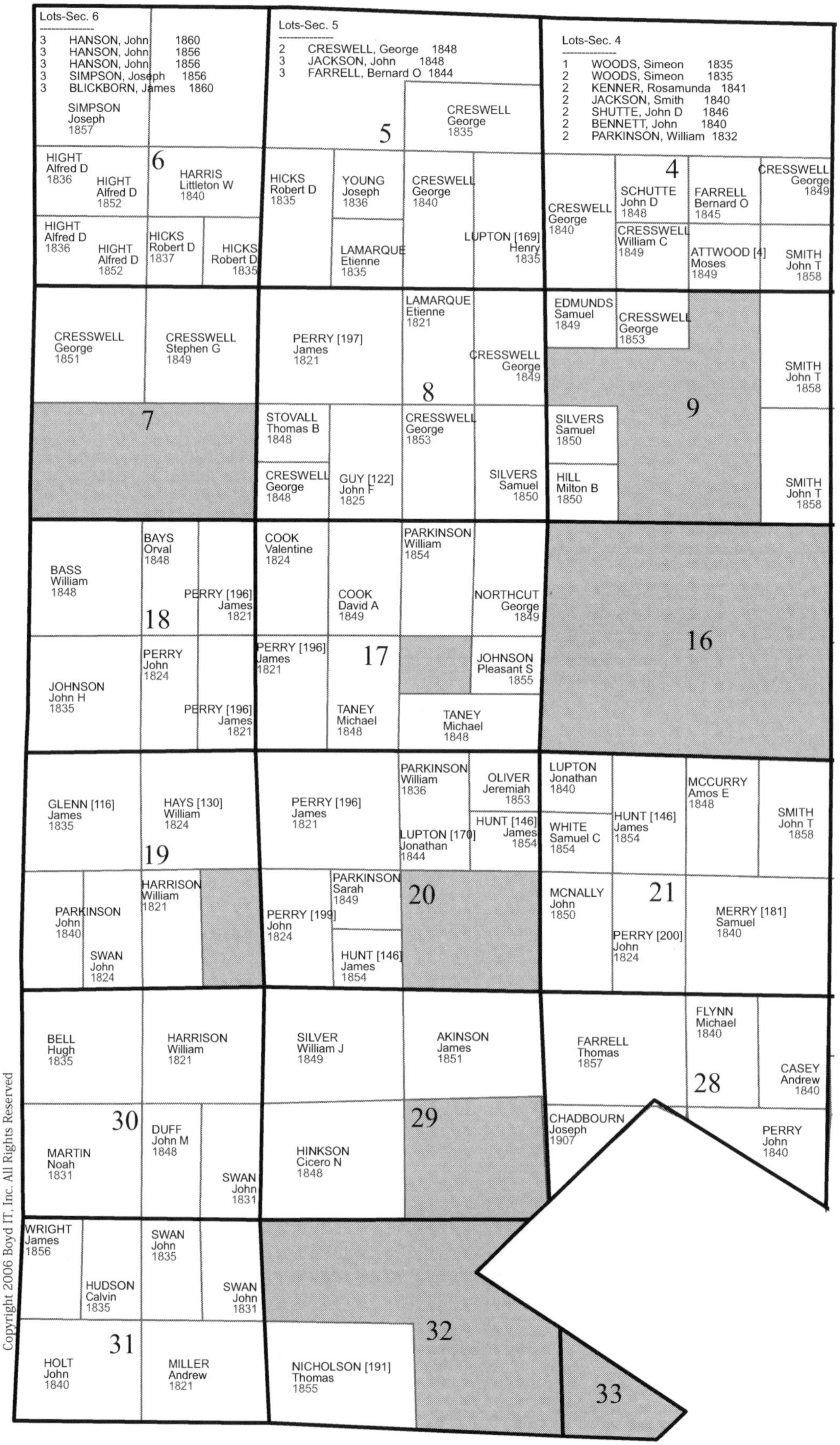

Lots-Sec. 6
3 HANSON, John 1860
3 HANSON, John 1856
3 HANSON, John 1856
3 SIMPSON, Joseph 1856
3 BLICKBORN, James 1860

Lots-Sec. 5
2 CRESWELL, George 1848
3 JACKSON, John 1848
3 FARRELL, Bernard O 1844

Lots-Sec. 4
1 WOODS, Simeon 1835
2 WOODS, Simeon 1835
2 KENNER, Rosamunda 1841
2 JACKSON, Smith 1840
2 SHUTTE, John D 1846
2 BENNETT, John 1840
2 PARKINSON, William 1832

SIMPSON Joseph 1857
6
HIGHT Alfred D 1836
HIGHT Alfred D 1852
HARRIS Littleton W 1840
HIGHT Alfred D 1836
HIGHT Alfred D 1852
HICKS Robert D 1837
HICKS Robert D 1835

5
CRESWELL George 1835
HICKS Robert D 1835
YOUNG Joseph 1836
CRESWELL George 1840
LAMARQUE Etienne 1835
LUPTON [169] Henry 1835

4
CRESWELL George 1840
SCHUTTE John D 1848
FARRELL Bernard O 1845
CRESSWELL George 1849
CRESSWELL William C 1849
ATTWOOD [4] Moses 1849
SMITH John T 1858

7
CRESSWELL George 1851
CRESSWELL Stephen G 1849

8
PERRY [197] James 1821
LAMARQUE Etienne 1821
CRESSWELL George 1849
STOVALL Thomas B 1848
CRESSWELL George 1853
CRESWELL George 1848
GUY [122] John F 1825
SILVERS Samuel 1850

9
EDMUNDS Samuel 1849
CRESSWELL George 1853
SMITH John T 1858
SILVERS Samuel 1850
HILL Milton B 1850
SMITH John T 1858

18
BASS William 1848
BAYS Orval 1848
PERRY [196] James 1821
JOHNSON John H 1835
PERRY John 1824
PERRY [196] James 1821

17
COOK Valentine 1824
COOK David A 1849
PARKINSON William 1854
NORTHCUT George 1849
PERRY [196] James 1821
JOHNSON Pleasant S 1855
TANEY Michael 1848
TANEY Michael 1848

16

19
GLENN [116] James 1835
HAYS [130] William 1824
PARKINSON John 1840
HARRISON William 1821
SWAN John 1824

20
PERRY [196] James 1821
PARKINSON William 1836
OLIVER Jeremiah 1853
HUNT [146] James 1854
LUPTON [170] Jonathan 1844
PARKINSON Sarah 1849
PERRY [199] John 1824
HUNT [146] James 1854

21
LUPTON Jonathan 1840
WHITE Samuel C 1854
HUNT [146] James 1854
MCCURRY Amos E 1848
SMITH John T 1858
MCNALLY John 1850
PERRY [200] John 1824
MERRY [181] Samuel 1840

30
BELL Hugh 1835
HARRISON William 1821
MARTIN Noah 1831
DUFF John M 1848
SWAN John 1831

29
SILVER William J 1849
AKINSON James 1851
HINKSON Cicero N 1848

28
FARRELL Thomas 1857
FLYNN Michael 1840
CASEY Andrew 1840
CHADBOURN Joseph 1907
PERRY John 1840

31
WRIGHT James 1856
HUDSON Calvin 1835
SWAN John 1835
SWAN John 1831
HOLT John 1840
MILLER Andrew 1821

32
NICHOLSON [191] Thomas 1855

33

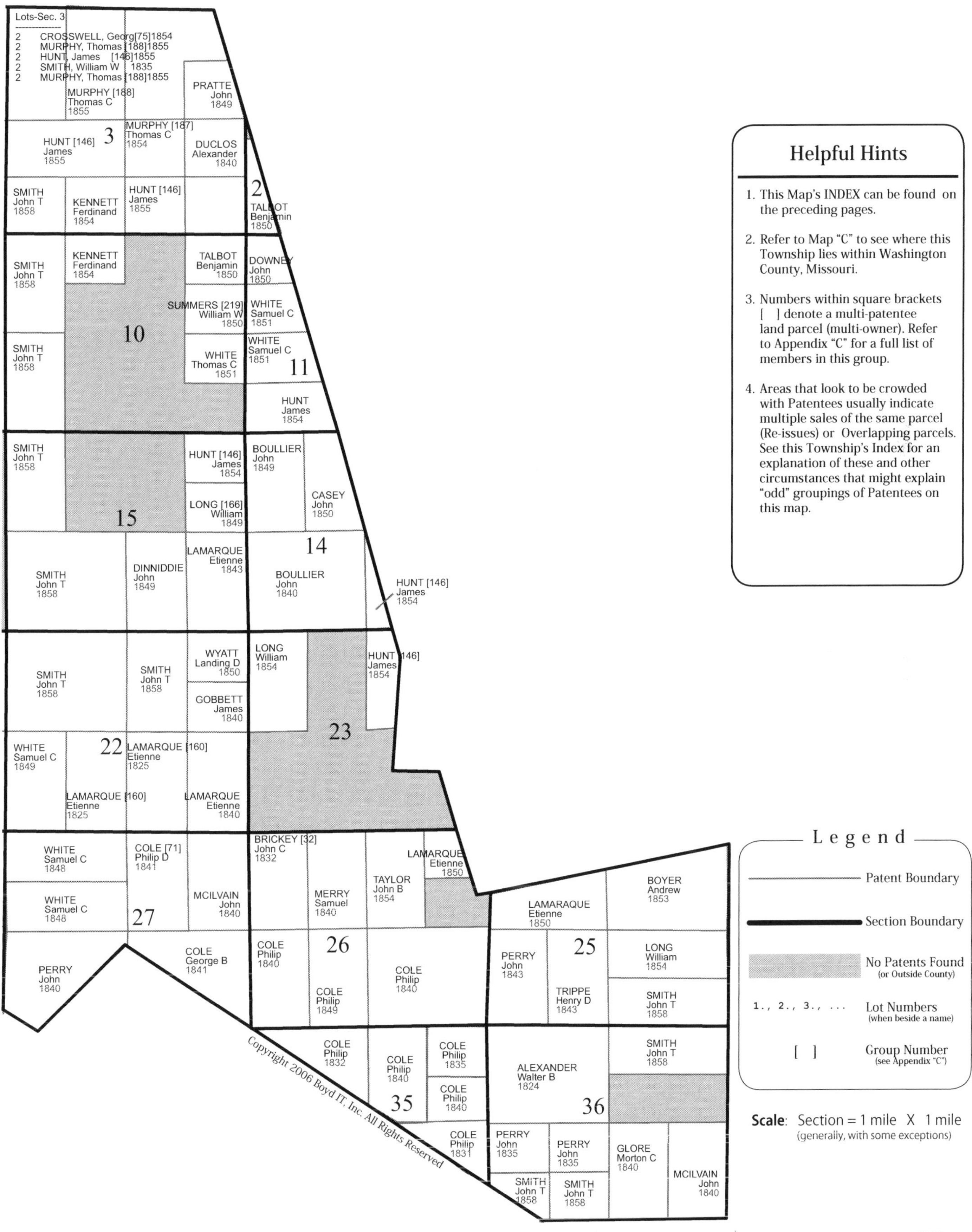

Helpful Hints

1. This Map's INDEX can be found on the preceding pages.
2. Refer to Map "C" to see where this Township lies within Washington County, Missouri.
3. Numbers within square brackets [ ] denote a multi-patentee land parcel (multi-owner). Refer to Appendix "C" for a full list of members in this group.
4. Areas that look to be crowded with Patentees usually indicate multiple sales of the same parcel (Re-issues) or Overlapping parcels. See this Township's Index for an explanation of these and other circumstances that might explain "odd" groupings of Patentees on this map.

Road Map

T38-N R2-E
5th PM Meridian

Map Group 14

Cities & Towns

- Aptus
- Frogtown
- Latty
- Old Mines
- Racola
- Robidoux

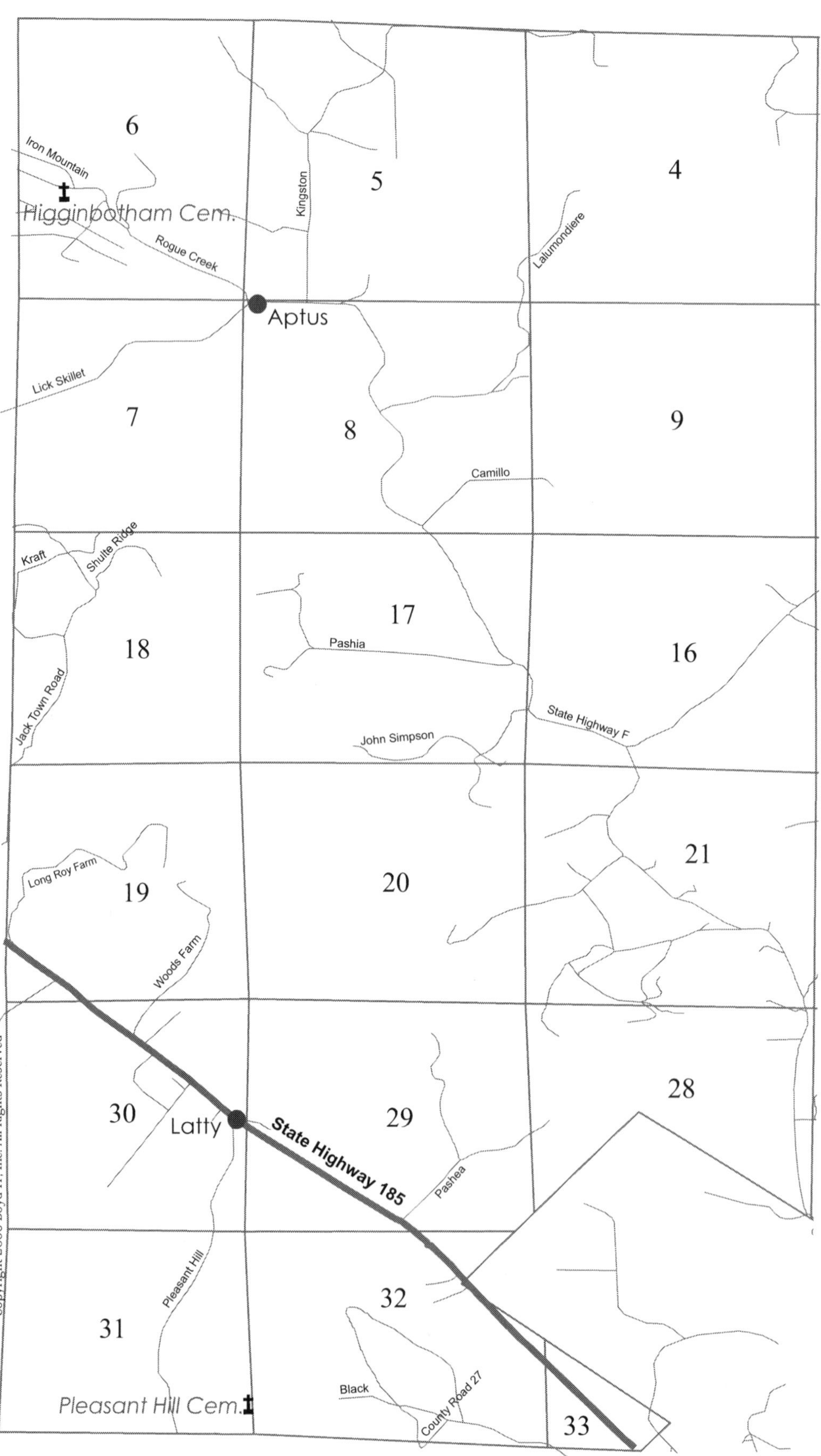

Cemeteries

- Higginbotham Cemetery
- Pleasant Hill Cemetery
- Old Baptist Church Cemetery
- Saint Joachim Cemetery Number 1
- Saint Joachim Cemetery Number 2
- Saint Joachim Cemetery Number 3

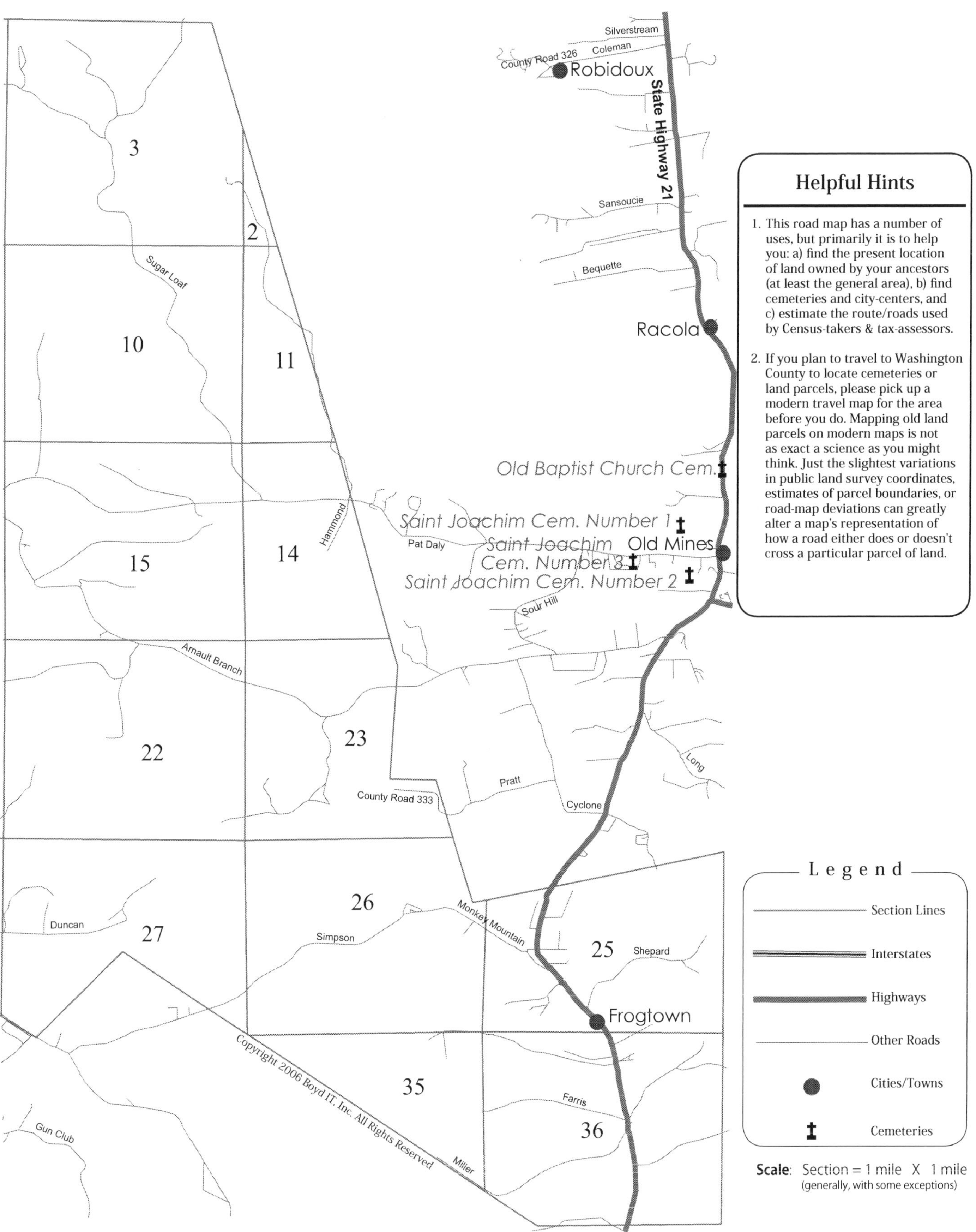

Helpful Hints

1. This road map has a number of uses, but primarily it is to help you: a) find the present location of land owned by your ancestors (at least the general area), b) find cemeteries and city-centers, and c) estimate the route/roads used by Census-takers & tax-assessors.

2. If you plan to travel to Washington County to locate cemeteries or land parcels, please pick up a modern travel map for the area before you do. Mapping old land parcels on modern maps is not as exact a science as you might think. Just the slightest variations in public land survey coordinates, estimates of parcel boundaries, or road-map deviations can greatly alter a map's representation of how a road either does or doesn't cross a particular parcel of land.

Legend

- Section Lines
- Interstates
- Highways
- Other Roads
- Cities/Towns
- Cemeteries

Scale: Section = 1 mile X 1 mile (generally, with some exceptions)

Historical Map

T38-N R2-E
5th PM Meridian

Map Group 14

Cities & Towns
- Aptus
- Frogtown
- Latty
- Old Mines
- Racola
- Robidoux

Cemeteries
- Higginbotham Cemetery
- Pleasant Hill Cemetery
- Old Baptist Church Cemetery
- Saint Joachim Cemetery Number 1
- Saint Joachim Cemetery Number 2
- Saint Joachim Cemetery Number 3

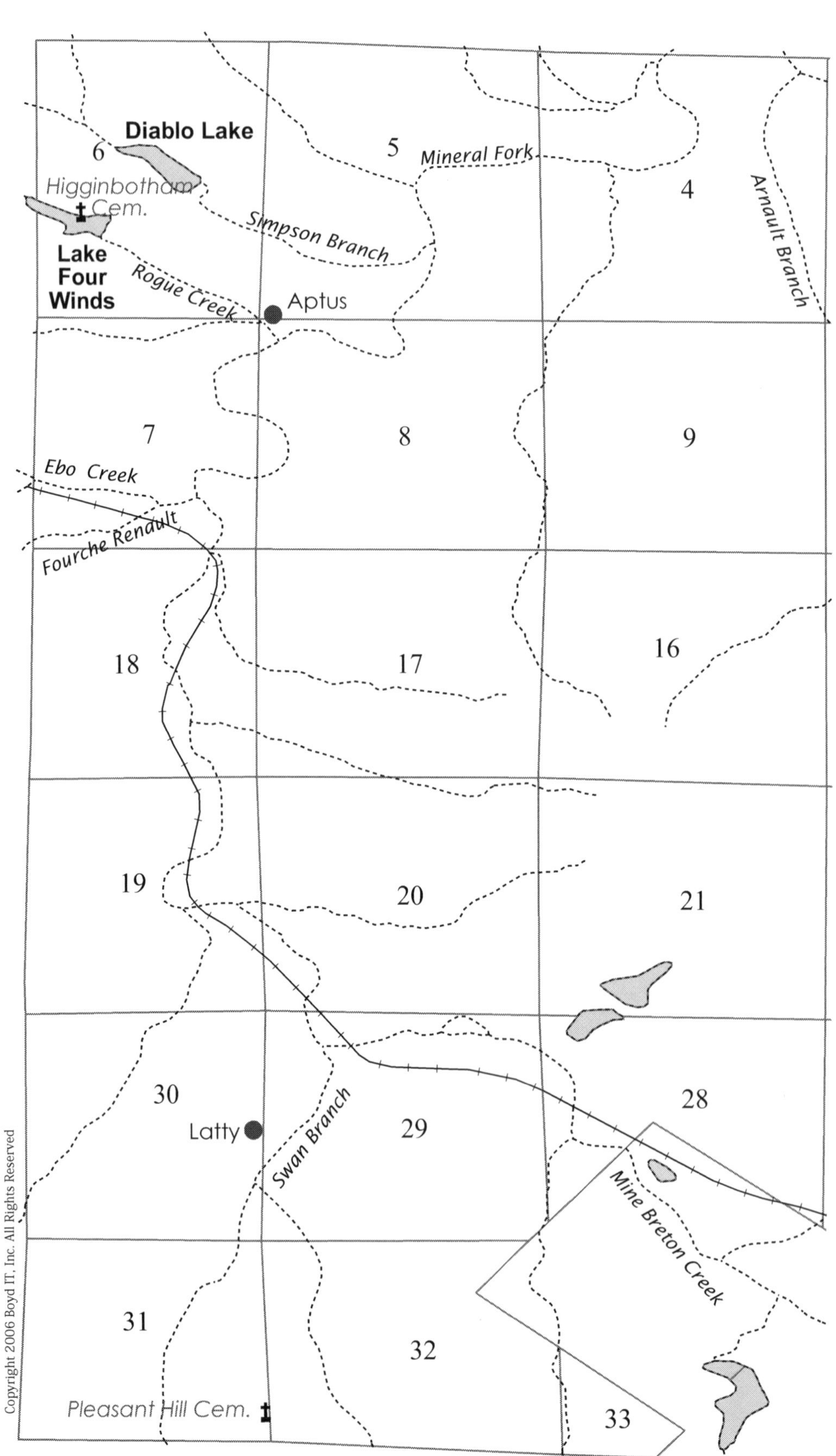

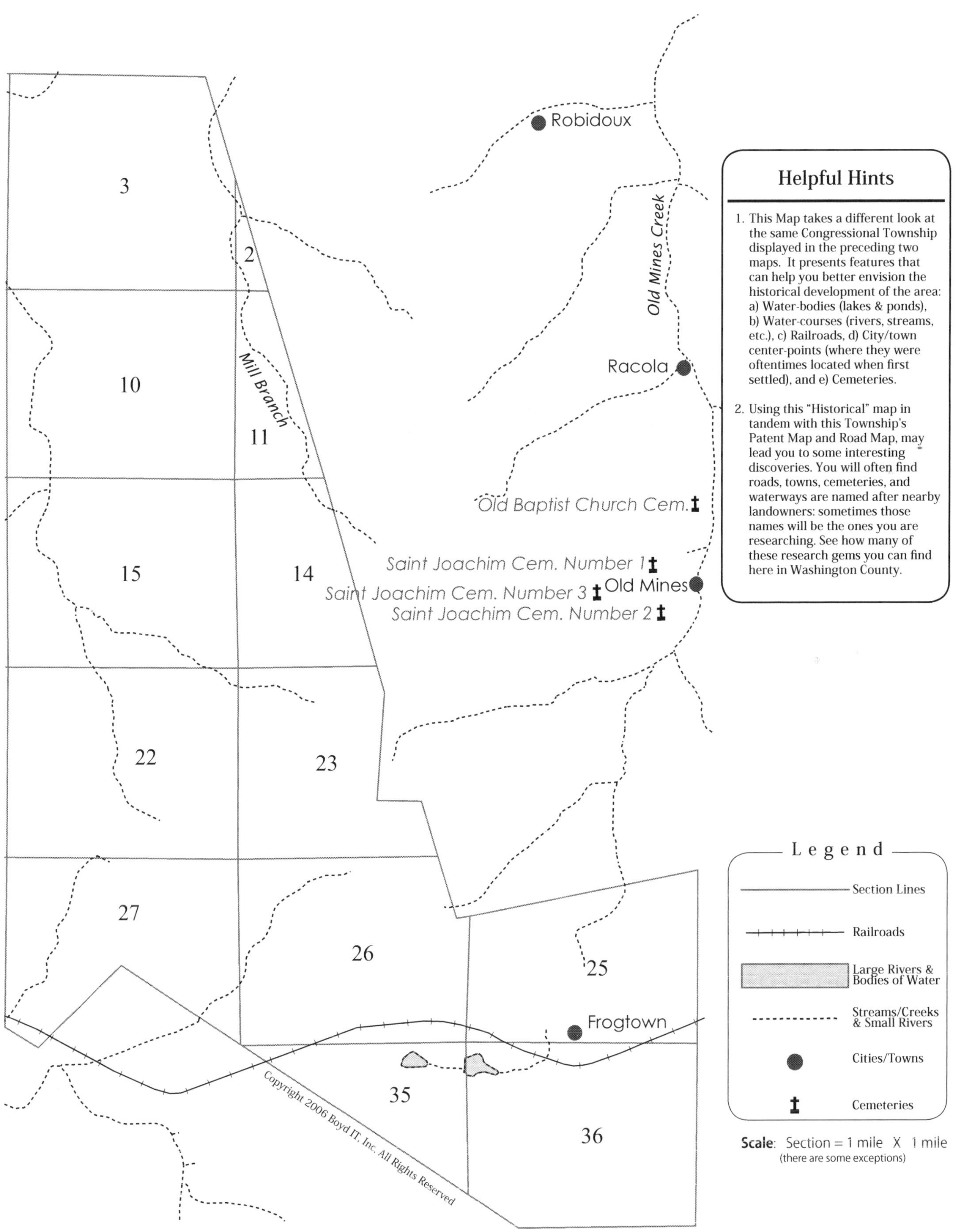

Helpful Hints

1. This Map takes a different look at the same Congressional Township displayed in the preceding two maps. It presents features that can help you better envision the historical development of the area: a) Water-bodies (lakes & ponds), b) Water-courses (rivers, streams, etc.), c) Railroads, d) City/town center-points (where they were oftentimes located when first settled), and e) Cemeteries.
2. Using this "Historical" map in tandem with this Township's Patent Map and Road Map, may lead you to some interesting discoveries. You will often find roads, towns, cemeteries, and waterways are named after nearby landowners: sometimes those names will be the ones you are researching. See how many of these research gems you can find here in Washington County.

Map Group 15: Index to Land Patents

Township 38-North Range 3-East (5th PM)

After you locate an individual in this Index, take note of the Section and Section Part then proceed to the Land Patent map on the pages immediately following. You should have no difficulty locating the corresponding parcel of land.

The "For More Info" Column will lead you to more information about the underlying Patents. See the *Legend* at right, and the "How to Use this Book" chapter, for more information.

LEGEND

"For More Info . . . " column

A = Authority (Legislative Act, See Appendix "A")
B = Block or Lot (location in Section unknown)
C = Cancelled Patent
F = Fractional Section
G = Group (Multi-Patentee Patent, see Appendix "C")
V = Overlaps another Parcel
R = Re-Issued (Parcel patented more than once)

(A & G items require you to look in the Appendixes referred to above. All other Letter-designations followed by a number require you to locate line-items in this index that possess the ID number found after the letter).

ID	Individual in Patent	Sec.	Sec. Part	Date Issued	Other Counties	For More Info . . .
2018	AUBUCHON, Napoleon	28	S½NW	1849-06-01		A1
1899	BEQUETTE, Derville	4	SESW	1848-07-01		A1 G16
1900	" "	4	W½SW	1848-07-01		A1 G16
2030	BLACKWELL, Robert	35	NWNE	1838-09-07		A1
2029	" "	25	SWSW	1840-10-01		A1
2031	BLACKWELL, Robert M	35	NENE	1840-10-01		A1
1925	BOAS, Jacob	30	NESE	1849-06-01		A1
1926	" "	30	SWSE	1849-06-01		A1
1924	" "	27	E½NW	1862-07-01		A1
1856	BOYER, Antoine	14	NWNE	1837-04-01		A1 F
1901	BOYER, Edmond	20	W½SW	1854-11-15		A1 F
1905	BOYER, Francis	11	SESE	1836-01-14		A1
1906	" "	5	SE	1848-05-04		A1
1999	BOYER, Justin	12	NWNE	1850-06-01		A1
2004	BOYER, Louis	14	NENE	1836-01-14		A1
2005	" "	14	SWNE	1841-12-10		A1
2003	" "	11	NESE	1848-07-01		A1 F
2012	BOYER, Michael	13	W½NW	1840-10-01		A1 G27
2019	BOYER, Nicholas	12	E½NE	1841-12-10		A1
2054	BOYER, Thomas L	11	NE	1856-11-01		A1 F
2074	BOYER, Xavia	11	SWSE	1854-11-15		A1 F
2012	BOYLE, Peter	13	W½NW	1840-10-01		A1 G27
2032	BROWN, Robert T	28	SE	1824-05-01		A1
1922	CAMPBELL, Isaac	27	SWNW	1848-06-01		A1
2050	CAMPBELL, Thomas	27	NESE	1854-03-01		A1
2051	" "	27	SENE	1854-03-01		A1
1946	CARPENTER, James M	35	N½SW	1854-11-15		A1 G47
1947	" "	36	SWSE	1854-11-15		A1 G48
1929	CATLETT, James	28	N½SW	1848-05-04		A1
1930	" "	29	N½SE	1848-05-04		A1
1902	CHEATHAM, Edward	4	2NE	1840-10-01		A1
1884	COBURN, Charles H	12	SESW	1854-11-15		A1 G70
1885	" "	12	SWSE	1854-11-15		A1 G70
1886	" "	23	NWSW	1854-11-15		A1 G70
1881	" "	26	S½SW	1854-11-15		A1 G69
1882	" "	27	SESE	1854-11-15		A1 G69
1883	" "	33	SESE	1854-11-15		A1 G69
1887	" "	34	S½NE	1854-11-15		A1 G70
1946	" "	35	N½SW	1854-11-15		A1 G47
1888	" "	35	SWNW	1854-11-15		A1 G70
1948	COBURN, James M	14	SENE	1854-03-01		A1 F
1860	COLE, Aquilla	33	E½SW	1831-10-01		A1
1861	" "	33	W½SW	1840-10-01		A1
1997	COLE, Joseph C	35	SWSW	1853-10-10		A1
2011	COLE, Micajah	3	2NE	1837-04-01		A1
2038	COLE, Samuel	23	NWSE	1840-10-01		A1

ID	Individual in Patent	Sec.	Sec. Part	Date Issued	Other Counties	For More Info . . .
2039	COLE, Samuel (Cont'd)	23	W½NE	1840-10-01		A1
2040	" "	27	W½NE	1840-10-01		A1
2037	" "	23	NESW	1843-04-10		A1
1843	COLEMAN, Adrian	5	2NW	1848-12-01		A1
1845	" "	5	W½1NE	1848-12-01		A1
1841	" "	4	W½1NW	1856-10-01		A1
1842	" "	4	W½2NW	1856-10-01		A1
1844	" "	5	3NE	1856-10-01		A1
1862	CULTON, Arthur H	34	NENE	1840-10-01		A1
2017	CULTON, Nancy	35	N½NW	1840-10-01		A1
2052	CUMMINGS, Thomas	13	SWSW	1853-10-10		A1
2042	CUMMINS, Samuel	13	NESW	1837-04-01		A1 G77
2041	" "	13	NWSW	1837-04-01		A1
1893	DUNKLIN, Daniel	33	N½NE	1824-05-10		A1
2025	ENGLEDOW, Randolph	27	SWSE	1840-10-01		A1
2026	" "	34	NWNE	1840-10-01		A1
1953	EVANS, James S	29	E½NW	1839-01-07		A1 R1964
1954	" "	29	W½NE	1839-01-07		A1
1967	EVENS, John	32	SW	1843-04-10		A1
2000	FLYNN, Leo T	15	SWNE	1921-02-07		A1 F
2008	FRISSELL, Mason	34	E½SW	1854-03-01		A1
2009	" "	34	SE	1854-03-01		A1
2010	" "	34	SWSW	1854-03-01		A1
1919	GARRETT, Hezekiah	30	S½1SW	1840-10-01		A1
1920	" "	30	S½2SW	1840-10-01		A1
1921	" "	31	1NW	1840-10-01		A1
1890	GEZZI, Damasr	15	NWSW	1854-03-01		A1
1891	" "	17	NE	1854-03-01		A1 F
1892	" "	22	SWNE	1854-03-01		A1
2001	GLORE, Lisbon	20	NE	1848-07-01		A1 F
2058	GOFF, William	15	SE	1826-05-01		A1 F
2059	" "	15	SESW	1838-09-07		A1 C R2060
2056	" "	15	NESW	1840-10-01		A1 C R2057
2061	" "	3	SE	1840-10-01		A1 F
2057	" "	15	NESW	1852-01-28		A1 R2056
2060	" "	15	SESW	1852-01-28		A1 R2059
2002	HARRIS, Littleton W	30	SENW	1849-06-01		A1
1863	HAWKINS, Augustus	35	SESW	1851-11-01		A1
1864	" "	35	SWSE	1853-10-10		A1
1995	HIBBARD, Jonathan P	30	N½1NW	1838-09-07		A1
1996	" "	30	N½2NW	1838-09-07		A1
2053	HIGGENBOTHAM, Thomas	26	E½NE	1836-01-14		A1
1917	HIGGINBOTHAM, George W	3	NW	1840-10-01		A1
1918	" "	3	SW	1843-04-10		A1
1993	HOPKINS, John W	26	E½SE	1824-05-01		A1
2047	HOUK, Solomon	20	SE	1831-02-15		A1
1931	HUNT, James	5	3NW	1854-03-01		A1
2022	HYPOLITE, Peter	13	SENW	1835-09-09		A1
2042	" "	13	NESW	1837-04-01		A1 G77
1907	HYPOTITE, Francis	13	NENE	1837-04-01		A1
1916	JAMISON, George	34	NW	1824-05-01		A1
1915	" "	27	W½SW	1826-05-01		A1
1899	KELLY, Michael	4	SESW	1848-07-01		A1 G16
1900	" "	4	W½SW	1848-07-01		A1 G16
2048	LAMARQUE, Stephen	1	NEN½SE	1849-05-01		A1 G161 F
2049	" "	1	SW	1849-05-01		A1 G161 F
1936	LANCASTER, James	10	NE	1844-08-01		A1 C F R1937
1938	" "	10	NENW	1844-08-01		A1 C F R1939
1940	" "	10	SENW	1844-08-01		A1 C F R1941
1943	" "	25	SWSE	1848-02-01		A1
1942	" "	25	SESW	1849-06-01		A1
1937	" "	10	NE	1852-01-28		A1 F R1936
1939	" "	10	NENW	1852-01-28		A1 R1938
1941	" "	10	SENW	1852-01-28		A1 F R1940
1944	" "	36	NENW	1853-10-10		A1
1945	" "	36	SWNW	1854-03-01		A1
2043	LATIMER, Samuel	13	W½NE	1840-10-01		A1
1849	LONG, Alfred	25	NWSE	1848-07-01		A1
1847	" "	25	NESE	1849-06-01		A1
1851	" "	25	SESE	1853-04-15		A1
1846	" "	25	NENW	1853-10-10		A1
1848	" "	25	NESW	1853-10-10		A1
1850	" "	25	S½NE	1853-10-10		A1

ID	Individual in Patent	Sec.	Sec. Part	Date Issued	Other Counties	For More Info . . .
1873	LONG, Branfield	36	NESW	1849-06-01		A1 G163
1874	" "	36	NWSE	1849-06-01		A1 G163
1877	LONG, Brumfield	25	NWNE	1851-11-01		A1
1876	" "	25	NENE	1853-10-10		A1
1880	" "	36	SWNE	1853-10-10		A1 G165
1875	" "	24	SWSE	1854-03-01		A1
1878	" "	36	NENE	1854-03-01		A1 G165
1879	" "	36	SESW	1854-03-01		A1 G165
2015	LONG, Milton	36	NESE	1848-02-01		A1
2016	" "	36	SESE	1853-10-10		A1
1873	LONG, William	36	NESW	1849-06-01		A1 G163
1874	" "	36	NWSE	1849-06-01		A1 G163
1880	" "	36	SWNE	1853-10-10		A1 G165
1878	" "	36	NENE	1854-03-01		A1 G165
1879	" "	36	SESW	1854-03-01		A1 G165
2064	" "	5	2NE	1854-03-01		A1
2065	" "	5	E½1NE	1854-03-01		A1
2062	" "	14	NW	1854-11-15		A1 F
2063	" "	19		1854-11-15		A1 F
2066	" "	9	N½NE	1865-03-15		A1
2067	" "	9	NENW	1865-03-15		A1
2048	MADDEN, Malichi	1	NEN½SE	1849-05-01		A1 G161 F
2049	" "	1	SW	1849-05-01		A1 G161 F
2006	" "	1	SWSE	1849-05-01		A1 F
1889	MANWARING, Charles H	12	NWSE	1835-09-09		A1
1865	MCANULTY, Bernard	12	SESE	1854-11-15		A1
1866	" "	13	S½SE	1854-11-15		A1
1867	" "	13	SESW	1854-11-15		A1
1868	" "	24	E½SW	1854-11-15		A1
1869	" "	24	NWNE	1854-11-15		A1
1870	" "	24	SWSW	1854-11-15		A1
1871	" "	36	NWNE	1854-11-15		A1
1872	" "	36	NWNW	1854-11-15		A1
1955	MCILVAIN, Jesse H	32	SE	1840-10-01		A1
1968	MCILVAIN, John	31	2NW	1840-10-01		A1
1956	MCILVAINE, Jesse H	28	S½SW	1841-07-01		A1
1957	" "	29	S½SE	1841-07-01		A1
1958	" "	32	NE	1841-07-01		A1
1959	" "	33	NW	1841-07-01		A1
1853	MINCK, Amos	4	E½1NW	1840-10-01		A1
1854	" "	4	NESW	1840-10-01		A1
1852	MITCHELL, Alfred	1	SESE	1848-02-01		A1 F
1949	MOULTRAY, James	12	NW	1824-05-20		A1 F
2068	MURPHEY, William S	8	2N½	1875-04-10		A1
2069	" "	8	3N½	1875-04-10		A1
2070	" "	8	4N½	1875-04-10		A1
2071	" "	9	NWNW	1875-04-10		A1
1923	OBUCHON, Isaac	14	SESE	1848-02-01		A1
1857	OWENS, Aquilla C	25	NWSW	1854-03-01		A1
1858	" "	26	NWSE	1854-03-01		A1 R1904
1859	" "	26	SWNE	1854-03-01		A1
1951	OWENS, James	25	SWNW	1840-10-01		A1
1952	" "	33	NESE	1840-10-01		A1
1950	" "	25	NWNW	1853-10-10		A1
1961	PAGE, John B	14	NWSE	1835-09-09		A1
1962	" "	14	SWSE	1840-10-01		A1
1894	PENYMAN, David E	26	NESW	1854-03-01		A1
1895	" "	26	SENW	1854-03-01		A1
1969	PERRY, John	3	1NE	1825-07-15		A1
1897	PERRYMAN, David E	35	SENW	1849-06-01		A1
1896	" "	26	SWSE	1853-10-10		A1
2023	PORTEL, Peter J	12	NESE	1840-10-01		A1
2024	" "	12	SWNE	1840-10-01		A1
1970	PORTELL, John	30	S½2NW	1854-11-15		A1
1998	PORTELL, Joseph	20	SESW	1854-11-15		A1 F
1960	RACINE, Joffroid	5	SW	1848-12-01		A1 F
1927	RAMBO, Jacob H	4	1NE	1825-07-15		A1
1881	RAY, Frederick	26	S½SW	1854-11-15		A1 G69
1882	" "	27	SESE	1854-11-15		A1 G69
1883	" "	33	SESE	1854-11-15		A1 G69
1914	REANDEAU, Francois	22	E½NE	1848-02-01		A1
1855	REANDO, Antoin	26	NWNW	1853-04-15		A1
1971	REANDO, John	23	SWSW	1848-07-01		A1

ID	Individual in Patent	Sec.	Sec. Part	Date Issued	Other Counties	For More Info . . .
1972	REANDO, John (Cont'd)	26	NENW	1854-03-01		A1
1964	REED, John C	29	E½NW	1840-10-01		A1 R1953
1965	" "	30	NWNE	1840-10-01		A1
1966	" "	30	SWNE	1840-10-01		A1
2007	RICHARDSON, Mary	23	SESW	1854-03-01		A1
1908	RIENDO, Francis	14	NESE	1840-10-01		A1
2021	ROBERT, Peter E	22	NWNE	1848-07-01		A1
2013	ROBERTS, Michael	12	NESW	1840-10-01		A1
2014	" "	13	NENW	1840-10-01		A1
1884	SAUNDERS, Thomas P	12	SESW	1854-11-15		A1 G70
1885	" "	12	SWSE	1854-11-15		A1 G70
1886	" "	23	NWSW	1854-11-15		A1 G70
1887	" "	34	S½NE	1854-11-15		A1 G70
1888	" "	35	SWNW	1854-11-15		A1 G70
2055	" "	36	W½SW	1854-11-15		A1 G206
1898	SCOTT, David H	27	NWSE	1854-03-01		A1
1974	SCOTT, John	33	S½NE	1824-05-01		A1
1973	" "	27	E½SW	1826-05-01		A1
1975	" "	33	W½SE	1832-02-11		A1
2020	SHURTLEFF, Oliver	17	SE	1848-07-01		A1 F
1903	SIMS, Elisha	27	NENE	1838-09-07		A1
2055	SMITH, Alexander H	36	W½SW	1854-11-15		A1 G206
1928	SMITH, James C	32	E½NW	1849-07-23		A1
1976	SMITH, John	22	SE	1834-05-20		A1
1977	" "	23	E½SE	1858-03-02		A1
1978	" "	24	NWSW	1858-03-02		A1
1979	SMITH, John T	10	SW	1858-03-02		A1 F
1980	" "	10	SWNW	1858-03-02		A1 F
1981	" "	21		1858-03-02		A1 F
1982	" "	22	W½	1858-03-02		A1
1983	" "	27	NWNW	1858-03-02		A1
1984	" "	28	N½NW	1858-03-02		A1
1985	" "	28	NE	1858-03-02		A1
1986	" "	31	SW	1858-03-02		A1 F
1987	" "	9	S½NE	1858-03-02		A1
1988	" "	9	S½NW	1858-03-02		A1
1989	" "	9	SE	1858-03-02		A1
1990	" "	9	SW	1858-03-02		A1
2027	SMITH, Reuben	15	NW	1824-05-01		A1
2028	" "	2	NW	1824-05-01		A1 F
2045	TAUSSIG, Seligman	13	N½SE	1854-03-01		A1
2046	" "	13	SENE	1854-03-01		A1
1992	TRIMBLE, John	29	W½NW	1840-10-01		A1
1991	" "	29	SW	1849-07-23		A1
1963	TRUDAU, John B	34	NWSW	1851-11-01		A1
2044	VAN REED, SAMUEL	30	E½NE	1838-09-07		A1
1909	VILLMARE, Francis	8	1NE	1854-03-01		A1 F
1910	" "	8	NWSE	1854-03-01		A1 F
1911	VILMAIN, Francis	12	W½SW	1840-10-01		A1
1912	VILMAR, Francis	8	NESE	1850-09-09		A1 F
1913	" "	8	S½SE	1850-09-09		A1 F
1947	WADE, George W	36	SWSE	1854-11-15		A1 G48
1994	WARDEN, Johnson	31	S½SE	1849-07-23		A1
1840	WEIDLE, Addison T	14	SW	1854-03-01		A1 F
2034	WHITE, Samuel C	30	N½2SW	1848-02-01		A1
2033	" "	30	N½1SW	1848-07-01		A1
2035	" "	30	NWSE	1849-06-01		A1
2036	" "	36	SENE	1849-06-01		A1
1934	WILKINSON, James J	31	W½NE	1840-10-01		A1
1932	" "	30	SESE	1849-06-01		A1
1933	" "	31	E½NE	1849-06-01		A1
1935	" "	32	NWNW	1849-06-01		A1
1904	WINEOUR, Elizabeth	26	NWSE	1854-03-01		A1 R1858
2072	WINEOUR, William	26	NWSW	1854-11-15		A1
2073	" "	26	SWNW	1854-11-15		A1

Patent Map

T38-N R3-E
5th PM Meridian

Map Group 15

Township Statistics

Parcels Mapped	:	235
Number of Patents	:	184
Number of Individuals	:	117
Patentees Identified	:	116
Number of Surnames	:	88
Multi-Patentee Parcels	:	22
Oldest Patent Date	:	5/1/1824
Most Recent Patent	:	2/7/1921
Block/Lot Parcels	:	27
Parcels Re - Issued	:	7
Parcels that Overlap	:	0
Cities and Towns	:	11
Cemeteries	:	5

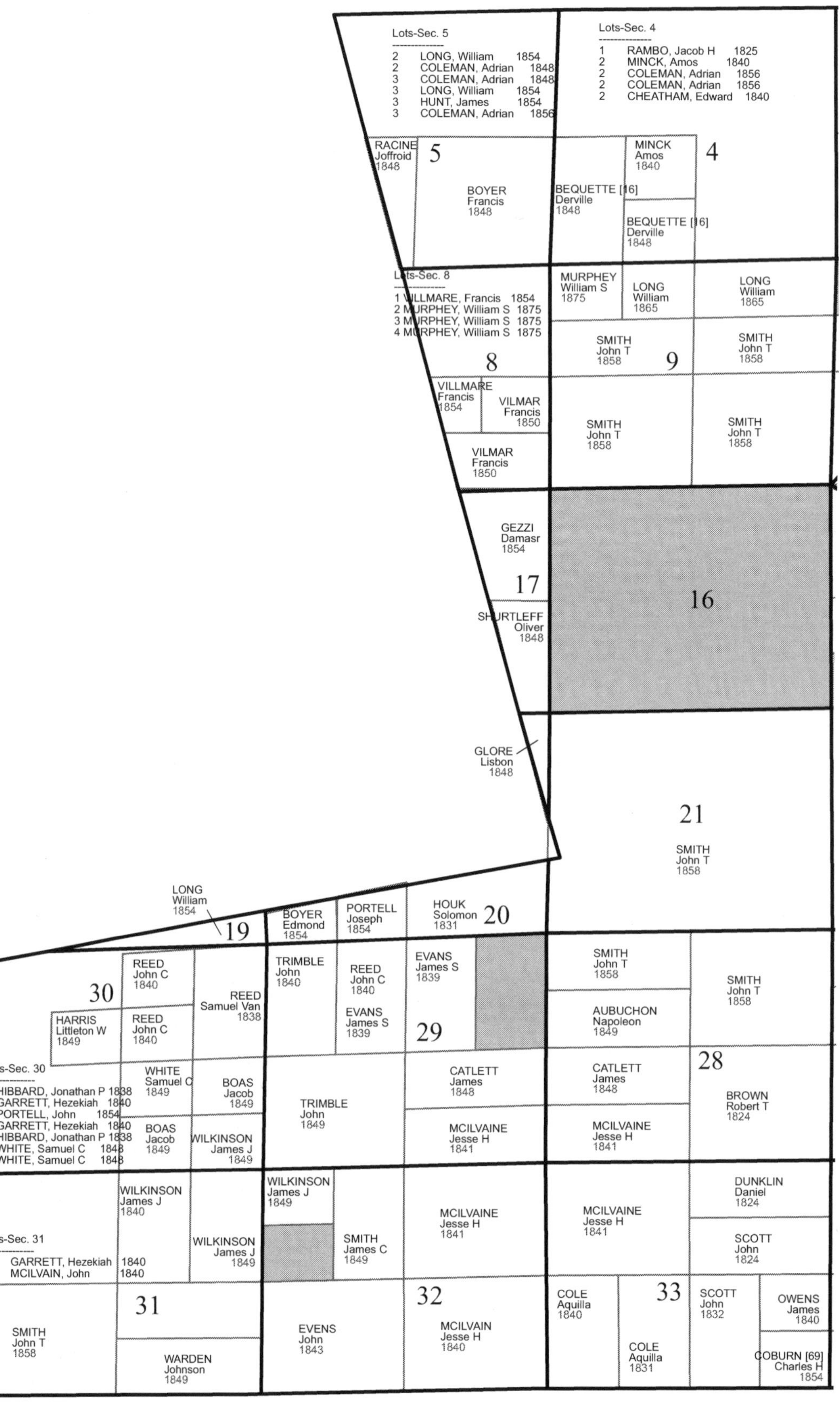

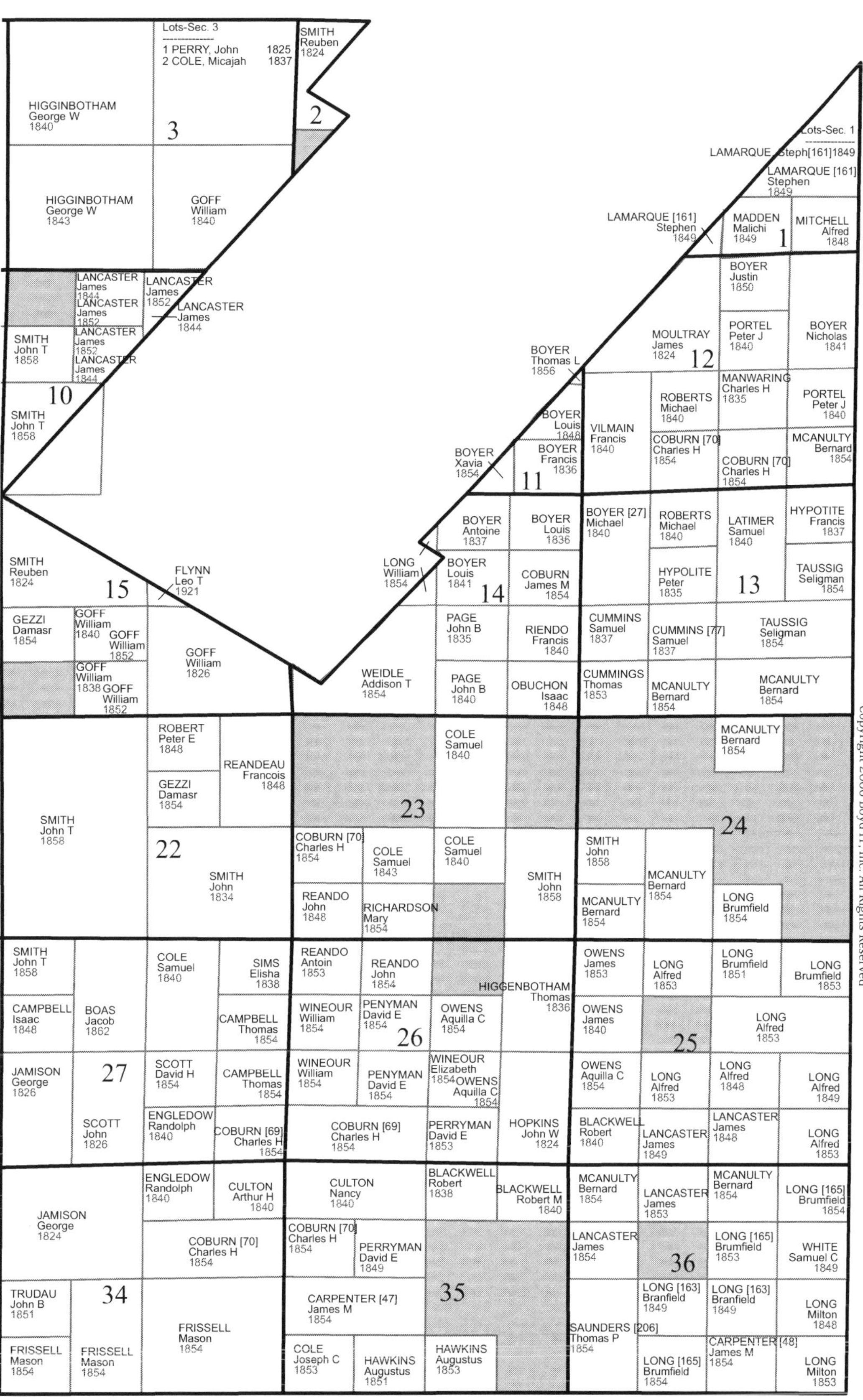

Helpful Hints

1. This Map's INDEX can be found on the preceding pages.
2. Refer to Map "C" to see where this Township lies within Washington County, Missouri.
3. Numbers within square brackets [ ] denote a multi-patentee land parcel (multi-owner). Refer to Appendix "C" for a full list of members in this group.
4. Areas that look to be crowded with Patentees usually indicate multiple sales of the same parcel (Re-issues) or Overlapping parcels. See this Township's Index for an explanation of these and other circumstances that might explain "odd" groupings of Patentees on this map.

Legend

- Patent Boundary
- Section Boundary
- No Patents Found (or Outside County)
- 1., 2., 3., ... Lot Numbers (when beside a name)
- [ ] Group Number (see Appendix "C")

Scale: Section = 1 mile X 1 mile (generally, with some exceptions)

Road Map

T38-N R3-E
5th PM Meridian

Map Group 15

Cities & Towns

- Adelbert (historical)
- Bellefontaine
- Cadet
- Cannon Mines
- Fountain Farm
- Shibboleth
- Tiff
- White (historical)
- Happy Hollow
- Mud Town
- Theabeau Town

Cemeteries

- Aquilla Cole Cemetery
- Barlow Cemetery
- Brick Cemetery
- Saint Joseph Cemetery
- Goff Cemetery

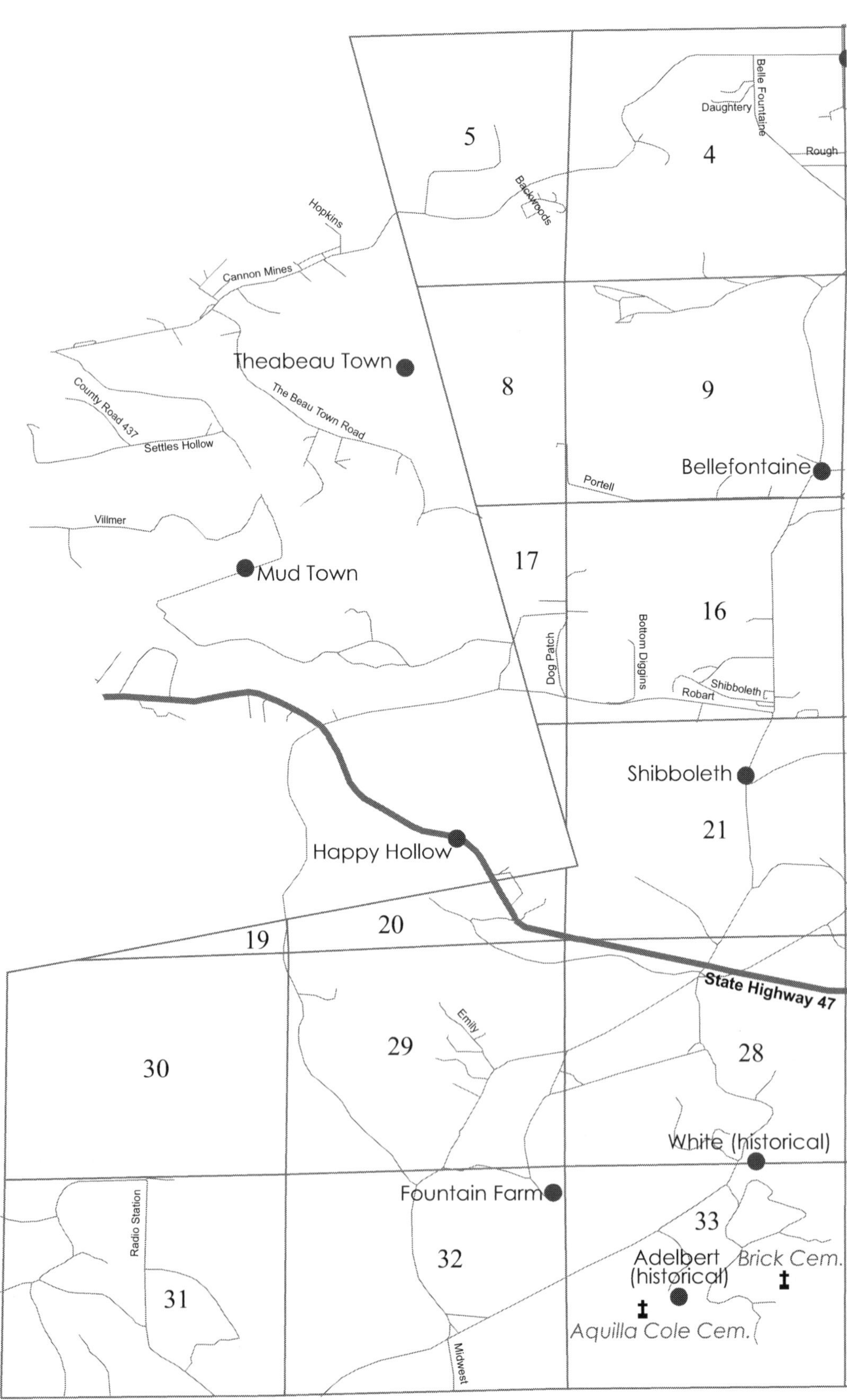

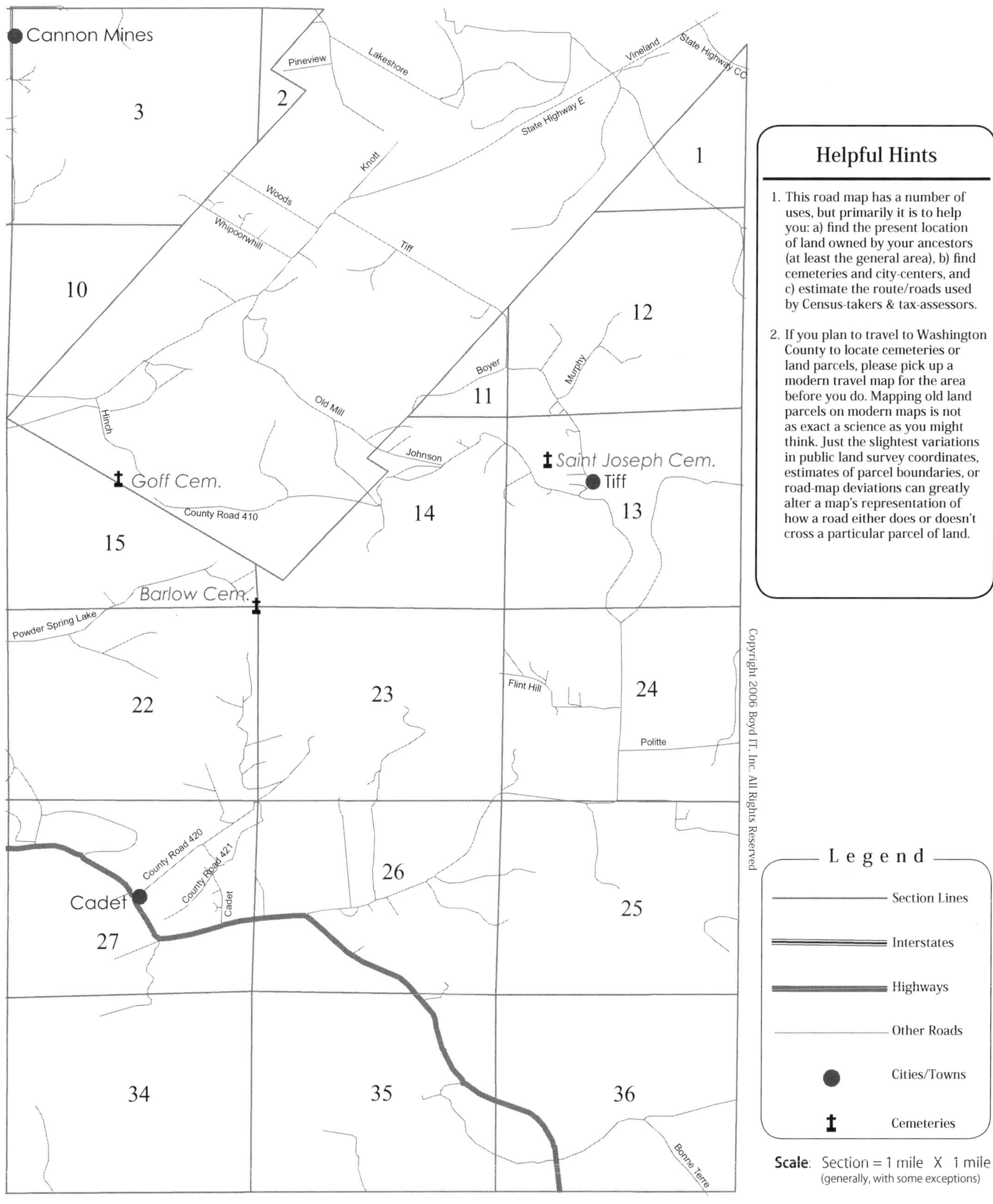
Cannon Mines
3
2
1
10
11
12
13
14
15
22
23
24
25
26
27
34
35
36
Pineview
Lakeshore
Vineland
State Highway CC
State Highway E
Knott
Woods
Whipoorwhill
Tiff
Murphy
Boyer
Old Mill
Hinch
Johnson
Saint Joseph Cem.
Tiff
Goff Cem.
County Road 410
Barlow Cem.
Powder Spring Lake
Flint Hill
Politte
County Road 420
County Road 421
Cadet
Cadet
Bonne Terre
Helpful Hints
1. This road map has a number of uses, but primarily it is to help you: a) find the present location of land owned by your ancestors (at least the general area), b) find cemeteries and city-centers, and c) estimate the route/roads used by Census-takers & tax-assessors.
2. If you plan to travel to Washington County to locate cemeteries or land parcels, please pick up a modern travel map for the area before you do. Mapping old land parcels on modern maps is not as exact a science as you might think. Just the slightest variations in public land survey coordinates, estimates of parcel boundaries, or road-map deviations can greatly alter a map's representation of how a road either does or doesn't cross a particular parcel of land.
Legend
Section Lines
Interstates
Highways
Other Roads
Cities/Towns
Cemeteries
Scale: Section = 1 mile X 1 mile
(generally, with some exceptions)

Historical Map

T38-N R3-E
5th PM Meridian

Map Group 15

Cities & Towns
- Adelbert (historical)
- Bellefontaine
- Cadet
- Cannon Mines
- Fountain Farm
- Shibboleth
- Tiff
- White (historical)
- Happy Hollow
- Mud Town
- Theabeau Town

Cemeteries
- Aquilla Cole Cemetery
- Barlow Cemetery
- Brick Cemetery
- Saint Joseph Cemetery
- Goff Cemetery

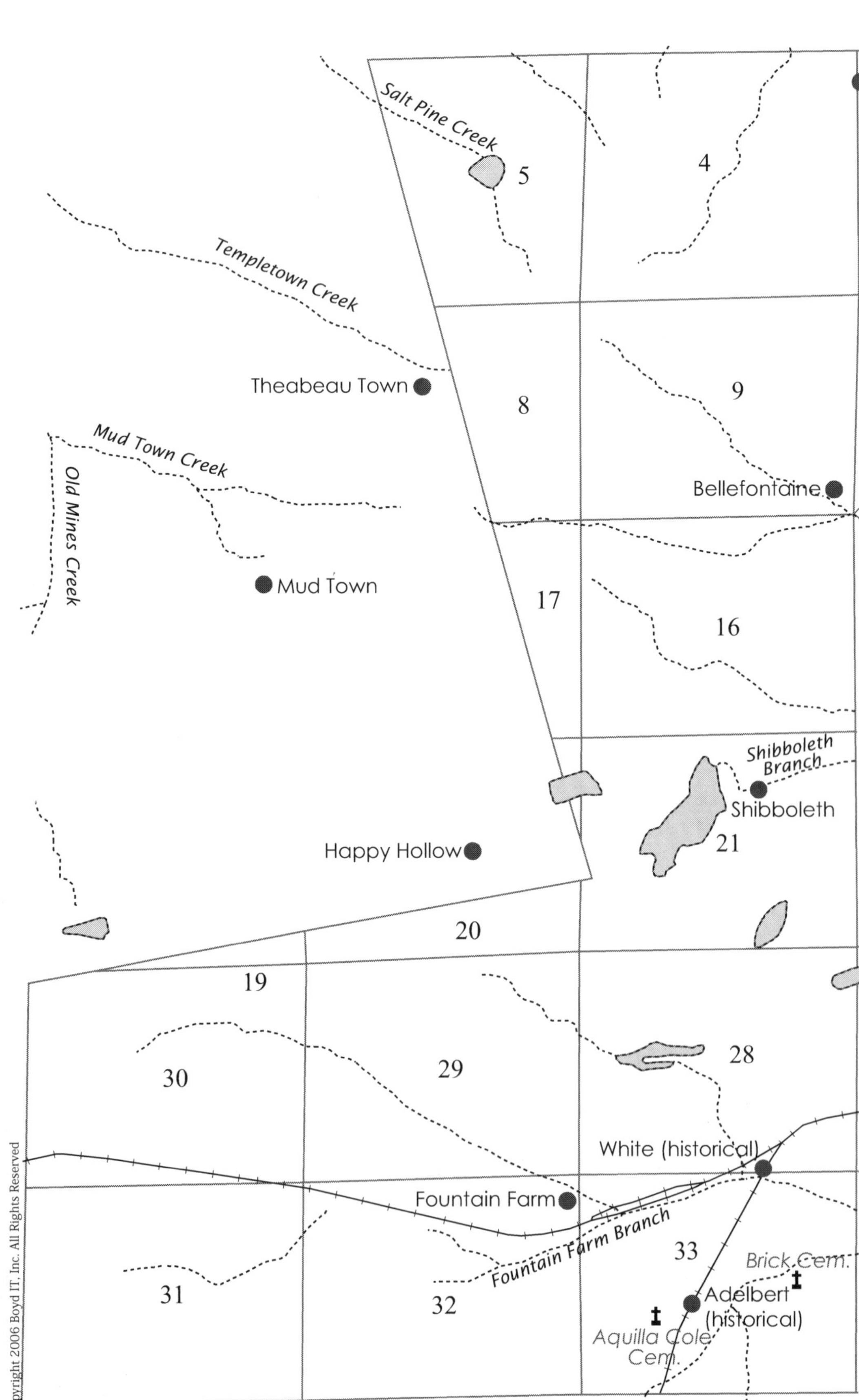

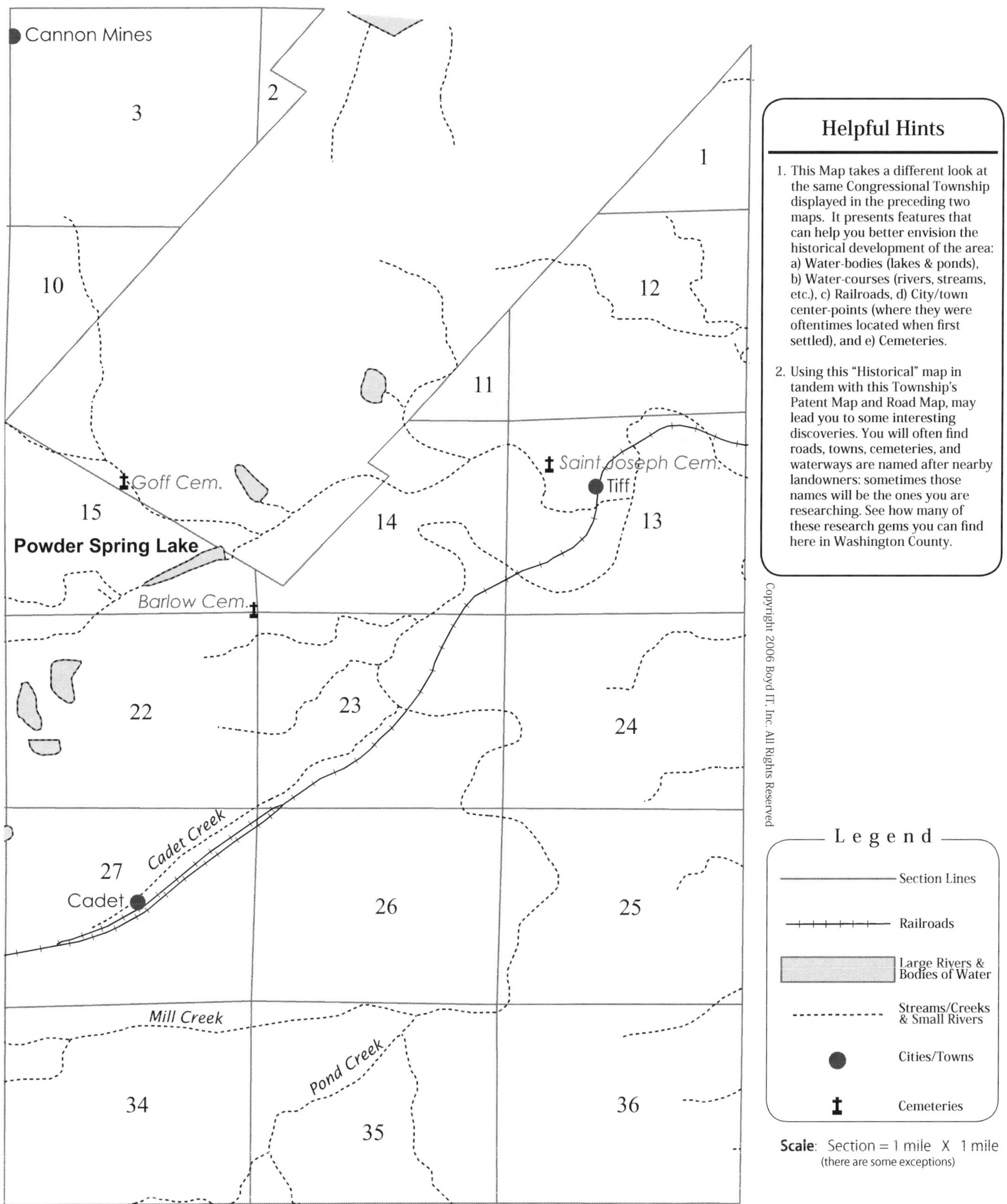
Cannon Mines
3
2
1
10
12
11
Goff Cem.
Saint Joseph Cem.
Tiff
15
14
13
Powder Spring Lake
Barlow Cem.
22
23
24
Cadet Creek
27
Cadet
26
25
Mill Creek
Pond Creek
34
35
36
Helpful Hints
1. This Map takes a different look at the same Congressional Township displayed in the preceding two maps. It presents features that can help you better envision the historical development of the area: a) Water-bodies (lakes & ponds), b) Water-courses (rivers, streams, etc.), c) Railroads, d) City/town center-points (where they were oftentimes located when first settled), and e) Cemeteries.
2. Using this "Historical" map in tandem with this Township's Patent Map and Road Map, may lead you to some interesting discoveries. You will often find roads, towns, cemeteries, and waterways are named after nearby landowners: sometimes those names will be the ones you are researching. See how many of these research gems you can find here in Washington County.
Copyright 2006 Boyd IT, Inc. All Rights Reserved
Legend
Section Lines
Railroads
Large Rivers & Bodies of Water
Streams/Creeks & Small Rivers
Cities/Towns
Cemeteries
Scale: Section = 1 mile X 1 mile
(there are some exceptions)

Map Group 16: Index to Land Patents

Township 37-North Range 2-West (5th PM)

After you locate an individual in this Index, take note of the Section and Section Part then proceed to the Land Patent map on the pages immediately following. You should have no difficulty locating the corresponding parcel of land.

The "For More Info" Column will lead you to more information about the underlying Patents. See the *Legend* at right, and the "How to Use this Book" chapter, for more information.

LEGEND

"For More Info . . . " column

- **A** = Authority (Legislative Act, See Appendix "A")
- **B** = Block or Lot (location in Section unknown)
- **C** = Cancelled Patent
- **F** = Fractional Section
- **G** = Group (Multi-Patentee Patent, see Appendix "C")
- **V** = Overlaps another Parcel
- **R** = Re-Issued (Parcel patented more than once)

(A & G items require you to look in the Appendixes referred to above. All other Letter-designations followed by a number require you to locate line-items in this index that possess the ID number found after the letter).

ID	Individual in Patent	Sec.	Sec. Part	Date Issued	Other Counties	For More Info . . .
2090	ANDERSON, John	25	SESE	1859-09-10	Crawford	A1
2091	" "	36	E½NE	1859-09-10	Crawford	A1
2075	BEACH, Asahel	36	N½SW	1859-09-01	Crawford	A1
2076	" "	36	NW	1859-09-01	Crawford	A1
2077	" "	36	W½NE	1859-09-01	Crawford	A1
2117	BELEW, William	25	SWSE	1876-06-20	Crawford	A3
2082	BELL, Daniel W	25	W½	1859-09-01	Crawford	A1
2087	BERRYMAN, J W	13	NESE	1892-08-01	Crawford	A1
2104	BOLLINGER, Moses	24	NENE	1837-11-07	Crawford	A1
2118	BUSCH, William	12	NENW	1892-08-01	Crawford	A1
2126	CAMPBELL, Zachariah	1	SESE	1857-12-15	Crawford	A1
2100	DEVALIN, Martha	1	E½2NW	1859-09-01	Crawford	A1
2101	" "	1	N½SE	1859-09-01	Crawford	A1
2102	" "	1	NE	1859-09-01	Crawford	A1
2103	" "	1	SWSE	1859-09-01	Crawford	A1
2108	DEVALIN, Rebecca	1	1NW	1859-09-01	Crawford	A1
2109	" "	1	SW	1859-09-01	Crawford	A1
2110	" "	1	W½2NW	1859-09-01	Crawford	A1
2097	DOBKINS, Joshua T	24	NWNE	1876-01-10	Crawford	A1
2095	DOYLE, Joseph	12	SE	1859-09-01	Crawford	A1
2096	" "	13	NE	1859-09-01	Crawford	A1
2084	ESTES, Henry	24	NESW	1856-01-03	Crawford	A1
2086	" "	24	SWSE	1856-01-03	Crawford	A1
2085	" "	24	SESW	1857-10-30	Crawford	A1
2113	FLYNN, Timothy	36	SE	1860-08-01	Crawford	A1
2106	FOGARTY, Oliver S	12	SESW	1860-10-01	Crawford	A1
2107	" "	13	NENW	1860-10-01	Crawford	A1
2092	GARRISON, John	13	SWSW	1833-10-15	Crawford	A1
2093	GARRISSON, John	13	NWSW	1837-01-17	Crawford	A1
2112	HARRISON, Thomas C	24	N½NE	1851-12-01	Crawford	A1 F
2088	HENSLEY, James	24	E½NW	1837-11-07	Crawford	A1
2094	HENSLEY, John	24	NWSE	1841-06-25	Crawford	A1
2123	HUDSPETH, William	12	W½SW	1837-11-14	Crawford	A1
2121	" "	12	SENW	1856-01-03	Crawford	A1
2122	" "	12	W½NE	1856-01-03	Crawford	A1
2120	" "	12	NESW	1857-12-15	Crawford	A1
2119	" "	12	NENE	1859-01-01	Crawford	A1
2081	NORTRUP, Conrad	36	SWSW	1860-10-01	Crawford	A1
2114	POWER, Walter	12	SENE	1906-06-30	Crawford	A1
2105	SCOTT, Moses	13	W½NW	1833-10-15	Crawford	A1
2089	SERVICE, James	24	W½SW	1860-10-01	Crawford	A1
2124	STAPLES, William	24	SESE	1837-03-15	Crawford	A1
2125	" "	25	NENE	1837-03-15	Crawford	A1
2083	SWIER, David	13	SENW	1837-11-14	Crawford	A1
2098	THOMPSON, Lovel	24	W½NW	1824-05-31	Crawford	A1
2111	TUCKER, Robert	13	SESE	1837-11-07	Crawford	A1

ID	Individual in Patent	Sec.	Sec. Part	Date Issued	Other Counties	For More Info . . .
2115	TUCKER, Walter W	13	E½SW	1837-01-24	Crawford	A1
2116	" "	13	W½SE	1837-01-24	Crawford	A1
2099	WALKER, Mark	12	NWNW	1856-01-03	Crawford	A1
2078	WOOD, Austin E	24	SENE	1876-01-10	Crawford	A1
2079	WOOD, Bruce	25	N½SE	1858-01-15	Crawford	A1
2080	" "	25	W½NE	1858-01-15	Crawford	A1

Patent Map

T37-N R2-W
5th PM Meridian

Map Group 16

Township Statistics

Parcels Mapped	:	52
Number of Patents	:	39
Number of Individuals	:	33
Patentees Identified	:	33
Number of Surnames	:	29
Multi-Patentee Parcels	:	0
Oldest Patent Date	:	5/31/1824
Most Recent Patent	:	6/30/1906
Block/Lot Parcels	:	3
Parcels Re - Issued	:	0
Parcels that Overlap	:	0
Cities and Towns	:	1
Cemeteries	:	0

Note: the area contained in this map amounts to far less than a full Township. Therefore, its contents are completely on this single page (instead of a "normal" 2-page spread).

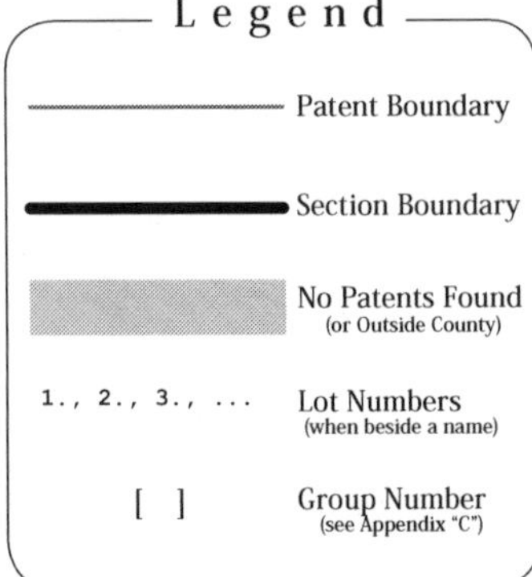

Scale: Section = 1 mile X 1 mile
(generally, with some exceptions)

Lots-Sec. 1
1 DEVALIN, Rebecca 1859
1 DEVALIN, Martha 1859
1 DEVALIN, Rebecca 1859

DEVALIN Martha 1859

1

DEVALIN Martha 1859

DEVALIN Rebecca 1859

DEVALIN Martha 1859

CAMPBELL Zachariah 1857

WALKER Mark 1856

BUSCH William 1892

HUDSPETH William 1856

HUDSPETH William 1859

HUDSPETH William 1856

12

POWER Walter 1906

HUDSPETH William 1837

HUDSPETH William 1857

FOGARTY Oliver S 1860

DOYLE Joseph 1859

Washington County

SCOTT Moses 1833

FOGARTY Oliver S 1860

SWIER David 1837

DOYLE Joseph 1859

13

GARRISSON John 1837

GARRISON John 1833

TUCKER Walter W 1837

TUCKER Walter W 1837

BERRYMAN J W 1892

TUCKER Robert 1837

THOMPSON Lovel 1824

HENSLEY James 1837

DOBKINS Joshua T 1876

HARRISON Thomas C 1851

BOLLINGER Moses 1837

24

WOOD Austin E 1876

SERVICE James 1860

ESTES Henry 1856

ESTES Henry 1857

HENSLEY John 1841

ESTES Henry 1856

STAPLES William 1837

Crawford County

WOOD Bruce 1858

STAPLES William 1837

25

BELL Daniel W 1859

WOOD Bruce 1858

BELEW William 1876

ANDERSON John 1859

BEACH Asahel 1859

BEACH Asahel 1859

ANDERSON John 1859

36

BEACH Asahel 1859

NORTRUP Conrad 1860

FLYNN Timothy 1860

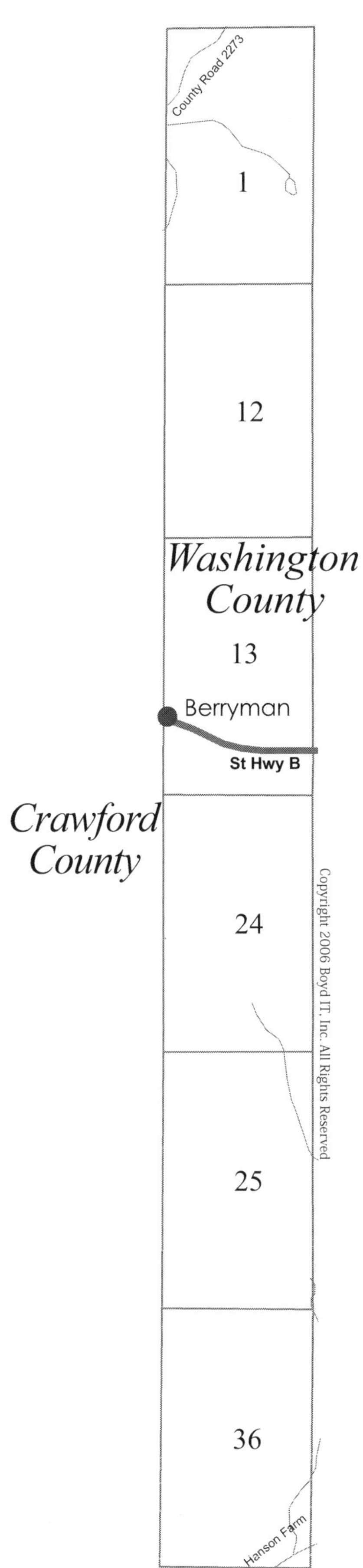

Road Map

T37-N R2-W
5th PM Meridian

Map Group 16

Note: the area contained in this map amounts to far less than a full Township. Therefore, its contents are completely on this single page (instead of a "normal" 2-page spread).

Cities & Towns

Berryman

Cemeteries

None

Legend

- Section Lines
- Interstates
- Highways
- Other Roads
- Cities/Towns
- Cemeteries

Scale: Section = 1 mile X 1 mile
(generally, with some exceptions)

Historical Map

T37-N R2-W
5th PM Meridian

Map Group 16

Note: the area contained in this map amounts to far less than a full Township. Therefore, its contents are completely on this single page (instead of a "normal" 2-page spread).

Cities & Towns
Berryman

Cemeteries
None

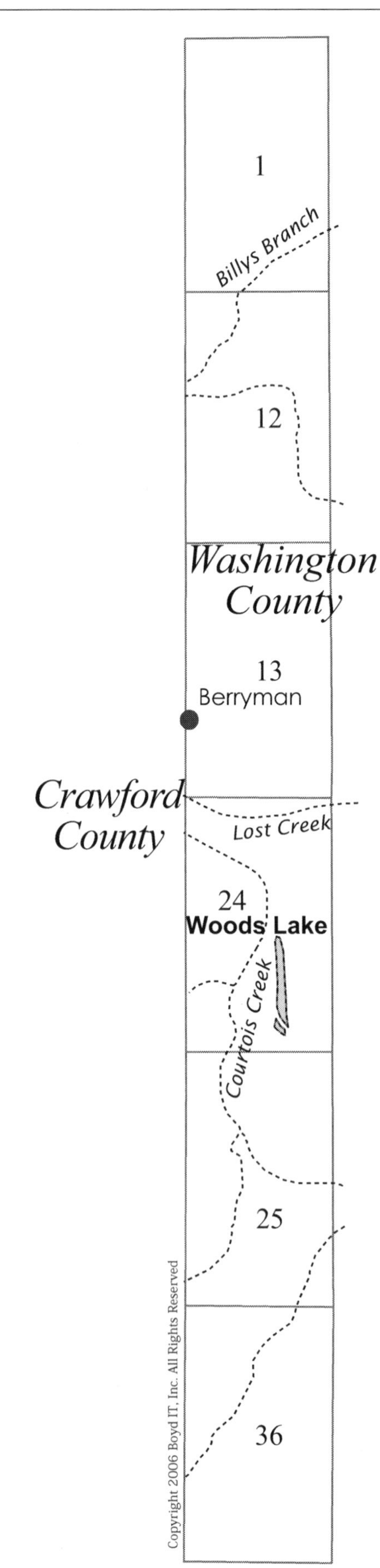

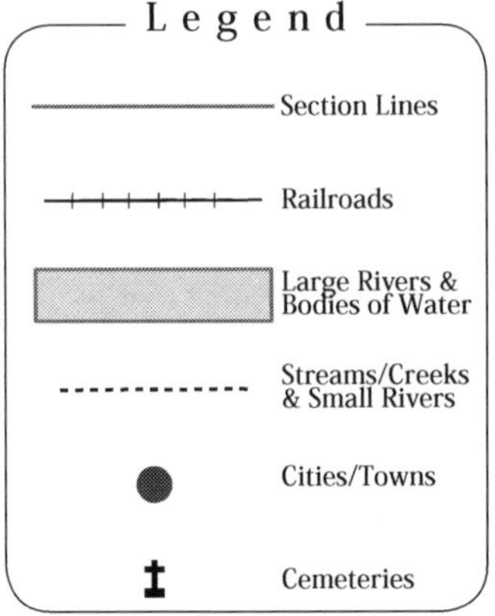

Scale: Section = 1 mile X 1 mile
(there are some exceptions)

Map Group 17: Index to Land Patents

Township 37-North Range 1-West (5th PM)

After you locate an individual in this Index, take note of the Section and Section Part then proceed to the Land Patent map on the pages immediately following. You should have no difficulty locating the corresponding parcel of land.

The "For More Info" Column will lead you to more information about the underlying Patents. See the *Legend* at right, and the "How to Use this Book" chapter, for more information.

LEGEND

"For More Info . . . " column

A = Authority (Legislative Act, See Appendix "A")
B = Block or Lot (location in Section unknown)
C = Cancelled Patent
F = Fractional Section
G = Group (Multi-Patentee Patent, see Appendix "C")
V = Overlaps another Parcel
R = Re-Issued (Parcel patented more than once)

(A & G items require you to look in the Appendixes referred to above. All other Letter-designations followed by a number require you to locate line-items in this index that possess the ID number found after the letter).

ID	Individual in Patent	Sec.	Sec. Part	Date Issued	Other Counties	For More Info . . .
2270	BALEW, William	31	SWNW	1869-07-01		A1 G6
2204	BERRYMAN, Josias	31	2SW	1851-12-01		A1 C
2205	" "	31	N½1SW	1851-12-01		A1 C
2206	" "	31	N½2NW	1851-12-01		A1
2207	" "	31	NWNE	1851-12-01		A1
2181	BLOUNT, James P	6	E½1NW	1859-09-01		A1
2279	BLUNT, Yancey	20	E½SE	1875-04-15		A3
2280	BLUNT, Yancy	20	NWSE	1892-07-11		A3
2232	BOAS, Robert J	32	E½SW	1837-11-07		A1
2214	BOLLINGER, Moses	18	S½1SW	1837-11-07		A1
2165	BOOTHE, George W	30	SESE	1837-11-07		A1 V2238
2166	" "	30	W½SE	1837-11-07		A1 V2238
2167	" "	31	NENE	1837-11-14		A1
2224	BRICKEY, Preston P	31	1NW	1837-11-07		A1
2177	BROCK, James	24	NWNE	1841-07-01		A1
2140	BRUEL, Chr	33	NWSW	1862-05-15		A1
2141	" "	33	S½SE	1862-05-15		A1
2142	" "	33	S½SW	1862-05-15		A1
2188	BUNYARD, John S	21	S½SE	1859-09-01		A1
2189	" "	21	S½SW	1859-09-01		A1
2190	" "	28	NWNW	1859-09-01		A1
2182	CARR, Jason	5	W½1NW	1848-03-01		A1
2217	CHALFANT, Presley G	20	E½SW	1859-09-01		A1
2218	" "	20	SWNW	1859-09-01		A1
2219	" "	20	SWSE	1859-09-01		A1
2220	" "	29	NENW	1859-09-01		A1
2221	" "	29	NWNE	1859-09-01		A1
2222	CHALFANT, Presly G	28	NENW	1859-01-01		A1
2128	COMPTON, Aley C	24	NWNW	1857-10-30		A1
2174	COMPTON, Henry S	13	SESW	1854-11-15		A1
2175	" "	24	NENW	1854-11-15		A1
2183	DINWIDDIE, John	26	NENE	1837-11-07		A1
2184	" "	26	NENW	1837-11-07		A1
2271	EASOM, William	13	SWSW	1856-06-03		A2
2143	FINISON, Daniel	20	N½NW	1837-11-07		A1
2178	FINISON, James	19	NENE	1837-11-07		A1
2127	FLEMING, Alexander	35	W½SE	1838-08-01		A1 G105
2185	FORESTER, John	36	SENE	1859-09-01		A1
2155	GHOLSON, Felix G	22	SWNW	1837-11-07		A1
2241	GILMORE, Solomon	15	NWNW	1859-09-10		A1
2242	" "	15	S½NW	1875-08-10		A3
2196	GREGORY, Joseph	20	NWNE	1854-11-15		A1
2197	" "	21	NWNW	1854-11-15		A1
2198	" "	21	SWNW	1854-11-15		A1
2272	HAGGARD, William	18	N½1SW	1900-02-02		A3
2273	" "	18	N½2SW	1900-02-02		A3

ID	Individual in Patent	Sec.	Sec. Part	Date Issued	Other Counties	For More Info . . .
2172	HALL, Harrison	25	NENE	1874-06-15		A1
2274	HARRIS, William	21	N½NE	1859-09-10		A1
2275	" "	21	NENW	1859-09-10		A1
2164	HARVEY, George P	23	NESE	1874-06-15		A1
2187	HOFF, John P	23	NWNE	1858-04-01		A1
2186	HOLMES, John	8	SESE	1841-06-25		A1
2260	HUDSON, Thomas O	19	SENE	1898-04-11		A3
2246	HUDSPETH, Theodore T	32	NWNW	1837-11-14		A1
2168	JINKERSON, George W	25	NWSW	1867-05-01		A1
2169	" "	26	SWSE	1867-05-01		A1
2192	JOHNSON, John W	32	SENW	1837-11-07		A1
2193	" "	32	SWNW	1837-11-14		A1
2261	JOHNSON, Uriah P	6	NENE	1848-03-01		A1
2254	KELLY, Thomas	21	N½SE	1837-01-24		A1
2133	LEAGUE, Charles C	22	NESW	1853-12-01		A1
2135	" "	22	NWSE	1854-11-15		A1
2134	" "	22	NWNW	1859-01-01		A1
2161	LONDON, George M	1	2NE	1904-11-22		A1
2162	" "	22	SWSW	1904-11-22		A1
2163	" "	34	NWNE	1904-11-22		A1
2270	LOOMIS, Levi S	31	SWNW	1869-07-01		A1 G6
2127	MANNING, Foreman	35	W½SE	1838-08-01		A1 G105
2156	" "	34	E½SE	1841-07-01		A1 G174
2157	" "	35	W½SW	1841-07-01		A1 G174
2158	" "	35	E½SE	1858-01-15		A1 G171
2210	MANNING, Lewis	29	E½NE	1875-04-01		A3
2211	" "	29	SENW	1875-04-01		A3
2212	" "	29	SWNE	1875-04-01		A3
2233	MANNING, Robert	26	SESW	1873-11-01		A3
2229	MARSHALL, Robert F	17	NENE	1859-09-10		A1
2230	" "	17	S½NE	1859-09-10		A1
2231	" "	17	SE	1859-09-10		A1
2247	MATHEWS, Thomas B	22	SESE	1854-11-15		A1
2129	MATTHEWS, Ambrose P	17	NWNW	1865-06-10		A1
2130	" "	8	SWSW	1865-06-10		A1
2151	MATTHEWS, Elijah B	25	SESE	1837-11-07		A1
2152	" "	25	W½SE	1837-11-07		A1
2148	" "	21	S½NE	1854-11-15		A1
2149	" "	21	SENW	1854-11-15		A1
2150	" "	22	NWSW	1859-09-01		A1
2153	MATTHEWS, Ezekiel	21	N½SW	1841-06-25		A1
2154	" "	23	SWSW	1854-11-15		A1
2173	MATTHEWS, Henry	36	N½SE	1871-11-01		A3
2195	MATTHEWS, Jonas	36	NENW	1872-07-01		A3
2225	MATTHEWS, Ralph	18	SWSE	1837-11-07		A1
2226	" "	19	NWNE	1837-11-07		A1
2239	MATTHEWS, Sarah B	24	NENE	1837-11-14		A1
2255	MATTHEWS, Thomas	22	SENW	1848-09-01		A1
2256	" "	22	SWNE	1848-09-01		A1
2250	MATTHEWS, Thomas B	26	NWNW	1858-01-15		A1
2251	" "	26	S½NE	1858-01-15		A1
2249	" "	26	NWNE	1858-12-01		A1
2252	" "	26	S½NW	1859-01-01		A1
2253	" "	27	NENE	1859-01-01		A1
2248	" "	17	SWNW	1865-06-10		A1
2264	MATTHEWS, William A	20	SENW	1837-11-14		A1
2265	" "	20	SWNE	1837-11-14		A1
2266	" "	23	NWNW	1848-03-01		A1
2267	MATTHEWS, William B	18	S½2SW	1837-11-07		A1
2268	" "	19	1NW	1837-11-07		A1
2269	" "	19	N½2NW	1837-11-07		A1
2259	MAXWELL, Thomas	13	SWSE	1854-11-15		A1
2257	" "	13	NESE	1856-06-16		A1
2258	" "	13	SESE	1869-07-01		A1
2158	MCKEE, Thomas S	35	E½SE	1858-01-15		A1 G171
2276	MCMILLEN, William M	6	W½1NW	1900-11-12		A3
2277	MCMURTREY, William M	20	E½NE	1837-11-07		A1
2234	MERRY, Samuel	17	E½SW	1837-11-07		A1 G183
2179	MOUTRAY, James H	5	W½2NW	1848-02-01		A1
2180	" "	6	N½2SW	1857-10-30		A1
2215	MURPHY, Newton	6	S½2SW	1906-06-20		A1
2216	" "	6	W½2NW	1907-05-10		A1
2144	OLIVER, David	32	SWSE	1838-08-01		A1

ID	Individual in Patent	Sec.	Sec. Part	Date Issued	Other Counties	For More Info . . .
2223	PAUL, Presly	22	SENE	1837-11-14		A1
2262	PEARSON, Wesley R	25	NESE	1874-06-15		A1
2263	" "	36	NESW	1875-03-05		A1
2147	PETTIGREW, Edwin	15	NENW	1859-09-10		A1
2146	" "	10	SESW	1875-08-10		A3
2131	POWELL, Ambrose	26	SESE	1837-11-07		A1
2132	" "	36	NWNW	1837-11-07		A1
2176	SAWYER, J M	4	W½2NW	1890-08-13		A1
2213	SCOTT, Lyndor D	14	SESE	1859-01-01		A1
2243	SHORE, Stephen D	31	S½NE	1860-10-01		A1
2244	" "	31	SESE	1860-10-01		A1
2245	" "	31	W½SE	1860-10-01		A1
2191	SILVEY, John	14	W½SE	1898-04-06		A3
2240	SIMMONS, Seth	10	SESE	1904-06-27		A1 R2136
2137	SMITH, Charles D	25	SWNE	1874-06-15		A1
2136	" "	10	SESE	1892-08-01		A1 R2240
2138	" "	29	NWNW	1892-08-01		A1
2139	" "	9	SWSW	1902-12-09		A1
2145	SMITH, Dorcas	17	SENW	1875-04-15		A3
2159	SMITH, Frederick	28	N½SW	1873-11-01		A3
2160	" "	28	S½NW	1873-11-01		A3
2209	SMITH, Laurence	23	NENW	1857-10-30		A1
2156	SMITH, Reuben	34	E½SE	1841-07-01		A1 G174
2157	" "	35	W½SW	1841-07-01		A1 G174
2237	STAPLES, Samuel	30	NESW	1838-08-01		A1
2238	" "	30	S½SE	1838-08-01		A1 V2165, 2166
2270	STAPPLES, Samuel O	31	SWNW	1869-07-01		A1 G6
2278	STEPHENS, William M	24	S½NW	1904-01-28		A1
2234	STONE, Samuel L	17	E½SW	1837-11-07		A1 G183
2235	STONE, Samuel P	35	E½SW	1837-11-07		A1
2236	" "	34	W½SE	1838-08-01		A1 G216
2156	" "	34	E½SE	1841-07-01		A1 G174
2157	" "	35	W½SW	1841-07-01		A1 G174
2170	WALTON, George	24	NESW	1858-12-01		A1
2171	" "	25	W½NW	1859-01-01		A1
2194	WALTON, John	32	SESE	1877-11-10		A1
2156	WHITE, James M	34	E½SE	1841-07-01		A1 G174
2157	" "	35	W½SW	1841-07-01		A1 G174
2199	WHITENER, Joseph L	17	NWNE	1905-04-05		A1
2200	" "	19	S½2NW	1905-04-05		A1
2201	" "	19	SWNE	1905-04-05		A1
2202	" "	20	W½SW	1905-04-05		A1
2203	" "	29	SWNW	1905-04-05		A1
2208	WICKERS, Julius	31	S½1SW	1856-06-03		A2
2236	WILKINSON, Jeremiah	34	W½SE	1838-08-01		A1 G216
2227	WILSON, Robert E	1	1NW	1905-03-30		A3
2228	" "	1	E½2NW	1905-03-30		A3

Patent Map

T37-N R1-W
5th PM Meridian

Map Group 17

Township Statistics

Parcels Mapped	:	154
Number of Patents	:	122
Number of Individuals	:	91
Patentees Identified	:	86
Number of Surnames	:	68
Multi-Patentee Parcels	:	7
Oldest Patent Date	:	1/24/1837
Most Recent Patent	:	5/10/1907
Block/Lot Parcels	:	23
Parcels Re - Issued	:	1
Parcels that Overlap	:	3
Cities and Towns	:	0
Cemeteries	:	3

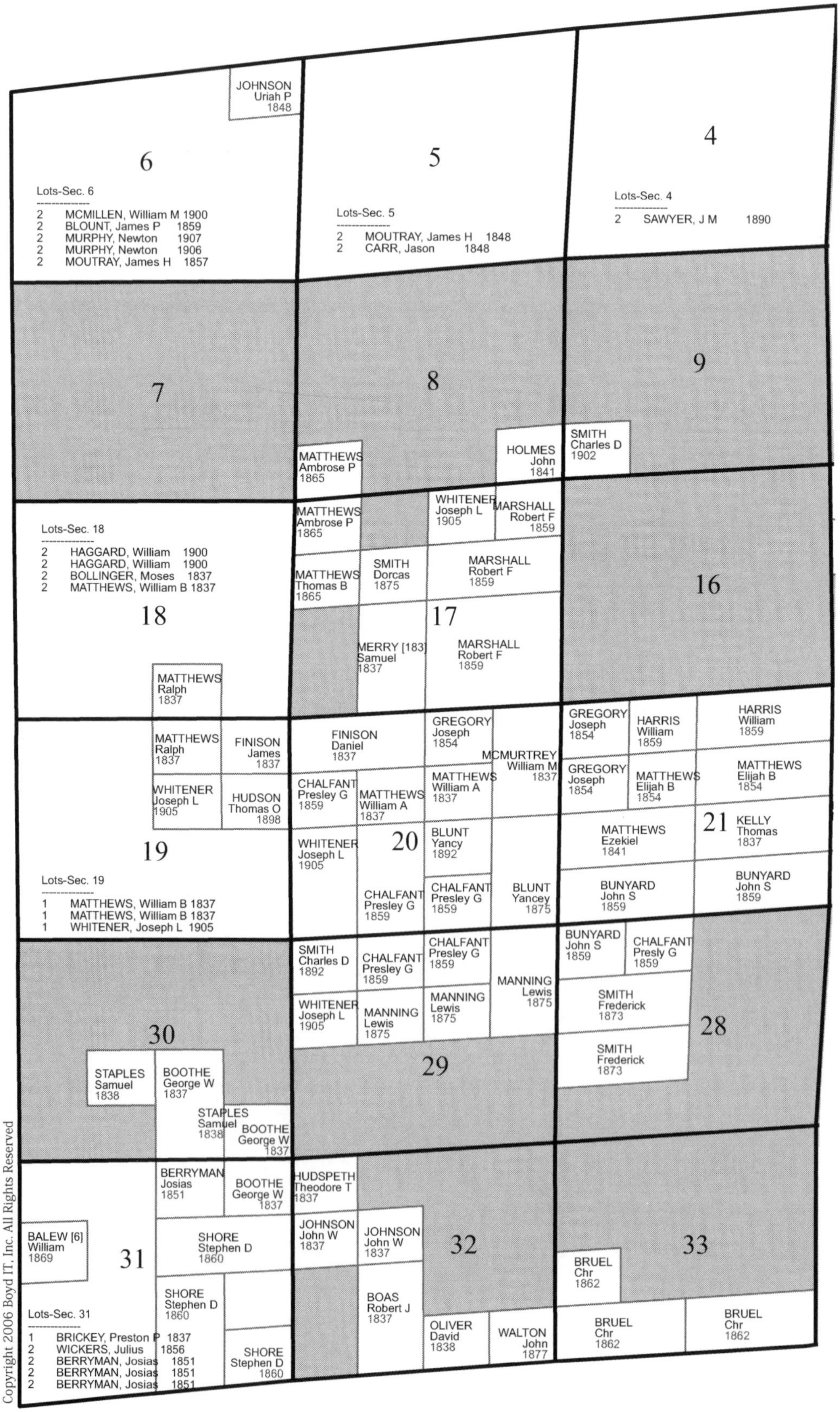

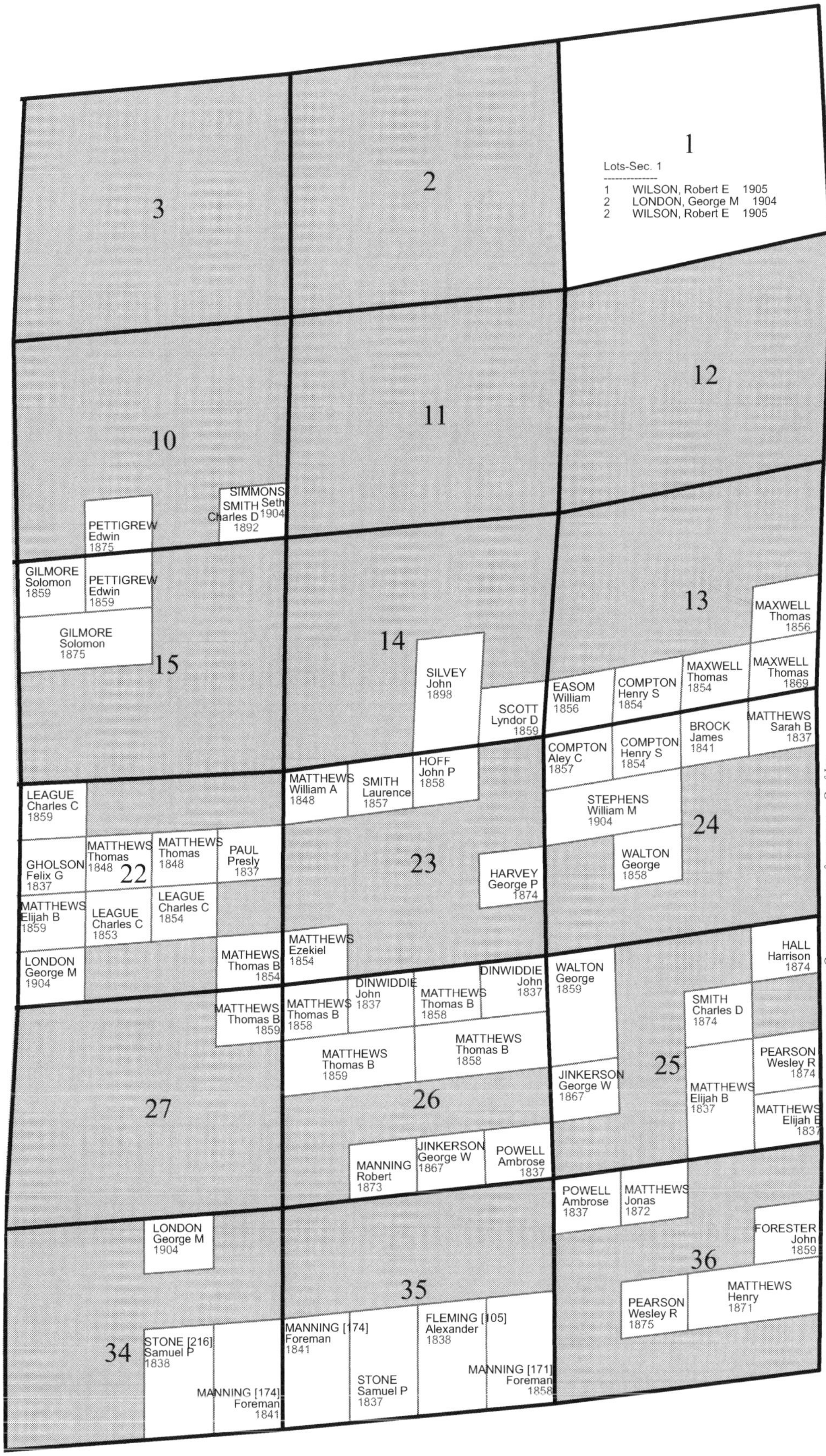

1
Lots-Sec. 1
1 WILSON, Robert E 1905
2 LONDON, George M 1904
2 WILSON, Robert E 1905
2
3
10
11
12
SIMMONS
SMITH Seth 1904
Charles D
1892
PETTIGREW Edwin 1875
GILMORE Solomon 1859
PETTIGREW Edwin 1859
GILMORE Solomon 1875
15
14
13
MAXWELL Thomas 1856
SILVEY John 1898
SCOTT Lyndor D 1859
EASOM William 1856
COMPTON Henry S 1854
MAXWELL Thomas 1854
MAXWELL Thomas 1869
COMPTON Aley C 1857
COMPTON Henry S 1854
BROCK James 1841
MATTHEWS Sarah B 1837
HOFF John P 1858
MATTHEWS William A 1848
SMITH Laurence 1857
STEPHENS William M 1904
24
LEAGUE Charles C 1859
MATTHEWS Thomas 1848
MATTHEWS Thomas 1848
PAUL Presly 1837
GHOLSON Felix G 1837
22
23
HARVEY George P 1874
WALTON George 1858
MATTHEWS Elijah B 1859
LEAGUE Charles C 1853
LEAGUE Charles C 1854
LONDON George M 1904
MATHEWS Thomas B 1854
MATTHEWS Ezekiel 1854
HALL Harrison 1874
DINWIDDIE John 1837
DINWIDDIE John 1837
WALTON George 1859
MATTHEWS Thomas B 1859
MATTHEWS Thomas B 1858
MATTHEWS Thomas B 1858
SMITH Charles D 1874
MATTHEWS Thomas B 1859
MATTHEWS Thomas B 1858
PEARSON Wesley R 1874
JINKERSON George W 1867
25
MATTHEWS Elijah B 1837
MATTHEWS Elijah B 1837
27
26
MANNING Robert 1873
JINKERSON George W 1867
POWELL Ambrose 1837
POWELL Ambrose 1837
MATTHEWS Jonas 1872
LONDON George M 1904
FORESTER John 1859
36
35
MATTHEWS Henry 1871
PEARSON Wesley R 1875
FLEMING [105] Alexander 1838
MANNING [174] Foreman 1841
34
STONE [216] Samuel P 1838
MANNING [174] Foreman 1841
STONE Samuel P 1837
MANNING [171] Foreman 1858

Helpful Hints

1. This Map's INDEX can be found on the preceding pages.
2. Refer to Map "C" to see where this Township lies within Washington County, Missouri.
3. Numbers within square brackets [ ] denote a multi-patentee land parcel (multi-owner). Refer to Appendix "C" for a full list of members in this group.
4. Areas that look to be crowded with Patentees usually indicate multiple sales of the same parcel (Re-issues) or Overlapping parcels. See this Township's Index for an explanation of these and other circumstances that might explain "odd" groupings of Patentees on this map.

Legend
Patent Boundary
Section Boundary
No Patents Found
(or Outside County)
1., 2., 3., ...
Lot Numbers
(when beside a name)
[ ]
Group Number
(see Appendix "C")

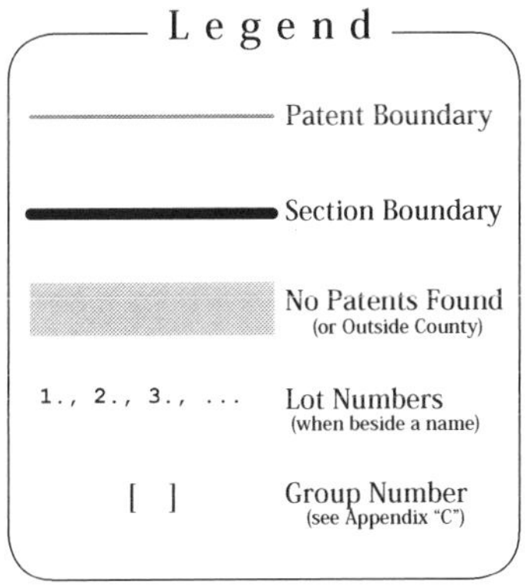

Scale: Section = 1 mile X 1 mile
(generally, with some exceptions)

Road Map

T37-N R1-W
5th PM Meridian

Map Group 17

Cities & Towns

None

Cemeteries

Cresswell Cemetery
Lost Creek Cemetery
Whitby-Ellis Cemetery

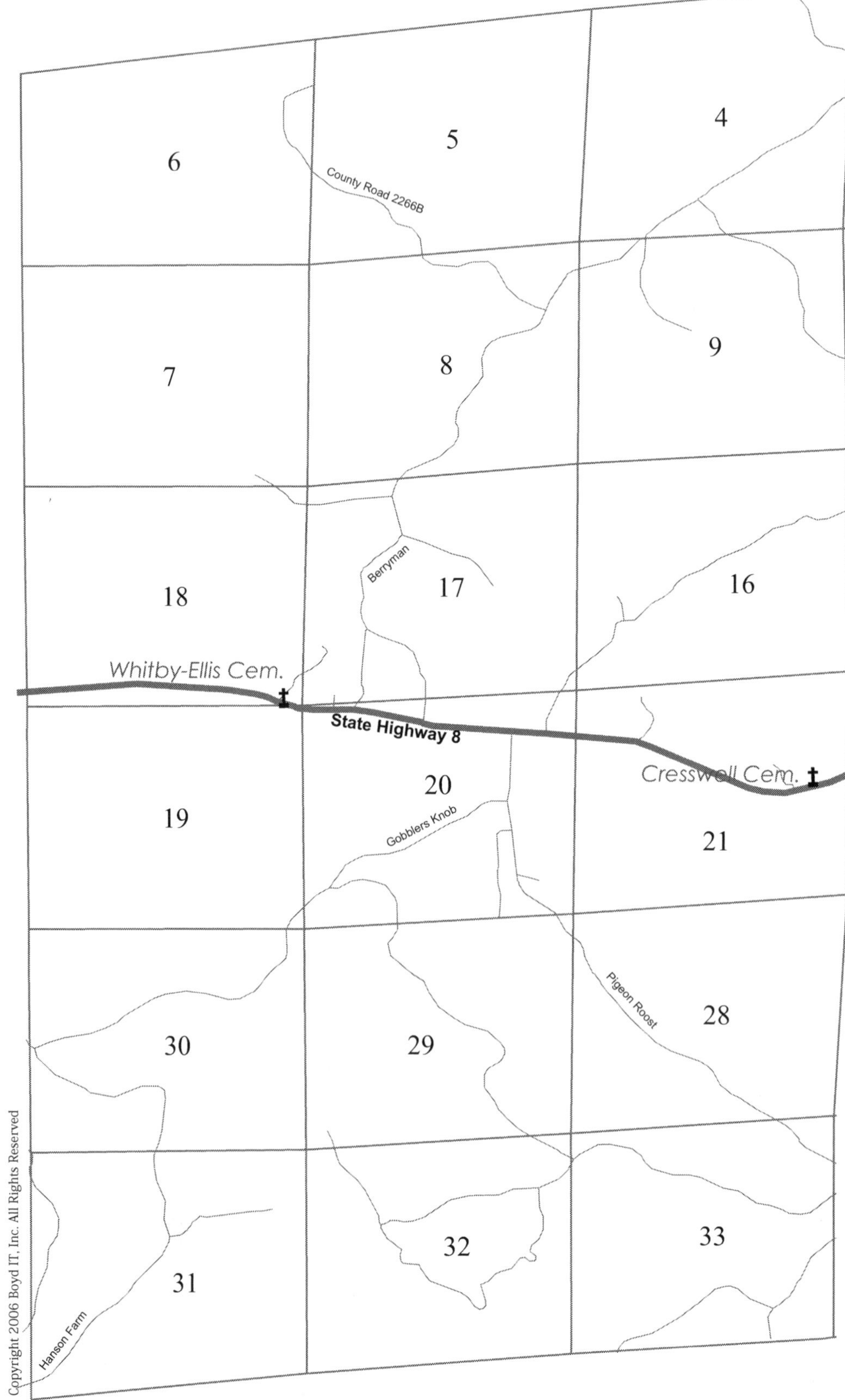

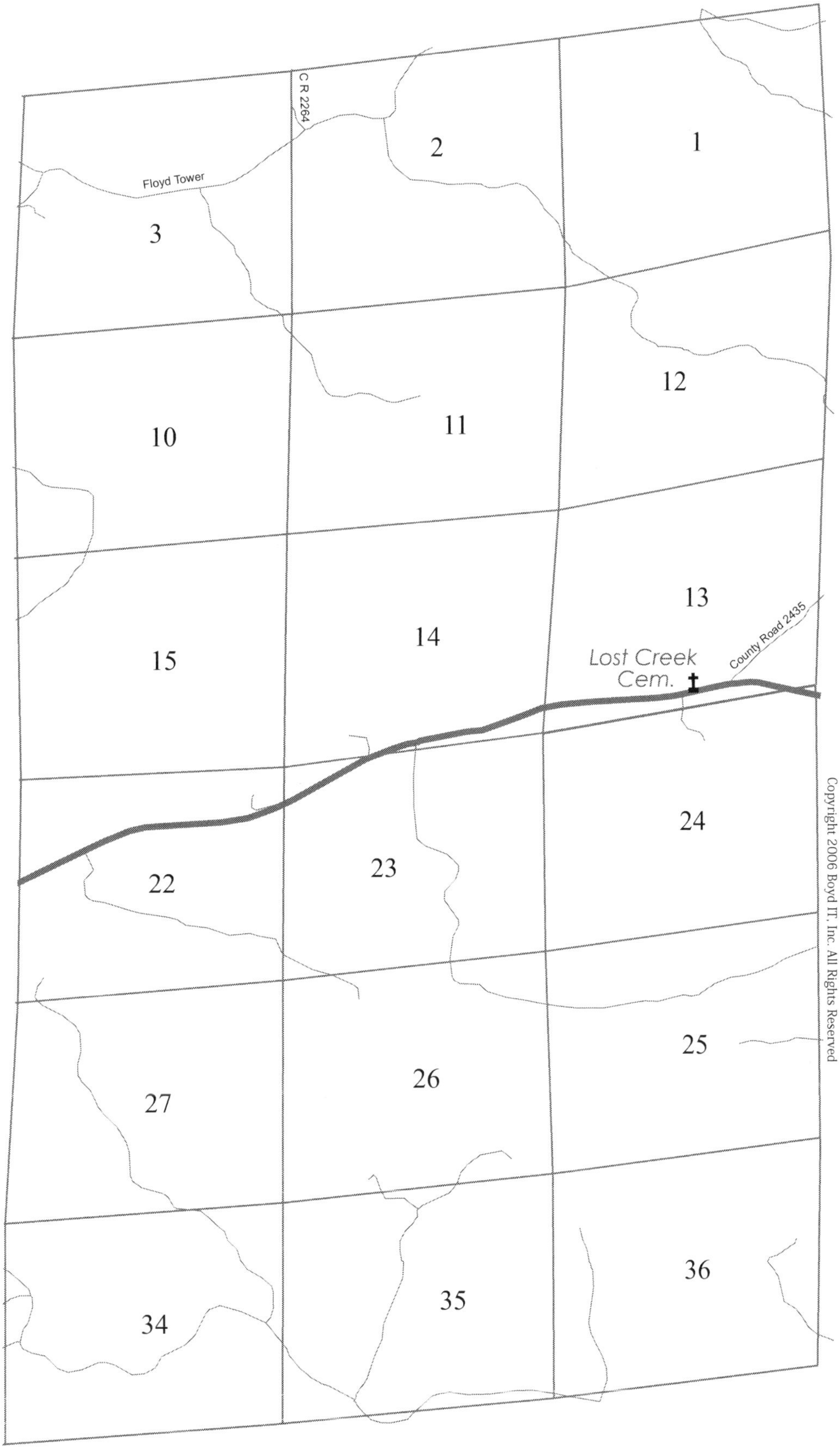

C R 2264
Floyd Tower
County Road 2435
Lost Creek Cem.

1 2 3 10 11 12 13 14 15 22 23 24 25 26 27 34 35 36

Helpful Hints

1. This road map has a number of uses, but primarily it is to help you: a) find the present location of land owned by your ancestors (at least the general area), b) find cemeteries and city-centers, and c) estimate the route/roads used by Census-takers & tax-assessors.
2. If you plan to travel to Washington County to locate cemeteries or land parcels, please pick up a modern travel map for the area before you do. Mapping old land parcels on modern maps is not as exact a science as you might think. Just the slightest variations in public land survey coordinates, estimates of parcel boundaries, or road-map deviations can greatly alter a map's representation of how a road either does or doesn't cross a particular parcel of land.

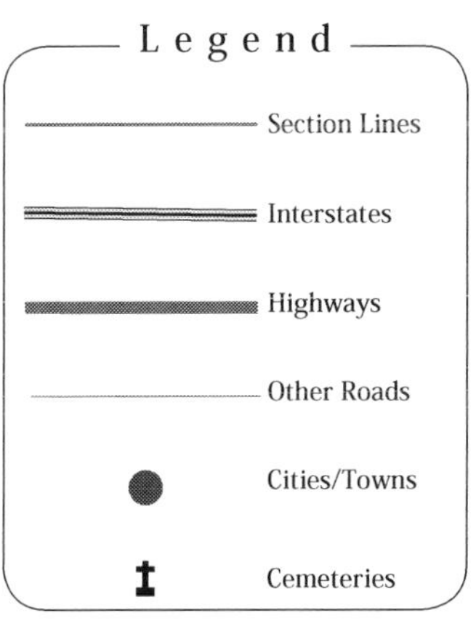

Scale: Section = 1 mile X 1 mile
(generally, with some exceptions)

Historical Map

T37-N R1-W
5th PM Meridian

Map Group 17

Cities & Towns
None

Cemeteries
Cresswell Cemetery
Lost Creek Cemetery
Whitby-Ellis Cemetery

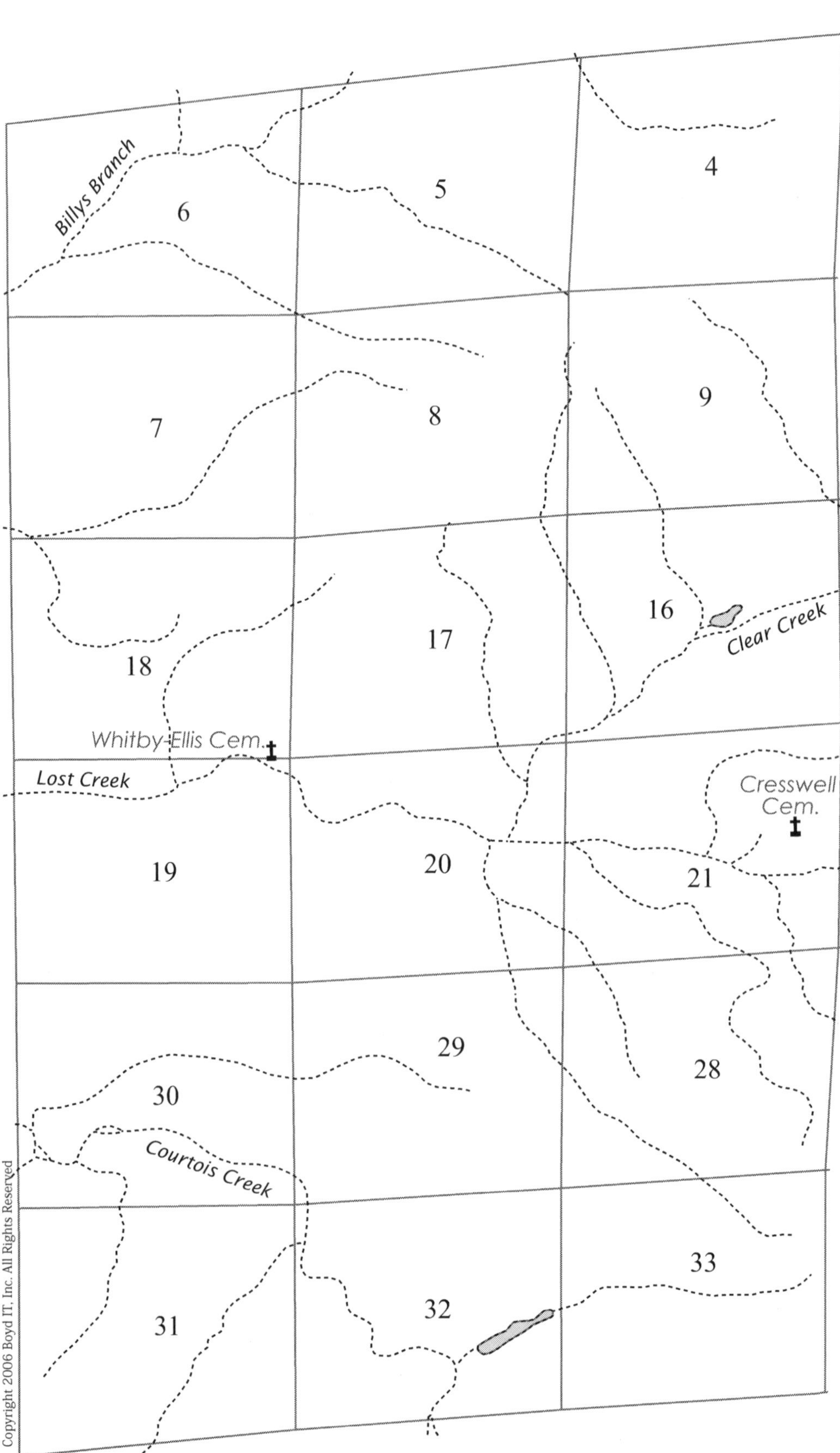

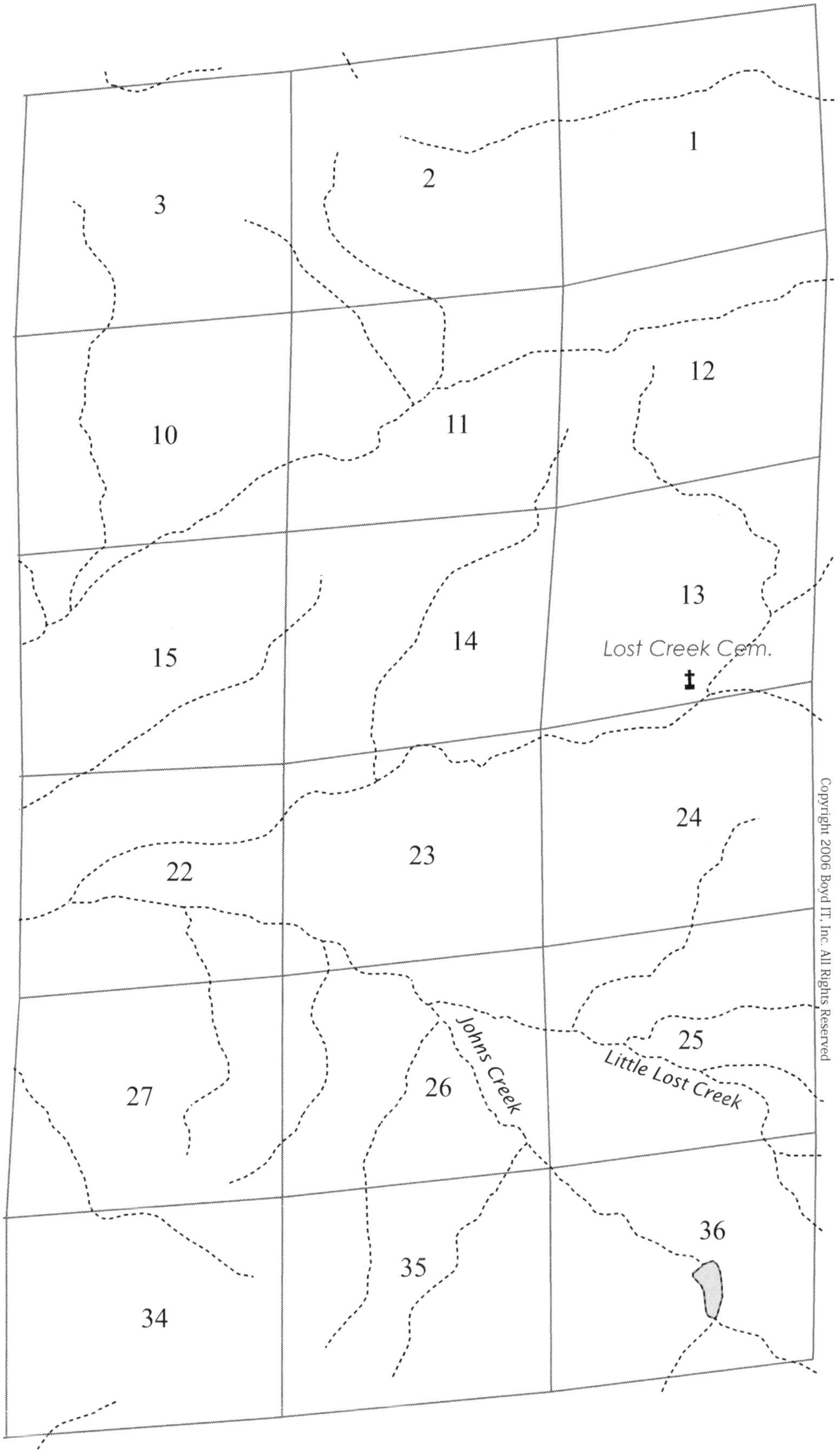

1 2 3 12 11 10 13 14 15 24 23 22 25 26 27 36 35 34

Lost Creek Cem.

Johns Creek

Little Lost Creek

Helpful Hints

1. This Map takes a different look at the same Congressional Township displayed in the preceding two maps. It presents features that can help you better envision the historical development of the area: a) Water-bodies (lakes & ponds), b) Water-courses (rivers, streams, etc.), c) Railroads, d) City/town center-points (where they were oftentimes located when first settled), and e) Cemeteries.
2. Using this "Historical" map in tandem with this Township's Patent Map and Road Map, may lead you to some interesting discoveries. You will often find roads, towns, cemeteries, and waterways are named after nearby landowners: sometimes those names will be the ones you are researching. See how many of these research gems you can find here in Washington County.

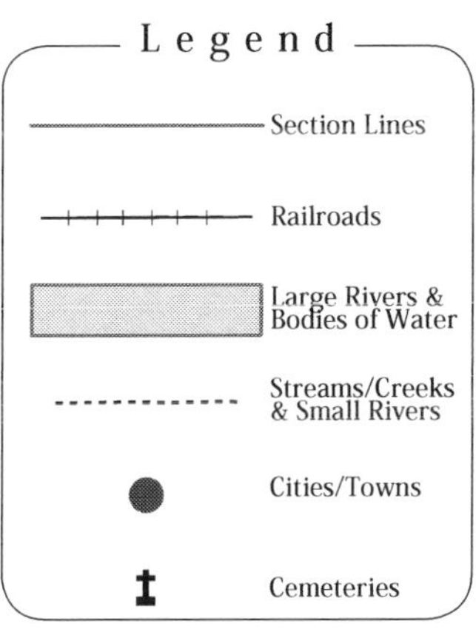

Scale: Section = 1 mile X 1 mile
(there are some exceptions)

Map Group 18: Index to Land Patents

Township 37-North Range 1-East (5th PM)

After you locate an individual in this Index, take note of the Section and Section Part then proceed to the Land Patent map on the pages immediately following. You should have no difficulty locating the corresponding parcel of land.

The "For More Info" Column will lead you to more information about the underlying Patents. See the *Legend* at right, and the "How to Use this Book" chapter, for more information.

LEGEND

"For More Info . . . " column

A = Authority (Legislative Act, See Appendix "A")
B = Block or Lot (location in Section unknown)
C = Cancelled Patent
F = Fractional Section
G = Group (Multi-Patentee Patent, see Appendix "C")
V = Overlaps another Parcel
R = Re-Issued (Parcel patented more than once)

(A & G items require you to look in the Appendixes referred to above. All other Letter-designations followed by a number require you to locate line-items in this index that possess the ID number found after the letter).

ID	Individual in Patent	Sec.	Sec. Part	Date Issued	Other Counties	For More Info . . .
2281	ALLEN, A N	12	NWSE	1869-07-01		A1 G2
2282	" "	12	SENE	1869-07-01		A1 G2
2381	ATKINSON, James	11	SE	1858-04-01		A1
2382	" "	11	SENE	1858-04-01		A1
2383	" "	12	SWNW	1858-04-01		A1
2384	" "	12	W½SW	1858-04-01		A1
2385	BAIZE, James	23	NWSE	1854-11-15		A1
2386	" "	23	SENE	1854-11-15		A1
2417	BARRON, John	2	W½1NW	1853-08-01		A1 G9
2418	BENNETT, John	2	E½SW	1837-11-07		A1 G14
2419	" "	2	W½SW	1837-11-07		A1 G14
2481	BLEDSOE, Monroe L	20	SENE	1912-03-28		A1 F
2482	BLOUNT, Peter D	29	SENW	1858-01-15		A1
2494	BLOUNT, Robert L	33	SESW	1906-06-21		A3
2448	BLUNT, John P	33	W½NE	1876-09-25		A3
2483	BLUNT, Peter D	29	N½SW	1841-07-01		A1
2484	" "	29	SWNW	1854-11-15		A1
2485	" "	31	NENE	1859-09-01		A1 V2474
2545	BOHANNAN, Zachariah	30	N½1SW	1872-07-01		A3
2546	" "	30	N½2SW	1872-07-01		A3
2306	BOHANNON, Elliott	30	NWSE	1875-12-20		A3
2516	BOHANNON, Urith	31	N½2NW	1885-12-19		A3
2505	BOOTHE, Sarah	20	SWSE	1858-01-15		A1
2283	BRAGG, Addison G	27	SESW	1858-04-01		A1 G28
2387	BROCK, James	4	SWNE	1841-07-01		A1
2389	" "	4	W½NW	1841-12-10		A1 G33
2388	" "	6	1NW	1859-01-01		A1
2296	BURGESS, Edward	2	NESE	1858-01-15		A1
2297	" "	2	SWSE	1858-01-15		A1
2479	BURROWES, Michael	32	NWNW	1858-04-01		A1
2473	CARROLL, Laurence	31	E½1SE	1859-09-10		A1
2474	" "	31	NE	1859-09-10		A1 V2485
2475	" "	32	NW	1859-09-10		A1 F
2476	" "	32	W½1SW	1859-09-10		A1 F
2394	CLARKSON, James L	13	W½NW	1866-09-01		A1
2395	" "	15	SWNW	1869-07-01		A1
2396	" "	21	NWNW	1869-07-01		A1
2397	" "	21	SWNE	1869-07-01		A1
2390	COMFORT, James H	6	2NW	1859-01-01		A1
2391	" "	6	3NE	1859-01-01		A1
2366	COMPTON, Henry S	19	NENW	1853-12-01		A1
2365	" "	18	S½2SW	1856-01-03		A1
2363	" "	17	S½SE	1859-09-10		A1
2364	" "	17	SESW	1859-09-10		A1
2367	" "	20	W½NE	1859-09-10		A1
2420	COMPTON, John	3	W½NW	1837-11-07		A1

ID	Individual in Patent	Sec.	Sec. Part	Date Issued	Other Counties	For More Info . . .
2421	COMPTON, John (Cont'd)	4	W½SE	1837-11-07		A1
2389	" "	4	W½NW	1841-12-10		A1 G33
2520	CRABTREE, William	10	NENW	1859-09-01		A1
2398	ELLIOTT, James M	5	SWSE	1849-04-10		A1
2424	EVANS, John	8	SWSE	1858-04-01		A1 G92
2422	" "	9	S½SW	1866-09-01		A1 G91
2423	" "	9	SWSE	1866-09-01		A1 G91
2429	EVENS, John	21	E½NE	1837-01-24		A1 G98
2439	" "	22	W½NW	1837-01-24		A1 G97
2425	" "	4	E½SW	1837-11-07		A1
2426	" "	9	E½NE	1837-11-07		A1
2427	" "	9	NWSE	1837-11-07		A1
2428	" "	9	SESE	1837-11-07		A1
2431	" "	7	NESE	1854-11-15		A1 G99
2433	" "	7	SENE	1854-11-15		A1 G99
2434	" "	8	E½NE	1854-11-15		A1 G99
2435	" "	8	NWSW	1854-11-15		A1 G99
2436	" "	8	W½NW	1854-11-15		A1 G99
2437	" "	9	NWSW	1854-11-15		A1 G99
2438	" "	9	W½NW	1854-11-15		A1 G99
2430	" "	18	NWNE	1857-10-30		A1 G99
2432	" "	7	NWSE	1857-10-30		A1 G99
2471	EYE, Laben	23	NESW	1888-12-08		A3
2472	" "	23	SWNE	1888-12-08		A3
2441	FIFER, John	8	NENW	1858-12-01		A1
2442	" "	8	NWNE	1858-12-01		A1
2295	FITCH, Charles W	26	SESE	1869-07-01		A1
2480	FLYNN, Michael M	11	N½NW	1904-01-28		A1
2443	FORD, John	31	NESW	1837-11-07		A1
2322	FRENCH, George R	21	S½SE	1859-09-01		A1
2323	" "	28	N½NE	1859-09-01		A1
2324	" "	28	N½NW	1859-09-01		A1
2325	" "	28	SENW	1859-09-01		A1
2326	" "	29	NENE	1859-09-01		A1
2315	GALE, George B	18	SESE	1904-12-29		A1
2316	" "	19	NWSE	1904-12-29		A1
2317	" "	19	SWNE	1904-12-29		A1
2318	" "	8	N½SE	1904-12-29		A1
2319	" "	8	SENW	1904-12-29		A1
2320	" "	8	SWNE	1904-12-29		A1
2307	GIBSON, Ellis	23	SESW	1860-10-01		A1
2487	GIBSON, Robert	23	NESE	1850-01-01		A1
2490	" "	24	NWSW	1853-12-01		A1
2493	" "	22	NESE	1854-11-15		A1 G110
2491	" "	24	SWSW	1858-01-15		A1
2489	" "	24	NESW	1859-09-01		A1
2488	" "	23	S½SE	1860-10-01		A1
2492	" "	26	NENE	1860-10-01		A1
2477	GLORE, Lisbon	26	NWNW	1857-04-15		A1
2470	HAEFNER, Joseph W	7	S½1NW	1854-11-15		A1
2469	" "	4	NENW	1859-09-01		A1
2416	HAIGH, John B	15	SWSE	1841-06-25		A1
2361	HALL, Harrison	19	S½1SW	1854-11-15		A1
2362	" "	30	N½1NW	1856-09-01		A1
2360	" "	19	2SW	1875-05-10		A3
2506	HANCOCK, Shaderick B	1	1NW	1858-04-01		A1
2507	" "	1	N½SW	1858-04-01		A1
2508	HANCOCK, Shadrach B	2	W½2NW	1859-09-01		A1
2509	" "	2	W½3NW	1859-09-01		A1
2288	HARRIS, Andrew J	19	SESE	1858-01-15		A1
2289	" "	30	NENE	1858-01-15		A1
2418	HIGHT, Alfred D	2	E½SW	1837-11-07		A1 G14
2419	" "	2	W½SW	1837-11-07		A1 G14
2290	HILL, Benjamin F	14	NENW	1904-06-02		A3
2291	" "	14	NWSW	1904-06-02		A3
2292	" "	14	W½NW	1904-06-02		A3
2299	HOLLINGSWORTH, Eli	11	NENE	1857-03-10		A1
2300	" "	2	SESE	1857-03-10		A1
2298	HOLLINSWORTH, Edward E	20	E½SE	1905-03-30		A3
2301	HOLLINSWORTH, Eli	19	SWSE	1859-09-01		A1
2302	" "	29	NWNW	1859-09-01		A1
2444	HOLT, John	4	E½NE	1841-06-25		A1
2528	HUDSON, William	1	W½2NE	1859-09-01		A1

ID	Individual in Patent	Sec.	Sec. Part	Date Issued	Other Counties	For More Info . . .
2529	HUDSON, William (Cont'd)	4	NWNE	1866-06-01		A1 G138
2512	JENKINS, Thomas J	21	NENW	1909-09-13		A3 F
2513	" "	21	NWNE	1909-09-13		A3 F
2377	JOHNSON, Isaac C	18	SWSE	1859-09-01		A1
2378	" "	19	NWNE	1859-09-01		A1
2466	KIRBY, Joseph	26	SWSW	1895-05-28		A3
2468	" "	27	SESE	1895-05-28		A3
2467	" "	27	NESE	1904-01-28		A1
2312	LEFFLER, Franklin	35	E½NW	1896-08-28		A3
2313	" "	35	W½NE	1896-08-28		A3
2446	LONG, John O	10	NWSW	1902-03-29		A1
2439	LORE, John	22	W½NW	1837-01-24		A1 G97
2314	MADDY, Gabriel	15	NWNW	1841-08-10		A1
2404	MASON, James	34	NWNE	1859-09-01		A1
2405	" "	34	S½NE	1859-09-01		A1
2287	MATTHEWS, Ambrose P	19	NWNW	1837-11-14		A1
2303	MATTHEWS, Elijah B	31	SWNW	1837-11-07		A1
2429	MCCABE, Alpheus	21	E½NE	1837-01-24		A1 G98
2379	MCGRADY, Israel	10	SWSW	1837-11-07		A1
2380	" "	9	NESE	1837-11-07		A1
2422	" "	9	S½SW	1866-09-01		A1 G91
2423	" "	9	SWSE	1866-09-01		A1 G91
2431	MCGREADY, Israel	7	NESE	1854-11-15		A1 G99
2433	" "	7	SENE	1854-11-15		A1 G99
2434	" "	8	E½NE	1854-11-15		A1 G99
2435	" "	8	NWSW	1854-11-15		A1 G99
2436	" "	8	W½NW	1854-11-15		A1 G99
2437	" "	9	NWSW	1854-11-15		A1 G99
2438	" "	9	W½NW	1854-11-15		A1 G99
2430	" "	18	NWNE	1857-10-30		A1 G99
2432	" "	7	NWSE	1857-10-30		A1 G99
2424	" "	8	SWSE	1858-04-01		A1 G92
2445	MCGREADY, John	4	SWSW	1837-11-14		A1
2406	MONTGOMERY, James	22	SENW	1860-10-01		A1
2407	" "	22	SWNE	1860-10-01		A1
2411	MONTGOMERY, John A	27	NWNE	1858-04-01		A1
2410	" "	27	NENW	1858-12-01		A1
2412	" "	27	NWSE	1858-12-01		A1
2413	" "	27	SWNW	1858-12-01		A1
2414	" "	27	W½SW	1858-12-01		A1
2415	" "	34	NWNW	1858-12-01		A1
2515	NICHOLSON, Thomas	1	E½2NE	1858-12-01		A1
2531	NICHOLSON, William	12	N½NE	1859-09-01		A1
2447	ORME, John	1	3NW	1848-03-01		A1
2408	OWENS, James	18	S½2NW	1857-10-30		A1
2532	PARKIN, William	31	NWSE	1856-01-03		A1
2535	" "	31	SENW	1856-01-03		A1
2533	" "	31	S½SE	1858-01-15		A1
2534	" "	31	S½SW	1860-09-01		A1
2517	PAUL, William A	4	SENW	1848-02-01		A1
2497	PEARSHALL, Samuel	10	NWNW	1858-04-01		A1
2498	" "	3	SENW	1858-04-01		A1
2504	PERSHALL, Samuel	2	NWSE	1837-11-07		A1
2499	" "	10	E½SW	1859-09-01		A1
2500	" "	10	NENE	1859-09-01		A1
2501	" "	10	S½NW	1859-09-01		A1
2502	" "	10	SWSE	1859-09-01		A1
2503	" "	10	W½NE	1859-09-01		A1
2529	PERSHALL, Samuel E	4	NWNE	1866-06-01		A1 G138
2392	PETTIGREW, James H	29	NENW	1885-02-25		A3
2393	" "	29	NWNE	1885-02-25		A3
2285	REVES, Albert	36	NESW	1838-08-01		A1
2286	" "	36	SWSE	1838-08-01		A1
2283	RICHARDSON, George B	27	SESW	1858-04-01		A1 G28
2284	ROBINSON, Agnes	1	E½SE	1852-01-01		A1
2451	ROBINSON, John T	36	NENE	1857-10-30		A1
2450	" "	25	SWNW	1858-12-01		A1
2452	" "	36	NWNE	1858-12-01		A1
2495	ROOT, S D	26	SESW	1869-07-01		A1
2496	" "	34	NENW	1869-07-01		A1
2305	SCOTT, Elisha J	3	E½3NE	1857-04-15		A1
2304	" "	3	E½2NE	1858-04-01		A1
2519	SCOTT, William C	5	W½1NE	1858-01-15		A1

ID	Individual in Patent	Sec.	Sec. Part	Date Issued	Other Counties	For More Info . . .
2358	SEYMOUR, Gideon	19	E½NE	1882-05-20		A3
2518	SEYMOUR, William B	3	SWSE	1869-07-01		A1
2308	SHEPHERD, Forrest	3	1NE	1873-11-01		A3
2309	" "	3	NENW	1873-11-01		A3
2310	" "	3	W½2NE	1873-11-01		A3
2311	" "	3	W½3NE	1873-11-01		A3
2281	SHEPHERD, G R	12	NWSE	1869-07-01		A1 G2
2282	" "	12	SENE	1869-07-01		A1 G2
2401	SILVEY, James M	9	SENW	1859-01-01		A1
2399	" "	9	NENW	1866-09-01		A1
2400	" "	9	NESW	1866-09-01		A1
2440	SILVEY, John F	15	NE	1888-12-08		A3
2536	SILVEY, William	15	NESW	1848-03-01		A1
2543	SILVEY, William W	15	NWSE	1853-04-15		A1
2544	" "	15	SESW	1853-04-15		A1
2542	" "	15	NESE	1858-04-01		A1
2402	SILVY, James M	9	NWNE	1856-06-16		A1
2403	" "	9	SWNE	1856-09-01		A1
2374	SMITH, Henry	21	NWSE	1875-05-10		A3
2493	SMITH, Hiram M	22	NESE	1854-11-15		A1 G110
2375	" "	25	SESW	1854-11-15		A1
2376	" "	36	NENW	1857-10-30		A1
2409	SMITH, Jesse B	4	E½SE	1825-07-15		A1
2486	SMITH, Robert F	1	2NW	1904-12-29		A1
2538	SMITH, William	36	SENW	1853-04-15		A1
2493	" "	22	NESE	1854-11-15		A1 G110
2537	" "	36	NWSE	1854-11-15		A1
2539	" "	36	SESE	1857-10-30		A1
2540	" "	36	SESW	1857-10-30		A1
2541	" "	36	SWNE	1857-10-30		A1
2449	STAPLES, John	23	SENW	1856-01-03		A1
2417	STEWART, William	2	W½1NW	1853-08-01		A1 G9
2527	STEWART, William H	2	E½NE	1847-02-11		A1 G215
2525	" "	2	E½NW	1847-02-11		A1
2526	" "	2	W½NE	1847-02-11		A1
2321	STROTHER, George F	3	W½SW	1825-07-15		A1
2514	TULLOCK, Thomas M	27	SWSE	1913-12-10		A3
2530	VALENTIN, William M	19	NESE	1915-03-30		A1
2478	VARNER, Mary	33	NENW	1854-11-15		A1
2464	VERNER, Jonathan	33	SENW	1857-04-15		A1
2293	WALTON, Benjamin F	22	NWSE	1869-07-01		A1
2294	WALTON, C C	28	NWSW	1870-10-15		A1
2333	WALTON, George	15	E½NW	1837-11-07		A1
2334	" "	15	W½SW	1837-11-07		A1
2339	" "	21	NESE	1837-11-07		A1
2336	" "	20	NESW	1853-08-01		A1
2327	" "	13	NWSW	1854-11-15		A1
2329	" "	14	NESE	1854-11-15		A1
2330	" "	14	NESW	1854-11-15		A1
2331	" "	14	SESW	1854-11-15		A1
2332	" "	14	W½NE	1854-11-15		A1
2335	" "	20	NENE	1854-11-15		A1
2338	" "	20	SWSW	1854-11-15		A1
2340	" "	22	E½SW	1854-11-15		A1
2341	" "	23	NENE	1854-11-15		A1
2342	" "	23	NENW	1854-11-15		A1
2343	" "	23	W½SW	1854-11-15		A1
2344	" "	24	NE	1854-11-15		A1
2346	" "	26	NENW	1854-11-15		A1
2352	" "	28	SWSW	1854-11-15		A1
2353	" "	29	NESE	1854-11-15		A1
2357	" "	30	NWNE	1854-11-15		A1
2337	" "	20	NWSW	1856-01-03		A1
2350	" "	27	SENW	1856-01-03		A1
2351	" "	28	SWNW	1856-01-03		A1
2355	" "	29	SWNE	1856-01-03		A1
2356	" "	29	W½SE	1856-01-03		A1
2345	" "	26	N½SW	1857-10-30		A1
2347	" "	26	S½NE	1857-10-30		A1
2348	" "	26	S½NW	1857-10-30		A1
2349	" "	27	S½NE	1857-10-30		A1
2328	" "	13	SWSW	1858-04-01		A1
2354	" "	29	SESE	1858-12-01		A1

ID	Individual in Patent	Sec.	Sec. Part	Date Issued	Other Counties	For More Info . . .
2459	WALTON, John	22	NWNE	1841-07-01		A1
2460	" "	22	SENE	1841-07-01		A1
2462	" "	23	SWNW	1853-08-01		A1
2453	" "	14	E½NE	1858-01-15		A1
2454	" "	14	S½SE	1858-01-15		A1
2455	" "	14	SENW	1858-01-15		A1
2456	" "	14	SWSW	1858-01-15		A1
2457	" "	15	SESE	1858-01-15		A1
2458	" "	22	NENW	1858-01-15		A1
2461	" "	23	NWNE	1860-10-01		A1
2465	WALTON, Joseph H	27	NESW	1854-11-15		A1
2359	WARNER, Green	31	NWSW	1874-11-05		A3
2368	WHITENER, Henry S	13	NESE	1904-12-29		A1
2369	" "	14	NWSE	1904-12-29		A1
2370	" "	21	S½NW	1904-12-29		A1
2371	" "	26	NWNE	1904-12-29		A1
2372	" "	27	NWNW	1904-12-29		A1
2373	" "	35	E½SE	1904-12-29		A1
2463	WILSON, John	5	SWSW	1858-01-15		A1
2524	WILSON, William F	5	SESW	1853-12-01		A1
2521	" "	4	NWSW	1856-10-10		A1
2522	" "	5	E½SE	1857-04-15		A1
2523	" "	5	NWSE	1858-12-01		A1
2510	WISDOM, Sloman	1	1NE	1903-06-08		A3
2511	" "	1	W½SE	1903-06-08		A3
2527	WOOLSAY, James	2	E½NE	1847-02-11		A1 G215

Patent Map

T37-N R1-E
5th PM Meridian

Map Group 18

Township Statistics

Parcels Mapped	:	266
Number of Patents	:	186
Number of Individuals	:	116
Patentees Identified	:	115
Number of Surnames	:	87
Multi-Patentee Parcels	:	24
Oldest Patent Date	:	7/15/1825
Most Recent Patent	:	3/30/1915
Block/Lot Parcels	:	29
Parcels Re - Issued	:	0
Parcels that Overlap	:	2
Cities and Towns	:	4
Cemeteries	:	7

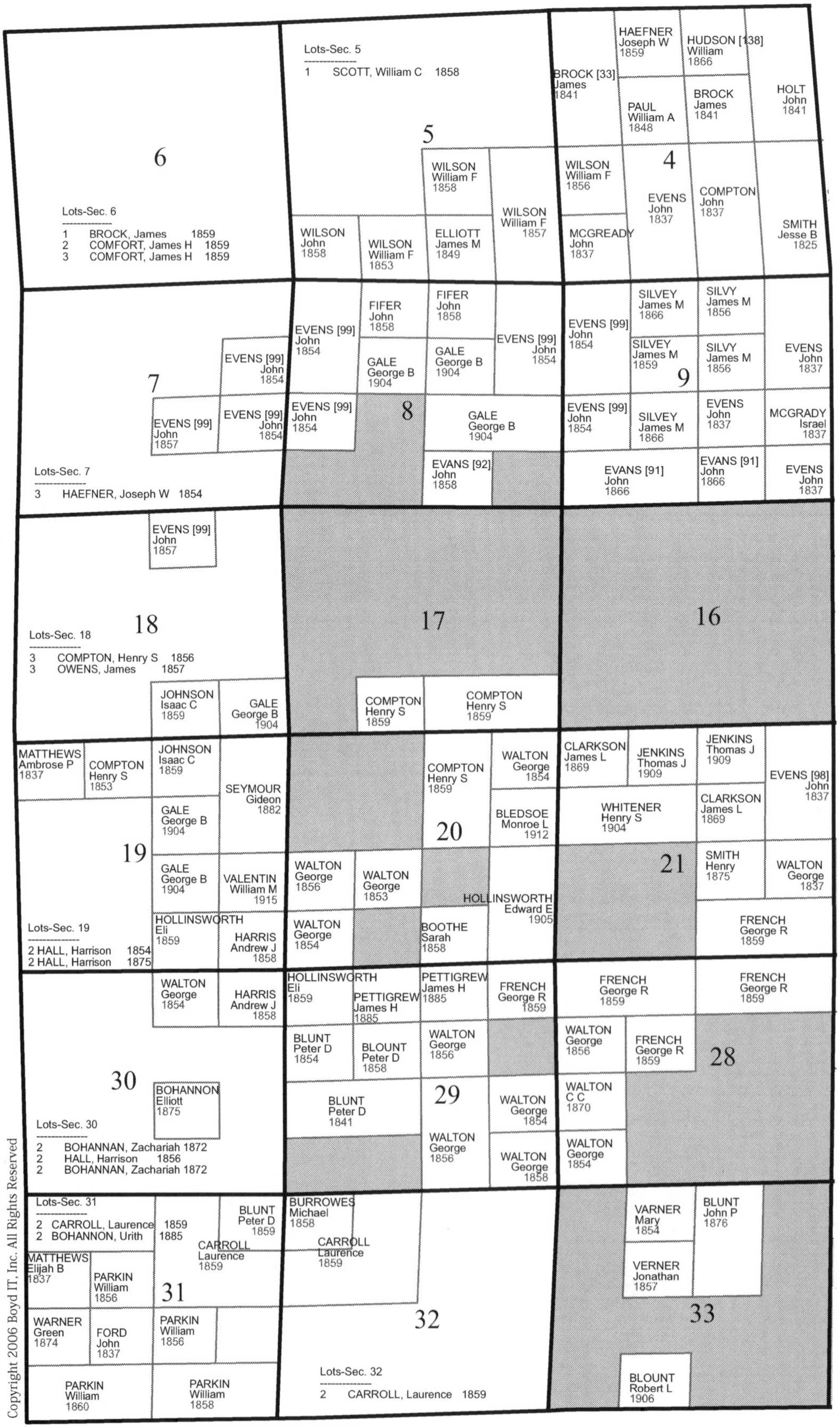

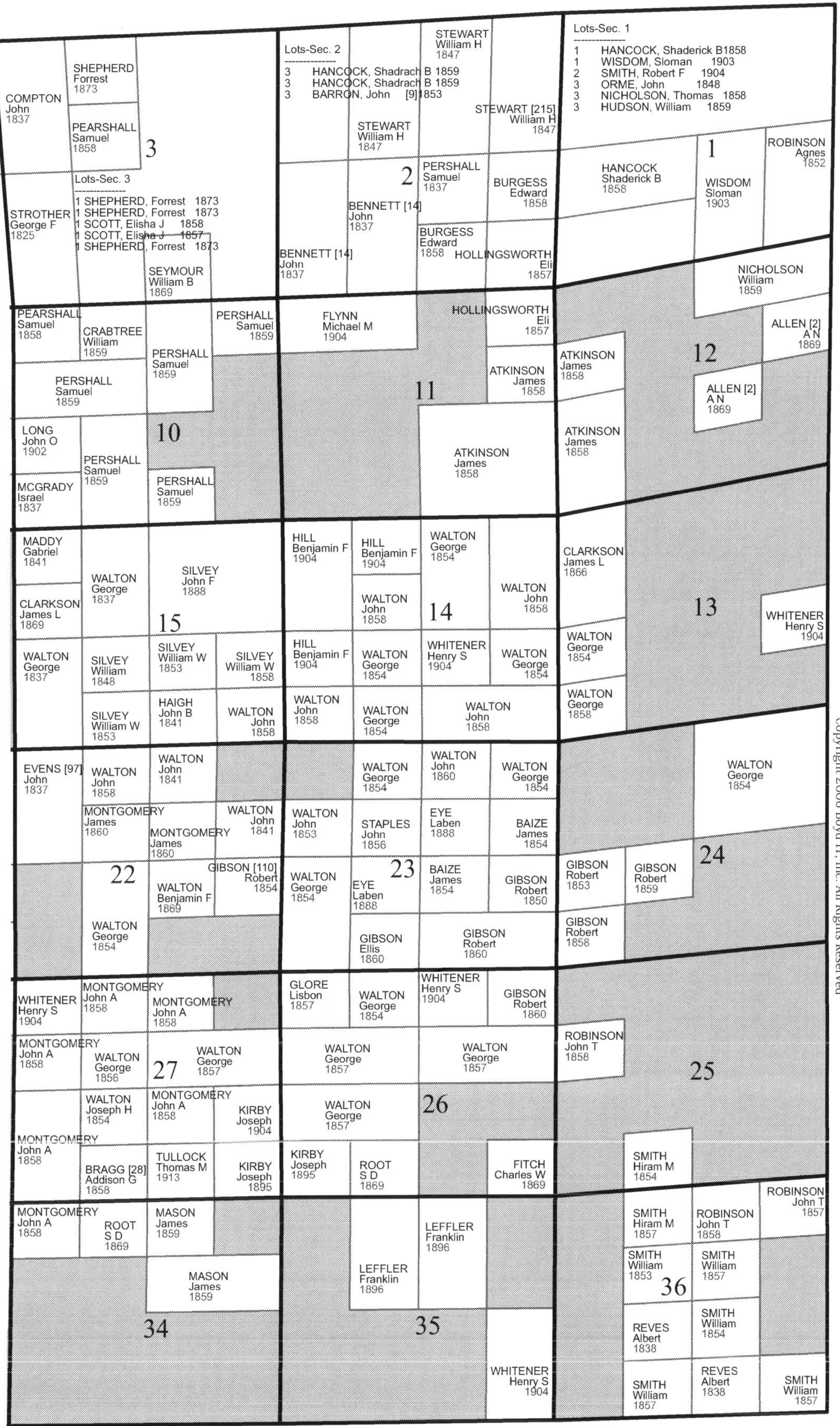

Helpful Hints

1. This Map's INDEX can be found on the preceding pages.
2. Refer to Map "C" to see where this Township lies within Washington County, Missouri.
3. Numbers within square brackets [ ] denote a multi-patentee land parcel (multi-owner). Refer to Appendix "C" for a full list of members in this group.
4. Areas that look to be crowded with Patentees usually indicate multiple sales of the same parcel (Re-issues) or Overlapping parcels. See this Township's Index for an explanation of these and other circumstances that might explain "odd" groupings of Patentees on this map.

Legend

(thin line)	Patent Boundary
(thick line)	Section Boundary
(shaded)	No Patents Found (or Outside County)
1., 2., 3., ...	Lot Numbers (when beside a name)
[ ]	Group Number (see Appendix "C")

Scale: Section = 1 mile X 1 mile (generally, with some exceptions)

Road Map

T37-N R1-E
5th PM Meridian

Map Group 18

Cities & Towns
- Camp Lakewood
- Floyd
- Levy
- Shirley

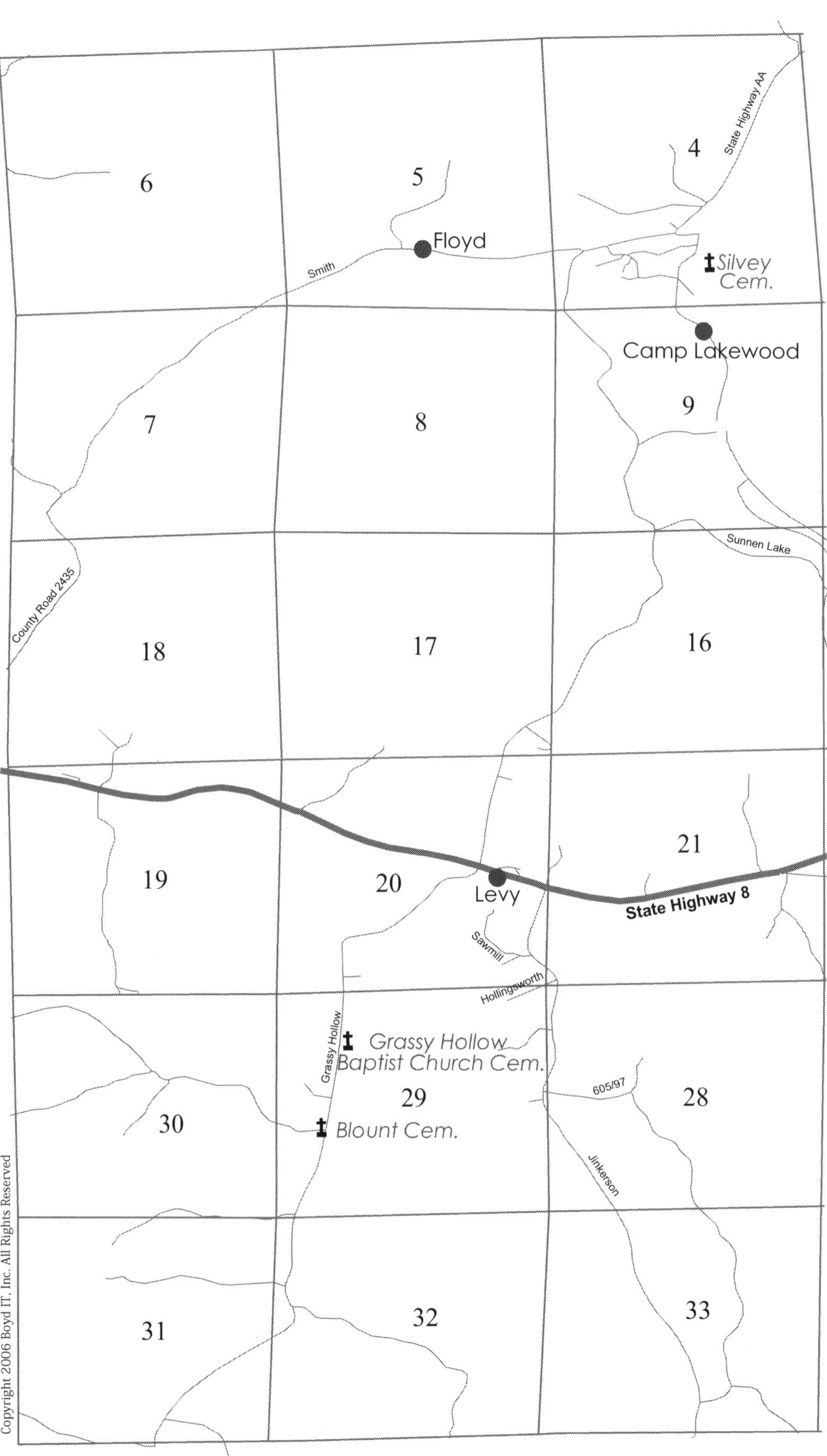

Cemeteries
- Blount Cemetery
- Grassy Hollow Baptist Church Cemetery
- High Point-Missionary Ridge Cemetery
- Shirley Union Church Cemetery
- Silvey Cemetery
- White Oak Grove Cemetery
- Wilson Family Cemetery

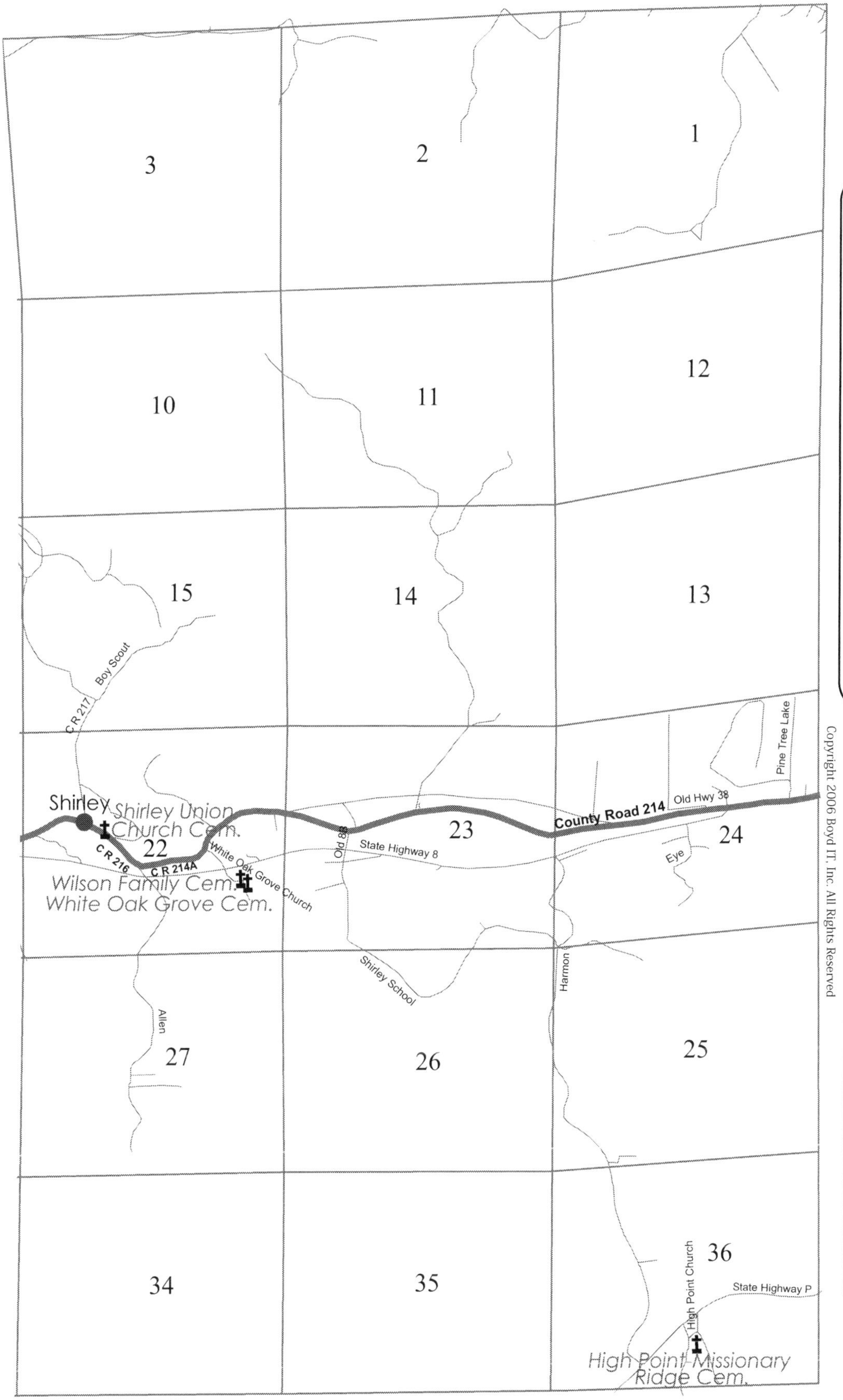

3
2
1
10
11
12
15
14
13
22
23
24
27
26
25
34
35
36

Boy Scout
CR 217
Shirley
Shirley Union Church Cem.
CR 216
CR 214A
White Oak Grove Church
Wilson Family Cem.
White Oak Grove Cem.
Old 88
State Highway 8
County Road 214
Old Hwy 38
Pine Tree Lake
Eye
Shirley School
Allen
Harmon
High Point Church
State Highway P
High Point Missionary Ridge Cem.

Helpful Hints

1. This road map has a number of uses, but primarily it is to help you: a) find the present location of land owned by your ancestors (at least the general area), b) find cemeteries and city-centers, and c) estimate the route/roads used by Census-takers & tax-assessors.
2. If you plan to travel to Washington County to locate cemeteries or land parcels, please pick up a modern travel map for the area before you do. Mapping old land parcels on modern maps is not as exact a science as you might think. Just the slightest variations in public land survey coordinates, estimates of parcel boundaries, or road-map deviations can greatly alter a map's representation of how a road either does or doesn't cross a particular parcel of land.

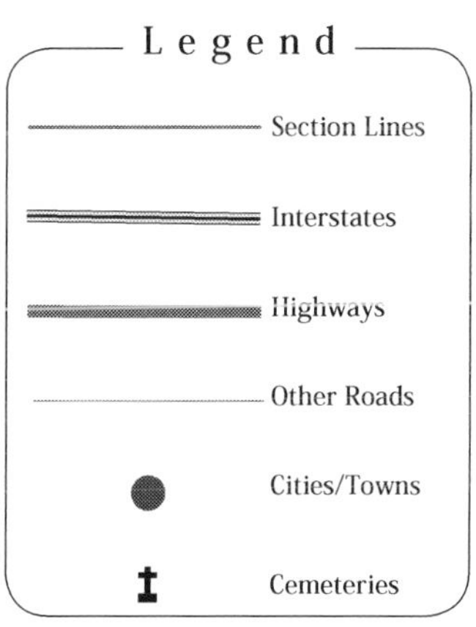

Scale: Section = 1 mile X 1 mile
(generally, with some exceptions)

Historical Map

T37-N R1-E
5th PM Meridian

Map Group 18

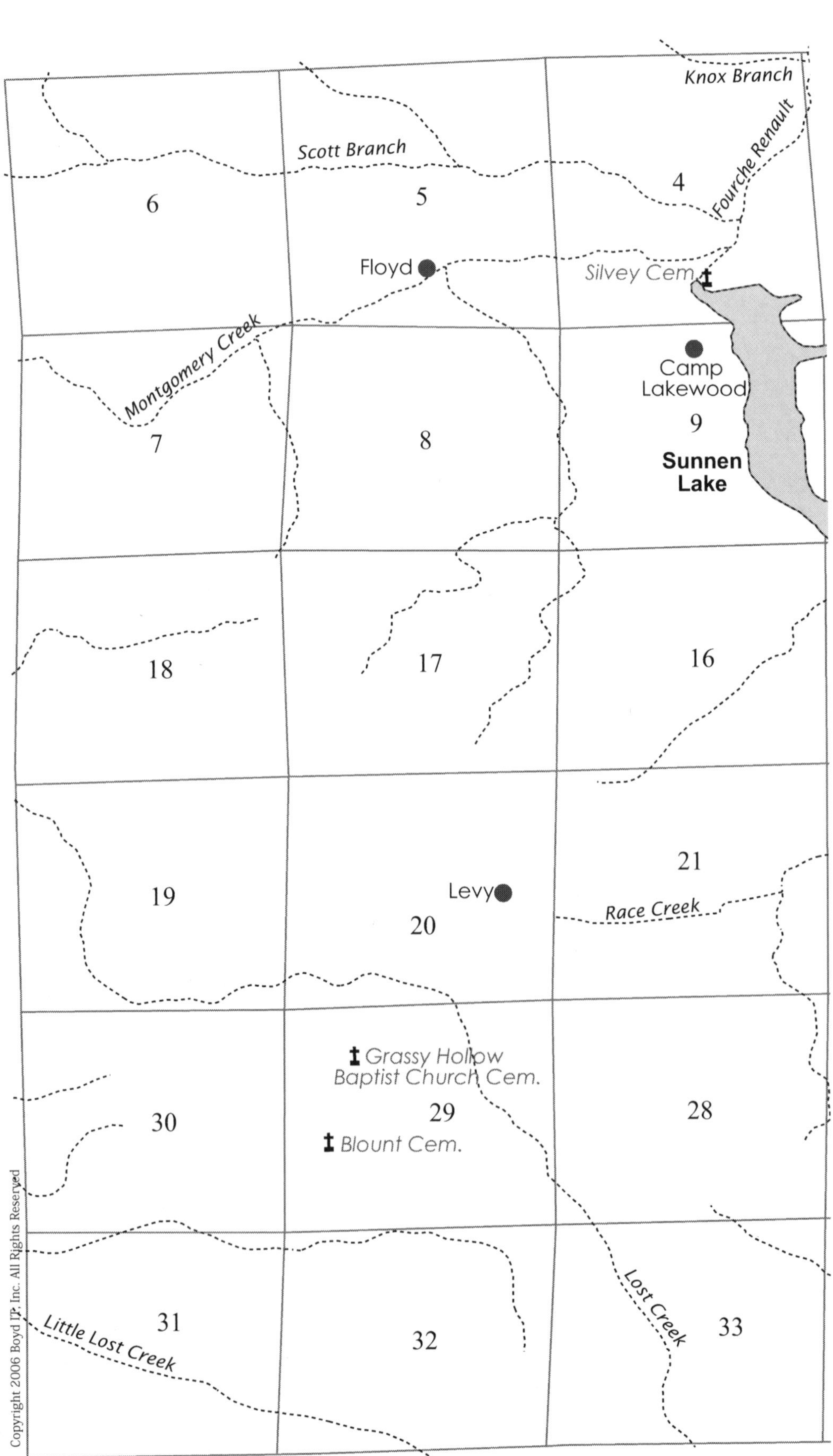

Cities & Towns

- Camp Lakewood
- Floyd
- Levy
- Shirley

Cemeteries

- Blount Cemetery
- Grassy Hollow Baptist Church Cemetery
- High Point-Missionary Ridge Cemetery
- Shirley Union Church Cemetery
- Silvey Cemetery
- White Oak Grove Cemetery
- Wilson Family Cemetery

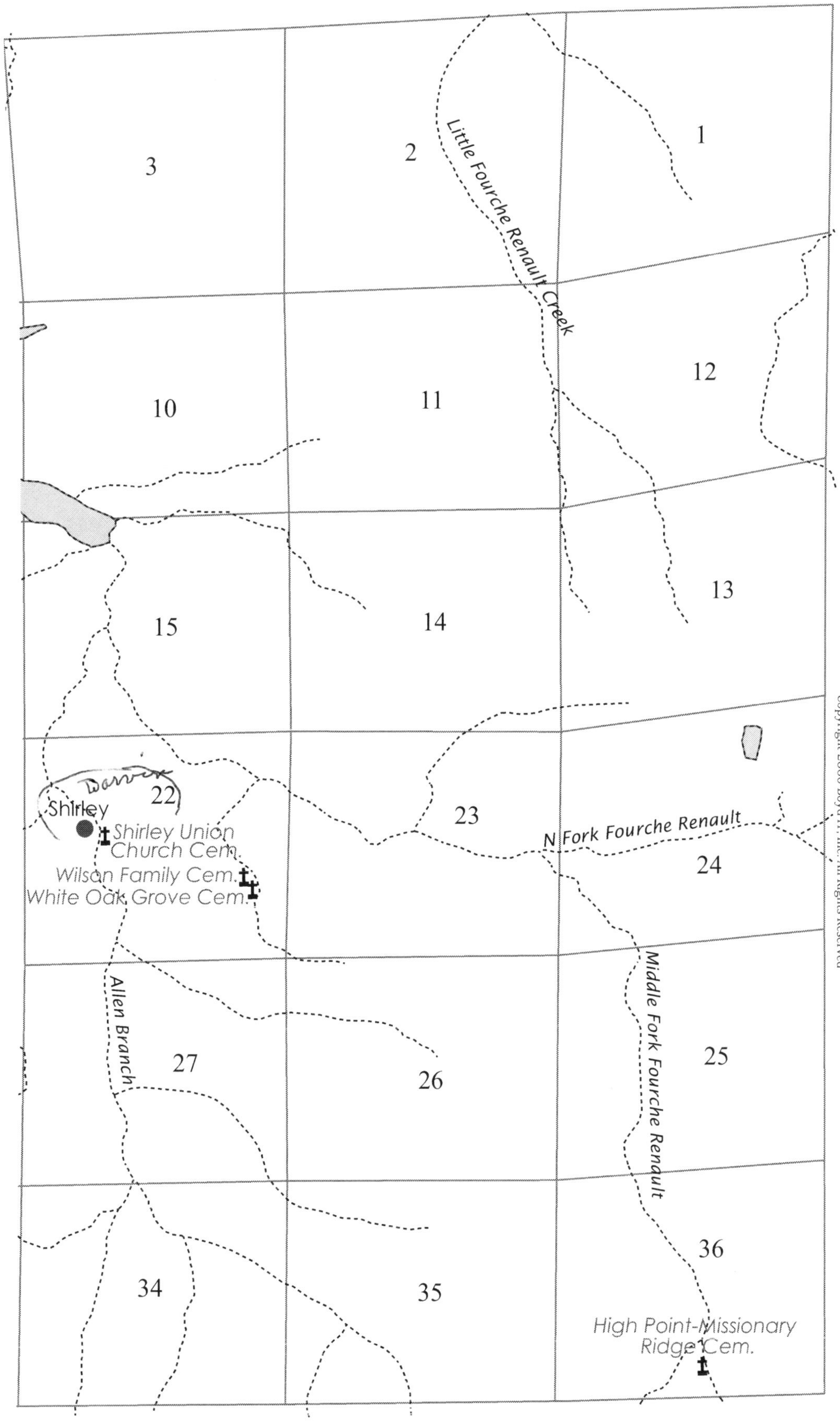

3
2
1
Little Fourche Renault Creek
10
11
12
15
14
13
22
Shirley
Shirley Union Church Cem.
Wilson Family Cem.
White Oak Grove Cem.
23
N Fork Fourche Renault
24
Allen Branch
27
26
Middle Fork Fourche Renault
25
34
35
36
High Point-Missionary Ridge Cem.

Helpful Hints

1. This Map takes a different look at the same Congressional Township displayed in the preceding two maps. It presents features that can help you better envision the historical development of the area: a) Water-bodies (lakes & ponds), b) Water-courses (rivers, streams, etc.), c) Railroads, d) City/town center-points (where they were oftentimes located when first settled), and e) Cemeteries.
2. Using this "Historical" map in tandem with this Township's Patent Map and Road Map, may lead you to some interesting discoveries. You will often find roads, towns, cemeteries, and waterways are named after nearby landowners: sometimes those names will be the ones you are researching. See how many of these research gems you can find here in Washington County.

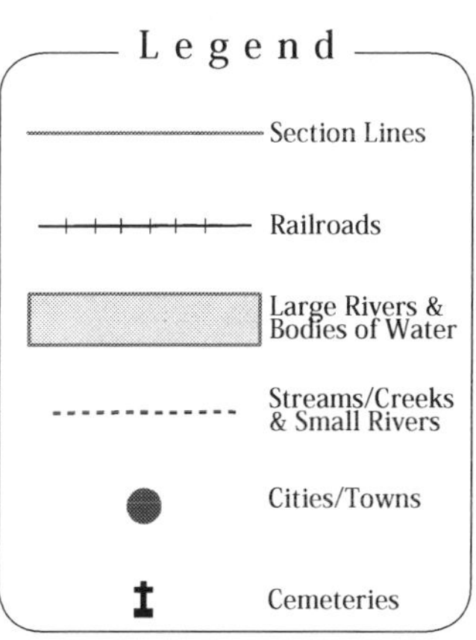

Scale: Section = 1 mile X 1 mile
(there are some exceptions)

Map Group 19: Index to Land Patents

Township 37-North Range 2-East (5th PM)

After you locate an individual in this Index, take note of the Section and Section Part then proceed to the Land Patent map on the pages immediately following. You should have no difficulty locating the corresponding parcel of land.

The "For More Info" Column will lead you to more information about the underlying Patents. See the *Legend* at right, and the "How to Use this Book" chapter, for more information.

LEGEND

"For More Info . . . " column

A = Authority (Legislative Act, See Appendix "A")
B = Block or Lot (location in Section unknown)
C = Cancelled Patent
F = Fractional Section
G = Group (Multi-Patentee Patent, see Appendix "C")
V = Overlaps another Parcel
R = Re-Issued (Parcel patented more than once)

(A & G items require you to look in the Appendixes referred to above. All other Letter-designations followed by a number require you to locate line-items in this index that possess the ID number found after the letter).

ID	Individual in Patent	Sec.	Sec. Part	Date Issued	Other Counties	For More Info . . .
2660	ALLEN, John W	32	SW	1858-01-15		A1
2700	BOGGS, Robert W	36	NESE	1837-11-14		A1
2650	BRICKEY, John S	23	NWSE	1854-11-15		A1 F
2591	BROLASKI, Henry L	25	NWSW	1856-10-10		A1
2592	" "	26	SESE	1856-10-10		A1
2593	" "	35	NWNE	1856-10-10		A1
2594	" "	35	SWNW	1856-10-10		A1
2595	" "	36	SESE	1856-10-10		A1
2641	BUGG, John P	15	E½SW	1860-08-01		A1
2642	" "	15	W½SE	1860-08-01		A1
2727	CAIN, William M	2	SESW	1848-09-01		A1
2685	CAMPBELL, Michael	20	SWSW	1858-01-15		A1
2689	CAMPBELL, Neal	28	NW	1857-04-15		A1
2552	CASEY, Andrew	8	SE	1837-11-14		A1
2621	CASEY, John	26	E½NW	1837-11-14		A1
2607	CLARKSON, James L	27	S½SE	1859-09-01		A1
2610	" "	34	NENW	1859-09-01		A1
2611	" "	34	NWNE	1859-09-01		A1
2615	" "	33	S½SE	1860-08-01		A1 G66
2617	" "	34	W½SW	1860-08-01		A1 G66
2616	" "	33	S½SW	1864-03-10		A1 G66
2612	" "	29	S½SE	1865-06-10		A1 G66
2614	" "	32	S½SE	1865-06-10		A1 G66
2608	" "	28	SWSE	1866-06-01		A1
2613	" "	32	NESE	1866-06-01		A1 G66
2609	" "	33	N½SE	1866-06-01		A1
2723	COOK, William C	5	SWSE	1870-05-10		A1 F
2587	DAVIS, Greer W	14	1	1860-08-01		A1 F
2588	" "	14	3	1860-08-01		A1 F
2622	DEANE, John	35	SWSE	1864-03-10		A1
2557	DEGURRIA, Antwine	36	NENW	1853-08-01		A1
2577	DESLOGE, Fermin	26	W½NW	1838-08-01		A1 G80
2576	" "	27	E½NE	1838-08-01		A1 G79
2684	DOLL, Mathias	24	N½SW	1871-11-01		A3 F
2719	DOWNARD, Volney	28	NWSE	1857-04-15		A1
2718	" "	28	NESW	1857-10-13		A1
2547	EATON, Absalom	21	E½SW	1838-08-01		A1 G84
2602	FICKES, Jacob	8	NWSW	1856-09-01		A1 F
2604	" "	8	S½SW	1856-09-01		A1
2601	" "	8	NESW	1856-10-10		A1
2600	" "	7	SENE	1857-04-15		A1
2603	" "	8	S½NW	1857-04-15		A1
2605	" "	8	SENE	1857-04-15		A1 F
2606	" "	8	W½NE	1857-04-15		A1 F
2586	FITCH, Gideon	34	SENE	1872-02-05		A1
2674	FRISSELL, Mason	20	N½SE	1858-12-01		A1

ID	Individual in Patent	Sec.	Sec. Part	Date Issued	Other Counties	For More Info . . .
2675	FRISSELL, Mason (Cont'd)	20	SWSE	1858-12-01		A1
2676	" "	21	NWSW	1858-12-01		A1
2677	" "	21	W½NW	1858-12-01		A1
2678	" "	29	W½NE	1858-12-01		A1
2701	GATY, Samuel	5	3NE	1866-06-01		A1 G107
2702	" "	5	6NE	1866-06-01		A1 G107
2668	GILCHRIST, Malcolm	9	NW	1837-11-07		A1 F
2669	" "	9	SW	1837-11-07		A1
2724	HALL, William	19	S½SE	1857-10-30		A1
2725	" "	30	N½NW	1857-10-30		A1
2726	" "	30	NE	1857-10-30		A1
2589	HARRIS, Henry	22	NWSW	1838-08-01		A1
2590	" "	22	SWSW	1838-08-01		A1
2578	HATHORN, George	21	SWSE	1837-11-07		A1
2619	HILL, James S	34	E½SW	1860-08-01		A1
2625	HOLT, John	5	SWNW	1837-11-07		A1 F
2626	" "	6	E½NW	1837-11-07		A1
2627	" "	6	NESE	1837-11-07		A1
2628	" "	6	SW	1837-11-07		A1
2623	" "	24	E½SE	1911-09-25		A1
2624	" "	24	NWSE	1911-09-25		A1
2695	HORNSEY, Robert	22	SWSE	1864-03-10		A1
2696	" "	5	SESW	1864-03-10		A1
2577	HOUSE, Adam	26	W½NW	1838-08-01		A1 G80
2576	" "	27	E½NE	1838-08-01		A1 G79
2716	HOWELL, Timothy W	23	SWSE	1857-04-15		A1 F
2670	HUFSTETTER, Mary	5	2NE	1853-04-15		A1
2717	HULL, Uriah	17	W½SE	1838-08-01		A1 G145
2615	JOHNSON, William J	33	S½SE	1860-08-01		A1 G66
2617	" "	34	W½SW	1860-08-01		A1 G66
2616	" "	33	S½SW	1864-03-10		A1 G66
2612	" "	29	S½SE	1865-06-10		A1 G66
2614	" "	32	S½SE	1865-06-10		A1 G66
2613	" "	32	NESE	1866-06-01		A1 G66
2620	JONES, Jesse	5	NWSW	1892-04-16		A3
2553	KEARNS, Andrew	25	W½NW	1859-09-01		A1
2734	KENDALL, Wilson A	5	5NE	1870-05-10		A1 F
2558	LACY, Benjamin	33	N½NW	1859-09-01		A1
2559	" "	33	NE	1859-09-01		A1
2550	LEWIS, Albert	17	NWNW	1856-10-10		A1
2548	LEWIS, Albert A	17	NENW	1854-11-15		A1
2549	" "	17	NESW	1857-10-30		A1
2690	MARTIN, Noah B	5	SENW	1869-07-01		A1
2556	MAUL, Antoine	34	W½NW	1837-11-14		A1
2618	MCCLOWNY, James	24	SESW	1860-03-01		A1
2703	MCCREARY, Samuel	21	E½NE	1838-08-01		A1 G178
2599	MCGREADY, Israel	12	NE	1866-06-01		A1 F
2633	MCILVAINE, John	1	W½	1837-11-07		A1 F
2632	" "	1	E½	1838-08-01		A1 F
2563	MCLANE, Charles	25	NENE	1853-04-15		A1
2634	MCMANUS, John	12	SE	1854-11-15		A1
2704	MERRY, Samuel	17	NE	1837-11-07		A1 G181
2554	MILLER, Andrew	6	NE	1821-09-24		A1
2579	MILLER, George	22	NE	1871-11-01		A3 F
2580	" "	22	NENW	1871-11-01		A3
2671	MOLLY, Mary	28	SESW	1864-03-10		A1
2574	MONDAY, Felix	28	NE	1838-08-01		A1
2555	MONTGOMERY, Andrew	17	E½SE	1838-08-01		A1 G185
2551	MORELAND, Alexander L	13	1	1860-08-01		A1 F
2573	MUNDAY, Felex	20	SESW	1838-08-01		A1
2635	MUNDY, John	15	NE	1847-06-04		A1 F
2691	MUNDY, Patrick	15	NW	1848-03-01		A1 F
2629	MYERS, John M	35	N½NW	1884-11-01		A3
2630	" "	35	SENW	1884-11-01		A3
2631	" "	35	SWNE	1884-11-01		A3
2662	MYERS, Joseph H	26	NESW	1857-10-30		A1
2663	" "	26	NWSW	1896-02-10		A1
2664	" "	27	NESE	1896-02-10		A1
2665	" "	27	NWSE	1896-02-10		A1
2672	MYERS, Mary	27	E½SW	1858-04-01		A1
2673	" "	27	SENW	1858-04-01		A1
2636	NICHOLSON, John	6	W½NW	1849-04-10		A1 G190
2636	NICHOLSON, Thomas	6	W½NW	1849-04-10		A1 G190

ID	Individual in Patent	Sec.	Sec. Part	Date Issued	Other Counties	For More Info . . .
2712	NICHOLSON, Thomas (Cont'd)	5	N½NW	1856-01-03		A1 F
2710	" "	5	1NE	1858-12-01		A1 F
2711	" "	5	4NE	1858-12-01		A1 F
2636	NICHOLSON, William	6	W½NW	1849-04-10		A1 G190
2728	" "	6	NWSE	1856-10-10		A1
2729	" "	6	SESE	1857-10-30		A1
2730	" "	6	SWSE	1859-09-01		A1
2581	NUESE, George	29	W½SW	1857-10-30		A1
2582	" "	30	E½SE	1857-10-30		A1
2583	" "	31	N½NE	1857-10-30		A1
2584	" "	31	SENE	1857-10-30		A1
2585	" "	32	SWNW	1857-10-30		A1
2567	OBRIEN, Daniel	14	SW	1848-03-01		A1 F
2637	OBRIEN, John	15	E½SE	1854-05-04		A1 F
2686	OBUCHON, Morelle	34	W½SE	1838-08-01		A1
2687	OBUCHON, Napoleon	34	SENW	1838-08-01		A1
2688	" "	34	SWNE	1838-08-01		A1
2638	OHANLIN, John	5	SWSW	1858-01-15		A1 F
2639	" "	8	NENE	1858-04-01		A1 F
2640	OHANLON, John	17	SENW	1854-11-15		A1
2713	OHANLON, Thomas	10		1847-04-10		A1 F
2714	" "	11		1847-04-10		A1 F
2572	OMARA, Eugene	11	W½SE	1850-04-29		A1 F
2571	PATTERSON, Elizabeth	23	SW	1837-03-15		A1 F
2643	PATTERSON, John P	23	NW	1871-11-01		A3 F
2555	PEASE, Henry	17	E½SE	1838-08-01		A1 G185
2717	" "	17	W½SE	1838-08-01		A1 G145
2703	" "	21	E½NE	1838-08-01		A1 G178
2547	" "	21	E½SW	1838-08-01		A1 G84
2596	" "	27	W½SW	1838-08-01		A1
2597	" "	28	E½SE	1838-08-01		A1
2697	PEEBLES, Robert	11	E½SE	1856-01-03		A1 F
2698	" "	12	W½	1856-01-03		A1 F
2699	" "	14	NE	1856-01-03		A1 F
2649	PERRY, John	21	E½NW	1824-05-01		A1 G198
2648	" "	9	SE	1824-05-20		A1
2704	" "	17	NE	1837-11-07		A1 G181
2644	" "	10	SE	1906-02-05		A1 F
2645	" "	11	SW	1906-02-05		A1 F
2646	" "	14		1906-02-05		A1 F
2647	" "	15		1906-02-05		A1 F
2649	PERRY, Samuel	21	E½NW	1824-05-01		A1 G198
2649	PERRY, William M	21	E½NW	1824-05-01		A1 G198
2706	REED, Samuel	20	NWNE	1848-02-01		A1
2705	" "	20	NENE	1850-01-01		A1
2708	" "	20	SENW	1854-11-15		A1
2707	" "	20	S½NE	1858-01-15		A1
2709	" "	20	SWNW	1860-08-01		A1
2651	ROBINSON, John T	18	S½NW	1857-10-30		A1
2652	" "	30	S½NW	1858-04-01		A1
2655	" "	8	NENW	1858-04-01		A1 F
2653	" "	31	SWNE	1865-06-10		A1
2654	" "	32	NWNW	1865-06-10		A1
2575	ROZIER, Ferdinand	26	NE	1837-11-07		A1
2577	ROZIER, Francis C	26	W½NW	1838-08-01		A1 G80
2570	RUSS, Eliza	24	SWSW	1857-04-15		A1 F
2715	RUSSELL, Thomas	22	SWNW	1860-08-01		A1
2720	SEYMOUR, William B	20	NESW	1866-06-01		A1
2568	SHIMIN, Edward C	34	NENE	1893-06-24		A1
2598	SINEX, Henry	21	NWSE	1838-08-01		A1
2560	SMITH, Charles D	19	N½1SW	1867-05-01		A1
2561	" "	29	NENW	1867-05-01		A1
2562	" "	33	SWNW	1867-05-01		A1
2566	SMITH, Daniel J	30	W½SE	1858-04-01		A1
2656	SMITH, John T	13	2	1857-03-02		A1 F
2657	" "	24	NW	1857-03-02		A1 F
2658	" "	24	SENE	1857-03-02		A1 F
2659	" "	24	W½NE	1857-03-02		A1 F
2666	SMITH, Lawrence	13	SESE	1871-07-25		A3 F
2667	" "	24	NENE	1871-07-25		A3 F
2731	SMITH, William	31	2SW	1857-10-30		A1
2732	" "	31	N½1SW	1857-10-30		A1
2569	TODD, Eliza A	23	E½SE	1837-11-07		A1 G220 F

ID	Individual in Patent	Sec.	Sec. Part	Date Issued	Other Counties	For More Info . . .
2569	TODD, Emily J	23	E½SE	1837-11-07		A1 G220 F
2569	TODD, Mary A	23	E½SE	1837-11-07		A1 G220 F
2569	TODD, Mathew A	23	E½SE	1837-11-07		A1 G220 F
2679	" "	20	SESE	1858-04-01		A1
2680	" "	21	SWSW	1858-04-01		A1
2681	" "	28	W½SW	1858-04-01		A1
2682	" "	29	E½NE	1858-04-01		A1
2683	" "	29	N½SE	1858-04-01		A1
2569	TODD, William A	23	E½SE	1837-11-07		A1 G220 F
2564	ULLMAN, Charles	33	N½SW	1892-08-01		A1
2565	" "	33	SENW	1892-08-01		A1
2661	VERNER, Jonathan	14	NW	1847-04-10		A1 F
2701	WARE, Joseph E	5	3NE	1866-06-01		A1 G107
2702	" "	5	6NE	1866-06-01		A1 G107
2692	WIGGER, Philip	25	SENE	1859-09-01		A1
2693	" "	25	W½NE	1859-09-01		A1
2694	WIGGER, Phillip	24	SWSE	1862-04-10		A1
2733	WILLOUGHBY, William	15	W½SW	1848-03-01		A1 F
2721	WOODS, William B	19	2SW	1857-04-15		A1
2722	" "	19	S½NW	1857-04-15		A1

Patent Map

T37-N R2-E
5th PM Meridian

Map Group 19

Township Statistics

Parcels Mapped	:	188
Number of Patents	:	138
Number of Individuals	:	107
Patentees Identified	:	101
Number of Surnames	:	82
Multi-Patentee Parcels	:	18
Oldest Patent Date	:	9/24/1821
Most Recent Patent	:	9/25/1911
Block/Lot Parcels	:	14
Parcels Re - Issued	:	0
Parcels that Overlap	:	0
Cities and Towns	:	3
Cemeteries	:	14

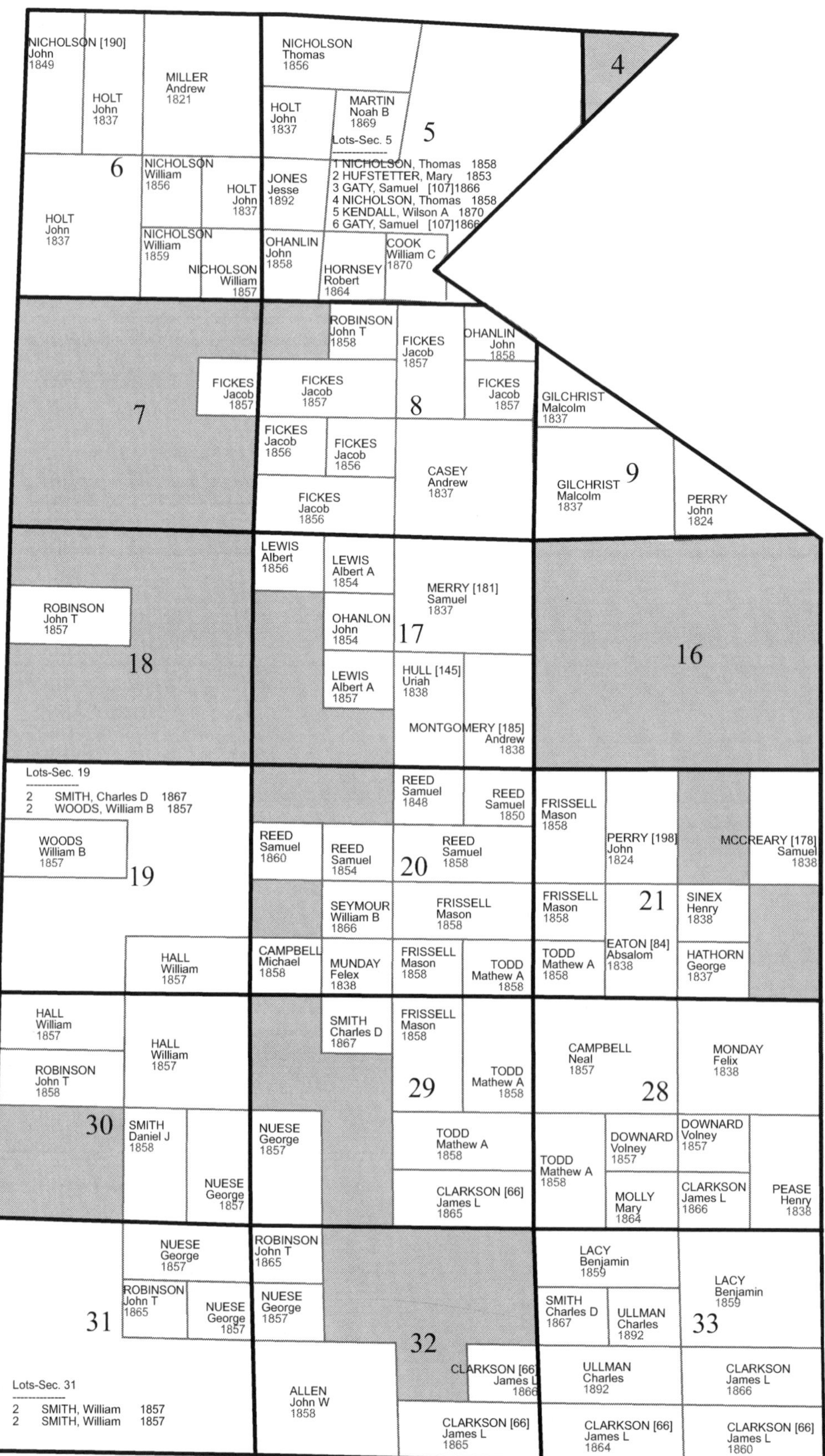

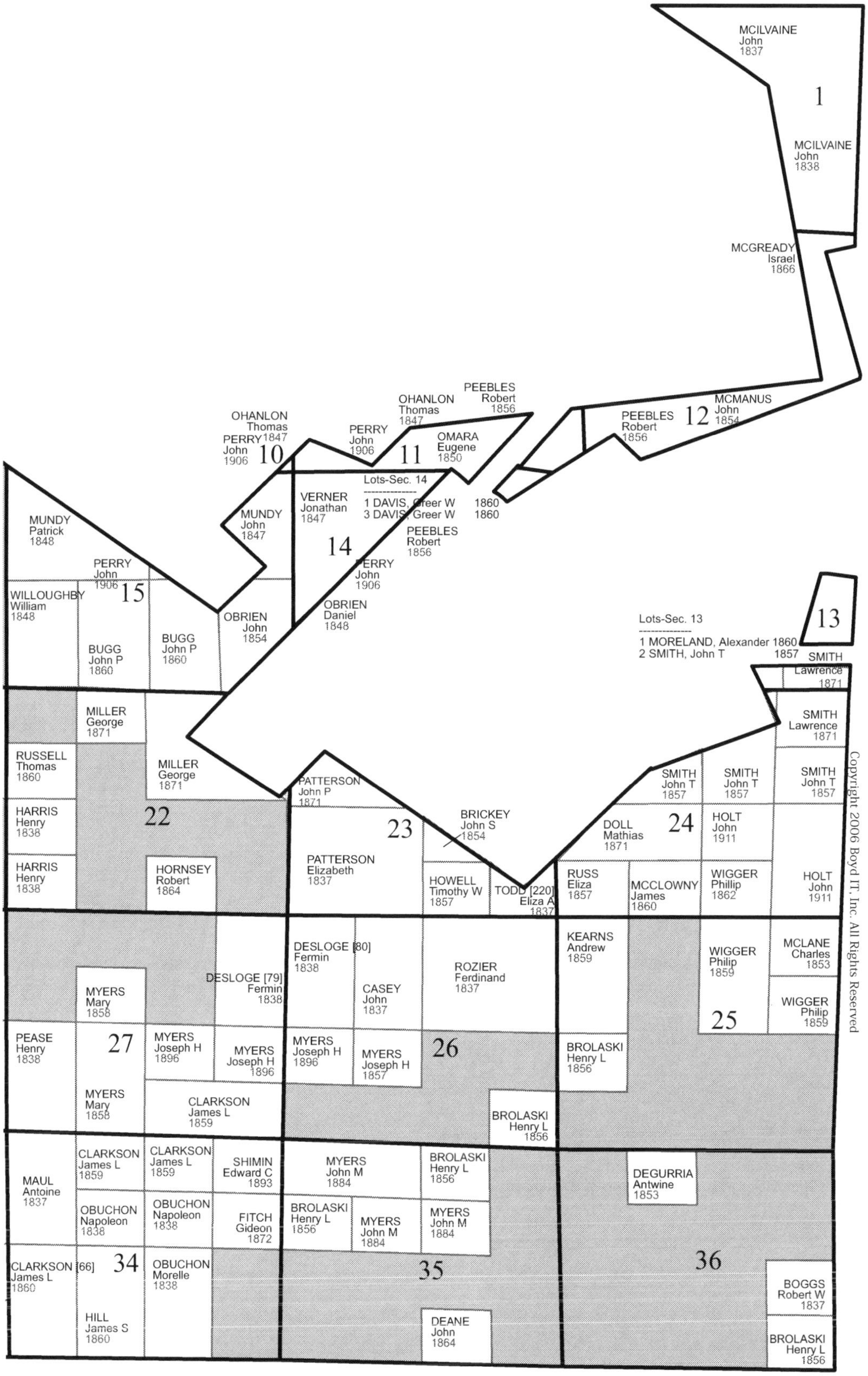

MCILVAINE John 1837

1

MCILVAINE John 1838

MCGREADY Israel 1866

OHANLON Thomas 1847

PEEBLES Robert 1856

OHANLON Thomas 1847

PERRY John 1906

PERRY John 1906

10

11

OMARA Eugene 1850

PEEBLES Robert 1856

12

MCMANUS John 1854

Lots-Sec. 14
1 DAVIS, Greer W 1860
3 DAVIS, Greer W 1860

VERNER Jonathan 1847

MUNDY John 1847

MUNDY Patrick 1848

14

PEEBLES Robert 1856

PERRY John 1906

PERRY John 1906

15

WILLOUGHBY William 1848

OBRIEN John 1854

OBRIEN Daniel 1848

BUGG John P 1860

BUGG John P 1860

Lots-Sec. 13
1 MORELAND, Alexander 1860
2 SMITH, John T 1857

13

SMITH Lawrence 1871

SMITH Lawrence 1871

MILLER George 1871

RUSSELL Thomas 1860

MILLER George 1871

HARRIS Henry 1838

22

HARRIS Henry 1838

HORNSEY Robert 1864

PATTERSON John P 1871

23

BRICKEY John S 1854

PATTERSON Elizabeth 1837

HOWELL Timothy W 1857

TODD [220] Eliza A 1837

SMITH John T 1857

SMITH John T 1857

SMITH John T 1857

DOLL Mathias 1871

24

HOLT John 1911

RUSS Eliza 1857

MCCLOWNY James 1860

WIGGER Phillip 1862

HOLT John 1911

DESLOGE [80] Fermin 1838

ROZIER Ferdinand 1837

KEARNS Andrew 1859

WIGGER Philip 1859

MCLANE Charles 1853

DESLOGE [79] Fermin 1838

CASEY John 1837

MYERS Mary 1858

25

WIGGER Philip 1859

PEASE Henry 1838

27

MYERS Joseph H 1896

MYERS Joseph H 1896

MYERS Joseph H 1896

MYERS Joseph H 1857

26

BROLASKI Henry L 1856

MYERS Mary 1858

CLARKSON James L 1859

BROLASKI Henry L 1856

CLARKSON James L 1859

CLARKSON James L 1859

SHIMIN Edward C 1893

MYERS John M 1884

BROLASKI Henry L 1856

MAUL Antoine 1837

DEGURRIA Antwine 1853

OBUCHON Napoleon 1838

OBUCHON Napoleon 1838

FITCH Gideon 1872

BROLASKI Henry L 1856

MYERS John M 1884

MYERS John M 1884

CLARKSON [66] James L 1860

34

OBUCHON Morelle 1838

35

36

BOGGS Robert W 1837

HILL James S 1860

DEANE John 1864

BROLASKI Henry L 1856

Helpful Hints

1. This Map's INDEX can be found on the preceding pages.
2. Refer to Map "C" to see where this Township lies within Washington County, Missouri.
3. Numbers within square brackets [ ] denote a multi-patentee land parcel (multi-owner). Refer to Appendix "C" for a full list of members in this group.
4. Areas that look to be crowded with Patentees usually indicate multiple sales of the same parcel (Re-issues) or Overlapping parcels. See this Township's Index for an explanation of these and other circumstances that might explain "odd" groupings of Patentees on this map.

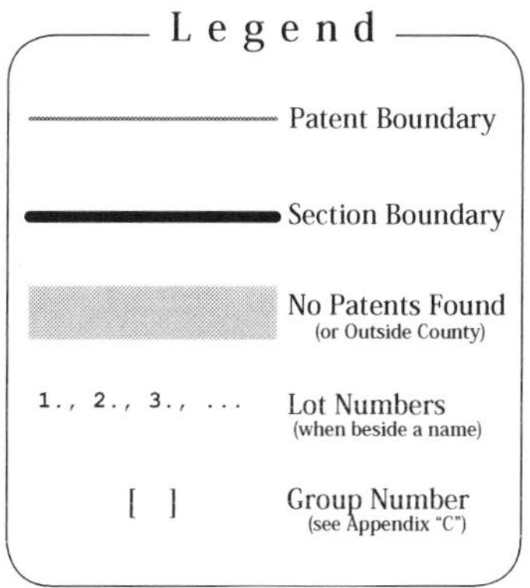

Scale: Section = 1 mile X 1 mile
(generally, with some exceptions)

Road Map

T37-N R2-E
5th PM Meridian

Map Group 19

Cities & Towns
- Bates Creek Camp
- Potosi
- Springtown

Cemeteries
- Bates Creek Cemetery
- Chadbourne Cemetery
- Nicholson Cemetery
- Calvary Cemetery
- City Cemetery
- Perry-McGready Cemetery
- Potosi Colored Cemetery
- Potosi New Masonic Cemetery
- Potosi Old Masonic Cemetery
- Potosi Presbyterian Cemetery
- Redbud Memorial Gardens
- Saint James Catholic Cemetery
- Sunset Hill Cemetery
- Trinity Cemetery

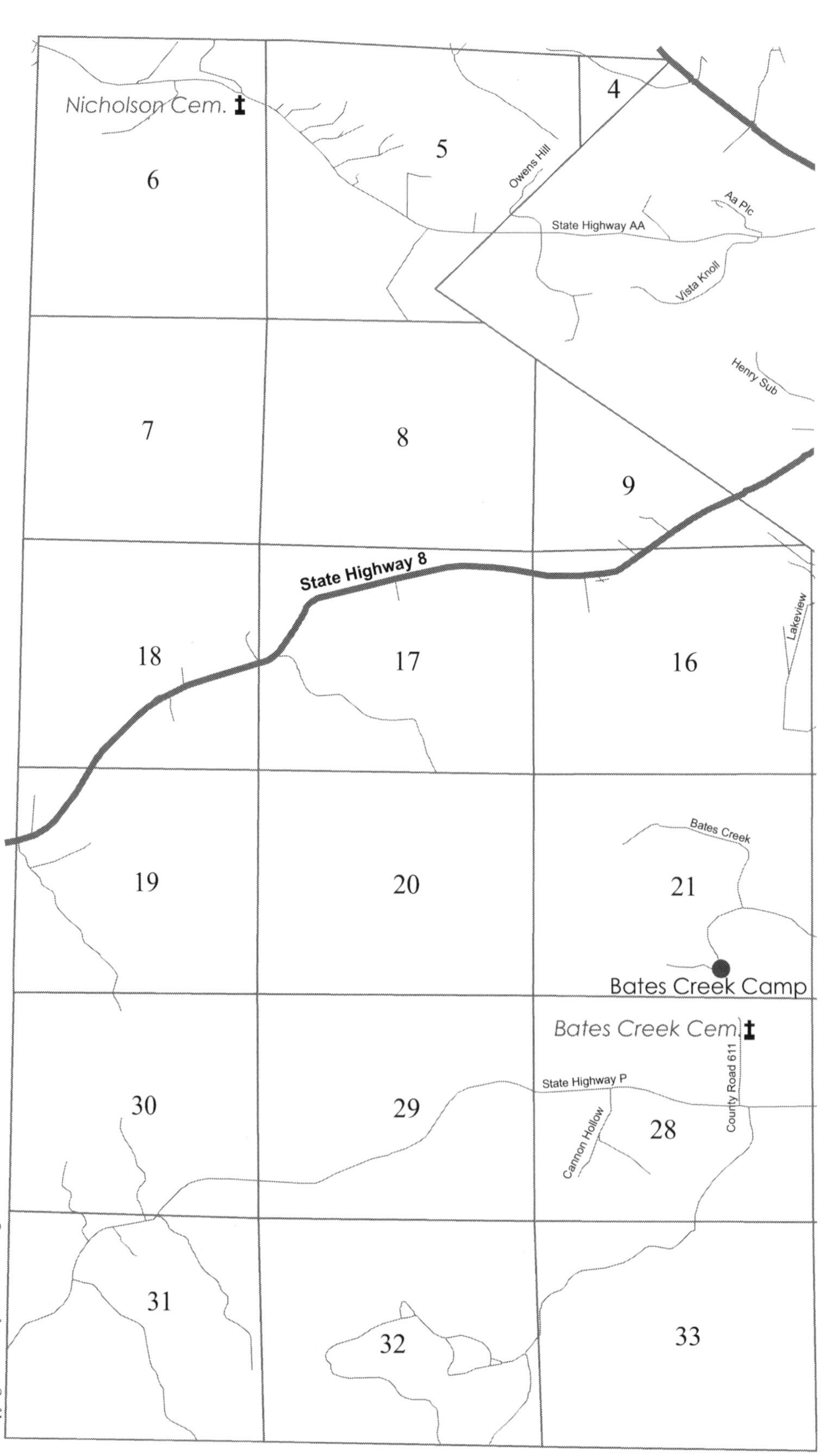

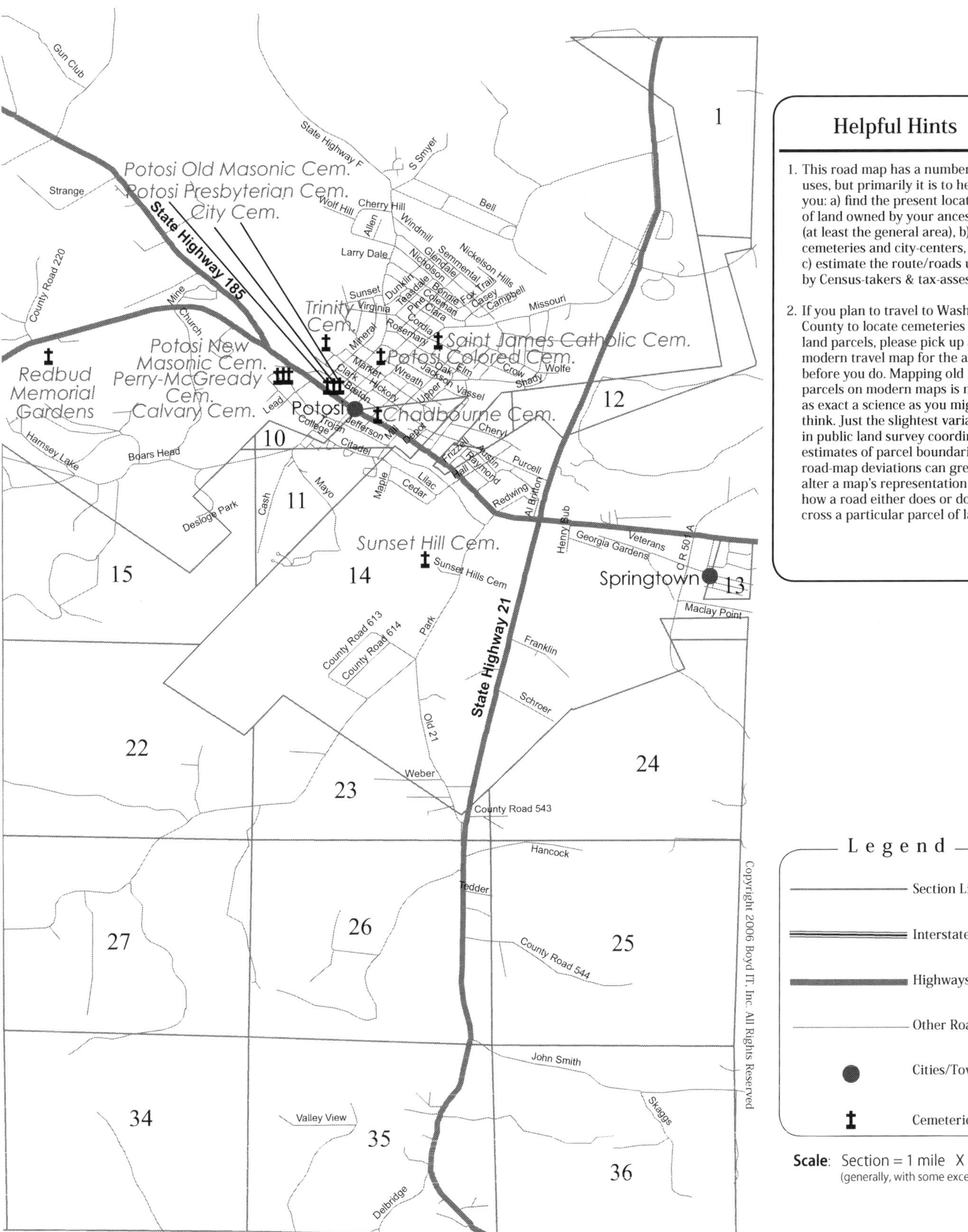

Helpful Hints

1. This road map has a number of uses, but primarily it is to help you: a) find the present location of land owned by your ancestors (at least the general area), b) find cemeteries and city-centers, and c) estimate the route/roads used by Census-takers & tax-assessors.
2. If you plan to travel to Washington County to locate cemeteries or land parcels, please pick up a modern travel map for the area before you do. Mapping old land parcels on modern maps is not as exact a science as you might think. Just the slightest variations in public land survey coordinates, estimates of parcel boundaries, or road-map deviations can greatly alter a map's representation of how a road either does or doesn't cross a particular parcel of land.

Legend

- Section Lines
- Interstates
- Highways
- Other Roads
- Cities/Towns
- Cemeteries

Scale: Section = 1 mile X 1 mile
(generally, with some exceptions)

Historical Map

T37-N R2-E
5th PM Meridian

Map Group 19

Cities & Towns

Bates Creek Camp
Potosi
Springtown

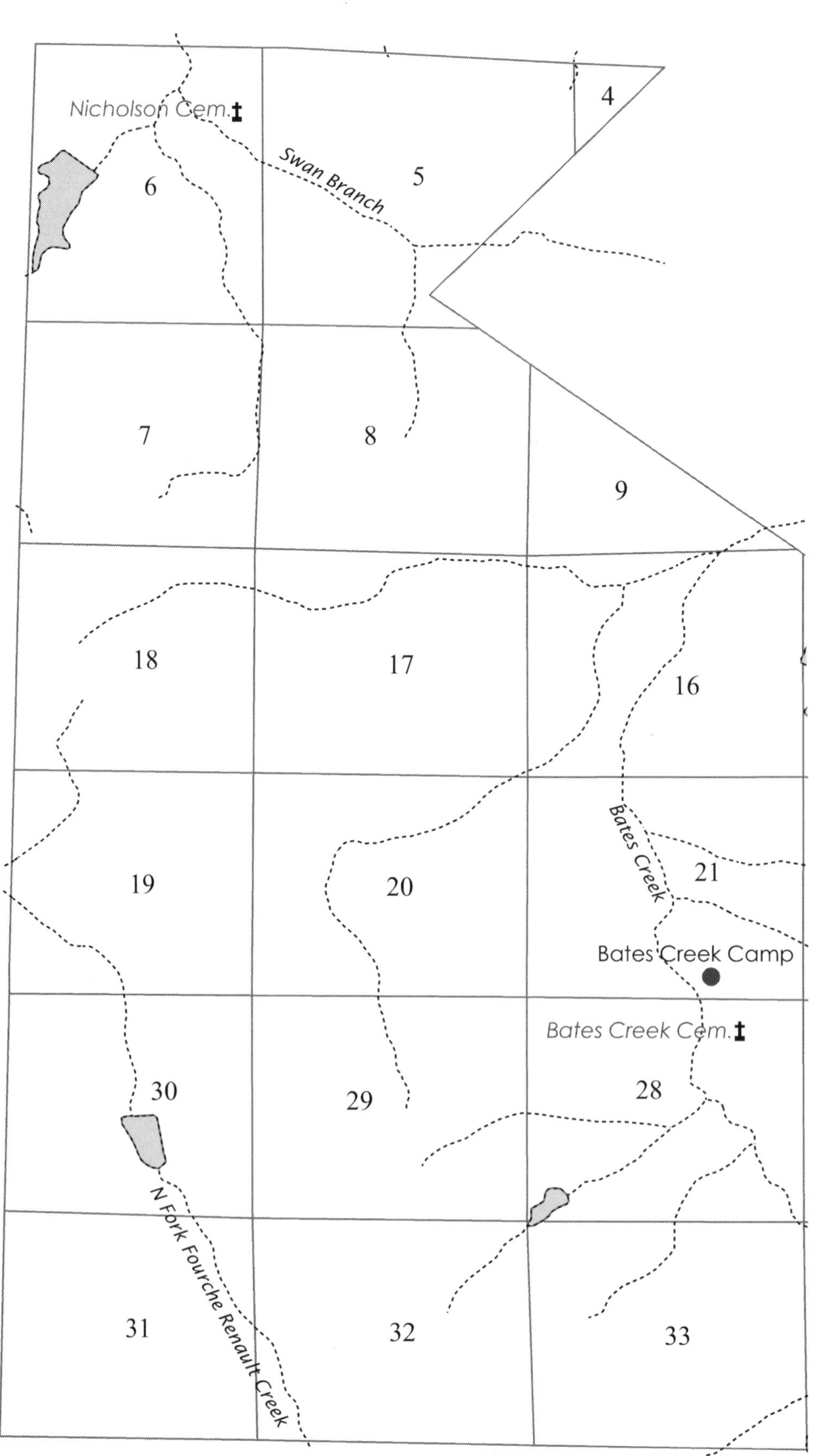

Cemeteries

Bates Creek Cemetery
Chadbourne Cemetery
Nicholson Cemetery
Calvary Cemetery
City Cemetery
Perry-McGready Cemetery
Potosi Colored Cemetery
Potosi New Masonic Cemetery
Potosi Old Masonic Cemetery
Potosi Presbyterian Cemetery
Redbud Memorial Gardens
Saint James Catholic Cemetery
Sunset Hill Cemetery
Trinity Cemetery

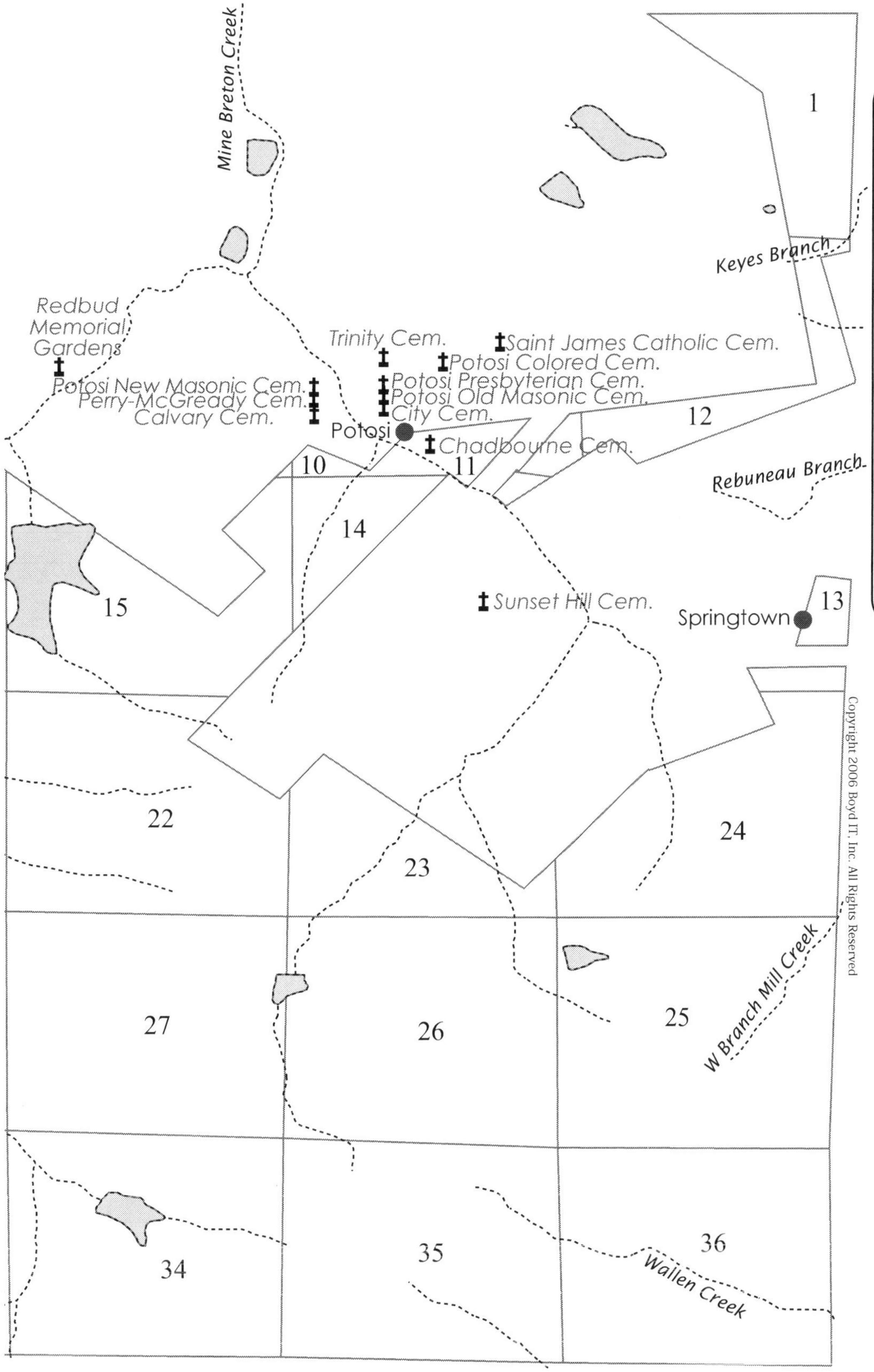

Mine Breton Creek
1
Keyes Branch
Redbud Memorial Gardens
Trinity Cem.
Saint James Catholic Cem.
Potosi Colored Cem.
Potosi New Masonic Cem.
Perry-McGready Cem.
Calvary Cem.
Potosi Presbyterian Cem.
Potosi Old Masonic Cem.
City Cem.
Potosi
Chadbourne Cem.
12
10
11
Rebuneau Branch
14
15
Sunset Hill Cem.
Springtown
13
22
24
23
27
26
25
W Branch Mill Creek
34
35
36
Wallen Creek

Helpful Hints

1. This Map takes a different look at the same Congressional Township displayed in the preceding two maps. It presents features that can help you better envision the historical development of the area: a) Water-bodies (lakes & ponds), b) Water-courses (rivers, streams, etc.), c) Railroads, d) City/town center-points (where they were oftentimes located when first settled), and e) Cemeteries.

2. Using this "Historical" map in tandem with this Township's Patent Map and Road Map, may lead you to some interesting discoveries. You will often find roads, towns, cemeteries, and waterways are named after nearby landowners: sometimes those names will be the ones you are researching. See how many of these research gems you can find here in Washington County.

Legend
Section Lines
Railroads
Large Rivers & Bodies of Water
Streams/Creeks & Small Rivers
Cities/Towns
Cemeteries

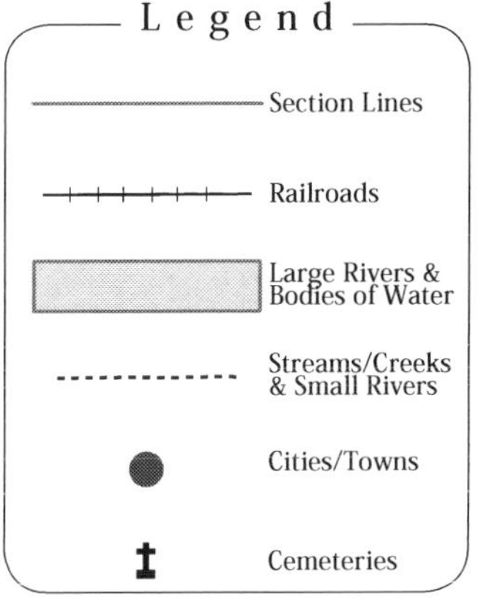

Scale: Section = 1 mile X 1 mile
(there are some exceptions)

Map Group 20: Index to Land Patents

Township 37-North Range 3-East (5th PM)

After you locate an individual in this Index, take note of the Section and Section Part then proceed to the Land Patent map on the pages immediately following. You should have no difficulty locating the corresponding parcel of land.

The "For More Info" Column will lead you to more information about the underlying Patents. See the *Legend* at right, and the "How to Use this Book" chapter, for more information.

LEGEND

"For More Info . . ." column

A = Authority (Legislative Act, See Appendix "A")
B = Block or Lot (location in Section unknown)
C = Cancelled Patent
F = Fractional Section
G = Group (Multi-Patentee Patent, see Appendix "C")
V = Overlaps another Parcel
R = Re-Issued (Parcel patented more than once)

(A & G items require you to look in the Appendixes referred to above. All other Letter-designations followed by a number require you to locate line-items in this index that possess the ID number found after the letter).

ID	Individual in Patent	Sec.	Sec. Part	Date Issued	Other Counties	For More Info . . .
2954	ARNOLD, William C	13	N½SW	1875-02-15		A3
2955	" "	13	SENW	1875-02-15		A3
2956	" "	13	SESW	1875-02-15		A3
2933	BAKER, Stephen J	13	NWNW	1872-07-01		A3
2786	BARROW, Gabriel	35	N½NE	1854-11-15		A1
2787	" "	35	SENE	1856-01-03		A1
2937	BELFIELD, Thomas	28	NWNE	1850-01-01		A1
2938	BELLFIELD, Thomas	28	NENE	1856-01-03		A1
2738	BLAIN, Albert	33	SWSW	1837-11-14		A1
2784	BOAS, Francis M	5	SE	1873-04-10		A3 F R2838
2819	BOAS, Jacob	10	E½NE	1837-01-24		A1 G23
2820	" "	10	W½NE	1837-01-24		A1 G24
2818	" "	5	1NE	1837-11-07		A1
2815	" "	15	W½NW	1848-03-01		A1
2814	" "	12	SESE	1856-01-03		A1
2816	" "	2	SWSW	1856-01-03		A1
2821	" "	21	SWSE	1856-06-16		A1 G25
2817	" "	3	SWSE	1858-12-01		A1
2922	BOGGS, Robert W	31	2SW	1837-11-07		A1
2923	" "	31	S½1SW	1837-11-14		A1
2779	BONE, Francis	36	NWNW	1841-08-10		A1
2780	" "	36	NWSW	1841-08-10		A1
2777	" "	25	SWSW	1857-03-10		A1
2778	" "	26	SESE	1857-03-10		A1
2799	BORING, Henry E	3	2NE	1837-11-07		A1
2863	BRICKEY, John J	36	SWSW	1837-11-07		A1
2920	BRICKEY, Preston P	17	SE	1837-11-07		A1 F
2800	BROLASKI, Henry L	31	2NW	1856-10-10		A1
2801	" "	34	SESW	1856-10-10		A1
2745	BRONSON, Arthur	5	2NE	1841-02-26		A1
2746	" "	5	W½NW	1841-02-26		A1
2893	BURTON, Levi G	34	SENE	1858-04-01		A1
2894	" "	35	NWSW	1858-04-01		A1
2895	" "	35	SWNW	1858-04-01		A1
2790	CAIN, George	11	NWNE	1837-11-14		A1
2791	" "	2	SWSE	1837-11-14		A1
2789	CAIN, George C	3	NWSE	1849-04-10		A1
2961	CAIN, William M	11	NESW	1848-09-01		A1
2792	CASEY, George	31	W½SE	1837-11-14		A1
2841	CASEY, John	31	NESE	1837-11-14		A1
2856	CASEY, John H	31	E½1SW	1853-12-01		A1
2859	" "	31	SWNE	1853-12-01		A1
2860	" "	32	SWNW	1853-12-01		A1
2855	" "	30	SWSE	1856-01-03		A1
2857	" "	31	NWNE	1856-01-03		A1
2858	" "	31	SENE	1859-01-01		A1

ID	Individual in Patent	Sec.	Sec. Part	Date Issued	Other Counties	For More Info . . .
2861	CAYCE, John H	31	SESE	1837-11-14		A1
2842	CLEUFF, John	11	SWNW	1848-09-01		A1
2843	CLUFF, John	3	SESE	1874-11-05		A3
2743	COLE, Aquilla	2	W½1NW	1838-08-01		A1
2744	" "	2	W½2NW	1838-08-01		A1
2807	COLE, Isaac S	1	NWSW	1856-01-03		A1
2808	" "	1	SWSW	1859-01-01		A1
2809	" "	12	E½NW	1859-01-01		A1
2810	" "	12	W½NW	1860-08-01		A1
2887	COLE, Joseph C	2	NWSW	1856-09-01		A1
2891	COLE, Joshua	1	S½SE	1837-01-24		A1
2890	" "	1	NESE	1849-04-10		A1
2892	COLE, Juliet	11	SWSE	1848-03-01		A1
2944	COLE, Thomas J	11	NWSE	1843-04-10		A1
2946	" "	11	SWNE	1848-03-01		A1
2942	" "	11	NENW	1849-04-10		A1
2945	" "	11	SENE	1853-08-01		A1
2943	" "	11	NESE	1856-01-03		A1
2947	" "	12	S½SW	1859-01-01		A1
2948	" "	12	SWSE	1859-01-01		A1
2935	COLEMAN, Thomas B	12	N½SW	1882-08-30		A3
2793	DAY, George	33	NESE	1852-01-01		A1
2794	" "	34	SWNW	1852-01-01		A1
2868	DUFF, John M	28	SENW	1837-11-14		A1
2869	" "	33	NENW	1837-11-14		A1
2921	DURHAM, Rhody	5	E½1NW	1838-08-01		A1
2844	ENDLY, John	20	SWSW	1859-09-01		A1
2761	EVANS, Charles	15	SW	1848-03-01		A1 G89 V2912, 2870...
2847	EVANS, John	34	NESW	1841-12-10		A1
2849	" "	21	E½NE	1848-02-01		A1 G94
2848	" "	22	W½NW	1848-02-01		A1 G93
2761	" "	15	SW	1848-03-01		A1 G89 V2912, 2870...
2846	" "	33	NWNE	1852-01-01		A1
2845	" "	27	NESE	1857-10-30		A1
2851	EVENS, John	28	SWNE	1853-08-01		A1
2852	" "	34	SWNE	1853-08-01		A1
2853	" "	4	E½2NE	1854-11-15		A1
2850	" "	26	SWSW	1857-10-30		A1
2798	FERGUSON, George W	17	NESW	1856-09-01		A1 G103 F
2906	FRISSELL, Mason	26	NWSE	1854-11-15		A1
2965	GLORE, William W	30	S½2SW	1853-12-01		A1
2964	" "	25	SWSE	1854-11-15		A1
2767	GUSHEE, Edward	30	1NW	1859-09-01		A1
2768	" "	30	1SW	1859-09-01		A1
2769	" "	30	NWSE	1859-09-01		A1
2770	" "	30	S½NE	1859-09-01		A1
2813	HAEFNER, J W	21	E½SW	1853-12-01		A1
2771	HARRISON, Edwin	24	E½SE	1869-07-01		A1
2772	" "	25	NENE	1869-07-01		A1
2773	" "	25	NWSE	1869-07-01		A1
2774	" "	26	SWSE	1869-07-01		A1
2775	" "	35	SWNE	1869-10-15		A1
2907	HARRISON, Meeke A	22	SENE	1854-11-15		A1
2761	HARRISON, Samuel	15	SW	1848-03-01		A1 G89 V2912, 2870...
2924	" "	25	NENW	1854-11-15		A1
2926	" "	25	SENW	1854-11-15		A1
2928	" "	25	SWNE	1854-11-15		A1
2925	" "	25	NESW	1856-01-03		A1
2927	" "	25	SESW	1856-01-03		A1
2747	HAWKINS, Augustus	2	W½2NE	1848-03-01		A1
2749	HAWKINS, Austin H	17	SESW	1848-03-01		A1
2750	" "	17	W½SW	1848-03-01		A1
2751	" "	20	NENW	1848-03-01		A1
2753	" "	20	W½NW	1848-03-01		A1
2752	" "	20	NWNE	1853-08-01		A1
2748	" "	17	NW	1854-11-15		A1 F
2755	" "	21	SENW	1857-10-30		A1
2756	" "	21	SWNE	1857-10-30		A1
2754	" "	21	N½NW	1858-01-15		A1
2822	HAWKINS, James H	1	W½2NW	1853-08-01		A1
2823	" "	2	SENW	1854-11-15		A1
2826	HAWKINS, James K	2	E½2NE	1841-07-01		A1
2761	HAY, David A	15	SW	1848-03-01		A1 G89 V2912, 2870...

ID	Individual in Patent	Sec.	Sec. Part	Date Issued	Other Counties	For More Info . . .
2862	HOLT, John	20	N½SE	1848-03-01		A1
2735	HOUSE, Adam	14	SESE	1856-09-01		A1
2934	HOUSE, Thomas A	13	SWSW	1857-04-15		A1
2900	HUDLESTON, Luke	20	SESW	1854-11-15		A1
2760	HUFF, Catharine	28	SESE	1837-11-14		A1
2805	HUFF, Isaac	26	E½NE	1873-02-01		A3
2806	" "	26	NESE	1873-02-01		A3
2833	HUFF, James W	25	NWSW	1882-03-30		A3
2834	" "	25	W½NW	1882-03-30		A3
2957	INGE, William	6	1NE	1837-01-24		A1
2958	" "	6	2NE	1837-01-24		A1
2824	JAMISON, James H	33	SESW	1837-11-07		A1
2825	" "	33	SWSE	1837-11-07		A1
2865	JAMISON, John	30	E½SE	1824-05-10		A1 G149
2795	JENKINS, George	26	NENW	1848-02-01		A1
2941	JOHNSON, Thomas C	26	NWNW	1849-04-10		A1
2939	" "	22	SESW	1851-12-01		A1
2940	" "	23	N½SW	1859-09-01		A1
2762	JOLLIN, Charles	36	SWNW	1857-03-10		A1
2864	KANE, John J	1	W½1NW	1886-04-10		A3
2781	LECLARE, Francis	32	SESE	1837-11-14		A1
2782	" "	32	W½NE	1837-11-14		A1
2783	LECLERE, Francis	22	W½NE	1837-11-07		A1
2898	LECLERE, Louis	31	NENE	1838-08-01		A1
2899	" "	32	NWNW	1838-08-01		A1
2796	LITTLE, George	5	E½SW	1838-08-01		A1
2759	LONG, Brumfield	1	E½2NE	1849-04-10		A1 G164
2759	LONG, Milton	1	E½2NE	1849-04-10		A1 G164
2908	" "	1	E½1NE	1854-11-15		A1
2909	" "	1	E½1NW	1859-01-01		A1
2910	" "	1	W½1NE	1859-01-01		A1
2911	" "	1	W½2NE	1859-01-01		A1
2759	LONG, William	1	E½2NE	1849-04-10		A1 G164
2959	" "	1	E½2NW	1859-01-01		A1
2960	" "	1	NWSE	1859-01-01		A1
2867	LORE, John	36	SE	1837-01-24		A1 G167
2866	" "	35	SWSE	1858-01-15		A1
2896	MARLE, Levi	15	SWNE	1848-02-01		A1
2897	MARLEE, Levi	10	NWSE	1856-06-16		A1
2828	MARLER, James	19	SENE	1871-10-20		A1
2836	MARLER, Joel	2	N½SE	1861-02-01		A1
2837	" "	2	SESE	1861-02-01		A1
2819	MARLER, John	10	E½NE	1837-01-24		A1 G23
2888	MARLER, Joseph	12	W½NE	1860-03-01		A1
2820	MARLER, Michael	10	W½NE	1837-01-24		A1 G24
2952	MATHEWS, William A	23	NWSE	1854-11-15		A1
2953	MATTHEWS, William A	30	NWNE	1856-01-03		A1
2867	MCCABE, Alpheus	36	SE	1837-01-24		A1 G167
2742	" "	36	SESW	1837-11-14		A1
2905	MCCABE, Marvin	36	NESW	1856-01-03		A1
2848	MCGREADY, Israel	22	W½NW	1848-02-01		A1 G93
2849	MCGREADY, Susan	21	E½NE	1848-02-01		A1 G94
2875	MCILVAINE, John	6	W½	1837-01-24		A1 F
2788	MCNEAL, George A	22	NWSW	1848-02-01		A1
2876	MCNEAL, John	21	NESE	1848-02-01		A1
2757	MESPLAY, Basille	4	E½SW	1825-07-15		A1 G184
2758	" "	9	E½NW	1825-07-15		A1 G184
2949	MESPLAY, Vetal	4	W½SW	1854-11-15		A1 F
2950	MISPLAY, Victor B	9	W½NE	1848-02-01		A1
2870	MOORE, John M	15	E½SW	1848-03-01		A1 V2761
2871	" "	15	NWSW	1848-03-01		A1 V2761
2872	" "	9	E½NE	1848-03-01		A1
2873	" "	9	E½SE	1848-03-01		A1
2874	" "	9	W½SE	1848-03-01		A1
2912	MOORE, Nancy J	15	SWSW	1848-02-01		A1 V2761
2929	MOORE, Samuel W	28	SWSW	1850-01-01		A1
2739	MORELAND, Alexander L	19	N½1SW	1860-08-01		A1
2740	" "	19	S½2SW	1860-08-01		A1
2854	MUDD, John F	2	E½2NW	1838-08-01		A1
2821	MURPHEY, Peter	21	SWSE	1856-06-16		A1 G25
2915	MURPHY, Peter W	14	E½SW	1848-03-01		A1
2916	" "	14	SENE	1848-03-01		A1
2917	" "	14	W½SW	1848-03-01		A1

ID	Individual in Patent	Sec.	Sec. Part	Date Issued	Other Counties	For More Info . . .
2918	MURPHY, Peter W (Cont'd)	15	SENW	1848-03-01		A1
2962	NEVES, William	4	1NE	1837-11-07		A1
2785	OBUCHON, Francis T	10	NESW	1848-02-01		A1
2877	PERRY, John	32	W½SW	1837-11-07		A1 G201
2765	PERRYMAN, David E	32	SENE	1856-10-10		A1
2901	RONGEY, Marshal	10	SESW	1848-03-01		A1
2903	RONGEY, Marshall	15	NENW	1854-11-15		A1
2902	RONGY, Marshal	10	W½SW	1849-04-10		A1
2757	ROZIER, Ferdinand	4	E½SW	1825-07-15		A1 G184
2758	" "	9	E½NW	1825-07-15		A1 G184
2827	SCOTT, James M	23	SWSW	1849-02-01		A1
2879	SCOTT, John	10	NW	1829-05-12		A1
2838	SCOTT, John C	5	SE	1825-07-15		A1 F R2784
2840	" "	8	NW	1825-07-15		A1 F
2839	" "	6	SE	1828-05-12		A1 F
2951	SHOLAR, Whitmell	4	W½2NE	1837-11-07		A1
2802	SMITH, Hiram	3	1NE	1837-11-07		A1
2804	" "	3	NESE	1837-11-07		A1
2803	" "	3	E½1NW	1849-04-10		A1
2829	SMITH, James	7	NW	1908-11-19		A1 F
2880	SMITH, John T	19	N½2SW	1857-03-02		A1 F
2881	" "	19	NENE	1857-03-02		A1 F
2882	" "	19	NW	1857-03-02		A1 F
2883	" "	19	W½NE	1857-03-02		A1 F
2913	SMITH, Peter	4	1NW	1841-06-25		A1
2914	" "	4	2NW	1841-06-25		A1
2811	STOW, Isaac	28	NWSE	1843-04-10		A1
2761	" "	15	SW	1848-03-01		A1 G89 V2912, 2870...
2878	SWENDT, John R	35	SESW	1850-01-01		A1
2830	THOMPSON, James	32	NENE	1851-12-01		A1 C
2831	" "	33	SENW	1851-12-01		A1 C
2832	" "	33	W½NW	1851-12-01		A1 C
2930	THOMPSON, Sebern	26	NESW	1857-10-30		A1
2931	" "	26	SENW	1857-10-30		A1
2932	" "	26	W½NE	1860-08-01		A1
2736	TIFFT, Alanson W	30	2NW	1859-09-01		A1
2737	" "	30	N½2SW	1859-09-01		A1
2904	TURPIN, Martin	25	NESE	1856-01-03		A1
2812	VALLE, J B	29	E½NW	1846-08-24		A1
2835	VALLE, Jean B	29	SW	1824-05-10		A1
2919	VAN FRANK, PHILIP R	9	W½NW	1865-06-10		A1 F
2963	VANDIVER, William	13	NENW	1854-11-15		A1
2741	VILLEMAR, Alexis	15	NENE	1856-01-03		A1
2936	WALTHALL, Thomas B	17	NE	1824-05-10		A1 F
2763	WALTON, Christopher	33	NENE	1837-11-14		A1
2764	" "	34	NWNW	1837-11-14		A1
2798	WATKINS, John C	17	NESW	1856-09-01		A1 G103 F
2776	WAUGH, Elizabeth	9	SW	1852-01-01		A1 F
2766	WEIGHER, David	34	E½NW	1838-08-01		A1
2797	WESTOVER, George T	34	W½SE	1841-08-10		A1
2865	WESTOVER, Job	30	E½SE	1824-05-10		A1 G149
2877	WHEALEY, William	32	W½SW	1837-11-07		A1 G201
2966	" "	35	SESE	1837-11-07		A1
2849	WHITE, James M	21	E½NE	1848-02-01		A1 G94
2848	" "	22	W½NW	1848-02-01		A1 G93
2967	WHITE, William	11	SENW	1854-11-15		A1
2884	WIATT, John	27	N½NW	1854-11-15		A1
2885	" "	29	W½NE	1854-11-15		A1
2886	WILDMAN, John	17	NENW	1837-11-07		A1 F
2889	WILDMAN, Joseph	20	E½NE	1837-11-07		A1

Patent Map

T37-N R3-E
5th PM Meridian

Map Group 20

Township Statistics

Parcels Mapped	:	233
Number of Patents	:	198
Number of Individuals	:	140
Patentees Identified	:	136
Number of Surnames	:	95
Multi-Patentee Parcels	:	13
Oldest Patent Date	:	5/10/1824
Most Recent Patent	:	11/19/1908
Block/Lot Parcels	:	38
Parcels Re - Issued	:	1
Parcels that Overlap	:	4
Cities and Towns	:	4
Cemeteries	:	3

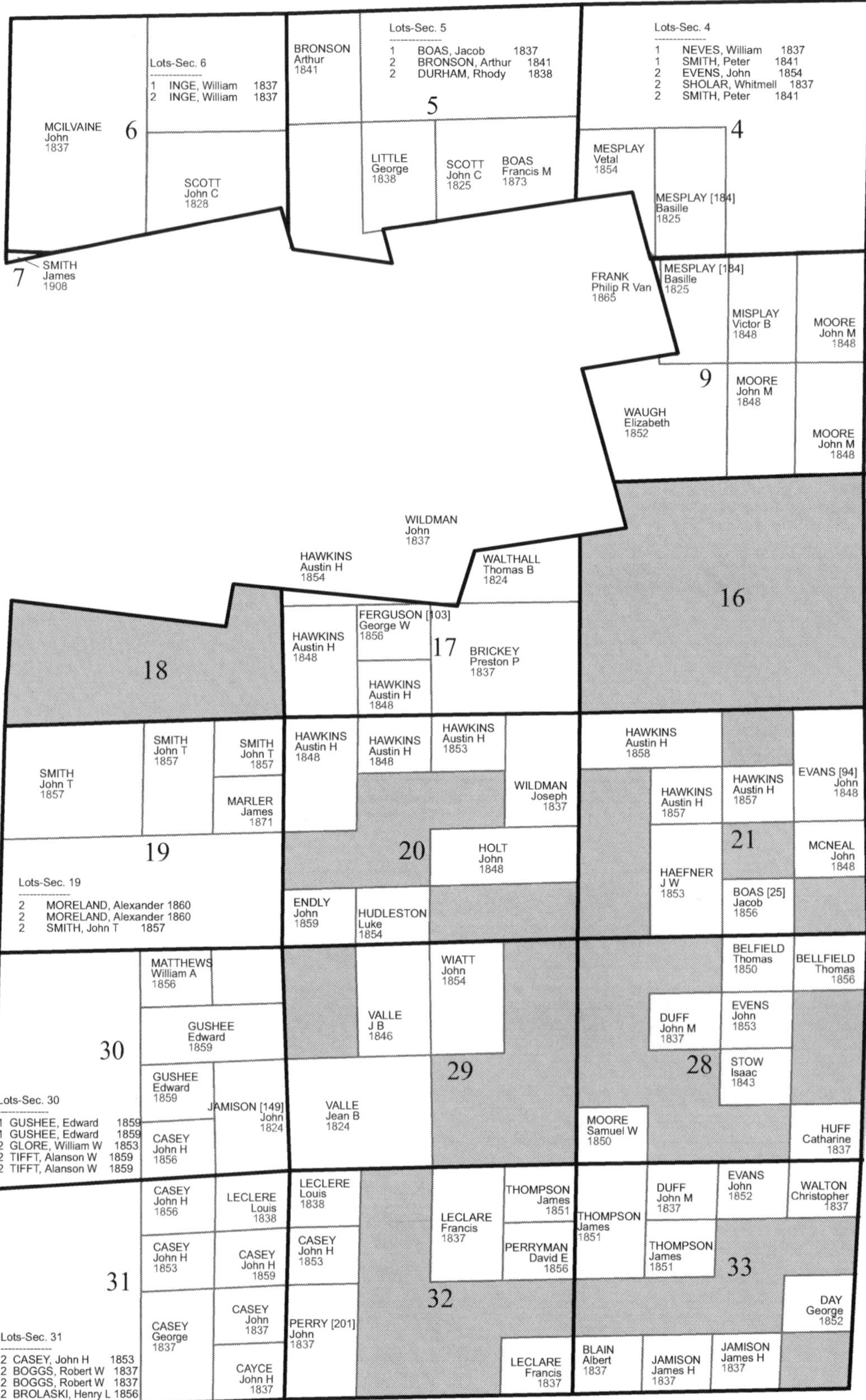

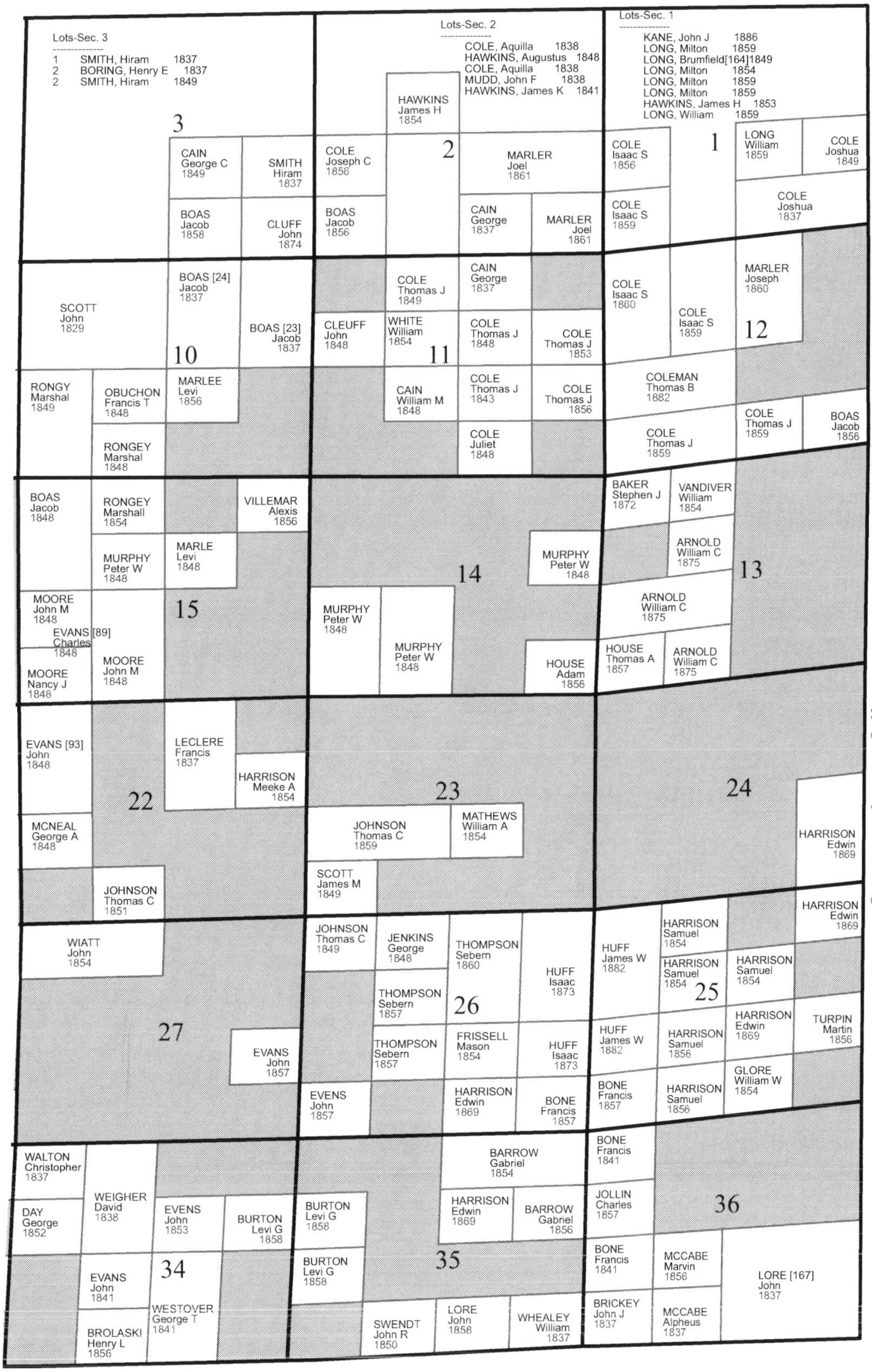

Lots-Sec. 3

1 SMITH, Hiram 1837
2 BORING, Henry E 1837
2 SMITH, Hiram 1849

3

CAIN George C 1849
SMITH Hiram 1837
BOAS Jacob 1858
CLUFF John 1874

Lots-Sec. 2

COLE, Aquilla 1838
HAWKINS, Augustus 1848
COLE, Aquilla 1838
MUDD, John F 1838
HAWKINS, James K 1841

HAWKINS James H 1854

2

COLE Joseph C 1856
MARLER Joel 1861
BOAS Jacob 1856
CAIN George 1837
MARLER Joel 1861

Lots-Sec. 1

KANE, John J 1886
LONG, Milton 1859
LONG, Brumfield[164]1849
LONG, Milton 1854
LONG, Milton 1859
LONG, Milton 1859
HAWKINS, James H 1853
LONG, William 1859

1

COLE Isaac S 1856
LONG William 1859
COLE Joshua 1849
COLE Joshua 1837
COLE Isaac S 1859

SCOTT John 1829
BOAS [24] Jacob 1837
BOAS [23] Jacob 1837

10

RONGY Marshal 1849
OBUCHON Francis T 1848
MARLEE Levi 1856
RONGEY Marshal 1848

COLE Thomas J 1849
CAIN George 1837
CLEUFF John 1848
WHITE William 1854

11

COLE Thomas J 1848
COLE Thomas J 1853
CAIN William M 1848
COLE Thomas J 1843
COLE Thomas J 1856
COLE Juliet 1848

COLE Isaac S 1860
COLE Isaac S 1859
MARLER Joseph 1860

12

COLEMAN Thomas B 1882
COLE Thomas J 1859
BOAS Jacob 1856
COLE Thomas J 1859

BOAS Jacob 1848
RONGEY Marshall 1854
VILLEMAR Alexis 1856
MURPHY Peter W 1848
MARLE Levi 1848
MOORE John M 1848

15

EVANS [89] Charles 1848
MOORE Nancy J 1848
MOORE John M 1848

14

MURPHY Peter W 1848
MURPHY Peter W 1848
MURPHY Peter W 1848
HOUSE Adam 1856

BAKER Stephen J 1872
VANDIVER William 1854
ARNOLD William C 1875

13

ARNOLD William C 1875
HOUSE Thomas A 1857
ARNOLD William C 1875

EVANS [93] John 1848
LECLERE Francis 1837
HARRISON Meeke A 1854

22

MCNEAL George A 1848
JOHNSON Thomas C 1851

23

JOHNSON Thomas C 1859
MATHEWS William A 1854
SCOTT James M 1849

24

HARRISON Edwin 1869

WIATT John 1854

27

EVANS John 1857

JOHNSON Thomas C 1849
JENKINS George 1848
THOMPSON Sebern 1860
HUFF Isaac 1873
THOMPSON Sebern 1857

26

THOMPSON Sebern 1857
FRISSELL Mason 1854
HUFF Isaac 1873
EVENS John 1857
HARRISON Edwin 1869
BONE Francis 1857

HARRISON Edwin 1869
HUFF James W 1882
HARRISON Samuel 1854
HARRISON Samuel 1854

25

HARRISON Samuel 1854
HUFF James W 1882
HARRISON Samuel 1856
HARRISON Edwin 1869
TURPIN Martin 1856
BONE Francis 1857
HARRISON Samuel 1856
GLORE William W 1854

WALTON Christopher 1837
DAY George 1852
WEIGHER David 1838
EVENS John 1853
BURTON Levi G 1858

34

EVANS John 1841
WESTOVER George T 1841
BROLASKI Henry L 1856

BURTON Levi G 1858
BARROW Gabriel 1854
HARRISON Edwin 1869
BARROW Gabriel 1856
BURTON Levi G 1858

35

SWENDT John R 1850
LORE John 1858
WHEALEY William 1837

BONE Francis 1841
JOLLIN Charles 1857

36

BONE Francis 1841
MCCABE Marvin 1856
LORE [167] John 1837
BRICKEY John J 1837
MCCABE Alpheus 1837

Helpful Hints

1. This Map's INDEX can be found on the preceding pages.
2. Refer to Map "C" to see where this Township lies within Washington County, Missouri.
3. Numbers within square brackets [ ] denote a multi-patentee land parcel (multi-owner). Refer to Appendix "C" for a full list of members in this group.
4. Areas that look to be crowded with Patentees usually indicate multiple sales of the same parcel (Re-issues) or Overlapping parcels. See this Township's Index for an explanation of these and other circumstances that might explain "odd" groupings of Patentees on this map.

Legend

Patent Boundary

Section Boundary

No Patents Found (or Outside County)

1., 2., 3., ... Lot Numbers (when beside a name)

[ ] Group Number (see Appendix "C")

Scale: Section = 1 mile X 1 mile (generally, with some exceptions)

Road Map

T37-N R3-E
5th PM Meridian

Map Group 20

Cities & Towns

French Town
Hopewell
Summit
Mineral Point

Cemeteries

Jarvis Farm Cemetery
McGready Family Cemetery
Boas Cemetery

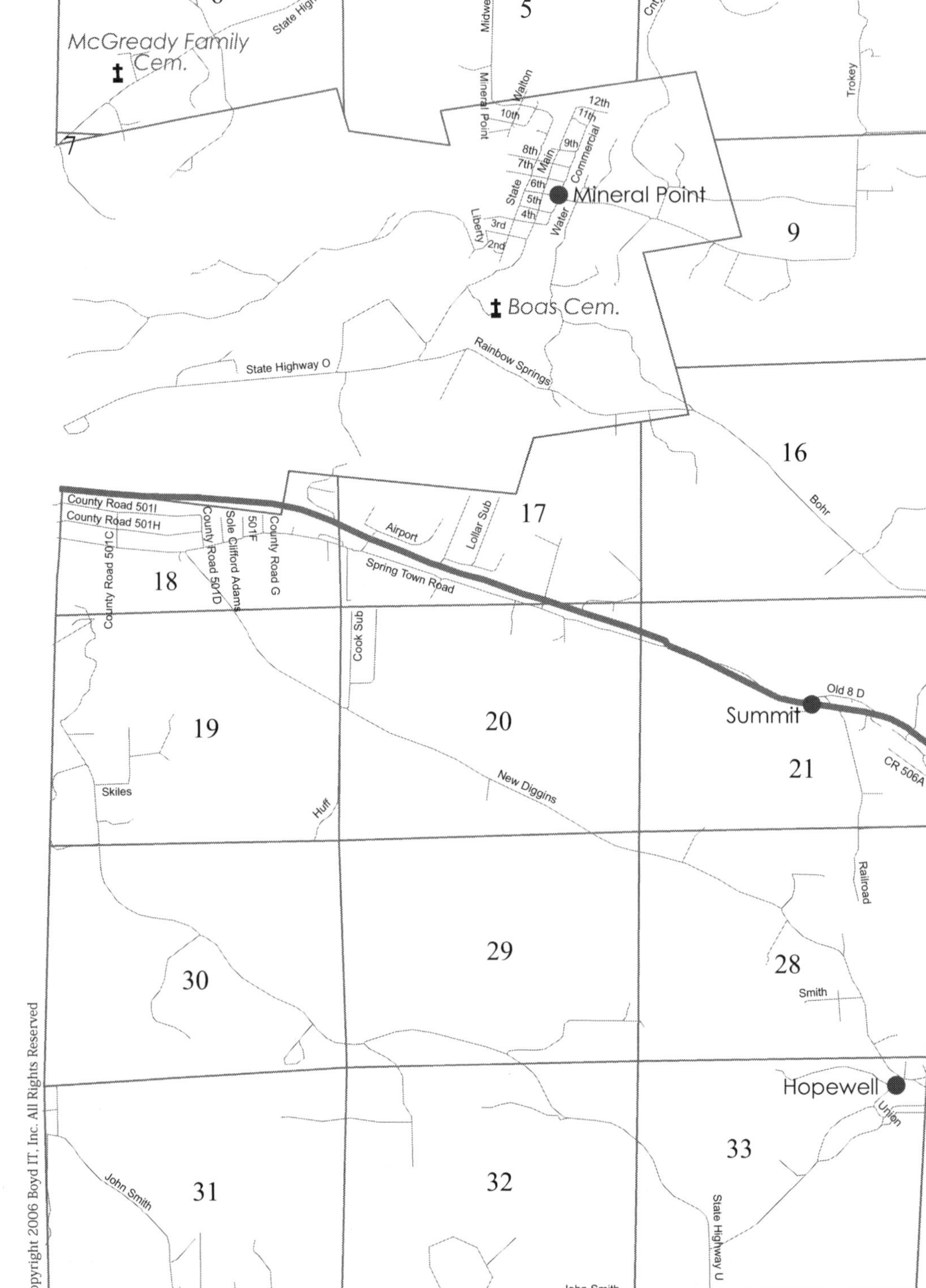

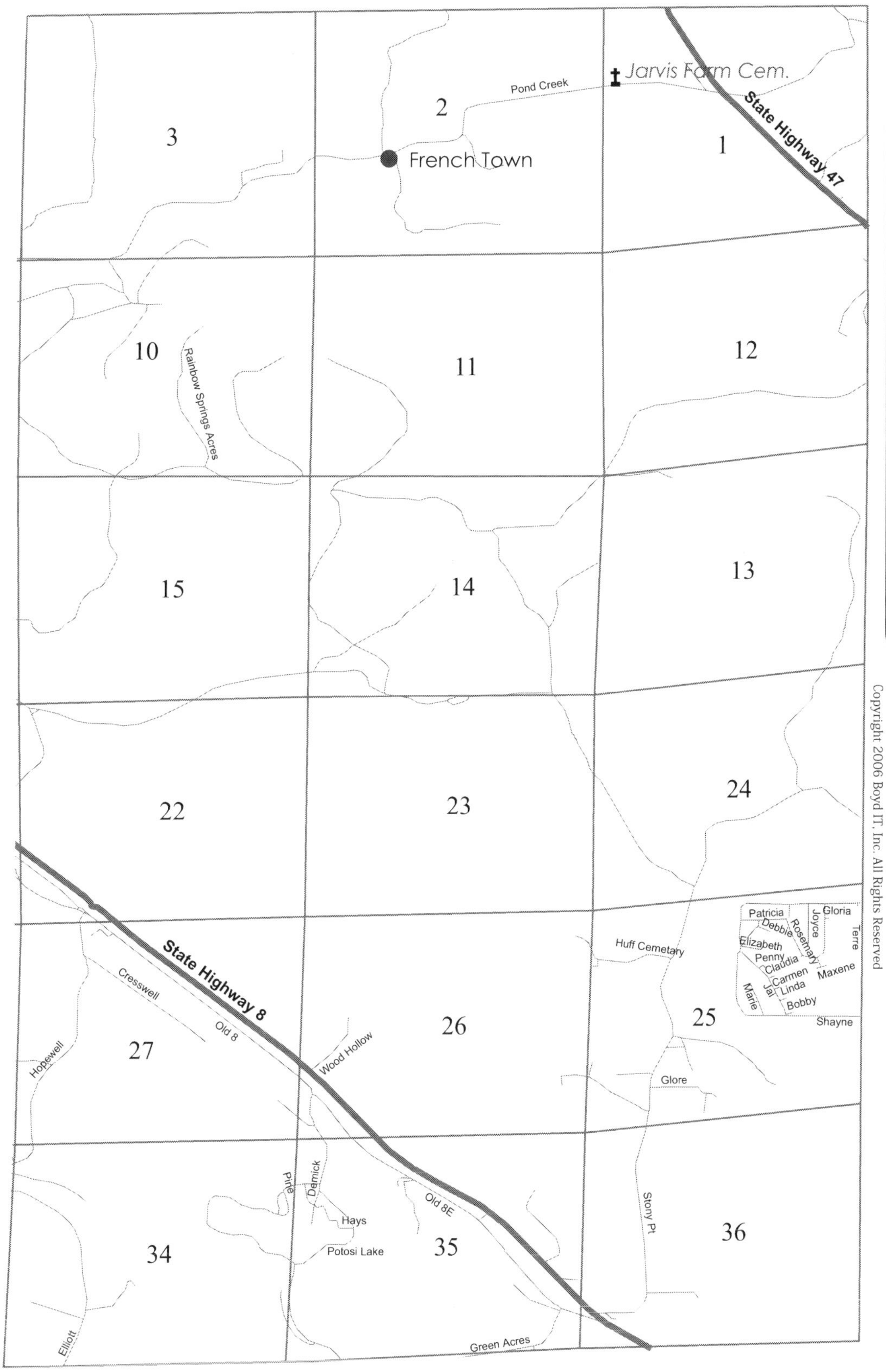

3
2
Pond Creek
Jarvis Farm Cem.
French Town
1
State Highway 47
10
Rainbow Springs Acres
11
12
15
14
13
22
23
24
State Highway 8
Cresswell
Old 8
Hopewell
27
Wood Hollow
26
Huff Cemetary
Patricia
Debbie
Rosemary
Joyce
Gloria
Terre
Elizabeth
Penny
Claudia
Carmen
Linda
Jai
Marie
Maxene
Bobby
Shayne
25
Glore
Pine
Damick
Hays
Potosi Lake
Old 8E
34
35
Stony Pt
36
Elliott
Green Acres

Helpful Hints

1. This road map has a number of uses, but primarily it is to help you: a) find the present location of land owned by your ancestors (at least the general area), b) find cemeteries and city-centers, and c) estimate the route/roads used by Census-takers & tax-assessors.

2. If you plan to travel to Washington County to locate cemeteries or land parcels, please pick up a modern travel map for the area before you do. Mapping old land parcels on modern maps is not as exact a science as you might think. Just the slightest variations in public land survey coordinates, estimates of parcel boundaries, or road-map deviations can greatly alter a map's representation of how a road either does or doesn't cross a particular parcel of land.

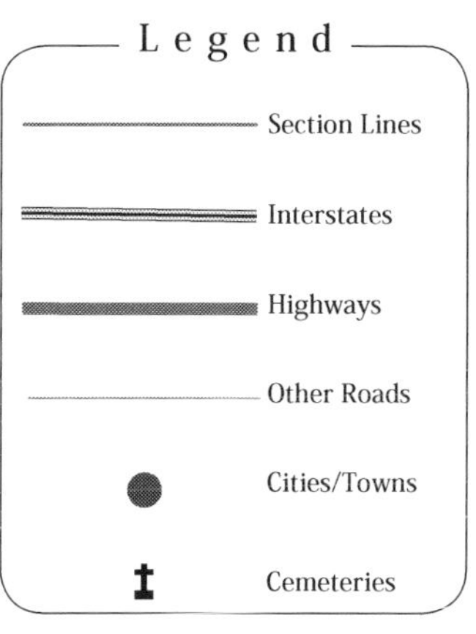

Scale: Section = 1 mile X 1 mile
(generally, with some exceptions)

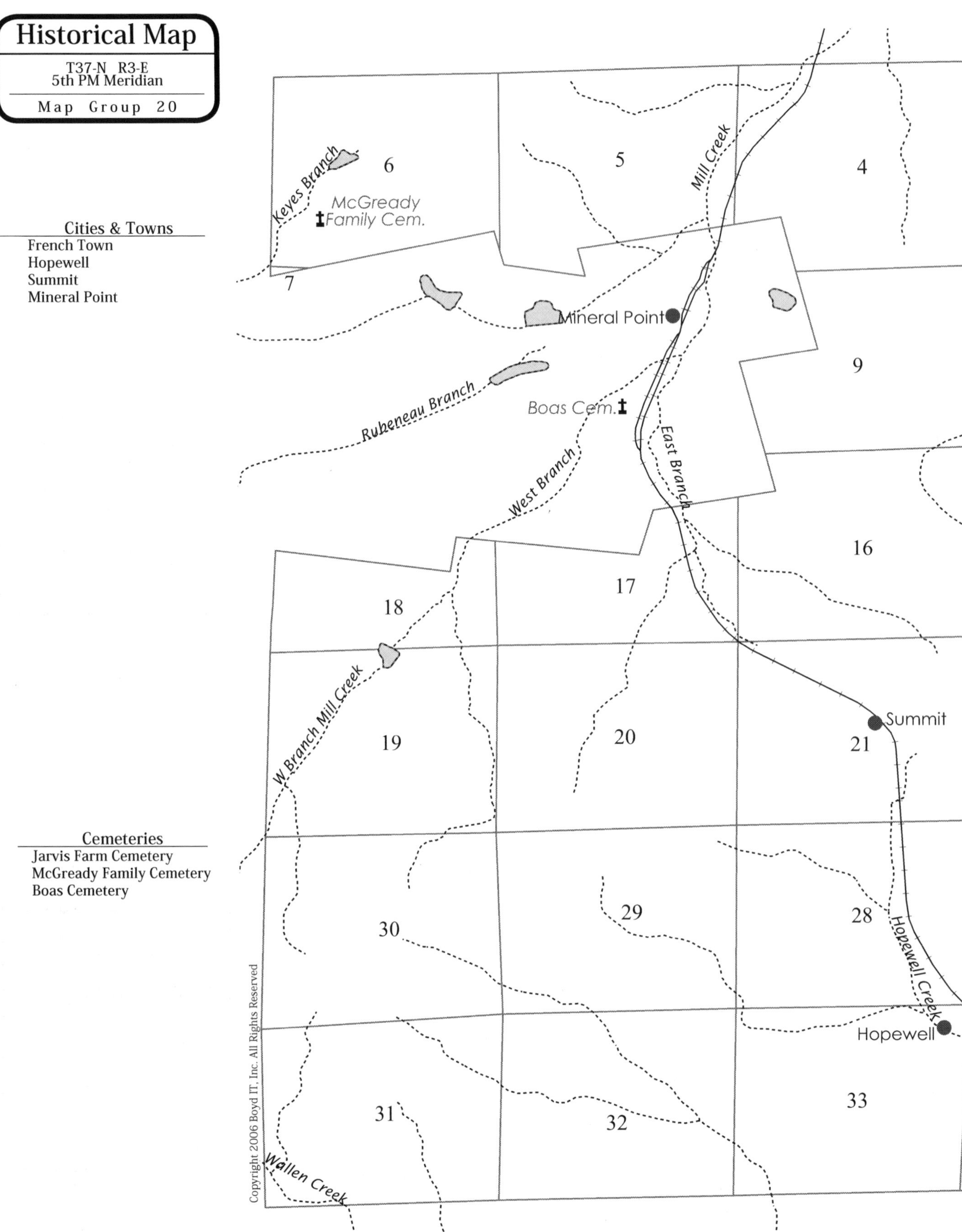
Historical Map
T37-N R3-E
5th PM Meridian
Map Group 20
Cities & Towns
French Town
Hopewell
Summit
Mineral Point
Cemeteries
Jarvis Farm Cemetery
McGready Family Cemetery
Boas Cemetery
6
5
4
7
9
16
17
18
19
20
21
28
29
30
31
32
33
Keyes Branch
McGready Family Cem.
Mill Creek
Mineral Point
Ruberieau Branch
Boas Cem.
East Branch
West Branch
W Branch Mill Creek
Summit
Hopewell Creek
Hopewell
Wallen Creek
Copyright 2006 Boyd IT, Inc. All Rights Reserved

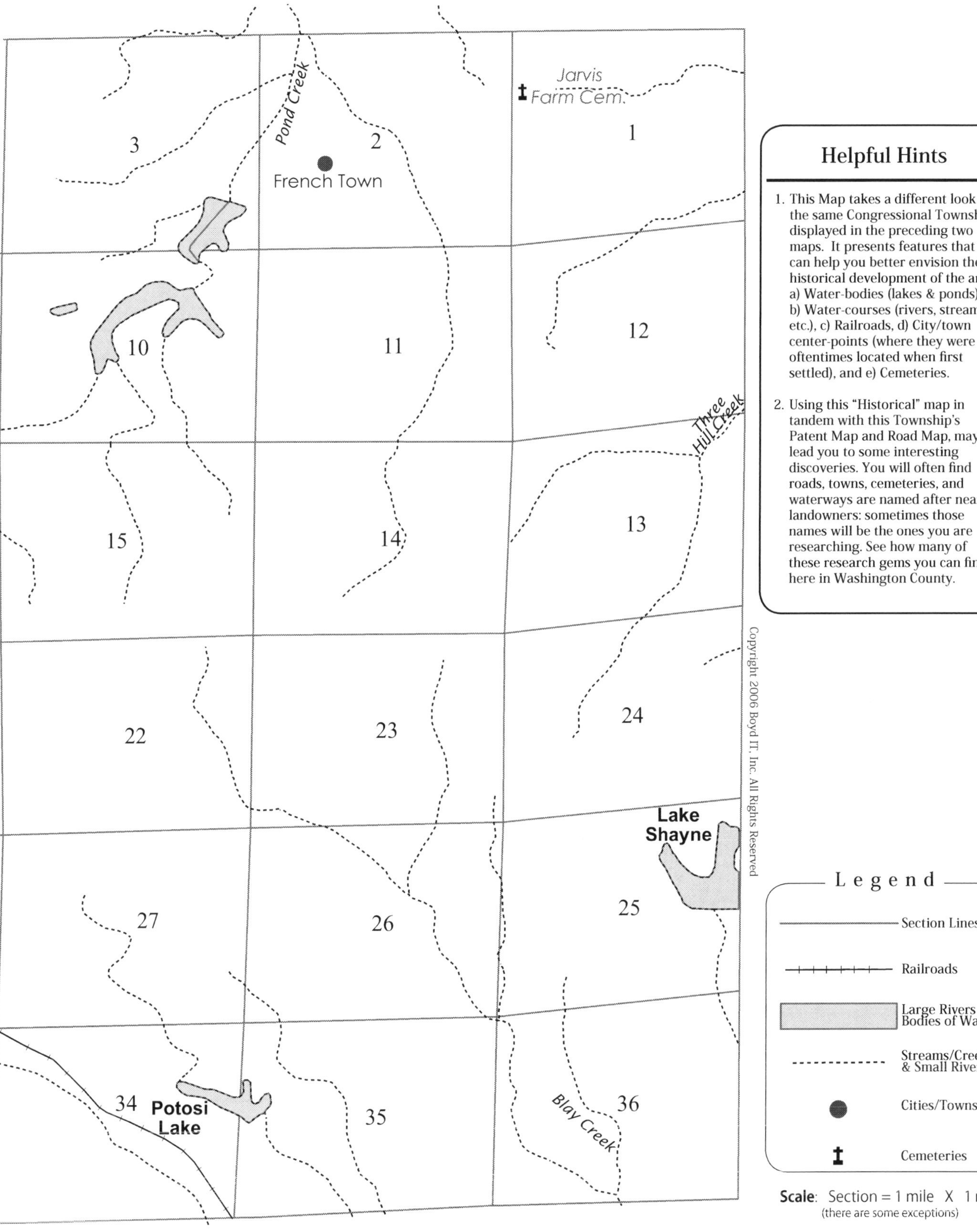

Helpful Hints

1. This Map takes a different look at the same Congressional Township displayed in the preceding two maps. It presents features that can help you better envision the historical development of the area: a) Water-bodies (lakes & ponds), b) Water-courses (rivers, streams, etc.), c) Railroads, d) City/town center-points (where they were oftentimes located when first settled), and e) Cemeteries.
2. Using this "Historical" map in tandem with this Township's Patent Map and Road Map, may lead you to some interesting discoveries. You will often find roads, towns, cemeteries, and waterways are named after nearby landowners: sometimes those names will be the ones you are researching. See how many of these research gems you can find here in Washington County.

Legend

- Section Lines
- Railroads
- Large Rivers & Bodies of Water
- Streams/Creeks & Small Rivers
- Cities/Towns
- Cemeteries

Scale: Section = 1 mile X 1 mile
(there are some exceptions)

Map Group 21: Index to Land Patents

Township 36-North Range 2-West (5th PM)

After you locate an individual in this Index, take note of the Section and Section Part then proceed to the Land Patent map on the pages immediately following. You should have no difficulty locating the corresponding parcel of land.

The "For More Info" Column will lead you to more information about the underlying Patents. See the *Legend* at right, and the "How to Use this Book" chapter, for more information.

LEGEND

"For More Info . . . " column

A = Authority (Legislative Act, See Appendix "A")
B = Block or Lot (location in Section unknown)
C = Cancelled Patent
F = Fractional Section
G = Group (Multi-Patentee Patent, see Appendix "C")
V = Overlaps another Parcel
R = Re-Issued (Parcel patented more than once)

(A & G items require you to look in the Appendixes referred to above. All other Letter-designations followed by a number require you to locate line-items in this index that possess the ID number found after the letter).

ID	Individual in Patent	Sec.	Sec. Part	Date Issued	Other Counties	For More Info . . .
2972	BATEMAN, Clarkson W	25	E½SW	1859-09-01	Crawford	A1
2973	" "	25	SE	1859-09-01	Crawford	A1
2974	" "	25	SWSW	1859-09-01	Crawford	A1
3000	BRUCE, William	13	SESW	1857-04-15	Crawford	A1
3001	" "	13	W½SE	1857-04-15	Crawford	A1
3002	" "	24	NENW	1857-04-15	Crawford	A1
2968	FINLEY, Alexander	24	E½SW	1859-09-01	Crawford	A1
2969	" "	24	SE	1859-09-01	Crawford	A1
2970	" "	24	SWSW	1859-09-01	Crawford	A1
2971	" "	25	NWNW	1859-09-01	Crawford	A1
2986	GIBSON, John B	25	E½NW	1859-09-01	Crawford	A1
2987	" "	25	NE	1859-09-01	Crawford	A1
2988	" "	25	NWSW	1859-09-01	Crawford	A1
2989	" "	25	SWNW	1859-09-01	Crawford	A1
2978	GRIMES, James	36	E½SE	1860-08-01	Crawford	A1
2979	" "	36	NWSE	1860-08-01	Crawford	A1
2990	HARPER, Joseph S	13	E½SE	1861-05-01	Crawford	A1
2980	JACO, James	13	SWNW	1858-12-01	Crawford	A1
2981	KNIGHT, James K	1	SE	1859-09-10	Crawford	A1
2982	" "	12	NE	1859-09-10	Crawford	A1
3003	KNIGHT, William G	1	N½	1860-02-16	Crawford	A1
2999	MARTIN, Owen S	12	NWNW	1857-04-15	Crawford	A1
2995	NICHOLS, Joshua D	1	SW	1859-09-01	Crawford	A1
2983	PALMATORY, James T	24	NE	1859-09-01	Crawford	A1
2984	" "	24	SENW	1859-09-01	Crawford	A1
2985	" "	24	W½NW	1859-09-01	Crawford	A1
2976	STATLER, Conrad	13	SENW	1856-10-10	Crawford	A1
2975	" "	13	NESW	1857-12-15	Crawford	A1
2977	" "	13	W½SW	1857-12-15	Crawford	A1
2991	TURNBAUGH, Joseph	36	SWNW	1858-04-01	Crawford	A1
2992	TURNBOUGH, Joseph	36	SESW	1857-12-15	Crawford	A1
2993	" "	36	SWSE	1857-12-15	Crawford	A1
2994	" "	36	W½SW	1857-12-15	Crawford	A1
2996	WARD, Moses W	12	N½SW	1859-09-10	Crawford	A1
2997	" "	12	NENW	1859-09-10	Crawford	A1
2998	" "	12	S½NW	1859-09-10	Crawford	A1
3004	WATERS, William H	12	S½SW	1859-09-10	Crawford	A1
3005	" "	12	SE	1859-09-10	Crawford	A1
3006	" "	13	N½NW	1859-09-10	Crawford	A1

KNIGHT William G 1860

1

NICHOLS Joshua D 1859

KNIGHT James K 1859

MARTIN Owen S 1857

WARD Moses W 1859

KNIGHT James K 1859

12

WARD Moses W 1859

WARD Moses W 1859

WATERS William H 1859

WATERS William H 1859

WATERS William H 1859

Washington County

JACO James 1858

STATLER Conrad 1856

13

STATLER Conrad 1857

STATLER Conrad 1857

BRUCE William 1857

HARPER Joseph S 1861

BRUCE William 1857

PALMATORY James T 1859

BRUCE William 1857

PALMATORY James T 1859

PALMATORY James T 1859

24

Crawford County

FINLEY Alexander 1859

FINLEY Alexander 1859

FINLEY Alexander 1859

FINLEY Alexander 1859

GIBSON John B 1859

GIBSON John B 1859

25

GIBSON John B 1859

GIBSON John B 1859

BATEMAN Clarkson W 1859

BATEMAN Clarkson W 1859

BATEMAN Clarkson W 1859

36

TURNBAUGH Joseph 1858

GRIMES James 1860

GRIMES James 1860

TURNBOUGH Joseph 1857

TURNBOUGH Joseph 1857

TURNBOUGH Joseph 1857

Patent Map

T36-N R2-W
5th PM Meridian

Map Group 21

Township Statistics

Parcels Mapped	:	39
Number of Patents	:	18
Number of Individuals	:	17
Patentees Identified	:	17
Number of Surnames	:	16
Multi-Patentee Parcels	:	0
Oldest Patent Date	:	10/10/1856
Most Recent Patent	:	5/1/1861
Block/Lot Parcels	:	0
Parcels Re - Issued	:	0
Parcels that Overlap	:	0
Cities and Towns	:	0
Cemeteries	:	0

Note: the area contained in this map amounts to far less than a full Township. Therefore, its contents are completely on this single page (instead of a "normal" 2-page spread).

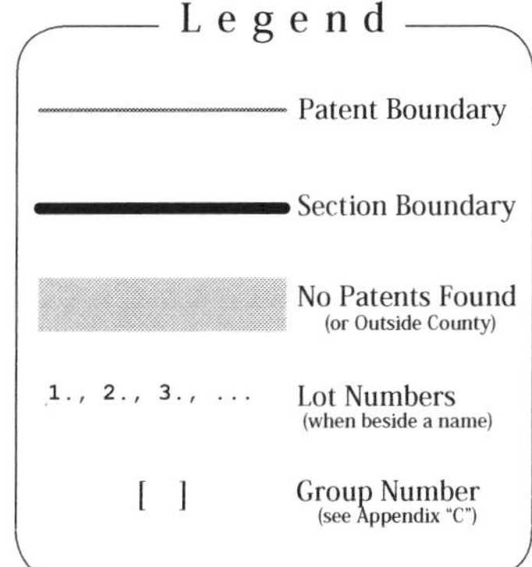

Scale: Section = 1 mile X 1 mile
(generally, with some exceptions)

Road Map

T36-N R2-W
5th PM Meridian

Map Group 21

Note: the area contained in this map amounts to far less than a full Township. Therefore, its contents are completely on this single page (instead of a "normal" 2-page spread).

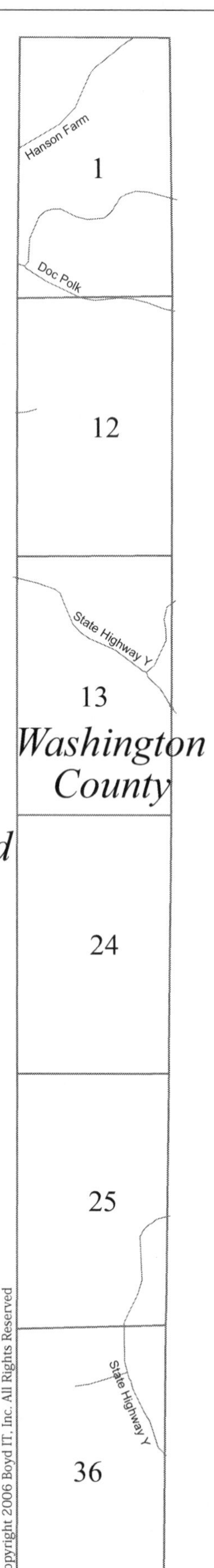

Cities & Towns

None

Cemeteries

None

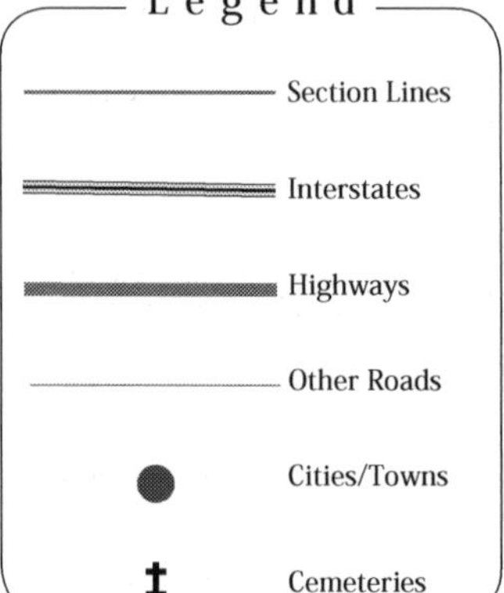

Scale: Section = 1 mile X 1 mile
(generally, with some exceptions)

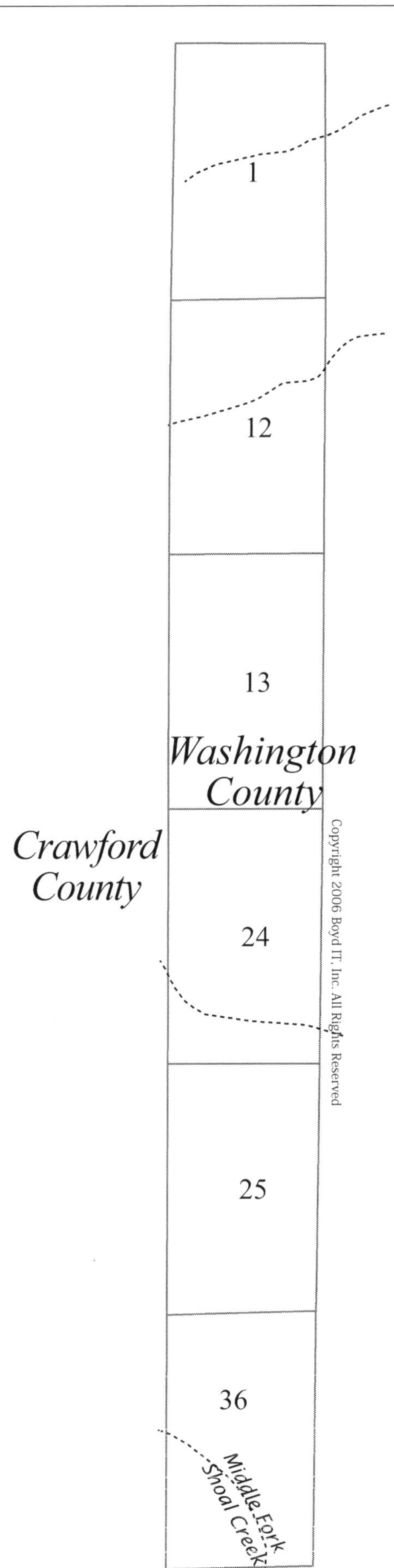

Historical Map

T36-N R2-W
5th PM Meridian

Map Group 21

Note: the area contained in this map amounts to far less than a full Township. Therefore, its contents are completely on this single page (instead of a "normal" 2-page spread).

Cities & Towns

None

Cemeteries

None

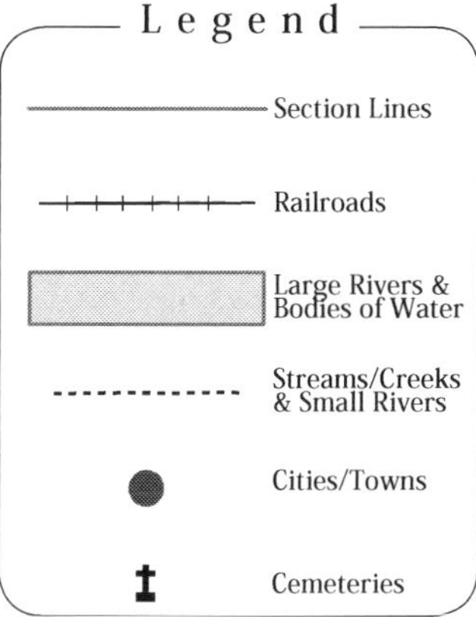

Scale: Section = 1 mile X 1 mile
(there are some exceptions)

Map Group 22: Index to Land Patents

Township 36-North Range 1-West (5th PM)

After you locate an individual in this Index, take note of the Section and Section Part then proceed to the Land Patent map on the pages immediately following. You should have no difficulty locating the corresponding parcel of land.

The "For More Info" Column will lead you to more information about the underlying Patents. See the *Legend* at right, and the "How to Use this Book" chapter, for more information.

LEGEND

"For More Info . . . " column

A = Authority (Legislative Act, See Appendix "A")
B = Block or Lot (location in Section unknown)
C = Cancelled Patent
F = Fractional Section
G = Group (Multi-Patentee Patent, see Appendix "C")
V = Overlaps another Parcel
R = Re-Issued (Parcel patented more than once)

(A & G items require you to look in the Appendixes referred to above. All other Letter-designations followed by a number require you to locate line-items in this index that possess the ID number found after the letter).

ID	Individual in Patent	Sec.	Sec. Part	Date Issued	Other Counties	For More Info . . .
3056	BACON, George H	36	W½	1859-09-01		A1
3151	BAIRD, Samuel	13	W½NE	1837-11-07		A1
3009	BEAN, Abner	1	1NW	1838-08-01		A1 G11
3096	BEAN, John	10	W½NE	1838-08-01		A1 G12
3115	BEAR, Joseph	14	E½NW	1838-08-01		A1
3170	BELL, William	1	2NE	1865-06-10		A1
3171	" "	1	E½2NW	1865-06-10		A1
3172	" "	10	NENW	1865-06-10		A1
3173	" "	10	NESE	1865-06-10		A1
3174	" "	11	NWSW	1865-06-10		A1
3175	" "	15	SESE	1865-06-10		A1
3176	" "	15	SESW	1865-06-10		A1
3177	" "	17	N½NW	1865-06-10		A1
3178	" "	17	SWNW	1865-06-10		A1
3179	" "	17	W½SW	1865-06-10		A1
3180	" "	21	E½SE	1865-06-10		A1
3181	" "	21	NE	1865-06-10		A1
3182	" "	21	SENW	1865-06-10		A1
3183	" "	21	SW	1865-06-10		A1
3184	" "	22	NESW	1865-06-10		A1
3185	" "	22	NWNE	1865-06-10		A1
3186	" "	22	S½SW	1865-06-10		A1
3187	" "	22	SE	1865-06-10		A1
3188	" "	23	N½NW	1865-06-10		A1
3189	" "	23	SENE	1865-06-10		A1
3190	" "	24	NESW	1865-06-10		A1
3191	" "	25	W½	1865-06-10		A1
3192	" "	26	E½SW	1865-06-10		A1
3193	" "	26	NW	1865-06-10		A1
3194	" "	26	NWSW	1865-06-10		A1
3195	" "	26	SE	1865-06-10		A1
3196	" "	27	NWNE	1865-06-10		A1
3197	" "	27	S½	1865-06-10		A1
3198	" "	27	S½NE	1865-06-10		A1
3199	" "	27	S½NW	1865-06-10		A1
3200	" "	28	E½	1865-06-10		A1
3201	" "	3	1NE	1865-06-10		A1
3202	" "	3	1NW	1865-06-10		A1
3203	" "	3	E½SW	1865-06-10		A1
3204	" "	3	SE	1865-06-10		A1
3205	" "	34	E½	1865-06-10		A1
3206	" "	34	E½NW	1865-06-10		A1
3207	" "	34	NESW	1865-06-10		A1
3208	" "	4	1NE	1865-06-10		A1
3209	" "	4	2NE	1865-06-10		A1
3210	" "	4	2NW	1865-06-10		A1

ID	Individual in Patent	Sec.	Sec. Part	Date Issued	Other Counties	For More Info . . .
3211	BELL, William (Cont'd)	4	N½SE	1865-06-10		A1
3212	" "	5	W½2NW	1865-06-10		A1
3213	" "	6	E½2NE	1865-06-10		A1
3214	" "	6	NWSW	1865-06-10		A1
3215	" "	7	S½NE	1865-06-10		A1
3216	" "	7	SE	1865-06-10		A1
3217	" "	8	SESW	1865-06-10		A1
3218	" "	8	W½NW	1865-06-10		A1
3219	" "	8	W½SW	1865-06-10		A1
3119	BERRYMAN, Josias	6	2NW	1851-12-01		A1 C
3136	BLACKWELL, Robert	3	W½2NE	1846-09-21		A1 G19
3135	" "	2	E½SW	1858-01-15		A1 G19
3069	BOAS, Jacob	10	E½NE	1837-01-24		A1 G23
3070	" "	11	W½NW	1837-01-24		A1 G24
3139	BOAS, Robert J	1	E½SE	1837-01-24		A1 G26
3138	" "	6	SWSW	1837-11-07		A1
3139	BRADSHAW, William	1	E½SE	1837-01-24		A1 G26
3150	BRAKEFIELD, Sam	19	N½1NW	1920-04-28		A1
3034	BROWN, Elisha	1	1NE	1838-08-01		A1 G35
3060	BROWN, George W	36	E½	1859-09-01		A1
3160	BROWN, Sloman	20	E½SE	1841-08-10		A1
3220	BROWN, William D	12	NW	1837-01-24		A1 G36
3055	CAMPBELL, George	12	W½NE	1837-01-24		A1 G44
3091	CAMPBELL, Jeremiah	2	W½SE	1838-08-01		A1 G45
3154	CAMPBELL, Samuel	12	E½SE	1838-08-01		A1 G46
3137	CARPENTER, Robert	11	E½NW	1838-08-01		A1 G49
3116	CASWELL, Joseph	14	E½SW	1838-08-01		A1 G55
3064	CLARK, Gotham	11	E½NE	1838-08-01		A1 G59
3120	CLARK, Jotham	14	E½NE	1838-08-01		A1
3054	COLE, Frederick B	23	NENE	1859-09-01		A1
3065	COVER, Henry B	29	N½SW	1894-12-17		A3
3066	" "	30	N½SE	1894-12-17		A3
3071	COVER, Jacob F	30	1SW	1894-12-17		A3
3072	" "	30	SWSE	1894-12-17		A3
3073	" "	31	N½1NW	1894-12-17		A3
3040	CRUMP, Fendoll P	7	NENE	1898-05-16		A1
3133	DONNA, Peter Charles	1	W½2NW	1838-08-01		A1 G81
3076	DUNCAN, James	21	NENW	1860-08-01		A1
3077	" "	21	W½NW	1860-08-01		A1
3126	EATON, Lazarus	2	W½SW	1837-01-24		A1 G85
3081	FLOWERS, James M	34	S½SW	1904-11-15		A3
3093	FLOWERS, Jesse	28	N½SW	1872-03-15		A3
3094	" "	28	S½NW	1872-03-15		A3
3109	FLOWERS, John W	33	NESE	1861-02-09		A1
3110	" "	33	S½SE	1872-03-15		A3
3111	" "	34	NWSW	1872-03-15		A3
3009	FORD, John	1	1NW	1838-08-01		A1 G11
3133	" "	1	W½2NW	1838-08-01		A1 G81
3067	GALLAUGHER, Henry	14	W½SE	1838-08-01		A1
3068	" "	23	W½NE	1838-08-01		A1
3155	GALLOWAY, Samuel	12	SW	1837-01-24		A1
3038	GHOLSON, Felix G	1	W½SW	1838-08-01		A1 G108
3039	" "	2	E½SE	1838-08-01		A1 G108
3025	GILLAM, Benjamin	2	W½2NW	1858-01-15		A1 G112
3078	GILLAM, James	35	E½NW	1904-04-08		A3
3079	" "	35	SWNW	1904-04-08		A3
3223	GILLAM, William	2	E½2NW	1841-06-25		A1 G113
3026	GILLIAM, Benjamin	9	W½NE	1838-08-01		A1
3224	GILLIAM, William	9	E½NE	1838-08-01		A1 G114
3018	GLENN, Alexander	17	E½NE	1838-08-01		A1
3019	" "	17	E½SE	1838-08-01		A1
3080	GLENN, James	34	W½NW	1835-12-30		A1 G115
3147	GOADE, Robert R	19	S½1NW	1859-09-01		A1
3148	" "	19	W½NE	1859-09-01		A1
3161	GOADE, Thomas A	17	SESW	1859-09-01		A1
3162	" "	20	NENW	1859-09-01		A1
3163	" "	20	SENE	1859-09-01		A1
3164	GRADE, Thomas	20	NWNE	1856-01-03		A1
3024	GRIFFITH, Ben M	9	SENW	1902-03-29		A1
3027	GRIFFITH, Benjamin M	4	W½1NW	1902-01-15		A1
3228	HEWIT, William	32	SESE	1859-09-01		A1
3229	" "	33	SWSW	1859-09-01		A1
3237	HOPKINS, William W	32	SWSE	1899-05-12		A3

ID	Individual in Patent	Sec.	Sec. Part	Date Issued	Other Counties	For More Info . . .
3008	HUDSPETH, Abijah W	15	W½SE	1848-09-01		A1 G140
3007	" "	3	2NW	1848-09-01		A1 G139
3012	HUDSPETH, Ahijah W	11	SWSW	1837-11-07		A1
3015	" "	15	NESE	1837-11-07		A1
3016	" "	15	W½NE	1837-11-07		A1
3017	" "	8	W½SE	1837-11-07		A1
3014	" "	14	W½NW	1838-08-01		A1
3013	" "	12	E½NE	1841-06-25		A1
3032	HUDSPETH, Drusillar R	20	NENE	1841-06-25		A1
3058	HUDSPETH, George R	15	NESW	1837-11-14		A1
3059	" "	8	SWNE	1837-11-14		A1
3102	HUDSPETH, John D	32	NWSE	1837-11-07		A1
3230	HUDSPETH, William	15	E½NE	1825-07-15		A1 R3231
3232	" "	32	SESW	1837-11-07		A1
3231	" "	15	E½NE	1917-05-04		A1 R3230
3127	HUITT, Margaret E	32	NESE	1904-07-15		A3 G143
3127	HUITT, William	32	NESE	1904-07-15		A3 G143
3149	HUTCHISON, S M	25	S½SE	1869-07-01		A1
3038	JANNEY, Nathan	1	W½SW	1838-08-01		A1 G108
3039	" "	2	E½SE	1838-08-01		A1 G108
3035	JARVIS, Eliza	33	SESW	1901-03-23		A3
3089	JARVIS, Jasper N	19	E½NE	1892-03-07		A3
3090	" "	20	W½NW	1892-03-07		A3
3128	JARVIS, Marion	32	SENW	1906-03-31		A3
3010	JETT, Abraham	1	W½SE	1838-08-01		A1 G151
3011	" "	14	W½NE	1838-08-01		A1 G152
3238	JINKINS, Zara F	20	N½SW	1892-03-07		A3
3239	" "	20	SESW	1892-03-07		A3
3240	" "	20	SWSE	1892-03-07		A3
3105	KEAUGH, John	9	NENW	1837-11-14		A1
3106	KEOUGH, John	4	S½SW	1838-08-01		A1
3159	LANCASTER, Semira C	15	NWNW	1853-08-01		A1
3235	LONG, William	6	1SW	1861-02-09		A1
3074	MALLOW, Jacob	4	NESW	1859-09-01		A1
3075	" "	4	SENW	1859-09-01		A1
3220	MANNING, Foreman	12	NW	1837-01-24		A1 G36
3041	" "	13	NW	1837-01-24		A1
3010	" "	1	W½SE	1838-08-01		A1 G151
3096	" "	10	W½NE	1838-08-01		A1 G12
3064	" "	11	E½NE	1838-08-01		A1 G59
3042	" "	11	W½SE	1838-08-01		A1 G172
3116	" "	14	E½SW	1838-08-01		A1 G55
3043	" "	14	W½SW	1838-08-01		A1 G175
3224	" "	9	E½NE	1838-08-01		A1 G114
3223	" "	2	E½2NW	1841-06-25		A1 G113
3044	" "	33	E½NE	1841-12-10		A1 G173
3136	" "	3	W½2NE	1846-09-21		A1 G19
3045	" "	17	W½NE	1848-02-01		A1 G174
3046	" "	17	W½SE	1848-02-01		A1 G174
3135	" "	2	E½SW	1858-01-15		A1 G19
3025	" "	2	W½2NW	1858-01-15		A1 G112
3047	" "	3	E½2NE	1858-01-15		A1 G171
3080	MANNING, Forman	34	W½NW	1835-12-30		A1 G115
3048	" "	13	SW	1837-11-07		A1
3052	" "	22	E½NW	1849-02-01		A1 G176
3053	" "	9	S½SW	1852-01-01		A1 G176
3049	" "	20	NWSE	1859-01-01		A1
3050	" "	20	SWNE	1859-01-01		A1
3051	" "	21	W½SE	1859-01-01		A1
3069	MARLER, John	10	E½NE	1837-01-24		A1 G23
3070	MARLER, Michael	11	W½NW	1837-01-24		A1 G24
3023	MARSHALL, Austin	33	W½NE	1869-07-01		A1
3030	MARTIN, Dabney	7	NENW	1857-04-15		A1
3031	" "	7	NWNE	1857-04-15		A1
3233	MARTIN, William J	7	S½1NW	1905-06-28		A3
3234	" "	7	S½2NW	1905-06-28		A3
3142	MASON, Robert	29	SWNE	1857-10-30		A1
3140	" "	20	SWSW	1859-09-01		A1
3141	" "	29	NWNE	1873-02-01		A3
3167	MATCHELL, William B	8	E½SE	1904-11-01		A3
3033	MATTHEWS, Elijah B	11	W½NE	1837-11-14		A1
3047	MCKEE, Thomas S	3	E½2NE	1858-01-15		A1 G171
3083	MIDGETT, James R	29	W½SE	1904-11-01		A3

ID	Individual in Patent	Sec.	Sec. Part	Date Issued	Other Counties	For More Info . . .
3082	MIDYETT, James	32	NESW	1859-09-01		A1
3143	MIDYETT, Robert	29	SWSW	1912-06-14		A3
3144	" "	30	SESE	1912-06-14		A3
3145	" "	31	NENE	1912-06-14		A3
3146	" "	32	NWNW	1912-06-14		A3
3061	MOSES, George W	30	2SW	1910-07-18		A3
3062	" "	31	2NW	1910-07-18		A3
3137	MURPHY, Jesse	11	E½NW	1838-08-01		A1 G49
3095	" "	9	SESE	1838-08-01		A1
3221	MURPHY, William D	10	S½NW	1838-08-01		A1
3222	" "	10	W½SW	1838-08-01		A1
3042	NEUSE, George	11	W½SE	1838-08-01		A1 G172
3057	" "	24	W½SE	1838-08-01		A1 G189
3130	NORVELL, Napoleon B	12	W½SE	1838-08-01		A1
3131	" "	2	1NW	1838-08-01		A1 G192
3107	ORCHARD, John	4	NWNW	1837-11-07		A1
3108	" "	5	NESE	1837-11-07		A1
3011	ORCHARDS, James	14	W½NE	1838-08-01		A1 G152
3236	PICKERING, William	13	SWSE	1865-06-10		A1
3020	POWELL, Ambrose	1	E½SW	1837-11-14		A1
3124	PULLAM, Kinchen	8	NESW	1859-09-01		A1
3125	PULLIAM, Kinchen	19	2NW	1860-08-01		A1
3103	PYATT, John E	29	SESW	1909-06-03		A3
3104	" "	32	NENW	1909-06-03		A3
3225	PYATT, William H	31	NWNE	1904-04-08		A3
3226	" "	31	S½1NW	1904-04-08		A3
3227	" "	31	S½NE	1904-04-08		A3
3132	ROBINSON, Norman F	32	W½NE	1904-04-08		A3
3084	SANDERS, James	8	E½NW	1837-11-07		A1
3085	" "	5	SW	1848-09-01		A1 G205
3118	SANDERS, Joshua	6	SESE	1837-11-07		A1
3117	" "	5	W½1NW	1837-11-14		A1
3063	SCOTT, George W	28	N½NW	1889-01-12		A3
3097	SCOTT, John C	10	E½SW	1838-08-01		A1
3099	" "	10	S½SE	1838-08-01		A1
3098	" "	10	NWSE	1841-06-25		A1
3100	" "	5	E½1NW	1843-04-10		A1
3101	" "	5	E½2NW	1843-04-10		A1
3168	SEYMOUR, William B	17	NESW	1869-07-01		A1
3169	" "	17	SENW	1869-07-01		A1
3021	SHIRLEY, Andrew J	26	SWSW	1860-08-01		A1
3022	" "	35	NWNW	1860-08-01		A1
3129	SHOTWELL, N T	28	S½SW	1869-07-01		A1
3028	SHOULTS, Catharine	15	E½NW	1838-08-01		A1 G207
3055	SMITH, Reuben	12	W½NE	1837-01-24		A1 G44
3134	" "	11	E½SW	1838-08-01		A1 G210
3154	" "	12	E½SE	1838-08-01		A1 G46
3028	" "	15	E½NW	1838-08-01		A1 G207
3131	" "	2	1NW	1838-08-01		A1 G192
3044	" "	33	E½NE	1841-12-10		A1 G173
3045	" "	17	W½NE	1848-02-01		A1 G174
3046	" "	17	W½SE	1848-02-01		A1 G174
3052	" "	22	E½NW	1849-02-01		A1 G176
3053	" "	9	S½SW	1852-01-01		A1 G176
3007	SPEAR, Charles	3	2NW	1848-09-01		A1 G139
3085	" "	5	SW	1848-09-01		A1 G205
3029	SPEERS, Charles	7	NWNW	1837-11-07		A1
3134	STAMM, Mary	11	E½SW	1838-08-01		A1 G210
3156	STEERMAN, Samuel P	11	E½SE	1838-08-01		A1 G212
3166	STEERMAN, Thomas	24	E½NW	1838-08-01		A1 G214
3156	STEERMAN, Thomas Jefferson	11	E½SE	1838-08-01		A1 G212
3165	" "	24	W½NW	1838-08-01		A1 G213
3091	STEVENSON, Joseph M	2	W½SE	1838-08-01		A1 G45
3126	STONE, Samuel P	2	W½SW	1837-01-24		A1 G85
3157	" "	2	2NE	1837-11-07		A1
3034	" "	1	1NE	1838-08-01		A1 G35
3166	" "	24	E½NW	1838-08-01		A1 G214
3158	" "	24	E½SE	1838-08-01		A1 G216
3165	" "	24	W½NW	1838-08-01		A1 G213
3057	" "	24	W½SE	1838-08-01		A1 G189
3044	" "	33	E½NE	1841-12-10		A1 G173
3045	" "	17	W½NE	1848-02-01		A1 G174
3046	" "	17	W½SE	1848-02-01		A1 G174

ID	Individual in Patent	Sec.	Sec. Part	Date Issued	Other Counties	For More Info . . .
3086	SWOFFORD, James	5	SWSE	1837-11-14		A1
3008	" "	15	W½SE	1848-09-01		A1 G140
3043	TEAS, Henry	14	W½SW	1838-08-01		A1 G175
3036	TINKERSON, Ezekiel	3	W½SW	1859-09-01		A1
3037	" "	4	S½SE	1859-09-01		A1
3087	WHEALAN, James	5	1NE	1838-08-01		A1
3088	" "	5	2NE	1838-08-01		A1
3044	WHITE, James H	33	E½NE	1841-12-10		A1 G173
3080	WHITE, James M	34	W½NW	1835-12-30		A1 G115
3045	" "	17	W½NE	1848-02-01		A1 G174
3046	" "	17	W½SE	1848-02-01		A1 G174
3152	WHITE, Samuel C	14	E½SE	1837-11-07		A1
3153	" "	2	1NE	1837-11-07		A1
3121	WICKERS, Julius	13	SESE	1856-06-03		A2
3122	" "	22	SWNE	1856-06-03		A2
3123	" "	27	NENE	1856-06-03		A2
3112	WILKERSON, John	25	NWSE	1872-07-01		A3
3113	" "	25	SENE	1872-07-01		A3
3114	" "	25	W½NE	1872-07-01		A3
3158	WILKINSON, Jeremiah	24	E½SE	1838-08-01		A1 G216
3092	" "	25	NENE	1860-08-01		A1

Patent Map

T36-N R1-W
5th PM Meridian

Map Group 22

Township Statistics

Parcels Mapped	:	234
Number of Patents	:	162
Number of Individuals	:	126
Patentees Identified	:	125
Number of Surnames	:	89
Multi-Patentee Parcels	:	45
Oldest Patent Date	:	7/15/1825
Most Recent Patent	:	4/28/1920
Block/Lot Parcels	:	38
Parcels Re - Issued	:	1
Parcels that Overlap	:	0
Cities and Towns	:	4
Cemeteries	:	1

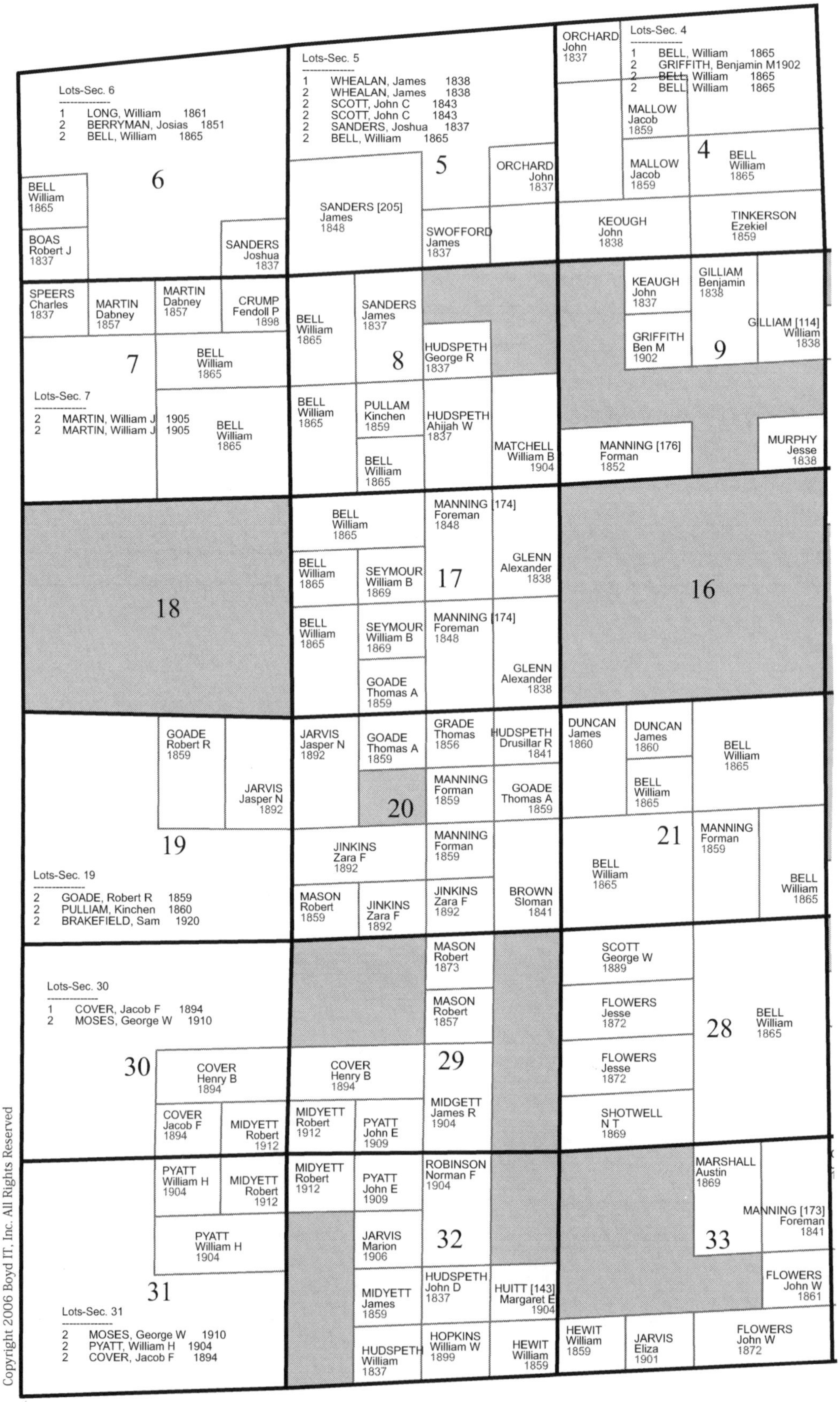

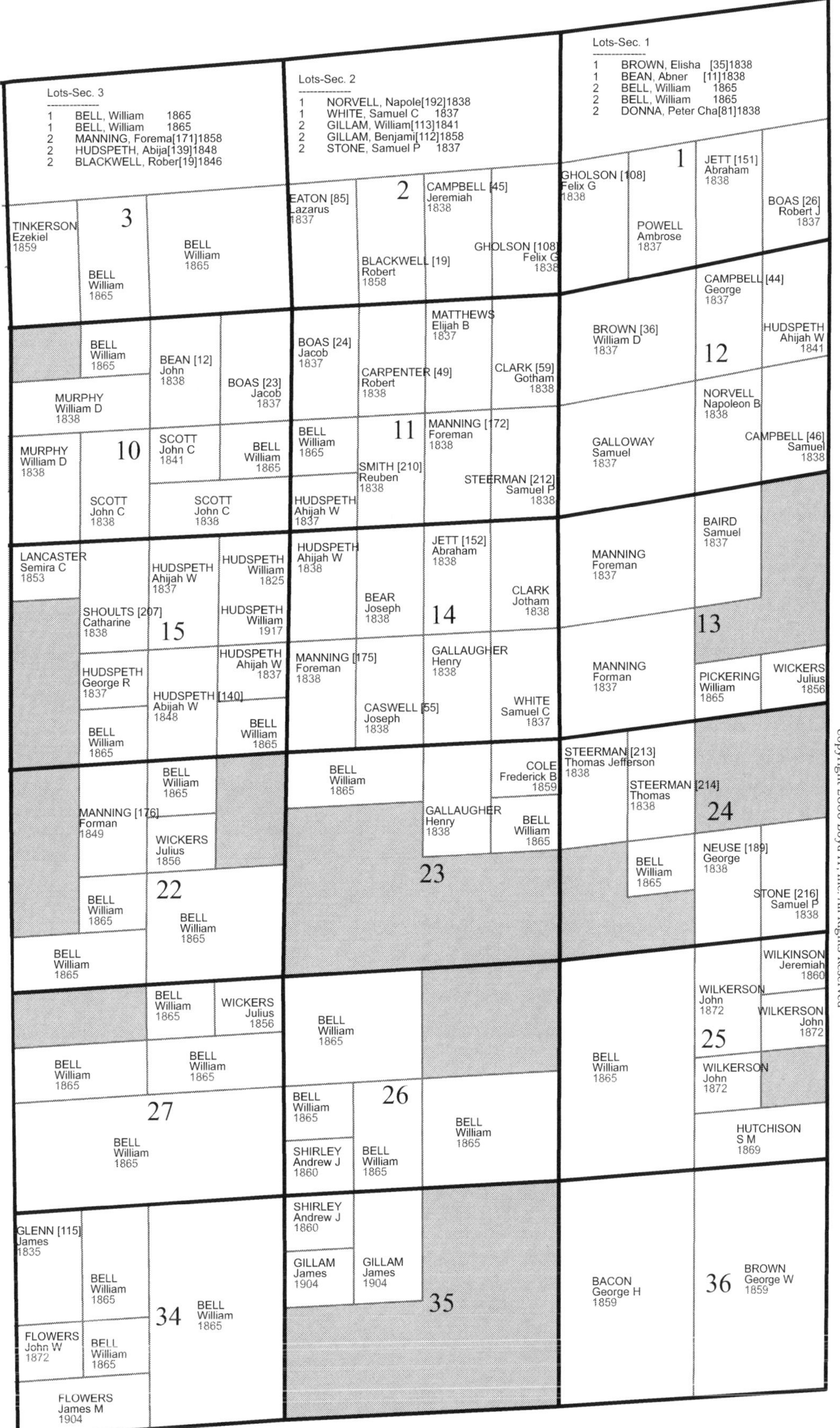

Helpful Hints

1. This Map's INDEX can be found on the preceding pages.
2. Refer to Map "C" to see where this Township lies within Washington County, Missouri.
3. Numbers within square brackets [ ] denote a multi-patentee land parcel (multi-owner). Refer to Appendix "C" for a full list of members in this group.
4. Areas that look to be crowded with Patentees usually indicate multiple sales of the same parcel (Re-issues) or Overlapping parcels. See this Township's Index for an explanation of these and other circumstances that might explain "odd" groupings of Patentees on this map.

Legend

- Patent Boundary
- Section Boundary
- No Patents Found (or Outside County)
- 1., 2., 3., ... Lot Numbers (when beside a name)
- [ ] Group Number (see Appendix "C")

Scale: Section = 1 mile X 1 mile (generally, with some exceptions)

Road Map

T36-N R1-W
5th PM Meridian

Map Group 22

Cities & Towns
- Brazil
- Delbridge
- Ishmael
- Palmer

Cemeteries
- Palmer Cemetery

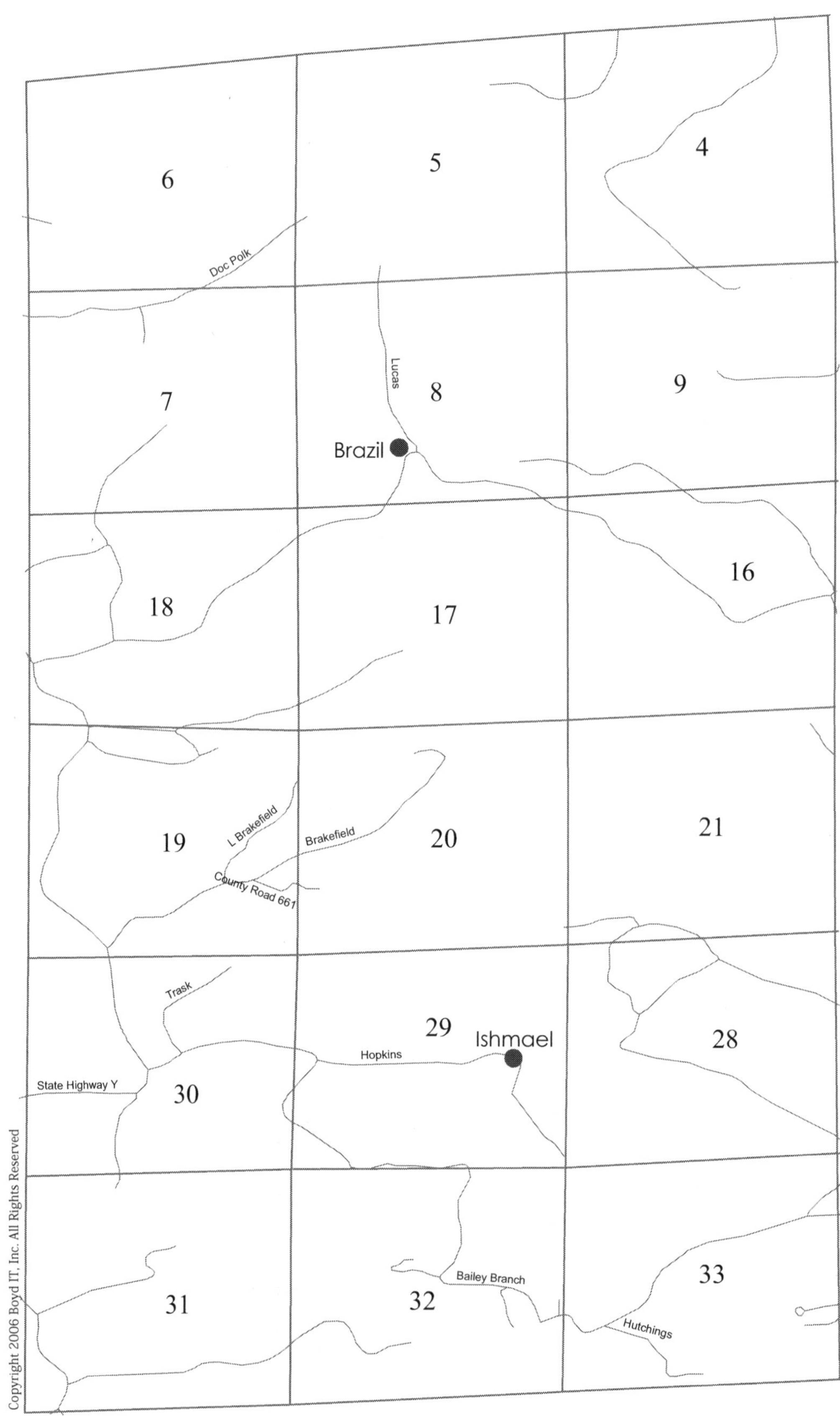

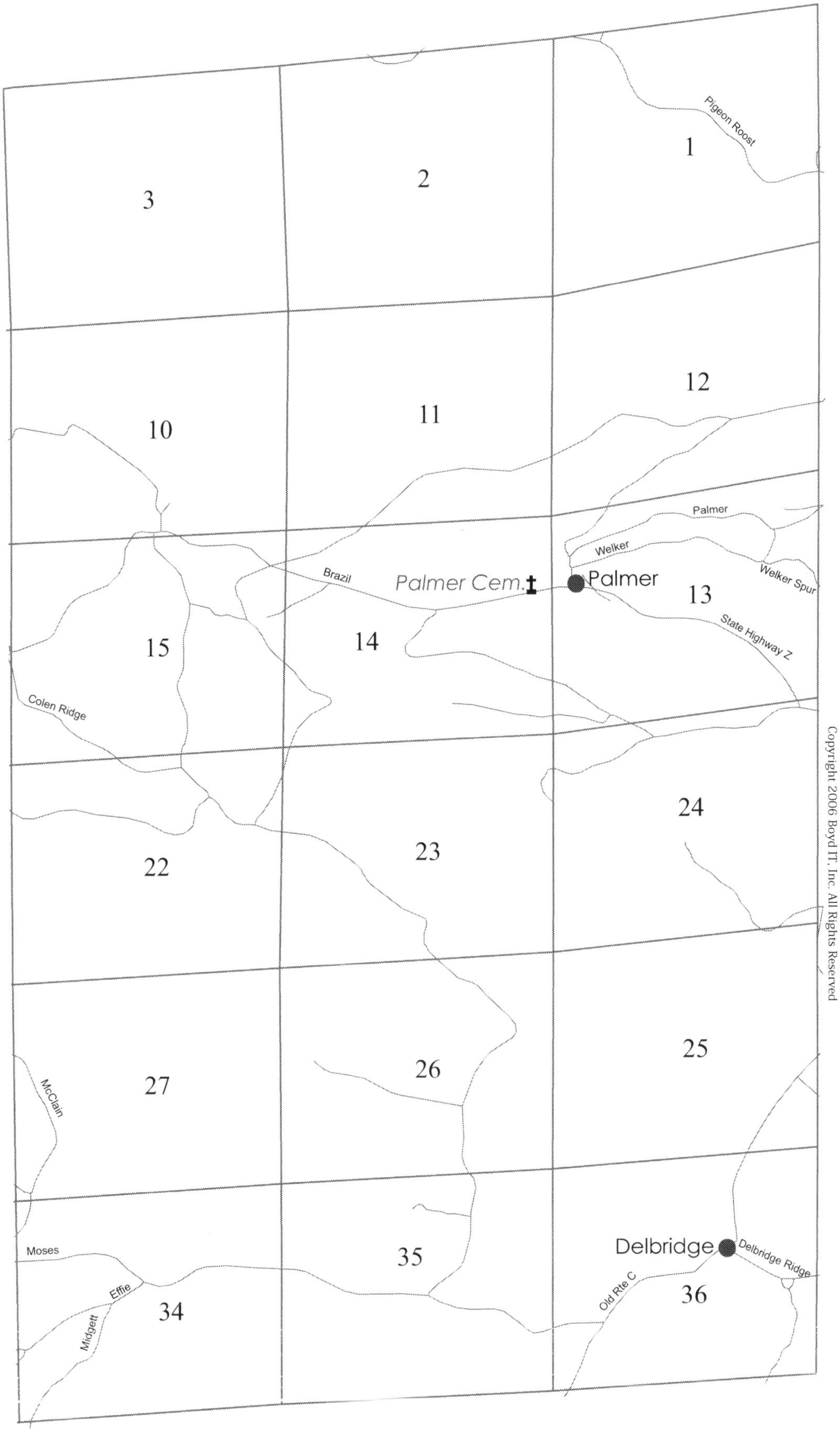

1 2 3
Pigeon Roost
12 11 10
Palmer
Welker
Brazil
Palmer Cem.
Palmer
13 14 15
Welker Spur
State Highway Z
Colen Ridge
24 23 22
25 26 27
McClain
Moses
Effie
Midgett
34 35 36
Delbridge
Delbridge Ridge
Old Rte C

Helpful Hints

1. This road map has a number of uses, but primarily it is to help you: a) find the present location of land owned by your ancestors (at least the general area), b) find cemeteries and city-centers, and c) estimate the route/roads used by Census-takers & tax-assessors.

2. If you plan to travel to Washington County to locate cemeteries or land parcels, please pick up a modern travel map for the area before you do. Mapping old land parcels on modern maps is not as exact a science as you might think. Just the slightest variations in public land survey coordinates, estimates of parcel boundaries, or road-map deviations can greatly alter a map's representation of how a road either does or doesn't cross a particular parcel of land.

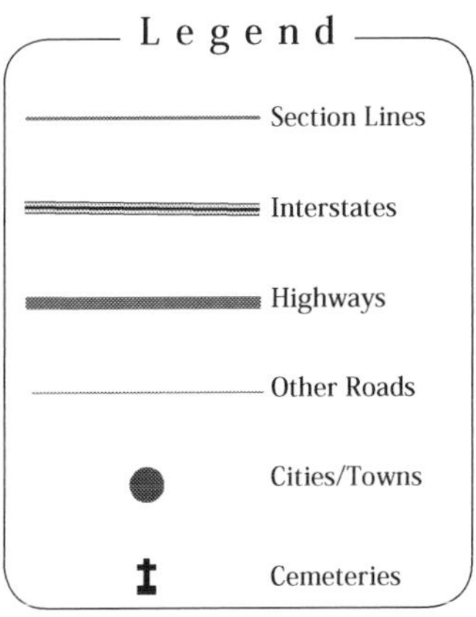

Scale: Section = 1 mile X 1 mile
(generally, with some exceptions)

Historical Map

T36-N R1-W
5th PM Meridian

Map Group 22

Cities & Towns

Brazil
Delbridge
Ishmael
Palmer

Cemeteries

Palmer Cemetery

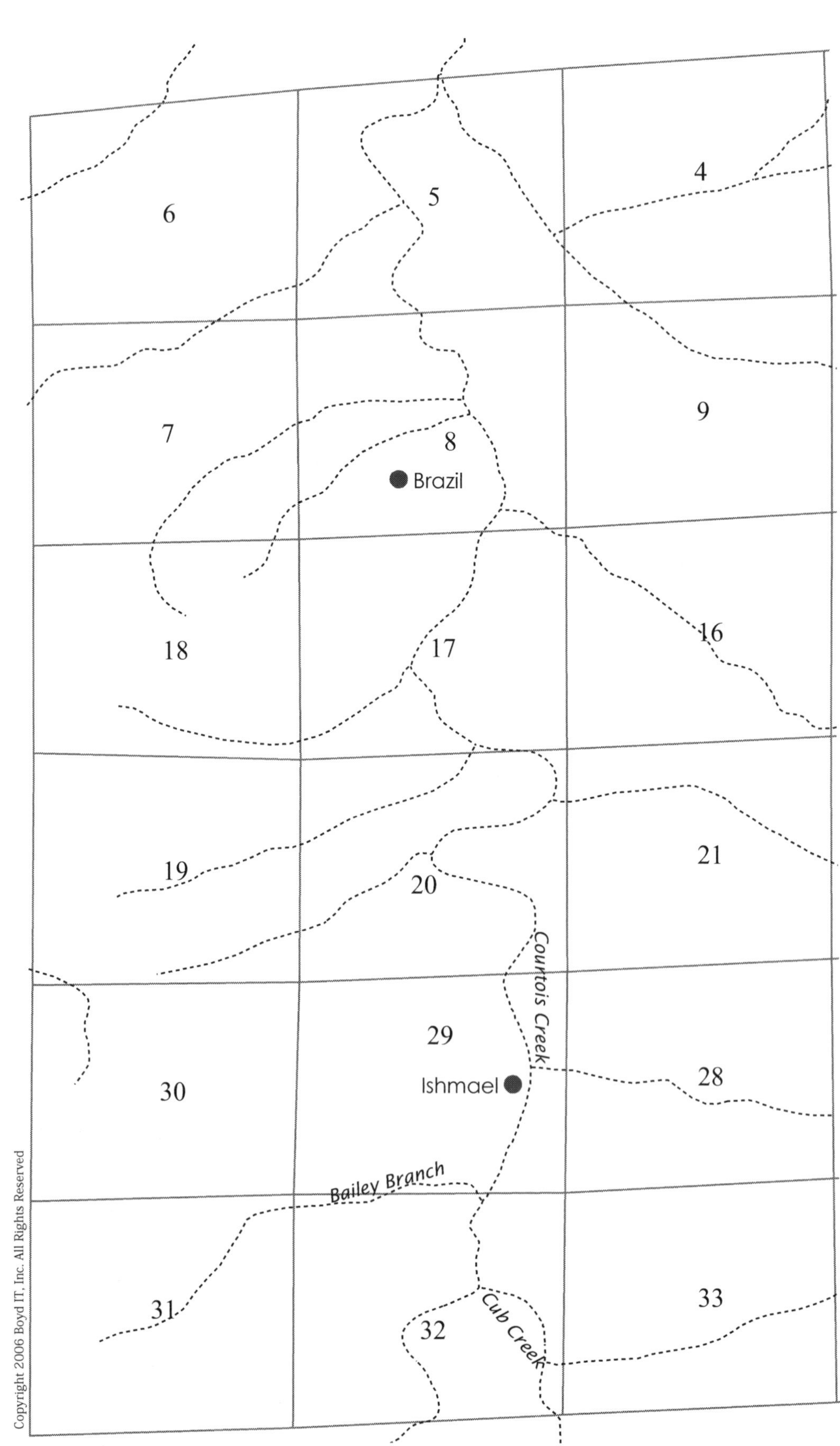

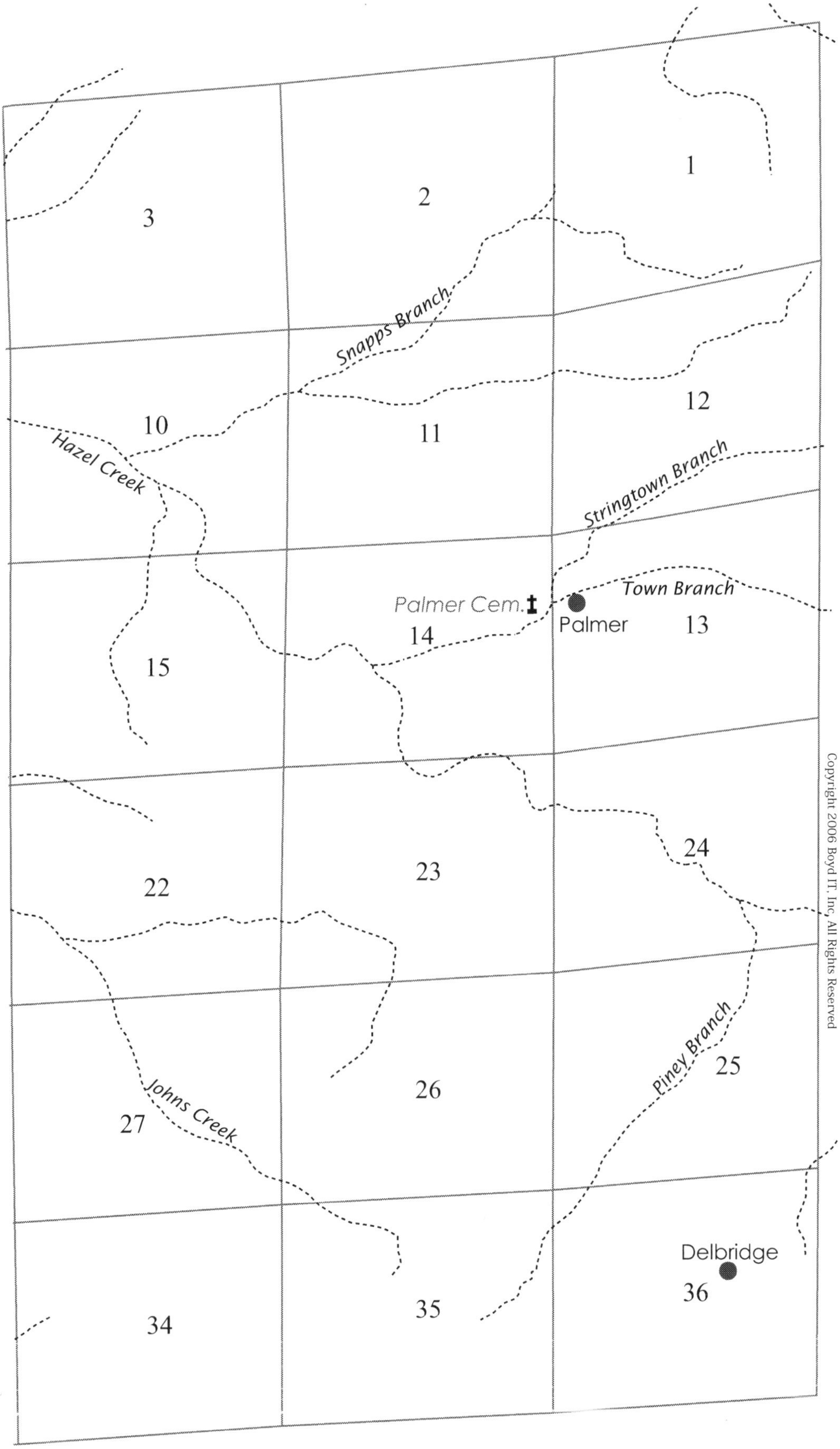

1
2
3
10
11
12
13
14
15
22
23
24
25
26
27
34
35
36
Snapps Branch
Hazel Creek
Stringtown Branch
Town Branch
Palmer Cem.
Palmer
Piney Branch
Johns Creek
Delbridge

Helpful Hints

1. This Map takes a different look at the same Congressional Township displayed in the preceding two maps. It presents features that can help you better envision the historical development of the area: a) Water-bodies (lakes & ponds), b) Water-courses (rivers, streams, etc.), c) Railroads, d) City/town center-points (where they were oftentimes located when first settled), and e) Cemeteries.
2. Using this "Historical" map in tandem with this Township's Patent Map and Road Map, may lead you to some interesting discoveries. You will often find roads, towns, cemeteries, and waterways are named after nearby landowners: sometimes those names will be the ones you are researching. See how many of these research gems you can find here in Washington County.

Legend
Section Lines
Railroads
Large Rivers & Bodies of Water
Streams/Creeks & Small Rivers
Cities/Towns
Cemeteries

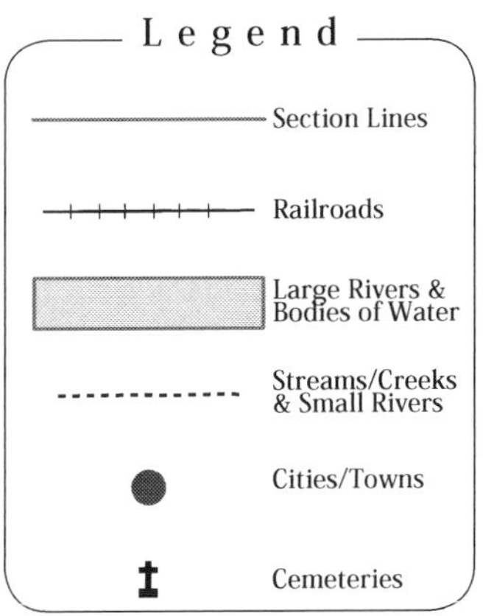

Scale: Section = 1 mile X 1 mile
(there are some exceptions)

Map Group 23: Index to Land Patents

Township 36-North Range 1-East (5th PM)

After you locate an individual in this Index, take note of the Section and Section Part then proceed to the Land Patent map on the pages immediately following. You should have no difficulty locating the corresponding parcel of land.

The "For More Info" Column will lead you to more information about the underlying Patents. See the *Legend* at right, and the "How to Use this Book" chapter, for more information.

LEGEND

"For More Info . . . " column

A = Authority (Legislative Act, See Appendix "A")
B = Block or Lot (location in Section unknown)
C = Cancelled Patent
F = Fractional Section
G = Group (Multi-Patentee Patent, see Appendix "C")
V = Overlaps another Parcel
R = Re-Issued (Parcel patented more than once)

(A & G items require you to look in the Appendixes referred to above. All other Letter-designations followed by a number require you to locate line-items in this index that possess the ID number found after the letter).

ID	Individual in Patent	Sec.	Sec. Part	Date Issued	Other Counties	For More Info . . .
3343	ADAMS, Francis M	25	NWSE	1869-07-01		A1
3344	" "	26	SENE	1888-05-07		A1
3534	ALDRIDGE, William	36	NWNE	1837-11-07		A1
3535	" "	36	SENE	1837-11-07		A1
3536	" "	36	W½SE	1837-11-07		A1
3488	AUGHEY, Samuel	4	NESW	1859-09-01		A1
3489	" "	4	SE	1859-09-01		A1
3490	BAIRD, Samuel	19	E½NE	1913-02-08		A1 G5
3248	BATCHELDER, Alvan J	11	SESE	1859-09-01		A1
3249	" "	12	W½SW	1859-09-01		A1
3250	" "	13	W½NW	1859-09-01		A1
3251	" "	14	E½NE	1859-09-01		A1
3486	BEAR, Robert J	8	W½NE	1838-08-01		A1
3282	BENNING, Benjamin P	26	SWNW	1845-06-01		A1 G15
3282	BENNING, Isaac G	26	SWNW	1845-06-01		A1 G15
3460	BLUNT, Peter D	7	W½SE	1837-01-24		A1 G22
3461	" "	8	E½NE	1837-01-24		A1 G22
3530	BOISAUBIN, Vincent	11	NESE	1859-09-01		A1
3531	" "	11	SENE	1859-09-01		A1
3532	" "	12	NW	1859-09-01		A1
3533	" "	12	W½NE	1859-09-01		A1
3491	BOSWELL, Samuel	20	NWNE	1837-01-24		A1
3490	BRICKEY, John Colwell	19	E½NE	1913-02-08		A1 G5
3455	BRONDAMOUR, Napoleon B	32	SENW	1859-09-01		A1
3456	" "	32	SW	1859-09-01		A1
3457	" "	32	SWSE	1859-09-01		A1
3458	" "	32	W½NW	1859-09-01		A1
3540	BROWN, William H	30	S½1SW	1859-09-01		A1
3541	" "	31	1NW	1859-09-01		A1
3542	" "	31	1SW	1859-09-01		A1
3543	" "	31	2NW	1859-09-01		A1
3544	" "	31	2SW	1859-09-01		A1
3474	BURDION, Reuben	17	E½NW	1838-08-01		A1 G38
3449	BURROWES, Michael	12	S½SE	1858-04-01		A1
3450	" "	12	SESW	1858-04-01		A1
3451	" "	13	N½NE	1858-04-01		A1
3452	" "	13	NENW	1858-04-01		A1
3523	BYRD, Thomas	24	W½NE	1837-11-14		A1
3345	CAMPBELL, George	7	E½SE	1837-01-24		A1 G44
3370	CAMPBELL, Jeremiah	17	E½SW	1838-08-01		A1 G45
3493	CAMPBELL, Samuel	6	W½SW	1838-08-01		A1 G46
3328	CARSON, Elizabeth	25	E½SW	1896-02-10		A1
3329	" "	25	NWSW	1896-02-10		A1
3330	" "	25	SWSE	1896-02-10		A1
3359	CARSON, James A	24	N½SW	1859-09-01		A1
3360	" "	24	NWSE	1859-09-01		A1

ID	Individual in Patent	Sec.	Sec. Part	Date Issued	Other Counties	For More Info . . .
3361	CARSON, James A (Cont'd)	24	S½NW	1859-09-01		A1
3524	CARSON, Thomas	36	E½SE	1837-11-07		A1
3539	CASH, William	19	2NW	1859-09-01		A1
3453	COFFMAN, Michael	30	N½1SW	1888-12-08		A3
3454	" "	30	N½2SW	1888-12-08		A3
3482	COMPTON, Richard	20	SWNE	1837-01-17		A1
3481	" "	20	SENE	1837-03-15		A1
3519	COMPTON, Stephen	18	S½2NW	1866-06-01		A1
3525	CROZIER, Thomas	19	1NW	1860-08-01		A1
3526	" "	19	N½1SW	1860-08-01		A1
3527	" "	19	N½2SW	1860-08-01		A1
3520	CUMPTON, Stephen	18	SW	1859-09-01		A1 F
3521	" "	18	W½SE	1859-09-01		A1
3302	DELAFIELD, Clarence	13	E½SW	1858-04-01		A1
3303	" "	13	NWSE	1858-04-01		A1
3304	" "	13	NWSW	1858-04-01		A1
3305	" "	13	S½NE	1858-04-01		A1
3306	" "	13	S½SE	1858-04-01		A1
3331	DESLOGE, Firmin	24	NESE	1854-11-15		A1
3332	" "	25	NESE	1854-11-15		A1
3333	" "	25	SWNE	1854-11-15		A1
3262	DICKEY, Andrew S	21	SESE	1853-04-15		A1
3263	" "	28	NENE	1854-11-15		A1
3265	" "	28	SENE	1856-01-03		A1
3264	" "	28	NWNE	1857-10-30		A1
3266	" "	28	SWNE	1859-01-01		A1
3385	DOUGLASS, John H	27	SENE	1859-01-01		A1
3386	" "	27	W½NE	1859-01-01		A1
3384	" "	27	SE	1859-09-10		A1
3280	DUNKIN, Benjamin F	17	E½NE	1860-08-01		A1
3281	" "	17	E½SE	1860-08-01		A1
3371	EARS, John	1	E½2NE	1856-06-03		A2
3363	EIDSON, James	36	SE	1854-11-15		A1 F
3372	EUSTIS, John	2	1NW	1859-09-01		A1
3373	" "	2	E½2NW	1859-09-01		A1
3374	" "	2	N½SW	1859-09-01		A1
3375	" "	3	E½1NE	1859-09-01		A1
3376	" "	3	N½SE	1859-09-01		A1
3379	FARRELL, John	4	W½1NW	1866-06-01		A1
3380	" "	4	W½SW	1866-06-01		A1
3381	" "	5	1NE	1866-06-01		A1
3382	" "	5	S½	1866-06-01		A1 G101
3383	" "	6	E½SE	1866-06-01		A1 G101
3377	" "	18	1NW	1866-09-01		A1
3378	" "	18	N½2NW	1866-09-01		A1
3258	FINK, Andrew H	32	N½SE	1859-09-01		A1
3259	" "	32	SESE	1859-09-01		A1
3260	" "	33	NESW	1859-09-01		A1
3261	" "	33	S½SW	1859-09-01		A1
3352	FISHER, Henry	23	SESW	1860-10-01		A1
3353	" "	23	SWSE	1860-10-01		A1
3354	" "	26	NENW	1860-10-01		A1
3445	GILCHRIST, Malcolm	8	E½SW	1837-11-07		A1
3446	" "	8	W½SW	1837-11-07		A1
3447	" "	9	SW	1837-11-07		A1
3448	" "	9	W½SE	1837-11-07		A1
3278	GROOM, Benjamin A	21	NESE	1877-11-10		A1
3279	" "	21	SENE	1877-11-10		A1
3244	HELLIARD, Alexander	24	SWSE	1852-01-01		A1
3245	" "	25	NWNE	1852-01-01		A1
3252	HENDERSON, Amariah	26	N½SW	1859-01-01		A1
3253	" "	26	NESE	1859-01-01		A1
3254	" "	26	S½SE	1859-01-01		A1
3255	" "	26	SENW	1859-01-01		A1
3256	" "	26	SESW	1859-01-01		A1
3257	" "	26	SWNE	1859-01-01		A1
3546	HILL, William	27	W½	1857-04-15		A1
3316	HILLEN, David C	14	SE	1857-10-30		A1
3317	" "	23	N½NE	1857-10-30		A1
3318	" "	24	N½NW	1857-10-30		A1
3387	HILLEN, John J	23	SESE	1857-04-15		A1
3388	" "	24	SWSW	1857-04-15		A1
3389	" "	25	NW	1857-04-15		A1

ID	Individual in Patent	Sec.	Sec. Part	Date Issued	Other Counties	For More Info . . .
3390	HILLEN, John J (Cont'd)	26	N½NE	1857-04-15		A1
3537	HILLEN, William B	21	W½SE	1857-04-15		A1
3358	HIRSH, J	17	W½SW	1866-09-01		A1 G133
3293	HUTCHINGS, Charles	20	NWSW	1837-01-24		A1
3294	" "	20	SWNW	1837-01-24		A1
3310	JARVIS, Cornelius	29	NWSW	1860-09-01		A1
3311	" "	29	S½SW	1860-09-01		A1
3312	" "	30	NESE	1860-09-01		A1
3313	" "	32	NENW	1860-09-01		A1
3314	" "	32	NWNE	1860-09-01		A1
3315	" "	32	S½NE	1860-09-01		A1
3337	JARVIS, Foster M	28	SESW	1857-10-30		A1
3338	" "	28	W½SE	1857-10-30		A1
3339	" "	33	E½NW	1857-10-30		A1
3341	" "	33	NWSW	1857-10-30		A1
3342	" "	33	SWNW	1857-10-30		A1
3340	" "	33	NWNW	1858-12-01		A1
3505	JARVIS, Silvester	30	1NW	1857-10-30		A1
3506	" "	30	2NW	1857-10-30		A1
3507	" "	30	NWSE	1857-10-30		A1
3508	" "	30	SWNE	1857-10-30		A1
3522	JARVIS, Sylvester	19	SESW	1856-01-03		A1
3443	JOHNSON, Louisa	4	E½1NW	1866-09-01		A1
3444	" "	4	W½1NE	1866-09-01		A1
3433	LASWELL, Joseph	7	W½NW	1838-08-01		A1 G162
3382	LIBBY, James C	5	S½	1866-06-01		A1 G101
3383	" "	6	E½SE	1866-06-01		A1 G101
3362	" "	17	W½NE	1866-09-01		A1
3355	LONG, Horris M	34	N½NE	1859-01-01		A1
3356	" "	34	NENW	1859-01-01		A1
3357	" "	34	SWNE	1859-01-01		A1
3334	MANNING, Foreman	7	W½NE	1838-08-01		A1 G175
3433	" "	7	W½NW	1838-08-01		A1 G162
3335	MANNING, Forman	6	W½SE	1837-11-07		A1
3336	" "	7	E½NE	1837-11-07		A1
3274	MARSHALL, Austin	23	NESE	1869-07-01		A1
3275	" "	23	SENE	1869-07-01		A1
3276	" "	25	SWSW	1869-07-01		A1
3277	" "	28	SWSW	1869-07-01		A1
3549	MARSHALL, William S	32	NENE	1869-07-01		A1
3392	MASON, John	1	E½1NW	1858-04-01		A1
3393	" "	1	E½2NW	1858-04-01		A1
3394	" "	1	E½3NW	1858-04-01		A1
3395	" "	1	E½SW	1858-04-01		A1
3396	" "	1	W½1NE	1858-04-01		A1
3397	" "	1	W½SE	1858-04-01		A1
3327	MATTHEWS, Elijah B	6	W½NW	1838-08-01		A1
3430	MATTHEWS, Johnson	6	E½1NW	1871-02-10		A3
3431	" "	6	E½2NW	1871-02-10		A3
3432	" "	6	W½1NE	1871-02-10		A3
3286	MAXWELL, Catharine	25	SESE	1837-11-07		A1
3436	MAXWELL, Joseph	36	NENE	1837-11-07		A1
3246	MCPHAILL, Alexander	22	E½SW	1833-10-15		A1 G179
3494	MERRY, Samuel	22	E½NW	1837-11-07		A1 G182
3495	" "	22	NE	1837-11-07		A1 G182
3496	" "	22	W½SE	1837-11-07		A1 G182
3497	" "	22	W½SW	1837-11-07		A1 G182
3246	MONTGOMERY, Nathan	22	E½SW	1833-10-15		A1 G179
3459	" "	22	W½NW	1913-02-08		A1 G186
3547	PARKIN, William	5	3NE	1866-04-13		A1
3548	" "	5	W½2NE	1866-04-13		A1
3406	PERRY, John	8	W½SE	1837-11-07		A1
3307	PORTER, Clarina P	29	SE	1896-02-10		A1
3308	" "	29	SENE	1896-02-10		A1
3309	" "	29	W½NE	1896-02-10		A1
3358	PRUDEN, E	17	W½SW	1866-09-01		A1 G133
3404	RAMSEY, John P	35	SESW	1856-01-03		A1
3405	" "	35	SWSW	1856-01-03		A1 F
3528	RENFRO, Thomas F	15	SWSE	1833-10-15		A1
3325	RICE, Edward C	31	E½	1859-09-01		A1
3366	ROBERSON, James	21	N½NW	1856-09-01		A1
3367	" "	21	SW	1856-09-01		A1
3368	ROBINSON, James	36	E½NW	1837-11-07		A1

ID	Individual in Patent	Sec.	Sec. Part	Date Issued	Other Counties	For More Info . . .
3369	ROBINSON, James (Cont'd)	36	SWNE	1837-11-07		A1
3407	ROBINSON, John T	1	NWSW	1859-09-01		A1
3408	" "	1	W½1NW	1859-09-01		A1
3409	" "	1	W½2NW	1859-09-01		A1
3412	" "	2	1NE	1859-09-01		A1
3413	" "	2	N½SE	1859-09-01		A1
3411	" "	13	SENW	1866-06-01		A1
3414	" "	24	SESE	1866-06-01		A1
3415	" "	24	SESW	1866-06-01		A1
3410	" "	10	NWSE	1869-07-01		A1
3483	ROBINSON, Richard	21	SWNW	1837-01-24		A1
3500	ROBINSON, Samuel	21	SWNE	1856-10-10		A1
3498	" "	21	NENE	1857-12-15		A1
3499	" "	21	NWNE	1857-12-15		A1
3382	SEYMOUR, William B	5	S½	1866-06-01		A1 G101
3383	" "	6	E½SE	1866-06-01		A1 G101
3538	" "	29	NESW	1869-07-01		A1
3347	SITTON, Harvey	19	W½SE	1856-06-16		A1
3348	" "	20	E½SW	1856-06-16		A1
3349	" "	20	NENE	1856-06-16		A1
3350	" "	20	NENW	1856-06-16		A1
3351	" "	29	NENW	1859-09-01		A1
3288	SMITH, Charles D	13	NESE	1869-07-01		A1
3289	" "	13	SWSW	1869-07-01		A1
3290	" "	14	W½NE	1869-07-01		A1
3287	" "	12	NESE	1869-10-15		A1
3291	" "	4	E½3NE	1873-04-01		A1
3292	" "	5	E½2NE	1873-04-01		A1
3416	SMITH, John W	1	W½3NW	1857-10-30		A1
3417	" "	2	2NE	1857-10-30		A1
3418	" "	2	3NE	1857-10-30		A1
3419	" "	2	E½3NW	1857-10-30		A1
3480	SMITH, Reuben	20	SE	1837-01-24		A1 G211
3345	" "	7	E½SE	1837-01-24		A1 G44
3476	" "	7	SW	1837-01-24		A1
3460	" "	7	W½SE	1837-01-24		A1 G22
3461	" "	8	E½NE	1837-01-24		A1 G22
3494	" "	22	E½NW	1837-11-07		A1 G182
3495	" "	22	NE	1837-11-07		A1 G182
3496	" "	22	W½SE	1837-11-07		A1 G182
3497	" "	22	W½SW	1837-11-07		A1 G182
3475	" "	6	E½SW	1837-11-07		A1
3477	" "	8	E½NW	1837-11-07		A1
3478	" "	8	E½SE	1837-11-07		A1
3479	" "	8	W½NW	1837-11-07		A1
3493	" "	6	W½SW	1838-08-01		A1 G46
3459	" "	22	W½NW	1913-02-08		A1 G186
3246	SMITH, Reubin	22	E½SW	1833-10-15		A1 G179
3550	SMITH, William	1	W½2NE	1857-10-30		A1 F
3529	STEERMAN, Thomas	7	E½NW	1838-08-01		A1 G214
3434	STEPHENSON, Joseph M	18	E½SE	1837-11-14		A1
3490	STEPHENSON, Joseph Milas	19	E½NE	1913-02-08		A1 G5
3435	STEVENSON, Joseph M	17	W½SE	1837-11-07		A1
3370	" "	17	E½SW	1838-08-01		A1 G45
3480	STONE, Samuel	20	SE	1837-01-24		A1 G211
3474	STONE, Samuel P	17	E½NW	1838-08-01		A1 G38
3529	" "	7	E½NW	1838-08-01		A1 G214
3241	STONER, Abraham	11	W½SW	1859-09-01		A1
3242	" "	14	NW	1859-09-01		A1
3243	" "	15	N½NE	1859-09-01		A1
3509	STONER, Simon	10	E½SE	1859-09-01		A1
3247	SUMPTER, Alexander	4	W½2NE	1853-08-01		A1
3487	SWAIN, Rufus	33	E½	1859-09-10		A1
3334	TEAS, Henry	7	W½NE	1838-08-01		A1 G175
3267	TENISON, Archibald	35	NESE	1849-04-10		A1
3511	TENNESON, Solomon	36	NWNW	1837-11-14		A1
3510	" "	35	SENE	1841-07-01		A1
3272	TENNISON, Archibald	36	E½SW	1856-01-03		A1
3268	" "	34	SENE	1857-10-30		A1
3269	" "	35	N½SW	1857-10-30		A1
3270	" "	35	NWSE	1857-10-30		A1
3271	" "	35	SWNW	1857-10-30		A1
3545	TENNISON, William H	35	SWSE	1862-05-15		A1

ID	Individual in Patent	Sec.	Sec. Part	Date Issued	Other Counties	For More Info . . .
3484	THOMPSON, Richard	34	NWNW	1860-10-01		A1
3485	" "	34	S½NW	1860-10-01		A1
3326	THORP, Eliakim	10	W½NW	1860-03-01		A1
3514	TINISON, Solomon	35	NENE	1856-01-03		A1
3518	" "	36	SWNW	1856-01-03		A1 F
3512	" "	26	SWSW	1859-01-01		A1
3513	" "	35	N½NW	1859-01-01		A1
3515	" "	35	NWNE	1859-01-01		A1
3516	" "	35	SENW	1859-01-01		A1
3517	" "	35	SWNE	1859-01-01		A1
3295	ULLMAN, Charles	4	E½2NW	1901-04-22		A1
3296	" "	4	SESW	1901-04-22		A1
3298	WALTON, Christopher	2	W½3NW	1856-06-10		A1
3299	" "	3	3NE	1856-06-10		A1
3300	" "	3	3NW	1856-06-10		A1
3301	" "	3	W½2NW	1856-06-10		A1
3297	" "	2	W½2NW	1857-04-15		A1
3346	WALTON, George	4	W½3NE	1853-12-01		A1
3437	WALTON, Joseph	4	E½1NE	1856-06-10		A1
3438	" "	5	1NW	1856-06-10		A1
3439	" "	5	2NE	1856-06-10		A1
3440	" "	5	E½2NW	1856-06-10		A1
3441	" "	5	NESW	1856-06-10		A1 V3382
3442	" "	5	W½1NE	1856-06-10		A1
3391	WARNER, John M	34	S½	1859-09-10		A1
3467	WELKER, Peter	20	NWNW	1843-04-10		A1
3462	" "	14	NWSW	1857-04-15		A1
3463	" "	15	N½SE	1857-04-15		A1
3464	" "	15	N½SW	1857-04-15		A1
3465	" "	15	S½NE	1857-04-15		A1
3466	" "	15	SWSW	1857-04-15		A1
3246	WHALEY, William	22	E½SW	1833-10-15		A1 G179
3364	WHITE, James M	19	NESE	1837-11-14		A1
3365	" "	20	SENW	1837-11-14		A1
3492	WHITE, Samuel C	17	W½NW	1837-11-07		A1
3501	WIGGER, Sidney	1	E½1NE	1856-09-01		A1
3502	" "	1	NESE	1856-09-01		A1
3503	" "	1	SESE	1857-10-30		A1
3504	" "	12	E½NE	1857-10-30		A1
3398	WILLARD, John N	19	SESE	1859-09-01		A1
3399	" "	20	SWSW	1859-09-01		A1
3400	" "	29	SENW	1859-09-01		A1
3401	" "	29	W½NW	1859-09-01		A1
3402	" "	30	N½NE	1859-09-01		A1
3403	" "	30	SENE	1859-09-01		A1
3273	WILSON, Arthur D	26	NWSE	1860-08-01		A1
3420	WOODARD, John	11	E½NW	1859-09-01		A1
3421	" "	11	E½SW	1859-09-01		A1
3422	" "	11	W½NE	1859-09-01		A1
3423	" "	11	W½SE	1859-09-01		A1
3283	WRIGHT, Brazillar	14	E½SW	1859-09-01		A1
3284	" "	23	NW	1859-09-01		A1
3285	" "	23	SWNE	1859-09-01		A1
3319	WRIGHT, David	10	NENE	1857-10-30		A1
3320	" "	11	NWNW	1857-10-30		A1
3321	" "	2	S½SW	1857-10-30		A1
3322	" "	3	S½SE	1857-10-30		A1
3323	" "	3	S½SW	1857-10-30		A1
3424	WRIGHT, John	10	E½NW	1857-04-15		A1
3425	" "	10	N½SW	1857-04-15		A1
3426	" "	10	SENE	1857-04-15		A1
3427	" "	10	W½NE	1857-04-15		A1
3428	" "	11	SWNW	1857-04-15		A1
3468	WRIGHT, Phineas B	22	E½SE	1859-09-01		A1
3469	" "	23	NESW	1859-09-01		A1
3470	" "	23	NWSE	1859-09-01		A1
3471	" "	23	W½SW	1859-09-01		A1
3472	" "	26	NWNW	1859-09-01		A1
3473	" "	27	NENE	1859-09-01		A1
3324	YOUNT, David	19	SWSW	1837-01-24		A1
3429	ZENT, John	28	E½SE	1869-07-01		A1

Patent Map

T36-N R1-E
5th PM Meridian

Map Group 23

Township Statistics

Parcels Mapped	:	310
Number of Patents	:	163
Number of Individuals	:	126
Patentees Identified	:	119
Number of Surnames	:	94
Multi-Patentee Parcels	:	21
Oldest Patent Date	:	10/15/1833
Most Recent Patent	:	2/8/1913
Block/Lot Parcels	:	57
Parcels Re - Issued	:	0
Parcels that Overlap	:	1
Cities and Towns	:	0
Cemeteries	:	5

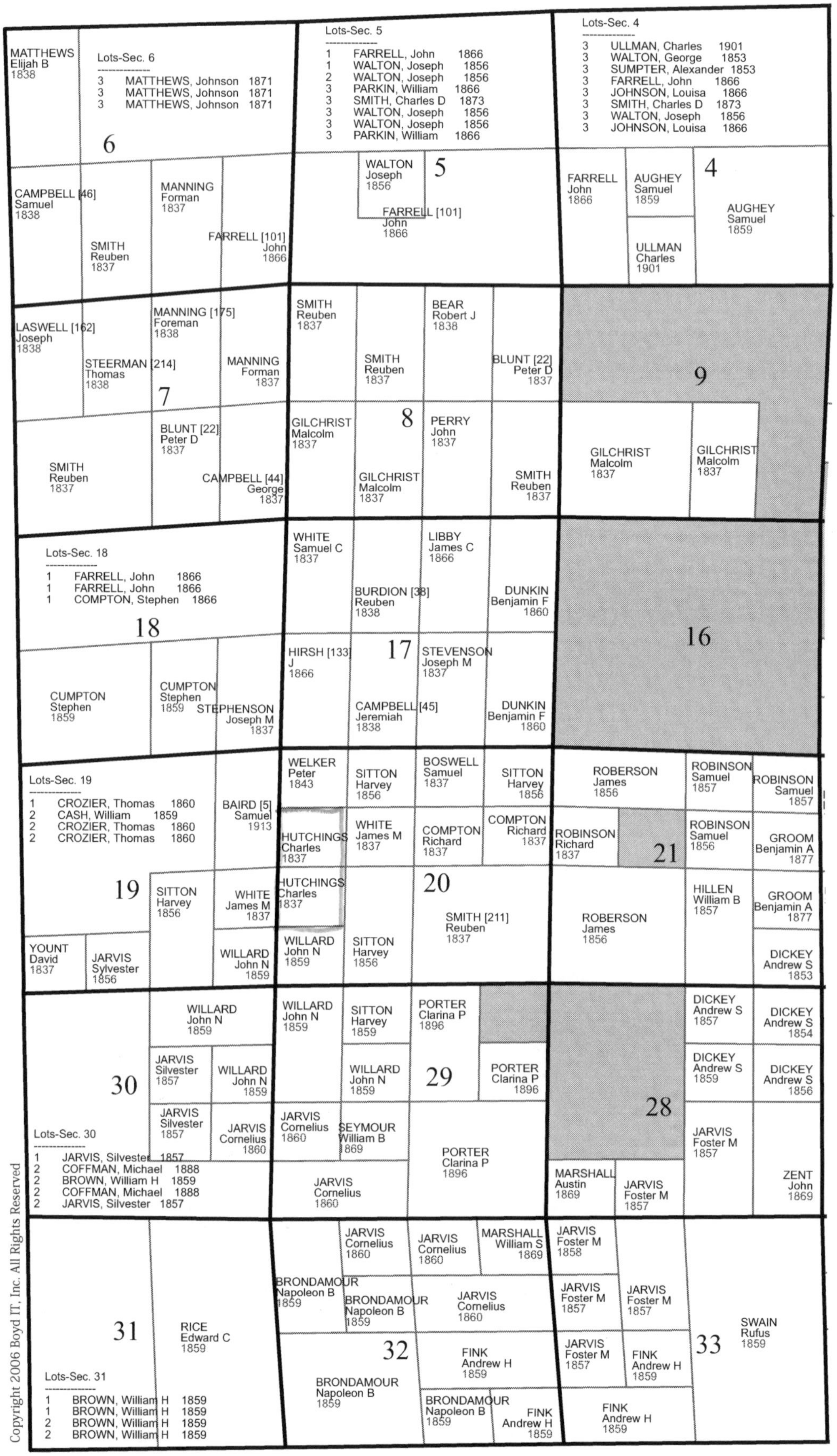

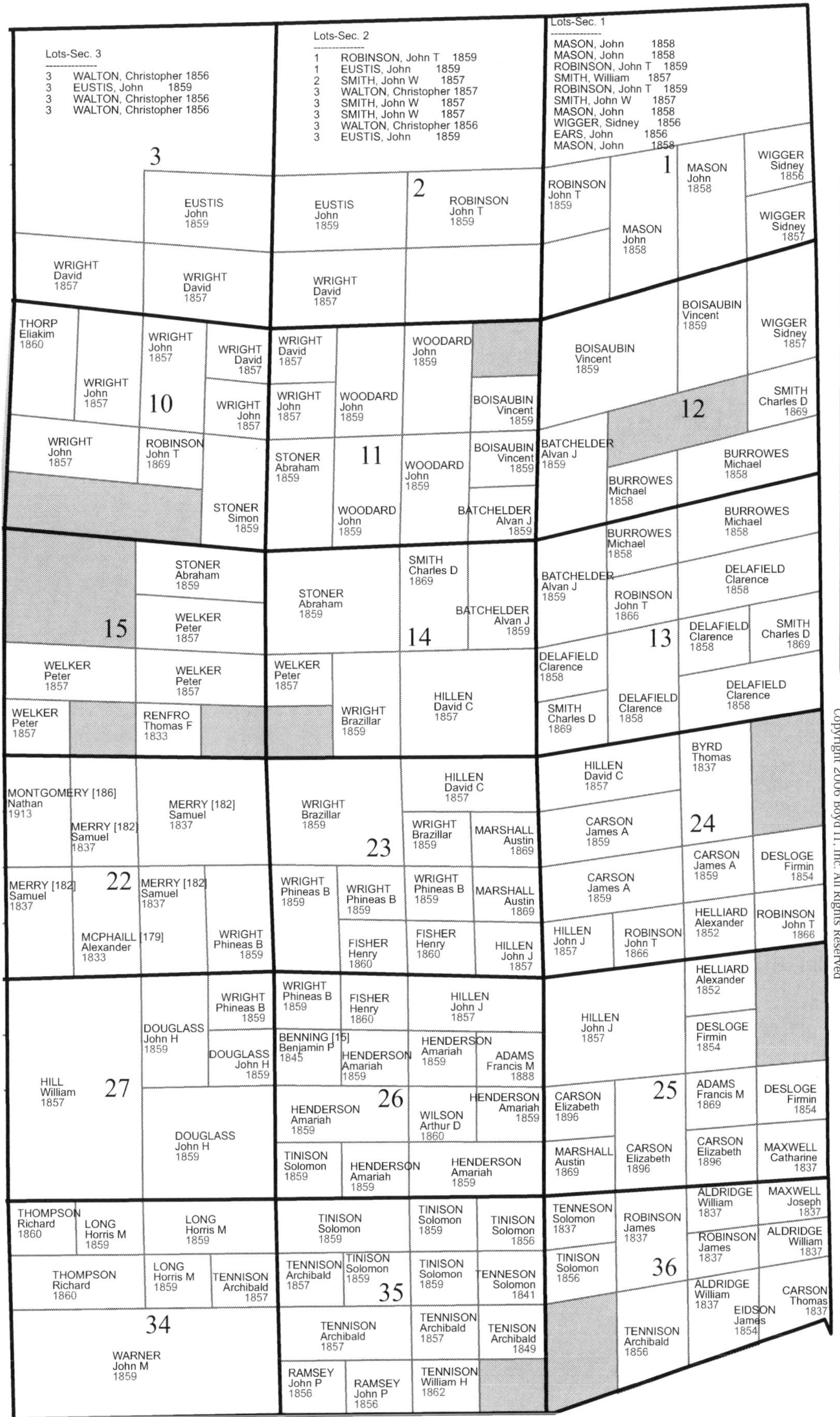

Helpful Hints

1. This Map's INDEX can be found on the preceding pages.
2. Refer to Map "C" to see where this Township lies within Washington County, Missouri.
3. Numbers within square brackets [ ] denote a multi-patentee land parcel (multi-owner). Refer to Appendix "C" for a full list of members in this group.
4. Areas that look to be crowded with Patentees usually indicate multiple sales of the same parcel (Re-issues) or Overlapping parcels. See this Township's Index for an explanation of these and other circumstances that might explain "odd" groupings of Patentees on this map.

Legend

- Patent Boundary
- Section Boundary
- No Patents Found (or Outside County)
- 1., 2., 3., ... Lot Numbers (when beside a name)
- [ ] Group Number (see Appendix "C")

Scale: Section = 1 mile X 1 mile (generally, with some exceptions)

Road Map

T36-N R1-E
5th PM Meridian

Map Group 23

Cities & Towns
None

Cemeteries
Hazel Creek Cemetery
Jenkins Family Cemetery
Scott Cemetery
Sitton Cemetery
Wright Cemetery

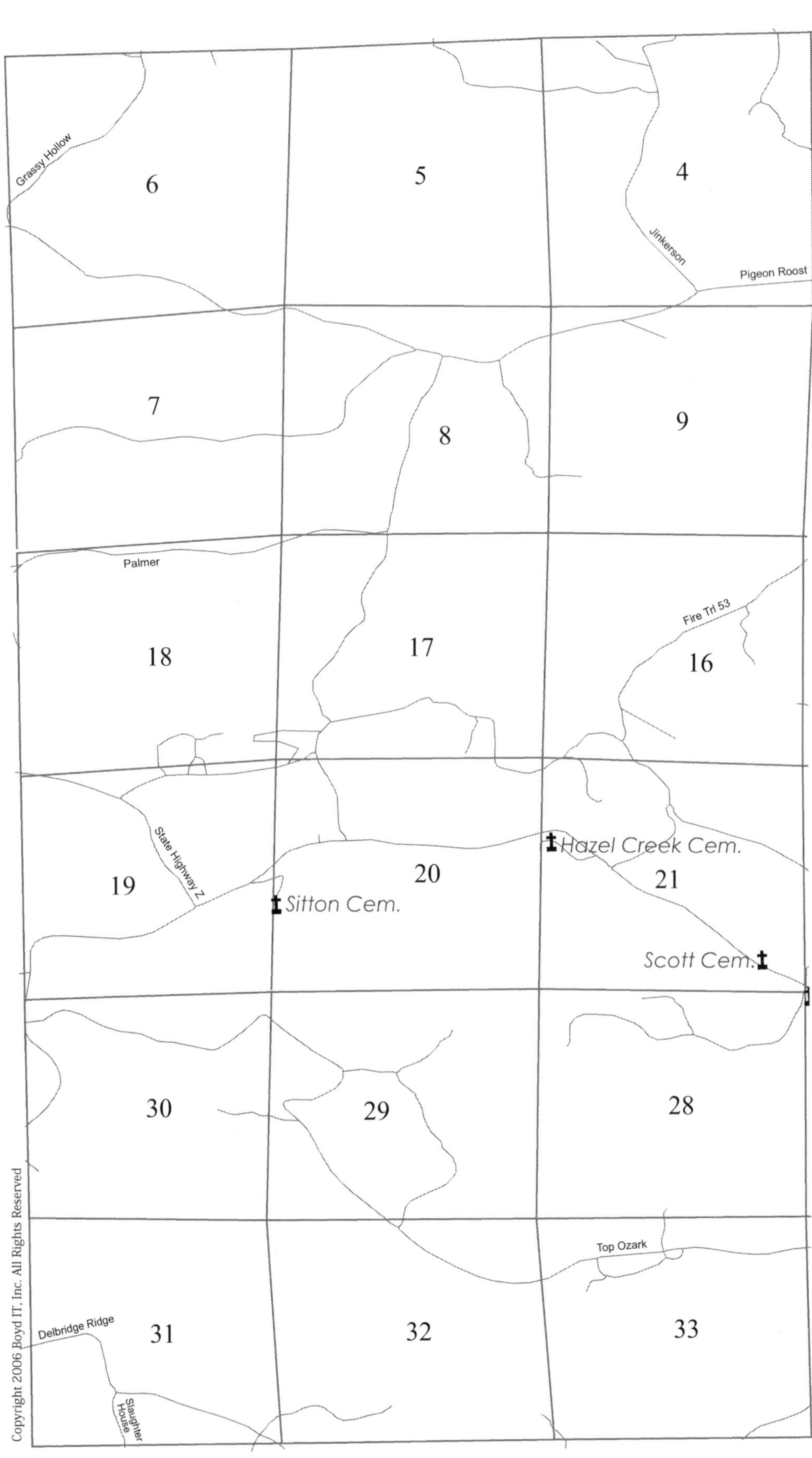

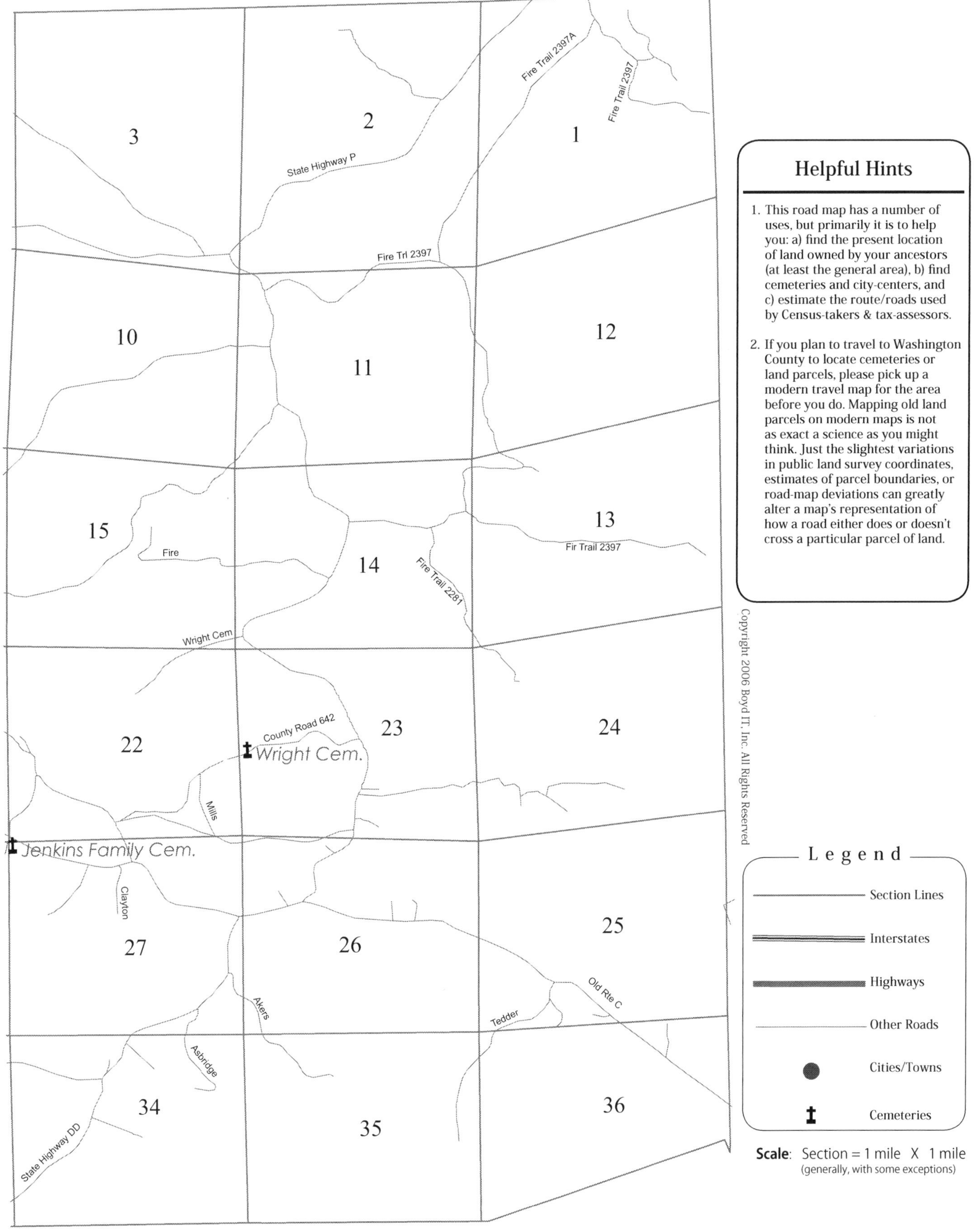

Helpful Hints

1. This road map has a number of uses, but primarily it is to help you: a) find the present location of land owned by your ancestors (at least the general area), b) find cemeteries and city-centers, and c) estimate the route/roads used by Census-takers & tax-assessors.

2. If you plan to travel to Washington County to locate cemeteries or land parcels, please pick up a modern travel map for the area before you do. Mapping old land parcels on modern maps is not as exact a science as you might think. Just the slightest variations in public land survey coordinates, estimates of parcel boundaries, or road-map deviations can greatly alter a map's representation of how a road either does or doesn't cross a particular parcel of land.

Historical Map

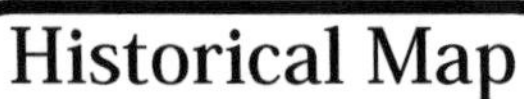

T36-N R1-E
5th PM Meridian

Map Group 23

Cities & Towns

None

Cemeteries

Hazel Creek Cemetery
Jenkins Family Cemetery
Scott Cemetery
Sitton Cemetery
Wright Cemetery

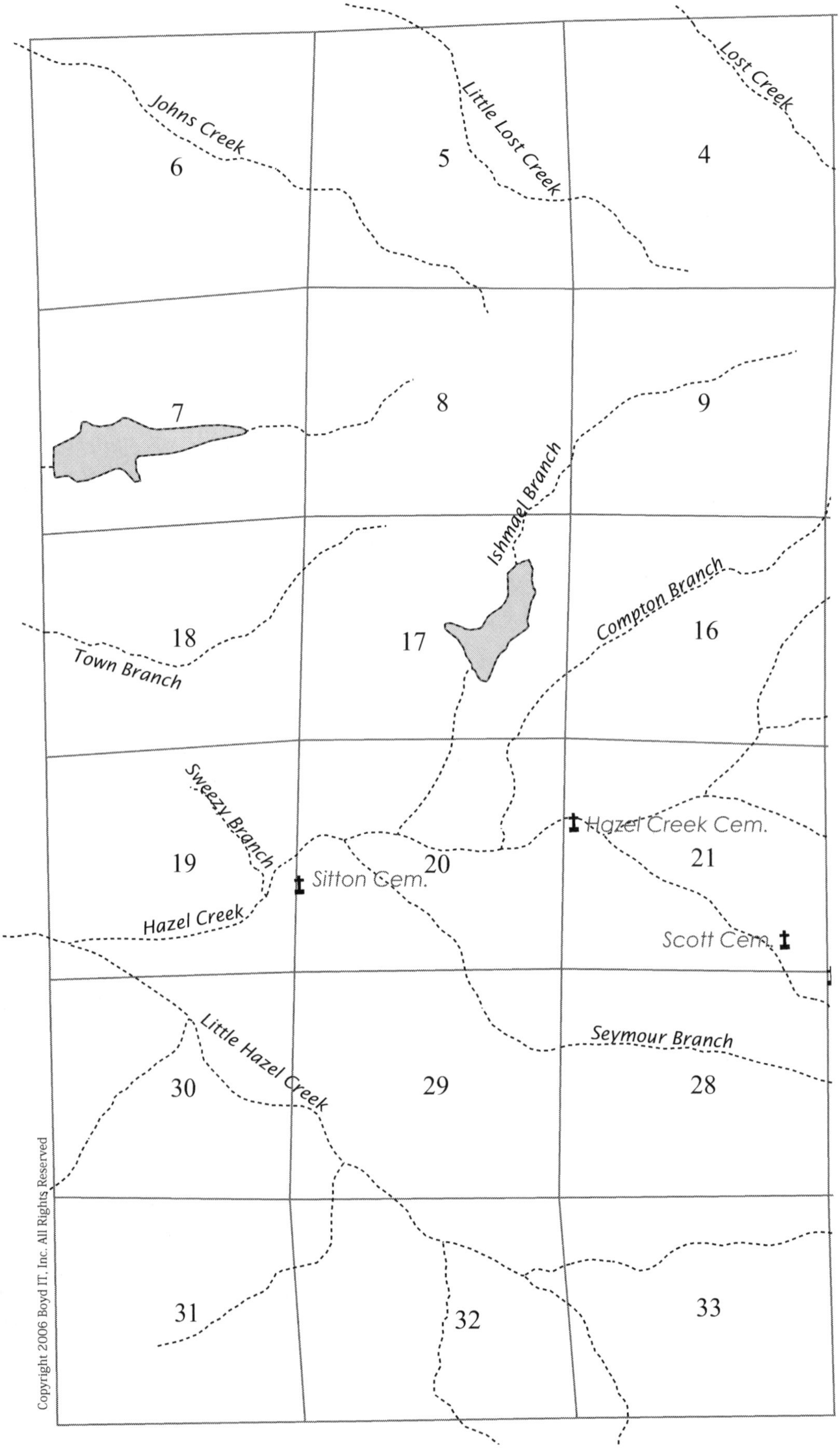

Johns Creek
Little Lost Creek
Lost Creek
6
5
4
7
8
9
Ishmael Branch
18
17
16
Compton Branch
Town Branch
Sweezy Branch
Hazel Creek Cem.
19
20
21
Sitton Cem.
Hazel Creek
Scott Cem.
Little Hazel Creek
Seymour Branch
30
29
28
31
32
33

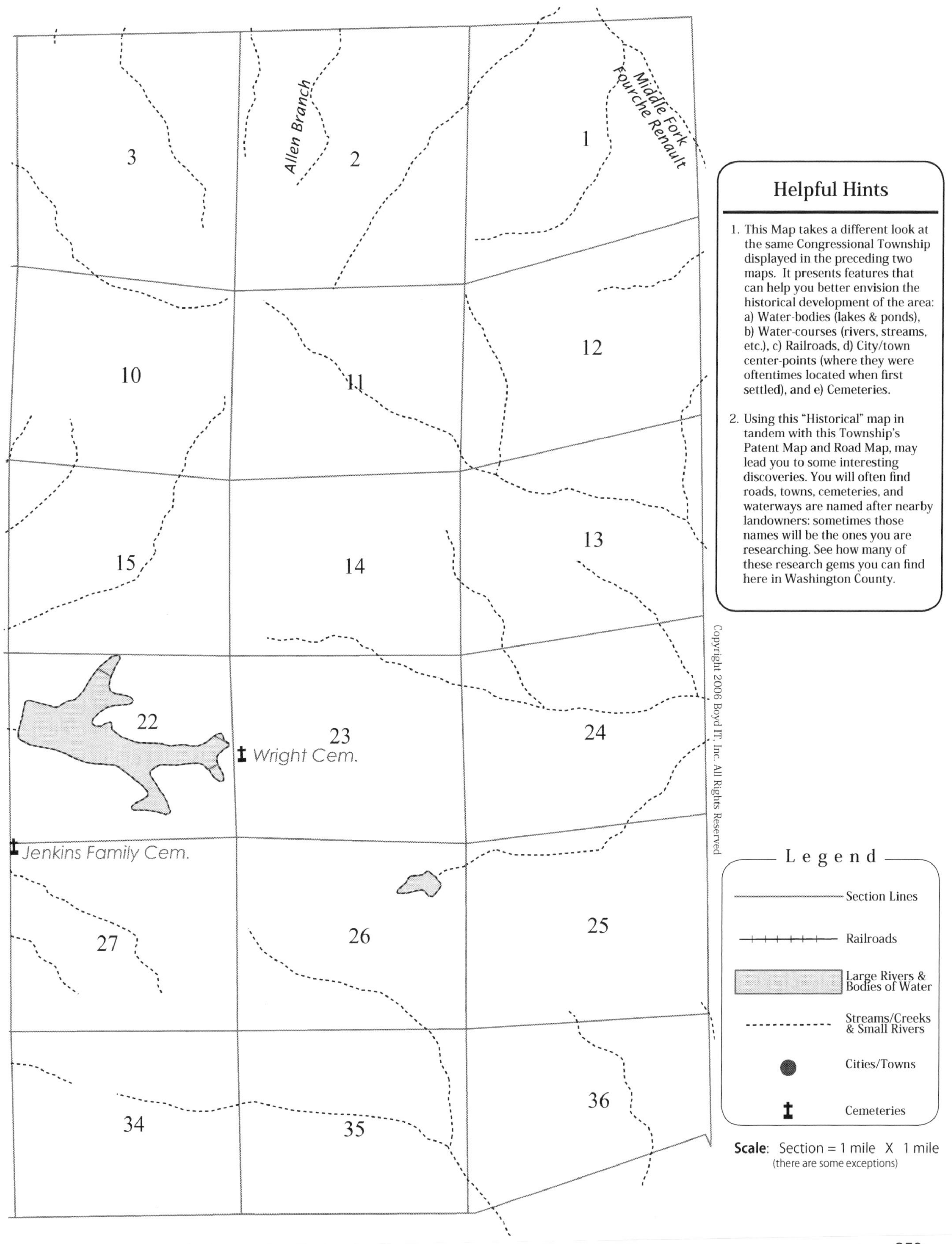

Helpful Hints

1. This Map takes a different look at the same Congressional Township displayed in the preceding two maps. It presents features that can help you better envision the historical development of the area: a) Water-bodies (lakes & ponds), b) Water-courses (rivers, streams, etc.), c) Railroads, d) City/town center-points (where they were oftentimes located when first settled), and e) Cemeteries.

2. Using this "Historical" map in tandem with this Township's Patent Map and Road Map, may lead you to some interesting discoveries. You will often find roads, towns, cemeteries, and waterways are named after nearby landowners: sometimes those names will be the ones you are researching. See how many of these research gems you can find here in Washington County.

Legend

- Section Lines
- Railroads
- Large Rivers & Bodies of Water
- Streams/Creeks & Small Rivers
- Cities/Towns
- Cemeteries

Scale: Section = 1 mile X 1 mile
(there are some exceptions)

Map Group 24: Index to Land Patents

Township 36-North Range 2-East (5th PM)

After you locate an individual in this Index, take note of the Section and Section Part then proceed to the Land Patent map on the pages immediately following. You should have no difficulty locating the corresponding parcel of land.

The "For More Info" Column will lead you to more information about the underlying Patents. See the *Legend* at right, and the "How to Use this Book" chapter, for more information.

LEGEND

"For More Info . . . " column

A = Authority (Legislative Act, See Appendix "A")
B = Block or Lot (location in Section unknown)
C = Cancelled Patent
F = Fractional Section
G = Group (Multi-Patentee Patent, see Appendix "C")
V = Overlaps another Parcel
R = Re-Issued (Parcel patented more than once)

(A & G items require you to look in the Appendixes referred to above. All other Letter-designations followed by a number require you to locate line-items in this index that possess the ID number found after the letter).

ID	Individual in Patent	Sec.	Sec. Part	Date Issued	Other Counties	For More Info . . .
3725	ALDRIDGE, William	19	E½NE	1837-11-14		A1
3642	AMONETT, John	26	NENE	1880-10-01		A1 F
3643	BELL, John B	10	SENE	1856-09-01		A1 G13
3644	" "	23	NENW	1856-09-01		A1 G13
3645	" "	23	SWNE	1856-09-01		A1 G13
3613	BENNING, Isaac	31	NE	1825-07-15		A1 F
3612	" "	30	SE	1838-08-01		A1 F
3614	BOAS, Jacob	12	SENW	1854-11-15		A1 V3621
3615	" "	12	SWNE	1854-11-15		A1
3551	BRAGG, Addison G	18	2SW	1859-01-01		A1
3600	BROLASKI, Henry L	1	2NE	1856-10-10		A1
3604	" "	10	SESE	1856-10-10		A1 R3730
3605	" "	10	W½1NW	1856-10-10		A1
3601	" "	10	E½NW	1857-04-15		A1
3602	" "	10	NENE	1857-04-15		A1
3603	" "	10	NWNW	1857-04-15		A1
3606	" "	10	W½NE	1857-04-15		A1
3607	" "	3	S½SW	1857-04-15		A1
3704	BRYAN, Robert	20	NW	1837-11-07		A1 G37
3705	" "	31	NW	1837-11-07		A1 G37 F
3703	" "	28	NW	1850-01-01		A1
3716	BRYAN, Susan	21	SESE	1875-12-01		A3
3729	BRYAN, William	28	SE	1824-05-31		A1 F
3704	" "	20	NW	1837-11-07		A1 G37
3705	" "	31	NW	1837-11-07		A1 G37 F
3728	" "	27	NW	1838-08-01		A1 F
3697	BURROWES, Michael	18	2NW	1858-04-01		A1
3712	BUXTON, Stephen A	21	E½NE	1860-03-01		A1
3713	" "	21	NESE	1860-03-01		A1
3714	" "	22	NWSW	1860-08-01		A1 R3566
3577	BYRD, Benjamin H	34	NE	1867-05-01		A1 F
3583	CAMPBELL, Colin C	11	W½NW	1837-11-14		A1 G43
3619	CAMPBELL, James	21	SESW	1850-01-01		A1
3620	" "	21	SWSE	1853-04-15		A1
3646	CAMPBELL, John C	11	E½NW	1837-11-14		A1
3647	" "	11	NE	1837-11-14		A1
3741	CAMPBELL, William D	1	SESW	1894-05-18		A3
3742	" "	12	NENW	1894-05-18		A3 V3621
3743	" "	12	W½NW	1894-05-18		A3
3718	CARSON, Thomas M	31	S½	1858-01-15		A1 F
3732	CARSON, William	18	SE	1837-11-14		A1
3733	" "	19	W½NE	1837-11-14		A1
3675	CARVER, Joseph	13	W½SW	1829-05-12		A1
3643	CASTLEMAN, Thomas D	10	SENE	1856-09-01		A1 G13
3644	" "	23	NENW	1856-09-01		A1 G13
3645	" "	23	SWNE	1856-09-01		A1 G13

ID	Individual in Patent	Sec.	Sec. Part	Date Issued	Other Counties	For More Info . . .
3648	CHANDLER, John	29	SWNE	1841-12-10		A1
3584	CHAPPEL, Edward	5	E½1SW	1859-09-01		A1
3585	" "	5	N½SE	1859-09-01		A1
3586	" "	5	NESW	1859-09-01		A1
3587	" "	5	W½1NE	1859-09-01		A1
3628	CLARKSON, James L	4	1NE	1860-08-01		A1 G66
3630	" "	4	E½2NE	1860-08-01		A1 G66
3627	" "	3	W½1NW	1864-03-10		A1 G66
3629	" "	4	1NW	1864-03-10		A1 G66
3631	" "	4	N½SE	1865-06-10		A1 G66
3632	" "	5	SESW	1866-06-01		A1 G66
3633	" "	5	SWSE	1866-06-01		A1 G66
3634	" "	8	N½SE	1866-06-01		A1 G66
3635	" "	8	SWSE	1866-06-01		A1 G66
3636	" "	9	N½SW	1866-06-01		A1 G66
3637	" "	9	SWNE	1866-06-01		A1 G66
3638	" "	9	W½SE	1866-06-01		A1 G66
3676	CLARKSON, Joseph G	5	3NW	1869-07-01		A1 G67
3677	" "	6	3NE	1869-07-01		A1 G67
3678	" "	8	SWSW	1869-07-01		A1 G67
3740	COLE, William	26	SWNE	1842-08-01		A1 F
3739	" "	26	N½NE	1853-04-15		A1 F
3737	" "	23	W½NW	1856-09-01		A1
3738	" "	23	W½SW	1856-09-01		A1
3735	" "	22	SESE	1858-12-01		A1
3736	" "	23	SESW	1858-12-01		A1
3734	" "	22	NESE	1861-02-09		A1
3751	COLEMAN, Wilson	14	SWSE	1862-12-10		A1
3752	" "	23	NWNE	1862-12-10		A1
3726	COWAN, William B	12	SE	1837-11-07		A1
3681	DAVIS, Juda	20	SE	1850-01-01		A1
3686	DAVIS, Luke	28	SW	1834-11-04		A1
3689	DAVIS, Luke H	21	SWSW	1850-01-01		A1
3690	" "	29	NE	1850-01-01		A1 F
3687	" "	20	NENE	1856-10-10		A1
3688	" "	20	W½NE	1856-10-10		A1
3744	DAVIS, William	20	E½SW	1837-11-07		A1 V3723
3745	" "	20	NWSW	1837-11-07		A1
3582	DELAFIELD, Clarence	18	N½1SW	1858-04-01		A1
3591	DESLOGE, Firmin	20	SWSW	1854-11-15		A1
3592	" "	29	NW	1854-11-15		A1 F
3573	DUNKLIN, Anthony	22	NESW	1884-02-15		A3
3706	EDMONDS, Samuel	24	W½NW	1829-05-12		A1 G86
3583	EVANS, James S	11	W½NW	1837-11-14		A1 G43
3649	EVANS, John	10	E½SW	1857-10-30		A1
3650	" "	10	SWSW	1866-09-01		A1
3651	EVENS, John	14	W½NW	1845-10-27		A1 G100
3652	" "	14	W½SW	1845-10-27		A1 G100
3653	" "	15	E½NE	1845-10-27		A1 G100
3654	" "	15	E½SW	1845-10-27		A1 G100
3655	" "	15	SE	1845-10-27		A1 G100
3656	" "	15	W½NE	1845-10-27		A1 G100
3746	EVENS, William H	10	NWSE	1901-06-29		A1
3747	" "	10	SWNW	1901-06-29		A1
3748	" "	9	SENE	1902-09-02		A1
3622	FARQUHAR, James	13	NW	1825-07-15		A1
3621	" "	12	E½NW	1837-11-07		A1 V3614, 3742
3663	FARRIS, John J	13	NESE	1854-11-15		A1
3669	FARRIS, John W	13	S½NE	1866-09-01		A1
3670	" "	24	NENW	1866-09-01		A1
3671	FARRISS, John W	13	E½SW	1856-09-01		A1 F
3672	" "	13	NENW	1856-09-01		A1 F
3673	" "	13	W½NE	1856-09-01		A1 F
3699	FICKES, Morgan	2	E½1NW	1856-09-01		A1
3616	FISHER, Jacob	21	W½NW	1825-07-15		A1 G104
3696	FRISSELL, Mason	22	S½SW	1854-11-15		A1
3717	GARVIN, Thomas	25	NW	1824-05-20		A1 F
3691	GILCHRIST, Malcolm	11	E½SE	1837-11-07		A1 G111
3692	" "	11	W½SE	1837-11-07		A1 G111
3693	" "	14	E½NE	1837-11-07		A1 G111
3707	GRAVES, Samuel	21	NENW	1859-09-10		A1
3708	" "	21	W½NE	1859-09-10		A1
3580	GRIDER, Christopher	29	NESW	1841-12-10		A1

ID	Individual in Patent	Sec.	Sec. Part	Date Issued	Other Counties	For More Info . . .
3581	GRIDER, Christopher (Cont'd)	29	NWSE	1841-12-10		A1
3680	HAEFNER, Joseph W	13	N½NE	1854-11-15		A1
3611	HAENSSLER, Herman A	17	NWNE	1889-05-29		A1
3608	HARPER, Henry W	5	NWSW	1906-06-21		A3
3609	" "	5	W½1NW	1906-06-21		A3
3610	" "	5	W½2NW	1906-06-21		A3
3720	HARRIS, Thomas R	29	SE	1824-05-10		A1 F
3721	" "	36	NE	1824-05-10		A1 F R3665
3719	" "	15	NWSW	1845-10-27		A1
3676	HENSON, Samuel P	5	3NW	1869-07-01		A1 G67
3677	" "	6	3NE	1869-07-01		A1 G67
3678	" "	8	SWSW	1869-07-01		A1 G67
3626	HICKERSON, James	23	E½NE	1838-08-01		A1
3597	HICKS, Henry G	4	W½2NE	1860-08-01		A1
3722	HOWE, Thomas W	13	SESE	1856-09-01		A1
3552	HUDSPETH, Ahijah W	32	NE	1824-05-10		A1 F
3553	" "	33	NW	1824-05-10		A1 F
3749	HUGHES, William	26	SE	1824-05-10		A1 F
3706	HUNT, Edward	24	W½NW	1829-05-12		A1 G86
3572	HUNTER, Andrew	36	SW	1837-01-17		A1 F
3570	" "	14	E½SE	1837-11-07		A1
3571	" "	24	SESE	1838-08-01		A1
3640	HUNTER, John A	23	NESE	1858-01-15		A1 F
3641	" "	24	SENW	1869-10-15		A1
3709	HUNTER, Samuel	27	SW	1824-05-31		A1 F
3566	HUTCHINGS, Allen S	22	NWSW	1860-08-01		A1 R3714
3567	" "	22	S½NE	1860-08-01		A1
3568	" "	22	SENW	1860-08-01		A1
3569	" "	22	SWSE	1860-08-01		A1
3660	HUTCHINGS, John	26	SW	1821-09-24		A1 F
3661	" "	33	NE	1821-09-24		A1
3662	" "	34	NW	1821-09-24		A1
3659	" "	26	S½NW	1852-01-01		A1 F
3616	IMBODEN, David	21	W½NW	1825-07-15		A1 G104
3598	JANIS, Henry	14	NWSE	1851-11-01		A1 G150
3599	" "	14	SENW	1851-11-01		A1 G150
3617	JOHNSON, James C	23	NESW	1874-06-15		A1 G153
3618	" "	23	NWSE	1874-06-15		A1 G153
3617	JOHNSON, William C	23	NESW	1874-06-15		A1 G153
3618	" "	23	NWSE	1874-06-15		A1 G153
3628	JOHNSON, William J	4	1NE	1860-08-01		A1 G66
3630	" "	4	E½2NE	1860-08-01		A1 G66
3627	" "	3	W½1NW	1864-03-10		A1 G66
3629	" "	4	1NW	1864-03-10		A1 G66
3631	" "	4	N½SE	1865-06-10		A1 G66
3632	" "	5	SESW	1866-06-01		A1 G66
3633	" "	5	SWSE	1866-06-01		A1 G66
3634	" "	8	N½SE	1866-06-01		A1 G66
3635	" "	8	SWSE	1866-06-01		A1 G66
3636	" "	9	N½SW	1866-06-01		A1 G66
3637	" "	9	SWNE	1866-06-01		A1 G66
3638	" "	9	W½SE	1866-06-01		A1 G66
3657	LINK, John F	25	N½SE	1853-12-01		A1 F
3593	LONDON, George M	6	3NW	1904-11-22		A1
3594	" "	6	W½2NE	1904-11-22		A1
3560	LUCAS, Alexander C	21	NWSW	1853-04-15		A1 G168
3556	" "	17	NWSE	1854-11-15		A1 G168
3557	" "	18	N½1NW	1854-11-15		A1 G168
3558	" "	18	NENE	1854-11-15		A1 G168
3554	" "	17	E½SE	1857-10-30		A1
3555	" "	17	SWSE	1857-10-30		A1
3559	" "	18	SENE	1857-10-30		A1 G168
3561	" "	9	NENW	1857-10-30		A1 G168
3562	" "	9	SENW	1859-04-13		A1 G168
3563	" "	9	W½NW	1859-04-13		A1 G168
3560	LUCAS, William	21	NWSW	1853-04-15		A1 G168
3556	" "	17	NWSE	1854-11-15		A1 G168
3557	" "	18	N½1NW	1854-11-15		A1 G168
3558	" "	18	NENE	1854-11-15		A1 G168
3559	" "	18	SENE	1857-10-30		A1 G168
3561	" "	9	NENW	1857-10-30		A1 G168
3562	" "	9	SENW	1859-04-13		A1 G168
3563	" "	9	W½NW	1859-04-13		A1 G168

ID	Individual in Patent	Sec.	Sec. Part	Date Issued	Other Counties	For More Info . . .
3684	MACKENZIE, Kenneth	12	W½SW	1854-11-15		A1
3750	MARTIN, William	10	NESE	1862-05-15		A1
3731	MARTIN, William C	3	SESE	1865-06-10		A1
3730	" "	10	SESE	1867-05-01		A1 R3604
3598	MATHEWS, Ezekiel C	14	NWSE	1851-11-01		A1 G150
3599	" "	14	SENW	1851-11-01		A1 G150
3683	MAXWELL, Katharine	30	S½SW	1838-08-01		A1 F
3664	MCCAUSLAND, John	36	N½NW	1859-09-01		A1
3665	" "	36	NE	1859-09-01		A1 R3721
3666	" "	36	NESW	1859-09-01		A1
3667	" "	36	SENW	1859-09-01		A1
3727	MCGREW, William B	22	SWNW	1888-12-08		A3
3596	MOREL, Hagan And	15	NW	1825-07-15		A1
3698	OBUCHON, Morelle	3	N½NE	1838-08-01		A1
3724	PEARSON, Wesley R	6	E½2NE	1875-05-15		A1
3639	PEERY, Jane	25	N½NW	1835-02-10		A1
3691	RELFE, James H	11	E½SE	1837-11-07		A1 G111
3623	" "	11	E½SW	1837-11-07		A1
3692	" "	11	W½SE	1837-11-07		A1 G111
3624	" "	11	W½SW	1837-11-07		A1
3693	" "	14	E½NE	1837-11-07		A1 G111
3625	" "	2	SW	1837-11-14		A1
3679	REYBURN, Joseph N	19	N½SW	1837-11-07		A1
3575	ROBINSON, Archibald	28	W½NE	1824-05-01		A1
3574	" "	28	E½NE	1824-05-31		A1
3576	" "	35	NW	1859-09-01		A1 F
3668	ROBINSON, John T	5	SWSW	1857-10-30		A1
3702	ROBINSON, Preston M	23	S½SE	1860-08-01		A1
3583	ROLFE, James H	11	W½NW	1837-11-14		A1 G43
3694	RUGGLES, Martin	14	W½NE	1821-09-24		A1
3695	" "	24	W½SW	1821-09-24		A1
3588	SIMONS, Eli L	6	1NE	1875-11-01		A3
3595	SIMPSON, George	14	NENW	1850-01-01		A1
3598	" "	14	NWSE	1851-11-01		A1 G150
3599	" "	14	SENW	1851-11-01		A1 G150
3658	SLOAN, John H	23	SENW	1859-09-01		A1 G209
3658	SLOAN, Thomas J	23	SENW	1859-09-01		A1 G209
3579	SMITH, Charles D	7	2SW	1869-07-01		A1
3578	" "	19	SESW	1869-10-15		A1
3682	SPENCER, Julius	14	E½SW	1867-05-01		A1
3715	THOMPSON, Stephen	10	E½NE	1852-01-01		A1 F
3564	TROXELL, Alexander	12	N½NE	1869-07-01		A1
3565	" "	12	SENE	1869-07-01		A1
3685	TUCKER, Lewis	25	SWSW	1856-01-03		A1 F
3589	WALLEN, Elisha	2	NESE	1858-01-15		A1 G221
3590	" "	2	SWSE	1858-04-01		A1 G221
3589	WALLEN, Nelson	2	NESE	1858-01-15		A1 G221
3590	" "	2	SWSE	1858-04-01		A1 G221
3651	WALTON, Christopher	14	W½NW	1845-10-27		A1 G100
3652	" "	14	W½SW	1845-10-27		A1 G100
3653	" "	15	E½NE	1845-10-27		A1 G100
3654	" "	15	E½SW	1845-10-27		A1 G100
3655	" "	15	SE	1845-10-27		A1 G100
3656	" "	15	W½NE	1845-10-27		A1 G100
3723	WHITEHEAD, Thomas	20	NESW	1841-12-10		A1 V3744
3674	WIATT, John	1	S½SE	1854-11-15		A1
3710	WIGGER, Sidney	6	2SW	1857-10-30		A1
3711	" "	6	N½1SW	1857-10-30		A1
3701	WILLIAMS, Mortimer F	25	SWSE	1837-01-17		A1 F
3700	" "	25	SESE	1837-01-24		A1

Patent Map

T36-N R2-E
5th PM Meridian

Map Group 24

Township Statistics

Parcels Mapped	:	202
Number of Patents	:	151
Number of Individuals	:	110
Patentees Identified	:	99
Number of Surnames	:	86
Multi-Patentee Parcels	:	47
Oldest Patent Date	:	9/24/1821
Most Recent Patent	:	6/21/1906
Block/Lot Parcels	:	25
Parcels Re - Issued	:	3
Parcels that Overlap	:	5
Cities and Towns	:	1
Cemeteries	:	5

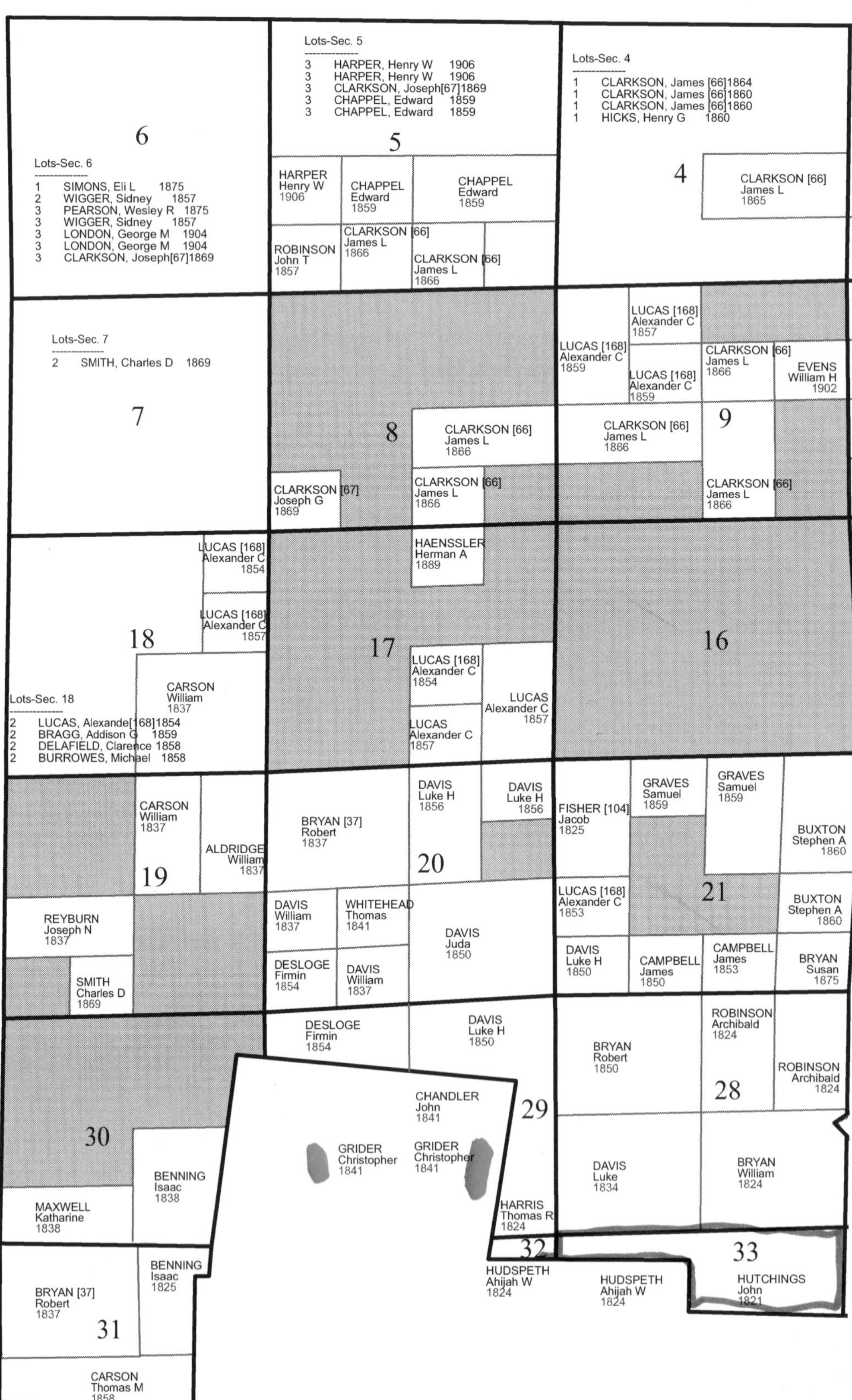

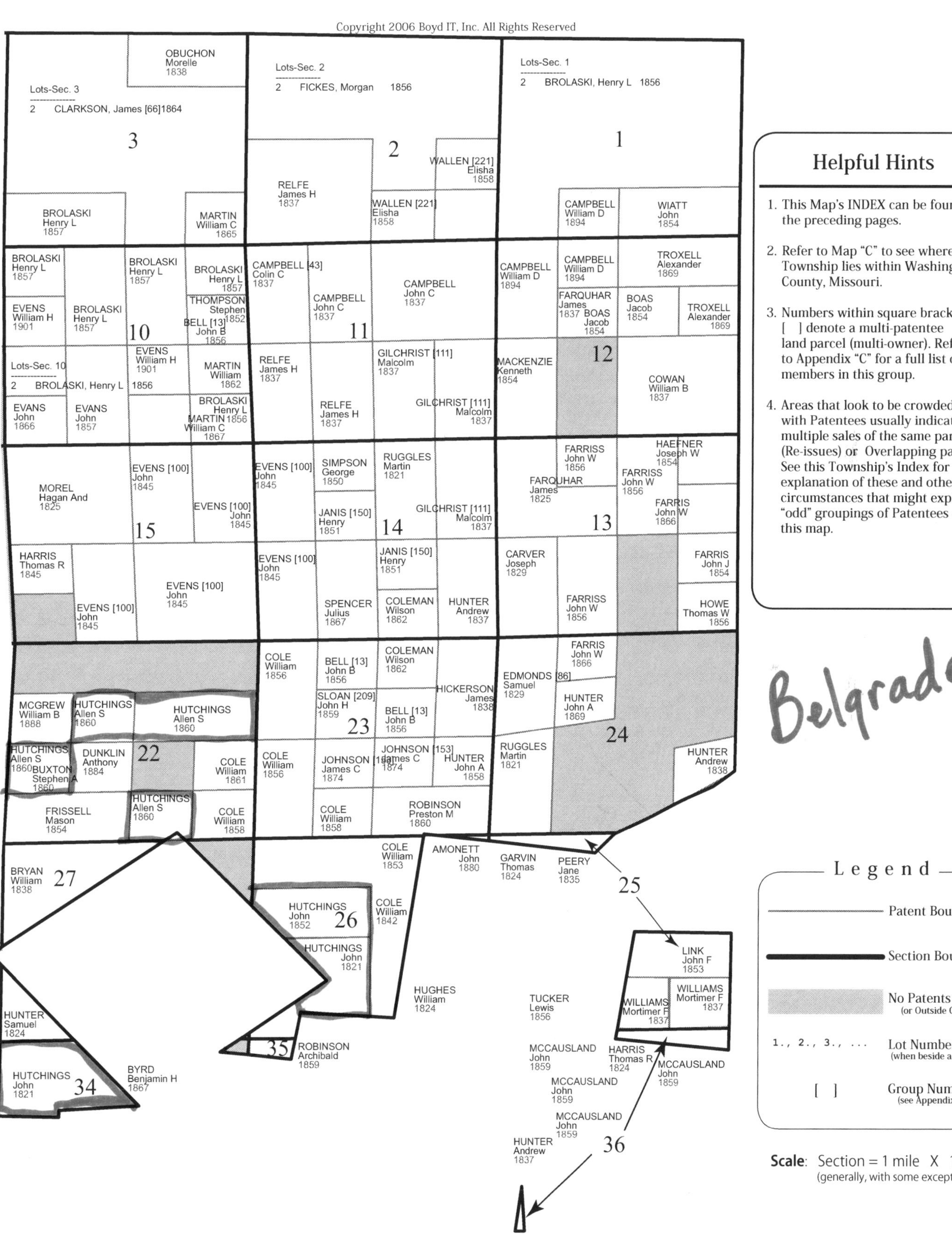

Helpful Hints

1. This Map's INDEX can be found on the preceding pages.
2. Refer to Map "C" to see where this Township lies within Washington County, Missouri.
3. Numbers within square brackets [ ] denote a multi-patentee land parcel (multi-owner). Refer to Appendix "C" for a full list of members in this group.
4. Areas that look to be crowded with Patentees usually indicate multiple sales of the same parcel (Re-issues) or Overlapping parcels. See this Township's Index for an explanation of these and other circumstances that might explain "odd" groupings of Patentees on this map.

Legend

Patent Boundary

Section Boundary

No Patents Found (or Outside County)

1., 2., 3., ... Lot Numbers (when beside a name)

[ ] Group Number (see Appendix "C")

Scale: Section = 1 mile X 1 mile (generally, with some exceptions)

Road Map

T36-N R2-E
5th PM Meridian

Map Group 24

Cities & Towns

Belgrade

Cemeteries

Bennett Bryan Cemetery
Davis Cemetery
Furnace Creek Cemetery
Belgrade Methodist Cemetery
Jane Bryan Cemetery

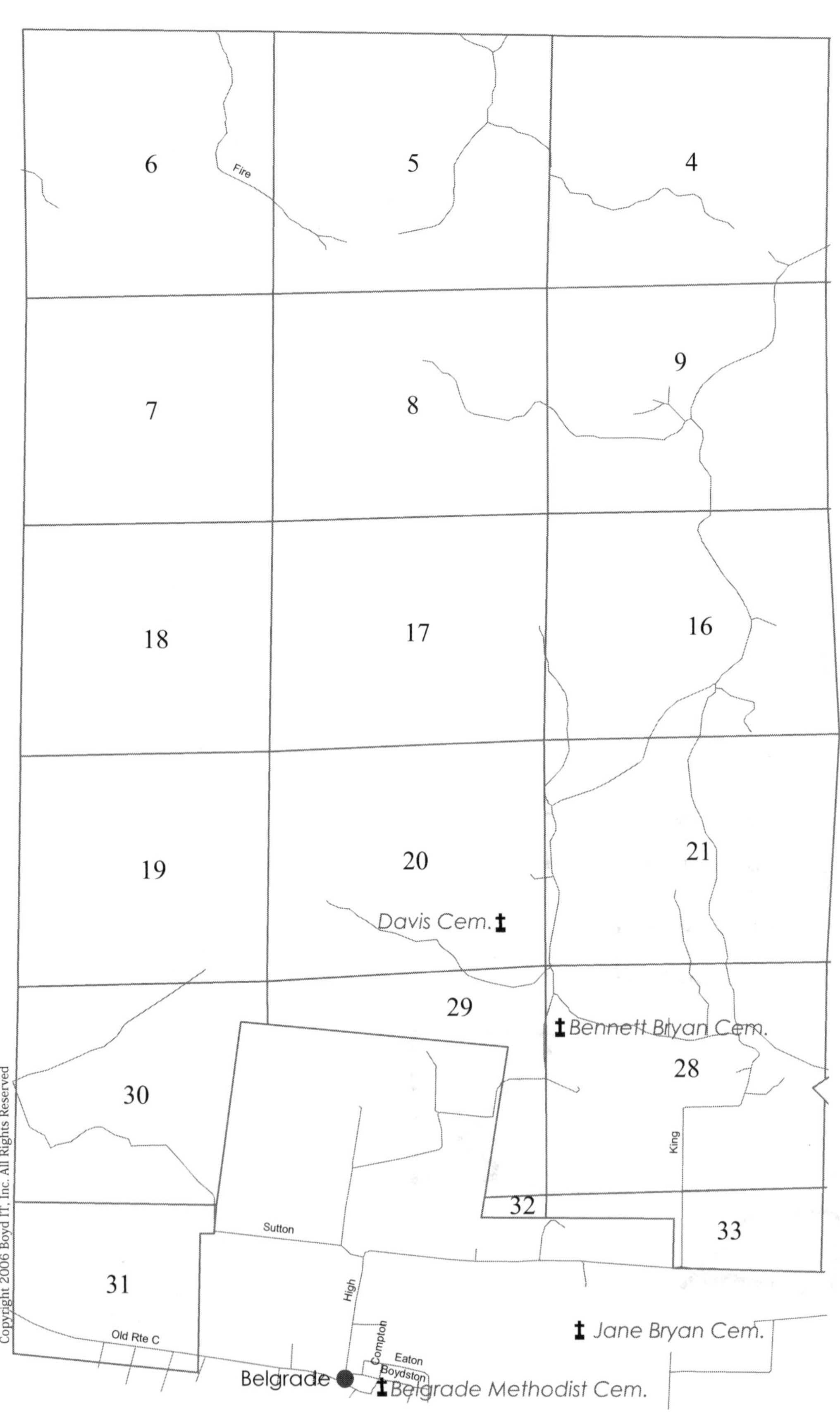

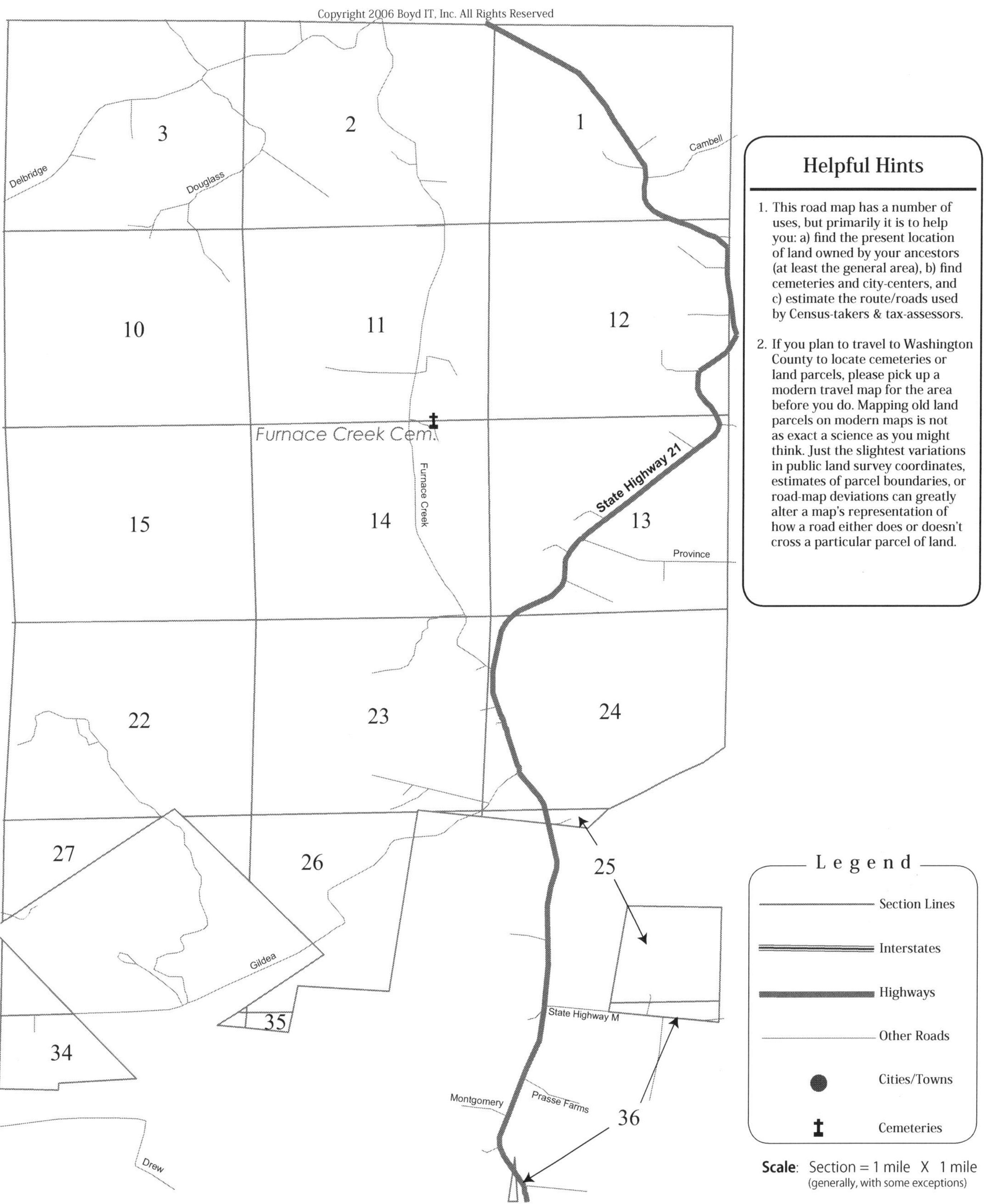

Helpful Hints

1. This road map has a number of uses, but primarily it is to help you: a) find the present location of land owned by your ancestors (at least the general area), b) find cemeteries and city-centers, and c) estimate the route/roads used by Census-takers & tax-assessors.

2. If you plan to travel to Washington County to locate cemeteries or land parcels, please pick up a modern travel map for the area before you do. Mapping old land parcels on modern maps is not as exact a science as you might think. Just the slightest variations in public land survey coordinates, estimates of parcel boundaries, or road-map deviations can greatly alter a map's representation of how a road either does or doesn't cross a particular parcel of land.

Scale: Section = 1 mile X 1 mile
(generally, with some exceptions)

Historical Map

T36-N R2-E
5th PM Meridian

Map Group 24

Cities & Towns
Belgrade

Cemeteries
Bennett Bryan Cemetery
Davis Cemetery
Furnace Creek Cemetery
Belgrade Methodist Cemetery
Jane Bryan Cemetery

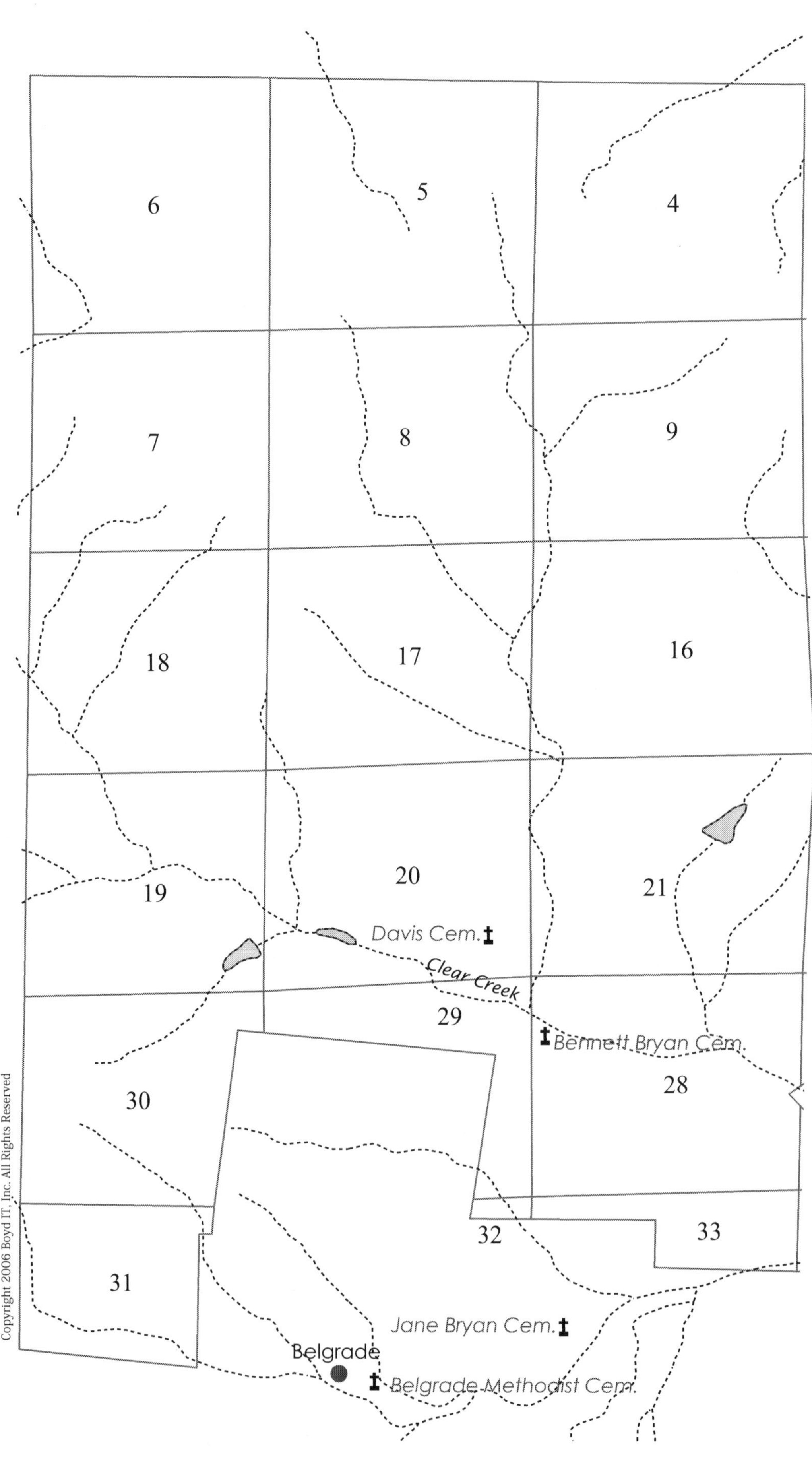

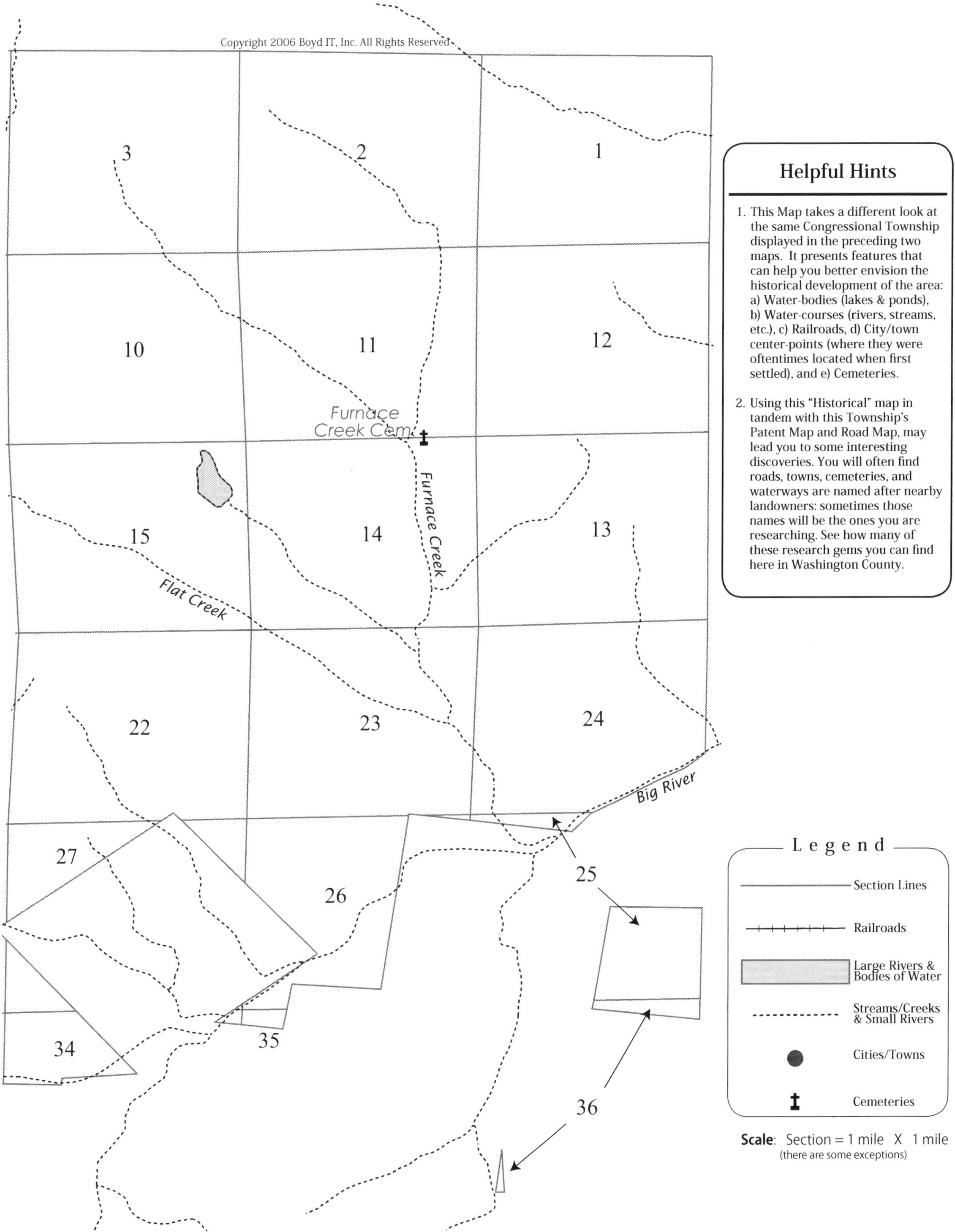

Helpful Hints

1. This Map takes a different look at the same Congressional Township displayed in the preceding two maps. It presents features that can help you better envision the historical development of the area: a) Water-bodies (lakes & ponds), b) Water-courses (rivers, streams, etc.), c) Railroads, d) City/town center-points (where they were oftentimes located when first settled), and e) Cemeteries.

2. Using this "Historical" map in tandem with this Township's Patent Map and Road Map, may lead you to some interesting discoveries. You will often find roads, towns, cemeteries, and waterways are named after nearby landowners: sometimes those names will be the ones you are researching. See how many of these research gems you can find here in Washington County.

Legend

- Section Lines
- Railroads
- Large Rivers & Bodies of Water
- Streams/Creeks & Small Rivers
- Cities/Towns
- Cemeteries

Scale: Section = 1 mile X 1 mile
(there are some exceptions)

Map Group 25: Index to Land Patents

Township 36-North Range 3-East (5th PM)

After you locate an individual in this Index, take note of the Section and Section Part then proceed to the Land Patent map on the pages immediately following. You should have no difficulty locating the corresponding parcel of land.

The "For More Info" Column will lead you to more information about the underlying Patents. See the *Legend* at right, and the "How to Use this Book" chapter, for more information.

LEGEND

"For More Info . . . " column

A = Authority (Legislative Act, See Appendix "A")
B = Block or Lot (location in Section unknown)
C = Cancelled Patent
F = Fractional Section
G = Group (Multi-Patentee Patent, see Appendix "C")
V = Overlaps another Parcel
R = Re-Issued (Parcel patented more than once)

(A & G items require you to look in the Appendixes referred to above. All other Letter-designations followed by a number require you to locate line-items in this index that possess the ID number found after the letter).

ID	Individual in Patent	Sec.	Sec. Part	Date Issued	Other Counties	For More Info . . .
3753	AGGUS, Abner	29	S½SE	1841-06-25		A1
3918	BOZARTH, Kilford	12	SWNW	1854-11-15		A1
3949	BRADLEY, Nathan	29	SENE	1877-11-10		A1
3865	BRINKER, John B	6	N½2NW	1837-11-14		A1
3832	BROLASKI, Henry L	6	N½3NW	1856-10-10		A1
3799	BROWN, Elisha	6	2NE	1838-08-01		A1 G34
3800	" "	6	E½1NE	1838-08-01		A1 G34
3873	BRYAN, John G	10	NENW	1862-04-10		A1 F
3874	" "	2	SW	1862-04-10		A1 F
3875	" "	3	SE	1862-04-10		A1 F
3799	BURDION, Reubin	6	2NE	1838-08-01		A1 G34
3800	" "	6	E½1NE	1838-08-01		A1 G34
3766	BUSH, Alexander G	25	NWNW	1837-11-14		A1
3765	" "	24	SWSW	1849-04-10		A1
3819	BUSH, George P	25	NENW	1852-01-01		A1
3820	" "	26	SENE	1852-01-01		A1
3866	CAMPBELL, John	17	NESE	1853-12-01		A1
4002	COWAN, William B	7	SW	1837-11-07		A1 G74
3785	DAVIDSON, Cosby	31	NENW	1841-06-25		A1 F
3786	" "	31	NWNW	1841-06-25		A1 F
3840	DAVIDSON, James	30	NE	1837-11-07		A1 F
4004	DAVIDSON, William	31	NWNE	1837-11-14		A1 F
3952	DAVISON, Paulina	29	NWSE	1841-08-10		A1 F
3850	DE BOW, JAMES M	17	W½NE	1837-11-07		A1
3851	" "	7	E½SE	1837-11-07		A1
3852	" "	7	W½SE	1837-11-07		A1
3983	DENTON, Stephen	25	SWSE	1854-11-15		A1
3953	DONNA, Peter C	18	N½1SW	1838-08-01		A1
3954	" "	18	N½2SW	1838-08-01		A1
3754	EATON, Abraham	9	SENE	1837-11-14		A1
3755	" "	9	W½NE	1837-11-14		A1
3757	EATON, Absalom	9	E½NW	1825-07-01		A1
3756	" "	11	W½NE	1838-08-01		A1
3919	EATON, Lazarus	10	E½SW	1837-01-24		A1
3920	" "	10	NESE	1837-11-07		A1
4006	EATON, William	10	SENW	1837-11-14		A1
3957	EDGAR, Reuben E	8	N½NE	1837-01-24		A1
3958	" "	9	W½NW	1837-01-24		A1
3956	" "	5	SESE	1841-07-01		A1
3816	EFFINGER, George M	17	NESW	1853-12-01		A1
3817	" "	17	NWSE	1853-12-01		A1
3818	" "	17	SENE	1853-12-01		A1
3849	EVANS, James L	36	SWSW	1854-11-15		A1
3857	EVANS, James S	20	NWNW	1853-12-01		A1 G90
3857	EVANS, Jesse R	20	NWNW	1853-12-01		A1 G90
3867	EVANS, John	17	E½NW	1845-06-01		A1 G95

ID	Individual in Patent	Sec.	Sec. Part	Date Issued	Other Counties	For More Info . . .
3868	EVANS, John (Cont'd)	1	SWSE	1849-04-10		A1 G96
3869	EVENS, John	3	NE2NW	1853-12-01		A1
3870	" "	6	N½2SW	1854-11-15		A1
3871	" "	6	N½3SW	1854-11-15		A1
3872	" "	6	S½3NW	1854-11-15		A1
3769	FARRIS, Anderson P	1	2NE	1848-09-01		A1 G102
3770	" "	1	3NE	1848-09-01		A1 G102
3769	FARRIS, Anthony P	1	2NE	1848-09-01		A1 G102
3770	" "	1	3NE	1848-09-01		A1 G102
3898	FARRIS, John J	18	3SW	1854-11-15		A1
3910	FARRIS, John W	19	W½NW	1866-09-01		A1 F
3763	FLEMMING, Alexander	18	S½1SW	1838-08-01		A1
3764	" "	18	S½2SW	1838-08-01		A1
3861	FRIZZLE, Jason	10	W½SE	1834-11-04		A1
3782	GELLENBECK, Casper H	34	SWNW	1871-10-20		A1
3959	GEORGE, Reyburn And	8	E½SW	1825-07-15		A1
3791	GIBSON, David	26	W½NW	1837-01-24		A1
3984	GOVRO, Stephen	1	1NE	1824-05-20		A1
3759	GREGORY, Absalom	35	NESE	1841-12-10		A1 V3761
3758	" "	25	SESE	1851-12-01		A1
3787	GREGORY, Darcus	26	W½SE	1838-08-01		A1
3788	GREGORY, Darius	26	SWNE	1837-11-14		A1
3935	GREGORY, Malachi	32	NESE	1853-04-12		A1
3923	GRINEA, Louis	2	1NW	1837-11-07		A1
3924	" "	2	W½1NE	1848-02-01		A1
3838	HAEFNER, J W	29	NW	1874-06-15		A1 F
3853	HARRINGTON, James M	18	S½NW	1859-09-01		A1
3760	HARRISON, Albert G	35	NENE	1837-03-03		A1 G127
3761	" "	35	SE	1837-03-03		A1 G127 V3759
3762	" "	35	W½NE	1837-03-03		A1 G127
3776	HAWKINS, Austin H	1	1NW	1843-04-10		A1
3778	" "	1	NWSW	1843-04-10		A1
3777	" "	1	NWSE	1848-03-01		A1
3792	HAYS, David	36	W½NW	1837-01-24		A1
3793	" "	5	W½SW	1837-01-24		A1 G128
3789	HAYS, David A	23	W½SW	1845-10-27		A1
3790	" "	25	SENW	1848-03-01		A1
3809	HAYS, Elizabeth	23	SESW	1845-10-27		A1
3839	HAYS, Jackson	36	NWSW	1841-08-10		A1
3844	HAYS, James	36	E½NW	1837-01-24		A1 V3886
3845	" "	5	E½SW	1837-01-24		A1 G129
3955	HAYS, Rachel	35	SENE	1837-03-15		A1
4010	HENDERSON, William	32	NW	1824-05-01		A1
3771	HENRY, Andrew	8	E½NW	1824-05-10		A1
3829	HICKS, Henrey	5	E½1NW	1848-09-01		A1
3830	" "	5	E½2NW	1848-09-01		A1
3887	HIGHLEY, John	14	SWNE	1853-08-01		A1
3888	" "	14	SWNW	1853-08-01		A1
3833	HORTON, Hezekiah W	35	W½NW	1837-01-24		A1 G134
3992	HOWE, Thomas W	19	E½NW	1853-12-01		A1 F
3993	" "	19	NE	1853-12-01		A1 F
3995	" "	20	SE	1853-12-01		A1 F
3996	" "	20	SWNW	1853-12-01		A1 F R3864
3994	" "	20	NE	1854-11-15		A1 F
3997	" "	29	NENE	1859-09-01		A1 F
3998	" "	29	SWNE	1859-09-01		A1 F
3767	HUGHES, Alexander	32	SWSW	1860-08-01		A1
3810	HUGHES, F M	28	SWSW	1874-11-05		A3 G141
3811	" "	33	NWNW	1874-11-05		A3 G141
3827	HUGHES, Hays	28	NENW	1860-03-01		A1
3846	HUGHES, James	28	W½NE	1825-07-15		A1
3892	HUGHES, John	27	SW	1824-05-01		A1
3893	" "	28	E½NE	1824-05-01		A1
3894	" "	28	NWNW	1837-03-15		A1
3889	" "	21	SE	1837-11-14		A1 F
3890	" "	22	SW	1837-11-14		A1 F
3891	" "	27	NW	1838-08-01		A1 F
3927	HUGHES, Mahlon	27	W½NE	1837-03-15		A1
3928	" "	27	W½SE	1837-03-15		A1
3929	" "	28	SESE	1856-01-03		A1
3931	" "	33	NENE	1856-01-03		A1
3934	" "	34	NWNW	1856-01-03		A1
3930	" "	28	SESW	1861-02-09		A1

ID	Individual in Patent	Sec.	Sec. Part	Date Issued	Other Counties	For More Info . . .
3932	HUGHES, Mahlon (Cont'd)	33	NENW	1861-02-09		A1
3933	" "	33	NWNE	1861-02-09		A1
3936	HUGHES, Mark	29	NESE	1861-02-09		A1
3810	HUGHES, Nancy E	28	SWSW	1874-11-05		A3 G141
3811	" "	33	NWNW	1874-11-05		A3 G141
3951	HUGHES, Parmelia	4	SWSW	1838-08-01		A1 G142
3961	HUGHES, Robert	14	W½SW	1824-05-01		A1 R3962
3963	" "	15	E½SE	1824-05-01		A1 R3964
3965	" "	15	W½SE	1834-11-04		A1 F
3966	" "	23	W½NE	1834-11-04		A1
3960	" "	14	E½SW	1837-03-15		A1 R3877
3962	" "	14	W½SW	1917-05-04		A1 R3961
3964	" "	15	E½SE	1917-05-04		A1 R3963
4011	HUGHES, William	29	NWNE	1842-08-01		A1 F
3999	HULL, Uriah	20	SW	1838-08-01		A1 G144 F
3774	HUNTER, Andrew	32	W½NE	1837-11-07		A1
3772	" "	19	SW	1838-08-01		A1 F
3773	" "	31	W½SW	1841-06-25		A1 F
3895	HUTCHINGS, John	31	E½SW	1841-06-25		A1 F
3896	" "	31	SENW	1841-06-25		A1 F
3897	" "	31	SWNW	1841-06-25		A1 F
3815	JAMISON, George	4	W½2NW	1837-11-14		A1
3834	JAMISON, Isaac W	3	NW2NW	1837-11-07		A1
3835	" "	4	1NW	1837-11-07		A1
3836	" "	4	E½2NW	1837-11-07		A1
3847	JAMISON, James	4	SE	1834-11-04		A1
3951	" "	4	SWSW	1838-08-01		A1 G142
3841	JAMISON, James H	4	1NE	1837-11-07		A1
3842	" "	4	2NE	1837-11-07		A1
3904	JAMISON, John	4	E½SW	1834-11-04		A1
3901	" "	3	SWSW	1841-07-01		A1
3902	" "	3	W½1NW	1841-07-01		A1
3899	" "	29	E½SW	1854-11-15		A1 F
3903	" "	32	NESW	1854-11-15		A1
3900	" "	3	SESW	1856-09-01		A1 F
3951	JAMISON, William	4	SWSW	1838-08-01		A1 G142
3905	JIMMERSON, John	7	E½NE	1825-07-15		A1
3760	JONES, Myers F	35	NENE	1837-03-03		A1 G127
3761	" "	35	SE	1837-03-03		A1 G127 V3759
3762	" "	35	W½NE	1837-03-03		A1 G127
3947	" "	26	E½SE	1837-10-09		A1 G157
3948	" "	26	E½SW	1837-10-09		A1 G157
3990	JORDAN, Thomas	1	SESE	1849-04-10		A1
3991	" "	12	NENE	1849-04-10		A1
3848	KINKAID, James	33	SESE	1837-11-14		A1
3783	KIRKPATRICK, Catharine	17	W½SW	1837-01-24		A1
3784	" "	18	E½SE	1837-01-24		A1
3794	KIRKPATRICK, David	17	SESW	1850-01-01		A1
3795	" "	20	NENW	1853-12-01		A1
3796	" "	20	SENW	1859-09-01		A1
3775	LATUNIO, Augustus	1	NESE	1837-11-14		A1
3989	LIGHTFOOT, Thomas J	28	W½SE	1877-01-15		A3
3760	LINN, Lewis F	35	NENE	1837-03-03		A1 G127
3761	" "	35	SE	1837-03-03		A1 G127 V3759
3762	" "	35	W½NE	1837-03-03		A1 G127
3854	MACKAY, James	33	S½NW	1856-06-03		A2
3855	" "	33	SWSE	1856-06-03		A2
4007	MAURICE, William H	28	NWSW	1866-06-01		A1 G177
4008	" "	28	S½NW	1866-06-01		A1 G177
4009	" "	8	SENE	1866-06-01		A1 G177
3913	MCCORMICK, Joseph	15	E½NW	1824-05-10		A1
3914	" "	15	SW	1837-11-07		A1 F
3916	" "	15	W½NW	1837-11-07		A1
3915	" "	15	W½NE	1838-08-01		A1
3974	MCCREARY, Samuel	2	NESE	1837-11-14		A1
3973	" "	11	E½NE	1838-08-01		A1
3975	" "	2	SESE	1845-10-27		A1
3862	MCILVAINE, Jesse H	9	E½SW	1854-11-15		A1
3999	MONTGOMERY, Andrew	20	SW	1838-08-01		A1 G144 F
3906	PERRY, John	5	2NE	1896-06-24		A1 G201
3907	" "	5	W½NW	1896-06-24		A1 G201
3967	PROFFETT, Robert R	36	NWSE	1857-10-30		A1
3968	PROFIT, Robert R	36	E½SW	1837-01-24		A1

ID	Individual in Patent	Sec.	Sec. Part	Date Issued	Other Counties	For More Info . . .
3797	PROFITT, David W	25	S½SW	1837-03-15		A1
3969	PROFITT, Robert R	36	SWSE	1837-11-07		A1
3917	PROVENCE, Joseph	3	S½2NW	1858-04-01		A1
3909	RATLEY, John	32	SESW	1883-06-30		A3
3937	REID, Matthew P	6	1SW	1859-09-01		A1
3938	" "	6	S½2SW	1859-09-01		A1
3939	" "	6	S½3SW	1859-09-01		A1
3760	RELFE, James H	35	NENE	1837-03-03		A1 G127
3761	" "	35	SE	1837-03-03		A1 G127 V3759
3762	" "	35	W½NE	1837-03-03		A1 G127
3947	" "	26	E½SE	1837-10-09		A1 G157
3948	" "	26	E½SW	1837-10-09		A1 G157
3843	" "	31	SE	1837-11-07		A1 G204 F
3856	ROBINSON, James	8	SWNE	1837-11-07		A1
3876	SCOTT, John G	13	NW	1853-12-01		A1
3877	" "	14	E½SW	1853-12-01		A1 C R3960
3878	" "	14	NESE	1853-12-01		A1 C R3977
3880	" "	21	NE	1853-12-01		A1 F
3881	" "	23	NENE	1853-12-01		A1 C R3980
3882	" "	23	NENW	1853-12-01		A1
3884	" "	32	SESE	1853-12-01		A1
3885	" "	32	W½SE	1853-12-01		A1
3886	" "	36	NENW	1853-12-01		A1 V3844
3883	" "	24	SWNW	1854-11-15		A1
3879	" "	17	NENE	1859-01-01		A1
3921	SELF, Lemuel	10	SWNW	1837-11-14		A1 R3922
3922	" "	10	SWNW	1837-11-14		A1 R3921
3981	SELF, Samuel	9	SE	1837-01-24		A1
3978	" "	15	E½NE	1837-11-07		A1
3979	" "	22	NE	1837-11-14		A1 F
3980	" "	23	NENE	1837-11-14		A1 R3881
3977	" "	14	NESE	1843-04-10		A1 R3878
3768	SLOAN, Amos	27	E½NW	1824-05-10		A1
3812	SLOAN, Fergues	22	SE	1834-11-04		A1 F
3813	" "	23	SWSE	1850-01-01		A1
3971	SLOAN, Robert	24	SE	1837-01-24		A1
3970	" "	23	SESE	1837-11-14		A1
3972	" "	24	SWNE	1850-01-01		A1
3985	SLOAN, Theodore	13	NESW	1853-12-01		A1
3986	SLOAN, Thomas I	26	N½NE	1837-11-14		A1
3987	SLOANE, Thomas I	23	W½NW	1825-07-15		A1 R3988
3988	" "	23	W½NW	1917-05-04		A1 R3987
3821	SMITH, George R	1	NESW	1837-11-14		A1
3779	STEVENSON, Benjamin	6	1NW	1837-11-14		A1
3780	" "	6	S½2NW	1837-11-14		A1
3781	" "	6	W½1NE	1837-11-14		A1
3814	STOLLE, George F	8	W½SE	1825-07-15		A1
3976	STONE, Samuel P	10	W½SW	1837-01-24		A1
3769	TAYLOR, John	1	2NE	1848-09-01		A1 G102
3770	" "	1	3NE	1848-09-01		A1 G102
3908	TAYLOR, John R	18	SESE	1857-04-15		A1 F
4002	THOMAS, Moses	7	SW	1837-11-07		A1 G74
3843	THOMPSON, Jane A	31	SE	1837-11-07		A1 G204 F
3860	" "	32	NWSW	1837-11-07		A1
3982	THOMPSON, Seaborn	5	E½1NE	1854-11-15		A1
4012	THOMPSON, William	34	NWSE	1856-06-16		A1
3831	TRIPP, Henry D	3	NE2NE	1841-08-10		A1
3926	TULLOCK, Magness	25	NWNE	1837-11-07		A1
3925	" "	25	NENE	1837-11-14		A1
3837	VALLE, J B	29	W½NW	1825-12-01		A1
3803	WALLEN, Elisha	34	E½SE	1829-05-12		A1
3833	" "	35	W½NW	1837-01-24		A1 G134
3845	" "	5	E½SW	1837-01-24		A1 G129
3793	" "	5	W½SW	1837-01-24		A1 G128
3802	" "	27	E½SE	1837-03-15		A1
3805	" "	35	E½NW	1837-03-15		A1
3801	" "	26	W½SW	1837-11-07		A1
3807	" "	5	NWSE	1837-11-14		A1
3808	" "	8	W½NW	1837-11-14		A1
3806	" "	35	SW	1841-06-25		A1
3804	" "	34	SENW	1859-01-01		A1
3911	WALLEN, John	5	W½1NE	1837-11-14		A1
3950	WALLEN, Nelson	5	SWSE	1841-07-01		A1

ID	Individual in Patent	Sec.	Sec. Part	Date Issued	Other Counties	For More Info . . .
3867	WALTON, Christopher	17	E½NW	1845-06-01		A1 G95
3822	WALTON, George	3	NW2NE	1841-08-10		A1
4007	WARE, Joseph E	28	NWSW	1866-06-01		A1 G177
4008	" "	28	S½NW	1866-06-01		A1 G177
4009	" "	8	SENE	1866-06-01		A1 G177
3798	WEIGER, David	1	2NW	1824-05-01		A1
3868	WESTOVER, George T	1	SWSE	1849-04-10		A1 G96
3912	WHAYLEY, John	2	W½2NE	1837-01-24		A1
3906	WHEALEY, William	5	2NE	1896-06-24		A1 G201
3907	" "	5	W½NW	1896-06-24		A1 G201
3858	WIATT, James	9	NENE	1854-11-15		A1
3859	WILDMAN, James	2	E½2NE	1841-08-10		A1
3828	WILLIAMS, Helen	30	SWSW	1841-06-25		A1 F
3944	WILLIAMS, Mortimer F	30	SWSE	1854-11-15		A1 F
3941	" "	30	NESW	1856-10-10		A1 F
3942	" "	30	NWSE	1856-10-10		A1 F
3946	" "	31	S½NE	1856-10-10		A1 F
3943	" "	30	SESE	1861-08-01		A1 F
3945	" "	31	NENE	1861-08-01		A1
3940	" "	29	SWSW	1866-09-01		A1 F
4003	WOLLIN, William B	34	NE	1824-05-01		A1
3826	WOOD, Gideon	26	SENW	1841-12-10		A1
3823	" "	25	NESW	1851-11-01		A1
3825	" "	25	SWNW	1851-11-01		A1
3824	" "	25	NWSW	1854-11-15		A1
4001	WOOD, Wiley	7	SWNE	1851-11-01		A1
4000	" "	7	NWNE	1853-08-01		A1
4005	WORTHAM, William E	18	NE	1859-09-01		A1
3863	ZOLMAN, Joel Z	20	NWSE	1838-08-01		A1
3864	" "	20	SWNW	1838-08-01		A1 R3996

Patent Map

T36-N R3-E
5th PM Meridian

Map Group 25

Township Statistics

Parcels Mapped	:	260
Number of Patents	:	215
Number of Individuals	:	147
Patentees Identified	:	137
Number of Surnames	:	97
Multi-Patentee Parcels	:	26
Oldest Patent Date	:	5/1/1824
Most Recent Patent	:	5/4/1917
Block/Lot Parcels	:	43
Parcels Re - Issued	:	8
Parcels that Overlap	:	4
Cities and Towns	:	1
Cemeteries	:	3

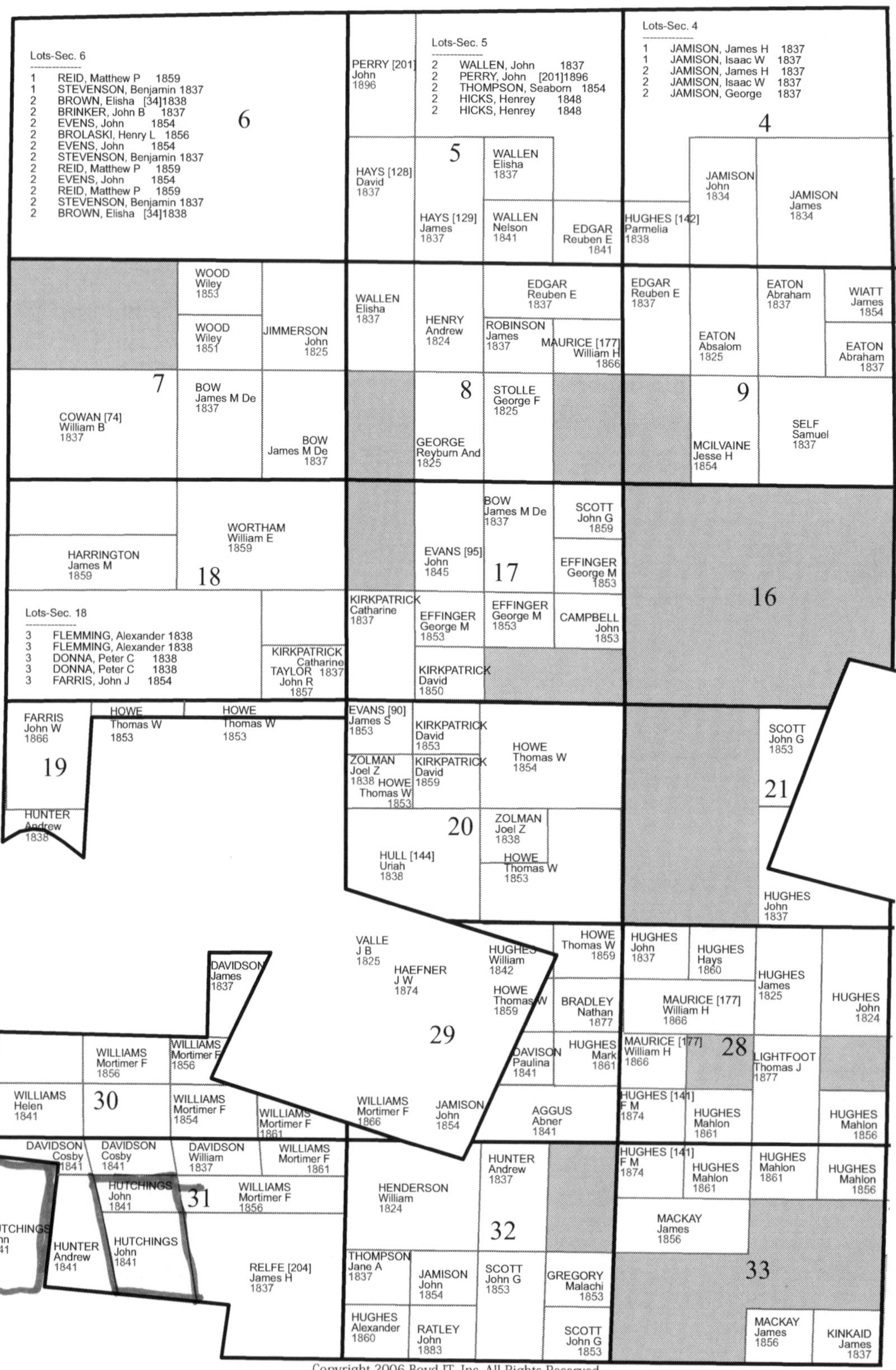

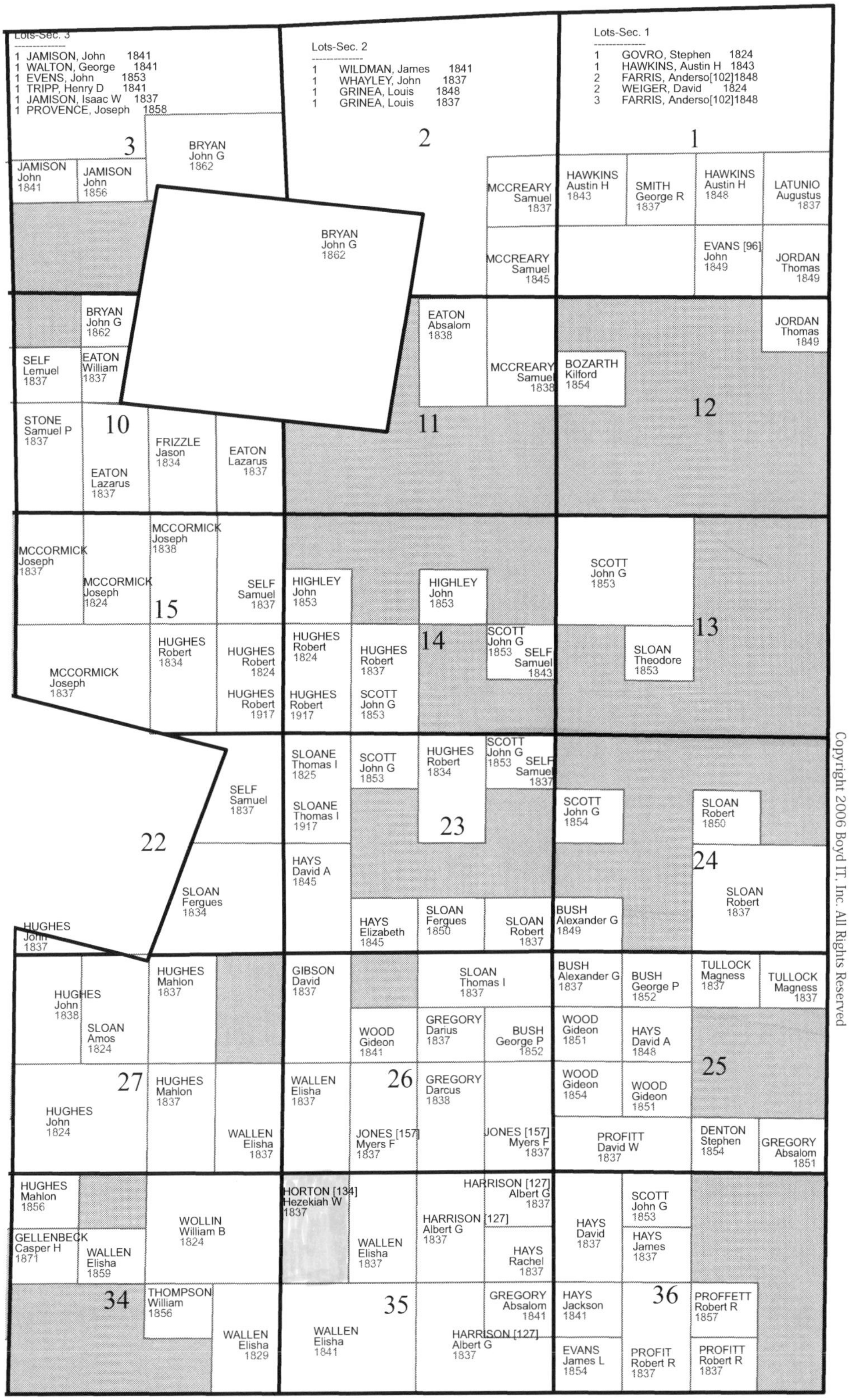

Lots-Sec. 3

1 JAMISON, John 1841
1 WALTON, George 1841
1 EVENS, John 1853
1 TRIPP, Henry D 1841
1 JAMISON, Isaac W 1837
1 PROVENCE, Joseph 1858

Lots-Sec. 2

1 WILDMAN, James 1841
1 WHAYLEY, John 1837
1 GRINEA, Louis 1848
1 GRINEA, Louis 1837

Lots-Sec. 1

1 GOVRO, Stephen 1824
1 HAWKINS, Austin H 1843
2 FARRIS, Anderso[102]1848
2 WEIGER, David 1824
3 FARRIS, Anderso[102]1848

3
JAMISON John 1841
JAMISON John 1856
BRYAN John G 1862

2
BRYAN John G 1862
MCCREARY Samuel 1837
MCCREARY Samuel 1845

1
HAWKINS Austin H 1843
SMITH George R 1837
HAWKINS Austin H 1848
LATUNIO Augustus 1837
EVANS [96] John 1849
JORDAN Thomas 1849

10
BRYAN John G 1862
SELF Lemuel 1837
EATON William 1837
STONE Samuel P 1837
FRIZZLE Jason 1834
EATON Lazarus 1837
EATON Lazarus 1837

11
EATON Absalom 1838
MCCREARY Samuel 1838

12
JORDAN Thomas 1849
BOZARTH Kilford 1854

15
MCCORMICK Joseph 1837
MCCORMICK Joseph 1838
MCCORMICK Joseph 1824
SELF Samuel 1837
MCCORMICK Joseph 1837
HUGHES Robert 1834
HUGHES Robert 1824
HUGHES Robert 1917

14
HIGHLEY John 1853
HIGHLEY John 1853
HUGHES Robert 1824
HUGHES Robert 1837
SCOTT John G 1853
SELF Samuel 1843
HUGHES Robert 1917
SCOTT John G 1853

13
SCOTT John G 1853
SLOAN Theodore 1853

22
SELF Samuel 1837
SLOAN Fergues 1834
HUGHES John 1837

23
SLOANE Thomas I 1825
SCOTT John G 1853
HUGHES Robert 1834
SCOTT John G 1853
SELF Samuel 1837
SLOANE Thomas I 1917
HAYS David A 1845
HAYS Elizabeth 1845
SLOAN Fergues 1850
SLOAN Robert 1837

24
SCOTT John G 1854
SLOAN Robert 1850
SLOAN Robert 1837
BUSH Alexander G 1849

27
HUGHES John 1838
SLOAN Amos 1824
HUGHES Mahlon 1837
HUGHES Mahlon 1837
HUGHES John 1824
WALLEN Elisha 1837

26
GIBSON David 1837
SLOAN Thomas I 1837
WOOD Gideon 1841
GREGORY Darius 1837
BUSH George P 1852
WALLEN Elisha 1837
GREGORY Darcus 1838
JONES [157] Myers F 1837
JONES [157] Myers F 1837

25
BUSH Alexander G 1837
BUSH George P 1852
TULLOCK Magness 1837
TULLOCK Magness 1837
WOOD Gideon 1851
HAYS David A 1848
WOOD Gideon 1854
WOOD Gideon 1851
PROFITT David W 1837
DENTON Stephen 1854
GREGORY Absalom 1851

34
HUGHES Mahlon 1856
WOLLIN William B 1824
GELLENBECK Casper H 1871
WALLEN Elisha 1859
THOMPSON William 1856
WALLEN Elisha 1829

35
HORTON [134] Hezekiah W 1837
WALLEN Elisha 1837
HARRISON [127] Albert G 1837
HARRISON [127] Albert G 1837
HAYS Rachel 1837
GREGORY Absalom 1841
WALLEN Elisha 1841
HARRISON [127] Albert G 1837

36
HAYS David 1837
SCOTT John G 1853
HAYS James 1837
HAYS Jackson 1841
PROFFETT Robert R 1857
EVANS James L 1854
PROFIT Robert R 1837
PROFITT Robert R 1837

Helpful Hints

1. This Map's INDEX can be found on the preceding pages.
2. Refer to Map "C" to see where this Township lies within Washington County, Missouri.
3. Numbers within square brackets [ ] denote a multi-patentee land parcel (multi-owner). Refer to Appendix "C" for a full list of members in this group.
4. Areas that look to be crowded with Patentees usually indicate multiple sales of the same parcel (Re-issues) or Overlapping parcels. See this Township's Index for an explanation of these and other circumstances that might explain "odd" groupings of Patentees on this map.

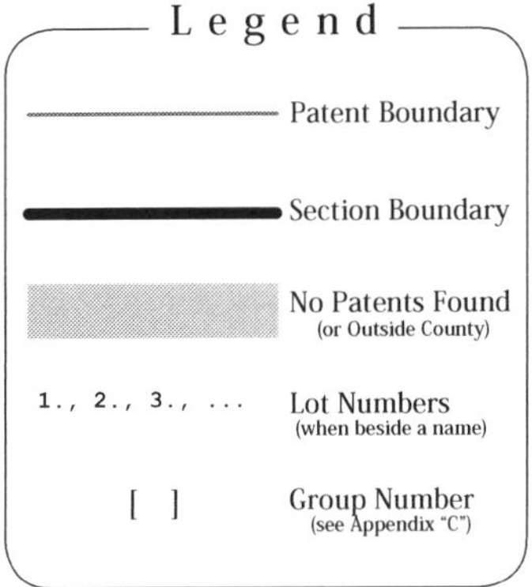

Scale: Section = 1 mile X 1 mile (generally, with some exceptions)

Road Map

T36-N R3-E
5th PM Meridian

Map Group 25

Cities & Towns

Irondale

Cemeteries

Big River Cemetery
Hickory Grove Cemetery
Hughes Cemetery

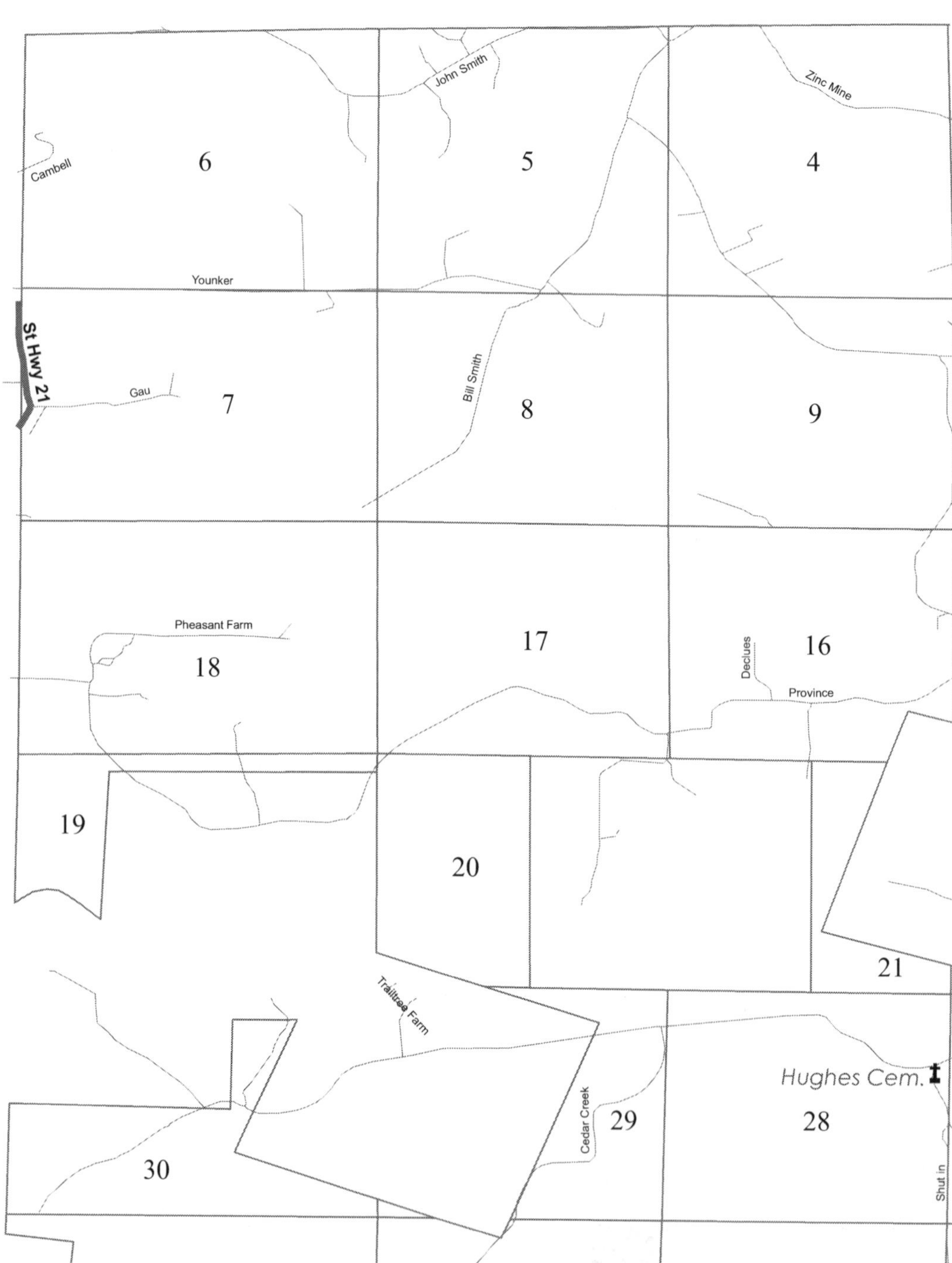

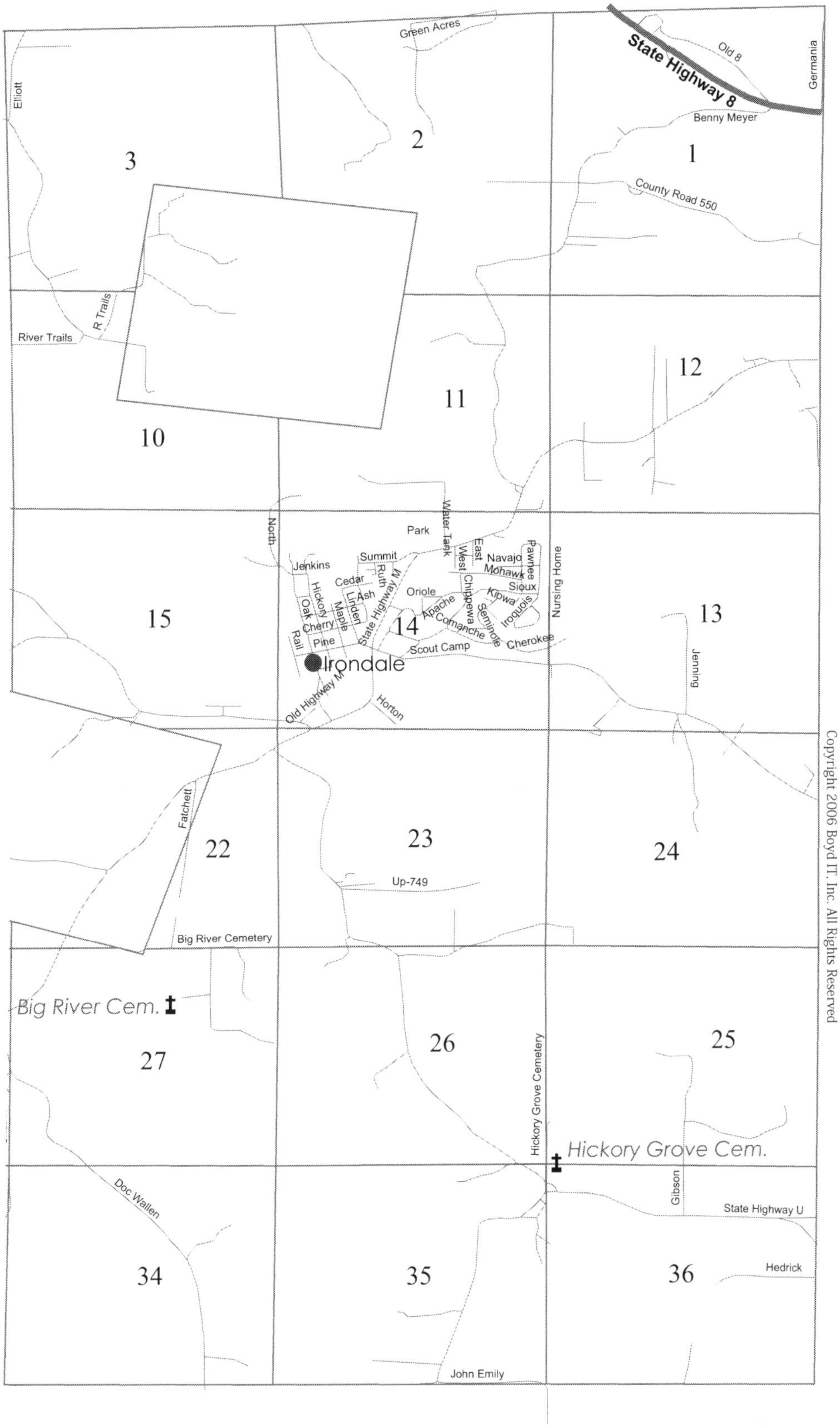

Green Acres
State Highway 8
Old 8
Germania
Elliott
Benny Meyer
3
2
1
County Road 550
R Trails
River Trails
12
11
10
Water Tank
North
Park
Jenkins
Summit
Cedar
Ruth
Ash
Hickory
Oak
Maple
Linden
Cherry
Pine
Rail
State Highway M
Oriole
Apache
Comanche
Chippewa
West
East
Navajo
Mohawk
Pawnee
Sioux
Kiowa
Seminole
Iroquois
Cherokee
Nursing Home
Scout Camp
15
14
13
Jenning
Irondale
Old Highway M
Horton

Fatchett
22
23
24
Up-749
Big River Cemetery
Big River Cem.
27
26
25
Hickory Grove Cemetery
Hickory Grove Cem.
Doc Wallen
Gibson
State Highway U
34
35
36
Hedrick
John Emily

Helpful Hints

1. This road map has a number of uses, but primarily it is to help you: a) find the present location of land owned by your ancestors (at least the general area), b) find cemeteries and city-centers, and c) estimate the route/roads used by Census-takers & tax-assessors.

2. If you plan to travel to Washington County to locate cemeteries or land parcels, please pick up a modern travel map for the area before you do. Mapping old land parcels on modern maps is not as exact a science as you might think. Just the slightest variations in public land survey coordinates, estimates of parcel boundaries, or road-map deviations can greatly alter a map's representation of how a road either does or doesn't cross a particular parcel of land.

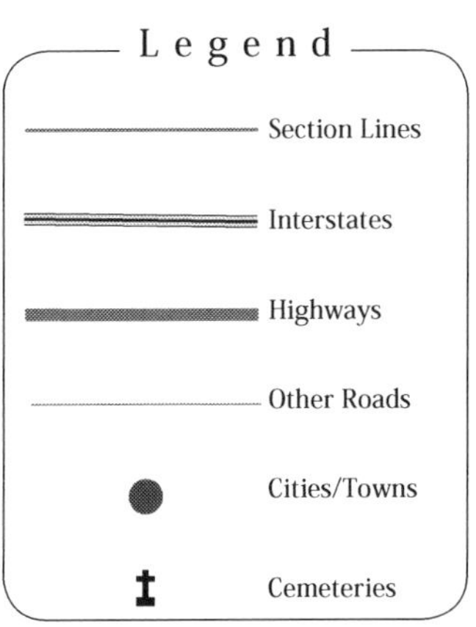

Scale: Section = 1 mile X 1 mile
(generally, with some exceptions)

Historical Map

T36-N R3-E
5th PM Meridian

Map Group 25

Cities & Towns
Irondale

Cemeteries
Big River Cemetery
Hickory Grove Cemetery
Hughes Cemetery

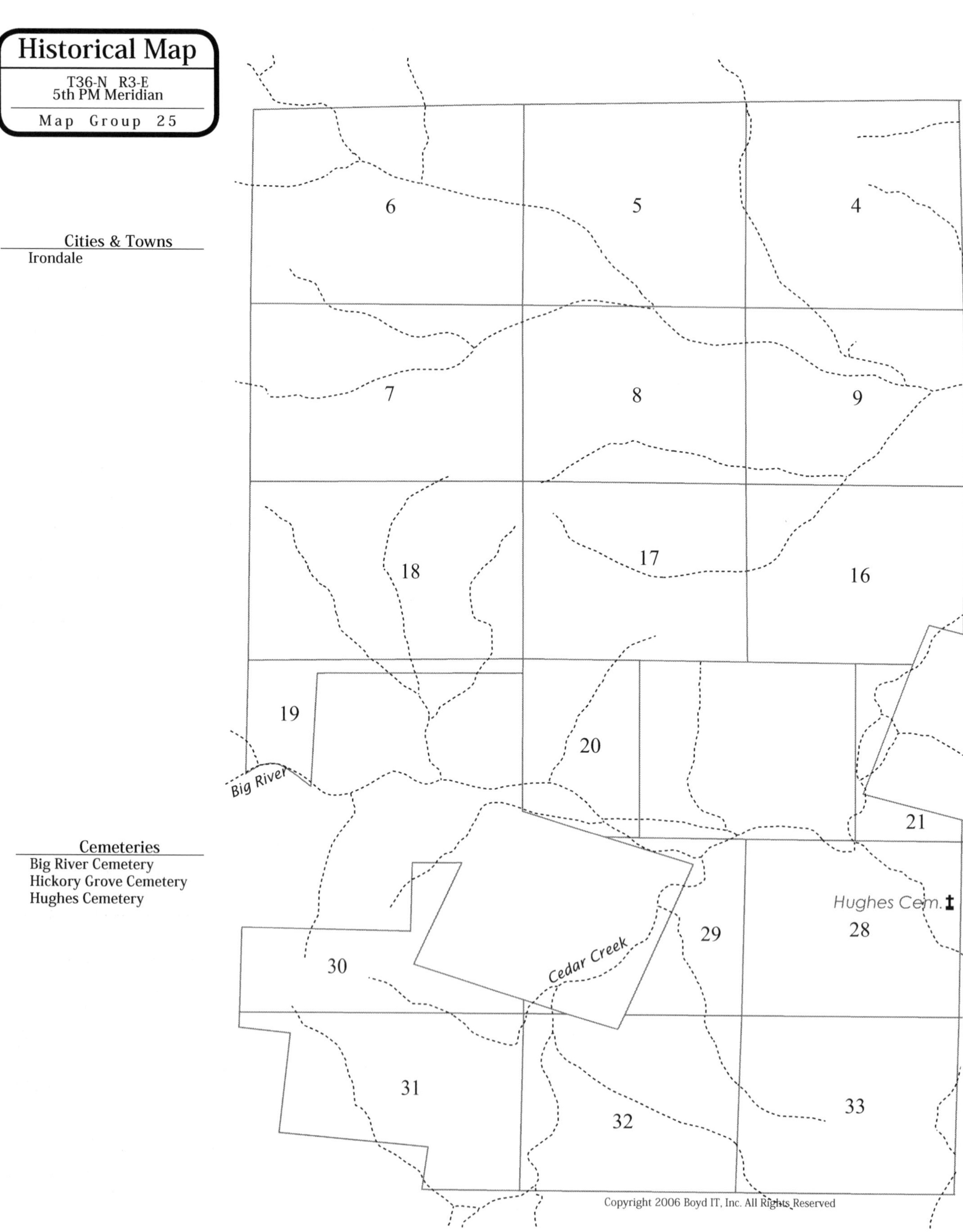

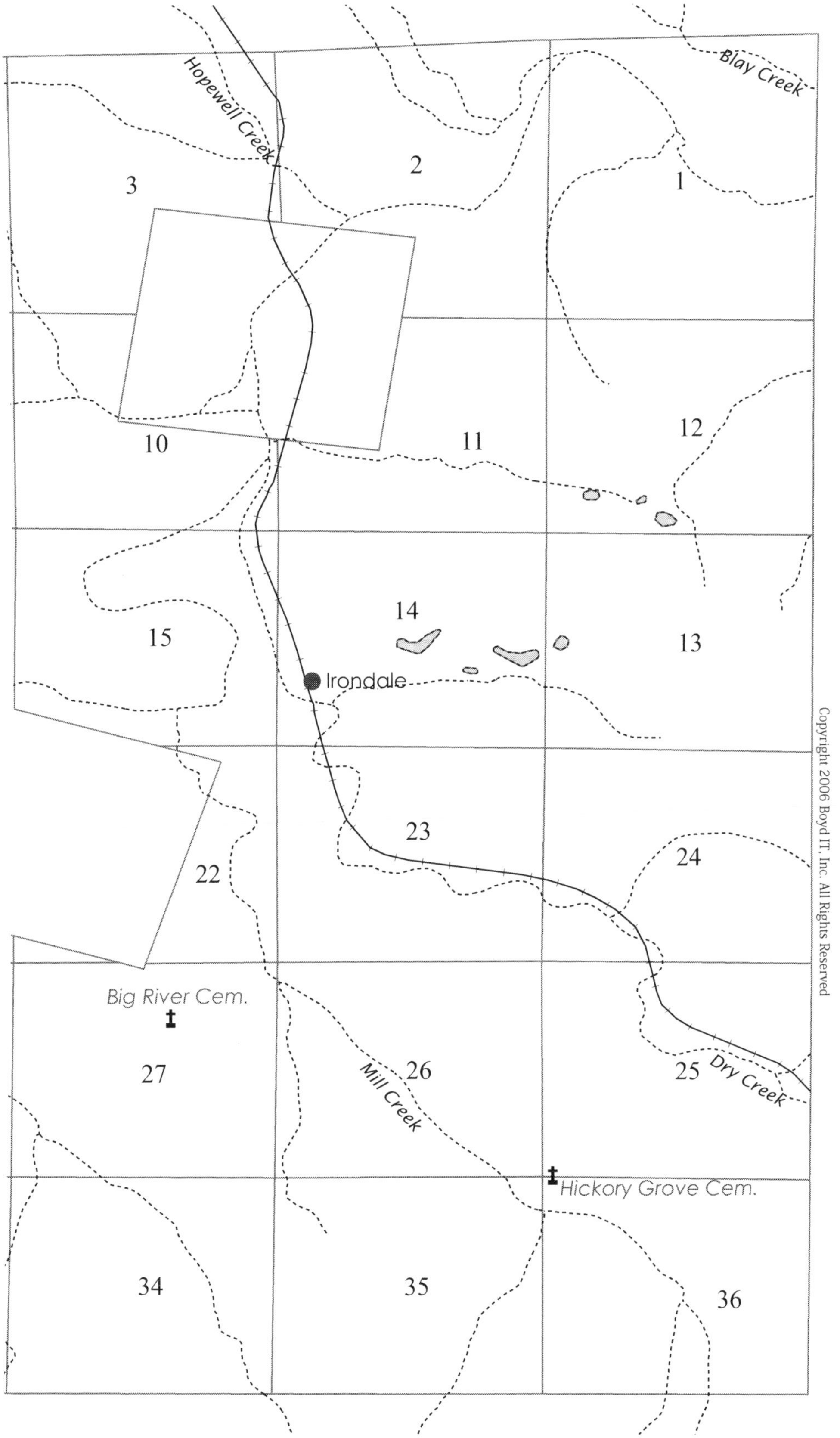

Hopewell Creek
Blay Creek
3
2
1
10
11
12
15
14
13
Irondale
22
23
24
Big River Cem.
27
26
25
Mill Creek
Dry Creek
Hickory Grove Cem.
34
35
36

Helpful Hints

1. This Map takes a different look at the same Congressional Township displayed in the preceding two maps. It presents features that can help you better envision the historical development of the area: a) Water-bodies (lakes & ponds), b) Water-courses (rivers, streams, etc.), c) Railroads, d) City/town center-points (where they were oftentimes located when first settled), and e) Cemeteries.
2. Using this "Historical" map in tandem with this Township's Patent Map and Road Map, may lead you to some interesting discoveries. You will often find roads, towns, cemeteries, and waterways are named after nearby landowners: sometimes those names will be the ones you are researching. See how many of these research gems you can find here in Washington County.

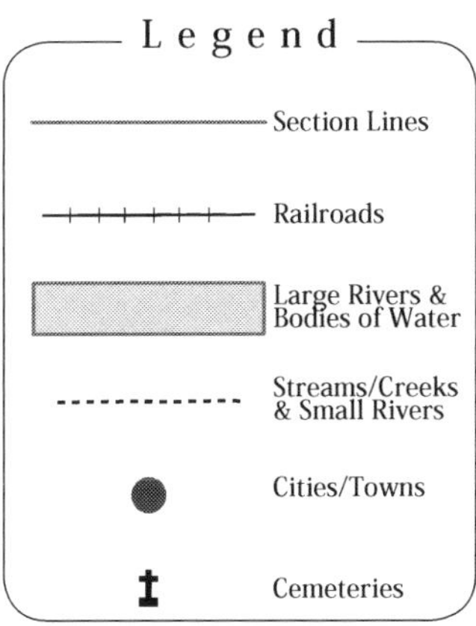

Scale: Section = 1 mile X 1 mile
(there are some exceptions)

Map Group 26: Index to Land Patents

Township 35-North Range 2-West (5th PM)

After you locate an individual in this Index, take note of the Section and Section Part then proceed to the Land Patent map on the pages immediately following. You should have no difficulty locating the corresponding parcel of land.

The "For More Info" Column will lead you to more information about the underlying Patents. See the *Legend* at right, and the "How to Use this Book" chapter, for more information.

LEGEND

"For More Info . . . " column

A = Authority (Legislative Act, See Appendix "A")
B = Block or Lot (location in Section unknown)
C = Cancelled Patent
F = Fractional Section
G = Group (Multi-Patentee Patent, see Appendix "C")
V = Overlaps another Parcel
R = Re-Issued (Parcel patented more than once)

(A & G items require you to look in the Appendixes referred to above. All other Letter-designations followed by a number require you to locate line-items in this index that possess the ID number found after the letter).

ID	Individual in Patent	Sec.	Sec. Part	Date Issued	Other Counties	For More Info . . .
4031	BAKER, James M	1	E½1NW	1860-03-01	Crawford	A1
4046	CASEBOLT, Riley E	1	SESW	1913-11-24	Crawford	A3
4014	DICKEY, Calvin	12	E½NW	1859-09-01	Crawford	A1
4015	" "	12	N½SW	1859-09-01	Crawford	A1
4016	" "	12	NWSE	1859-09-01	Crawford	A1
4017	" "	12	SWNE	1859-09-01	Crawford	A1
4018	" "	12	SWNW	1859-09-01	Crawford	A1
4019	" "	12	SWSW	1859-09-01	Crawford	A1
4038	DOTSON, Matthew H	12	E½SE	1859-09-10	Crawford	A1
4039	" "	12	SENE	1859-09-10	Crawford	A1
4040	" "	12	SESW	1859-09-10	Crawford	A1
4041	" "	12	SWSE	1859-09-10	Crawford	A1
4013	GILLIAM, Burrell B	1	W½2NE	1913-11-24	Crawford	A3
4030	GRIMES, James	1	E½2NE	1860-08-01	Crawford	A1
4042	HENSLEE, Obadiah	1	NWSW	1857-03-10	Crawford	A1
4043	HENSLEY, Obediah	1	NESW	1860-10-01	Crawford	A1
4044	" "	1	SWSW	1860-10-01	Crawford	A1
4045	" "	12	NWNW	1860-10-01	Crawford	A1
4036	HINDS, John F	1	2NW	1861-02-09	Crawford	A1
4037	" "	1	W½1NW	1861-02-09	Crawford	A1
4020	KING, Calvin M	13	NENE	1857-03-10	Crawford	A1
4021	" "	13	W½NE	1857-03-10	Crawford	A1
4029	KING, George W	13	SENE	1857-03-10	Crawford	A1
4028	" "	13	NESE	1859-09-01	Crawford	A1
4047	KING, Thomas B	13	NWNW	1860-08-01	Crawford	A1
4032	MASON, Jesse	13	E½NW	1859-01-01	Crawford	A1
4033	" "	13	NESW	1859-01-01	Crawford	A1
4034	" "	13	NWSE	1859-01-01	Crawford	A1
4035	" "	13	SWNW	1860-08-01	Crawford	A1
4022	SMITH, Charles	13	NWSW	1860-08-01	Crawford	A1
4023	" "	13	S½SE	1860-08-01	Crawford	A1
4024	" "	13	S½SW	1860-08-01	Crawford	A1
4025	SMITH, Elsworth F	1	1NE	1859-09-01	Crawford	A1
4026	" "	1	SE	1859-09-01	Crawford	A1
4027	" "	12	N½NE	1859-09-01	Crawford	A1

Lots-Sec. 1

Lot	Name	Year
1	SMITH, Elsworth F	1859
2	HINDS, John F	1861
2	GRIMES, James	1860
2	BAKER, James M	1860
2	HINDS, John F	1861
2	GILLIAM, Burrell B	1913

1

HENSLEE Obadiah 1857

HENSLEY Obediah 1860

SMITH Elsworth F 1859

HENSLEY Obediah 1860

CASEBOLT Riley E 1913

Washington County

HENSLEY Obediah 1860

SMITH Elsworth F 1859

DICKEY Calvin 1859

DICKEY Calvin 1859

DICKEY Calvin 1859

DOTSON Matthew H 1859

12

Crawford County

DICKEY Calvin 1859

DICKEY Calvin 1859

DICKEY Calvin 1859

DOTSON Matthew H 1859

DOTSON Matthew H 1859

DOTSON Matthew H 1859

KING Thomas B 1860

KING Calvin M 1857

KING Calvin M 1857

MASON Jesse 1859

MASON Jesse 1860

KING George W 1857

13

SMITH Charles 1860

MASON Jesse 1859

MASON Jesse 1859

KING George W 1859

SMITH Charles 1860

SMITH Charles 1860

Patent Map

T35-N R2-W
5th PM Meridian

Map Group 26

Township Statistics

Parcels Mapped	:	35
Number of Patents	:	17
Number of Individuals	:	15
Patentees Identified	:	15
Number of Surnames	:	12
Multi-Patentee Parcels	:	0
Oldest Patent Date	:	3/10/1857
Most Recent Patent	:	11/24/1913
Block/Lot Parcels	:	6
Parcels Re - Issued	:	0
Parcels that Overlap	:	0
Cities and Towns	:	0
Cemeteries	:	0

Note: the area contained in this map amounts to far less than a full Township. Therefore, its contents are completely on this single page (instead of a "normal" 2-page spread).

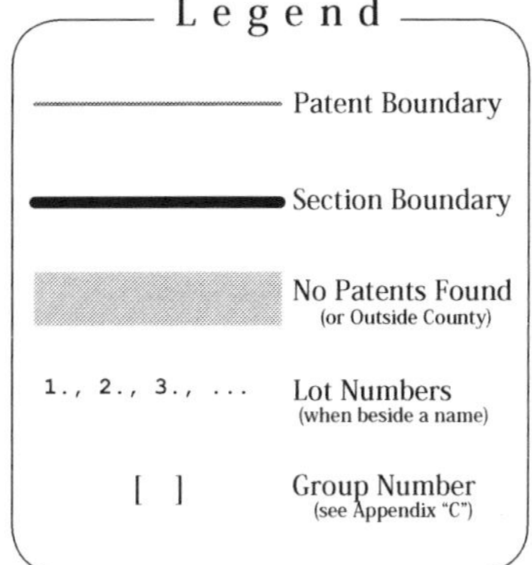

Scale: Section = 1 mile X 1 mile
(generally, with some exceptions)

Road Map

T35-N R2-W
5th PM Meridian

Map Group 26

Note: the area contained in this map amounts to far less than a full Township. Therefore, its contents are completely on this single page (instead of a "normal" 2-page spread).

Cities & Towns
None

Cemeteries
None

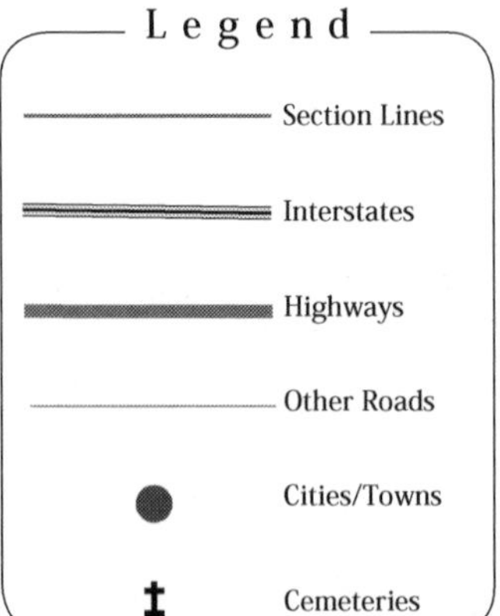

Scale: Section = 1 mile X 1 mile
(generally, with some exceptions)

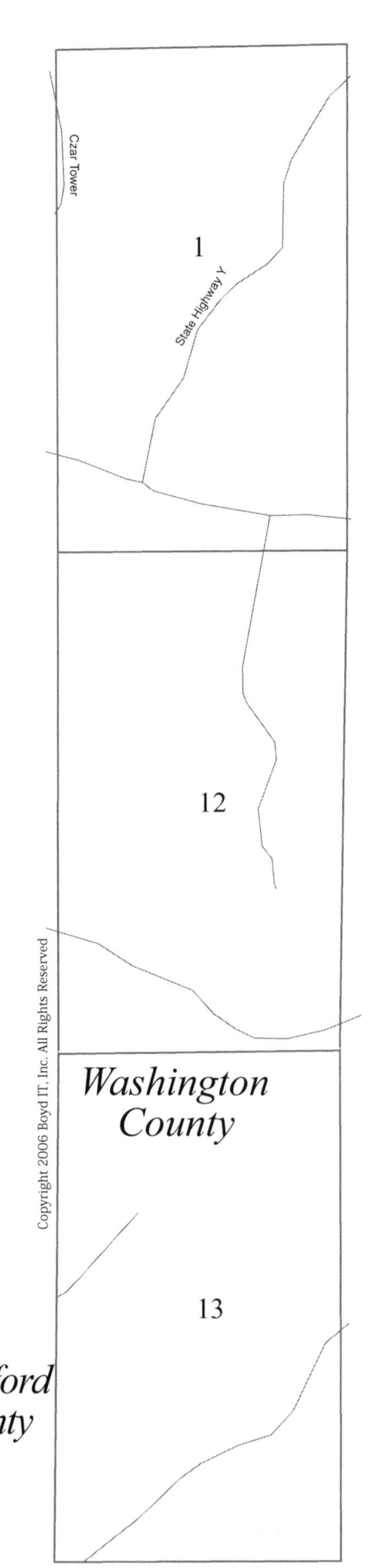

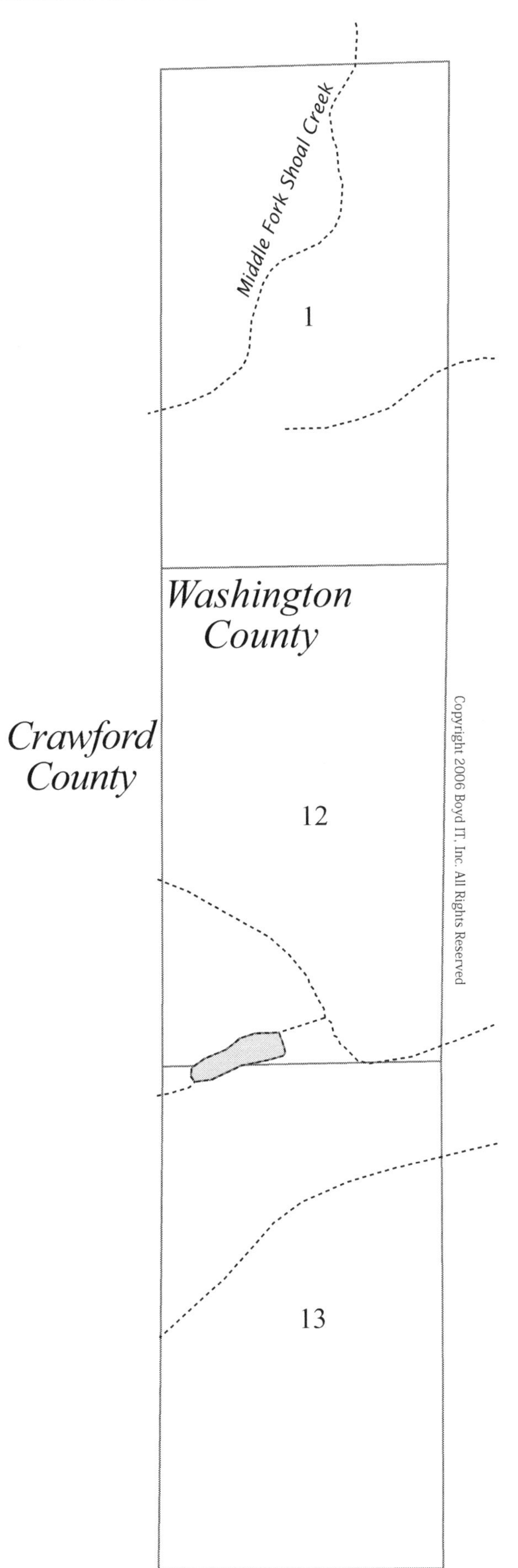

Historical Map

T35-N R2-W
5th PM Meridian

Map Group 26

Note: the area contained in this map amounts to far less than a full Township. Therefore, its contents are completely on this single page (instead of a "normal" 2-page spread).

Cities & Towns

None

Cemeteries

None

Legend

- Section Lines
- Railroads
- Large Rivers & Bodies of Water
- Streams/Creeks & Small Rivers
- Cities/Towns
- Cemeteries

Scale: Section = 1 mile X 1 mile
(there are some exceptions)

Map Group 27: Index to Land Patents

Township 35-North Range 1-West (5th PM)

After you locate an individual in this Index, take note of the Section and Section Part then proceed to the Land Patent map on the pages immediately following. You should have no difficulty locating the corresponding parcel of land.

The "For More Info" Column will lead you to more information about the underlying Patents. See the *Legend* at right, and the "How to Use this Book" chapter, for more information.

LEGEND

"For More Info . . . " column

A = Authority (Legislative Act, See Appendix "A")
B = Block or Lot (location in Section unknown)
C = Cancelled Patent
F = Fractional Section
G = Group (Multi-Patentee Patent, see Appendix "C")
V = Overlaps another Parcel
R = Re-Issued (Parcel patented more than once)

(A & G items require you to look in the Appendixes referred to above. All other Letter-designations followed by a number require you to locate line-items in this index that possess the ID number found after the letter).

ID	Individual in Patent	Sec.	Sec. Part	Date Issued	Other Counties	For More Info . . .
4121	ALMOND, John	1	2NE	1860-08-01		A1
4122	" "	1	3NW	1860-08-01		A1
4141	BATEMAN, Kersey	6	E½NW	1860-03-01		A1
4142	" "	6	NE	1860-03-01		A1
4143	" "	6	SWNW	1860-03-01		A1
4177	BLAIR, William H	10	E½SW	1905-12-30		A3
4123	BORMAN, John	13	SW	1859-09-01		A1
4064	BOTTO, Antonio	7	N½	1859-09-01		A1
4170	COLE, Watson	2	W½2NW	1856-06-10		A1
4171	" "	3	2NE	1856-06-10		A1
4172	" "	3	E½1NW	1856-06-10		A1
4168	" "	2	1NW	1859-01-01		A1
4173	" "	3	NWSE	1859-01-01		A1
4169	" "	2	E½2NW	1859-09-01		A1
4048	COUNTS, Adam	12	SENW	1837-11-14		A1
4128	CURRY, John J	13	NWNW	1859-09-01		A1
4129	" "	13	S½NW	1859-09-01		A1
4130	" "	13	SE	1859-09-01		A1
4131	" "	13	SWNE	1859-09-01		A1
4105	DAVIS, Henry C	3	1NE	1837-03-15		A1
4106	DIKEMAN, Henry	18	S½SE	1859-09-01		A1
4148	DOTSON, Matthew H	7	2SW	1859-09-10		A1
4149	" "	7	N½1SW	1859-09-10		A1
4076	ELLISON, Charles H	4	NESW	1861-05-01		A1
4077	" "	4	NWSE	1861-05-01		A1
4049	FASSETT, Alonzo D	14	E½NW	1859-09-01		A1
4050	" "	14	SW	1859-09-01		A1
4051	" "	14	SWNW	1859-09-01		A1
4052	" "	14	SWSE	1859-09-01		A1
4151	FENISON, Robert C	17	W½SW	1859-09-01		A1
4152	FENISON, Samuel	17	NESE	1858-12-01		A1
4153	FENNISON, Samuel	17	NWNE	1856-01-03		A1
4154	" "	17	S½SE	1856-01-03		A1
4097	FIELD, George H	10	E½NW	1859-09-01		A1
4098	" "	10	E½SE	1859-09-01		A1
4099	" "	10	NE	1859-09-01		A1
4156	FOSTER, Theodore S	8	NE	1859-09-01		A1
4157	" "	8	NENW	1859-09-01		A1
4158	" "	8	NESE	1859-09-01		A1
4159	" "	8	W½NW	1859-09-01		A1
4090	GAY, George	10	NWSW	1860-03-01		A1
4091	" "	10	W½NW	1860-03-01		A1
4092	" "	12	NENW	1860-03-01		A1
4093	" "	12	W½NW	1860-03-01		A1
4094	" "	12	W½SW	1860-03-01		A1
4075	GILLAM, Burrell B	5	SESE	1899-05-12		A3

ID	Individual in Patent	Sec.	Sec. Part	Date Issued	Other Counties	For More Info . . .
4068	GILLIAM, Benjamin	3	2NW	1859-01-01		A1
4070	" "	3	W½1NW	1859-01-01		A1
4069	" "	3	NWSW	1859-09-01		A1
4071	" "	4	E½2NE	1859-09-01		A1
4072	" "	4	NESE	1859-09-01		A1
4095	GILLIAM, George	4	E½1NW	1859-09-01		A1
4096	" "	4	W½1NE	1859-09-01		A1
4124	HEITZ, John	6	S½	1859-09-01		A1
4078	HENRY, David L	11	E½	1859-09-01		A1
4178	HEWIT, William	4	NWSW	1859-09-01		A1
4179	" "	4	S½SW	1859-09-01		A1
4180	" "	4	SWSE	1859-09-01		A1
4181	" "	4	W½1NW	1859-09-01		A1
4125	HOGAN, John	12	S½NE	1859-09-01		A1
4126	" "	12	SE	1859-09-01		A1
4127	" "	13	N½NE	1859-09-01		A1
4103	HUITT, Green	17	NWSE	1833-10-15		A1
4104	" "	17	SWNE	1833-10-15		A1
4155	HUITT, Samuel	2	W½1NE	1837-03-15		A1
4174	HUITT, William E	18	1SW	1857-10-30		A1
4175	" "	18	NWSE	1857-10-30		A1
4176	" "	18	S½2SW	1857-10-30		A1
4118	JARVIS, James M	5	W½2NW	1898-12-01		A3
4063	JOHNSTON, Andrew L	4	W½2NE	1908-11-12		A3
4163	JUDD, Thomas L	14	NWNW	1859-09-01		A1
4164	" "	15	NENE	1859-09-01		A1
4165	" "	15	S½NE	1859-09-01		A1
4166	" "	15	SE	1859-09-01		A1
4100	KING, George W	18	S½1NW	1857-03-10		A1
4101	" "	18	S½2NW	1857-03-10		A1
4102	" "	18	SWNE	1859-09-01		A1
4160	KING, Thomas B	18	N½1NW	1857-03-10		A1
4161	" "	18	N½2NW	1857-03-10		A1
4162	" "	7	S½1SW	1857-03-10		A1
4056	LARAMORE, Andrew H	8	E½SW	1857-03-10		A1
4053	" "	17	NENE	1859-09-01		A1
4054	" "	17	NENW	1859-09-01		A1
4055	" "	17	NWNW	1859-09-01		A1
4057	" "	8	NWSE	1859-09-01		A1
4058	" "	8	SESE	1859-09-01		A1
4059	" "	8	SWSE	1859-09-01		A1
4114	LARAMORE, James	18	N½NE	1857-03-10		A1
4117	" "	7	SE	1857-03-10		A1
4115	" "	18	NESE	1859-09-01		A1
4116	" "	18	SENE	1859-09-01		A1
4079	MACK, David	1	E½SW	1859-09-01		A1
4080	" "	1	SE	1859-09-01		A1
4081	" "	12	N½NE	1859-09-01		A1
4136	MCBRIDE, Joseph	2	W½SW	1859-09-01		A1
4137	" "	3	E½SE	1859-09-01		A1
4138	" "	3	E½SW	1859-09-01		A1
4139	" "	3	SWSE	1859-09-01		A1
4140	" "	3	SWSW	1859-09-01		A1
4132	MCCLAIN, John	12	NESW	1876-01-10		A3
4182	MCGINN, William	9	S½	1859-09-01		A1
4107	MORGAN, Henry	13	SENE	1859-03-01		A1
4119	NILEND, Joel	17	E½SW	1860-08-01		A1
4120	" "	17	S½NW	1860-08-01		A1
4087	PATCH, George A	14	N½SE	1859-09-01		A1
4088	" "	14	NE	1859-09-01		A1
4082	POWERS, Edward S	10	SWSW	1859-09-01		A1
4083	" "	15	SENW	1859-09-01		A1
4084	" "	15	SW	1859-09-01		A1
4085	" "	15	W½NW	1859-09-01		A1
4089	PRATT, George A	11	W½	1859-09-01		A1
4167	PRICE, Walter W	9	N½	1859-09-01		A1
4086	SCOTT, Frank A	8	W½SW	1861-05-01		A1
4133	STEWART, John	2	NESE	1856-06-03		A2
4134	" "	4	E½1NE	1856-06-03		A2
4135	TAYLOR, John T	17	SENE	1879-12-15		A3
4150	TOWNSEND, Montie L	14	SESE	1916-12-18		A1
4145	TURNER, Marion W	5	SW	1857-03-10		A1
4146	" "	5	W½1NW	1857-03-10		A1

ID	Individual in Patent	Sec.	Sec. Part	Date Issued	Other Counties	For More Info . . .
4144	TURNER, Marion W (Cont'd)	5	NESE	1859-09-01		A1
4147	" "	5	W½SE	1859-09-01		A1
4183	WALKER, William W	5	NE	1859-09-01		A1
4184	WILLARD, Willis	2	3NE	1860-10-01		A1
4185	" "	2	3NW	1860-10-01		A1
4186	" "	3	3NE	1860-10-01		A1
4187	" "	3	3NW	1860-10-01		A1
4073	WOODRUFF, Benjamin	12	SESW	1858-01-15		A1
4074	" "	13	NENW	1858-01-15		A1
4060	YODER, Andrew J	10	W½SE	1859-09-10		A1
4061	" "	15	NENW	1859-09-10		A1
4062	" "	15	NWNE	1859-09-10		A1
4065	YOUNT, Azariah	1	1NE	1859-09-01		A1
4066	" "	1	2NW	1859-09-01		A1
4067	" "	1	E½1NW	1859-09-01		A1
4108	YOUNT, Ira	1	W½SW	1856-01-03		A1
4109	" "	2	2NE	1856-01-03		A1
4110	" "	2	E½SW	1859-09-01		A1
4111	" "	2	NWSE	1859-09-01		A1
4112	" "	2	SESE	1859-09-01		A1
4113	YOUNT, Jacob	4	SESE	1908-11-12		A3

Patent Map

T35-N R1-W
5th PM Meridian

Map Group 27

Township Statistics

Parcels Mapped	:	140
Number of Patents	:	71
Number of Individuals	:	58
Patentees Identified	:	58
Number of Surnames	:	50
Multi-Patentee Parcels	:	0
Oldest Patent Date	:	10/15/1833
Most Recent Patent	:	12/18/1916
Block/Lot Parcels	:	36
Parcels Re - Issued	:	0
Parcels that Overlap	:	0
Cities and Towns	:	2
Cemeteries	:	4

Note: the area contained in this map amounts to far less than a full Township. Therefore, its contents are completely on this single page (instead of a "normal" 2-page spread).

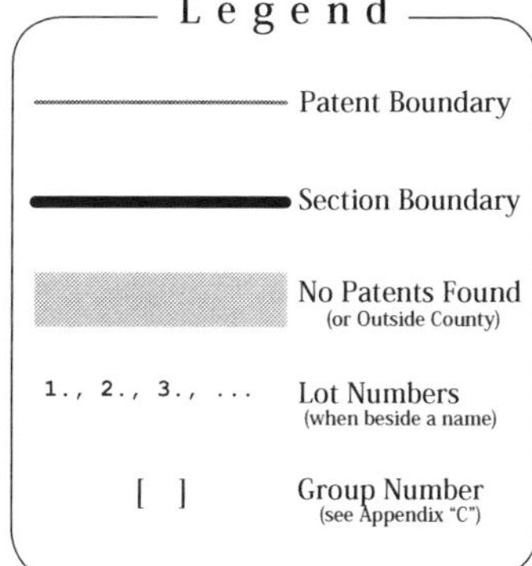

Scale: Section = 1 mile X 1 mile
(generally, with some exceptions)

Road Map

T35-N R1-W
5th PM Meridian

Map Group 27

Note: the area contained in this map amounts to far less than a full Township. Therefore, its contents are completely on this single page (instead of a "normal" 2-page spread).

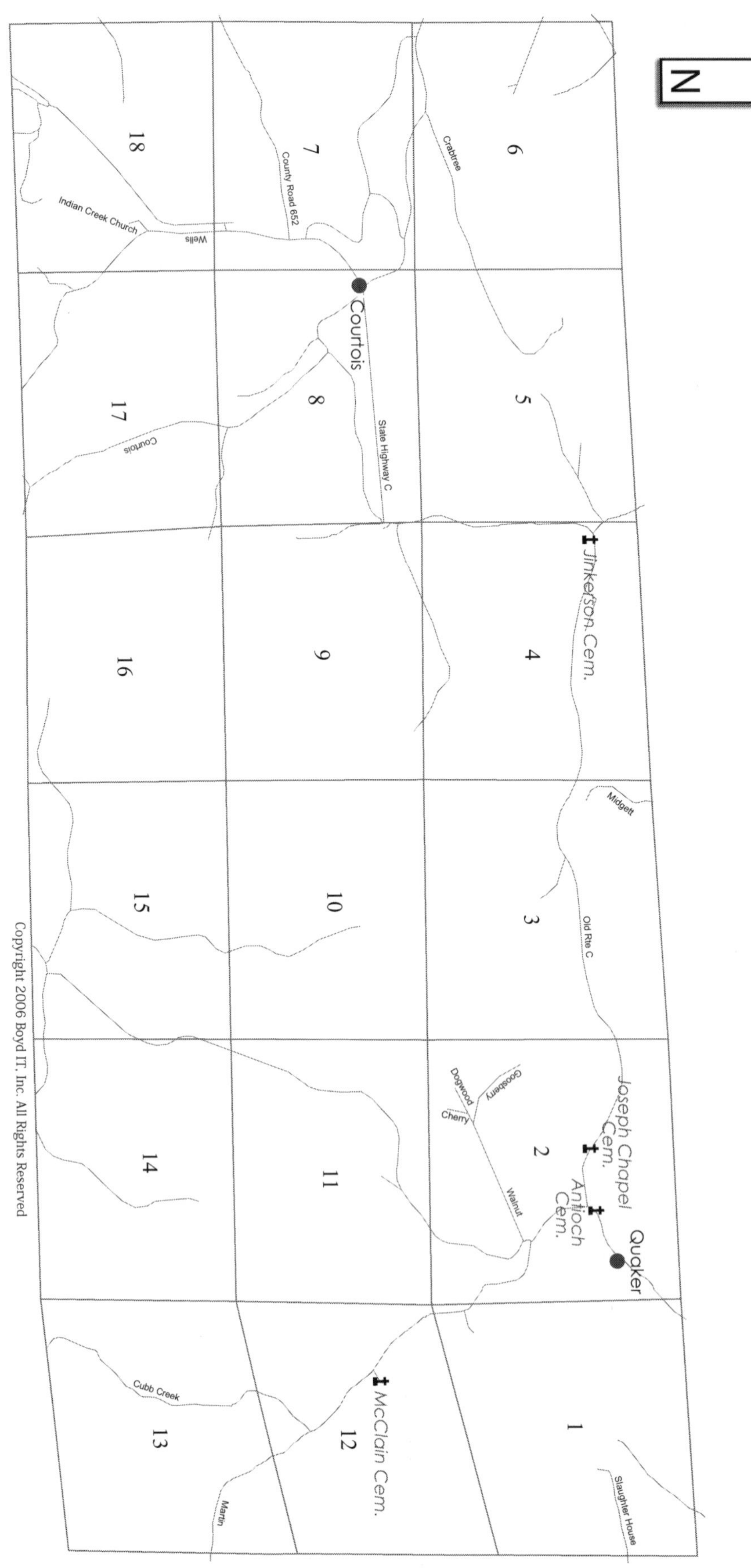

Cities & Towns

Courtois
Quaker

Cemeteries

Antioch Cemetery
Jinkerson Cemetery
Joseph Chapel Cemetery
McClain Cemetery

Legend

Section Lines
Interstates
Highways
Other Roads
Cities/Towns
Cemeteries

Scale: Section = 1 mile X 1 mile
(generally, with some exceptions)

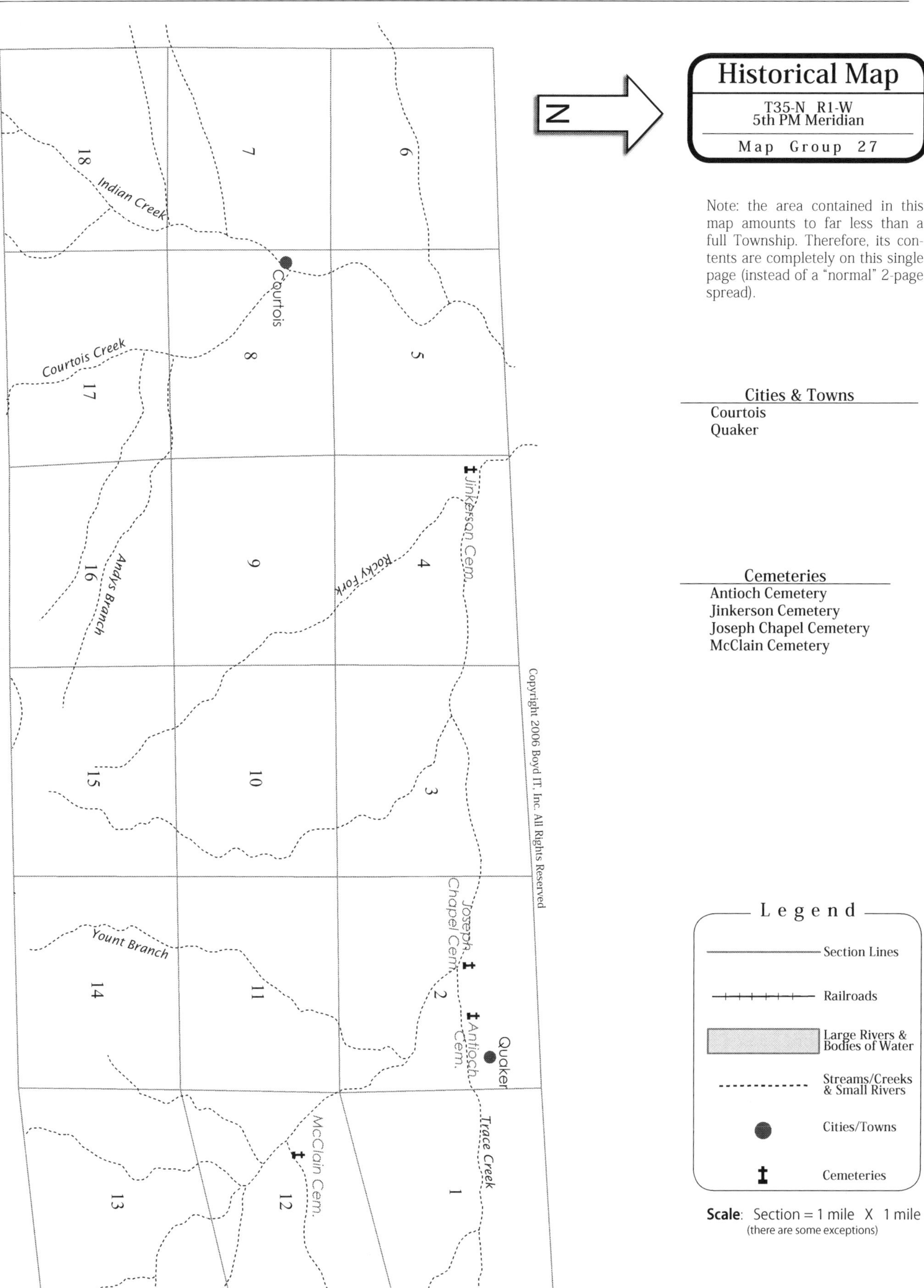

N
Historical Map
T35-N R1-W
5th PM Meridian
Map Group 27
Note: the area contained in this map amounts to far less than a full Township. Therefore, its contents are completely on this single page (instead of a "normal" 2-page spread).
Cities & Towns
Courtois
Quaker
Cemeteries
Antioch Cemetery
Jinkerson Cemetery
Joseph Chapel Cemetery
McClain Cemetery
Legend
Section Lines
Railroads
Large Rivers & Bodies of Water
Streams/Creeks & Small Rivers
Cities/Towns
Cemeteries
Scale: Section = 1 mile X 1 mile
(there are some exceptions)
18
7
6
Indian Creek
Courtois
Courtois Creek
8
5
17
Jinkerson Cem.
Rocky Fork
16
9
4
Andys Branch
15
10
3
Copyright 2006 Boyd IT, Inc. All Rights Reserved
Joseph Chapel Cem.
Yount Branch
14
11
2
Antioch Cem.
Quaker
McClain Cem.
Trace Creek
13
12
1

Map Group 28: Index to Land Patents

Township 35-North Range 1-East (5th PM)

After you locate an individual in this Index, take note of the Section and Section Part then proceed to the Land Patent map on the pages immediately following. You should have no difficulty locating the corresponding parcel of land.

The "For More Info" Column will lead you to more information about the underlying Patents. See the *Legend* at right, and the "How to Use this Book" chapter, for more information.

LEGEND

"For More Info . . . " column

- **A** = Authority (Legislative Act, See Appendix "A")
- **B** = Block or Lot (location in Section unknown)
- **C** = Cancelled Patent
- **F** = Fractional Section
- **G** = Group (Multi-Patentee Patent, see Appendix "C")
- **V** = Overlaps another Parcel
- **R** = Re-Issued (Parcel patented more than once)

(A & G items require you to look in the Appendixes referred to above. All other Letter-designations followed by a number require you to locate line-items in this index that possess the ID number found after the letter).

ID	Individual in Patent	Sec.	Sec. Part	Date Issued	Other Counties	For More Info . . .
4202	ALDRIDGE, Charles	14	W½NE	1851-12-01		A1 G1
4197	" "	12	SWNW	1852-01-01		A1
4200	" "	14	SWNW	1856-01-03		A1
4198	" "	14	NWNW	1856-10-10		A1
4199	" "	14	NWSE	1858-12-01		A1
4194	" "	10	N½SE	1859-01-01		A1
4196	" "	11	W½SW	1859-01-01		A1
4195	" "	10	SWSW	1859-09-01		A1
4201	" "	15	NWNW	1859-09-01		A1
4227	ALDRIDGE, James	15	E½NE	1857-04-15		A1
4228	" "	15	NWNE	1857-04-15		A1
4202	ALDRIDGE, William	14	W½NE	1851-12-01		A1 G1
4233	ARNOLD, James R	2	E½3NE	1870-05-10		A1 F
4264	AUSTIN, Lora E	10	N½NW	1859-09-01		A1
4265	" "	10	SENW	1859-09-01		A1
4266	" "	3	SWSW	1859-09-01		A1
4267	" "	9	E½NE	1859-09-01		A1
4268	" "	9	E½SE	1859-09-01		A1
4220	BARGER, H L	12	SE	1869-07-01		A1 F
4327	BARGER, William S	11	E½SW	1882-06-30		A3
4329	BARKER, William T	4	W½2NE	1860-10-01		A1
4307	BASSNETT, Thomas	3	E½SW	1896-12-26		A1
4308	" "	3	W½1NE	1896-12-26		A1
4313	BATTERSON, William H	13	E½SW	1859-09-01		A1
4314	" "	13	SENW	1859-09-01		A1
4315	" "	13	SWSW	1859-09-01		A1
4246	BLACK, John H	11	NWSE	1856-06-10		A1
4247	" "	11	S½NE	1856-06-10		A1
4248	" "	11	SWSE	1856-09-01		A1
4217	BREMAN, George	7	E½NE	1860-10-01		A1
4192	CONAWAY, Archibald	17	SW	1859-01-01		A1
4213	CORNELL, Enos B	5	1NE	1860-03-01		A1 R4281
4214	" "	5	E½SW	1860-03-01		A1 V4252
4215	" "	5	SE	1860-03-01		A1 R4283
4203	DENNING, Charles L	3	NWSW	1859-09-01		A1
4204	" "	3	W½1NW	1859-09-01		A1
4205	" "	4	1NE	1859-09-01		A1
4206	" "	4	SE	1859-09-01		A1
4191	DICKEY, Andrew S	15	SESW	1833-10-15		A1 V4216
4230	DUTY, James M	15	E½NW	1857-04-15		A1
4231	" "	15	NESW	1857-04-15		A1
4232	" "	15	SWNE	1857-04-15		A1
4226	FARMER, J Riley	3	E½1NW	1908-08-17		A3
4306	FORTUNE, Stephen L	1	N½	1874-11-05		A3 F
4326	GIPSON, William P	11	NENW	1856-01-03		A1
4188	GOFORTH, Allen M	13	NWSW	1857-04-15		A1

ID	Individual in Patent	Sec.	Sec. Part	Date Issued	Other Counties	For More Info . . .
4189	GOFORTH, Andrew	13	W½NW	1824-05-20		A1
4190	" "	14	NENE	1837-11-14		A1
4269	GOFORTH, Lydia	14	SENE	1858-12-01		A1
4271	GOFORTH, Martin	3	E½1NE	1896-01-14		A3
4272	" "	3	N½SE	1896-01-14		A3
4245	GRAGG, John	13	S½SE	1859-01-01		A1 F
4216	GRISHAM, Francis G	15	S½SW	1904-01-28		A1 V4191
4276	GUINN, Mary	17	N½NW	1859-09-01		A1
4277	" "	18	1NW	1859-09-01		A1
4278	" "	18	N½NE	1859-09-01		A1
4279	" "	18	NWSE	1859-09-01		A1
4280	" "	18	SWNE	1859-09-01		A1
4300	HARGRAVE, Samuel	2	E½3NW	1845-10-27		A1
4299	" "	2	3NE	1897-09-20		A1
4316	HELMICK, William	17	SE	1860-08-01		A1
4301	HENDERSON, Samuel	12	E½NW	1821-09-24		A1
4249	HILL, John H	10	E½NE	1877-10-10		A3
4221	HOLDEN, Harris R	18	S½SE	1859-09-01		A1
4222	" "	18	SW	1859-09-01		A1
4207	HORTON, Christopher C	11	SENW	1896-06-15		A1
4242	HORTON, John C	1	NWSW	1872-06-15		A1
4298	HORTON, Rufus	11	SWNW	1898-12-01		A3
4229	JARRELL, James B	15	SWNW	1910-01-24		A1
4250	JONES, John	5	1NW	1859-09-01		A1
4251	" "	5	2NW	1859-09-01		A1
4252	" "	5	SW	1859-09-01		A1 V4214
4321	LEONARD, William	9	W½NE	1860-08-01		A1
4322	" "	9	W½SE	1860-08-01		A1
4323	LUCAS, William	8	E½NE	1859-09-10		A1
4324	" "	8	E½SE	1859-09-10		A1
4325	" "	9	SW	1859-09-10		A1
4290	MANEY, Robert	4	3NW	1860-08-01		A1
4291	" "	5	3NE	1860-08-01		A1
4292	" "	5	3NW	1860-08-01		A1
4293	" "	6	3NE	1860-08-01		A1
4302	MCMURTREY, Samuel M	13	E½NE	1859-01-01		A1 F
4303	" "	13	N½SE	1859-01-01		A1 F
4309	MESPLAY, Vetal	17	NE	1860-09-01		A1
4310	" "	17	S½NW	1860-09-01		A1
4311	" "	18	NESE	1860-09-01		A1
4312	" "	18	SENE	1860-09-01		A1
4223	MORGAN, Henry	18	2NW	1859-03-01		A1
4212	PAINE, Edward	6	E½3NW	1859-09-01		A1
4211	" "	6	2NW	1859-09-10		A1
4243	PEAK, John F	2	S½SW	1875-08-10		A3
4244	" "	3	S½SE	1875-08-10		A3
4224	PECK, Horace M	7	SE	1859-09-01		A1
4225	" "	8	SW	1859-09-01		A1
4304	PHILPOT, Samuel	12	NENE	1867-08-20		A1 F
4305	PRYOR, Samuel W	2	SE	1850-01-01		A1 F
4235	RAMSEY, James	3	E½3NE	1849-04-10		A1
4234	" "	1	SE	1854-11-15		A1 F
4241	RAMSEY, Jasper N	10	W½NE	1857-04-15		A1
4253	RAMSEY, John L	11	NWNE	1854-11-15		A1
4259	RAMSEY, John P	3	W½3NE	1849-04-10		A1
4257	" "	2	W½2NW	1856-01-03		A1 F
4258	" "	3	E½2NE	1856-01-03		A1 F
4254	" "	2	E½2NW	1860-08-01		A1
4255	" "	2	NWSW	1876-05-15		A3
4256	" "	2	W½1NW	1876-05-15		A3
4262	RAMSEY, Leah	3	E½3NW	1856-01-03		A1
4263	" "	3	W½2NE	1856-01-03		A1
4208	RICE, Edward P	6	1NE	1859-09-01		A1
4209	" "	6	2NE	1859-09-01		A1
4210	" "	6	SE	1859-09-01		A1
4273	RICE, Martin	8	NW	1859-09-01		A1
4274	" "	8	W½NE	1859-09-01		A1
4275	" "	8	W½SE	1859-09-01		A1
4281	SHONBACKER, Michael	5	1NE	1859-09-01		A1 R4213
4282	" "	5	2NE	1859-09-01		A1
4283	" "	5	SE	1859-09-01		A1 R4215
4287	SMITH, Robert H	4	1NW	1859-09-01		A1
4288	" "	4	2NW	1859-09-01		A1

ID	Individual in Patent	Sec.	Sec. Part	Date Issued	Other Counties	For More Info . . .
4289	SMITH, Robert H (Cont'd)	4	SW	1859-09-01		A1
4193	STEPHENS, Benjamin F	14	SESE	1888-12-08		A3
4218	STEPHENS, George W	14	SESW	1876-09-30		A1
4219	" "	14	SWSE	1876-09-30		A1
4328	STEVENS, William S	15	NWSW	1902-02-21		A1
4260	STEWART, John	12	NWNW	1856-06-03		A2 F
4261	" "	2	W½3NW	1856-06-03		A2
4294	STUDLEY, Robert P	6	1NW	1859-09-01		A1
4295	" "	6	SW	1859-09-01		A1
4296	" "	7	N½1NW	1859-09-01		A1
4297	" "	7	N½2NW	1859-09-01		A1
4284	TAYLOR, Richard S	10	S½SE	1860-10-01		A1
4285	" "	10	SESW	1860-10-01		A1
4237	TEDDER, James	3	W½3NW	1856-06-16		A1
4239	" "	4	E½2NE	1856-06-16		A1
4236	" "	3	E½2NW	1860-08-01		A1
4238	" "	4	3NE	1860-08-01		A1
4270	TEDDER, Martha	3	W½2NW	1853-04-12		A1
4240	VINEYARD, James	11	NENE	1856-09-01		A1
4317	WILLIAMS, William L	7	S½1NW	1859-09-01		A1
4318	" "	7	S½2NW	1859-09-01		A1
4319	" "	7	SW	1859-09-01		A1
4320	" "	7	W½NE	1859-09-01		A1
4330	WOODS, William	12	SW	1825-07-15		A1 F
4286	WORTHAM, Robert A	14	NESW	1907-05-10		A1

Patent Map

T35-N R1-E
5th PM Meridian

Map Group 28

Township Statistics

Parcels Mapped	:	143
Number of Patents	:	83
Number of Individuals	:	69
Patentees Identified	:	69
Number of Surnames	:	54
Multi-Patentee Parcels	:	1
Oldest Patent Date	:	9/24/1821
Most Recent Patent	:	1/24/1910
Block/Lot Parcels	:	45
Parcels Re - Issued	:	2
Parcels that Overlap	:	4
Cities and Towns	:	3
Cemeteries	:	2

Note: the area contained in this map amounts to far less than a full Township. Therefore, its contents are completely on this single page (instead of a "normal" 2-page spread).

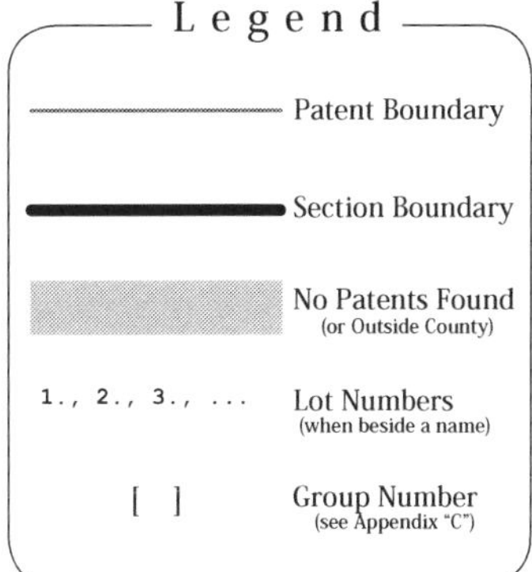

Scale: Section = 1 mile X 1 mile
(generally, with some exceptions)

Road Map

T35-N R1-E
5th PM Meridian

Map Group 28

Note: the area contained in this map amounts to far less than a full Township. Therefore, its contents are completely on this single page (instead of a "normal" 2-page spread).

Cities & Towns

Horton Town
Sunlight
Peoria

Cemeteries

Horton Cemetery
Sunlight Cemetery

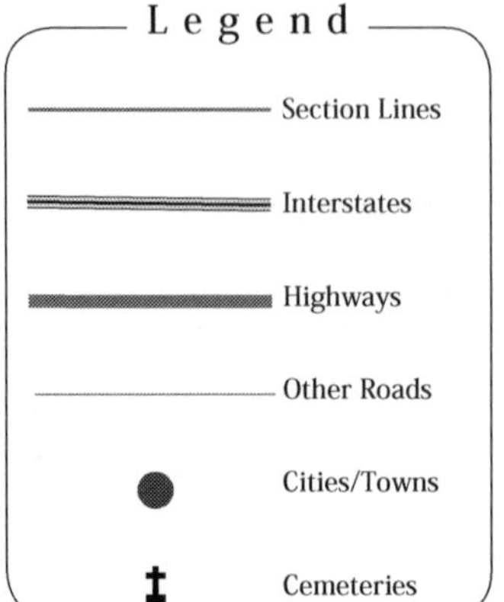

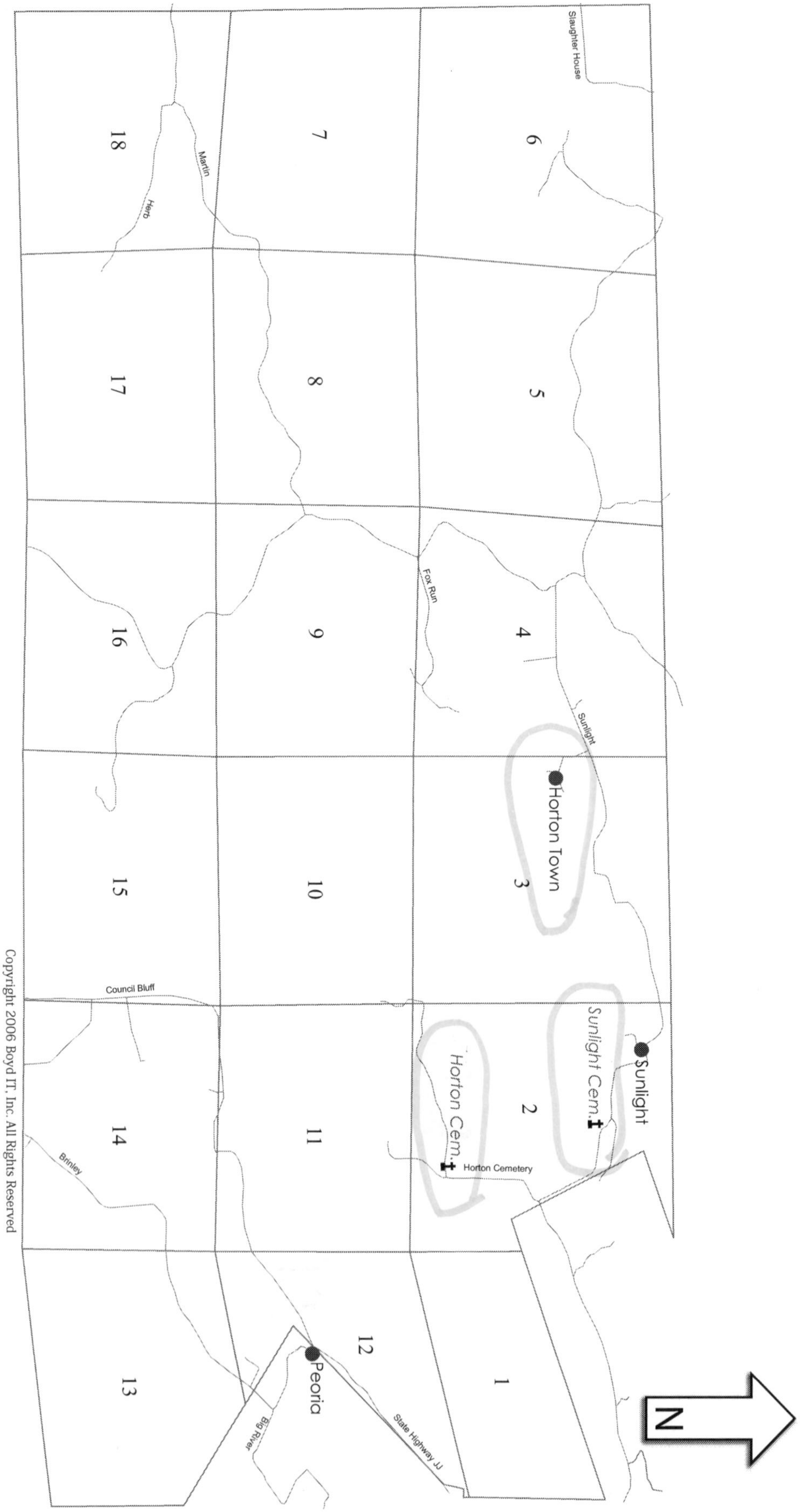

Scale: Section = 1 mile X 1 mile
(generally, with some exceptions)

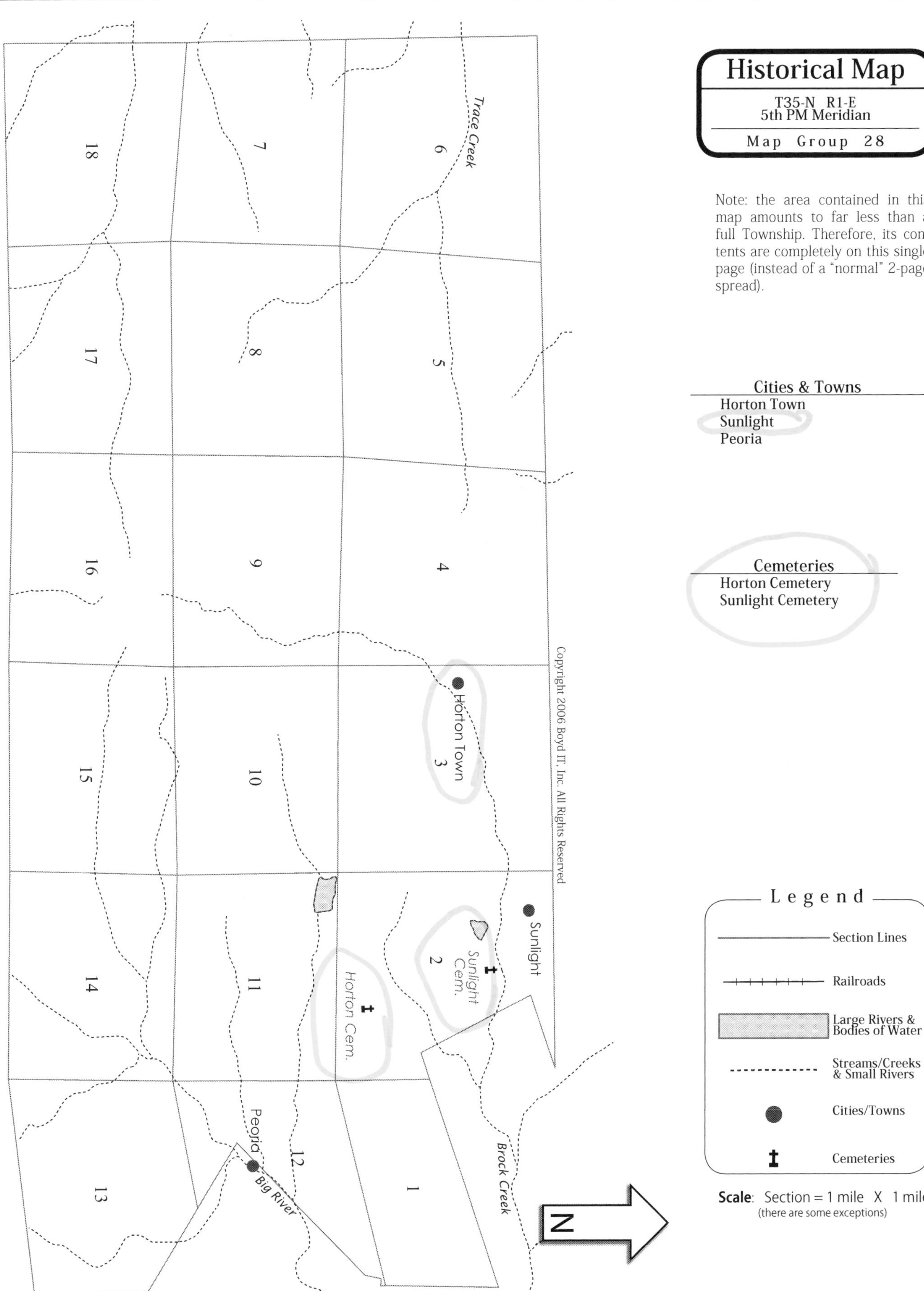
Historical Map
T35-N R1-E
5th PM Meridian
Map Group 28
Note: the area contained in this map amounts to far less than a full Township. Therefore, its contents are completely on this single page (instead of a "normal" 2-page spread).
Cities & Towns
Horton Town
Sunlight
Peoria
Cemeteries
Horton Cemetery
Sunlight Cemetery
Legend
Section Lines
Railroads
Large Rivers & Bodies of Water
Streams/Creeks & Small Rivers
Cities/Towns
Cemeteries
Scale: Section = 1 mile X 1 mile
(there are some exceptions)
Trace Creek
Horton Town
Sunlight
Sunlight Cem.
Horton Cem.
Peoria
Big River
Brock Creek
N
18
7
6
17
8
5
16
9
4
15
10
3
14
11
2
13
12
1

Map Group 29: Index to Land Patents

Township 35-North Range 2-East (5th PM)

After you locate an individual in this Index, take note of the Section and Section Part then proceed to the Land Patent map on the pages immediately following. You should have no difficulty locating the corresponding parcel of land.

The "For More Info" Column will lead you to more information about the underlying Patents. See the *Legend* at right, and the "How to Use this Book" chapter, for more information.

LEGEND

"For More Info . . . " column

A = Authority (Legislative Act, See Appendix "A")
B = Block or Lot (location in Section unknown)
C = Cancelled Patent
F = Fractional Section
G = Group (Multi-Patentee Patent, see Appendix "C")
V = Overlaps another Parcel
R = Re-Issued (Parcel patented more than once)

(A & G items require you to look in the Appendixes referred to above. All other Letter-designations followed by a number require you to locate line-items in this index that possess the ID number found after the letter).

ID	Individual in Patent	Sec.	Sec. Part	Date Issued	Other Counties	For More Info . . .
4390	BLACKFORD, Nathaniel G	8	SENE	1857-10-30		A1 F
4391	" "	8	W½NE	1857-10-30		A1 F
4412	BLANTON, William O	17	NENW	1837-11-14		A1
4331	BRINKER, Abraham	12	SE	1821-09-24		A1
4385	BROOKS, Moses	10	W½SW	1850-01-01		A1
4384	" "	10	NESW	1856-01-03		A1 V4360
4386	" "	9	SESE	1856-01-03		A1
4404	BUFORD, William	14	NW	1824-05-10		A1 F
4389	BUXTON, Nathaniel	2	SWSE	1854-11-15		A1
4405	CARSON, William	5	SE	1837-11-07		A1 F
4406	" "	8	NENE	1837-11-07		A1 F
4338	DUDLEY, David P	13	NE	1860-08-01		A1 G82 F
4336	EVANS, Clabourn W	4	E½SE	1850-01-01		A1 F
4335	" "	3	NWSW	1856-10-10		A1
4353	EVANS, James	10	SENW	1856-01-03		A1
4359	EVANS, James S	10	E½SE	1837-11-07		A1
4360	" "	10	E½SW	1837-11-07		A1 V4384
4361	" "	10	W½NE	1837-11-07		A1
4362	" "	11	E½NW	1837-11-07		A1
4363	" "	11	SW	1837-11-07		A1 F
4377	EVANS, Joseph	15	E½NW	1841-06-25		A1
4378	" "	15	NWNW	1841-06-25		A1
4388	EVENS, Nancy	3	W½1NW	1870-09-20		A1
4407	EVERSOLE, William G	3	NESW	1857-10-30		A1
4408	FORRESTER, William M	15	SW	1857-04-15		A1
4409	" "	15	SWNW	1857-04-15		A1
4413	GIBSON, William P	17	E½NE	1858-04-01		A1
4339	GRAGG, Elijah	9	NE	1850-01-01		A1 F
4367	GRAGG, John	17	SWSW	1859-01-01		A1
4333	GREEN, Austin	3	E½1NW	1873-11-01		A3
4340	GREGG, Elijah	10	W½NW	1850-01-01		A1
4341	" "	9	NESE	1851-12-01		A1
4368	GREGG, John	18	S½SW	1854-11-15		A1
4369	GROGG, John	18	N½SW	1856-06-10		A1
4349	GROSS, Jacob S	10	E½NE	1837-11-07		A1 G121
4350	" "	11	W½NW	1837-11-07		A1 G121 F
4392	HANGER, Peter A	10	NENW	1850-01-01		A1
4393	" "	3	SESW	1850-01-01		A1
4338	HARRIS, Oliver	13	NE	1860-08-01		A1 G82 F
4355	HAYS, James M	17	NWSE	1856-01-03		A1
4356	" "	8	NWSE	1856-01-03		A1
4358	" "	8	SESE	1856-09-01		A1
4357	" "	8	S½NW	1867-08-20		A1
4382	HERSHEY, Merritt D	18	SENE	1911-02-09		A1 R4383
4383	HERSHEY, Merritt W	18	SENE	1910-12-19		A1 C R4382
4387	JONES, Myers	15	E½NE	1824-05-10		A1

ID	Individual in Patent	Sec.	Sec. Part	Date Issued	Other Counties	For More Info . . .
4346	LANINS, Jacob	1	NW	1821-09-24		A1 F
4347	" "	2	NE	1821-09-24		A1 F
4348	LANIUS, Jacob	1	SW	1824-05-01		A1 F
4379	LUTS, Joseph	2	1NW	1856-01-03		A1 F
4380	" "	2	E½2NW	1856-01-03		A1 F
4411	MAXWELL, William	13	SE	1850-01-01		A1 F
4334	MCNABB, Chester C	3	W½1NE	1906-03-16		A1
4395	MORGAN, Silas G	17	NESE	1860-08-01		A1
4396	" "	17	S½SE	1860-08-01		A1
4337	MORRIS, Curtis	3	SESE	1856-06-03		A2
4397	PAGE, Stephen L	15	NWSE	1856-09-01		A1
4398	" "	15	W½NE	1856-09-01		A1
4332	PEERY, Andrew	2	SE	1824-05-01		A1 F
4342	PREWETT, Gabriel	17	E½SW	1837-11-07		A1
4343	" "	8	NESE	1837-11-07		A1
4344	PREWITT, Gabriel	17	NWNE	1841-07-01		A1
4381	PRUETT, Mary J	9	W½SW	1850-01-01		A1
4345	QUEEN, Harrison	2	W½2NW	1874-11-05		A3 F
4349	RELFE, James H	10	E½NE	1837-11-07		A1 G121
4354	" "	11	NE	1837-11-07		A1 F
4350	" "	11	W½NW	1837-11-07		A1 G121 F
4399	SLOAN, Theodore F	14	SW	1857-04-15		A1 F
4400	" "	15	E½SE	1857-04-15		A1
4401	" "	15	SWSE	1857-04-15		A1
4394	STEPHENSON, Robert M	1	SE	1821-09-24		A1 F
4376	THOMAS, John	7	SE	1826-12-20		A1 F
4370	" "	17	SENW	1837-11-14		A1
4371	" "	17	SWNE	1837-11-14		A1
4373	" "	18	NWNE	1856-06-16		A1
4372	" "	18	NW	1856-10-10		A1 F
4374	" "	18	SE	1859-01-01		A1
4375	" "	18	SWNE	1859-01-01		A1
4410	THOMAS, William M	18	NENE	1837-11-14		A1
4365	THOMPSON, Jane A	3	SWSE	1854-11-15		A1
4364	" "	3	NWSE	1856-10-10		A1
4415	VINYARD, William	3	NESE	1850-01-01		A1
4414	" "	2	NWSW	1851-12-01		A1
4416	WOODS, William	11	SE	1821-09-24		A1 F
4418	" "	8	SW	1824-05-10		A1
4417	" "	17	W½NW	1825-07-15		A1
4419	" "	8	SWSE	1837-11-14		A1
4351	WOOLFORD, Jacob	2	NESW	1852-01-01		A1
4352	" "	2	S½SW	1853-08-01		A1
4402	WRIGHT, Thomas	9	SESW	1885-12-19		A3
4403	" "	9	SWSE	1885-12-19		A3
4366	YEATES, John C	17	NWSW	1860-08-01		A1

Patent Map

T35-N R2-E
5th PM Meridian

Map Group 29

Township Statistics

Parcels Mapped	:	89
Number of Patents	:	75
Number of Individuals	:	53
Patentees Identified	:	52
Number of Surnames	:	46
Multi-Patentee Parcels	:	3
Oldest Patent Date	:	9/24/1821
Most Recent Patent	:	2/9/1911
Block/Lot Parcels	:	6
Parcels Re - Issued	:	1
Parcels that Overlap	:	2
Cities and Towns	:	1
Cemeteries	:	5

Note: the area contained in this map amounts to far less than a full Township. Therefore, its contents are completely on this single page (instead of a "normal" 2-page spread).

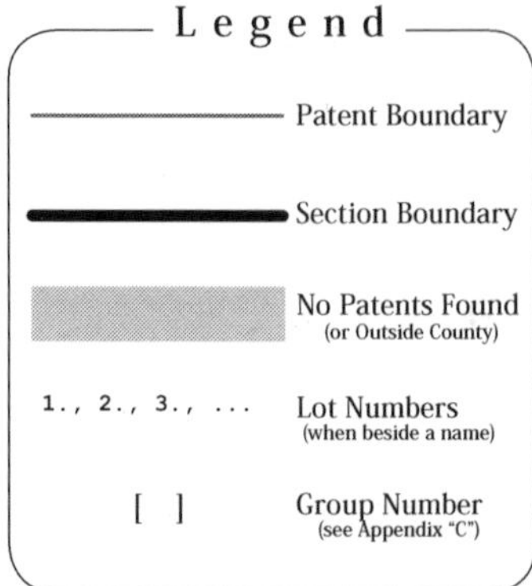

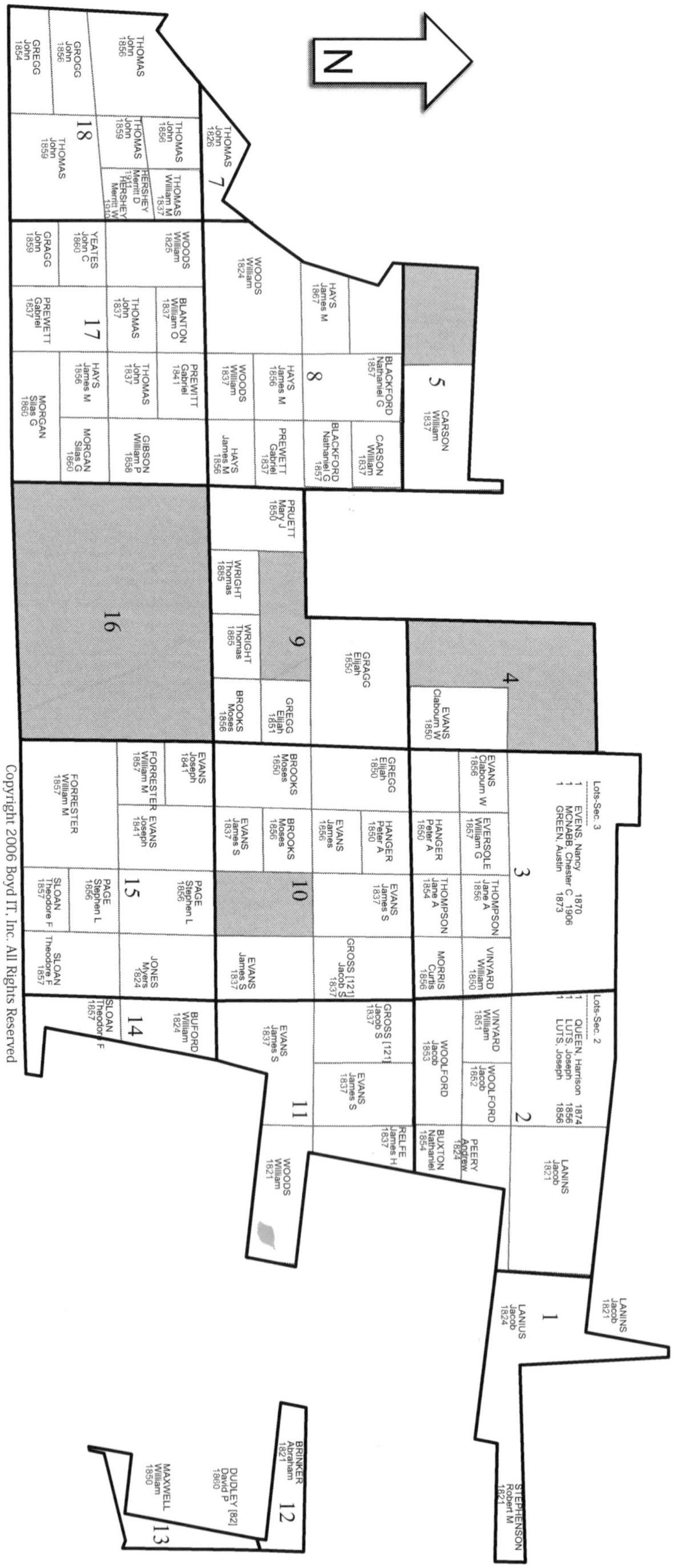

Scale: Section = 1 mile X 1 mile
(generally, with some exceptions)

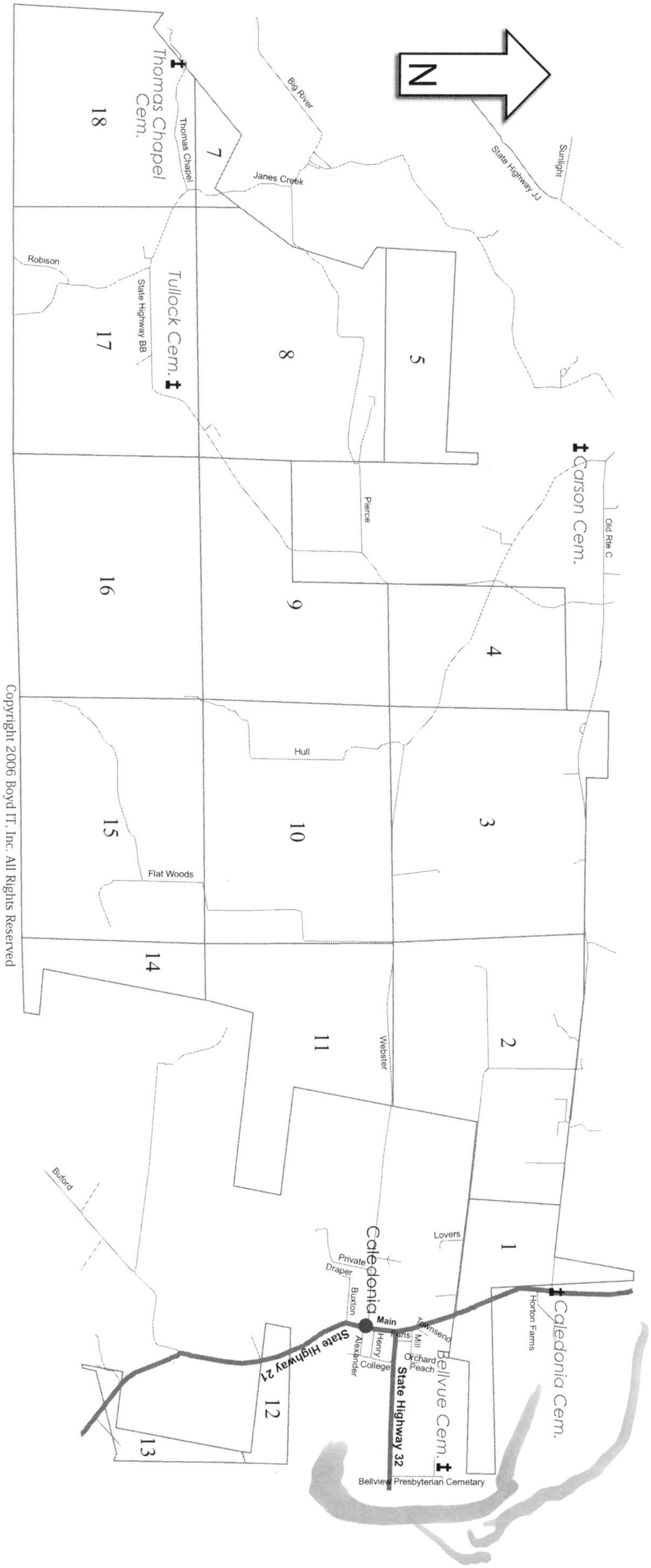

Road Map

T35-N R2-E
5th PM Meridian

Map Group 29

Note: the area contained in this map amounts to far less than a full Township. Therefore, its contents are completely on this single page (instead of a "normal" 2-page spread).

Cities & Towns

Caledonia

Cemeteries

Thomas Chapel Cemetery
Tullock Cemetery
Bellvue Cemetery
Caledonia Cemetery
Carson Cemetery

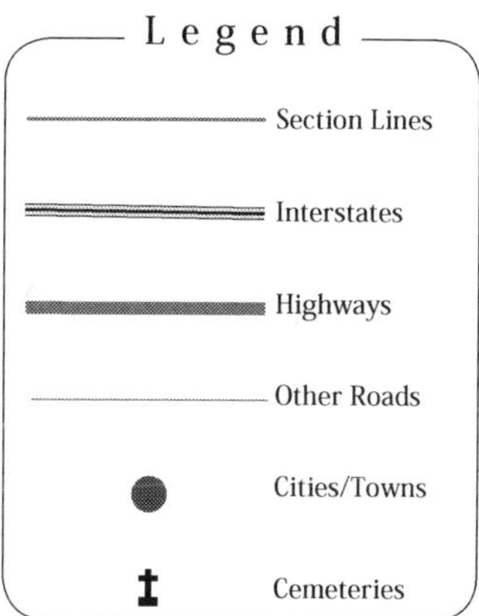

Scale: Section = 1 mile X 1 mile
(generally, with some exceptions)

Historical Map

T35-N R2-E
5th PM Meridian

Map Group 29

Note: the area contained in this map amounts to far less than a full Township. Therefore, its contents are completely on this single page (instead of a "normal" 2-page spread).

Cities & Towns

Caledonia

Cemeteries

Thomas Chapel Cemetery
Tullock Cemetery
Bellvue Cemetery
Caledonia Cemetery
Carson Cemetery

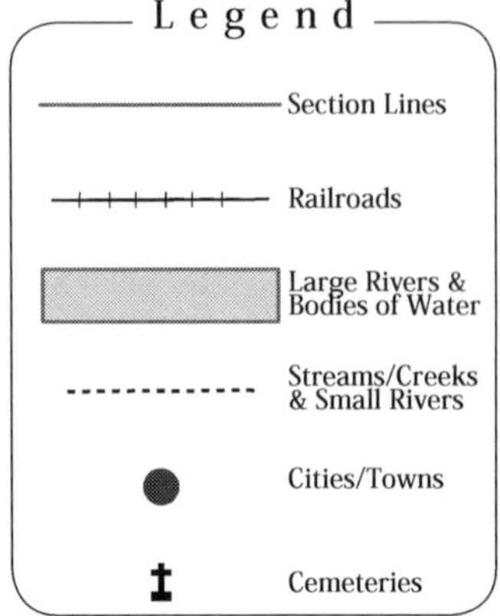

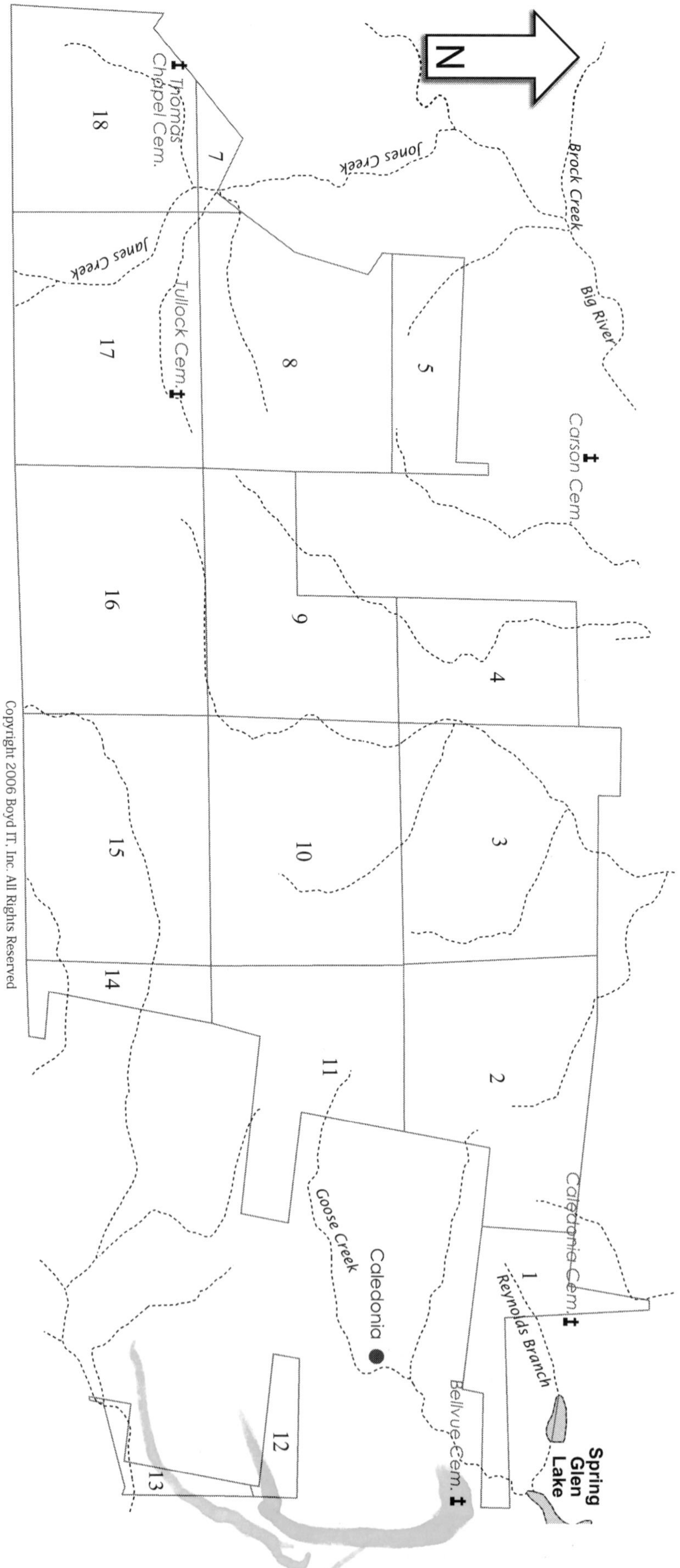

Scale: Section = 1 mile X 1 mile
(there are some exceptions)

Map Group 30: Index to Land Patents

Township 35-North Range 3-East (5th PM)

After you locate an individual in this Index, take note of the Section and Section Part then proceed to the Land Patent map on the pages immediately following. You should have no difficulty locating the corresponding parcel of land.

The "For More Info" Column will lead you to more information about the underlying Patents. See the *Legend* at right, and the "How to Use this Book" chapter, for more information.

LEGEND

"For More Info . . . " column

A = Authority (Legislative Act, See Appendix "A")
B = Block or Lot (location in Section unknown)
C = Cancelled Patent
F = Fractional Section
G = Group (Multi-Patentee Patent, see Appendix "C")
V = Overlaps another Parcel
R = Re-Issued (Parcel patented more than once)

(A & G items require you to look in the Appendixes referred to above. All other Letter-designations followed by a number require you to locate line-items in this index that possess the ID number found after the letter).

ID	Individual in Patent	Sec.	Sec. Part	Date Issued	Other Counties	For More Info . . .
4425	ALEXANDER, Alexander T	10	E½SW	1824-05-10		A1
4426	" "	10	NWSE	1837-03-15		A1
4427	" "	10	SWSE	1841-06-25		A1
4486	ALEXANDER, John	9	SWSE	1837-03-15		A1
4504	ALEXANDER, John P	9	W½NE	1824-05-10		A1
4503	" "	9	SENW	1837-11-14		A1
4505	ALEXANDER, John R	9	SENE	1837-11-14		A1
4515	ALEXANDER, Joseph E	10	NESE	1841-06-25		A1
4523	BACON, Ludwell	1	W½3NW	1856-06-03		A2
4524	" "	3	1NW	1856-06-03		A2
4525	" "	3	E½1NE	1856-06-03		A2
4526	" "	3	SE	1856-06-03		A2
4434	BLACK, David M	7	E½NE	1824-05-10		A1 G18
4464	BOAS, Jacob	7	W½NE	1837-11-07		A1
4430	BREWINGTON, Barney B	17	E½NW	1856-10-10		A1
4445	BREWINGTON, Evans	8	SESE	1853-12-01		A1
4488	BREWINGTON, John E	10	NWSW	1852-01-01		A1
4489	" "	9	NESE	1852-01-01		A1
4522	CASTLEMAN, Lewis	18	3SW	1848-09-01		A1 F
4438	DAY, Edward	18	SENE	1837-11-14		A1
4439	" "	8	NWNW	1837-11-14		A1
4528	DENT, Mark	17	NE	1824-05-01		A1
4435	DUDLEY, David P	18	S½2NW	1860-08-01		A1 G82
4436	" "	18	S½3NW	1860-08-01		A1 G82
4487	DUNCAN, John	5	E½	1859-09-10		A1
4446	ELMER, Francis B	18	NESE	1860-08-01		A1
4490	FORTNER, John	14	NESW	1872-07-01		A3
4485	FORTNER, John A	14	NESE	1896-01-14		A3
4468	GAN, James	14	NWNW	1857-10-30		A1
4469	" "	14	S½NW	1857-10-30		A1
4566	GARRITY, William E	11	NESW	1848-03-01		A1 G106
4540	GATES, Richard	2	W½5NW	1848-03-01		A1
4435	HARRIS, Oliver	18	S½2NW	1860-08-01		A1 G82
4436	" "	18	S½3NW	1860-08-01		A1 G82
4437	HENDERSON, Edward B	11	NENE	1860-08-01		A1
4496	HIGHLY, John	7	SESE	1857-10-30		A1
4497	" "	8	SWSW	1857-10-30		A1
4498	HORTON, John	2	SESE	1849-04-10		A1
4465	HOWARD, Jacob C	14	S½SW	1859-09-01		A1
4466	HOWARD, James B	14	NENW	1859-09-01		A1
4531	HOWARD, Mordecai	9	NENE	1859-09-01		A1
4532	HOWARD, Mordecai J	10	SWSW	1856-01-03		A1
4533	" "	15	N½NE	1856-01-03		A1
4536	" "	9	SESW	1856-01-03		A1
4534	" "	9	N½NW	1864-10-26		A1
4535	" "	9	NWSE	1864-10-26		A1

ID	Individual in Patent	Sec.	Sec. Part	Date Issued	Other Counties	For More Info . . .
4537	HOWARD, Mordica J	15	S½SW	1837-11-14		A1
4538	HOWARD, Mordicia	15	W½NW	1854-11-15		A1
4541	HOWARD, Richard M	10	NENE	1859-09-01		A1
4546	HUGHES, Samuel	6	1NE	1824-05-01		A1
4547	" "	6	E½SE	1824-05-10		A1
4459	IMBODEN, Henry	17	W½NW	1859-09-01		A1
4551	IMBODEN, Samuel	7	W½SE	1837-01-24		A1 F
4548	" "	7	NESE	1856-01-03		A1 F
4550	" "	7	NWSW	1856-01-03		A1 F
4552	" "	8	SWNW	1856-01-03		A1 F
4549	" "	7	NW	1857-04-15		A1 F R4470
4566	JOHNSON, Benjamin F	11	NESW	1848-03-01		A1 G106
4462	JOHNSON, Isaac	8	E½NE	1837-11-14		A1
4463	" "	8	SWNE	1841-07-01		A1
4461	" "	11	SWSW	1848-03-01		A1
4516	JOHNSON, Joseph	14	NENE	1848-03-01		A1
4514	JOHNSON, Joseph B	11	SESW	1848-03-01		A1
4472	KINKEAD, James	1	W½1NE	1841-07-01		A1
4556	KINKEAD, Susannah	1	W½2NE	1841-07-01		A1
4557	KINSEY, Thomas J	11	SESE	1848-03-01		A1
4553	LATTIMER, Samuel	6	SESW	1837-01-24		A1 F
4473	MACKAY, James	12	W½NW	1856-06-03		A2
4460	MARTINDALE, Howell	12	SESE	1848-02-01		A1
4474	MATHIS, James	9	NWSW	1856-01-03		A1
4475	" "	9	SWNW	1856-01-03		A1
4567	MEYERS, William J	11	N½NW	1859-09-10		A1
4568	" "	11	SENE	1859-09-10		A1
4569	" "	11	W½NE	1859-09-10		A1
4563	MOODY, William A	13	NWSW	1854-11-15		A1
4562	" "	13	NESW	1859-09-01		A1
4564	" "	14	SESE	1859-09-01		A1
4565	" "	14	SWSE	1859-09-01		A1
4477	MOORE, James	6	NWSW	1837-01-17		A1
4478	" "	6	S½NW	1837-01-17		A1
4476	" "	6	NESW	1837-01-24		A1 F
4433	MORRIS, Curtis	5	W½1NW	1856-06-03		A2
4434	NAVE, Jacob	7	E½NE	1824-05-10		A1 G18
4560	NICHOLAS, Walker	18	NWNE	1837-11-07		A1
4561	" "	18	S½1NW	1837-11-07		A1
4431	PARKER, Charles	8	SWSE	1856-06-16		A1
4481	PARKS, Jefferson	10	E½NW	1857-04-15		A1
4482	" "	10	W½NE	1857-04-15		A1
4527	PEEBLES, Marcus	17	E½SE	1860-08-01		A1
4554	PETERSON, Sterling	5	SW	1837-11-07		A1
4555	" "	5	W½SE	1837-11-07		A1 V4487
4447	PURSLEY, George	12	E½SW	1856-06-03		A2
4448	" "	12	SENW	1856-06-03		A2
4449	" "	13	SESE	1856-06-03		A2
4450	" "	2	1NE	1856-06-03		A2
4451	" "	2	SW	1856-06-03		A2
4452	" "	2	W½SE	1856-06-03		A2
4453	" "	3	SW	1856-06-03		A2
4572	RANDALL, William	8	N½SE	1837-01-24		A1
4571	RATLEY, William P	13	SWNW	1885-06-20		A3
4423	RELFE, Alexander C	7	E½SW	1856-09-01		A1
4424	" "	7	SWSW	1856-09-01		A1
4421	" "	18	N½2NW	1856-10-10		A1
4422	" "	18	N½3NW	1856-10-10		A1
4467	RELFE, James D	18	NENE	1854-11-15		A1
4470	RELFE, James H	7	NW	1837-01-24		A1 F R4549
4471	" "	7	SW	1837-01-24		A1 F
4420	RENN, Adolph	15	SENE	1905-08-26		A3
4539	REYNOLDS, Pleasant M	15	SWNE	1857-04-15		A1
4429	ROBINSON, Archibald	15	NWSW	1837-03-15		A1
4428	" "	15	NESW	1837-11-07		A1
4479	ROBINSON, James	13	NENE	1853-12-01		A1
4573	RUSSELL, William	18	1SW	1827-03-27		A1
4574	" "	18	2SW	1827-03-27		A1
4491	SCOTT, John G	4	1NW	1853-12-01		A1
4492	" "	4	W½3NE	1853-12-01		A1
4493	" "	5	2NE	1853-12-01		A1
4494	" "	5	3NE	1853-12-01		A1
4495	" "	5	E½1NW	1853-12-01		A1

ID	Individual in Patent	Sec.	Sec. Part	Date Issued	Other Counties	For More Info . . .
4517	SHERLOCK, Joseph	14	NWNE	1858-12-01		A1
4518	" "	14	NWSE	1859-09-01		A1
4519	" "	14	SENE	1859-09-01		A1
4520	" "	14	SWNE	1859-09-01		A1
4521	SHIRLOCK, Joseph	13	NWNW	1857-10-30		A1
4542	STEVENSON, Robert M	15	E½NW	1824-05-10		A1
4506	STEWART, John	10	SESE	1856-06-03		A2
4507	" "	11	NWSE	1856-06-03		A2
4508	" "	11	SWSE	1856-06-03		A2
4509	" "	18	SWNE	1856-06-03		A2
4510	" "	18	W½SE	1856-06-03		A2
4511	STOFER, John W	8	NENW	1841-06-25		A1
4483	SUTTON, Jeremiah	8	NWNE	1837-01-24		A1
4544	SUTTON, Robert	6	NE2NE	1835-12-30		A1
4545	" "	6	SE2NE	1837-03-15		A1
4543	" "	5	E½3NW	1853-04-12		A1
4558	SUTTON, Valentine	6	E½NE	1837-03-15		A1
4559	" "	6	SW2NE	1837-03-15		A1
4576	SUTTON, William	4	W½SW	1837-11-14		A1
4575	" "	4	SESW	1856-01-03		A1
4577	" "	8	E½SW	1856-01-03		A1
4578	" "	8	SENW	1856-01-03		A1
4570	SUTTON, William J	5	W½3NW	1837-11-14		A1
4432	TAYLOR, Chester T	9	NESW	1911-12-04		A1
4484	TAYLOR, Jesse J	18	N½1NW	1876-06-20		A3
4500	TAYLOR, John L	17	SESW	1856-10-10		A1
4502	" "	17	W½SE	1856-10-10		A1
4499	" "	17	N½SW	1857-04-15		A1
4501	" "	17	SWSW	1857-04-15		A1
4440	TEDDER, Elisha	9	SESE	1857-04-15		A1
4529	TRAMMELL, Martha	13	SENE	1854-11-15		A1
4480	WALKER, James	9	SWSW	1859-09-01		A1
4443	WALLEN, Elisha	2	3NW	1837-11-07		A1
4444	" "	3	E½3NE	1837-11-07		A1
4441	" "	13	SENW	1849-04-10		A1
4442	" "	13	W½NE	1859-09-01		A1
4454	WALLEN, Hays	1	W½1NW	1848-03-01		A1
4458	" "	3	E½2NE	1849-04-10		A1
4455	" "	2	E½1NW	1854-11-15		A1
4456	" "	2	E½2NW	1854-11-15		A1
4457	" "	2	W½1NW	1856-06-16		A1
4512	WALLEN, John	2	3NE	1837-11-07		A1
4513	" "	2	E½2NE	1848-03-01		A1
4530	WALLEN, Mary	2	W½2NE	1848-03-01		A1

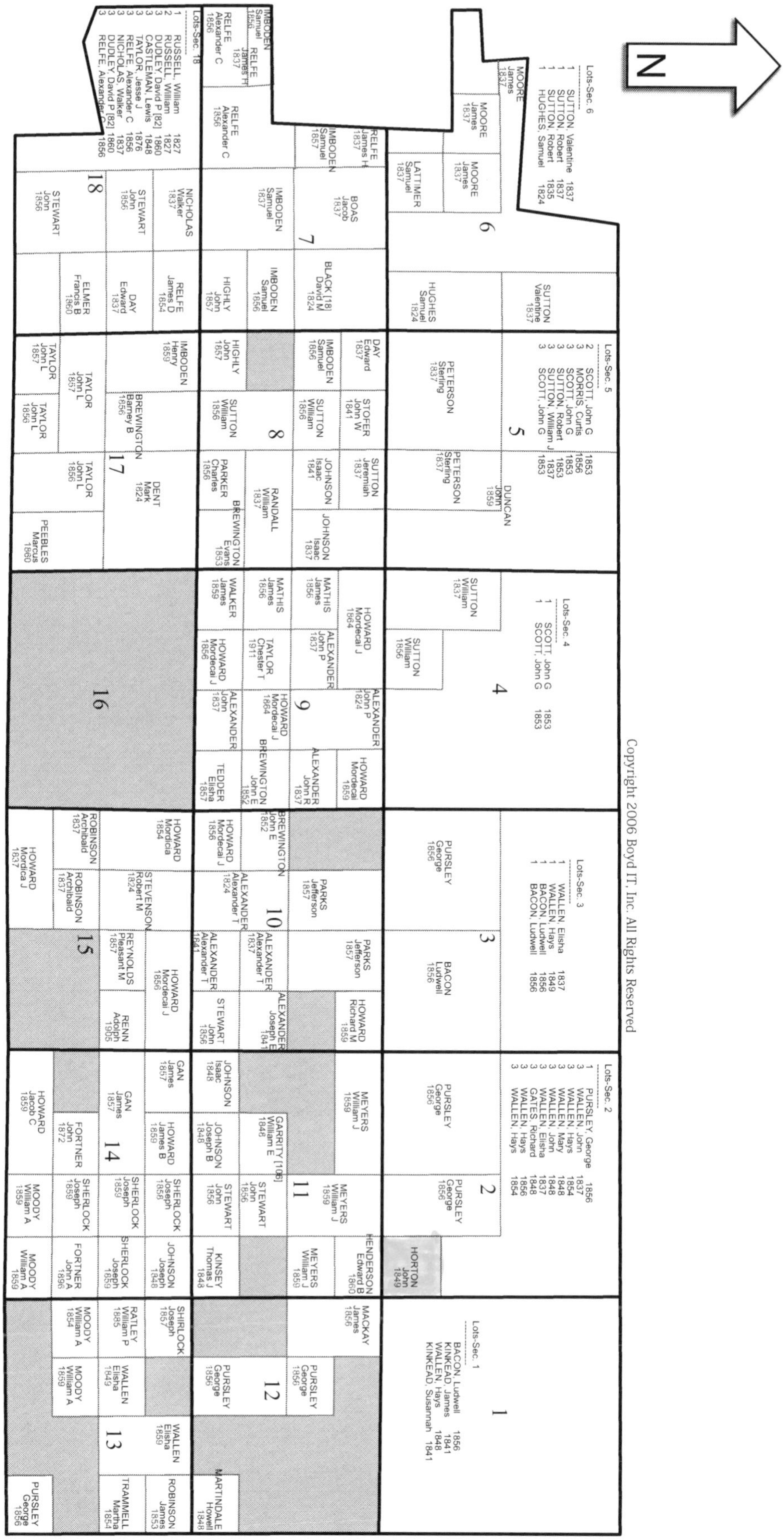

Patent Map

T35-N R3-E
5th PM Meridian

Map Group 30

Township Statistics

Parcels Mapped	:	159
Number of Patents	:	122
Number of Individuals	:	89
Patentees Identified	:	86
Number of Surnames	:	59
Multi-Patentee Parcels	:	4
Oldest Patent Date	:	5/1/1824
Most Recent Patent	:	12/4/1911
Block/Lot Parcels	:	38
Parcels Re - Issued	:	1
Parcels that Overlap	:	1
Cities and Towns	:	1
Cemeteries	:	2

Note: the area contained in this map amounts to far less than a full Township. Therefore, its contents are completely on this single page (instead of a "normal" 2-page spread).

Legend

——	Patent Boundary
▬▬	Section Boundary
(shaded)	No Patents Found (or Outside County)
1., 2., 3., ...	Lot Numbers (when beside a name)
[ ]	Group Number (see Appendix "C")

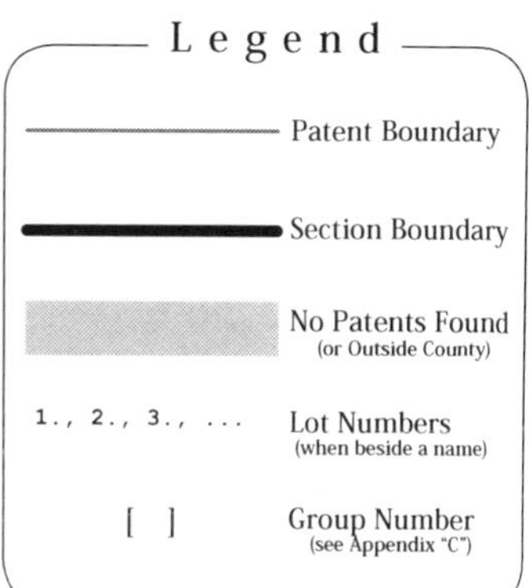

Scale: Section = 1 mile X 1 mile
(generally, with some exceptions)

Road Map

T35-N R3-E
5th PM Meridian

Map Group 30

Note: the area contained in this map amounts to far less than a full Township. Therefore, its contents are completely on this single page (instead of a "normal" 2-page spread).

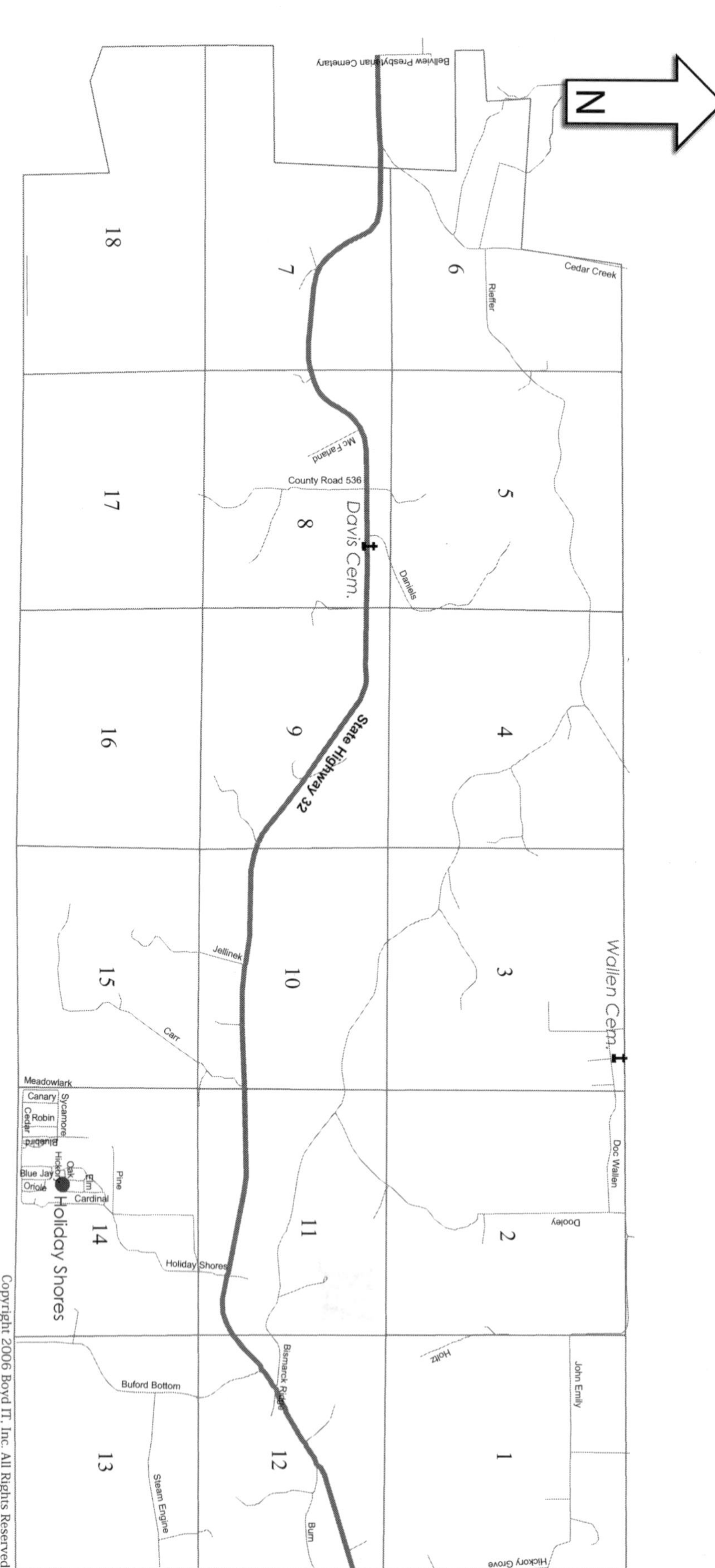

Cities & Towns

Holiday Shores

Cemeteries

Davis Cemetery
Wallen Cemetery

Legend

- Section Lines
- Interstates
- Highways
- Other Roads
- Cities/Towns
- Cemeteries

Scale: Section = 1 mile X 1 mile
(generally, with some exceptions)

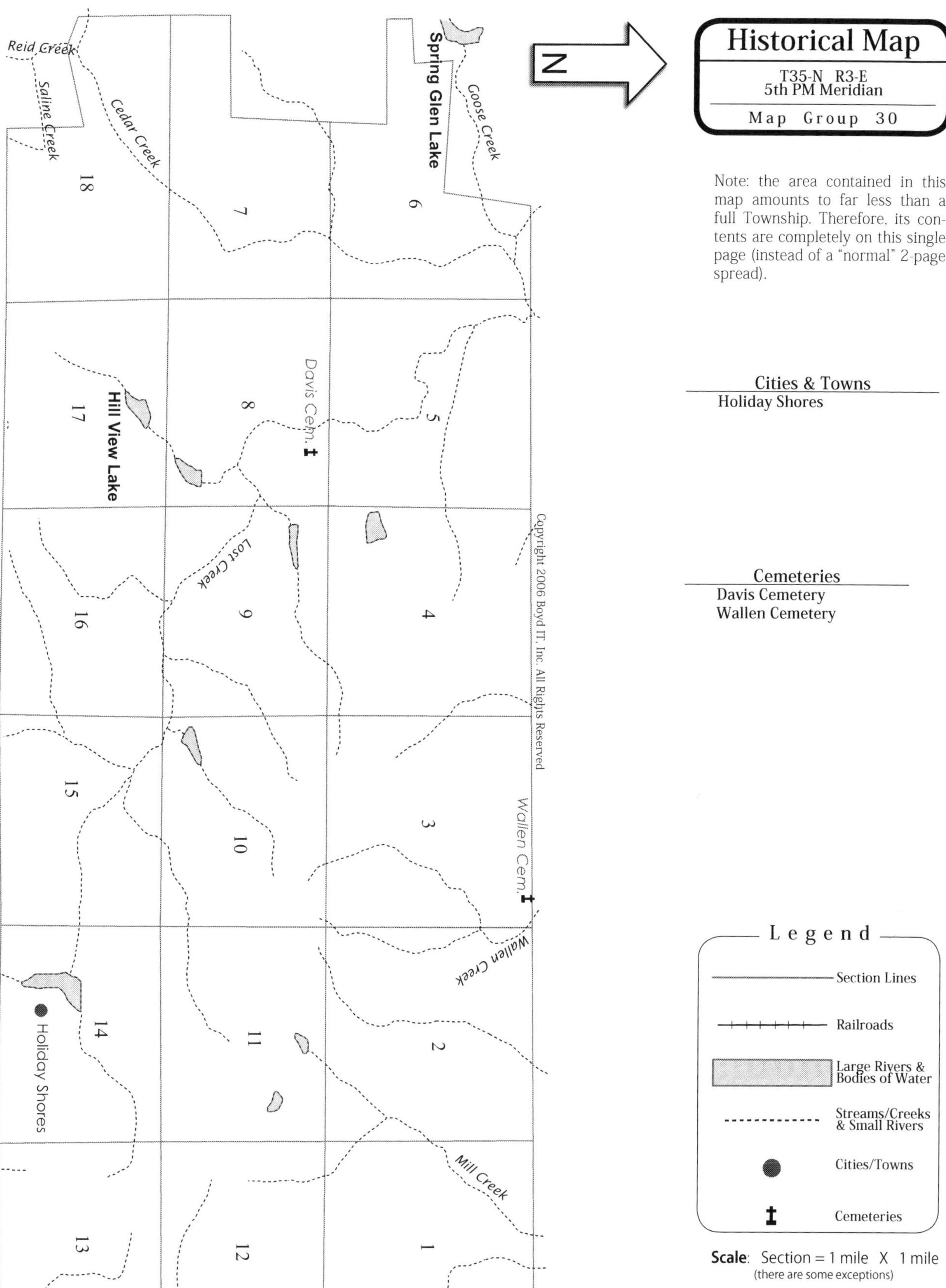
Historical Map
T35-N R3-E
5th PM Meridian
Map Group 30
N
Note: the area contained in this map amounts to far less than a full Township. Therefore, its contents are completely on this single page (instead of a "normal" 2-page spread).
Cities & Towns
Holiday Shores
Cemeteries
Davis Cemetery
Wallen Cemetery
Legend
Section Lines
Railroads
Large Rivers & Bodies of Water
Streams/Creeks & Small Rivers
Cities/Towns
Cemeteries
Scale: Section = 1 mile X 1 mile
(there are some exceptions)
Reid Creek
Saline Creek
Cedar Creek
Spring Glen Lake
Goose Creek
Hill View Lake
Davis Cem.
Lost Creek
Wallen Cem.
Wallen Creek
Holiday Shores
Mill Creek
Copyright 2006 Boyd IT, Inc. All Rights Reserved
18
7
6
17
8
5
16
9
4
15
10
3
14
11
2
13
12
1

Appendices

Appendix A - Acts of Congress Authorizing the Patents Contained in this Book

The following Acts of Congress are referred to throughout the Indexes in this book. The text of the Federal Statutes referred to below can usually be found on the web. For more information on such laws, check out the publishers's web-site at *www.arphax.com,* go to the "Research" page, and click on the "Land-Law" link.

Ref. No.	Date and Act of Congress	Number of Parcels of Land
1	April 24, 1820: Sale-Cash Entry (3 Stat. 566)	4326
2	March 17, 1842: Scrip or Nature of Scrip (5 Stat. 607)	56
3	May 20, 1862: Homestead EntryOriginal (12 Stat. 392)	196

Appendix B - Section Parts (Aliquot Parts)

The following represent the various abbreviations we have found thus far in describing the parts of a Public Land Section. Some of these are very obscure and rarely used, but we wanted to list them for just that reason. A full section is 1 square mile or 640 acres.

Section Part	Description	Acres
<none>	Full Acre (if no Section Part is listed, presumed a full Section)	640
<1-??>	A number represents a Lot Number and can be of various sizes	?
E½	East Half-Section	320
E½E½	East Half of East Half-Section	160
E½E½SE	East Half of East Half of Southeast Quarter-Section	40
E½N½	East Half of North Half-Section	160
E½NE	East Half of Northeast Quarter-Section	80
E½NENE	East Half of Northeast Quarter of Northeast Quarter-Section	20
E½NENW	East Half of Northeast Quarter of Northwest Quarter-Section	20
E½NESE	East Half of Northeast Quarter of Southeast Quarter-Section	20
E½NESW	East Half of Northeast Quarter of Southwest Quarter-Section	20
E½NW	East Half of Northwest Quarter-Section	80
E½NWNE	East Half of Northwest Quarter of Northeast Quarter-Section	20
E½NWNW	East Half of Northwest Quarter of Northwest Quarter-Section	20
E½NWSE	East Half of Northwest Quarter of Southeast Quarter-Section	20
E½NWSW	East Half of Northwest Quarter of Southwest Quarter-Section	20
E½S½	East Half of South Half-Section	160
E½SE	East Half of Southeast Quarter-Section	80
E½SENE	East Half of Southeast Quarter of Northeast Quarter-Section	20
E½SENW	East Half of Southeast Quarter of Northwest Quarter-Section	20
E½SESE	East Half of Southeast Quarter of Southeast Quarter-Section	20
E½SESW	East Half of Southeast Quarter of Southwest Quarter-Section	20
E½SW	East Half of Southwest Quarter-Section	80
E½SWNE	East Half of Southwest Quarter of Northeast Quarter-Section	20
E½SWNW	East Half of Southwest Quarter of Northwest Quarter-Section	20
E½SWSE	East Half of Southwest Quarter of Southeast Quarter-Section	20
E½SWSW	East Half of Southwest Quarter of Southwest Quarter-Section	20
E½W½	East Half of West Half-Section	160
N½	North Half-Section	320
N½E½NE	North Half of East Half of Northeast Quarter-Section	40
N½E½NW	North Half of East Half of Northwest Quarter-Section	40
N½E½SE	North Half of East Half of Southeast Quarter-Section	40
N½E½SW	North Half of East Half of Southwest Quarter-Section	40
N½N½	North Half of North Half-Section	160
N½NE	North Half of Northeast Quarter-Section	80
N½NENE	North Half of Northeast Quarter of Northeast Quarter-Section	20
N½NENW	North Half of Northeast Quarter of Northwest Quarter-Section	20
N½NESE	North Half of Northeast Quarter of Southeast Quarter-Section	20
N½NESW	North Half of Northeast Quarter of Southwest Quarter-Section	20
N½NW	North Half of Northwest Quarter-Section	80
N½NWNE	North Half of Northwest Quarter of Northeast Quarter-Section	20
N½NWNW	North Half of Northwest Quarter of Northwest Quarter-Section	20
N½NWSE	North Half of Northwest Quarter of Southeast Quarter-Section	20
N½NWSW	North Half of Northwest Quarter of Southwest Quarter-Section	20
N½S½	North Half of South Half-Section	160
N½SE	North Half of Southeast Quarter-Section	80
N½SENE	North Half of Southeast Quarter of Northeast Quarter-Section	20
N½SENW	North Half of Southeast Quarter of Northwest Quarter-Section	20
N½SESE	North Half of Southeast Quarter of Southeast Quarter-Section	20

Section Part	Description	Acres
N½SESW	North Half of Southeast Quarter of Southwest Quarter-Section	20
N½SESW	North Half of Southeast Quarter of Southwest Quarter-Section	20
N½SW	North Half of Southwest Quarter-Section	80
N½SWNE	North Half of Southwest Quarter of Northeast Quarter-Section	20
N½SWNW	North Half of Southwest Quarter of Northwest Quarter-Section	20
N½SWSE	North Half of Southwest Quarter of Southeast Quarter-Section	20
N½SWSE	North Half of Southwest Quarter of Southeast Quarter-Section	20
N½SWSW	North Half of Southwest Quarter of Southwest Quarter-Section	20
N½W½NW	North Half of West Half of Northwest Quarter-Section	40
N½W½SE	North Half of West Half of Southeast Quarter-Section	40
N½W½SW	North Half of West Half of Southwest Quarter-Section	40
NE	Northeast Quarter-Section	160
NEN½	Northeast Quarter of North Half-Section	80
NENE	Northeast Quarter of Northeast Quarter-Section	40
NENENE	Northeast Quarter of Northeast Quarter of Northeast Quarter	10
NENENW	Northeast Quarter of Northeast Quarter of Northwest Quarter	10
NENESE	Northeast Quarter of Northeast Quarter of Southeast Quarter	10
NENESW	Northeast Quarter of Northeast Quarter of Southwest Quarter	10
NENW	Northeast Quarter of Northwest Quarter-Section	40
NENWNE	Northeast Quarter of Northwest Quarter of Northeast Quarter	10
NENWNW	Northeast Quarter of Northwest Quarter of Northwest Quarter	10
NENWSE	Northeast Quarter of Northwest Quarter of Southeast Quarter	10
NENWSW	Northeast Quarter of Northwest Quarter of Southwest Quarter	10
NESE	Northeast Quarter of Southeast Quarter-Section	40
NESENE	Northeast Quarter of Southeast Quarter of Northeast Quarter	10
NESENW	Northeast Quarter of Southeast Quarter of Northwest Quarter	10
NESESE	Northeast Quarter of Southeast Quarter of Southeast Quarter	10
NESESW	Northeast Quarter of Southeast Quarter of Southwest Quarter	10
NESW	Northeast Quarter of Southwest Quarter-Section	40
NESWNE	Northeast Quarter of Southwest Quarter of Northeast Quarter	10
NESWNW	Northeast Quarter of Southwest Quarter of Northwest Quarter	10
NESWSE	Northeast Quarter of Southwest Quarter of Southeast Quarter	10
NESWSW	Northeast Quarter of Southwest Quarter of Southwest Quarter	10
NW	Northwest Quarter-Section	160
NWE½	Northwest Quarter of Eastern Half-Section	80
NWN½	Northwest Quarter of North Half-Section	80
NWNE	Northwest Quarter of Northeast Quarter-Section	40
NWNENE	Northwest Quarter of Northeast Quarter of Northeast Quarter	10
NWNENW	Northwest Quarter of Northeast Quarter of Northwest Quarter	10
NWNESE	Northwest Quarter of Northeast Quarter of Southeast Quarter	10
NWNESW	Northwest Quarter of Northeast Quarter of Southwest Quarter	10
NWNW	Northwest Quarter of Northwest Quarter-Section	40
NWNWNE	Northwest Quarter of Northwest Quarter of Northeast Quarter	10
NWNWNW	Northwest Quarter of Northwest Quarter of Northwest Quarter	10
NWNWSE	Northwest Quarter of Northwest Quarter of Southeast Quarter	10
NWNWSW	Northwest Quarter of Northwest Quarter of Southwest Quarter	10
NWSE	Northwest Quarter of Southeast Quarter-Section	40
NWSENE	Northwest Quarter of Southeast Quarter of Northeast Quarter	10
NWSENW	Northwest Quarter of Southeast Quarter of Northwest Quarter	10
NWSESE	Northwest Quarter of Southeast Quarter of Southeast Quarter	10
NWSESW	Northwest Quarter of Southeast Quarter of Southwest Quarter	10
NWSW	Northwest Quarter of Southwest Quarter-Section	40
NWSWNE	Northwest Quarter of Southwest Quarter of Northeast Quarter	10
NWSWNW	Northwest Quarter of Southwest Quarter of Northwest Quarter	10
NWSWSE	Northwest Quarter of Southwest Quarter of Southeast Quarter	10
NWSWSW	Northwest Quarter of Southwest Quarter of Southwest Quarter	10
S½	South Half-Section	320
S½E½NE	South Half of East Half of Northeast Quarter-Section	40
S½E½NW	South Half of East Half of Northwest Quarter-Section	40
S½E½SE	South Half of East Half of Southeast Quarter-Section	40

Section Part	Description	Acres
S½E½SW	South Half of East Half of Southwest Quarter-Section	40
S½N½	South Half of North Half-Section	160
S½NE	South Half of Northeast Quarter-Section	80
S½NENE	South Half of Northeast Quarter of Northeast Quarter-Section	20
S½NENW	South Half of Northeast Quarter of Northwest Quarter-Section	20
S½NESE	South Half of Northeast Quarter of Southeast Quarter-Section	20
S½NESW	South Half of Northeast Quarter of Southwest Quarter-Section	20
S½NW	South Half of Northwest Quarter-Section	80
S½NWNE	South Half of Northwest Quarter of Northeast Quarter-Section	20
S½NWNW	South Half of Northwest Quarter of Northwest Quarter-Section	20
S½NWSE	South Half of Northwest Quarter of Southeast Quarter-Section	20
S½NWSW	South Half of Northwest Quarter of Southwest Quarter-Section	20
S½S½	South Half of South Half-Section	160
S½SE	South Half of Southeast Quarter-Section	80
S½SENE	South Half of Southeast Quarter of Northeast Quarter-Section	20
S½SENW	South Half of Southeast Quarter of Northwest Quarter-Section	20
S½SESE	South Half of Southeast Quarter of Southeast Quarter-Section	20
S½SESW	South Half of Southeast Quarter of Southwest Quarter-Section	20
S½SESW	South Half of Southeast Quarter of Southwest Quarter-Section	20
S½SW	South Half of Southwest Quarter-Section	80
S½SWNE	South Half of Southwest Quarter of Northeast Quarter-Section	20
S½SWNW	South Half of Southwest Quarter of Northwest Quarter-Section	20
S½SWSE	South Half of Southwest Quarter of Southeast Quarter-Section	20
S½SWSE	South Half of Southwest Quarter of Southeast Quarter-Section	20
S½SWSW	South Half of Southwest Quarter of Southwest Quarter-Section	20
S½W½NE	South Half of West Half of Northeast Quarter-Section	40
S½W½NW	South Half of West Half of Northwest Quarter-Section	40
S½W½SE	South Half of West Half of Southeast Quarter-Section	40
S½W½SW	South Half of West Half of Southwest Quarter-Section	40
SE	Southeast Quarter Section	160
SEN½	Southeast Quarter of North Half-Section	80
SENE	Southeast Quarter of Northeast Quarter-Section	40
SENENE	Southeast Quarter of Northeast Quarter of Northeast Quarter	10
SENENW	Southeast Quarter of Northeast Quarter of Northwest Quarter	10
SENESE	Southeast Quarter of Northeast Quarter of Southeast Quarter	10
SENESW	Southeast Quarter of Northeast Quarter of Southwest Quarter	10
SENW	Southeast Quarter of Northwest Quarter-Section	40
SENWNE	Southeast Quarter of Northwest Quarter of Northeast Quarter	10
SENWNW	Southeast Quarter of Northwest Quarter of Northwest Quarter	10
SENWSE	Souteast Quarter of Northwest Quarter of Southeast Quarter	10
SENWSW	Southeast Quarter of Northwest Quarter of Southwest Quarter	10
SESE	Southeast Quarter of Southeast Quarter-Section	40
SESENE	SoutheastQuarter of Southeast Quarter of Northeast Quarter	10
SESENW	Southeast Quarter of Southeast Quarter of Northwest Quarter	10
SESESE	Southeast Quarter of Southeast Quarter of Southeast Quarter	10
SESESW	Southeast Quarter of Southeast Quarter of Southwest Quarter	10
SESW	Southeast Quarter of Southwest Quarter-Section	40
SESWNE	Southeast Quarter of Southwest Quarter of Northeast Quarter	10
SESWNW	Southeast Quarter of Southwest Quarter of Northwest Quarter	10
SESWSE	Southeast Quarter of Southwest Quarter of Southeast Quarter	10
SESWSW	Southeast Quarter of Southwest Quarter of Southwest Quarter	10
SW	Southwest Quarter-Section	160
SWNE	Southwest Quarter of Northeast Quarter-Section	40
SWNENE	Southwest Quarter of Northeast Quarter of Northeast Quarter	10
SWNENW	Southwest Quarter of Northeast Quarter of Northwest Quarter	10
SWNESE	Southwest Quarter of Northeast Quarter of Southeast Quarter	10
SWNESW	Southwest Quarter of Northeast Quarter of Southwest Quarter	10
SWNW	Southwest Quarter of Northwest Quarter-Section	40
SWNWNE	Southwest Quarter of Northwest Quarter of Northeast Quarter	10
SWNWNW	Southwest Quarter of Northwest Quarter of Northwest Quarter	10

Section Part	Description	Acres
SWNWSE	Southwest Quarter of Northwest Quarter of Southeast Quarter	10
SWNWSW	Southwest Quarter of Northwest Quarter of Southwest Quarter	10
SWSE	Southwest Quarter of Southeast Quarter-Section	40
SWSENE	Southwest Quarter of Southeast Quarter of Northeast Quarter	10
SWSENW	Southwest Quarter of Southeast Quarter of Northwest Quarter	10
SWSESE	Southwest Quarter of Southeast Quarter of Southeast Quarter	10
SWSESW	Southwest Quarter of Southeast Quarter of Southwest Quarter	10
SWSW	Southwest Quarter of Southwest Quarter-Section	40
SWSWNE	Southwest Quarter of Southwest Quarter of Northeast Quarter	10
SWSWNW	Southwest Quarter of Southwest Quarter of Northwest Quarter	10
SWSWSE	Southwest Quarter of Southwest Quarter of Southeast Quarter	10
SWSWSW	Southwest Quarter of Southwest Quarter of Southwest Quarter	10
W½	West Half-Section	320
W½E½	West Half of East Half-Section	160
W½N½	West Half of North Half-Section (same as NW)	160
W½NE	West Half of Northeast Quarter	80
W½NENE	West Half of Northeast Quarter of Northeast Quarter-Section	20
W½NENW	West Half of Northeast Quarter of Northwest Quarter-Section	20
W½NESE	West Half of Northeast Quarter of Southeast Quarter-Section	20
W½NESW	West Half of Northeast Quarter of Southwest Quarter-Section	20
W½NW	West Half of Northwest Quarter-Section	80
W½NWNE	West Half of Northwest Quarter of Northeast Quarter-Section	20
W½NWNW	West Half of Northwest Quarter of Northwest Quarter-Section	20
W½NWSE	West Half of Northwest Quarter of Southeast Quarter-Section	20
W½NWSW	West Half of Northwest Quarter of Southwest Quarter-Section	20
W½S½	West Half of South Half-Section	160
W½SE	West Half of Southeast Quarter-Section	80
W½SENE	West Half of Southeast Quarter of Northeast Quarter-Section	20
W½SENW	West Half of Southeast Quarter of Northwest Quarter-Section	20
W½SESE	West Half of Southeast Quarter of Southeast Quarter-Section	20
W½SESW	West Half of Southeast Quarter of Southwest Quarter-Section	20
W½SW	West Half of Southwest Quarter-Section	80
W½SWNE	West Half of Southwest Quarter of Northeast Quarter-Section	20
W½SWNW	West Half of Southwest Quarter of Northwest Quarter-Section	20
W½SWSE	West Half of Southwest Quarter of Southeast Quarter-Section	20
W½SWSW	West Half of Southwest Quarter of Southwest Quarter-Section	20
W½W½	West Half of West Half-Section	160

Appendix C - Multi-Patentee Groups

The following index presents groups of people who jointly received patents in Washington County, Missouri. The Group Numbers are used in the Patent Maps and their Indexes so that you may then turn to this Appendix in order to identify all the members of the each buying group.

Group Number 1
ALDRIDGE, Charles; ALDRIDGE, William

Group Number 2
ALLEN, A N; SHEPHERD, G R

Group Number 3
AMES, Edgar; AMES, Henry

Group Number 4
ATTWOOD, Moses; JACKSON, Smith; PIERCE, Charles

Group Number 5
BAIRD, Samuel; BRICKEY, John Colwell; STEPHENSON, Joseph Milas

Group Number 6
BALEW, William; LOOMIS, Levi S; STAPPLES, Samuel O

Group Number 7
BARBOUR, Gabriel H; COXE, Henry S; TAYLOR, Nathaniel P

Group Number 8
BARBOUR, James T; BARBOUR, William T; CHRISTY, Andrew

Group Number 9
BARRON, John; STEWART, William

Group Number 10
BASS, William; BRIGGS, Oliver

Group Number 11
BEAN, Abner; FORD, John

Group Number 12
BEAN, John; MANNING, Foreman

Group Number 13
BELL, John B; CASTLEMAN, Thomas D

Group Number 14
BENNETT, John; HIGHT, Alfred D

Group Number 15
BENNING, Benjamin P; BENNING, Isaac G

Group Number 16
BEQUETTE, Derville; KELLY, Michael

Group Number 17
BERRY, Moses; MCSPADEN, Moses M

Group Number 18
BLACK, David M; NAVE, Jacob

Group Number 19
BLACKWELL, Robert; MANNING, Foreman

Group Number 20
BLANTON, Absalom; BREDELL, Edward; CLARK, Jacob

Group Number 21
BLANTON, Absolom; KIMBERLIN, Renard

Group Number 22
BLUNT, Peter D; SMITH, Reuben

Group Number 23
BOAS, Jacob; MARLER, John

Group Number 24
BOAS, Jacob; MARLER, Michael

Group Number 25
BOAS, Jacob; MURPHEY, Peter

Group Number 26
BOAS, Robert J; BRADSHAW, William

Group Number 27
BOYER, Michael; BOYLE, Peter

Group Number 28
BRAGG, Addison G; RICHARDSON, George B

Group Number 29
BREDELL, Edward; COLLIER, George

Group Number 30
BREDELL, Edward; DUNKLIN, Stephen T

Group Number 31
BREDELL, Edward; GAMBLE, Archibald

Group Number 32
BRICKEY, John C; MCILVAIN, John

Group Number 33
BROCK, James; COMPTON, John

Group Number 34
BROWN, Elisha; BURDION, Reubin

Group Number 35
BROWN, Elisha; STONE, Samuel P

Group Number 36
BROWN, William D; MANNING, Foreman

Group Number 37
BRYAN, Robert; BRYAN, William

Group Number 38
BURDION, Reuben; STONE, Samuel P

Group Number 39
BURGESS, Sanders; HOOTER, Louis C

Group Number 40
CALVERD, Peter C; THURMOND, Bennett

Group Number 41
CALVERD, Peter; SULLIVAN, Stephen

Group Number 42
CAMP, William K; HUFF, Powell

Group Number 43
CAMPBELL, Colin C; EVANS, James S; ROLFE, James H

Group Number 44
CAMPBELL, George; SMITH, Reuben

Group Number 45
CAMPBELL, Jeremiah; STEVENSON, Joseph M

Group Number 46
CAMPBELL, Samuel; SMITH, Reuben

Group Number 47
CARPENTER, James M; COBURN, Charles H

Group Number 48
CARPENTER, James M; WADE, George W

Group Number 49
CARPENTER, Robert; MURPHY, Jesse

Group Number 50
CARTER, Harden T; CLARK, Jacob; CROW, William; HIBLER, Daniel

Group Number 51
CARTER, Harden T; CROW, Joseph; CROW, William; HARMAN, James

Group Number 52
CARTER, Hardin T; HORBISON, Thomas; POINDEXTER, Marcellus

Group Number 53
CARTER, Peggy; JONES, Peggy

Group Number 54
CASEY, John; CLAUSEY, John; HILL, Jonas M; HILL, Milton B

Group Number 55
CASWELL, Joseph; MANNING, Foreman

Group Number 56
CATLIFF, James; DOUGHERTY, Patrick; OBUCHAN, John M

Group Number 57
CHEATHAM, Archibald; JOHNSON, Calvin

Group Number 58
CLARK, Austin; CLARK, Jacob

Group Number 59
CLARK, Gotham; MANNING, Foreman

Group Number 60
CLARK, Jacob; HIBLER, Daniel

Group Number 61
CLARK, Jacob; HIBLER, Daniel; HIBLER, Isaac

Group Number 62
CLARK, Jacob; INGE, Chesley B

Group Number 63
CLARK, Jacob; MARTIN, Thomas J

Group Number 64
CLARK, Jacob; MCDOWELL, William; STEVENS, Richard H

Group Number 65
CLARK, Jacob; WHITMIRE, John

Group Number 66
CLARKSON, James L; JOHNSON, William J

Group Number 67
CLARKSON, Joseph G; HENSON, Samuel P

Group Number 68
CLOUDY, Norman S; JOHNSON, Uriah P

Group Number 69
COBURN, Charles H; RAY, Frederick

Group Number 70
COBURN, Charles H; SAUNDERS, Thomas P

Group Number 71
COLE, Philip D; SMITH, William W

Group Number 72
COMPTON, John; DUNKLIN, Stephen T

Group Number 73
COMPTON, Joseph; SMITHER, Joel

Group Number 74
COWAN, William B; THOMAS, Moses

Group Number 75
CROSSWELL, George; LUMPKINS, Charles B

Group Number 76
CROW, Joseph; CROW, William; HARMAN, James

Group Number 77
CUMMINS, Samuel; HYPOLITE, Peter

Group Number 78
DARBY, John F; JOHNSON, Isaac

Group Number 79
DESLOGE, Fermin; HOUSE, Adam

Group Number 80
DESLOGE, Fermin; HOUSE, Adam; ROZIER, Francis C

Group Number 81
DONNA, Peter Charles; FORD, John

Group Number 82
DUDLEY, David P; HARRIS, Oliver

Group Number 83
DUNKLIN, Stephen T; LERSHALL, Samuel

Group Number 84
EATON, Absalom; PEASE, Henry

Group Number 85
EATON, Lazarus; STONE, Samuel P

Group Number 86
EDMONDS, Samuel; HUNT, Edward

Group Number 87
EDWARDS, Charles A; WILCOX, William L

Group Number 88
ELLIOTT, Richard S; HUNT, James; LEFFINGWELL, Hiram W

Group Number 89
EVANS, Charles; EVANS, John; HARRISON, Samuel; HAY, David A; STOW, Isaac

Group Number 90
EVANS, James S; EVANS, Jesse R

Group Number 91
EVANS, John; MCGRADY, Israel

Group Number 92
EVANS, John; MCGREADY, Israel

Group Number 93
EVANS, John; MCGREADY, Israel; WHITE, James M

Group Number 94
EVANS, John; MCGREADY, Susan; WHITE, James M

Group Number 95
EVANS, John; WALTON, Christopher

Group Number 96
EVANS, John; WESTOVER, George T

Group Number 97
EVENS, John; LORE, John

Group Number 98
EVENS, John; MCCABE, Alpheus

Group Number 99
EVENS, John; MCGREADY, Israel

Group Number 100
EVENS, John; WALTON, Christopher

Group Number 101
FARRELL, John; LIBBY, James C; SEYMOUR, William B

Group Number 102
FARRIS, Anderson P; FARRIS, Anthony P; TAYLOR, John

Group Number 103
FERGUSON, George W; WATKINS, John C

Group Number 104
FISHER, Jacob; IMBODEN, David

Group Number 105
FLEMING, Alexander; MANNING, Foreman

Group Number 106
GARRITY, William E; JOHNSON, Benjamin F

Group Number 107
GATY, Samuel; WARE, Joseph E

Group Number 108
GHOLSON, Felix G; JANNEY, Nathan

Group Number 109
GIBSON, James R; GIBSON, Samuel D

Group Number 110
GIBSON, Robert; SMITH, Hiram M; SMITH, William

Group Number 111
GILCHRIST, Malcolm; RELFE, James H

Group Number 112
GILLAM, Benjamin; MANNING, Foreman

Group Number 113
GILLAM, William; MANNING, Foreman

Group Number 114
GILLIAM, William; MANNING, Foreman

Group Number 115
GLENN, James; MANNING, Forman; WHITE, James M

Group Number 116
GLENN, James; SMITH, Jesse B

Group Number 117
GODARD, Eugene; PAGE, John B

Group Number 118
GODAT, Eugene; HULSEY, William; PAGE, John B

Group Number 119
GREEN, Obediah; PARKINSON, John

Group Number 120
GREENE, Obadiah; PARKINSON, John

Group Number 121
GROSS, Jacob S; RELFE, James H

Group Number 122
GUY, John F; STEMBER, John

Group Number 123
HAEFNER, Joseph W; MATTHEWS, William A

Group Number 124
HALLIDAY, John; STANDEFER, David W

Group Number 125
HARLOW, Alden; HARLOW, Josiah

Group Number 126
HARMAN, James L; MCDOWELL, John

Group Number 127
HARRISON, Albert G; JONES, Myers F; LINN, Lewis F; RELFE, James H

Group Number 128
HAYS, David; WALLEN, Elisha

Group Number 129
HAYS, James; WALLEN, Elisha

Group Number 130
HAYS, William; PERRY, John

Group Number 131
HIBLER, Daniel; WESTOVER, George T

Group Number 132
HILL, Britton; HOUSEMAN, James; JACKSON, Smith; PIERCE, Charles; THOMAS, Elihu

Group Number 133
HIRSH, J; PRUDEN, E

Group Number 134
HORTON, Hezekiah W; WALLEN, Elisha

Group Number 135
HOUSEMAN, James D; IRVINE, Andrew; SCHARIT, Augustus W

Group Number 136
HOUSEMAN, James D; PIERCE, Charles; THOMAS, Elihu B

Group Number 137
HOUSEMAN, James; PIERCE, Charles; THOMAS, Elihu B

Group Number 138
HUDSON, William; PERSHALL, Samuel E

Group Number 139
HUDSPETH, Abijah W; SPEAR, Charles

Group Number 140
HUDSPETH, Abijah W; SWOFFORD, James

Group Number 141
HUGHES, F M; HUGHES, Nancy E

Group Number 142
HUGHES, Parmelia; JAMISON, James; JAMISON, William

Group Number 143
HUITT, Margaret E; HUITT, William

Group Number 144
HULL, Uriah; MONTGOMERY, Andrew

Group Number 145
HULL, Uriah; PEASE, Henry

Group Number 146
HUNT, James; JOHNSTON, Robert

Group Number 147
HUNT, James; READING, James N

Group Number 148
IRVINE, Andrew; SHOOK, Amos C

Group Number 149
JAMISON, John; WESTOVER, Job

Group Number 150
JANIS, Henry; MATHEWS, Ezekiel C; SIMPSON, George

Group Number 151
JETT, Abraham; MANNING, Foreman

Group Number 152
JETT, Abraham; ORCHARDS, James

Group Number 153
JOHNSON, James C; JOHNSON, William C

Group Number 154
JOHNSON, Jeptha B; JOHNSON, John H; JOHNSON, Joseph D; STACEY, Joseph

Group Number 155
JOHNSON, Jeptha B; JOHNSON, Joseph; THOMAS, John

Group Number 156
JOHNSON, Pleasant S; SHIELDS, James W

Group Number 157
JONES, Myers F; RELFE, James H

Group Number 158
KIRKPATRICK, Francis W; SOULARD, Benjamin A; SOULARD, James G

Group Number 159
KIRKPATRICK, Francis W; SOULARD, Benjamin S; SOULARD, James G

Group Number 160
LAMARQUE, Etienne; SMITH, Reuben

Group Number 161
LAMARQUE, Stephen; MADDEN, Malichi

Group Number 162
LASWELL, Joseph; MANNING, Foreman

Group Number 163
LONG, Branfield; LONG, William

Group Number 164
LONG, Brumfield; LONG, Milton; LONG, William

Group Number 165
LONG, Brumfield; LONG, William

Group Number 166
LONG, William; WHITE, Samuel

Group Number 167
LORE, John; MCCABE, Alpheus

Group Number 168
LUCAS, Alexander C; LUCAS, William

Group Number 169
LUPTON, Henry; LUPTON, Jonathan; LUPTON, Joseph

Group Number 170
LUPTON, Jonathan; PARKINSON, William

Group Number 171
MANNING, Foreman; MCKEE, Thomas S

Group Number 172
MANNING, Foreman; NEUSE, George

Group Number 173
MANNING, Foreman; SMITH, Reuben; STONE, Samuel P; WHITE, James H

Group Number 174
MANNING, Foreman; SMITH, Reuben; STONE, Samuel P; WHITE, James M

Group Number 175
MANNING, Foreman; TEAS, Henry

Group Number 176
MANNING, Forman; SMITH, Reuben

Group Number 177
MAURICE, William H; WARE, Joseph E

Group Number 178
MCCREARY, Samuel; PEASE, Henry

Group Number 179
MCPHAILL, Alexander; MONTGOMERY, Nathan; SMITH, Reubin; WHALEY, William

Group Number 180
MELVIN, Alfred; SULLIVAN, Stephen

Group Number 181
MERRY, Samuel; PERRY, John

Group Number 182
MERRY, Samuel; SMITH, Reuben

Group Number 183
MERRY, Samuel; STONE, Samuel L

Group Number 184
MESPLAY, Basille; ROZIER, Ferdinand

Group Number 185
MONTGOMERY, Andrew; PEASE, Henry

Group Number 186
MONTGOMERY, Nathan; SMITH, Reuben

Group Number 187
MURPHY, Thomas C; MURPHY, William

Group Number 188
MURPHY, Thomas C; MURPHY, William S

Group Number 189
NEUSE, George; STONE, Samuel P

Group Number 190
NICHOLSON, John; NICHOLSON, Thomas; NICHOLSON, William

Group Number 191
NICHOLSON, Thomas; NICHOLSON, William

Group Number 192
NORVELL, Napoleon B; SMITH, Reuben

Group Number 193
OCHELTREE, William; RECTOR, Elias

Group Number 194
PEIRCE, Charles; THOMAS, Elihu B

Group Number 195
PERRY, James F; PERRY, Samuel

Group Number 196
PERRY, James; PERRY, John; PERRY, Samuel; PERRY, William

Group Number 197
PERRY, James; PERRY, Samuel

Group Number 198
PERRY, John; PERRY, Samuel; PERRY, William M

Group Number 199
PERRY, John; PERRY, William

Group Number 200
PERRY, John; PERRY, William M

Group Number 201
PERRY, John; WHEALEY, William

Group Number 202
RANEY, Felix; RANEY, James; RANEY, Valentine

Group Number 203
REED, John C; WHITE, James M

Group Number 204
RELFE, James H; THOMPSON, Jane A

Group Number 205
SANDERS, James; SPEAR, Charles

Group Number 206
SAUNDERS, Thomas P; SMITH, Alexander H

Group Number 207
SHOULTS, Catharine; SMITH, Reuben

Group Number 208
SILVERS, Levi H; SILVERS, Washington

Group Number 209
SLOAN, John H; SLOAN, Thomas J

Group Number 210
SMITH, Reuben; STAMM, Mary

Group Number 211
SMITH, Reuben; STONE, Samuel

Group Number 212
STEERMAN, Samuel P; STEERMAN, Thomas Jefferson

Group Number 213
STEERMAN, Thomas Jefferson; STONE, Samuel P

Group Number 214
STEERMAN, Thomas; STONE, Samuel P

Group Number 215
STEWART, William H; WOOLSAY, James

Group Number 216
STONE, Samuel P; WILKINSON, Jeremiah

Group Number 217
SUMMERS, Valentine T; SUMMERS, William H

Group Number 218
SUMMERS, Valentine; SUMMERS, William

Group Number 219
SUMMERS, William W; WHITE, Thomas S

Group Number 220
TODD, Eliza A; TODD, Emily J; TODD, Mary A; TODD, Mathew A; TODD, William A

Group Number 221
WALLEN, Elisha; WALLEN, Nelson

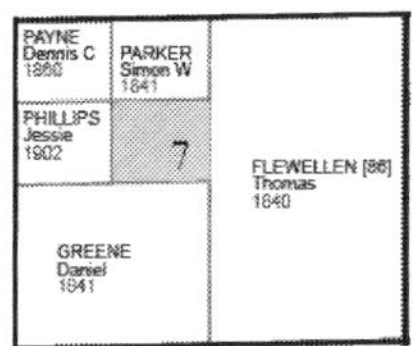

Extra! Extra! (about our Indexes)

We purposefully do not have an all-name index in the back of this volume so that our readers do not miss one of the best uses of this book: finding misspelled names among more specialized indexes.

Without repeating the text of our "How-to" chapter, we have nonetheless tried to assist our more anxious researchers by delivering a short-cut to the two county-wide Surname Indexes, the second of which will lead you to all-name indexes for each Congressional Township mapped in this volume :

For your convenience, the "How To Use this Book" Chart on page 2 is repeated on the reverse of this page.

We should be releasing new titles every week for the foreseeable future. We urge you to write, fax, call, or email us any time for a current list of titles. Of course, our web-page will always have the most current information about current and upcoming books.

Arphax Publishing Co.
2210 Research Park Blvd.
Norman, Oklahoma 73069
(800) 681-5298 toll-free
(405) 366-6181 local
(405) 366-8184 fax
info@arphax.com

www.arphax.com

How to Use This Book - A Graphical Summary

Part I
"The Big Picture"

Map A ▸ *Counties in the State*
Map B ▸ *Surrounding Counties*
Map C ▸ *Congressional Townships (Map Groups) in the County*
Map D ▸ *Cities & Towns in the County*
Map E ▸ *Cemeteries in the County*
Surnames in the County ▸ *Number of Land-Parcels for Each Surname*
Surname/Township Index ▸ Directs you to Township Map Groups in Part II

The Surname/Township Index can direct you to any number of **Township Map Groups**

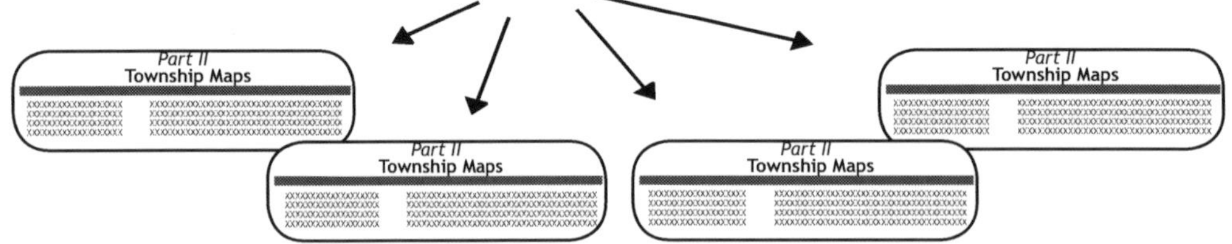

Part II
Township Map Groups
(1 for each Township in the County)

Each Township Map Group contains all four of of the following tools . . .

Land Patent Index ▸ *Every-name Index of Patents Mapped in this Township*
Land Patent Map ▸ *Map of Patents as listed in above Index*
Road Map ▸ *Map of Roads, City-centers, and Cemeteries in the Township*
Historical Map ▸ *Map of Railroads, Lakes, Rivers, Creeks, City-Centers, and Cemeteries*

Appendices

Appendix A ▸ *Congressional Authority enabling Patents within our Maps*
Appendix B ▸ *Section-Parts / Aliquot Parts (a comprehensive list)*
Appendix C ▸ *Multi-patentee Groups (Individuals within Buying Groups)*

Made in the USA
Columbia, SC
02 October 2018